California Central District

COURT AND CHAMBERS PRACTICE MANUAL

DISTRICT COURT
Selected General Orders
Procedures and Practices

INDIVIDUAL JUDGES
Procedures and Practices
Standing Orders
Case Management Orders and Forms
Scheduling Information
Chambers and Biographical Information

Mid-2012 Edition

Compiled by Practicing Attorneys
Meliora Law

Printed and bound in the United States of America.
ISBN: 978-0-9838302-0-7

Meliora Law LLC
19250 Stevens Creek Boulevard, Suite 100
Cupertino, CA 94015
www.melioralaw.com

PUBLISHER'S PREFACE

The information contained herein are current as received through March 2012.

THE PUBLISHER

March 2012

TABLE OF CONTENTS

This page intentionally left blank.

This page intentionally left blank.

PART I

DISTRICT COURT

SELECTED GENERAL ORDERS
PROCEDURES AND PRACTICES

I. General Orders

A. *General Order No. 06-06 – Wireless Communication Devices Within Courthouses and Federal Buildings*

IN THE UNITED STATES DISTICT COURT
FOR THE CENTRAL DISTRICT OF CALIFORNIA

IN THE MATTER OF:		
	)	**GENERAL ORDER NO. 06-06**
WIRELESS COMMUNICATION DEVICES WITHIN COURTHOUSES AND FEDERAL BUILDINGS	)	

IT IS HEREBY ORDERED that all wireless communication devices shall be turned off while in any courtroom or during any jury deliberation, unless the judge presiding otherwise orders.

Nonetheless, individual judges may elect to bar all wireless communication devices from their courtrooms.

Wireless communication devices are electronic devices that are capable of either sending or receiving data such as text messages, still images or movies. Such devices shall include, but are not limited to, mobile phones, laptop computers and personal digital assistants (PDAs) that are capable of sending or receiving text or pictures, or of recording or transmitting, sounds, images or movies.

DATED: November 16, 2006

II. Procedures Regarding Settlements

A. *Procedures for Implementing Settlement Options*

PROCEDURES FOR IMPLEMENTING SETTLEMENT OPTIONS

In every civil case, the parties, unless exempted by the trial judge, shall participate in one of the settlement procedures set forth in Local Rule 16-15 or as otherwise approved by the trial judge. No later than 45 days before the final Local Rule 16 pre-trial conference, the parties shall select and participate in one of the suggested settlement procedures as set forth in Local Rule 16-15 or as otherwise approved by the trial judge. Except as otherwise ordered by the Court, a Notice and Request of Settlement Procedure Selection (ADR-1), signed by counsel for both sides, shall be filed not later than 14 days after entry of the scheduling order under F.R.Civ.P. 16 (b).

If Settlement Procedure No. 1 (Local Rule 16-15.4) is selected: If the assigned district judge is to conduct the settlement procedure, the parties must contact that district judge's courtroom deputy and arrange a date and time for the settlement conference. The courtroom deputy will calendar the matter accordingly. If the assigned discovery magistrate judge is to conduct the settlement conference, the courtroom deputy shall refer the matter for settlement conference to that assigned magistrate judge. The magistrate judge's courtroom deputy will calendar the matter accordingly. Further questions regarding this option may be referred to the courtroom deputy for the assigned district judge or assigned discovery magistrate judge, as appropriate.

If Settlement Procedure No. 2 (Local Rule 16-15.4) is selected: The parties must access the Attorney Settlement Officer Panel List available from the website. There are two panel lists on the website, one alphabetical and the other by area of law. The website also contains personal profiles of those panel members who voluntarily provided such information. The Attorney Settlement Officer Panel List is updated periodically by the Panel Coordinator. If the parties do not have the ability to access the website, the parties may contact the courtroom deputy to the assigned judge for the case. The courtroom deputy will make a photocopy of the appropriate section of the list that relates to the type of case that the parties are litigating and fax or mail that appropriate section to the requesting party. The parties shall then make a selection from the list, obtain consent from the Attorney Settlement Officer selected and file a Stipulation Regarding Selection of Attorney Settlement Officer (ADR-2). The parties and the Attorney Settlement Officer shall arrange for an agreed upon date, time and place for a settlement conference and shall so notify the Panel Coordinator. If the parties cannot agree on an appropriate Attorney Settlement Officer from the list, they shall submit the ADR-2 requesting a random assignment of an Attorney Settlement Officer. The Panel Coordinator will perform the random assignment of an Attorney Settlement Officer from the particular area of law designated on the ADR-2 and will notify the parties by mail of the selection. Within five days after the conclusion of the settlement proceeding, the Attorney Settlement Officer shall file with the court and serve the parties and the Panel Coordinator an Attorney Settlement Officer Proceeding Report (ADR-3). Further questions regarding the Attorney Settlement Officer Panel may be referred to the ADR Program Office at (213) 894-2993.

If Settlement Procedure No. 3 (Local Rule 16-15.4) is selected: The parties shall appear before a retired judicial officer or other private or non-profit dispute resolution body for mediation-type settlement proceedings. The parties shall make any necessary arrangements in this regard and should file a notice with the court naming the person who will conduct the settlement conference and indicating the date set for the settlement conference.

If a "Notice to Parties of ADR Program" has been issued: Along with the Notice provided to plaintiff's counsel at the time of the filing of the complaint, plaintiff's counsel (or defense counsel if a removal case) will also be given an "ADR Program Questionnaire." This Questionnaire is to be completed jointly by the parties and filed concurrently with the report required under Federal Rules of Civil Procedure 26(f). After reviewing the Questionnaire, if the judge assigned to the case determines that the case is suitable for referral to the program the parties will receive an "Order/Referral to ADR Program." For further information on the program, please see General Order 07-01 which is available on the Court's website.

B. Procedures for Reserving Courthouse Facilities for Settlement Proceedings

PROCEDURES FOR RESERVING COURTHOUSE FACILITIES FOR SETTLEMENT PROCEEDINGS

Use of Courthouse Facilities for Settlement Proceedings

Attorney Settlement Officers may reserve court facilities for settlement proceedings conducted pursuant to their service as members of the Attorney Settlement Officer Panel. Court facilities may not be used for private mediations.

The following individuals are available to assist with room reservations for settlement conferences to be held at divisional courthouses:

- Los Angeles (Spring Street) – Grace Moon – (213) 894-1400
- Santa Ana – Adrian Delgado – (714) 338-4785
- Riverside – Kiry Gray – (951) 328-4451

FOR LOS ANGELES (SPRING STREET) ONLY: Due to the heavy use of facilities at the Los Angeles location, please observe the following procedures:

- When you arrive at the courthouse, please check-in with Grace so that she can escort you to the conference room(s) and open the room(s). Please advise counsel that both they and their client(s) should check-in with Grace as well. Grace is located in room 910 of the Spring Street courthouse. If Grace is not available, please contact Cecilia Gonda at (213) 894-4467. If neither Grace nor Cecilia is available, you may contact Dawn Osborne-Adams at (213) 894-1215.

- Please request conference room reservations as far in advance as possible. If you leave a voice mail with Grace, your message must include your e-mail address, your cellphone number, your contact telephone number, and the name of an alternate contact person in the event you are not available when she returns your call.

- Please be aware that the number of rooms you reserve will be the number of rooms available to you on the day of the settlement conference. Do not assume that any unoccupied rooms are available for your use.

- Occasionally, room locations will be changed. Grace will notify you of the new location as soon as she is aware of any change in room assignments.

- Should a settlement proceeding be canceled, please advise Grace as soon as possible so that she may cancel your room reservation.

- Please close and lock the door(s) to the conference room(s) once the settlement proceeding has concluded.

Thank you for your cooperation.

III. Other Procedures and Practices

A. Bill of Costs Handbook

BILL OF COSTS HANDBOOK

(January 1, 2010)

This handbook has been prepared to assist parties in properly completing and filing Bill of Costs.

The prevailing party is entitled to reasonable costs as incurred by the proceedings. No costs are allowed unless a party qualifies as, or is determined by the Court to be, the prevailing party. Pursuant to Local Civil Rule 54-2:

A. The plaintiff is the prevailing party when it recovers on the entire complaint;

B. The defendant is the prevailing party when the proceeding is terminated by court-ordered dismissal or judgment in favor of the defendant;

C. The Court shall determine the prevailing party when there is a partial recovery or a recovery by more than one party;

D. The Court shall determine the prevailing party when the case is voluntarily dismissed or otherwise voluntarily terminated.

Within (15) days after the entry of judgment, the party entitled to costs shall electronically file a Notice of Application to the Clerk to Tax Costs and shall attach a proposed Bill of Costs on Form CV-59. The Bill of Costs and the Notice of Application to the Clerk to Tax Costs shall be prepared as two separate documents. All costs shall be specified so that the nature of the claim can be readily understood. A courtesy hard copy of the application and Form CV-59 shall be submitted to the Clerk's designee within 24 hours after e-filing. The designee for Los Angeles and Riverside is Lydia Yurtchuk; courtesy copies for Los Angeles and Riverside shall be submitted at the Spring Street Courthouse, Civil Intake section. The designee for Santa Ana is Milli Borgarding; courtesy copies for Santa Ana shall be submitted at the Santa Ana Courthouse, Civil Intake section. The Bill of Costs will be electronically filed by the Clerk's designee once a determination of allowable costs are made.

The Notice of Application to the Clerk to Tax Costs shall state the hour and date the application will be made in the event a telephonic or personal appearance is deemed necessary. This date and time cannot be less than 14 days nor more than 21 days from the date that notice is given to other parties. **The moving party must select an appropriate hearing date and time.** It is not necessary to clear the date with the Court or the Clerk's designee. All Bill of Costs hearings or appearances are before the Clerk's designee and not the assigned district or magistrate judge.

For Los Angeles and Riverside, effective August 1, 2009, Bill of Costs hearings are scheduled on Thursdays at 9:00 a.m., 10:00 a.m., 11:00 a.m. and 1:00 p.m. In person appearances are no longer required. Hearings are conducted telephonically but in most instances, no telephonic hearing is necessary as the Bill of Costs is considered on the submitted documents. If a telephonic or in person appearance is necessary, the designee will contact the parties. To continue or take a scheduled Bill of Costs hearing off calendar, please call the appropriate telephone number below:

- for Los Angeles cases assigned to district and magistrate judges located at the Spring Street and Roybal Courthouses, call 213-894-0007 or 213-894-8249;

- for all cases assigned to Riverside district and magistrate judges, call 213-894-0007 or 213-894-8249.

For Santa Ana, Bill of Costs hearings are scheduled on Fridays at 10:00 a.m. or 2:00 p.m. in Room 1-053. To continue, take a scheduled Bill of Cots hearing off calendar or to ascertain the name of or speak to the person that will be hearing a particular Bill of Costs, call 714-338-4764 or 714-338-4760.

If the hearing date falls an a holiday, the next available date shall be used.

Please notify the appropriate Clerk's designee at least 24 hours in advance of the hearing date in the following instances: (1) where the matter has been settled, or (2) where one of the parties intends to submit the matter on the documentation filed and not make an appearance at the hearing.

Pursuant to Local Civil Rule 54-7, any party may file and serve written objections to any item specified in a Bill of Costs. The grounds for the objection must be specifically stated and must be filed and served no later than seven (7) days before the date noticed for the application. **No verbal objection will be considered.** A written response to filed objections may be filed and served no later than three (3) days before the date noticed for the application. A courtesy hard copy of the objection and responses shall be submitted to the Clerk's designee within 24 hours after e-filing.

After considering any objections to the Bill of Costs and any responses thereto, the Clerk shall tax costs. The Clerk's decision will be final unless modified by the Court upon review. As soon as practicable after the taxation of costs becomes final, the Clerk shall enter a notation on the docket sheet reflecting the award of costs.

A review by the Court can be obtained by a motion to retax costs filed and served within seven (7) days of the Clerk's decision. The review will be limited to the record made before the Clerk and will encompass only those items specifically identified in the motion.

ITEMS TAXABLE AS COSTS:

Pursuant to Local Rule 54-4, the following fees are taxable as costs:

A. The Clerk's filing fees (*pro hac vice* fees are not recoverable);

B. Fees for service of process (whether served by the U.S. Marshal or other persons authorized by F.R.Civ.P. 4) and for service of subpoenas pursuant to F.R.Civ.P. 45;

C. United States Marshal's fees include:

1. Fees paid according to 28 U.S.C. Section 1921;

2. Charges connected with caring for property attached, replevied libeled, or held pending stay of execution;

3. The United States Marshal's commission on collections paid to creditors. That commission shall be 1 percent of the amount up to $1,000.00, and ½ of 1 percent of the amount in excess of $1,000, but not less than $2.50 for any collection.

D. Clerk's fees for certification of documents necessary for preparation for a hearing or a trial;

E. Fees for reporter's transcripts, including the cost of the original transcript and one copy of all or any part of a trial transcript, daily transcript or a transcript of matters occurring before or after trial, **if requested by the Court or prepared pursuant to stipulation**;

F. Costs incurred with taking oral depositions, including:

1. The cost of the original deposition and one copy used for any purpose in the connection with the case, but not including the cost of videotaped or recorded depositions unless ordered by the Court. Deposition transcripts include non-expedited transcripts, the reporter's appearance fee, fees for binding, bates stamping, non-expedited shipping and handling, processing fee, ASCII disks, production and code compliance charge, electronic transmission charge, mini-scripts and witness handing charges;

2. The reasonable fees of a deposition reporter, including reporter fees when a deponent fails to appear at a scheduled deposition, the notary, and any other persons required to report or transcribe the deposition, but not including the costs of video or audio technicians unless otherwise ordered by the Court; expedited rates are not allowable unless ordered by the Court;

3. Reasonable witness fees paid to a deponent, including fees actually paid to an expert witness deponent pursuant to F.R.Civ.P. 26(b)(4)(c). However, such fees do not include expert witness fees paid to a trial witness in excess of the statutory witness fees unless otherwise ordered by the Court;

4. Reasonable fees paid to an interpreter whose presence is necessary when taking a deposition;

5. The cost of copying or reproducing exhibits used at the deposition and made a part of the deposition transcript.

G. Witness fees if required to attend by the opposing party or if the witnesses are employees of a corporation and are not parties in their individual capacities:

1. Attendance fees of $40.00 per day;

2. Mileage for transportation to and from the Court at the prevailing rate;

3. *Per diem* at the prevailing rate;

4. Miscellaneous fee at the prevailing rate.

H. Fees paid to interpreters and translators including:

1. The salaries, fees, expenses and costs of an interpreter as provided by 28 U.S.C. Sections 1827 and 1828;

2. Fees for translation of documents received in evidence, used as part of the proceeding or when otherwise reasonably necessary to the preparation of the case.

I. Docket fees according to 28 U.S.C. Section 1923 (if incurred);

J. The reasonable fees and expenses of masters, commissioners and receivers;

K. Document preparation costs including:

1. The costs of copies of an exhibit attached to a document necessarily filed and served; other than exhibits, the costs of copies of documents filed and served is generally not taxable;

2. The cost of copies of documents or records admitted into evidence when the original is not available or the copy is substituted for the original at the request of an opposing party;

3. Fees concerned with officially certifying that a document or record does not exist;

4. Patent Office charges for the patent file wrappers and prior art patents necessary to the prosecution or defense of a proceeding involving a patent;

5. Notary fees incurred in notarizing a documents when the cost of the document is taxable;

6. Fees for necessary certification or exemplification of any document or record.

L. Premiums paid on undertakings, bonds, security stipulations or substitutes where required by law, court order, or where necessary to enable a party to secure a right granted in the proceeding.

UPON ORDER OF THE COURT, these items may also be taxed as costs:

A. Summaries, computations, polls, surveys, statistical comparisons, maps, charts, diagrams, and other visual aids reasonably necessary to assist the jury or the Court in understanding the issues at trial;

B. Photographs, if admitted in evidence or attached to documents necessarily filed and served upon the opposing party;

C. The cost of models.

SPECIAL CASES:

A. Removed Cases – Costs incurred in State Court prior to removal, which are recoverable under state statutes, shall be recovered by the prevailing party in Federal Court;

B. Costs on Appeal – Costs on appeal taxable in the District Court shall be governed by F.R.App.P. 39(e). Such costs bill is to be filed no later than thirty (30) days after the date the mandate or judgment was issued by the Court of Appeals;

C. Costs on a Bankruptcy Appeal to the District Court - A cost bill on a bankruptcy appeal decided in the District Court is to be filed within fifteen (15) days of the entered date of the order deciding a bankruptcy appeal. The following are taxable as costs for bankruptcy appeals decided by the District Court:

1. The costs of printing or otherwise reproducing briefs or excerpts of the record. A statement by counsel that the cost is no higher than generally charged for such reproduction in the local area and that no more copies than what was actually necessary were reproduced shall be required;

2. The cost of the preparation and transmission of the record;

3. If supersedeas or other bonds were purchased in order to preserve rights pending appeal, the premium paid for such bonds;

4. Any clerk's fees which have actually been paid.

IMPORTANT:

Each item that is claimed in the Bill of Costs (Form CV-59) must be set forth separately. The prevailing party or attorney having knowledge of the facts shall complete the Declaration portion of the Bill of Costs verifying that:

A. The items claimed as costs are correct;

B. The costs have been necessarily incurred in the case;

C. The services for which fees have been charged were actually and necessarily performed;

Proper itemization and documentation of the actual expenses such as copies of receipts, returned checks, bills, etc. shall be attached as exhibits to the Bill of Costs.

WRIT OF EXECUTION:

Upon request, the Clerk will issue a Writ of Execution to recover attorney's fees included in the judgment and any separate award of costs by the Clerk when:

A. A certified copy of the final judgment and separate Bill of Costs (Form CV-59)and if appropriate, a certified copy of the order awarding attorney's fees, are presented in the District Court; or

B. A mandate of the Court of Appeals is presented to recover costs taxed by the Appellate Court.

ATTORNEY'S FEES:

Any motion or application for attorney's fees shall be served and filed within fourteen (14) days after the entry of judgment or other final order, unless otherwise ordered by the Court. The motions are heard only by the judge assigned to the case and must be filed separately from the Bill of Costs (see Local Civil Rule 7).

B. Disbursement Procedures

DISBURSEMENT PROCEDURES

To avoid some of the delays the clerk's office has experienced in disbursing funds, the following information is being provided to assist attorneys in preparing judgments and orders for disbursement.

Civil Disbursements

Amounts of $5,000.00 or more that are deposited as security with the Court are deposited into interest bearing accounts; therefore, orders for disbursements for amounts of $5,000.00 or more must include the following information:

(1) The amount of principal to be disbursed;

(2) If more than one payee, the name of each payee and the amount each payee is to receive;

(3) A provision that the Clerk of Court shall disburse any accrued interest;

(4) If more than one payee, the percentage of interest each payee is to receive.

Please note that if the security is deposited into an interest bearing account and the order does not mention disbursement of interest, only the principal amount will be released and a second order for disbursement of interest will be required.

In addition to the order, the IRS requires the completion of form W-9 (Request for Taxpayer Identification Number and Certification) when disbursements are made for money that is deposited into interest bearing accounts. The original W-9 form must be submitted to the Fiscal Department, along with a memorandum or note indicating the case name and number. The W-9 form should not be attached to the original judgment or order when submitted for to the Court for approval. The Fiscal Department will hold the W-9 until a signed copy of the judgment or the order is received. W-9 forms can be obtained from the IRS, the Fiscal Department, or from the Court's website at www.cacd.uscourts.gov.

Any amounts deposited as security with the Court that are less than $5,000.00 are deposited into the general registry which is a non-interest bearing account. Disbursements from that type of account do not require a W-9 form.

Criminal Disbursements

The disbursement requirements for Judgment and Probation/Commitment Orders are handled the same way as disbursements for orders and judgments. Since 1997, all amounts deposited as security in the amount of $5,000.00 or more are deposited into interest bearing accounts; therefore, when a bond is exonerated upon surrender or if a bond is ordered exonerated, and the deposit for that bond was placed in an interest bearing account, the order must include language that disbursement is for the principal amount, "together with any accrued interest, if applicable." An exact amount of interest is not required. Please note that prior to 1997, all money deposited as security, regardless of the amount, was deposited in the general, non-interest bearing, registry account.

Criminal form CR-7 (Affidavit re Appearance Bond, Cash Security) has been amended to include the social security number of the owner of the cash security. If an attorney or authorized agent of the owner of the cash security is making the deposit, the attorney or authorized agent must know the social security number of the owner of the cash security. The affidavit, which is completed at the Fiscal Department at the time the cash is deposited as security, is needed only if the cash security is placed into an interest bearing account. Form CR-7 can be obtained from the Court's website at www.cacd.uscourts.gov.

If you have any questions regarding disbursement orders please contact Regina Newcomer, Fiscal Assistant Supervisor, at 213-894-3676.

C. *Post Judgment Procedures*

POST JUDGMENT PROCEDURES

The following information is provided to assist judgment creditors in collecting monetary judgments. Please note that the number of copies mentioned in each of the categories below is the number of copies required by the Court; an additional copy is required for a conformed copy. All the forms mentioned in these procedures are available on the Court's website at www.cacd.uscourts.gov.

Writ of Execution – Bank Account

1. Submit to the clerk's office an original and one copy of Affidavit and Request for Issuance of Writ of Execution (form CV-24).

2. Submit to the clerk's office an original and three copies of Writ of Execution (form CV-23). For each additional judgment debtor, submit an additional copy of the writ.

3. The clerk will verify all information on the affidavit and the writ; there can be no blank spaces on the forms; additionally:

- if any monetary category does not apply, a zero amount must be inserted;
- the attorney fee category can only be completed with an amount after attorney fees have been awarded, and the costs category can only be complete with an amount after a bill of costs hearing or awarded by the Court; one writ may be submitted for the judgment, attorney fees, and costs;
- the judgment debtor's full name and address must be included on the writ;
- *see* 28 §1961 for allowable interest.

4. Within three days after the receipt of the affidavit and the writ, the clerk will sign the original writ and emboss it with the clerk's seal; the other two copies of the writ will be name stamped.

5. The requestor of the writ can either instruct the clerk's office to return the original writ to the requestor or request that a copy of the application and the writ be delivered to the U.S. Marshal's Service; if someone other than the U.S. Marshal's Service or a state or local law enforcement officer authorized by state law to effect service is going to serve the writ, the requestor must file a pleading with the Court entitled Request and Order for Appointment of Process Server; the Request and Order shall contain the name of the process server the requestor intends to use for service. For information and requirements regarding the U.S. Marshal's Service serving a writ, as well as inquiring about their service fees, please call (213)894-2485.

6. Should the original writ of execution be lost and another writ of execution be requested, a declaration must be submitted to the clerk's office stating the circumstances surrounding the loss of the original writ. Should a writ of execution be returned by the U.S. Marshal's Service because no money was collected, and the judgment creditor wants another writ in order to serve another bank, the original writ must be filed with the clerk's office before a second original writ will be issued. All writs issued after the first writ of execution, either because the original writ was lost or because another creditor is to be served, are known as alias writs. With each additional writ requested, the requestor must also file an Affidavit and Request for Alias Writ, and note the sequence number of writ requested. For example, an Affidavit and

Request for Third Alias Writ will accompany the request for a third writ of execution. There is no limitation to the number of alias writs that may be requested and issued.

Writ of Execution – Real Property

Follow the procedure for obtaining a writ of execution - bank levy, but submit to the clerk's office an original and four copies of the Writ of Execution (form CV-23).

Writ of Execution – Wages

Follow the procedure for obtaining a writ of execution - bank levy.

Abstract of Judgment – Real Property

1. In order to have an abstract of judgment recorded against real property, submit the appropriate fee to the clerk's office and one Abstract of Judgment (form G-18) for each abstract requested. The clerk's office does not issues copies of abstracts.

2. The clerk's office will verify the information on the abstract and will return the abstract to the requestor within three days.

3. The requestor must submit the abstract to the county recorder for recording. Please note that county recorders will not accept for recording any abstract that contains white outs or corrections.

Registering a Judgment from Another District

1. To register a judgment obtained in another district, submit the appropriate fee to the clerk's office, a Certification of Judgment for Registration in Another District (AO form 451) or other equivalent certification form from the other district certifying the appeal period, and one certified copy of the judgment.

2. Once the foreign judgment is registered, writs and abstracts can be issued by the Court.

Obtaining a Judgment for Registration in Another District

1. Request from the Clerk's Office a certified copy of the judgment. There is a per page charge for a copy of the judgment and a fee to certify the judgment. Please refer to the Schedule of Fees.

2. The Clerk's Office will prepare a Certification of Judgment for Registration in Another District (form CV-101) and attach it to the certified copy of the judgment. There is a fee to certify form CV-101. Please refer to the Schedule of Fees.

3. Submit the Certification of Judgment for Registration in Another District, the certified copy of the judgment, as well as any required filing fee, to the District Court Clerk's Office in the district where application will be made for writs of execution or abstracts of judgment.

D. ***Preparing Sealed Documents for Filing***

PREPARING SEALED DOCUMENTS FOR FILING

Pursuant to Local Rule 79-5.1 No case or document shall be filed under seal without prior approval by the Court. If a filing under seal is requested, a written application and proposed order shall be presented along with the document for filing under seal. The original and judge's copy of the document shall be sealed in separate envelopes with a copy of the title page attached to the front of each envelope (*see* sample attachment).

Application and Orders to Seal, along with the document to be placed under seal, shall not be electronically filed but shall be filed traditionally in the manner prescribed by Local Rule 79-5. Attorneys filing a document under this provision shall file electronically a Notice of Manual Filing (form G-92).

No case or document shall be filed under seal without prior approval by the Court. If a filing under seal is requested, a written application and proposed order shall be presented along with the document for filing under seal. The original and judge's copy of the document shall be sealed in separate envelopes with a copy of the title page attached to the front of each envelope. *See* sample attachment below.

All filings submitted under seal are to be made in an original and one copy, both blue-backed and two-hole punched, on 28 lined paper. The original shall be placed in a separate envelope with a copy of the title page attached to the front of the envelope designated as "ORIGINAL." The copy shall also be placed in a separate envelope with a copy of the title page attached to the front of the envelope designated as "COPY."

You must provide additional copies if you wish conformed copies. Conformed copies must be placed in separate sealed envelopes. They should not be placed in the envelope containing the original or judge's copy of the document.

If a Notice of Filing/Lodging Under Seal is submitted for filing, the sealed document must be presented in its proper form at the same time the Notice is filed. If the document is being filed under seal pursuant to a prior order of the Court, i.e. continuing protective order, counsel must submit either a copy of the protective order or, under the case number of the title page, type "Filed Under Seal Pursuant To Protective Order Dated _________." Otherwise, the Clerk's Office will not know whether there was a previous order allowing the document to be filed under seal.

To avoid confusion if the judge denies filing under seal, it is helpful to include language in the proposed order for optional dispositions of the underlying application, proposed order and document(s) requested to sealed. For example:

IF DENIED:

The underlying document and the sealing application shall be returned to ________ without filing. Or,

The underlying document and sealing application shall be filed, but not under seal.

<u>Sample Attachment</u>

IN THE UNITED STATES DISTICT COURT
FOR THE CENTRAL DISTRICT OF CALIFORNIA

	)	**(CASE NUMBER)**
Plaintiff(s),	)	**(DOCUMENT TITLE)**
v.	)	
Defendant(s).	)	**<u>FILED UNDER SEAL</u>**
______________________________	)	**(PURSUANT TO PROTECTIVE ORDER DATED ________ if applicable)**

E. Tips on Practice in Federal Court

TIPS ON PRACTICE IN FEDERAL COURT

- Documents may be delayed in reaching the assigned district and/or magistrate judge if the judges' initials on the document are incorrect. For a list of district and magistrate judge initials, see "Judges' Initials" which is located on this website under "Attorney Information" > "Attorney Assistance."
- Read and keep up with changes in the local rules as well as the judge's requirements. Both can be found on the court's website.
- Come to court prepared, and do not send an uninformed associate to handle a proceeding. Judges expect that lawyers appearing before them are prepared and know the case thoroughly. A "simple motion to dismiss" may be converted to a motion for summary judgment at the hearing. A "simple trial setting conference" may turn into a settlement conference.
- Learn from your adversary. If he or she does something that impresses you, adapt it for your own work, especially if the judge or jury seemed to like it.
- Federal court is formal. Your formality shows the court, the jurors, the witnesses, and your client that you respect the seriousness of events.
- Always stand up when you speak in court. Most judges want you to go to the lectern except to make very brief statements, such as objections.
- Address the judge only as "your honor" when addressing the judge in the courtroom. Refer to the judge as "the Court," "his honor," or "her honor" if you need to refer to the judge while addressing a witness or the jury.
- Stop speaking if the judge begins to speak. The court reporter will take down what the judge is saying. Don't worry that you were interrupted; the judge will usually give you an opportunity to finish your thought.
- Listen and respond to what the judge says or otherwise signals, as it may show that the judge needs evidence, argument, or explanation about a point that you thought was clear. Pay attention to the Courtroom Deputy Clerk, who also tries to give signals to assist counsel, such as directing counsel to go to the lectern or staying out of the well.
- Talk in plain language. Avoid cliches such as "For the record, your honor . . ."
- Never evade a judge's question. Answer the question, then explain -- not the reverse.
- Never interrupt the judge.
- Ask permission before entering the well area of the courtroom.
- Never speak directly to your opponent, unless you first get the court's permission to confer. Then confer quietly. The same goes for conferring with witnesses before you put them on the stand. When you speak aloud it should only be to address the judge, to question witnesses on the stand, or to address jurors in *voir dire*, opening statement or closing argument.
- Documents submitted to the court should be proofread by the signator for spelling

errors, for formal compliance with the rules, and for case citation accuracy. Each judge receives several inches, sometimes feet, of papers to read every day. The side that knows how to be clear, direct and concise is the one that may frame the issues in the judge's mind.

- Never resort to snide remarks or name-calling about the opposing counsel or his client, orally or in writing. A snide remark about an opponent in a lawyer's papers reflects more on the writer than the opponent. If the circumstances are such that you must make personal remarks about an opposing counsel, speak very objectively, describing factually what he or she did.

- Direct inquiries that cannot be resolved by reviewing the local rules can be made to the Courtroom Deputy Clerk assigned to the judge. Do not call chambers unless requested or authorized by the Court to do so, as it can be construed as an *ex parte* communication with the Court.

PART II

INDIVIDUAL JUDGES

PROCEDURES AND PRACTICES
STANDING ORDERS
CASE MANAGEMENT ORDERS AND FORMS
SCHEDULING INFORMATION
CHAMBERS AND BIOGRAPHICAL INFORMATION

District Judges

Hon. Percy Anderson

District Judge

<u>**Chambers Information**</u>

U.S. District Court, Central District of California
Courtroom 15, Spring Street Floor
312 N. Spring Street
Los Angeles, CA 90012

<u>**Scheduling Information**</u>

Courtroom Deputy: (213) 894-1795

Civil Law and Motion	Mondays at 1:30 p.m.
Criminal Law and Motion	Mondays at 3:30 p.m.

<u>**Biographical Information**</u>

Born 1948 in Long Beach, CA

Federal Judicial Service:

-Judge, U. S. District Court, Central District of California
-Nominated by George W. Bush on January 23, 2002, to a seat vacated by Kim McLane Wardlaw; Confirmed by the Senate on April 25, 2002, and received commission on May 1, 2002.

Education:

-University of California, Los Angeles, A.B., 1970
-University of California, Los Angeles, School of Law, J.D., 1975

Professional Career:

-Directing Attorney, San Fernando Valley Neighborhood Legal Services, Inc., California, 1975-1978
-Lecturer, University of California, Los Angeles, School of Law, 1977-1978
-Consultant, Legal Services Corporation, California, 1978-1979
-Assistant U.S. Attorney, Central District of California, 1979-1985

I. Judge Anderson's Procedures and Practices

A. *Procedures and Schedules*

1. Civil Motions are heard on **Mondays** at **1:30 p.m.**

   Criminal motions are heard on **Mondays** at **3:30 p.m.**

   (If Monday is a holiday, the next motion date is the following Monday.)

   It is not necessary to clear a motion date with the court clerk prior to filing the motion.

2. Discovery motions are to be calendared before the magistrate judge.

3. Tentative rulings are not issued.

4. Conformed mandatory chambers copies of all motions, opposition and reply papers shall be hand delivered to chambers (Room 163) on Spring Street and placed in a courtesy copy bin located on a wall outside the entry door to chambers.

   Mandatory chambers copies of e-filed documents shall be delivered to chambers.

5. *Ex parte* applications are for extraordinary relief. *See Mission Power Engineering Co. v. Continental Casualty Co., 883 F. Supp. 488 (C.D. Cal. 1995).* Applications must be in accordance with Local Rule 7-19 and any applicable General Order. Ex parte applications are normally considered on the papers and are rarely set for hearing. If a hearing is necessary the parties will be notified. Opposition papers are to be filed no later than 3:00 p.m. on the first business day following service of the application. A conformed mandatory chambers copy of moving, opposition, or notice of non-opposition papers are to be hand-delivered to the courtesy box outside the entrance to chambers on the Spring Street level of the U.S. Courthouse, 312 North Spring Street. Counsel will be notified by the clerk of the Court's ruling. Sanctions may be imposed for misuse of *ex parte* applications.

6. Continuances are granted only upon a showing of good cause. Requests for continuances must be by motion, stipulation or application accompanied by a declaration setting forth the reasons for the requested continuance. The declaration should also include whether there have been any prior requests for continuances and whether these requests were granted or denied by the Court. Stipulations extending dates set by this Court are not effective unless approved by the Court. Requests for continuance should be submitted well in advance of the requested relief. Requests for continuance not in compliance with this Order or the Local Rules of Practice for the Central District of California will be denied.

7. Counsel should not contact the judge's law clerk or secretary unless responding to an inquiry they initiated.

8. Calls will not be returned regarding the status of submitted motions, stipulations or proposed orders. Sufficient copies of any forms of order should be provided for conforming along with a self-addressed, stamped envelope. Counsel may also determine the status of any submitted motion, stipulation or proposed order by accessing the docket sheet through PACER.

9. If counsel have a calendar conflict, they should notify the deputy court clerk as soon as possible.

10. Contact the court clerk if you wish to bring electronic equipment into the courthouse.

11. For general information on how to order a transcript of any reported or digitally recorded proceeding, please contact 213-894-3015 or visit www.cacd.uscourts.gov > General Information > Court Reporter/Recorder Transcripts. If you require an estimate of cost for the preparation of a transcript, contact the court reporter/recorder for the desired proceeding.

To determine the court reporter/recorder for a particular proceeding, go to the Court Reporter Schedule web page and click on View by Date. Once you've determined the correct court reporter/recorder for the desired session, click on Court Reporter Phone and Email List for contact information.

12. Please call (213) 894-5774 if you have questions regarding law clerk or extern positions.

13. Trial Preparation

a. Court hours: Trials are conducted Tuesday through Friday. Trial is from 9:00 a.m. to 5:00 p.m. on the first day of trial and 8:00 a.m. to 1:30 p.m. each day thereafter.

b. Exhibit Lists and Witness Lists: The parties shall file their witness lists and exhibits lists in accordance with Local Rule 16. Counsel are to assemble their exhibits by placing them in three-ring binders labeled on the spine portion of the binder showing both the volume number and the exhibit numbers. Each exhibit shall be separated by a tabbed divider on the right side. Counsel shall provide original exhibits for the Courtroom Deputy Clerk and a duplicate set for the judge. The original exhibits shall be tagged with the appropriate exhibit tags in the upper or lower right corner of the first page of each exhibit. Each binder shall contain a Table of Contents. Counsel must comply with Local Rule 26-4 when numbering the exhibits. The Clerk's Office, Room G-8, 312 North Spring Street, Los Angeles, can supply counsel with appropriate exhibit tags.

The Court requires the following to be submitted to the Courtroom Deputy Clerk on the first day of trial:

1. The original exhibits with the Court's exhibit tags. Plaintiff shall use yellow tags; defendant shall use blue tags. Each tag shall be stapled to the front of the exhibit on the upper right corner and include the case number, case name, and exhibit number.

2. One bench book with a copy of each exhibit for the Court's use, tabbed as described above; a copy of the witness lists).

3. Three (3) copies of exhibit lists.

4. Three (3) copies of witness lists in the order in which the witnesses will be called to testify.

Lead trial counsel are to meet no later than ten (10) calendar days before trial to discuss and agree to the extent possible on issues including foundation, and which exhibits may be received into evidence.

c. Jury Instructions: Fourteen (14) calendar days prior to counsel's Rule 16-2 pre-trial meeting, counsel shall exchange proposed jury instructions(general and special) and special verdict forms (if applicable). Seven (7) calendar days prior to the Rule 16-2 meeting, counsel shall exchange any objections to the instructions and special verdict forms. Prior to, or at the time of the Rule 16-2 meeting, counsel shall meet and confer with the goal of reaching agreement on one set of joint jury instructions and one special verdict form.

The parties shall make every attempt to agree upon the jury instructions before submitting them to the Court. It is expected that counsel will agree on the substantial majority of jury instructions, particularly when pattern instructions provide a statement of applicable law. When the Manual of Model Civil Jury Instructions for the Ninth Circuit provides a version of an applicable requested instruction, the parties should submit the most recent version of the Model instruction, modified as necessary to fit the facts of the case (e.g., inserting names of parties to whom instruction applies). Where language appears in brackets in the model instruction, counsel shall select the appropriate text and eliminate the inapplicable bracketed text. Where California law applies, counsel are directed to use California Jury Instructions -- Civil (8th ed.) (BAJI.) If neither of the above sources is applicable, counsel should use the instructions from O'Malley, Grenig & Lee (formerly Levitt & Blackmar et al), Federal Jury Practice and Instructions (latest edition). Each requested jury instruction shall cover only one subject or principle of law and shall be numbered and set forth in full on a separate page, citing the authority or source of the requested instruction (except for the "clean" jury copy discussed below.)

When the parties disagree on an instruction, the party opposing the instruction must attach a short statement (one to two paragraphs) supporting the objection, and the party submitting the instruction must attach a short statement supporting the instruction. Each statement should be on a separate page and should follow directly after the disputed instruction.

The parties ultimately must submit one document or, if the parties disagree over any proposed jury instructions, two documents. If the parties submit two documents, those documents shall consist of: (1) a set of Joint Proposed Jury Instructions and (2) a set of Disputed Jury Instructions, along with reasons supporting and opposing each disputed instruction in the format set forth in previous paragraph.

The parties must file proposed jury instructions fourteen (14) calendar days before the Pre-trial Conference. If the court is closed that day, counsel shall file the proposed instructions the preceding Friday. No later than 5:00 p.m. on the date such instructions are due, the parties must submit conformed mandatory chambers copies to the Court's courtesy box located outside the entrance to chambers on the Spring Street level of the U.S. Courthouse. Counsel shall also provide the Court with a 3½ inch diskette in WordPerfect format containing the proposed jury instructions, in accordance with this paragraph and the next paragraph.

The Court will send a copy of the instructions into the jury room for the jury's use during deliberations. Accordingly, in addition to the file copies described above, the diskette submitted with the jury instructions shall contain a "clean set" of Joint Proposed and/or Disputed Jury Instructions, containing only the text of each instruction set forth in full on each page, with the caption "Court's Instruction No. __" (eliminating titles, supporting authority, indication of party proposing, etc.).

An index page shall accompany all jury instructions submitted to the Court. The index page shall indicate the following:

a. the number of the instruction;
b. a brief title of the instruction;
c. the source of the instruction and any relevant case citations; and
d. the page number of the instruction.

EXAMPLE:

Number	Title	Source	Page
1	Trademark-Defined (15 U.S.C. § 1127)	9th Cir.15.3.2	7

Along with the jury instructions, counsel shall submit any necessary special verdict form seven (7)calendar days before the Pre-trial Conference.

d. Summary of Expected Testimony: Counsel shall prepare a list of their witnesses, including a brief summary (two to three paragraphs) of each witness's expected testimony and an estimate of the length of time needed for direct examination. Counsel shall exchange these lists with opposing counsel. **Counsel shall jointly file a single list of witness testimony summaries, including estimates for direct examination of their own witnesses and estimates for cross-examination of opposing witnesses.** These statements shall be filed at the time counsel lodge the Proposed Pre-trial Conference Order, i.e., fourteen (14) days before the Pre-trial Conference.

e. Voir Dire: Counsel may, but need not, submit brief proposed voir dire questions for the jury seven (7) calendar days before the Pre-trial Conference. The Court will conduct its own voir dire after consulting any proposed voir dire submitted by counsel.

f. Joint Statement of the Case: Counsel shall prepare a joint statement of the case for the Court to read to the prospective panel of jurors prior to the commencement of voir dire. The statement should not exceed one page. The statement shall be filed with the Court seven (7) calendar days before the Pre-trial Conference.

14. Pursuant to Local Rule 16-14, the parties in every `case must elect a settlement procedure. The final meeting with the parties' settlement officer must take place no later than 45 days before the Pre-trial Conference.

If counsel has received a "Notice to Parties of Alternate Dispute Resolution (ADR) Program" - forms ADR-08, ADR-10, or ADR-11 with an attached "ADR Program Questionnaire" form ADR-09, please see General Order 02-07 which is located in the "General Orders" section on the home page of the Court's website. The Attorney Settlement Officer information is located in the section "Attorney Information, ADR.

II. Judge Anderson's Case Management Orders

A. *Civil Trial Order*

IN THE UNITED STATES DISTICT COURT
FOR THE CENTRAL DISTRICT OF CALIFORNIA

	)	Case No. ________
Plaintiff(s),	)	
v.	)	**CIVIL TRIAL ORDER**
Defendant(s).	)	
____________________	)	

This matter is set for trial before the Honorable Percy Anderson, Courtroom No. 15 (1st Floor, Spring Street level), United States Courthouse, 312 North Spring Street, Los Angeles, California. The Court's procedures and requirements for civil trials are set forth below:

FINAL TRIAL EXHIBIT STIPULATION

1. The parties shall prepare a final Trial Exhibit Stipulation which shall contain each party's numbered list of all trial exhibits, with objections, if any, to each exhibit including the basis of the objection and the offering party's response. All exhibits to which there is no objection shall be deemed admitted. All parties shall stipulate to the authenticity of exhibits whenever possible, and the final Trial Exhibit Stipulation shall identify any exhibits whose authenticity has not been stipulated to and the specific reasons for the party's failure to stipulate.

The Stipulation shall be substantially in the following form:

Trial Exhibit Stipulation

Plaintiff(s)' Exhibits

Number	Description	If Objection, State Grounds	Response to Objection

Defendant(s)' Exhibits

Number	Description	If Objection, State Grounds	Response to Objection

The final Trial Exhibit Stipulation shall be filed five days before trial. Failure to comply with this paragraph shall constitute a waiver of all objections.

MOTIONS *IN LIMINE*

1. Motions *in limine* are not to be used as disguised motions for summary judgment. Their purpose is limited to alerting the Court to significant evidentiary issues that can be addressed and resolved prior to trial.

2. Before filing any motion *in limine*, Counsel are to meet and confer regarding the potential evidentiary dispute, and the Court is to be advised in the motion that such meeting has occurred. If either party refuses to participate in the meet and confer process, the Court will impose sanctions including a resolution of the issue against the party refusing to cooperate.

THE COMMENCEMENT OF THE TRIAL

1. Counsel shall arrive in the Courtroom at 8:30 a.m. on the first day of trial for the purpose of handling logistical and administrative matters pertaining to the trial, including the submission of exhibits as discussed below.

2. Counsel shall present the Courtroom Deputy with the following documents on the first day of trial:

(a) All of the original exhibits, with official exhibit tags attached in the lower or upper right hand corner of the first page of each exhibit and bearing the same number shown on the exhibit list. Counsel shall assemble their Exhibits by placing them in 3-ring binders with each Exhibit separated by a tab divider on the right side. These exhibits shall be numbered in accordance with Local Rules 16-5 and 26-4. Each binder shall contain a Table of Contents.

(b) One bench book with a copy of each exhibit for the Court's use, tabbed as described above.

(c) In addition to the exhibit binders, Counsel shall bring with them to the first day of trial three (3) copies of their exhibit list; three (3) copies of their final witness list in the order in which the witnesses will be called to testify and (3) copies of the Joint Trial Witness Time Estimate Form. A copy of the exhibit list with all admitted exhibits will be given to the jury during deliberations. Counsel shall review and approve the exhibit list with the Courtroom Deputy before it is given to the jury.

(d) Not later than ten (10) calendar days before trial, all counsel shall meet to stipulate to the extent possible to foundation, and which exhibits may be received into evidence at the start of trial. Counsel shall note the exhibits to be received into evidence on the exhibit list.

3. If Counsel need to arrange for the installation of their own additional equipment, such as video monitors, overhead projectors, etc., notify the Courtroom Deputy no later than 4:30 p.m. the Thursday BEFORE trial so that the necessary arrangements can be made.

4. Trials are conducted Tuesday through Friday from 8:00 a.m. to 1:30 p.m., with two fifteen (15) minute breaks.

5. Counsel in advance of trial, or at least before the witness testifies, is to notify the clerk – preferably in writing – what exhibits the witness will be asked to testify about. The clerk then places those exhibits before the witness at the beginning of that witness' testimony, each clearly labeled.

6. Before trial commences, the Court will give Counsel an opportunity to discuss administrative matters and anticipated procedural or legal issues. On the first day of trial, this will include a final discussion of voir dire questions and the content of the joint statement. During the trial, the court will not hold bench or chambers conferences, it is the intention of the court that trial testimony will be presented without interruption for five or six hours each day, and all legal issues of importance must be raised in advance of trial by written noticed motions. If there are any matters Counsel wish to discuss, inform the Courtroom Deputy and the matter can be heard at the next recess or the next day.

WITNESSES

1. The parties are to exchange final witness lists in the order in which the witnesses will be called to testify together with a final joint trial witness time estimate form five (5) days prior to trial. Courtesy copies of the final witness lists and final joint trial witness estimate form shall be delivered to the courtesy box on the wall outside the entrance to chambers on the Spring Street level of the U.S. Courthouse, 312 North Spring Street, by 4:00 p.m. on the date due.

2. Plaintiff must advise defendant, no later than noon on the Friday before the commencement of trial, the names of the witnesses in the order in which they will be called to testify on the first Tuesday and Wednesday of trial. Failure to adhere to this provision of the

Court's order may result in the Court precluding the witness from testifying at trial.

TIME LIMITS

1. The Court will, in every case, impose time limits on the amount of time each side will have for opening statement, witness examination and closing argument.

COURT TRIALS

The Court orders that counsel comply with the following in their preparation for trial.

1. All counsel are to be completely familiar with the Federal Rules of Civil Procedure and the Local Rules of this Court.

2. All counsel are to prepare proposed findings of fact and conclusions of law (the original and one copy are to be lodged with the Court and three copies are to be served on opposing counsel). These findings of fact and conclusions of law are to be lodged with the court and served on or before twenty-one (21) days prior to trial. Upon receiving these proposed findings of fact and conclusions of law from opposing counsel, each party shall:

(A) Underline with red pencil those portions which it disputes.

(B) Underline with blue pencil those portions which it admits.

(C) Underline with yellow pencil those portions which it does not dispute but deems irrelevant.

3. In this connection, counsel are to note that they ***need not come to a uniform conclusion*** as to the entire proposed finding or, indeed, an entire sentence within a proposed finding. They may agree with part of it, disagree with part of it and/or consider a portion of it irrelevant.

4. Upon completion of the foregoing, each counsel shall file two (2) marked copies of opposing counsel's proposed findings of fact and conclusions of law with the court and return one marked copy to opposing counsel no later than seven (7) days prior to trial.

5. The parties shall be prepared to submit to the court, and to exchange among themselves, supplemental findings of fact and conclusions of law during the course of the trial, with respect to which the same underlining procedure may be ordered.

6. Counsel in non-jury trials shall submit the direct testimony of their witnesses in writing in a declaration executed under penalty of perjury. These declarations shall be in admissible form with appropriate foundation established for the declarant's statements. Paragraphs in each declaration shall be numbered consecutively to facilitate the identification of paragraphs for evidentiary objections.

7. Counsel are to exchange and file these declarations with the Court at least ten calendar days before trial, unless otherwise ordered by the Court. Five calendar days before trial, Counsel may file a separate document stating any evidentiary objections to those declarations. Courtesy copies of the evidentiary objections shall be delivered to the courtesy box on the wall outside the entrance to chambers on the Spring Street level of the U.S. Courthouse, 312 North Spring Street, by 4:00 p.m. on the date due.

8. At trial, the Court will rule on the evidentiary objections and, depending upon the ruling, the declarations will be received in evidence, either in whole or in part, or rejected. Counsel will then conduct the cross-examination and re-direct examination at trial. This order does not apply to rebuttal witnesses.

9. Failure to comply with the literal terms of this Order will result in sanctions or the

Court may refuse to allow that witness to testify.

VOIR DIRE AND JURY SELECTION

1. The Court will conduct *voir dire* after conferring with Counsel regarding potential areas of questioning. A portion of the *voir dire* may be based on written questions given to the jurors when they arrive at Court.

2. In most cases, the Court will conduct its initial *voir dire* of 14 prospective jurors who will be seated in the jury box. Normally the Court selects a jury of eight.

3. Except in an unusual case, each side will have three peremptory challenges. Therefore, if 14 jurors are in the box and all six peremptories are exercised, the remaining eight jurors will constitute the jury panel. If fewer than six peremptories are exercised, the eight low-numbered jurors (by seat number in the jury box) will constitute the jury panel.

INSTRUCTIONS GOVERNING PROCEDURE DURING TRIAL

1. Counsel are expected to cooperate with each other during trial to insure the efficient and expeditious use of court and juror time.

2. Counsel shall not refer to their clients or any witness over 14 years of age by their first names during trial.

3. Do not discuss the law or argue the case in opening statements.

4. Do not use objections for purposes of making a speech, recapitulating testimony, or attempting to guide the witness. When objecting, state only that you are objecting and the specific legal ground of the objection, *e.g.*, hearsay, irrelevant, etc. The court will not hear arguments on ordinary evidentiary issues. Most unusual or complex evidentiary issues can be foreseen and disposed of in advance; those that cannot ordinarily will be disposed of at the next recess, with the witness retained until the issue is resolved.

5. Counsel should not paraphrase the witness' answer into a new question which asks the same thing. For example:

   (a) Do I understand you to mean that . . .
   (b) Is it your testimony then that . . .
   (c) Is it fair to say that . . .
   (d) Can we assume then that . . .
   (e) So that I am clear . . .

There is no need to hear the testimony of the witness two or three times. In addition having been asked and answered, often these questions are argumentative.

6. Counsel are to have their witnesses review all exhibits about which they will be questioned.

7. In multi-party cases, Counsel are expected to coordinate their cross-examination. The Court will not permit each party's counsel to repeat previous cross-examination questions.

8. Do not allow witnesses either to draw diagrams or put markings on exhibits while the jury is in the box. Diagrams or exhibits should be drawn or marked by the witness before getting to the stand. The witness may then adopt the diagrams and markings and tell the jury what they represent.

9. Do not approach the Courtroom Deputy or the witness box without the Court's permission. Please return to the lectern when your purpose has been accomplished. Do not enter the well of the Court without the Court's permission.

10. Please rise when addressing the Court, and when the jury enters or leaves the courtroom.

11. Address all remarks to the Court. Do not directly address the Courtroom Deputy, the reporter or opposing counsel. If you wish to speak with opposing counsel, ask permission to talk to counsel off the record. All requests to re-read questions or answers, or to have an exhibit placed in front of a witness, shall be addressed to the Court.

12. Although the Court encourages the parties to stipulate to facts that are not reasonably in dispute, do not offer a stipulation unless you have previously conferred with opposing counsel and reached an agreement.

13. All depositions to be used in the trial, either as evidence or for impeachment, must be signed and lodged with the Courtroom Deputy on the first day of trial or such earlier date as the Court may order. If deposition transcripts available on diskette or (C.D. CAL., they should be lodged with the hard copy.

14. Whenever Counsel expects to offer a group of answers to interrogatories or requests for admissions, extracted from one or more lengthy documents, Counsel shall prepare a new document listing each question and answer and identifying the document from which it was extracted. Copies of this new document should be given to the Court and opposing counsel.

15. While court is in session, do not leave the counsel table to confer with investigators, secretaries, or witnesses unless permission is granted in advance.

16. When a party has more than one lawyer, only one may conduct the examination of a given witness and only that lawyer may handle objections during the testimony of that witness.

17. If a witness was on the stand at a recess or adjournment, have the witness back on the stand and ready to proceed when court resumes.

18. Do not run out of witnesses. If you are out of witnesses and there is more than a brief delay, the Court may deem that you have rested.

19. Counsel are advised to be on time as the Court starts promptly.

POST TRIAL EXHIBIT LIST

1. At or before the conclusion of the evidence, counsel of reach party shall submit a "clean" list of only those exhibits offered by such party that have been admitted into evidence. Such lists shall be in a form suitable for submission to the jury and shall set forth the following information with respect to each exhibit to the extent applicable:

(A) Exhibit Number

(B) Date

(C) A brief description of the exhibit that will enable jurors to identify it but which does not characterize the exhibits or its contents (*e.g.*, letter from A to B, photograph of 100 Main Street).

IT IS SO ORDERED.

DATED: ___________________

PERCY ANDERSON
United States District Judge

B. Order Regarding Criminal Trial

IN THE UNITED STATES DISTICT COURT
FOR THE CENTRAL DISTRICT OF CALIFORNIA

UNITED STATES OF AMERICA, Plaintiff, v. Defendant(s). ______________________	)))))	Case No. ____________ **ORDER RE CRIMINAL TRIAL**

The above matter is set for trial before the Honorable Percy Anderson, Courtroom No. 15, United States Courthouse.

PRE-TRIAL AND TRIAL DATES

1. Pretrial motions, including motions *in limine*, shall be filed on: ______________.
Oppositions shall be filed on: ____________________.
Replies (optional) shall be filed on: ________________.
Status Conference/Hearing is set for: ____________ at 3:00 p.m.
Trial is set for Tuesday at 9:00 A.M. on: ___________________.

2. As of January 1, 2007, the United States District Court for the Central District of California has implemented the mandatory electronic filing of documents in all new and pending criminal cases. Information about the Court's Electronic Case Filing system ("ECF") is available on the Court's website at www.cacd.uscourts.gov/cmecf.

The electronic filing of all documents required to be filed electronically in this matter shall be completed by 4:00 p.m. on the date due. Documents filed electronically after 4:00 p.m. on the date due will be considered untimely and may result in the striking of the document and the imposition of other sanctions.

All manually filed documents (those documents excused from the electronic filing requirements by General Order 06-07, section VII) shall be served personally on opposing counsel or faxed to opposing counsel no later than 4:30 p.m. on the day of filing.

3. Counsel are ORDERED to serve courtesy copies of all electronically filed documents, and conformed courtesy copies of manually filed documents, to Chambers at the United States Courthouse, 312 North Spring Street, Courtroom 15, Los Angeles, California 90012 by 5:00 p.m. on the day of filing.

4. Counsel are ORDERED to list their facsimile transmission numbers along with their address and telephone numbers on all papers submitted to the Court in order to facilitate communication by the Court.

DISCOVERY & NOTICE

5. Counsel for the government and counsel for defendant shall comply promptly with discovery and notice pursuant to Fed. R. Crim. P. 12, 12.1, 12.2, 12.3, 15, and 16. Upon government counsel's discovery of any evidence within the scope of *Brady v. Maryland*, 373 U.S. 83 (1963), such evidence shall be produced forthwith to counsel for the defendant. Counsel for the government shall also disclose to counsel for defendant the existence or non-existence of: (1) evidence obtained by electronic surveillance; and (2) testimony by a government informer.

APPLICATIONS AND STIPULATIONS TO EXTEND TIME

1. Applications to extend the time to file any required document or to continue any hearing, status conference or trial date must set forth the following:

(a) the existing due date or hearing date, as well as the status conference and the trial date;

(b) specific, concrete reasons supporting good cause for granting the extension; and

(c) whether there have been prior requests for extensions, and whether those requests were granted or denied by the Court.

MOTIONS *IN LIMINE*

1. Before filing any motion *in limine*, counsel for the parties shall confer in a good faith effort to eliminate the necessity for hearing the motion *in limine* or to eliminate as many of the disputes as possible. It shall be the responsibility of counsel for the moving party to arrange for this conference. The conference shall take place in person within five calendar days of service upon opposing counsel of a letter requesting such conference. Unless counsel agree otherwise, the conference shall take place at the office of the counsel for the government. If both counsel are not located in the same county in the Central District, the conference may take place by telephone. The moving party's letter shall identify the testimony, exhibits, or other specific matters alleged to be inadmissible and/or prejudicial, shall state briefly with respect to each such matter the moving party's position (and provide any legal authority which the moving party believes is dispositive), and specify the terms of the order to be sought.

2. If counsel are unable to resolve their differences, they shall prepare a Joint Motion *in Limine*. The Joint Motion *in Limine* shall consist of one document signed by all counsel. The Joint Motion *in Limine* shall contain a clear identification of the testimony, exhibits, or other specific matters alleged to be inadmissible and/or prejudicial and a statement of the specific prejudice that will be suffered by the moving party if the motion is not granted. The identification of the matters in dispute shall be followed by each party's contentions and each party's memorandum of points and authorities. The title page of the Joint Motion *in Limine* must state the hearing date for the motions *in limine* and the trial date.

3. Joint Motions *in Limine* made for the purpose of precluding the mention or display of inadmissible and/or prejudicial matter in the presence of the jury shall be accompanied by a declaration from the moving party that includes the following: (a) a clear identification of the specific matter alleged to be inadmissible and/or prejudicial; (b) a representation to the Court that the subject of the motion *in limine* has been discussed with opposing counsel, and that opposing counsel has either indicated that such matter will be mentioned or displayed in the presence of the jury before it is admitted in evidence or that counsel has refused to stipulate that such matter will not be mentioned or displayed in the presence of the jury unless and until it is admitted in evidence; and (c) a statement of the specific prejudice that will be suffered by the moving party if the motion *in limine* is not granted.

4. Unless ordered by the Court, no supplemental or separate memorandum of points and authorities shall be filed by either party in connection with any motion *in limine*.

5. The Court will not consider any motion *in limine* in the absence of a joint motion or a declaration from counsel for the moving party establishing that opposing counsel: (a) failed to confer in a timely manner; (b) failed to provide the opposing party's portion of the joint motion in a timely manner; or (c) refused to sign and return the joint motion after the opposing party's portion was added.

6. Unless otherwise ordered by the Court, motions *in limine* will be heard at the Final Status Conference. Unless the Court in its discretion otherwise allows, no motions *in limine* shall be filed or heard on an *ex parte* basis, absent a showing of irreparable injury or prejudice

not attributable to the lack of diligence of the moving party.

7. The failure of any counsel to comply with or cooperate in the foregoing procedures will result in the imposition of sanctions, including a resolution of the issue against the party refusing to cooperate.

TRIAL

1. Counsel for the government shall file with the Court in camera (under seal) all statements of all witnesses to be called by the government in its case-in-chief. Such statements shall be filed at least five (5) calendar days before trial.

2. Counsel shall arrive at the Courtroom promptly on the first day of trial.

3. Counsel for the government shall present the Courtroom Deputy with the following documents on the first day of trial:

(a) THREE copies of the government's witness list.

(b) THREE copies of the government's exhibit list in the form specified in Local Rule 9.9 (Civil).

(c) ALL of the government's exhibits, with official exhibit tags attached and bearing the same number shown on the exhibit list. Defendant's counsel does not have to deliver his or her exhibits to the Courtroom Deputy on the first day of trial; however, Defendant's counsel is responsible for affixing completed exhibit tags with the case name and case number to his or her exhibits which are intended to be used in the defendant's case. Exhibit tags can be obtained from the receptionist in the main Clerk's Office, located at 312 North Spring Street, Room G-8. Exhibits shall be numbered 1, 2, 3, 4, *etc.*, NOT 1.1, 1.50 *etc.* If a blow up is an enlargement of an existing exhibit, it shall be designated with the number of the original exhibit followed by an "A." Counsel for the government should be aware that the Court will order that exhibits such as firearms, narcotics, etc., remain in the custody of the agents during the pendency of the trial. The agent will be required to sign the appropriate form in order to take custody of such exhibits. It shall be the responsibility of the agents to produce said items for court, secure them at night and guard them at all times while in the courtroom.

(d) A bench book containing a copy of all exhibits that can be reproduced. Each exhibit shall be tabbed with the exhibit number for easy referral. Defendant's counsel shall provide the Court with a copy of their exhibits as they are introduced during trial.

(e) A floppy disk containing the exhibit list. A copy of the exhibit list with all admitted exhibits will be given to the jury during deliberations. Government and defense counsel shall review and approve the exhibit list with the Courtroom Deputy prior to it being given to the jury.

9. If counsel need to arrange for the installation of their own additional equipment, such as video monitors, overhead projectors, etc., notify the Courtroom Deputy no later than 4:30 p.m. two days BEFORE trial so that the necessary arrangements can be made.

10. Trials commence on Tuesday at 8:30 a.m. Trials are conducted Tuesday through Friday from 8:00 a.m. to 1:30 p.m., with two fifteen (15) minute breaks normally at 10:00 a.m. and 12:00 p.m.

11. The Court reserves the time from 7:30 a.m. to 8:00 a.m. to handle legal and administrative matters outside of the presence of the jury. The trial before the jury will commence promptly at 8:00 a.m. Counsel is urged to anticipate matters which may need discussion or hearing outside of the presence of the jury and to raise them during this period, during breaks or at the end of the day.

JURY INSTRUCTIONS & VERDICT FORMS

1. Jury instructions in the form described below are to be submitted not later than the Wednesday of the week prior to trial. The parties must submit JOINT jury instructions, a JOINT proposed verdict form and, if necessary, special interrogatories. The parties shall meet and confer sufficiently in advance of the required filing date with the objective of submitting one set of agreed upon instructions, verdict form and, if necessary, special interrogatories. The parties shall submit a copy of these filings to the Court by e-mailing them to pa_chambers@cacd.uscourts.gov in the manner provided for by General Order 06-07, section VIII, for proposed orders, proposed judgments, and other proposed documents requiring a judge's signature.

2. If the parties cannot agree upon one complete set of instructions, verdict form and/or special interrogatories, they shall file two documents with the Court: a joint document reflecting the agreed upon instructions, verdict form and/or special interrogatories; and a second document in the form of a joint statement regarding the disputed instructions, verdict form, and/or special interrogatories in the following format for each instruction, verdict form and/or special interrogatories in issue:

(a) A separate page containing the text of the disputed language with an identification of the party proposing it;

(b) Following the text of the disputed language, the opposing party's statement of objections to the disputed language along with legal authority in support of the argument (not to exceed one page) and proposed alternative language where appropriate; and

(c) The proposing party's response to the objection with legal authority supporting the proposed language, not to exceed one page. Both the agreed on set, and the joint statement re: disputed instructions, verdict form, and/or special interrogatories shall be filed at least five calendar days before the trial.

3. All proposed jury instructions shall be in the format specified by Local Rule 51-2 (civil). The Court will send a copy of the instructions into the jury room for the jury's use during deliberations. Accordingly, in addition to the file copies described above, the diskette submitted with the jury instructions shall contain a "clean set" of Joint Proposed and/or Disputed Jury Instructions, containing only the text of each instruction set forth in full on each page, with the caption "Court's Instruction No. ___" (eliminating titles, supporting authority, indication of party proposing, etc.).

4. A Table of Contents shall be included with all jury instructions submitted to the Court. The Table of Contents shall set forth the following:

(a) The number of the instruction;
(b) A brief title of the instruction;
(c) The source of the instruction; and
(d) The page number of the instruction.

EXAMPLE:

Number	Title	Source	Page Number
1	Duty of the Jury	9th Cir. 1.01	1

5. Each requested jury instruction shall be numbered and set forth in full on a separate page, citing the authority or source of the requested instruction.

6. The Court prefers counsel to use the instructions from the Manual of Model Criminal

Jury Instructions for the Ninth Circuit (West Publishing, current edition). Another suggested source is Federal Jury Practice and Instructions, Devitt, Blackmar, Wolff and O'Malley (West Publishing, current edition).

7. Modifications of instructions from the foregoing sources (or any other form instructions) must specifically state the modification made to the original form instruction and the authority supporting the modification.

INSTRUCTIONS GOVERNING PROCEDURE DURING TRIAL

1. Counsel are expected to cooperate with each other during trial to insure the efficient and expeditious use of court and juror time.

2. Counsel shall not refer to their clients or any witness over 14 years of age by their first names during trial.

3. Do not discuss the law or argue the case in opening statements.

4. Do not use objections for purposes of making a speech, recapitulating testimony, or attempting to guide the witness. When objecting, state only that you are objecting and the specific legal ground of the objection, *e.g.*, hearsay, irrelevant, etc. The court will not hear arguments on ordinary evidentiary issues. Most unusual or complex evidentiary issues can be foreseen and disposed of in advance; those that cannot ordinarily will be disposed of at the next recess, with the witness retained until the issue is resolved. During the trial, the court will not hold bench or chambers conferences, it is the intention of the court that trial testimony will be presented without interruption for five or six hours each day, and all legal issues of importance must be raised in advance of trial by written noticed motions. If there are any matters Counsel wish to discuss, inform the Courtroom Deputy and the matter can be heard at the next recess or the next day.

5. Counsel should not paraphrase the witness' answer into a new question which asks the same thing. For example:

(a) Do I understand you to mean that . . .
(b) Is it your testimony then that . . .
(c) Is it fair to say that . . .
(d) Can we assume then that . . .
(e) So that I am clear . . .

There is no need to hear the testimony of the witness two or three times. In addition having been asked and answered, often these questions are argumentative.

6. Counsel are to have their witnesses review all exhibits about which they will be questioned.

7. In multi-party cases, Counsel are expected to coordinate their cross-examination. The Court will not permit each party's counsel to repeat previous cross-examination questions.

8. Do not allow witnesses either to draw diagrams or put markings on exhibits while the jury is in the box. Diagrams or exhibits should be drawn or marked by the witness before getting to the stand. The witness may then adopt the diagrams and markings and tell the jury what they represent.

9. Do not approach the Courtroom Deputy or the witness box without the Court's permission. Please return to the lectern when your purpose has been accomplished. Do not enter the well of the Court without the Court's permission.

10. Please rise when addressing the Court, and when the jury enters or leaves the courtroom.

11. Address all remarks to the Court. Do not directly address the Courtroom Deputy, the reporter or opposing counsel. If you wish to speak with opposing counsel, ask permission to talk to counsel off the record. All requests to re-read questions or answers, or to have an exhibit placed in front of a witness, shall be addressed to the Court.

12. While court is in session, do not leave the counsel table to confer with investigators, secretaries, or witnesses unless permission is granted in advance.

13. When a party has more than one lawyer, only one may conduct the examination of a given witness and only that lawyer may handle objections during the testimony of that witness.

14. If a witness was on the stand at a recess or adjournment, have the witness back on the stand and ready to proceed when court resumes.

15. Do not run out of witnesses. If you are out of witnesses and there is more than a brief delay, the Court may deem that you have rested.

16. Counsel are advised to be on time as the Court starts promptly.

17. Do not make an offer of stipulation unless you have conferred with opposing counsel and reached an agreement. Any stipulation of fact will require the defendant's personal concurrence and shall be submitted to the Court in writing for approval. A proposed stipulation should be explained to the defendant in advance.

18. Counsel should not by facial expression, nodding, or other conduct exhibit any opinion, adverse or favorable, concerning any testimony being given by a witness. Counsel must admonish counsel's own clients and witnesses to avoid such conduct.

19. Counsel are admonished to not state in summation, "I am reading from the reporter's transcript." Counsel may, however, refer to "notes" [which may include a partial transcript] and proceed to deliver the recounted in a "question and answer" format. Counsel are not to suggest to the jury that they may request rereading of testimony. That subject will be covered with the jury in the jury charge as follows:

> Re-reading of testimony is possible, but I must review all of what is to be re-read – *there is no transcript made up.* And, even if there were, I would have to have it re-read due to objections, side-bars, and other proceedings outside the jury's presence. Moreover, I or the attorneys might feel that other matters should be included in the same read-back. Preparing for a re-read of testimony takes time. Please understand that, so that if a request is made, we will gladly arrange to do so, but the jury should keep deliberating until we are able to make sure that we have everything ready.

Dated: ____________________

____
PERCY ANDERSON
United States District Judge

C. *Order Setting Scheduling Conference*

IN THE UNITED STATES DISTICT COURT
FOR THE CENTRAL DISTRICT OF CALIFORNIA

Plaintiff(s),	Case No. _______________
v.	**SCHEDULING MEETING OF COUNSEL**
Defendant(s).	[FRCP 16, 26(f)] SCHEDULING CONFERENCE set for ____________, at 10:30 a.m. [FRCP 26(f)]

This action has been assigned to the calendar of United States District Judge Percy Anderson. The responsibility for the progress of litigation in the federal courts falls not only upon the attorneys in the action, but upon the court as well.

In order "to secure the just, speedy, and inexpensive determination of every action," (Fed. R. Civ. P. 1), all counsel are hereby ordered to familiarize themselves with the Federal Rules of Civil Procedure and the Local Rules of the Central District of California.

Counsel please note the changes made to former Local Rule 6, now superseded, by Fed. R. Civ. P. 16 and 26(f), effective December 1, 2000. A Scheduling Conference is set for the date and time set forth in the caption.[1] Counsel shall meet at least twenty-one (21) days in advance of the Scheduling Conference to prepare a jointly signed report for the court to be submitted no less than fourteen (14) days before the Scheduling Conference. The report is to contain the items set forth below. Pursuant to Fed. R. Civ. P. 16(c), the parties shall be represented by counsel with authority to enter into stipulations regarding all matters pertaining to conduct of the case.

The joint report to be submitted shall contain the items listed in Fed. R. Civ. P. 26(f), the parties' recommendations and agreements, if any, about the final scheduling order as listed in Fed. R. Civ. P. 16(b)(1) through (6), and those items listed in Fed. R. Civ. P. 16(c) which counsel believe will be useful to discuss at the Scheduling Conference. Items which must be listed are the following:

(1) a listing and proposed schedule of written discovery, depositions, and a proposed discovery cut-off date;

(2) a listing and proposed schedule of law and motion matters, and a proposed dispositive motion cut-off date;

(3) a statement of what efforts have been made to settle or resolve the case to date and what settlement procedure is recommended pursuant to Local Rule 16-14.4 (specifically excluding any

---

[1] Unless there is a likelihood that upon motion by a party the Court would order that any or all discovery is premature, it is advisable for counsel to begin to conduct discovery actively before the Scheduling Conference required by Fed. R. Civ. P. 16(b). At the very least, the parties shall comply fully with the letter and spirit of Fed. R. Civ. P. 26(a) and thereby obtain and produce most of what would be produced in the early stage of discovery, because at the Scheduling Conference the Court will impose tight deadlines to complete discovery.

statement of the terms discussed);

(4) an estimated length of trial and a proposed date for the Final Pretrial Conference and for Trial;

(5) a discussion of other parties likely to be added;

(6) whether trial will be by jury or to the court;

(7) any other issues affecting the status or management of the case; and

(8) proposals regarding severance, bifurcation or other ordering of proof.

In addition, the Scheduling Conference Report shall contain the following:

(1) a short synopsis of the principal issues in the case;

(2) a statement of whether pleadings are likely to be amended;

(3) a statement as to issues which any party believes may be determined by motion.

At the Scheduling Conference, the court will set a date for discovery cut-off,[2] a final date by which dispositive motions must be set for hearing, a Final Pretrial Conference date, and a trial date. The parties should also be aware that pursuant to Fed. R. Civ. P. 26(f), no later than fourteen (14) days after the Scheduling Conference, the parties must submit an agreed discovery plan to the court for approval; this subject will be discussed at the Scheduling Conference. The parties should recommend to the court whether or not the requirement of a discovery plan should be waived.

A continuance of the Scheduling Conference will be granted only for good cause. (Counsel are informed that continuance of the Scheduling Conference causes commensurate delay in the trial date.) **The failure to submit a joint report in advance of the Scheduling Conference or the failure to attend the Scheduling Conference may result in the dismissal of the action, striking the answer and entering a default, and/or the imposition of sanctions.**

A settlement procedure appropriate to the particular case will be used in every civil action pursuant to Local Rule 16-15.1. In the Scheduling Conference Report, counsel are to recommend a specific settlement procedure provided for in Local Rule 16-15 which will be utilized in this case. This Court participates in the Alternative Dispute Resolution Pilot Program. See General Order 02-07. Accordingly, except in extraordinary circumstances, the Court will not refer the parties to the Magistrate Judge assigned to this action to conduct the settlement conference. As a result, in most instances, the available alternatives for consideration are:

Settlement Procedure No. 2:

The parties shall appear before an attorney selected from the Attorney Settlement Officer Panel (Local Rule 16-15.4(2); or

---

2 This is not the date by which discovery requests must be served; but the date by which all discovery is to be completed. Any motion challenging the adequacy of discovery responses must be filed timely, served and calendared sufficiently in advance of the discovery cutoff date to permit the responses to be obtained before that date, if the motion is granted. The Court requires compliance with Local Rule 37-1 and 37-2 in the preparation and filing of discovery motions. Except in the case of an extreme emergency which was not created by the lawyer bringing the motion, discovery motions may not be heard on an *ex parte* basis.

Settlement Procedure No. 3:

> The parties shall participate in a non-judicial dispute resolution proceeding (Local Rule 16-15.4(3).

The Court does not utilize Settlement Procedure No. 1 (Local Rule 16-15.4(1), but the parties are free to seek the Court's approval to engage in an alternative settlement mechanism not listed in Local Rule 16-15.4.

The report to the Court as to the above items should be preceded by a thorough and frank discussion among the attorneys for the parties. A Joint Scheduling Report which does not comply with FRCP 16, 26(f) and this Order may cause continuance of the Scheduling Conference and possible award of sanctions under FRCP 16(f) against the party or parties responsible. A courtesy copy of the Joint Report shall be delivered to the courtesy box next to the entrance to chambers on the Spring Street level of the U.S. Courthouse, 312 North Spring Street, by 12:00 noon of the business day following filing.

Motions shall be filed in accordance with Local Rule 7; the next available motion date can be obtained from the Filing Window.[3] This Court hears motions on **Mondays, commencing at 1:30 p.m. No supplemental brief shall be filed without prior leave of Court.** Courtesy copies of **opposition and reply papers** shall be delivered to the courtesy box next to the entrance to chambers on the Spring Street level of the U.S. Courthouse, 312 North Spring Street, by 12:00 noon of the business day following filing. Adherence to the timing requirements is mandatory for chambers' preparation of motion matters.

Counsel should take note of the changes to the Local Rules affecting motion practice in the Central District. Among other things, Local Rule 7-3 requires counsel to engage in a pre-filing conference "to discuss thoroughly . . . the substance of the contemplated motion and any potential resolution." Counsel should discuss the issues sufficiently that if a motion is still necessary, the briefing may be directed to those substantive issues requiring resolution by the Court. Counsel should resolve minor procedural or other nonsubstantive matters during the conference.

Memoranda of Points and Authorities in support of or in opposition to motions shall not exceed 25 pages. Replies shall not exceed 12 pages. Only in rare instances and for good cause shown will the Court grant an application to extend these page limitations. **Typeface shall comply with Local Rule 11-3.1.1. <u>NOTE:</u> If Times Roman font is used, the size must be no less than 14; if Courier is used, the size must be no less than 12.** Footnotes shall be in typeface no more than one size smaller than text size and shall be used sparingly. Filings which do not conform to the Local Rules and this Order will not be considered.

Counsel shall deliver a courtesy copy of all **opposition and reply papers** in motion matters to the courtesy box next to the entrance to chambers on the Spring Street level of the U.S. Courthouse, 312 North Spring Street, by 12:00 noon of the business day following filing.

Each party filing or opposing a motion or seeking the determination of any matter shall file a Proposed Order setting forth the relief or action sought and a brief statement of the rationale for the decision with appropriate citations. If the Proposed Order exceeds two pages, the proposing party shall also submit a copy of the Proposed Order to the Court's ECF e-mail address, in WordPerfect format (X3 or earlier versions) or Microsoft Word (Word 2003

---

[3] All law and motion matters, except for motions *in limine*, must be set for hearing (not filing) by the motion cutoff date.

or earlier versions).

Counsel are reminded *ex parte* applications are solely for extraordinary relief. *See Mission Power Engineering Co. v. Continental Casualty Co.*, 883 F. Supp. 488 (C.D. Cal. 1995).

Counsel for plaintiff shall immediately serve this Order on all parties, including any new parties to the action.

IT IS SO ORDERED.

Date: ______________________

____
PERCY ANDERSON
United States District Judge

D. *Scheduling Order*

IN THE UNITED STATES DISTICT COURT
FOR THE CENTRAL DISTRICT OF CALIFORNIA

)	Case No. _______________
Plaintiff(s),)	
v.)	**SCHEDULING ORDER [FED. R. CIV. P. 16(b)]**
Defendant(s).)	
___________________________________)	

1. Establishing a Discovery Cut-off Date of _______.
2. Setting Motion Cutoff date of _______.
3. Setting Final Pretrial Conference for _______ at 1:30 p.m.
4. Setting Jury/Court Trial Date of at _______ 9:00 a.m.

1. **Discovery Cut-Off.** This is the last date to complete discovery, including expert discovery, and the resolution of any discovery motions before the magistrate judge. If expert witnesses are to be called at trial, the parties shall designate experts to be called at trial and provide reports required by Fed. R. Civ. P. 26(a)(2)(B), not later than eight weeks prior to the discovery cutoff date. Rebuttal expert witnesses shall be designated and reports provided as required by Fed. R. Civ. P. 26(a)(2)(B), not later than five weeks prior to the discovery cutoff date. Failure to timely comply with this deadline may result in the expert being excluded at trial as a witness. The Court requires compliance with Local Rule 37-1 and 37-2 in the preparation and filing of discovery motions. Discovery motions may not be heard on an *ex parte* basis.

2. **Joinder of Parties and Amendment of Pleadings.** The deadline for joining parties and amending pleadings is ninety (90) days after the date of this Order. Any motions to join other parties or for leave to amend the pleadings shall be filed within sixty (60) days of the date of this Order so that they can be heard and decided prior to the deadline. This deadline does not apply if the deadline for joining parties or amending pleadings has already been calendared or occurred by virtue of an order issued by another Judge.

In addition to the requirements of Local Rule 15-1, all motions to amend the pleadings shall (1) state the effect of the amendment; (2) be serially numbered to differentiate the amendment from previous amendments and (3) state the page, line number(s), and wording of any proposed change or addition of material.

For the Court's ease of reference, the moving party shall submit to chambers a redlined version of the amended pleading.

3. **Motion Filing Cut-Off.** The Court hears motions on Mondays at 1:30 p.m. The motion filing cut-off date is the last day motions may be heard (not filed). The Court will not decide late motions. Issues left undetermined by the passage of the motion cut-off date should be listed as issues for trial in the Final Pretrial Conference Order. As an exception to the above, motions in limine dealing with evidentiary matters may be heard at or before trial; however, summary judgment motions disguised as motions in limine will not be heard. Parties need not wait until the discovery cut off to bring motions for summary judgment or partial summary judgment. However, in the usual case, the Court expects that more than the minimum notice

will be provided to counsel opposing motions for summary judgment. In the usual case, the parties should confer and agree on the date for setting such motions.

Ex parte applications are entertained solely for extraordinary relief. *See Mission Power Eng. Co. v. Continental Casualty Co.*, 883 F.Supp. 488 (C.D. Cal. 1995). Strict adherence to proper *ex parte* procedures is required for any *ex parte* application filed with the Court.

4. **Stipulations to Extend Time.** Stipulations to extend the time to file any required document or to continue any pretrial or trial date must set forth:

(a) the existing due date or hearing date;

(b) the current pretrial conference date and trial date;

(c) the specific reasons supporting good cause for granting the extension or continuance. For example, a statement that a continuance "will promote settlement" or that the parties decided to suspend discovery while engaging is settlement discussions is insufficient.

(d) whether there have been any prior requests for extensions or continuances, and whether these were granted or denied by the Court.

5. **Summary Judgment Motions.** The Separate Statement of Undisputed Facts is to be prepared in a two column format. The left hand column should set forth the allegedly undisputed fact. The right hand column should set forth the evidence that supports the factual statement. The fact statements should be set forth in sequentially numbered paragraphs. Each paragraph should contain a narrowly focused statement of fact. Each numbered paragraph should address a single subject in as concise a manner as possible.

The opposing party's statement of genuine issues must be in two columns and track the movant's separate statement exactly as prepared. The document must be in two columns; the left hand column must restate the allegedly undisputed fact, and the right hand column must indicate either undisputed, or disputed. The opposing party may dispute all or only a portion of the statement, but if disputing only a portion, must clearly indicate what part is being disputed. Where the opposing party is disputing the fact in whole or part, the opposing party must, in the right hand column, label and restate the moving party's evidence in support of the fact, followed by the opposing party's evidence controverting the fact. Where the opposing party is disputing the fact on the basis of an evidentiary objection, the party must cite to the evidence alleged to be objectionable and state the ground of the objection and nothing more. **No argument should be set forth in this document.**

The opposing party may submit additional material facts that bear on or relate to the issues raised by the movant, which shall follow the format described above for the moving party's separate statement. These additional facts shall follow the movant's facts, shall continue in sequentially numbered paragraphs (i.e., if movant's last statement of fact was set forth in paragraph 30, then the first new fact will be set forth in paragraph 31), and shall set forth in the right hand column the evidence that supports that statement.

The moving party, in its reply, shall respond to the additional facts in the same manner and format that the opposition party is required to adhere to in responding to the statement of undisputed facts, as described above.

(a) Supporting Evidence. No party should submit any evidence other than the specific items of evidence or testimony necessary to support or controvert a proposed statement of undisputed fact. Thus, for example, the entire transcript of a deposition, entire sets of interrogatory responses, and documents that do not specifically support or controvert material in the separate statements, should not be submitted in support or opposition to a motion for summary judgment. Any such material will not be considered.

Evidence submitted in support or opposition to a motion should be submitted either by way of stipulation or as exhibits to declarations sufficient to authenticate the proffered evidence, and should not be attached to the Memorandum of Points and Authorities. The Court will accept counsel's authentication of deposition transcript, of written discovery responses, and of the receipt of documents in discovery ***if the fact that the document was in the opponent's possession is of independent significance***. Documentary evidence as to which there is no stipulation regarding foundation must be accompanied by the testimony, either by declaration or properly authenticated deposition transcript, of a witness who can establish its authenticity.

If evidence in support of or in opposition to a motion exceeds twenty pages, the evidence must be in a separate bound volume and include a Table of Contents.

(b) Objections to Evidence. If a party disputes a fact based in whole or in part on an evidentiary objection, the ground of the objection, as indicated above, should be stated in the separate statement but not argued in that document. Evidentiary objections are to be addressed in a separate memorandum to be filed with the opposition or reply brief of the party. This memorandum should be organized **to track the paragraph numbers of the separate statement in sequence**. It should identify the specific item of evidence to which objection is made, the ground of the objection, and a very brief argument with citation to authority as to why the objection is well taken. The following is an example of the format contemplated by the Court:

> Separate Statement Paragraph 1: Objection to the supporting deposition transcript of Jane Smith at 60:1-10 on the grounds that the statement constitutes inadmissible hearsay and no exception is applicable. To the extent it is offered to prove her state of mind, it is irrelevant since her state of mind is not in issue.
> Fed. R. Evid. 801, 802.

Do not submit blanket or boilerplate objections to the opponent's statements of undisputed fact: these will be disregarded and overruled.

(c) The Memorandum of Points and Authorities. The movant's memorandum of points and authorities should be in the usual form required under Local Rule 7 and should contain a narrative statement of facts as to those aspects of the case that are before the Court. All facts should be supported with citations to the paragraph number in the Separate Statement that supports the factual assertion and not to the underlying evidence.

Unless the case involves some unusual twist on Rule 56, the motion need only contain a brief statement of the Rule 56 standard; the Court is familiar with the Rule and with its interpretation under *Celotex* and its progeny. If at all possible, the argument should be organized to focus on the pertinent elements of the cause(s) of action or defense(s) in issue, with the purpose of showing the existence or non-existence of a genuine issue of material fact for trial on that element of the claim or defense. Likewise, the opposition memorandum of points and authorities should be in the usual form required by Local Rule 7, and where the opposition memorandum sets forth facts, the memorandum should cite to paragraphs in the separate statement if they are not in dispute, to the evidence that contravenes the fact where the fact is in dispute, or, if the fact is contravened by an additional fact in the statement of genuine issues, the citation should be to such fact by paragraph number.

(d) Timing. In virtually every case, the Court expects that the moving party will provide more than the minimum twenty-one (21) day notice for such motions. The moving party shall submit a copy of the Statement of Uncontroverted Facts and Conclusions of Law to the Court's ECF e-mail address, in WordPerfect format (X3 or earlier versions) or Microsoft Word (Word 2003 or earlier versions).

6. Motions *in Limine.* Before filing any motion *in limine*, counsel for the parties shall confer pursuant to Local Rule 7-3 in a good faith effort to eliminate the necessity for hearing the motion *in limine* or to eliminate as many of the disputes as possible. It shall be the responsibility of counsel for the moving party to arrange for this conference. The conference shall take place in person within five calendar days of service upon opposing counsel of a letter requesting such conference. Unless counsel agree otherwise, the conference shall take place at the office of the moving party. If both counsel are not located in the same county in the Central District, the conference may take place by telephone. The moving party's letter shall identify the testimony, exhibits, or other specific matters alleged to be inadmissible and/or prejudicial, shall state briefly with respect to each such matter the moving party's position (and provide any legal authority which the moving party believes is dispositive), and specify the terms of the order to be sought.

(a) If counsel are unable to resolve their differences, they shall prepare a Joint Motion *in Limine*. The Joint Motion *in Limine* shall consist of one document signed by all counsel. The Joint Motion *in Limine* shall contain a clear identification of the testimony, exhibits, or other specific matters alleged to be inadmissible and/or prejudicial and a statement of the specific prejudice that will be suffered by the moving party if the motion is not granted. The identification of the matters in dispute shall be followed by each party's contentions and each party's memorandum of points and authorities. The title page of the Joint Motion *in Limine* must state the hearing date for the motions *in limine* and the trial date.

(b) Unless otherwise ordered by the Court, motions *in limine* will be heard on the date indicated in the Schedule of Trial and Pretrial Dates issued by the Court. Unless the Court in its discretion otherwise allows, no motions *in limine* shall be filed or heard on an *ex parte* basis absent a showing of irreparable injury or prejudice not attributable to the lack of diligence of the moving party. The moving party shall serve its portion of the Joint Motion *in Limine* on the responding party fourteen (14) days prior to the date for filing of motions *in limine* indicated in the Schedule of Trial and Pretrial Dates. The responding party shall then serve the opposition portion of the Joint Motion *in Limine* on the moving party both on paper and in an electronic format seven (7) days prior to the date for the filing of motions *in limine*. The moving party shall incorporate the responding party's portion into the Joint Motion *in Limine*, add its arguments in reply, and file and serve the Joint Motion *in Limine*. Neither party's portions of a Joint Motion *in Limine* shall exceed eight (8) pages.

(c) Joint Motions *in Limine* made for the purpose of precluding the mention or display of inadmissible and/or prejudicial matter in the presence of the jury shall be accompanied by a declaration from the moving party that includes the following: (1) a clear identification of the specific matter alleged to be inadmissible and/or prejudicial; (2) a representation to the Court that the subject of the motion *in limine* has been discussed with opposing counsel, and that opposing counsel has either indicated that such matter will be mentioned or displayed in the presence of the jury before it is admitted in evidence or that counsel has refused to stipulate that such matter will not be mentioned or displayed in the presence of the jury unless and until it is admitted in evidence; and (3) a statement of the specific prejudice that will be suffered by the moving party if the motion *in limine* is not granted.

(d) Unless ordered by the Court, no supplemental or separate memorandum of points and authorities shall be filed by either party in connection with any motion *in limine.*

(e) The Court will not consider any motion in limine in the absence of a joint motion or a declaration from counsel for the moving party establishing that opposing counsel: (1) failed to confer in a timely manner; (2) failed to provide the opposing party's portion of the joint motion in a timely manner; or (3) refused to sign and return the joint motion after the opposing party's portion was added.

(f) The failure of any counsel to comply with or cooperate in the foregoing procedures will result in the imposition of sanctions, including a resolution of the issue against the party refusing to cooperate.

7. **Pretrial Conference and Trial Setting.** Compliance with the requirements of Local Rule 16 is mandatory. Counsel shall submit carefully prepared Memoranda of Contentions of Fact and Law (which may also serve as the trial briefs) and Proposed Pre-Trial Conference Order ("PTCO") in accordance with the provisions of Local Rules 16-2.8 through 16-6. The Proposed Pre-Trial Conference Order shall conform to the example set forth in Appendix A to the Local Rules, modified as necessary to comply with this order.

The Memoranda of Contentions of Fact and Law, Exhibit Lists, and Witness Lists shall be served and filed no later than fourteen (14) calendar days before the Pre-Trial Conference. The Proposed Pre-Trial Conference Order shall be filed fourteen (14) calendar days before the Pre-Trial Conference.

The Proposed Pre-Trial Conference Order must contain a Table of Contents. Place in all capital letters and in bold the separately numbered headings for each category in the PTCO. Under paragraph 1, list each claim, counterclaim, or defense that has been dismissed or abandoned. In multiple party cases where not all claims or counterclaims will be prosecuted against all remaining parties on the other side, please specify to which party each claim or counterclaim directed. The factual issues in dispute should track the elements of a claim or defense upon which the jury would be required to make findings. Counsel should state issues in ultimate fact form, not as evidentiary fact issues (*i.e.*, "was the defendant negligent," "was defendant's negligence the proximate cause of plaintiff's injury;" not "was the plaintiff standing on the corner of 5th and Spring at 10:00 a.m. on May 3"). Issues of law should state legal issues upon which the Court will be required to rule after the Pre-Trial Conference, including during the trial, and should not list ultimate fact issues to be submitted to the trier of fact.

In drafting the PTCO, the Court expects that counsel will attempt to agree on and set forth as many non-contested facts as possible. The Court will normally read the uncontested facts to the jury at the start of the trial. Carefully drafted and comprehensively stated stipulation of facts will reduce the length of trial and increase jury understanding of the case.

If expert witnesses are to be called at trial, each party must list and identify its respective expert witnesses, both retained and non-retained. ***Failure of a party to list and identify an expert witness in the Proposed Pre-Trial Conference Order shall preclude a party from calling that expert witness at trial.***

This case has been placed on calendar for a Final Pretrial Conference ("PTC") pursuant to F. R. Civ. P. 16 and Local Rule 16-1, unless the PTC was expressly waived at the Scheduling Conference by the Court. Unless excused for good cause, each party appearing in this action shall be represented at the PTC and all pretrial meetings of counsel, by lead trial counsel. The failure to attend the PTC or to submit the required pretrial documents may result in the dismissal of the action, striking the answer and entering a default, and/or the imposition of sanctions.

A continuance of the Final Pretrial Conference at counsel's request or stipulation is highly unlikely. Counsel should plan to do the necessary pretrial work on a schedule which will insure its completion with time to spare before the Final Pretrial Conference. Specifically, failure to complete discovery work, including expert discovery, is not a ground for a continuance.

Compliance with the requirements of Local Rules 16-1 to 16-13 is required by the Court. Carefully prepared Memoranda of Contentions of Fact (which may also serve as the trial brief) and a proposed Final Pretrial Conference Order shall be submitted in accordance with the provisions of Local Rule 16-6 and the form of the proposed Final Pretrial Conference Order shall be in conformity with the format set forth in Appendix A to the Local Rules.

At the PTC, counsel should be prepared to discuss means of streamlining the trial, including, but not limited to: bifurcation, presentation of non-critical testimony by deposition excerpts, stipulations as to the content of testimony, presentation of testimony on direct examination by declaration subject to cross-examination, and qualification of experts by admitted resumes. In rare cases where the PTC is waived by the Court, counsel must follow Local Rule 16-10.

8. **Summary of Witness Testimony and Time Estimates.** Counsel shall prepare a list of their witnesses, including a brief summary (two to three paragraphs) of each witness' expected testimony and an estimate of the length of time needed for direct examination; and whether the witness will testify by deposition or in person. **Counsel shall exchange these lists with opposing counsel. Counsel shall jointly file a single list of witness testimony summaries, including estimates for direct examination of their own witnesses and estimates for cross-examination of opposing witnesses.** These statements shall be filed at the time counsel file the Proposed Pre-Trial Conference Order, *i.e.*, fourteen (14) days before the Pre-Trial Conference. A copy of the Joint Trial Witness Form is attached to this Order.

If a party desires to offer deposition testimony into evidence at trial, he shall designate only those relevant portions of same which he wishes to read at trial and advise opposing counsel of same. Opposing counsel shall then designate those relevant portions of such deposition which he wishes to offer in evidence. All objections to any such testimony shall be made in writing and filed at the same time counsel file the Proposed Pre-Trial Conference Order so the Court may consider whether ruling on such objections will either facilitate the conduct of the trial or result in the disposition of certain evidentiary matters that may assist continuing settlement negotiations.

9. **Jury Instructions and Verdict Forms.** Fourteen (14) calendar days prior to counsel's Rule 16 pre-trial meeting, counsel shall exchange proposed jury instructions (general and special) and special verdict forms (if applicable). Seven (7) calendar days prior to the Rule 16-2 meeting, counsel shall exchange any objections to the instructions and special verdict forms. Prior to, or at the time of the Rule 16 meeting, counsel shall meet and confer with the goal of reaching agreement on one set of joint jury instructions and one special verdict form.

The parties should make every attempt to agree upon the jury instructions before submitting them to the Court. The Court expects counsel to agree on the substantial majority of jury instructions, particularly when pattern instructions provide a statement of applicable law. When the Manual of Model Civil Jury Instructions for the Ninth Circuit provides a version of an applicable requested instruction, the parties should submit the most recent version of the Model instruction. Where language appears in brackets in the model instruction, counsel shall select the appropriate text and eliminate the inapplicable bracketed text. Where California law applies, counsel should use California Jury Instructions – Civil (8th ed.) ("BAJI"). If neither of the above sources is applicable, counsel are directed to use the instructions from O'Malley, Grenig & Lee (formerly Devitt, et al.), Federal Jury Practice and Instructions (latest edition). Each requested jury instruction shall cover only one subject or principle of law and shall be numbered and set forth in full on a separate page, citing the authority or source of the requested instruction (except for the "clean" jury copy discussed below).

When the parties disagree on an instruction, the party opposing the instruction must attach a short statement (one to two paragraphs) supporting the objection, and the party submitting the instruction must attach a short statement supporting the instruction. Each statement should be on a separate page and should follow directly after the disputed instruction.

The parties ultimately must submit one document or, if the parties disagree over any proposed jury instructions, two documents. If the parties submit two documents, those documents shall consist of: (1) a set of Joint Proposed Jury Instructions and (2) a set of Disputed Jury Instructions, along with reasons supporting and opposing each disputed instruction in the format set forth in the previous paragraph.

The parties must file proposed jury instructions fourteen (14) calendar days before the Pre-Trial Conference. If the court is closed that day, counsel shall file the proposed instructions the preceding Friday. No later than 5:00 p.m. on the date such instructions are due, the parties must submit conformed courtesy copies to the Court's courtesy box located outside the entrance to chambers on the Spring Street level of the U.S. Courthouse. Counsel shall also submit a copy of the proposed jury instructions to the Court's ECF e-mail address in WordPerfect format (X3 or earlier versions) or Microsoft Word (Word 2003 or earlier versions) in accordance with this paragraph and the previous paragraph.

The Court will send a copy of the instructions into the jury room for the jury's use during deliberations. Accordingly, in addition to the file copies described above, the e-mail containing the jury instructions shall contain a "clean set" of Joint Proposed and/or Disputed Jury Instructions, containing only the text of each instruction set forth in full on each page, with the caption "Court's Instruction No. __" (eliminating titles, supporting authority, indication of party proposing, etc.).

An index page shall accompany all jury instructions submitted to the Court. The index page shall indicate the following:

(a) The number of the instruction;
(b) A brief title of the instruction;
(c) The source of the instruction and any relevant case citations; and
(d) The page number of the instruction.

EXAMPLE:

Number	Title	Source	Page
1	Trademark-Defined (15 U.S.C. § 1127)	9th Cir. 15.3.2	7

Along with the jury instructions, counsel shall submit any necessary special verdict form fourteen (14) calendar days before the Pre-Trial Conference and e-mail any such proposed special verdict form in WordPerfect format (X3 or earlier versions) or Microsoft Word (Word 2003 or earlier versions) to the Court's ECF e-mail address.

10. ***Voir Dire* Questions.** Counsel may, but need not, submit brief proposed *voir dire* questions for the jury at the Pre-Trial Conference. The Court will conduct its own *voir dire* after consulting any proposed *voir dire* submitted by counsel.

11. **Joint Statement of the Case.** Counsel shall submit a joint statement of the case at the Pretrial Conference. The joint statement of the case will be read to the prospective panel of jurors prior to the commencement of *voir dire*. The statement should not exceed one page. The statement shall be filed with the Court at the Pre-Trial Conference.

12. **Exhibits.** The parties shall file their witness lists and exhibits lists in accordance with Local Rule 16. Counsel are to assemble their exhibits by placing them in three-ring binders labeled on the spine portion of the binder showing both the volume number and the exhibit numbers. Each exhibit shall be separated by a tabbed divider on the right side. Counsel shall provide original exhibits for the Courtroom Deputy Clerk and a duplicate set for the judge. The original exhibits shall be tagged with the appropriate exhibit tags in the upper or lower right corner of the first page of each exhibit. Each binder shall contain a Table of Contents. Counsel must comply with Local Rule 26-4 when numbering the exhibits. The Clerk's Office, Room G-8, 312 North Spring Street, Los Angeles, California can supply counsel with appropriate exhibit tags.

13. **Pre-Trial Exhibit Stipulation.** The parties shall prepare a Pre-Trial Exhibit Stipulation which shall contain each party's numbered list of trial exhibits, with objections, if any, to each exhibit including the basis of the objection and the offering party's response. All exhibits to which there is no objection shall be deemed admitted. All parties shall stipulate to the authenticity of exhibits whenever possible, and the Pre-Trial Exhibit Stipulation shall identify any exhibits whose authenticity has not been stipulated to and the specific reasons for the party's failure to stipulate.

The Stipulation shall be substantially in the following form:

Pre-Trial Exhibit Stipulation

Plaintiff's Exhibits

Number	Description	Objection	Response to Objection

Defendant's Exhibits

Number	Description	Objection	Response to Objection

The Pre-Trial Exhibit Stipulation shall be filed at the same time as counsel files the Proposed Pre-Trial Conference Order. Failure to comply with this paragraph shall constitute a waiver of all objections.

The Court requires the following to be submitted to the Courtroom Deputy Clerk on the first day of trial:

(1) The original exhibits with the Court's exhibit tags. Plaintiff shall use yellow tags; defendant shall use blue tags. Each tag shall be stapled to the front of the exhibit on the upper right corner and include the case number, case name, and exhibit number.

(2) One bench book with a copy of each exhibit for the Court's use, tabbed as described above; a copy of the witness lists).

(3) Three (3) copies of exhibit lists and a floppy disk containing the exhibit list.

(4) Three (3) copies of witness lists in the order in which the witnesses will be called to testify.

All counsel are to meet no later than ten (10) calendar days before trial to discuss and agree to the extent possible on issues including foundation and admissibility.

14. <u>Findings of Fact and Conclusions of Law.</u> For a non-jury trial, counsel for each party shall file and serve proposed findings of fact and conclusions of law fourteen days before trial. The parties should also e-mail these proposed findings of fact and conclusions of law in WordPerfect format (X3 or earlier versions) or Microsoft Word (Word 2003 or earlier versions) to the Court's ECF e-mail address. Counsel for each party shall then:

(1) Underline or highlight in red the portions which it disputes;

(2) Underline or highlight in blue the portions which it admits; and

(3) Underline or highlight in yellow the portions which it does not dispute, but deems irrelevant.

Counsel may agree with a part of a finding or conclusion, disagree with a part of it and/or consider a part of it irrelevant.

The parties should then file and serve their respective objections to the other party's proposed findings of fact and conclusions of law. Courtesy copies of the marked copies shall be delivered to the courtesy box next to the entrance to chambers on the Spring Street level of the U.S. Courthouse, 312 North Spring Street, by 12:00 noon of the business day following filing.

15. <u>Settlement.</u> Local Rule 16-15.2 provides that the Settlement Conference shall be conducted not later than 45 days before the Pretrial Conference. The Court believes that in most cases completion of all discovery and dispositive motions will help the parties assess their positions before they embark on the costly pre-trial process. However, in many cases, the parties find it more difficult to settle after they have incurred the cost of all discovery and motion practice. Accordingly, the Court strongly encourages counsel and the parties to pursue settlement earlier.

The Court has a keen interest in helping the parties achieve settlement. If the parties believe that it would be more likely that a settlement would be reached if they conduct settlement conference at an earlier time than that specified by the Court, they should conduct it at that time. In any event, the parties must file a Status Report re Settlement at the time they file the Proposed Pretrial Order.

The Court will not conduct settlement conferences in non-jury cases which the Court will try. In jury cases, the Court will conduct a settlement conference at the parties' request if three conditions exist:

1. The parties are satisfied that the fact issues in the case will be tried to a jury;

2. All significant pre-trial rulings which Court must make have been made; and

3. The parties desire the Court to conduct the conference, understanding that if settlement fails, the Court will preside over the trial of the case.

16. Sanctions. The failure to attend the pretrial conference or to submit in conformity with this order, the jury instructions, pre-trial exhibit stipulation, joint statement of the case, voir dire questions, summary of witness testimony and times estimates, proposed Pretrial Conference Order or the memorandum of contentions of fact and law may result in the dismissal of the action, striking the answer and entering default and/or the imposition of sanctions.

IT IS SO ORDERED.

Date: ______________________ ____________________

PERCY ANDERSON
United States District Judge

JOINT TRIAL WITNESS ESTIMATE FORM

CASE: ____________________ TRIAL DATE: __________________

	WITNESS NAME	PARTY CALLING WITNESS AND ESTIMATE	X-EXAMINER'S ESTIMATE	DESCRIPTION OF TESTIMONY	COMMENTS
1					
2					
3					
4					
	TOTAL ESTIMATE S THIS PAGE:				

Instructions:

(1) List witnesses (last name first);
(2) For description, be extremely brief, *e.g.*, "eyewitness to accident." Or "expert on standard of care."
(3) Use estimates within fractions of an hour, rounded off to closest quarter of an hour. *E.g.*, if you estimate 20 minutes, make it .25. An estimate of one and one-half hours would be 1.5. An estimate of three-quarters of an hour would be .75;
(4) Note special factors in "Comments" column. *E.g.*, "Needs interpreter." (5) Entries may be in handwriting if very neat and legible.

E. ***Standing Order***

IN THE UNITED STATES DISTICT COURT
FOR THE CENTRAL DISTRICT OF CALIFORNIA

	)	Case No. ____________
Plaintiff(s),	)	
v.	)	**STANDING ORDER**
Defendant(s).	)	
____________________	)	

READ THIS ORDER CAREFULLY. IT CONTROLS THE CASE AND DIFFERS IN SOME RESPECTS FROM THE LOCAL RULES.

This action has been assigned to the calendar of Judge Percy Anderson. Both the Court and the attorneys bear responsibility for the progress of litigation in the Federal Courts. To secure the just, speedy, and inexpensive determination of every action, Fed. R. Civ. P. 1, all counsel are ordered to familiarize themselves with the Federal Rules of Civil Procedure and the Local Rules of the Central District of California.

IT IS HEREBY ORDERED:

1. **Service of the Complaint:** The Plaintiff shall promptly serve the Complaint in accordance with Fed. R. Civ. P. 4 and file the proofs of service pursuant to Local Rule 5-3.1.

2. **Presence of Lead Counsel:** Lead trial counsel shall attend all proceedings before this Court, including all status and settlement conferences.

3. **Discovery:**

(a) All discovery matters have been referred to a United States Magistrate Judge, who will hear all discovery disputes. (The Magistrate Judge's initials follow the Judge's initials next to the case number.) All discovery documents must include the words "DISCOVERY MATTER" in the caption to ensure proper routing. Counsel are directed to contact the Magistrate Judge's Courtroom Deputy Clerk to schedule matters for hearing. Please do not deliver courtesy copies of these documents to this Court.

The decision of the Magistrate Judge shall be final, subject to modification by the District Court only where it has been shown that the Magistrate Judge's Order is clearly erroneous or contrary to law. Any party may file and serve a motion for review and reconsideration before this Court. The moving party must file and serve the motion within ten (10) days of service of a written ruling or within ten (10) days of an oral ruling that the Magistrate Judge states will not be followed by a written ruling. The motion must specify which portions of the ruling are clearly erroneous or contrary to law and support the contention with points and authorities. Counsel shall deliver a conformed copy of the moving papers and responses to the Magistrate Judge's clerk at the time of filing.

(b) Unless there is a likelihood that upon motion by a party the Court would order that any or all discovery is premature, it is advisable for counsel to begin to conduct discovery actively before the Scheduling Conference. At the very least, the parties shall comply fully with the letter and spirit of Fed. R. Civ. P. 26(a) and thereby obtain and produce most of what would be produced in the early stage of discovery, because at the Scheduling Conference the Court will impose tight deadlines to complete discovery.

(c) If expert witnesses are to be called at trial, the parties shall designate experts to be called at trial and provide reports required by Fed. R. Civ. P. 26(a)(2)(B), not later than eight weeks prior to the discovery cutoff date. Rebuttal expert witnesses shall be designated and reports provided as required by Fed. R. Civ. P. 26(a)(2)(B), not later than five weeks prior to the discovery cutoff date. Failure to timely comply with this deadline may result in the expert being excluded at trial as a witness.

4. Electronic Filing: As of November 1, 2007 for patent, trademark, and copyright cases, and January 1, 2008 for all other cases, the United States District Court for the Central District of California requires electronic filing of documents in all new and pending civil cases. Information about the Court's Electronic Case Filing system ("ECF") is available on the Court's website at www.cacd.uscourts.gov/cmecf.

All manually filed documents (those documents excused from the electronic filing requirements by General Order 08-02, Section V) shall be served on the person as otherwise required by the Federal Rules of Civil Procedure or the Local Rules.

5. **Courtesy Copies:** Counsel are ordered to serve courtesy copies of all electronically filed documents, and conformed courtesy copies of all manually filed documents, to the courtesy box next to the entrance to chambers on the Spring Street level of the U.S. Courthouse, 312 North Spring Street, by 12:00 noon of the business day following filing. Courtesy copies may be delivered to chambers by either personally delivering them to the courtesy box or sending them by guaranteed overnight delivery. If a courtesy copy is sent to chambers by guaranteed overnight delivery, the sender shall notify the delivery service that the signature of the recipient is not required.

6. **Motions:**

(a) Time for Filing and Hearing Motions: Motions shall be filed in accordance with Local Rule 7.1.[1] This Court hears motions on **Mondays, commencing at 1:30 p.m. No supplemental brief shall be filed without prior leave of Court.** Many motions to dismiss or to strike could be avoided if the parties confer in good faith (as they are required to do under L.R. 7-3), especially for perceived defects in a complaint, answer or counterclaim which could be corrected by amendment. *See Chang v. Chen,* 80 F.3d 1293, 1296 (9th Cir. 1996) (where a motion to dismiss is granted, a district court should provide leave to amend unless it is clear that the complaint could not be saved by *any* amendment). Moreover, a party has the right to amend his complaint "once as a matter of course at any time before a responsive pleading is served." Fed. R. Civ. P. 15(a). A 12(b)(6) motion is not a responsive pleading and therefore plaintiff might have a right to amend. *See Nolen v. Fitzharris*, 450 F.2d 958, 958-59 (9th Cir. 1971); *St. Michael's Convalescent Hospital v. California*, 643 F.2d 1369, 1374 (9th Cir. 1981). And even where a party has amended his Complaint once or a responsive pleading has been served, the Federal Rules provide that leave to amend should be "freely given when justice so requires." F.R.Civ.P. 15(a). The Ninth Circuit requires that this policy favoring amendment be applied with "extreme liberality." *Morongo Band of Mission Indians v. Rose*, 893 F.2d 1074, 1079 (9th Cir. 1990).

These principles require that counsel for the plaintiff should carefully evaluate the

---

1 Among other things, Local Rule 7-3 requires counsel to engage in a pre-filing conference "to discuss thoroughly . . . the substance of the contemplated motion and any potential resolution." Counsel should discuss the issues sufficiently so that if a motion is still necessary, the briefing may be directed to those substantive issues requiring resolution by the Court. Counsel should resolve minor procedural or other non-substantive matters during the conference.

defendant's contentions as to the deficiencies in the complaint and in many instances, the moving party should agree to any amendment that would cure a curable defect.

In the unlikely event that motions under Fed. R. Civ. P. 12 challenging pleadings are filed after the Rule 16 Scheduling Conference, the moving party shall attach a copy of the challenged pleading to the Memorandum of Points and Authorities in support of the motion. The foregoing provisions apply as well to motions to dismiss a counterclaim, answer or affirmative defense, which a plaintiff might file.

(b) Length and Format of Motion Papers: **Memoranda of Points and Authorities in support of or in opposition to motions shall not exceed 25 pages. Replies shall not exceed 12 pages.** Only in rare instances and for good cause shown will the Court grant an application to extend these page limitations.

Typeface shall comply with Local Rule 11-3.1.1. NOTE: If Times Roman font is used, the size must be no less than 14; if Courier is used, the size must be no less than 12. Footnotes shall be in typeface no more than one size smaller than text size and shall be used sparingly.

Filings which do not conform to the Local Rules and this Order will not be considered.

(c) Citations to Case Law: Citations to case law **must** identify not only the case being cited, but the specific page being referenced. Certain kinds of authority are considered more useful – or authoritative – than others. If more than one authority is cited in support of a proposition, these supporting authorities are to be listed such that the more authoritative ones appear first.

(d) Citations to Other Sources: Counsel are reminded that the basic purpose of a legal citation is to allow the reader to locate a cited source accurately and efficiently. Accordingly, statutory references should identify, with specificity, which sections and subsections are being referenced (*e.g.*, Jurisdiction over this cause of action may appropriately be found in 47 U.S.C. § 33, which grants the district courts jurisdiction over all offenses of the Submarine Cable Act, whether the infraction occurred within the territorial waters of the United States or on board a vessel of the United States outside said waters). Statutory references which do not indicate specifically which section and subsection are being referred to (*e.g.*, Plaintiffs allege conduct in violation of the Federal Electronic Communication Privacy Act, 18 U.S.C. § 2511, *et seq.*) are to be **avoided**. Citations to treatises, manuals, and other materials should similarly include the volume and the section being referenced.

7. Proposed Orders: Each party filing or opposing a motion or seeking the determination of any matter shall serve and lodge a Proposed Order setting forth the relief or action sought and a brief statement of the rationale for the decision with appropriate citations. If the Proposed Order exceeds two pages, the proposing party shall also submit a copy of the Proposed Order to the Court's ECF e-mail address, in WordPerfect format (X3 or earlier versions) or Microsoft Word (Word 2003 or earlier versions).

8. *Ex Parte* Applications: Counsel are reminded ex parte applications are solely for extraordinary relief. *See Mission Power Engineering Co. v. Continental Casualty Co.*, 883 F. Supp. 488 (C.D. Cal. 1995). Applications which fail to conform with Local Rules 7-19 and 7-19.1, including a statement of opposing counsel's position, will not be considered. Any opposition must be filed not later than 24 hours after service. If counsel do not intend to oppose the *ex parte* application, counsel must inform the court clerk by telephone. The Court considers *ex* *parte* applications on the papers and usually does not set these matters for hearing. Counsel shall deliver a courtesy copy of moving, opposition, or notice of non-opposition papers to the courtesy box outside the entrance to chambers on the Spring Street level of the U.S. Courthouse, 312 North Spring Street. The Courtroom Deputy Clerk will notify counsel of the Court's ruling or a hearing date and time, if the Court determines a hearing is necessary.

9. Applications or Stipulations to Extend the Time to File any Required Document or to Continue any Pretrial or Trial Date: No stipulations extending scheduling requirements or modifying applicable rules are effective until and unless the Court approves them. Both applications and stipulations must be filed in advance of the date due and set forth:

(a) the existing due date or hearing date as well as the discovery cutoff date, the last date for hearing motions, the pre-trial conference date and the trial date;

(b) specific, concrete reasons supporting good cause for granting the extension. In this regard, a statement that an extension "will promote settlement" is insufficient. The requesting party or parties must indicate the status of ongoing negotiations: (*i.e.*, have written proposals been exchanged? Is counsel in the process of reviewing a draft settlement agreement? Has a mediator been selected?);

(c) whether there have been prior requests for extensions, and whether these were granted or denied by the Court.

10. TROs and Injunctions: Parties seeking emergency or provisional relief shall comply with Fed. R. Civ. P. 65 and Local Rule 65. The Court will not rule on any application for such relief for at least 24 hours after the party subject to the requested order has been served; such party may file opposing or responding papers in the interim. The parties shall lodge a courtesy copy, conformed to reflect that it has been filed, of all papers relating to TROs and injunctions. The courtesy copy shall be placed in the courtesy box outside the entrance to chambers. All such papers shall be filed "loose" – *i.e.*, not inside envelopes.

11. Cases Removed From State Court: All documents filed in state court, including documents appended to the complaint, answers and motions, must be refiled in this Court as a supplement to the Notice of Removal, if not already included. *See* 28 U.S.C. § 1447(a)(b). If the defendant has not yet responded, the answer or responsive pleading filed in this Court must comply with the Federal Rules of Civil Procedure and the Local Rules of the Central District. If a motion was pending in state court before the case was removed, it must be re-noticed in accordance with Local Rule 7.

12. ERISA Cases: Absent an agreed upon statement of facts, the court will not hear motions for summary judgment, but will hear motions to determine the standard of review and the scope of the administrative record. *See Kearney v. Standard Ins. Co.*, 175 F.3d 1084 (9th Cir. 1999). There will be a court trial (usually confined to oral argument) on the administrative record.

13. Consent to Magistrate Judge: The parties may consent to have a United States Magistrate Judge preside over the entire case, including trial. The parties are free to select from amongst all the magistrate judges available for this purpose, not just the magistrate judge assigned to this case. (Please consult the court's website for the list of the available magistrate judges.)

14. Status of Fictitiously Named Defendants: This Court intends to adhere to the following procedures where a matter is removed to this Court on diversity grounds with fictitiously named defendants referred to in the complaint. *See* 28 U.S.C. §§ 1441(a), 1447.

(a) Plaintiff is normally expected to ascertain the identity of and serve any fictitiously named defendants within 120 days of the removal of the action to this Court.

(b) If plaintiff believes (by reason of the necessity for discovery or otherwise) that fictitiously named defendants cannot be fully identified within the 120-day period, an *ex parte* application requesting permission to extend that period to effectuate service may be filed with this Court. Such application shall state the reasons therefor, and may be granted upon a showing of good cause. The ex parte application shall be served upon all appearing parties, and shall state that appearing parties may comment within seven (7) days of the filing of the *ex parte* application.

(c) If plaintiff desires to substitute a named defendant for one of the fictitiously named parties, plaintiff first shall seek to obtain consent from counsel for the previously-identified defendants (and counsel for the fictitiously named party, if that party has separate counsel). If consent is withheld or denied, plaintiff may apply *ex parte* requesting such amendment, with notice to all appearing parties. Each party shall have seven calendar days to respond. The *ex parte* application and any response should comment not only on the substitution of the named party for a fictitiously named defendant, but on the question of whether the matter should thereafter be remanded to the Superior Court if diversity of citizenship is destroyed by the addition of the new substituted party. *See* 28 U.S.C. § 1447(c)(d).

15. **Bankruptcy Appeals:** Counsel shall comply with the Notice Regarding Appeal from Bankruptcy Court issued at the time the appeal is filed in the District Court. The matter is considered submitted upon the filing of the appellant's reply brief. No oral argument is held unless otherwise ordered by this Court.

16. **Communications with Chambers:** Counsel shall not attempt to contact the Court or its chambers staff by telephone or by any other *ex parte* means, although counsel may contact the Courtroom Deputy, at (213) 894-1795, with appropriate inquiries. To facilitate communication with the Courtroom Deputy, counsel should list their facsimile transmission numbers along with their telephone numbers on all papers.

17. **Notice of this Order:** Counsel for plaintiff shall immediately serve this Order on all parties, including any new parties to the action. If this case came to the Court by noticed removal, defendant shall serve this Order on all other parties.

IT IS SO ORDERED.

Dated: October 31, 2008

PERCY ANDERSON
United States District Judge

Hon. Cormac J. Carney
District Judge

Chambers Information
U.S. District Court, Central District of California
Courtroom 9B
411 West Fourth Street
Santa Ana, CA 92701

Scheduling Information
Courtroom Deputy: (714) 338-2849

Civil Law and Motion	Mondays at 1:30 p.m.
Criminal Law and Motion	Mondays at 9:00 a.m.

Judge's Biography
Born 1959 in Detroit, MI

Federal Judicial Service:
-Judge, U. S. District Court, Central District of California
-Nominated by George W. Bush on January 7, 2003, to a seat vacated by Carlos R. Moreno; Confirmed by the Senate on April 7, 2003, and received commission on April 9, 2003.

Education:
-University of California, Los Angeles, B.A., 1983
-Harvard Law School, J.D., 1987

Professional Career:
-U.S. Air Force, 1979-1983
-Private Practice, California, 1987-2001
-Judge, Superior Court, Orange County, California, 2001-2003

I. Judge Carney's Procedures and Practices

A. *Procedures and Schedules*

1. Civil motions are heard on: **Monday**, Time: **1:30 p.m.**

   Criminal motions and hearings are heard on: **Monday**, Time: **9:00 a.m.**

   (If Monday is a holiday, next motion date is the **following Monday**)

   It is not necessary to clear or reserve a motion date with the court clerk prior to filing the motion, but must be in compliance with all Local and Federal Rules regarding service.

2. Discovery motions are to be calendared before the Magistrate Judge.

3. Are tentative rulings issued?
   Please inquire of the court clerk when checking in immediately prior to the court hearing.

4. Mandatory Chambers Copies of all e-filed documents shall be delivered to the mandatory chambers copy box on the 9th Floor. It is imperative that the mandatory chambers copies be delivered by noon following the date of filing as required by General Order 10-07.IV.D. Failure to deliver timely mandatory chambers copies may result in a delay in hearing a motion or ordering the matter off calendar.

5. Procedures for filing an ex parte application: It is the practice of Judge Carney that ALL Ex -Parte applications are submitted on the papers. If the Court finds that a hearing is necessary, counsel will be notified and given a hearing date and time. The same procedure is followed on an application for a temporary restraining order.

6. To request a continuance of any scheduled court proceeding: Only **written applications or stipulations** for continuances will be considered by the Court. Continuances are only granted upon a showing of good cause, particularly focusing upon evidence of diligent work by the party seeking delay and of prejudice that may result from the denial of a continuance. Counsel requesting the continuance **MUST** submit a **DETAILED** declaration as to their reason. Any continuances requested not accompanied by said declaration, or not in compliance with this Order or the Local Rules of the Central District of California will automatically be rejected without notice to the parties. The Court sets FIRM trial dates and will not change them without good cause having been shown. Stipulations or applications MUST be submitted well in advance of the relief requested. Counsel is not to assume the request is granted without notification from the Court.

7. Are counsel allowed to contact the judge's law clerks or secretary? NO.

8. Inquiries regarding the status of a motion, stipulation or proposed order: Pursuant to Local Rules 7-1 and 11-4.5.

9. Calendar conflicts: Counsel shall notify both of the Judges' court clerks. Counsel should go to the most senior of the judges. A priority before that Judge should be requested.

10. Procedures for bringing electronic equipment into the courtroom: Counsel must petition the Court in writing at the earliest possible date and obtain an Order of Authorization, as the Courthouse regulations require a property pass to deliver or

remove equipment from the building.

11. To order an audio tape or transcript: For general information on how to order a transcript of any reported or digitally recorded proceeding, please contact 213-894-3015 or visit www.cacd.uscourts.gov > General Information > Court Reporter/Recorder Transcripts. If you require an estimate of cost for the preparation of a transcript, contact the court reporter/recorder for the desired proceeding.

To determine the court reporter/recorder for a particular proceeding, go to the Court Reporter Schedule web page and click on View by Date. Once you've determined the correct court reporter/recorder for the desired session, click on Court Reporter Phone and Email List for contact information.

12. Questions regarding law clerk positions: Should be directed to Judge Carney's chambers. Judge Carney does not accept extern applications.

13. Trial preparation:

a. Court hours: Tuesday through Friday, 9:00 a.m.- 5:00 p.m.

b. Exhibit preparation: A joint exhibit list shall be prepared in compliance with Local Rules 11-5.3 & 16-5. All exhibits shall be placed in loose leaf binders with official exhibit tags attached. Exhibits are to be delivered to Courtroom Deputy Clerk not later than 8:30 a.m. on the first day of trial. Special arrangements for voluminous exhibits should be made with the Courtroom Deputy Clerk by Wednesday of the prior week. A separate exhibit number shall NOT be given to each page of an exhibit.

c. Jury instructions: In a jury trial, jury instructions are to be submitted no later than 5 court days prior to the Pre-Trial Conference or 1 week prior to the trial if Pre-Trial Conference is waived. The parties MUST submit JOINT jury instructions. In order to produce these joint instructions, the parties SHALL MEET AND CONFER sufficiently in advance of the required submission date. The instructions should be submitted in the order in which the parties wish to have the instructions read. This order should reflect a single organized sequence agreed to by all of the parties. The Court INSISTS upon receiving lucid and accurate instructions setting forth the elements of each party's claims and defenses. The instructions should be tailored to the facts of each case.

Procedures for Instructions Upon Which Agreement Cannot be Reached: Counsel will submit three (3) sets (with an extra copy for the Court's law clerks) in the following form:

1. The agreed upon instructions.
2. Those instructions propounded by plaintiff, opposed by defendant.
3. Those instructions propounded by defendant, opposed by plaintiff.

Instructions upon which agreement cannot be reached should reflect the basic disagreements among the parties as to the law. While the Court recognizes that such disagreements arise in almost every case, the Court also recognizes that parties ultimately disagree over only a limited number of issues. The disputed instructions should be equally so limited.

The disputed instructions should be presented to the Court within the framework of the overall set of instructions. The parties should put forth differing versions of disputed instructions, and the Court will select one version.

The instructions submitted to the Court MUST be numbered, and the parties must also submit an unnumbered index. Attribution and case citation for each instruction shall be placed on pages following a proposed instruction. For disputed instructions, a party should note its objections to a proposed instruction and its reasons for putting forth its alternative on pages placed after its own alternative instruction.

INSTRUCTIONS SHALL BE BRIEF, CLEAR, CONCISE, WRITTEN IN PLAIN ENGLISH, FREE OF ARGUMENT AND SHALL BE ORGANIZED IN A LOGICAL FASHION SO AS TO AID JURY COMPREHENSION. Standard or form instructions, if used, must be revised to address the particular facts and issues of this case.

The following list contains some suggested sources for jury instructions:

1. Ninth Circuit Model Jury Instructions (updated yearly)
2. Federal Jury Practice and Instructions (Devitt and Blackmar (4th Edition)
3. Modern Federal Jury Instructions (Mathew Bender)
4. California Forms of Jury Instructions (Mathew Bender)

d. Verdict forms: Counsel are to prepare and submit verdict form(s) in accordance with the same procedures as those required for jury instructions. Counsel are to use best efforts to agree upon a joint verdict form and then submit it to the Court no later than 5 court days prior to the Pre-Trial Conference or 1 week prior to the trial if the Pre-Trial Conference is waived. If counsel cannot agree as to the form of the verdict, the parties should submit their respective version to the Court on the submission date for the joint verdict form.

e. Motions in Limine: All Motions in Limine will be heard at the Pre-Trial Conference. All Motions in Limine must be filed and served in compliance with Local Rule 6-1. Opposition papers must be filed and served in compliance with Local Rule 7-9. Reply papers must be filed and served in compliance with Local Rule 7-10.

14. Procedures for obtaining the services of an interpreter on a civil case: Counsel shall make arrangements through the Court Interpreter's Office at 213-894-4599.

15. Other:

a. The Court does not permit telephonic appearances in any matter before it.

b. In the event of inconsistencies between the submission and lodging dates listed above and the Local Rules, the above dates shall govern.

II. Judge Carney's Case Management Orders

A. Order Regarding Criminal Pre-Trial Motions, Trials, and Sentencing

IN THE UNITED STATES DISTICT COURT
FOR THE CENTRAL DISTRICT OF CALIFORNIA

UNITED STATES OF AMERICA	)	Case No. ______________
Plaintiff(s),	)	
v.	)	**ORDER RE CRIMINAL PRE-TRIAL**
Defendant(s).	)	**MOTIONS, TRIALS, AND**
______________________________	)	**SENTENCING**

The above matter is set for trial before the Honorable Cormac J. Carney, United States District Judge, Courtroom 9B, Ronald Reagan Federal Building and United States Courthouse, 411 West Fourth Street, Santa Ana, CA 92701. Counsel preparing for trial before this Court shall comply with this Order. Failure to comply with this order may subject counsel to sanctions.

MOTION PRACTICE

1. Unless the Local Criminal Rules prescribe a different time for filing a particular motion, pre-trial motions must be filed and served not later than twenty-eight (28) days after arraignment and set for hearing not later than the Monday eight (8) days prior to the trial date at 9:30 a.m. Counsel's estimate of the time required for presentation of the motion must be set forth adjacent to the caption.

2. A party opposing a motion must file and serve an opposition not later than seven (7) days after service of the motion or as otherwise permitted by the Court. Counsel's estimate of the time required for presentation of the opposition to the motion must be set forth in the caption of the opposition.

3. Memoranda of Points and Authorities in support of or in opposition to motions shall not exceed 25 pages. Replies shall not exceed 12 pages. Only in rare instances and for good cause shown will the Court grant an application to extend these page limitations. No supplemental briefs shall be filed without prior leave of court.

4. Before filing any motion for discovery, counsel shall confer with opposing counsel to ascertain what discovery will be provided. Any discovery motion shall state with particularity what is requested, and whether such discovery has been declined. Motions made without prior consultation with opposing counsel or which fail to include the above information will not be heard.

DISCOVERY AND NOTICE

5. Counsel for the government and counsel for the defendant shall comply promptly with discovery and notice pursuant to Fed. R. Crim. P., Rules 12, 12.1, 12.2, 12.3, 15 and 16. Upon government counsel's discovery of any evidence within the scope of *Brady v. Maryland*, 373 U.S. 83 (1963), such evidence shall be produced forthwith to counsel for the defendant. Counsel for the government shall also disclose to counsel for the defendant the existence or non-existence of: (1) evidence obtained by electronic surveillance; and (2) testimony by a government informant.

TRIAL

8. Trials are held Tuesdays through Friday, 9:00 a.m. to 5:00 p.m.

9. Counsel shall arrive at the Courtroom at 8:30 a.m. on the first day of trial and present the Courtroom Deputy with the following documents:

a. Three copies of the government's witness list;

b. Three copies of the government's exhibit list;

c. All of the government's exhibits with official exhibit tags attached;

d. A bench book containing a copy of all reproducible exhibits, tabbed with exhibit numbers along the right hand side;

10. Defense counsel need not deliver the exhibits to the Courtroom Deputy on the first day of trial; however, defense counsel is responsible for affixing completed exhibit tags to the exhibits which are intended for use in defendant's case. Defense counsel shall provide the Court with a copy of their exhibits as they are introduced during trial.

11. *Voir Dire*: At least four (4) court days prior to trial, each counsel shall file with the clerk and serve on opposing counsel any special questions requested to be put to prospective jurors by the Court during *voir dire*.

12. Jury Instructions and Verdict Forms: In a jury trial, no later than one (1) week before trial, counsel shall submit **JOINT** jury instructions and a **JOINT** proposed verdict form (if a special verdict is desired). In order to produce these joint documents, counsel shall meet and confer sufficiently in advance of the required submission date with the goal of agreeing upon instructions and a verdict form. The instructions should be submitted in the order in which the parties wish to have the instructions read. This order should reflect a single organized sequence agreed to by all of the parties.

The jury instructions shall be submitted as follows:

a. Agreed upon JOINT jury instructions;

b. Instructions propounded by the government to which the defendant(s) objects; and

c. Instructions propounded by defendant(s) to which the government objects.

Instructions upon which agreement cannot be reached should reflect the basic disagreements among the parties as to the law.

Attribution and case citation for each instruction should be placed on pages following a proposed instruction. For disputed instructions, a party should note its objections to a proposed instruction and its reasons for putting forth its alternative on pages placed after its own alternative instruction.

INSTRUCTIONS SHALL BE BRIEF, CLEAR, CONCISE, WRITTEN IN PLAIN ENGLISH, FREE OF ARGUMENT, AND SHALL BE ORGANIZED IN LOGICAL FASHION AS TO AID JURY COMPREHENSION. Standard or form instructions, if used, must be revised to address the particular facts and issues of the case.

SENTENCING PROCEEDINGS

13. If a defendant is convicted, the sentencing proceedings will be conducted pursuant to Fed. Crim. Pro. Rule 32 and the Local Rules. If any party wishes to present material to the Court which has (a) not been previously filed with the Court or presented at trial, or (b) not been previously provided to the opposing party and the assigned United States Probation Officer, such party must file and serve the information or evidence no later than two (2) weeks before the scheduled sentencing hearing. Notwithstanding the foregoing, a statement of each party's position concerning sentencing shall be filed and served no later than two (2) weeks before the sentencing hearing, and the proof of service shall reflect service on the assigned United States Probation Officer. Timely filing is important to enable the Probation Officer sufficient time to prepare and disclose any addendum to the Probation Report that may be required in response to new information and/or evidence and/or a party's sentencing position. Failure to timely file and serve such information, evidence, or statement of position may result in such information not being considered by the Court in imposing defendant's sentence.

The Courtroom Deputy is directed to serve this Order on all counsel at the time of post-indictment arraignment proceedings.

IT IS SO ORDERED.

DATED: ____________________

____
CORMAC J. CARNEY
United States District Judge

B. Order Regarding Settlement Procedures, Pre-Trial Conference, and Trial

IN THE UNITED STATES DISTICT COURT
FOR THE CENTRAL DISTRICT OF CALIFORNIA

	)	Case No. _______________
Plaintiff(s),	)	
v.	)	**ORDER REGARDING**
Defendant(s).	)	**SETTLEMENT PROCEDURES,**
______________________________	)	**PRE-TRIAL CONFERENCE, AND TRIAL**

This matter is assigned for all purposes to the Honorable Cormac J. Carney, United States District Judge, Courtroom 9B, Ronald Reagan Federal Building and United States Courthouse, 411 West Fourth Street, Santa Ana, California, 92701-4516. The Court's mandatory procedures and requirements for Settlement, the Pre-Trial Conference and Trial are as follows:

SETTLEMENT PROCEDURES

1. It is the policy of the Court to encourage disposition of civil litigation by settlement when such is in the best interest of the parties. The Court favors any reasonable means to accomplish this goal. All settlement discussions will be conducted in compliance with Local Rule 16-15. The parties **must** elect one of the settlement procedures outlined in Local Rule 16-15.4. If the parties do not timely file a Notice of Settlement Procedure Selection, the Court may order the parties to participate in any of the settlement procedures set forth in the Local Rule. Unless otherwise ordered, no later than forty-five (45) days before the Pre-Trial Conference, the parties **must** participate in the selected settlement procedure. The Court may, on its own motion, order the parties to settlement following the Pre-Trial Conference. Given the high costs of litigation and the enormous commitment of resources that a trial requires, the parties must explore every option for resolving their disputes, short of trial. The failure of any party to comply with the local rules and engage in meaningful settlement discussions may result in the imposition of sanctions against that noncomplying party.

PRE-TRIAL CONFERENCE

2. Compliance with the requirements of Local Rule 16 is mandatory. Counsel will lodge carefully prepared Memoranda of Contentions of Fact and Law (which may also serve as the trial briefs) and a Final Pre-Trial Conference Order in accordance with the provisions of Local Rules 16-4 and 16-7. The Memoranda of Contentions of Fact and Law will be served no later than twenty-one (21) calendar days before the Pre-Trial Conference. The Final Pre-Trial Conference Order will be lodged five (5) court days before the Pre-Trial Conference. The form of the Final Pre-Trial Conference Order will be in conformity with the form set forth in Appendix A to the Local Rules.

MOTIONS *IN LIMINE*

3. All Motions *in Limine* will be heard at the Pre-Trial Conference. The purpose of these motions is to alert the Court to significant evidentiary issues that can be addressed and resolved prior to trial. All Motions *in Limine* must be filed and served in compliance with Local Rule 6-1. Opposition papers must be filed and served in compliance with Local Rule 7-9. Reply papers must be filed and served in compliance with Local Rule 7-10.

STATEMENT OF THE CASE

4. Counsel will prepare a joint statement of the case which will be read by the Court to the prospective panel of jurors prior to the commencement of voir dire. The statement should not be more than two or three paragraphs. The statement will be filed with the Court five (5) court days before the Pre-Trial Conference or one (1) week prior to the trial if the Pre-Trial Conference is waived.

EXHIBIT LIST AND EXHIBIT PREPARATION

5. A joint exhibit list will be prepared in compliance with Local Rule 16-6. The joint exhibit list will contain the information required by F.R.Civ.P. 26(a)(3)(C). The joint exhibit list will be filed no later than five (5) court days prior to the Pre-Trial Conference or one (1) week prior to the trial if the Pre-Trial Conference is waived. In order to produce the joint exhibit list, the parties **will** meet and confer sufficiently in advance of the required submission date.

6. Exhibits are to be delivered to the Courtroom Deputy Clerk not later than 8:30 a.m. on the first day of trial. All exhibits will be placed in loose leaf binders which are tabbed down the right side with exhibit numbers. The spine of the notebook is to be marked with the case name and number and the numbers of the exhibits contained therein. The notebooks are to be prepared with an original for the Clerk, which will be tagged with the appropriate exhibit tags in the upper right-hand corner of the first page of each exhibit, and one copy for the Court. Each notebook will contain a list of the included exhibits. The exhibits are to be numbered in accordance with Local Rule 26-3. Counsel may obtain exhibit tags (yellow for plaintiff and blue for defendant) at the Clerk's Office, Intake Window. Special arrangements for voluminous or over sized exhibits should be made with the Courtroom Deputy Clerk by Wednesday of the week before trial.

WITNESS LISTS

7. A witness list will be prepared in compliance with Local Rule 16-5. The witness list will be filed no later than five (5) court days prior to the Pre-Trial Conference or one (1) week prior to the trial if the Pre-Trial Conference is waived. Counsel will submit the names of the witnesses in the order that they are expected to testify, and provide, to the extent possible, an accurate estimate of the time needed for each witness for direct, cross, redirect and re-cross. Counsel will also provide a brief summary of what each witness will testify to. If more than one witness is offered on the same subject, the summary should be sufficiently detailed to allow the Court to determine if the testimony is cumulative.

JURY INSTRUCTIONS

8. In a jury trial, jury instructions are to be filed no later than five (5) court days prior to the Pre-Trial Conference or one (1) week prior to the trial if Pre-Trial Conference is waived. The parties must submit joint jury instructions. The parties **will** meet and confer sufficiently in advance of the required submission date, in order to prepare the joint jury instructions. The instructions should be submitted in the order in which the parties wish to have the instructions read. This order should reflect a single organized sequence agreed to by all of the parties. The Court insists upon receiving lucid and accurate instructions setting forth the elements of each party's claims and defenses. The instructions should be tailored to the facts of each case. INSTRUCTIONS WILL BE BRIEF, CLEAR, CONCISE, WRITTEN IN PLAIN ENGLISH, FREE OF ARGUMENT AND WILL BE ORGANIZED IN A LOGICAL FASHION SO AS TO AID JURY COMPREHENSION.

9. In the event that agreement cannot be reached, counsel will submit three (3) sets of

instructions (with an extra set for the Court's law clerks) in the following format: (1) the agreed upon instructions; (2) the instructions proposed by plaintiff and opposed by defendant; and (3) the instructions proposed by defendant and opposed by plaintiff. Instructions upon which agreement cannot be reached should reflect the basic disagreements among the parties as to the law. The disputed instructions should be presented to the Court within the framework of the overall set of instructions. The parties should put forth differing versions of disputed instructions, and the Court will select one version.

10. The instructions submitted to the Court must be numbered, and the parties must also submit an unnumbered index. Attribution and case citation for each instruction will be placed on pages following a proposed instruction. For disputed instructions, a party should note its objections to a proposed instruction and its reasons for putting forth its alternative on pages placed after its own alternative instruction.

VERDICT FORMS

11. Counsel are to prepare and file a verdict form in accordance with the same procedures as those required for jury instructions. Counsel are to use their best efforts to agree upon a joint verdict form and submit it to the Court no later than five (5) court days prior to the Pre-Trial Conference or one (1) week prior to the trial if the Pre-Trial Conference is waived. If counsel cannot agree as to the form of the verdict, the parties should submit their respective version to the Court on the submission date for the joint verdict form.

12. **Counsel are advised that if any inconsistencies exist between the submission and lodging dates provided in this Order and the Local Rules, the dates in this Order will govern and supercede the Local Rules.**

IT IS SO ORDERED.

IT IS FURTHER ORDERED that the Clerk of the Court shall serve, by United States mail, copies of this Order on counsel for the parties in this matter.

DATED: ____________________

____
CORMAC J. CARNEY
United States District Judge

Hon. David O. Carter

District Judge

Chambers Information
U.S. District Court, Central District of California
Courtroom 9D
411 West Fourth Street
Santa Ana, CA 92701

Scheduling Information
Courtroom Deputy: (714) 338-4543

Civil Law and Motion, Status Conferences, and Pre-Trial Conferences	Mondays at 8:30 a.m.
Criminal Law and Motion, Status Conferences, Pleas, and Sentencings	Mondays at 1:30 p.m.
Trials	Tuesday to Friday, from 8:30 a.m. until the Court recesses for the day.

Judge's Biography
Born 1944 in Providence, RI

Federal Judicial Service:
-Judge, U. S. District Court, Central District of California
-Nominated by William J. Clinton on June 25, 1998, to a seat vacated by William J. Rea; Confirmed by the Senate on October 21, 1998, and received commission on October 22, 1998.

Education:
-University of California, Los Angeles, B.A., 1967
-University of California, Los Angeles, School of Law, J.D., 1972

Professional Career:
-District Attorney, Orange County, California, 1972-1981
-Judge, Western Division, Orange County Municipal Court, California, 1981-1982
-Judge, Eastern Division, Orange County Municipal Court, California, 1982
-Judge, Orange County Superior Court, California, 1982-1998

I. Judge Carter's Procedures and Practices

A. *Procedures and Schedules*

I. SCHEDULING AND COURT HOURS

A. Motions. Motions are heard on Mondays. When Monday is a holiday, the next motion date is the following Monday. It is not necessary to clear or reserve a motion date with the court clerk prior to filing the motion, but the motion must be in compliance with all Local and Federal Rules regarding service.

1. **Civil Motions, Status Conferences, and Pre-Trial Conferences** are set for ***Mondays*** at ***8:30 a.m.***

2. **Criminal Motions, Status Conferences, Pleas, and Sentencings** are set for ***Mondays*** at ***1:30 p.m.***

B. Trials. Trials are held Tuesday to Friday, from 8:30 a.m. until the Court recesses for the day.

II. MOTION PRACTICE

A. Mandatory Chambers Copies and Filing in Santa Ana. Mandatory Chambers Copies of all e-filed documents shall be delivered to the mandatory chambers copy box on the 9th Floor by noon following the date of filing as required by General Order 10-07.IV.D. Counsel shall email any proposed order in WordPerfect or Microsoft Word to DOC_Chambers@cacd.uscourts.gov as required by General Order 10-07.VI.B. The Court does not accept mandatory chambers copies of sealed documents; counsel shall submit all under seal filings to the Southern Division Intake Section in Santa Ana as required by General Order 10-07.V.D.

B. Continuances. Continuances are rarely granted. To request a continuance of a hearing date, a stipulation signed by all parties should be filed, setting forth in detail the reason for the requested continuance. Ex parte applications for continuances will be granted only upon good cause shown.

C. Tentative rulings. The Court may issue a tentative ruling on a motion. If so, copies will be distributed to counsel the morning of the hearing.

D. Court appearances. Parties shall be represented at all court appearances by the counsel expected to be in charge of conducting trial on behalf of the parties. Under no circumstances should counsel, or a party if the party is appearing pro se, fail to appear at a court appearance unless their appearance has been waived by prior order of the Court. Even if a settlement has been reached, counsel for all parties, or the party if appearing pro se, must appear at court appearances until a stipulation of dismissal signed by all parties has been lodged with the Court.

E. Ex Parte Applications. Ex Parte applications are submitted on the papers. If the Court finds that a hearing is necessary, counsel will be notified and given a hearing date and time. The moving party shall serve the opposing party and shall notify the opposing party that any opposition must be filed no later than 24 hours after such service. If counsel does not intend to oppose the ex parte application, counsel must inform the Court as soon as possible.

III. THE COURT'S STANDARD ORDERS

Early in the litigation of a case, the Court sends out an Order Setting a Scheduling Conference. This Order provides important guidance regarding the procedures counsel should follow. At or after the Scheduling Conference, the Court provides counsel with a Scheduling Order. This Order confirms the dates selected by counsel and the Court and provides further guidance regarding the procedures that counsel should follow. Both Orders should be read and attended to carefully, as compliance with the Orders is required. Samples of the Orders can be obtained by clicking on the attachments below.

IV. LAW CLERK AND EXTERN APPLICATIONS

Law clerk and extern applications should be mailed to chambers (United States Courthouse, 411 West Fourth Street, Suite 9-160, Santa Ana, CA 92701-4516). Questions should be directed to the Judge's law clerks, who can be reached by calling 714-338-4545. Clerkship applicants should submit a cover letter, resume, transcript, brief writing sample (suggested length is under 15 pages), and 2-3 letters of recommendation. Externship applicants should submit the same materials, except that letters of recommendation are not required.

Other information: Counsel are directed to comply with all Local Rules. If counsel have received a "Notice to Parties of ADR Program" (form ADR-08, ADR-10, or ADR-11 with attached "ADR Program Questionnaire" form ADR-09), please see the section on the Court's website entitled "ADR," General Order 02-07, for further information. The ADR section also contains Attorney Settlement Officer information.

For general information on how to order a transcript of any reported or digitally recorded proceeding, please contact 213-894-3015 or visit www.cacd.uscourts.gov > General Information > Court Reporter/Recorder Transcripts. If you require an estimate of cost for the preparation of a transcript, contact the court reporter/recorder for the desired proceeding.

To determine the court reporter/recorder for a particular proceeding, go to the Court Reporter Schedule web page and click on View by Date. Once you've determined the correct court reporter/recorder for the desired session, click on Court Reporter Phone and Email List for contact information.

Mandatory Chambers Copies of all e-filed documents shall be delivered to the mandatory chambers copy box on the 9th Floor. It is imperative that the mandatory chambers copies be delivered by noon following the date of filing as required by General Order 10-07.IV.D. Failure to deliver timely mandatory chambers copies may result in a delay in hearing a motion or ordering the matter off calendar.

II. Judge Carter's Case Management Orders

A. *Order Setting Scheduling Conference*

IN THE UNITED STATES DISTICT COURT
FOR THE CENTRAL DISTRICT OF CALIFORNIA

Plaintiff(s),	Case No. ______________
v.	**ORDER SETTING SCHEDULING CONFERENCE FOR**
Defendant(s).	March 28, 2011 at 8:30 a.m., Courtroom 9-D
	READ IMMEDIATELY

This action has been assigned to the calendar of Judge David O. Carter. The responsibility for the progress of litigation in the federal courts falls not only upon the attorneys in the action, but upon the Court as well. Accordingly, the Court issues this Order.

In order "to secure the just, speedy, and inexpensive determination of every action," Fed. R. Civ. P. 1, all counsel shall familiarize themselves with the Federal Rules of Civil Procedure and the Local Rules of the Central District of California.[1] All civil actions or proceedings will be pre-tried according to Federal Rules of Civil Procedure 16 and 26 and applicable Local Rules.

Unless there is a likelihood that upon motion by a party the Court would order that any or all discovery is premature, the Court encourages the parties to begin discovery before the Scheduling Conference. The parties shall comply fully with the letter and spirit of Rule 26(a) and thereby obtain and produce most of what would be produced in the early stages of discovery, because at the Scheduling Conference the Court will impose tight deadlines to complete discovery.

RULE 26(f) CONFERENCE OF PARTIES

Counsel shall confer pursuant to Federal Rule of Civil Procedure 26(f). This conference shall occur at least twenty-one (21) days before the Scheduling Conference set by the Court.

RULE 26(f) REPORT

The parties shall file their Rule 26(f) report with the Court no later than fourteen (14) days prior to the Scheduling Conference set by the Court. The report shall contain the following:

(1) a short factual summary of the case and of claims and defenses;

(2) a short synopsis of the principal issues in the case;

(3) a statement of whether parties are likely to be added and whether the pleadings are likely to be amended (counsel should note that the Court sets a deadline of ninety (90) days after the date the Scheduling Order is issued for the joinder of parties and the amendment of pleadings; any motions to join parties or for leave to amend must be filed within sixty (60) days of the day the Scheduling Order is issued to allow them to be determined prior to the 90-day deadline);

(4) a statement as to issues which any party believes may be determined by motion and a listing of then contemplated law and motion matters;

[1] Copies of the Local Rules are available at: <www.cacd.uscourts.gov>.

(5) a statement of what settlement discussions have occurred and what settlement procedure is recommended, pursuant to Local Rules 16-15 through 16-15.9 (specifically excluding any statement of the terms discussed and specifically including, if mediation is chosen, the particular mediator who has been chosen);

(6) a discovery plan, which should set forth discovery phases, the order of discovery, and any limitations on discovery;

(7) a statement of whether trial will be by jury or to the Court and a realistic estimated length of trial (mindful that the Court generally conducts a **four (4) day timed jury trial**, where each side is given ten (10) hours, excluding jury selection, opening statement and closing argument);

(8) a statement of any other issues affecting the status or management of the case; and

(9) our **proposed, *specific* dates** as follows:

(a) a discovery cut-off date;

(b) a final motion cut-off date, **which should be a Monday and will be the last day on which motions will be heard** (counsel should note that motions will need to be filed several weeks in advance of this date as required by Local Rule 6; ordinarily the motion cut-off should be approximately forty-five (45) days after the discovery cutoff);

(c) a date for the Final Pretrial Conference, **which should be a Monday**; and

(d) a date for trial, **which should be a Tuesday**.

After the parties have selected these dates, ***continuances are rarely granted*** due to the Court's heavy case load and in fairness to other litigants before the Court.

A report that does not comply with Rule 26(f) and this Order may subject the party or parties responsible to sanctions under Local Rule 83-7. Counsel for all parties participating in the conference of parties should sign the report.

SCHEDULING CONFERENCE AND SCHEDULING ORDER

As indicated in this Order, this case has been placed on the Court's calendar for a Scheduling Conference pursuant to Rule 26(f) in this Court at 8:30 a.m. The parties shall be represented at the Scheduling Conference by **lead counsel**. A continuance of the Scheduling Conference will be granted rarely and only for good cause and will not be granted if a continuance would result in the Scheduling Conference being set after the time limit for the Court to issue a Scheduling Order under Rule 16(b).

The Court usually issues Scheduling Orders pursuant to Rule 16(b) at or after the Scheduling Conference.

SETTLEMENT PROCEDURES

A settlement procedure appropriate to the particular case will be used in every civil action. See Local R. 16-14.4. In their Rule 26(f) report, counsel are to recommend a specific settlement procedure provided for in Local Rule 16-14.4. Available alternatives include:

(1) appearance before a retired judicial officer or other private or non-profit dispute resolution body for settlement or mediation proceedings (if chosen, the particular mediator selected should be indicated);

(2) appearance before an attorney selected from the Attorney Settlement Officer Panel;

(3) if one of the parties is a public entity, a settlement conference before the magistrate judge assigned to this case; or

(4) such other settlement mechanism proposed by the parties and approved by the Court.

The report to the Court concerning settlement procedures should be preceded by a thorough and frank discussion among the attorneys for the parties.

MOTION MATTERS

In motion matters, counsel should note the timing and service requirements of Local Rules 6 and 7 and their sub-parts, including:

(1) Rule 6-1 (twenty-eight (28) days notice for all motions unless served by mail, in which case thirty-one (31) days is required) (notice of motion and moving papers to be filed twenty (28) days before the hearing date);

(2) Rule 7-9 (responses to all motions twenty-one (21) calendar days before the hearing date); and

(3) Rule 7-10 (reply, if any, to all responses fourteen (14) calendar days before the hearing date).

Counsel must comply with the timing requirements of the Local Rules so that chambers can properly prepare for motion matters.

COURT APPEARANCES

Parties shall be represented at **all** court appearances by lead counsel. Personal appearance is required at all court appearances.

Under no circumstances should counsel, or a party if the party is appearing pro se, fail to appear at a court appearance unless the appearance has been waived by prior order of the Court. Even if a settlement has been reached, counsel for all parties, or the party if appearing pro se, must appear at Court appearances until a stipulation of dismissal signed by all parties has been lodged with the Court.

OTHER

Counsel are required to electronically file all papers in accordance with General Order 10-07.

All appropriate inquiries should be directed to Kathy Peterson, Deputy Court Clerk, at (714) 338-4543. Counsel should not attempt to contact chambers directly. Counsel should list their facsimile transmission numbers and email addresses on their papers in order to facilitate communication by the Deputy Court Clerk.

Plaintiff shall serve a copy of this Order on any as-yet unserved Defendants when Plaintiff serves the Complaint on them.

IT IS SO ORDERED.

DATED: _______________

____
DAVID O. CARTER
United States District Judge

B. ***Scheduling Order***

IN THE UNITED STATES DISTICT COURT
FOR THE CENTRAL DISTRICT OF CALIFORNIA

Plaintiff(s), v. Defendant(s).	Case No. ___________ **SCHEDULING ORDER** 1. SETTING DISCOVERY CUT-OFF DATE: _______. 2. MOTION CUT-OFF DATE: _______. 3. SETTING FINAL PRETRIAL CONFERENCE: ________ (at 8:30 a.m.) 4. SETTING JURY TRIAL DATE: ______ (at 8:30 a.m.)

This Pretrial Scheduling Order governs the course of all pretrial proceedings in this case. For further guidance, consult the Federal Rules of Civil Procedure and the Local Rules.

JOINDER OF PARTIES AND AMENDMENT OF PLEADINGS

The deadline for joining parties and amending pleadings is ninety (90) days after the date of this Order. Any motions to join other parties or for leave to amend the pleadings shall be filed within sixty (60) days of the date of this Order so that they can be heard and decided prior to the deadline.

DISCOVERY CUT-OFF

The Court has established a cut-off date for discovery in this action. All discovery is to be completed on, or prior to, the cut-off date. Expert discovery must also be completed by the discovery cutoff date. Plan now to complete discovery on the schedule set; a continuance is *unlikely*. Accordingly, the following discovery schedule shall apply in this Court:

(1) Depositions: All depositions shall be scheduled to commence at least five (5) working days prior to the discovery cut-off date. A deposition which commences five (5) days prior to the discovery cut-off date may continue beyond the cut-off date, as necessary.

(2) Written Discovery: All interrogatories, requests for production of documents, and requests for admissions shall be served at least forty-five (45) days before the discovery cut-off date. The Court will not approve stipulations between counsel that permit responses to be served after the cut-off date except in unusual circumstances and upon a showing of good cause.

(3) Discovery Motions: Any motion regarding the inadequacy of responses to discovery must be filed and served no later than five (5) days after the discovery cut-off date. The Court requires compliance with the requirements of Local Rule 37 in the preparation and filing of discovery motions. Whenever possible, counsel should resolve discovery problems on their own in a courteous, reasonable, and professional manner. Assistance of the Court in the resolution of most discovery matters should not be necessary.

Parties shall follow the disclosure and timing rules of the Federal Rules of Civil

Procedure and the Local Rules. Routine discovery motions will be referred to the magistrate judge assigned to the case.

MOTION MATTERS

In motion matters, counsel should note the timing and service requirements of Local Rules 6 and 7 and its subparts including:

(1) Rule 6-1 (twenty-eight (28) days notice for all motions unless served by mail, in which case thirty-one (31) days is required) (notice of motion and moving papers to be filed twenty-eight (28) days before the hearing date);

(2) Rule 7-9 (responses to all motions twenty-one (21) calendar days before the hearing date); and

(3) Rule 7-10 (reply, if any, to all responses fourteen (14) calendar days before the hearing date).

Counsel must comply with the timing requirements of the Local Rules so that chambers can properly prepare for motion matters.

The motion cut-off date is the last day on which the Court will hear motions. Counsel should note that motions will need to be filed several weeks in advance of this date as required by Local Rule 6.

PRETRIAL CONFERENCE AND TRIAL SETTING

This case has been placed on calendar for a Pretrial Conference ("PTC") pursuant to Federal Rule of Civil Procedure 16 and the Local Rules. Unless excused for good cause, each party appearing in this action shall be represented at the PTC and all pretrial meetings of counsel by the attorney who is to have charge of the conduct of the trial on behalf of such party.

A continuance of the Pretrial Conference at counsel's request or stipulation is *highly unlikely*. Counsel should plan to do the necessary pretrial work on a schedule which will ensure its completion with time to spare before the Pretrial Conference. Failure to complete discovery work is not grounds for a continuance. The Court has a crowded docket and to displace another case already set for trial in favor of a case in which counsel have not been diligent in preparing their case would not be just.

Compliance with the requirements of Local Rule 16 is required by the Court. Carefully prepared Memoranda of Contentions of Fact and Law (which may also serve as the trial brief) and a proposed Pretrial Conference Order ("PTCO") shall be submitted in accordance with the provisions of Local Rules 16-6 through 16-7. and the form of the proposed Pretrial Conference Order shall be in conformity with the format set forth in Appendix A to Local Rules.

The Memoranda of Contentions of Fact and Law are due twenty-one (21) days before the PTC and the proposed PTCO is to be lodged eleven (11) days before the PTC. Adherence to the time requirements is necessary to provide the Court and its staff time to prepare the matter.

At the PTC, counsel should be prepared to discuss means of streamlining the trial, including, but not limited to: bifurcation, presentation of non-critical testimony by deposition excerpts, stipulations as to the content of testimony, presentation of testimony on direct examination by declaration subject to cross-examination, and qualification of experts by admitted resumes. In rare cases in which the Court waives the PTC, counsel must follow Local

Rules 16-10 through 16-10.1.

In drafting the PTCO, the Court expects that counsel will attempt to agree on and set forth as many uncontested facts as possible. The Court will normally read the uncontested facts to the jury at the start of the trial. A carefully drafted and comprehensively stated stipulation of facts will reduce the length of trial and increase jury understanding of the case.

All motions (except motions *in limine* dealing with admissibility of evidence) must be disposed of before the Pretrial Conference. A motion *in limine* may not be used as a substitute for a summary judgment motion. All motions *in limine* must be filed no later than the date on which the PTCO is lodged with the Court; oppositions to motions *in limine* must be filed no later than 7 days prior to the PTC.

JURY INSTRUCTIONS/FINDINGS OF FACT AND CONCLUSIONS OF LAW

Proposed jury instructions must be timely filed. The parties should exchange proposed jury instructions and agree as much as possible on the necessary instructions before filing them with the Court. In matters tried to the Court, the parties should prepare, serve, and lodge proposed findings of fact and conclusions of law as promptly as possible and in compliance with the Local Rules. Both parties should also submit their proposed jury instructions and findings of fact and conclusions of law on disk, preferably in Word Perfect format.

COURT APPEARANCES

Parties shall be represented at *all* court appearances by the counsel expected to be in charge of conducting trial on behalf of the parties.

Under no circumstances should counsel, or a party if the party is appearing *pro se*, fail to appear at a court appearance unless their appearance has been waived by prior order of the Court. Even if a settlement has been reached, counsel for all parties, or the party if appearing *pro se*, must appear at court appearances until a stipulation of dismissal signed by all parties has been lodged with the Court.

OTHER

Counsel are required to electronically file all papers in accordance with General Order 10-07.

All appropriate inquiries should be directed to Kathy Peterson, Deputy Court Clerk, at (714) 338-4543. Counsel should not attempt to contact chambers directly. Counsel should list their email addresses and facsimile transmission numbers on their papers in order to facilitate communication by the Deputy Court Clerk.

The Deputy Court Clerk is ordered to serve a copy of this Order on all parties to this action, if not personally handed to counsel at the Scheduling Conference.

IT IS SO ORDERED.

DATE: ________________

____
DAVID O. CARTER
United States District Judge

Hon. Audrey B. Collins

Chief District Judge

Chambers Information

U.S. District Court, Central District of California
Courtroom 680
255 East Temple Street
Los Angeles, CA 90012

Scheduling Information

Courtroom Deputy: (213) 894-6500

Civil Law and Motion	Mondays at 10:00 a.m.
Criminal Law and Motion	Mondays at 1:30 p.m.

Judge's Biography

Born 1945 in Chester, PA

Federal Judicial Service:

-Judge, U. S. District Court, Central District of California
-Nominated by William J. Clinton on January 27, 1994, to a seat vacated by Robert C. Bonner; Confirmed by the Senate on May 6, 1994, and received commission on May 9, 1994. Served as Chief Judge, 2009-present.

Education:

-Howard University, B.A., 1967
-American University, M.A., 1969
-University of California, Los Angeles, School of Law, J.D., 1977

Professional Career:

-Assistant Attorney, Legal Aid Foundation of Los Angeles, California, 1977
-Deputy District Attorney, Los Angeles County District Attorney's Office, California, 1978-1994
-Head Deputy, Torrance Branch Office, 1987-1988
-Assistant Director, Bureaus of Central and Special Operations, 1988-1992
-Assistant District Attorney, 1992-1994
-Deputy General Counsel, Office of the Special Advisor to the L.A.P.D. Board of
-Commissioners, California, 1992

I. Judge Collins' Procedures and Practices

A. *Procedures and Schedules*

1. Civil motions are heard on: Monday, time: 10:00 AM

   Criminal motions are heard on: Monday, time: 1:30 PM

   (If Monday is a holiday, motion date is the next Monday)

   It is not necessary to clear a motion date with the court clerk prior to filing the motion.

2. Discovery motions are to be scheduled before the Magistrate Judge.

3. Tentative rulings are issued only at the hearing prior to calling the case. For security reasons, paper copies of filings shall be removed from envelopes or folders before being placed in the chambers drop-box.

4. Efiling is mandatory as of January 2, 2008.

5. Two sets of mandatory chambers paper copies must be delivered directly to chambers by 12:00 p.m. (noon) of the court day following the efiling of any document. Counsel shall familiarize themselves with the Central District's General Order 08-02 and 08-11.

6. When it is necessary to file an ex parte application, counsel shall submit with the application a declaration indicating the necessity of the ex parte, that the opposing party(ies) have been notified and whether they oppose the application. The Court will notify counsel if a hearing is to be scheduled. See the Court's Order re: Pretrial Conference for additional information on the filing of ex parte applications.

7. Submit a stipulation if you are seeking a continuance or extension of time. See General Order 10-07 for the correct procedure to follow in submitting a stipulation and proposed order to the Court.

8. Counsel should for no reason contact chambers, law clerks or the secretary.

9. Inquiries re: status of motions, stipulations or proposed orders should be made by checking the docket sheet through PACER.

10. If counsel have a calendar conflict, they should contact the Court Clerk as soon as possible.

11. There are no occasions when electronic equipment is allowed in the courtroom without the Court's prior approval.

12. For general information on how to order a transcript of any reported or digitally recorded proceeding, please contact 213-894-3015 or visit www.cacd.uscourts.gov > General Information > Court Reporter/Recorder Transcripts. If you require an estimate of cost for the preparation of a transcript, contact the court reporter/recorder for the desired proceeding.

    To determine the court reporter/recorder for a particular proceeding, go to the Court Reporter Schedule web page and click on View by Date. Once you've determined the correct court reporter/recorder for the desired session, click on Court Reporter Phone and Email List for contact information.

13. Trial preparation: Court hours: 8:30 AM - 5:00 PM
    -have exhibit tags in place prior to bringing exhibits to Court

-only substantive instructions should be submitted
-counsel should prepare verdict forms in civil cases

14. It is the responsibility of counsel in a civil case to arrange the services of an interpreter - 213-894-4599.

If counsel has received a "Notice to Parties of Alternate Dispute Resolution (ADR) Program" - forms ADR-08, ADR-10, or ADR-11 with an attached "ADR Program Questionnaire" form ADR-09, please see General Order 07-01 which is located in the "General Orders" section on the home page of the Court's website. The Attorney Settlement Officer information is located in the section "Attorney Information, ADR."

II. Judge Collins' Case Management Orders

A. Civil Court Trial Order

IN THE UNITED STATES DISTICT COURT
FOR THE CENTRAL DISTRICT OF CALIFORNIA

Plaintiff(s),)	Case No. ______________
v.)	
Defendant(s).)	**CIVIL COURT TRIAL ORDER**

The above matter is set for trial before the Honorable Audrey B. Collins, Courtroom 680, Roybal Federal Building, 255 East Temple Street, Los Angeles, CA 90012.

PRETRIAL AND TRIAL DATES

1. The Court orders the following dates:

a. Cut-off date for filing motions to join other parties and amend the pleadings is ______________.

b. Discovery cut-off is ______________________.

c. Cut-off date for motions to be filed is Monday, ________________.

d. Final Pretrial Conference is set for Monday, ______________ at 10:00 a.m.

e. Trial is set for Tuesday, ______________________ at 8:30 a.m.

DISCOVERY

2. The Court has ordered the above cut-off date for discovery in this action. *The non-expert discovery cut-off date means the last day by which all depositions must be completed and responses to all previously served written discovery must be provided. It does not mean the last day to initiate discovery or to file a motion with the magistrate judge seeking to compel discovery.* A deposition commenced at least five (5) days before the cut-off date may continue beyond the cut-off date. Discovery should be kept to a minimum and focus only on issues genuinely in dispute. Counsel are expected to resolve substantially all discovery problems without the assistance of the court. If discovery disputes cannot be resolved, the court requires strict compliance with the requirements of Local Rule 37.

LAW AND MOTION

3. The Court has ordered the above cut-off date for the filing of motions in this action. **Two sets of mandatory chambers' paper copies must be delivered directly to chambers by 12:00 p.m. (noon) of the court day following the filing of any document. *For security reasons, paper copies of filings should be removed from envelopes or folders before being placed in the chambers drop-box.* Counsel should familiarize themselves with Central District General Orders 08-02 and 08-11.**

4. Counsel must comply with Local Rule 7, including Rule 7-3, Conference of Counsel Prior to Filing of Motions. See the detailed discussion in the Court's Order Re Pretrial Conference.

5. When filing motions for summary judgment, the Court encourages the moving party to provide more than the minimum twenty-eight (28) day notice.

6. If oral argument is not required, counsel will be advised the week before the hearing date. If oral argument is to be heard, a tentative ruling or an outline of issues on which argument should concentrate will generally be available 30 minutes before the time of hearing.

SETTLEMENT PROCEDURES

7. As set forth in Local Rule 16-15.1, a settlement procedure is required in every case. A Notice of Settlement Procedure shall be filed not later than 14 days after entry of the Scheduling Order (L.R. 16-15.2). Counsel should become familiar with the options presented by Local Rule 16-15.4. Counsel are responsible for conducting settlement procedures no later than forty-five (45) days before the Pretrial Conference and shall submit with the proposed Pretrial Conference Order a status report detailing what procedure has been followed (L.R. 16-15.2). If the parties do not file a timely Notice of Settlement Procedure Selection, the trial judge may order the parties to participate in any of the settlement procedures set forth in this rule (L.R. 16 – 15.3).

8. The undersigned will not conduct settlement conferences in non-jury cases which she is to try.

9. Unless otherwise ordered by the judge or magistrate judge conducting a settlement conference, the parties shall follow the "Requirements for Settlement Procedures" set forth in Local Rule 16-15.5.

10. If a settlement is reached, it shall be reported immediately to this court as required by Local Rule 16-15.7. In addition, the parties must file a Status Report re Settlement at the time that they lodge the Proposed Pre-Trial Conference Order, indicating whether they have conducted the Local Rule 16 Settlement Conference and/or what additional steps are being taken to achieve settlement.

PREPARATION FOR FINAL PRETRIAL CONFERENCE

11. Compliance with all requirements of Local Rule 16 is required by the Court. Carefully prepared Memoranda of Contentions of Fact (which may also serve as the trial brief), Witness Lists, Joint Exhibit Lists, and a Final Pretrial Conference Order ("FPTCO") shall be submitted in accordance with the time limits and other requirements of Local Rules 16 - 4 through 16 - 7. Note that service and filing of these documents begins 21 days before the Final Pretrial Conference. (L.R. 16 – 4). Also note that Rule 16 contains specific requirements for presentation of deposition testimony (L.R. 16 -2.7) and disclosure of graphic and illustrative material (L.R. 16 – 3).

12. As required by Local Rule 16 - 7.2, the FPTCO should follow the format shown in Pretrial Form No. 1 set forth in Appendix A to the Local Rules.

MOTIONS IN LIMINE

13. Motions in limine on classes of evidence which are appropriate for preliminary rulings must be filed no later than twenty-eight (28) days before the date of the Final Pretrial Conference. Oppositions shall be filed no later than twenty-one (21) days before the date of the Final Pretrial Conference. Reply briefs shall be filed no later than fourteen (14) days before the date of the Final Pretrial Conference. The Court does not appreciate mass filings of such motions and may limit those heard if parties abuse the process.

FINAL PRETRIAL CONFERENCE

14. This case has been placed on calendar for a Final Pretrial Conference ("FPTC"), as stated above, pursuant to Fed. R. Civ. P. 16 and Local Rule 16, unless the FPTC is exempted pursuant to L.R. 16-11 or was expressly waived at the Pretrial/Scheduling Conference by the Court. Unless excused for good cause, each party appearing in this action shall be represented at the FPTC and all pretrial meetings by the attorney who is to have charge of the conduct of the trial on behalf of such party.

15. No continuance of the FPTC shall be granted merely on stipulation of the parties. (Local Rule 16-9). Counsel should plan to do the necessary pretrial work on a schedule which will ensure its completion with time to spare before the FPTC, and in accordance with Local Rule 16. Specifically, failure to complete discovery is <u>not</u> a ground for a continuance.

16. At the FPTC, counsel should be prepared to discuss means of streamlining the trial, including, but not limited to, bifurcation, presentation of non-critical testimony by deposition excerpts, stipulations as to the content of testimony, and qualification of experts by admitted resumes. In rare cases where the PTC is waived by the Court, counsel must follow Local Rule 11-2.

TRIAL PREPARATION FOR COURT TRIAL - FINDINGS OF FACT AND CONCLUSIONS OF LAW, EXHIBITS AND LISTS

17. The Court orders that counsel comply with the following in their preparation for trial:

- **a.** Counsel for each party shall lodge and serve proposed Findings of Fact and Conclusions of Law at least seven (7) days before trial.
- **b.** The parties shall be prepared to submit to the Court, and to exchange among themselves, supplemental findings of fact and conclusions of law during the course of the trial.
- **c.** Counsel are to prepare their exhibits for presentation at the trial by placing them in 3-hole notebooks which are tabbed down the side with the exhibit numbers. These notebooks are to be prepared in an original for the Courtroom Deputy Clerk and two copies. The originals shall each be tagged with the appropriate exhibit tags in the upper or lower right-hand corner of the first page of each exhibit. Each notebook shall contain a list of each exhibit included. Counsel shall supply three extra copies of their individual or joint exhibit list and witness list to the Courtroom Deputy Clerk at the trial. The exhibits are to be numbered in accordance with Local Rule 16-6.
- **d.** All counsel are to meet not later than ten (10) calendar days before trial and to stipulate as far as is possible to foundation, waiver of the best evidence rule, and which exhibits may be received into evidence at the start of trial. The exhibits to be so received will be noted on the extra copies of the exhibit lists.

Dated: ____________________

____
AUDREY B. COLLINS
Chief United States District Judge

B. Civil Jury Trial Order

IN THE UNITED STATES DISTICT COURT
FOR THE CENTRAL DISTRICT OF CALIFORNIA

	)	Case No. _______________
Plaintiff(s),	)	
v.	)	
Defendant(s).	)	**CIVIL JURY TRIAL ORDER**
______________________	)	

The above matter is set for trial before the Honorable Audrey B. Collins, Courtroom 680, Roybal Federal Building, 255 East Temple Street, Los Angeles, CA 90012.

PRETRIAL AND TRIAL DATES

1. The Court orders the following dates:

a. Cut-off date for filing motions to join other parties and amending the pleadings is _______________.

b. Discovery cut-off is _________________________.

c. Cut-off date for motions **to be filed** is Monday, __________________.

d. Final Pretrial Conference is set for Monday, ________________ at 10:00 a.m. *Trial counsel must be present. Note: Counsel must comply with Local Rule 16.*

e. Trial is set for Tuesday, _______________________ at 8:30 a.m.

DISCOVERY

2. The Court has ordered the above cut-off date for discovery in this action. *The non-expert discovery cut-off date means the last day by which all depositions must be completed and responses to all previously served written discovery must be provided. It does not mean the last day to initiate discovery or to file a motion with the magistrate judge seeking to compel discovery.* A deposition commenced at least five (5) days before the cut-off date may continue beyond the cut-off date. Discovery should be kept to a minimum and focus only on issues genuinely in dispute. Counsel are expected to resolve substantially all discovery problems without the assistance of the court. If discovery disputes cannot be resolved, the parties are referred to the magistrate judge assigned to the case for resolution. The Court requires strict compliance with L.R. 7-3; including its Pre-Filing Conference of Counsel.

LAW AND MOTION

3. The Court has ordered the above cut-off date for the filing of motions in this action. **Two sets of mandatory chambers' paper copies must be delivered directly to chambers by 12:00 p.m. (noon) of the court day following the filing of any document.** ***For security reasons, paper copies of filings should be removed from envelopes or folders before placing them in the chambers drop-box.*** **Counsel should familiarize themselves with Central District General Orders 08-02 & 08-11.**

4. ***Counsel must comply with Local Rule 7, including L.R. 7-3, Conference of Counsel Prior to Filing of Motions. See the detailed discussion in the Court's Order Re Pretrial Conference.***

5. When filing motions for summary judgment, the Court encourages the moving party to provide more than the minimum twenty-eight (28) day notice.

6. If oral argument is not required, counsel will be advised the week before the hearing date. If oral argument is to be heard, a tentative ruling or an outline of issues on which argument should concentrate will generally be available 30 minutes before the time of hearing.

SETTLEMENT PROCEDURES

7. As set forth in Local Rule 16 - 15.1, a settlement procedure is required in every case. A Notice of Settlement Procedure shall be filed not later than 14 days after entry of the Scheduling Order. (L.R. 16 - 15.2). Counsel should become familiar with the options presented by L.R. 16 -15.4. Counsel are responsible for conducting settlement procedures no later than forty-five (45) days before the Pretrial Conference and shall submit with the proposed Pretrial Conference Order a status report detailing what procedure has been followed (L.R. 16 – 15.2).

8. If the parties do not file a timely Notice of Settlement Procedure Selection, the trial judge may order the parties to participate in any of the settlement procedures set forth in this rule (L.R. 16 – 15.3).

9. The undersigned will not conduct settlement conference in non-jury cases which she is to try. In jury cases, the undersigned will conduct a settlement conference if three conditions exist:
   a. Counsel are satisfied that the fact issues in the case will be tried to a jury;
   b. All significant pretrial rulings which the Court must make have been made; and
   c. All counsel desire the undersigned to conduct the conference, understanding that if settlement fails, the undersigned will try the case.

   If all three conditions exist, counsel must submit to this Court a proposed stipulation requesting a settlement conference date.

10. Unless otherwise ordered by the judge or magistrate judge conducting a settlement conference (whose procedures will apply if different than set forth here); the parties shall follow the "Requirements for Settlement Procedures" set forth in Local Rule 16 – 15.5.

11. If a settlement is reached, it shall be reported immediately to this Court as required by Local Rule 16 - 15.7. In addition, the parties must file a Status Report re Settlement at the time that they lodge the Proposed Pre-Trial Conference Order, indicating whether they have conducted the Local Rule 16 Settlement Conference and/or what additional steps are being taken to achieve settlement.

PREPARATION FOR FINAL PRETRIAL CONFERENCE

12. Compliance with all requirements of Local Rule 16 is required by the Court. Carefully prepared Memoranda of Contentions of Fact (which may also serve as the trial brief), Witness Lists, Joint Exhibit Lists, and a Final Pretrial Conference Order ("FPTCO") shall be submitted in accordance with the time limits and other requirements of Local Rules 16 - 4 through 16 – 7.

    Note that service and filing of these documents begins 21 days before the Final Pretrial Conference. (L.R. 16 – 4).

    Also note that Rule 16 contains specific requirements for presentation of deposition testimony (L.R. 16 -2.7) and disclosure of graphic and illustrative material (L.R. 16–3).

13. As required by Local Rule 16 - 7.2, the FPTCO should follow the format shown in Pretrial Form No. 1 set forth in Appendix A to the Local Rules.

MOTIONS IN LIMINE

14. Motions in limine on classes of evidence which are appropriate for preliminary rulings must be filed no later than twenty-eight (28) days before the date of the Final Pretrial Conference. Oppositions shall be filed no later than twenty-one (21) days before the date of the Final Pretrial Conference. Reply briefs shall be filed no later than fourteen (14) days before the date of the Final Pretrial Conference. The Court does not appreciate mass filings of such motions and may limit those heard if parties abuse the process.

FINAL PRETRIAL CONFERENCE

15. This case has been placed on calendar for a Final Pretrial Conference ("FPTC"), pursuant to Fed. R. Civ. P. 16 and Local Rule 16, unless the FPTC is exempted pursuant to L.R. 16-11 or was waived at the Pretrial/Scheduling Conference by the Court. Unless excused for good cause, each party appearing in this action shall be represented at the FPTC and all pretrial meetings by the attorney who is to have charge of the conduct of the trial on behalf of such party.

16. No continuance of the FPTC shall be granted merely on stipulation of the parties (Local Rule 16 - 9). Counsel should plan to do the necessary pretrial work on a schedule which will ensure its completion with time to spare before the FPTC, and in accordance with Local Rule 16. Specifically, failure to complete discovery is <u>not</u> a ground for a continuance.

17. At the FPTC, counsel should be prepared to discuss means of streamlining the trial, including, but not limited to, bifurcation, presentation of non-critical testimony by deposition excerpts, stipulations as to the content of testimony, and qualification of experts by admitted resumes. In rare cases where the FPTC is waived by the Court, counsel must follow Local Rule 16 - 11.2.

JURY INSTRUCTIONS & SPECIAL VERDICT FORMS

18. Seven (7) calendar days prior to the Rule 16 - 2 meeting of counsel, counsel shall exchange proposed jury instructions and special verdict forms (if applicable). Within seven (7) calendar days, Counsel shall exchange any objections to the instructions and special verdict forms. Counsel shall meet and confer prior to the Final Pretrial Conference with the goal of reaching agreement on a set of joint instructions and one special verdict form.

19. Three (3) calendar days before the Final Pretrial Conference itself, the parties shall file two copies of their JOINT jury instructions. The JOINT jury instructions shall be filed in the following form:

- **a.** The agreed upon instructions, acceptable to all parties, are to be listed (not copied), indicating source and number, which should conserve resources, time and the environment;
- **b.** Plaintiff's proposed instructions, objected to by defendant; and
- **c.** Defendant's proposed instructions, objected to by plaintiff.

Objections to disputed instructions shall be filed by the date of the Pretrial

Conference. Any and all objections and shall first set forth the proposed instruction in its entirety. The objection shall be specific, and contain citation to authority and/or a concise argument supporting the view that the instruction is improper. If applicable, the objecting party shall submit an alternative instruction on a separate page.

20. The Court prefers Counsel to use the instructions from the *Manual of Model Jury Instructions for the Ninth Circuit* (2007 Edition) where applicable. Where California law is to be applied and the above instructions are inapplicable, the Court expects counsel to agree on the use of CACI jury instructions. If neither of the above sources are applicable, counsel is directed to use the instructions from Devitt, Blackmar & Wolff, *Federal Jury Practice and Instructions or California Forms of Jury Instructions.* Each requested jury instruction shall be numbered and set forth in full on a separate page, citing the authority or source of the requested instruction (except for the jury copy discussed infra).

21. An index page shall accompany all jury instructions submitted to the Court. The index page shall indicate the following:

a. The number of the instruction;

b. A brief title of the instruction;

c. The source of the instruction and any relevant case citations; and

d. The page number of the instruction.

EXAMPLE:

Number	Title	Source	Page
1	Burden of Proof	9th Cir. 1.3	5

EXHIBITS

22. Counsel are to prepare their exhibits for presentation at the trial by placing them in 3-hole notebooks which are tabbed down the side with the exhibit numbers. These notebook exhibits are to be prepared for the Courtroom Deputy Clerk in an original, which shall be tagged with the appropriate exhibit tags in the lower or upper right hand corner of the first page of each exhibit, and two copies. Each notebook shall contain a list of each exhibit included. Counsel shall also supply three extra copies of their individual or joint exhibit list and witness list to the Courtroom Deputy Clerk at the start of the trial. The exhibits are to be prepared in accordance with Local Rule 16 -6.

23. In jury cases where a significant number of exhibits are to be admitted, the Court encourages counsel, preferably by agreement, to consider ways in which testimony about exhibits may be clarified for the jury while it is being presented. Counsel may consider such devices as ELMOs, computers, or enlargements of important exhibits. Counsel may not pass exhibits up and down the jury box while court is in session.

24. All counsel are to meet not later than ten (10) calendar days before trial and to stipulate as far as is possible to foundation, waiver of the best evidence rule, and which exhibits may be received into evidence at the start of trial. The exhibits to be so received will be noted on the extra copies of the exhibit lists.

INSTRUCTIONS GOVERNING PROCEDURE DURING TRIAL

25. If counsel need to arrange for the installation of their own additional equipment, such as video monitors, overhead projectors, etc., notify the Courtroom Deputy Clerk no later than 4:30 p.m. two days before trial so that the necessary arrangement may be made.

26. Trial days are Tuesday through Friday 9:00 a.m. to 4:30 p.m. with a morning and afternoon break and a lunch recess from approximately 12:00 p.m. to 1:15 p.m.

27. Before trial commences, the Court will give counsel an opportunity to discuss administrative matters and anticipated procedural or legal problems. During the trial, if there are any matters you wish to discuss, please inform my Courtroom Deputy Clerk.

28. Avoid discussing the law or arguing the case in opening statements.

29. When objecting, state only that you are objecting and the legal ground of the objection, e.g., hearsay, irrelevant, etc. If you wish to argue an objection, ask for permission to do so outside of the hearing of the jury.

30. The Court reserves the time from 8:30 a.m. to 9:00 a.m. to handle legal and administrative matters outside of the presence of the jury. The trial before the jury will commence promptly at 9:00 a.m. Counsel is urged to anticipate matters which may need discussion or hearing outside of the presence of the jury and to raise them during this period.

31. Do not approach the clerk or the witness box without the Court's permission. Please return to the lectern when your purpose has been accomplished.

32. Please rise when addressing the Court. In jury cases, please rise when the jury enters or leaves the courtroom.

33. Address all remarks to the Court. Do not directly address the clerk, the reporter or opposing counsel. If you wish to speak with opposing counsel, ask permission to talk to him or her off the record. All requests for the re-reading of questions or answers, or to have an exhibit placed in front of a witness, shall be addressed to the Court.

34. While court is in session, do not leave the counsel table to confer with investigators, secretaries, or witnesses in the back of the courtroom unless permission is granted in advance.

35. When a party has more than one lawyer, only one may conduct the examination of a given witness and only that same lawyer may handle objections during the testimony of that witness.

36. If a witness was on the stand at a recess or adjournment, have the witness back on the stand and ready to proceed when Court resumes.

37. Do not run out of witnesses. If you are out of witnesses and there is more than a brief delay, the Court may deem that you have rested.

38. The Court attempts to cooperate with doctors and other professional witnesses and will, except in extraordinary circumstances, accommodate them by permitting them to be put on out of sequence. Anticipate any such possibility and discuss it with opposing counsel. If there is an objection, confer with the Court in advance.

39. Counsel are advised to be on time as the Court starts promptly.

Dated: ________________

AUDREY B. COLLINS
Chief United States District Judge

C. Criminal Motion and Trial Order

IN THE UNITED STATES DISTICT COURT
FOR THE CENTRAL DISTRICT OF CALIFORNIA

UNITED STATES OF AMERICA, Plaintiff, v. Defendant(s).	)))))	Case No. ________ **CRIMINAL MOTION AND TRIAL ORDER**

The above matter is set for trial before the Honorable Audrey B. Collins, Courtroom 680, Roybal Federal Building, 255 E. Temple St., Los Angeles, CA 90012.

MOTIONS

1. Pre-Trial motions shall be filed on ______________. (Monday preceding four weeks before trial).
2. Opposition shall be filed on ______________. (Monday preceding three weeks before trial).
3. Replies shall be filed on ______________. (Monday preceding three weeks before trial).
4. Hearing and Pre-Trial Conference are set for __________ at ________. (Monday preceding two weeks before trial).
5. Trial is set for Tuesday, __________ at 8:30 a.m.
6. ***All pleadings shall be served personally on opposing counsel or faxed to opposing counsel no later than 4:30 p.m. on the day of filing. Two sets of mandatory chambers copies must be delivered directly to chambers by 12:00 p.m. (noon) of the court day following the filing of any document. For security reasons, paper copies of filings should be removed from envelopes or folders before being placed in the chambers drop-box. Counsel shall familiarize themselves with Central District General Orders 08-02 & 08-11.***

DISCOVERY & NOTICE

7. Counsel for the government and counsel for defendant shall comply promptly with discovery and notice matters pursuant to Fed. R. Crim. P. 12, 12.1, 12.2, 12.3, 15, and 16.

TRIAL PREPARATION

8. Counsel shall arrive at the Courtroom not later than 8:30 a.m. on the first day of trial.
9. Counsel for the Government shall present the Courtroom Deputy Clerk with the following documents:
   a. THREE copies of the Government's witness list;
   b. THREE copies of the Government's exhibit list in the form specified in Local Civil Rule 16-5;
   c. ALL of the Government's exhibits, with official exhibit tags attached, bearing the same number shown on the exhibit list. These shall be delivered to the Clerk not

later than 8:30 a.m. on the first day of trial. (Defendant's counsel does not have to deliver his or her exhibits to the Clerk on the first day of trial; however, Defendant's counsel is responsible for affixing completed exhibit tags with the case name and case number to the exhibits to be used in the Defendant's case.) Exhibits shall be numbered 1, 2, 3, 4, etc. If a blow up is an enlargement of an existing exhibit, it shall be designated with the number of the original exhibit followed by an "A." Counsel for the government should be aware that the Court will order that exhibits such as firearms, narcotics, etc., remain in the custody of the agents during the pendency of the trial. The agent will be required to sign the appropriate form in order to take custody of such exhibits. It shall be the responsibility of the agents to produce said items for court, secure them at night and guard them at all times while in the courtroom. Exhibit tags can be obtained from the receptionist in the main clerk's office, Room G-8; and

d. A bench book containing a copy of all exhibits that can be reproduced. Each exhibit shall be tabbed with the exhibit number for easy referral. (Defendant's counsel shall provide the Court with a copy of Defendant's exhibits as introduced).

10. If counsel need to arrange for the installation of their own additional equipment, such as video monitors, overhead projectors, etc., notify the Courtroom Deputy Clerk no later than 4:30 p.m. two days BEFORE trial so that the necessary arrangement may be made.

11. Trial days are usually Tuesday through Friday 9:00 a.m. to 5:00 p.m. with a morning and afternoon break and a lunch recess from approximately 12:00 to 1:15 p.m. 12. Before trial commences, the Court will give counsel an opportunity to discuss administrative matters and anticipated procedural or legal problems. During the trial, if there are any matters counsel wish to discuss, they must inform the Courtroom Deputy Clerk.

JURY INSTRUCTIONS & VERDICT FORMS

13. Jury instructions in the form described below are to be submitted not later than the Tuesday of the week prior to trial. Counsel need only submit proposed SUBSTANTIVE instructions. The Court will propound its own general instructions and will essentially follow the format set out in the Manual of Model Criminal Jury Instructions for the Ninth Circuit (Thompson West 2010 ed.). If a special verdict is desired, counsel shall submit a proposed verdict form with the jury instructions.

14. The parties must submit JOINT jury instructions and a JOINT proposed verdict form (if a special verdict is desired). In order to produce these joint instructions, the parties shall meet and confer sufficiently in advance of the required submission date with the goal of agreeing upon instructions and verdict forms. The jury instructions shall be submitted as follows: 1) JOINT jury instructions (those instructions which are agreed to by all parties); and 2) DISPUTED jury instructions (those instructions propounded by a party to which another party objects). Objections to disputed instructions shall be filed not later than the Friday before the trial. Each requested jury instruction shall be numbered and set forth in full on a separate page, citing the authority or source of the requested instruction.

15. The Court prefers that counsel use the instructions from the

Manual of Model Criminal Jury Instructions for the Ninth Circuit (Thompson West, 2010 ed.). Another suggested sources is Devitt, Blackmar and O'Malley, Federal Jury Practice and Instructions (West Publ'g Co., 4th ed.).

16. An index page shall accompany all jury instructions that are submitted to the Court. The index page shall indicate the following:

a. The number of the instruction;

b. A brief title of the instruction;

c. The source of the instruction; and

d. The page number of the instruction.

EXAMPLE:

Number	Title	Source	Page Number
1	Duty of the Jury	9th Cir. 1.1	1

INSTRUCTIONS GOVERNING PROCEDURE DURING TRIAL

17. Counsel shall not refer to their clients by their first names during trials.

18. Avoid discussing the law or arguing the case in opening statements.

19. When objecting, state only that you are objecting and the legal ground of the objection, e.g., hearsay, irrelevant, etc. If you wish to argue an objection, ask for permission to do so outside the hearing of the jury.

20. The Court reserves the time from 8:30 a.m. to 9:00 a.m. to handle legal and administrative matters outside the presence of the jury. The trial before the jury will commence promptly at 9:00 a.m. Counsel are urged to anticipate matters that may need discussion or hearing outside the presence of the jury and to raise them during this period.

21. Do not approach the clerk or the witness box without the Court's permission. Please return to the lectern when your purpose has been accomplished.

22. Please rise when addressing the Court. In jury cases, please rise when the jury enters or leaves the courtroom.

23. Address all remarks to the Court. Do not directly address the clerk, the reporter or opposing counsel. If you wish to speak with opposing counsel, ask permission to talk to him or her off the record. All requests for the re-reading of questions or answers, or to have an exhibit placed in front of a witness, shall be addressed to the Court.

24. Do not make an offer of stipulation unless you have conferred with opposing counsel and have reason to believe the stipulation will be accepted. Any stipulation of fact will require the Defendant's personal concurrence and shall be submitted to the Court in writing for approval. A proposed stipulation should be explained to the Defendant in advance.

25. While court is in session, do not leave the counsel table to confer with investigators, secretaries, or witnesses in the back of the Courtroom unless permission is granted in advance.

26. When a party has more than one lawyer, only one may conduct the examination of a given witness and only that same lawyer may handle objections during the testimony of that witness.

27. If a witness was on the stand at a recess or adjournment, have the witness back on the stand and ready to proceed when Court resumes.

28. Do not run out of witnesses. If you are out of witnesses and there is more than a brief delay, the Court may deem that you have rested.

29. The Court attempts to cooperate with doctors and other professional witnesses and will, except in extraordinary circumstances, accommodate them by permitting them to be put on out of sequence. Anticipate any such possibility and discuss it with opposing counsel. If there is an objection, confer with the Court in advance.

30. Counsel are advised to be on time as the Court starts promptly.

Date: ________________

____

AUDREY B. COLLINS
Chief United States District Judge

D. Order Regarding Pretrial Conference

IN THE UNITED STATES DISTICT COURT
FOR THE CENTRAL DISTRICT OF CALIFORNIA

)	Case No. _______________
Plaintiff(s),)	
v.)	**ORDER RE: PRETRIAL CONFERENCE:**
Defendant(s).)	1. PRETRIAL CONFERENCE PURSUANT TO FED.R. CIV. P. 16 and 26; AND LOCAL RULE 26
______________________________)	2. MOTIONS & *EX PARTE* APPLICATIONS
	3. EFILING – MANDATORY CHAMBERS PAPER COPIES

This action has been assigned to the calendar of Chief Judge Audrey B. Collins, Courtroom 680, Roybal Federal Building, 255 East Temple Street, Los Angeles, CA 90012.

The responsibility for the progress of litigation in the Federal Courts falls not only upon the attorneys in the action, but upon the Court as well. In order "to secure the just, speedy, and inexpensive determination of every action," Fed. R. Civ. P. 1, all counsel are hereby ordered to familiarize themselves with the Federal Rules of Civil Procedure and the Local Rules of the Central District of California.

NOTICE: Two sets of mandatory chambers paper copies must be delivered to chambers by 12:00 p.m. (noon) of the court day following the filing of any document. For security reasons, paper copies of filings shall be removed from envelopes or folders before being placed with chamber's drop box. Counsel shall familiarize themselves with Central District General Orders 08-02 and 08-11.

1. SCHEDULING CONFERENCE

This matter is set for a Pretrial/Scheduling Conference on __________ at a.m.

(a) The conference will be held pursuant to Fed. R. Civ. P. 16, 26(f), and Local Rule 26-1. The parties are reminded of their obligations to disclose information. The parties must confer on a discovery plan not later than 21 days prior to the scheduling conference and report to the Court by filing a Joint Rule 26(f) Report not later than 14 days after they confer as required by Fed. R. Civ. P. 26 and the Local Rules of this Court. Failure to comply with all applicable rules or to cooperate in the preparation of the Joint Rule 26(f) Report may lead to the imposition of sanctions.

(b) Counsel should begin to conduct discovery before the Scheduling Conference. This will expedite settlement discussions and early motion work on the litigation.

(c) If counsel for any party has his or her office outside Los Angeles County, the Court may in its discretion conduct the scheduling conference by conference telephone call. *Counsel requesting the telephonic conference shall contact the courtroom deputy at (213) 894-6500 for approval.* Opposing counsel who are outside of Los Angeles County may also participate by telephone. Counsel requesting the telephonic will be responsible for originating the conference call to the court after assembling all parties on the line. Counsel may be required to remain available on the telephone until the case number is called.

2. **FILING AND CONTENTS OF THE JOINT RULE 26(f) REPORT**
The Joint Rule 26(f) Report shall be filed not later than one week before the scheduling conference. Plaintiff is responsible for drafting the report, but it shall be submitted and signed jointly. The Joint Rule 26(f) Report shall include the following:

   (a) A short statement of the claims, counterclaims, and affirmative defenses, not to exceed three (3) pages;

   (b) A brief description of the key legal issues;

   (c) A discussion of the likelihood of motions seeking to add other parties or claims, file amended pleadings, or transfer venue;

   (d) A discussion of discovery and experts pursuant to Rule 26(f);

   (e) A description of any issues which may be resolved by motions for summary judgment;

   (f) A brief description of settlement discussions to date, and the settlement selection pursuant to Local Rule 16;

   (g) A realistic time estimate required for trial and whether it will be by jury or court;

   (h) Proposed dates for:
   - Motion and claims cut-off;
   - Discovery cut-off;
   - Motion cut-off;
   - Final Pre-Trial Conference;
   - Jury or court trial[1]; and

   (i) Any other matters affecting the status of the case.
   - ERISA cases. Note that the Court will not hear motions for summary judgment, see Kearney v. Standard Insurance Co., 175 F.3d 1084 (1999), but will hear motions to determine the standard of review and the scope of the administrative record. There will be a court trial (usually confined to oral argument) on the administrative record, along with any other expanded testimony.
   - Patent Cases. Counsel should propose dates for claim construction and Markman hearings.
   - Consent to Magistrate Judge. The parties may consent to have a magistrate judge preside over the entire case, including trial. The parties are free to select from among all the magistrate judges available for this purpose, not just the magistrate judge assigned to this case. (Please consult the court's website for the list of Magistrate Judges.)

3. MOTIONS
In motion matters, counsel should note the timing and service requirements of Local Rules 6 and 7, **as revised effective January 1, 2010**, which include:

   a. **Local Rule 6-1:** If mailed, the notice of motion shall be served not later than thirty-one (31) days before the hearing date designated in the notice. If served personally, the notice of motion shall be served not later than twenty-eight (28)

[1] All motion cut-off and pre-trial conference dates are on Mondays. Trials are always set on Tuesdays.

days before the hearing date designated in the notice.

b. **Local Rule 7-3:** Pre-Filing Conference of Counsel. Counsel should be familiar with this rule, which requires a pre-filing meeting to discuss the substance and potential resolution of non-discovery motions. Note that counsel for the moving party must notify the Court in any notice of motion that the meeting took place.

c. **Local Rule 7:** Note the requirements included in L.R. 7-4. The notice of motion shall include a concise statement of the relief or court action the movant seeks.

d. **Local Rule 7-9:** Opposing papers shall be served upon other parties and filed not later than twenty-one (21) days before the hearing date.

e. Local Rule 7-10: Reply papers, if any, shall be served and filed not later than fourteen (14) days before the motion hearing date.

Adherence to the timing requirements of all Local Rules is mandatory for proper chambers preparation of motion matters.

4. **DISCOVERY**
This Court refers all discovery motions and disputes to the magistrate judge assigned to the case. Note that the discovery cut-off date means the last day by which depositions must be completed and responses to all previously served written discovery must be provided. (See further discussion in the Court's Civil Jury and Court Trial Orders.)

5. **EX PARTE APPLICATIONS**
Ex parte applications are considered on the papers and are not usually set for hearing. Ex parte applications are to be reserved solely for extraordinary relief. This court may impose sanctions for misuse of ex parte applications. See Local Rule 7-19; In re Intermagnetics Am., Inc., 101 B.R. 191 (Bankr. C.D. Cal. 1989). Counsel are ordered to read and comply with the requirements of Mission Power Engineering, Co. v. Continental Casualty Co., 883 F. Supp. 488 (C.D. Cal. 1995), before filing an ex parte application with this court.

Counsel must comply with Local Rule 7-19 and 7-19.1. Applications which fail to conform with these rules, including a statement of opposing counsel's position, will not be considered. The moving party shall serve the opposing party by facsimile transmission. Opposing papers must be filed not later than twenty-four hours following such facsimile service. Counsel must inform the Courtroom Deputy Clerk, Angela Bridges, (213) 894-6500, if the ex parte application will not be opposed. Counsel must deliver two mandatory chambers paper copies of the ex parte application and opposing papers to chambers.

6. **SETTLEMENT PROCEDURE**
A settlement procedure appropriate to the particular case will be used in every civil action. Counsel must be familiar with the procedures and timing mandated by Local Rule 16-14. A Notice of Settlement Selection Procedure, signed by counsel for both sides, shall be filed no later than 10 days after entry of this order. Frank discussion of settlement options should begin now.

7. **NOTICE TO BE PROVIDED BY COUNSEL**
Plaintiff's counsel or, if plaintiff is appearing *pro se*, defendant's counsel, shall provide this Order to any parties who first appear after the date of this Order and to parties

who are known to exist but have not yet entered appearances.

8. <u>COURT'S WEBSITE</u>

Copies of this and all other orders of this Court that may become applicable to this case are available on the Central District of California website at www.cacd.uscourts.gov under "Judge's Procedures & Schedules." Copies of the Local Rules and General Orders are also available on the website.[2]

IT IS SO ORDERED.

Dated: ________________

____

AUDREY B. COLLINS
Chief United States District Judge

---

[2] Local Rules may be purchased from the following:

Los Angeles Daily Journal	West Publishing Co.	Metropolitan News
915 East First Street	50 West Kellogg Boulevard	210 South Spring Street
Los Angeles, CA 90012	St. Paul, MN 55164-9979	Los Angeles, CA 90012

E. *Order Regarding Settlement Conference*

IN THE UNITED STATES DISTICT COURT
FOR THE CENTRAL DISTRICT OF CALIFORNIA

	)	Case No. ______________
Plaintiff(s),	)	
v.	)	**ORDER RE: SETTLEMENT**
Defendant(s).	)	**CONFERENCE (Local Rule 16)**
______________________________	)	

This matter has been set for a settlement conference with **Judge Audrey B. Collins** at the above date, time, and place. The parties should read and follow the procedure set forth in Local Rules 16. In summary, the following procedure will be used:

1. **Settlement Conference Letters.** The parties shall submit confidential settlement conference letters, in accord with Local Rule 16-14.5, to the court **at least three (3) court days before the conference**, and shall exchange non-confidential letters with other counsel. The letters shall summarize the important issues and the party's position on each issue, shall contain information regarding damages in non-conclusionary form, and shall summarize the course of negotiations up to that point. The letters shall be brief (not to exceed five (5) pages) and to the point and shall not include mass numbers of exhibits; counsel are to keep in mind that the purpose of the letter is to familiarize the Court with the issues in the case, not to try the case. Proposals for settlement and counsel's own evaluation of the case not yet communicated to opposing counsel should be included in the separate confidential settlement letter.

2. **Persons Present.** *At the settlement conference, all persons whose consent is necessary to conclude settlement shall personally be present.* As an exception, out-of-district parties, or agents empowered to settle, may be available by telephone provided they are realistically in fact at the telephone, until released by counsel even if after normal business hours at the place where the party or agent is located. Counsel are responsible to see that this is done. In the case of a corporate party, the person who can say "yes" as well as "no" to a settlement proposal must be the person present. If the settlement proposal must be presented to a board or committee, the person whose recommendation is normally followed by the board or committee must be the person present. *Where an insurer will pay or contribute to a settlement, Insurance Representatives including all parties and their counsel must be present or available to participate by speaker phone in the conference.*

3. **Conduct of the Conference.** The Court will confer with the attorneys and claims representatives, if any, jointly and separately. Each party shall be prepared to negotiate for so long as prospects of settlement are not foreclosed, even after normal court hours. The Court may confer with the parties in the presence of their attorneys. If settlement is reached, it will be placed on the record at the conclusion of the conference.

4. **Optional Requirements.** The Court may require any of the procedures set forth in Rule 16-14.6.

Date: ______________

____
AUDREY B. COLLINS
Chief United States District Judge

Hon. Valerie Baker Fairbank

District Judge

Chambers Information

U.S. District Court, Central District of California
Courtroom 9, Spring Street Floor
312 N. Spring Street
Los Angeles, CA 90012

Scheduling Information

Courtroom Deputy: (213) 894-0066

Civil Law and Motion	Mondays at 1:30 p.m.
Criminal Law and Motion	Mondays at 10:00 a.m.

Judge's Biography

Born 1949 in Minneapolis, MN

Federal Judicial Service:

-Judge, U. S. District Court, Central District of California
-Nominated by George W. Bush on January 9, 2007, to a seat vacated by Consuelo B. Marshall; Confirmed by the Senate on February 1, 2007, and received commission on February 16, 2007.

Education:

-University of California, Santa Barbara, B.A., 1971
-University of California, Santa Barbara, M.A., 1972
-University of California, Los Angeles School of Law, 1975, J.D.

Professional Career:

-Private Practice, Los Angeles, California, 1975-1977, 1980-1986
-Assistant U.S. Attorney, U.S. Attorney's Office, Central District of California, 1977-1980
-Judge, Los Angeles Municipal Report, California, 1986-1987
-Judge, County of Los Angeles, Superior Court of California, 1987-2007

I. Judge Fairbank's Procedures and Practices

A. Patent Local Rules for Judge Fairbank's Court

PATENT LOCAL RULES

1. SCOPE OF RULES

1-1. Title.

These are the Local Rules of Practice for Patent Cases before the United States District Court for the Northern District of California. They should be cited as "Patent L.R._."

1-2. Scope and Construction.

These rules apply to all civil actions filed in or transferred to this Court which allege infringement of a utility patent in a complaint, counterclaim, cross-claim or third party claim, or which seek a declaratory judgment that a utility patent is not infringed, is invalid or is unenforceable. The Civil Local Rules of this Court shall also apply to such actions, except to the extent that they are inconsistent with these Patent Local Rules. If the filings or actions in a case do not trigger the application of these Patent Local Rules under the terms set forth herein, the parties shall, as soon as such circumstances become known, meet and confer for the purpose of agreeing on the application of these Patent Local Rules to the case and promptly report the results of the meet and confer to the Court.

1-3. Modification of these Rules.

The Court may modify the obligations or deadlines set forth in these Patent Local Rules based on the circumstances of any particular case, including, without limitation, the simplicity or complexity of the case as shown by the patents, claims, products, or parties involved. Such modifications shall, in most cases, be made at the initial case management conference, but may be made at other times upon a showing of good cause. In advance of submission of any request for a modification, the parties shall meet and confer for purposes of reaching an agreement, if possible, upon any modification.

1-4. Effective Date.

These Patent Local Rules take effect on March 1, 2008. They govern patent cases filed on or after that date. For actions pending prior to March 1, 2008, the provisions of the Patent Local Rules that were in effect on February 29, 2008, shall apply.

2. GENERAL PROVISIONS

2-1. Governing Procedure.

(a) Initial Case Management Conference. When the parties confer pursuant to FRCivP 26(f), in addition to the matters covered by FRCivP 26, the parties shall discuss and address in the Case Management Statement filed pursuant to FRCivP 26(f) and Civil L.R. 16-9, the following topics:

(1) Proposed modification of the obligations or deadlines set forth in these Patent Local Rules to ensure that they are suitable for the circumstances of the particular case (see Patent L.R. 1-3);

(2) The scope and timing of any claim construction discovery including disclosure of and discovery from any expert witness permitted by the court.;

(3) The format of the Claim Construction Hearing, including whether the Court will hear live testimony, the order of presentation, and the estimated length of the hearing; and

(4) How the parties intend to educate the court on the technology at issue.

* * *

2-3. Certification of Disclosures.

All statements, disclosures, or charts filed or served in accordance with these Patent Local Rules shall be dated and signed by counsel of record. Counsel's signature shall constitute a certification that to the best of his or her knowledge, information, and belief, formed after an inquiry that is reasonable under the circumstances, the information contained in the statement, disclosure, or chart is complete and correct at the time it is made.

2-4. Admissibility of Disclosures.

Statements, disclosures, or charts governed by these Patent Local Rules are admissible to the extent permitted by the Federal Rules of Evidence or Procedure. However, the statements and disclosures provided for in Patent L.R. 4-1 and 4-2 are not admissible for any purpose other than in connection with motions seeking an extension or modification of the time periods within which actions contemplated by these Patent Local Rules shall be taken.

2-5. Relationship to Federal Rules of Civil Procedure.

Except as provided in this paragraph or as otherwise ordered, it shall not be a ground for objecting to an opposing party's discovery request (*e.g.*, interrogatory, document request, request for admission, deposition question) or declining to provide information otherwise required to be disclosed pursuant to FRCivP 26(a)(1) that the discovery request or disclosure requirement is premature in light of, or otherwise conflicts with, these Patent Local Rules, absent other legitimate objection. A party may object, however, to responding to the following categories of discovery requests (or decline to provide information in its initial disclosures under FRCivP 26(a)(1)) on the ground that they are premature in light of the timetable provided in the Patent Local Rules:

(a) Requests seeking to elicit a party's claim construction position;

(b) Requests seeking to elicit from the patent claimant a comparison of the asserted claims and the accused apparatus, product, device, process, method, act, or other instrumentality;

(c) Requests seeking to elicit from an accused infringer a comparison of the asserted claims and the prior art; and

(d) Requests seeking to elicit from an accused infringer the identification of any advice of counsel, and related documents.

Where a party properly objects to a discovery request (or declines to provide information in its initial disclosures under FRCivP 26(a)(1)) as set forth above, that party shall provide the requested information on the date on which it is required to be provided to an opposing party under these Patent Local Rules or as set by the Court, unless there exists another legitimate ground for objection.

3. PATENT DISCLOSURES

3-1. Disclosure of Asserted Claims and Infringement Contentions.

Not later than 10 days after the Initial Case Management Conference, a party claiming patent infringement shall serve on all parties a "Disclosure of Asserted Claims and Infringement Contentions." Separately for each opposing party, the "Disclosure of Asserted Claims and Infringement Contentions" shall contain the following information:

(a) Each claim of each patent in suit that is allegedly infringed by each opposing party, including for each claim the applicable statutory subsections of 35 U.S.C. § 271 asserted;

(b) Separately for each asserted claim, each accused apparatus, product, device, process, method, act, or other instrumentality ("Accused Instrumentality") of each opposing party of which the party is aware. This identification shall be as specific as possible. Each product, device, and apparatus shall be identified by name or model number, if known. Each method or process shall be identified by name, if known, or by any product, device, or apparatus which, when used, allegedly results in the practice of the claimed method or process;

(c) A chart identifying specifically where each limitation of each asserted claim is found within each Accused Instrumentality, including for each limitation that such party contends is governed by 35 U.S.C. § 112(6), the identity of the structure(s), act(s), or material(s) in the Accused Instrumentality that performs the claimed function.

(d) For each claim which is alleged to have been indirectly infringed, an identification of any direct infringement and a description of the acts of the alleged indirect infringer that contribute to or are inducing that direct infringement. Insofar as alleged direct infringement is based on joint acts of multiple parties, the role of each such party in the direct infringement must be described.

(e) Whether each limitation of each asserted claim is alleged to be literally present or present under the doctrine of equivalents in the Accused Instrumentality;

(f) For any patent that claims priority to an earlier application, the priority date to which each asserted claim allegedly is entitled; and

(g) If a party claiming patent infringement wishes to preserve the right to rely, for any purpose, on the assertion that its own apparatus, product, device, process, method, act, or other instrumentality practices the claimed invention, the party shall identify, separately for each asserted claim, each such apparatus, product, device, process, method, act, or other instrumentality that incorporates or reflects that particular claim.

(h) If a party claiming patent infringement alleges willful infringement, the basis for such allegation.

3-2. Document Production Accompanying Disclosure.

With the "Disclosure of Asserted Claims and Infringement Contentions," the party claiming patent infringement shall produce to each opposing party or make available for inspection and copying:

(a) Documents (*e.g.*, contracts, purchase orders, invoices, advertisements, marketing materials, offer letters, beta site testing agreements, and third party or joint development agreements) sufficient to evidence each discussion with, disclosure to, or other manner of providing to a third party, or sale of or offer to sell, or any public use of, the claimed invention prior to the date of application for the patent in suit. A party's production of a document as required herein shall not constitute an admission that such document evidences or is prior art under 35 U.S.C. § 102;

(b) All documents evidencing the conception, reduction to practice, design, and development of each claimed invention, which were created on or before the date of application for the patent in suit or the priority date identified pursuant to Patent L.R. 3-1(f), whichever is earlier;

(c) A copy of the file history for each patent in suit; and

(d) All documents evidencing ownership of the patent rights by the party asserting patent infringement.

(e) If a party identifies instrumentalities pursuant to Patent L.R. 3-1(g), documents sufficient to show the operation of any aspects or elements of such instrumentalities the patent claimant relies upon as embodying any asserted claims.

The producing party shall separately identify by production number which documents correspond to each category.

3-3. Invalidity Contentions.

Not later than 45 days after service upon it of the "Disclosure of Asserted Claims and Infringement Contentions," each party opposing a claim of patent infringement, shall serve on all parties its "Invalidity Contentions" which shall contain the following information:

(a) The identity of each item of prior art that allegedly anticipates each asserted claim or renders it obvious. Each prior art patent shall be identified by its number, country of origin, and date of issue. Each prior art publication shall be identified by its title, date of publication, and where feasible, author and publisher. Prior art under 35 U.S.C. § 102(b) shall be identified by specifying the item offered for sale or publicly used or known, the date the offer or use took place or the information became known, and the identity of the person or entity which made the use or which made and received the offer, or the person or entity which made the information known or to whom it was made known. Prior art under 35 U.S.C. § 102(f) shall be identified by providing the name of the person(s) from whom and the circumstances under which the invention or any part of it was derived. Prior art under 35 U.S.C. § 102(g) shall be identified by providing the identities of the person(s) or entities involved in and the circumstances surrounding the making of the invention before the patent applicant(s);

(b) Whether each item of prior art anticipates each asserted claim or renders it obvious. If obviousness is alleged, an explanation of why the prior art renders the asserted claim obvious, including an identification of any combinations of prior art showing obviousness;

(c) A chart identifying where specifically in each alleged item of prior art each limitation of each asserted claim is found, including for each limitation that such party contends is governed by 35 U.S.C. § 112(6), the identity of the structure(s), act(s), or material(s) in each item of prior art that performs the claimed function; and

(d) Any grounds of invalidity based on 35 U.S.C. § 101, indefiniteness under 35 U.S.C. § 112(2) or enablement or written description under 35 U.S.C. § 112(1) of any of the asserted claims.

3-4. Document Production Accompanying Invalidity Contentions.

With the "Invalidity Contentions," the party opposing a claim of patent infringement shall produce or make available for inspection and copying:

(a) Source code, specifications, schematics, flow charts, artwork, formulas, or other documentation sufficient to show the operation of any aspects or elements of an Accused Instrumentality identified by the patent claimant in its Patent L.R. 3-1(c) chart; and

(b) A copy or sample of the prior art identified pursuant to Patent L.R. 3-3(a) which does not appear in the file history of the patent(s) at issue. To the extent any such item is not in English, an English translation of the portion(s) relied upon shall be produced.

The producing party shall separately identify by production number which documents correspond to each category.

3-5. Disclosure Requirement in Patent Cases for Declaratory Judgment of Invalidity.

(a) Invalidity Contentions If No Claim of Infringement. In all cases in which a party files a complaint or other pleading seeking a declaratory judgment that a patent is invalid Patent L.R. 3-1 and 3-2 shall not apply unless and until a claim for patent infringement is made by a party. If the defendant does not assert a claim for patent infringement in its answer to the complaint, no later than 10 days after the defendant serves its answer, or 10 days after the

Initial Case Management Conference, whichever is later, the party seeking a declaratory judgment of invalidity shall serve upon each opposing party its Invalidity Contentions that conform to Patent L.R. 3-3 and produce or make available for inspection and copying the documents described in Patent L.R. 3-4.

(b) Inapplicability of Rule. This Patent L.R. 3-5 shall not apply to cases in which a request for a declaratory judgment that a patent is invalid is filed in response to a complaint for infringement of the same patent.

3-6. Amendment to Contentions.

Amendment of the Infringement Contentions or the Invalidity Contentions may be made only by order of the Court upon a timely showing of good cause. Non-exhaustive examples of circumstances that may, absent undue prejudice to the nonmoving party, support a finding of good cause include: (a) a claim construction by the Court different from that proposed by the party seeking amendment; (b) recent discovery of material, prior art despite earlier diligent search; and (c) recent discovery of nonpublic information about the Accused Instrumentality which was not discovered, despite diligent efforts, before the service of the Infringement Contentions. The duty to supplement discovery responses does not excuse the need to obtain leave of court to amend contentions.

3-7. Advice of Counsel.

Not later than 50 days after service by the Court of its Claim Construction Ruling, each party relying upon advice of counsel as part of a patent-related claim or defense for any reason shall:

(a) Produce or make available for inspection and copying any written advice and documents related thereto for which the attorney-client and work product protection have been waived;

(b) Provide a written summary of any oral advice and produce or make available for inspection and copying that summary and documents related thereto for which the attorney-client and work product protection have been waived; and

(c) Serve a privilege log identifying any other documents, except those authored by counsel acting solely as trial counsel, relating to the subject matter of the advice which the party is withholding on the grounds of attorney-client privilege or work product protection.

A party who does not comply with the requirements of this Patent L.R. 3-7 shall not be permitted to rely on advice of counsel for any purpose absent a stipulation of all parties or by order of the Court.

4. CLAIM CONSTRUCTION PROCEEDINGS

4-1. Exchange of Proposed Terms for Construction.

(a) Not later than 10 days after service of the "Invalidity Contentions" pursuant to Patent L.R. 3-3, not later than 45 days after service upon it of the "Disclosure of Asserted Claims and Infringement Contentions" in those actions where validity is not at issue (and Patent L.R. 3-3 does not apply), or, in all cases in which a party files a complaint or other pleading seeking a declaratory judgment not based on validity, not later than 10 days after the defendant serves an answer that does not assert a claim for patent infringement (and Patent L.R. 3-1 does not apply), each party shall serve on each other party a list of claim terms which that party contends should be construed by the Court, and identify any claim term which that party contends should be governed by 35 U.S.C. § 112(6).

(b) The parties shall thereafter meet and confer for the purposes of limiting the terms in dispute by narrowing or resolving differences and facilitating the ultimate preparation of a

Joint Claim Construction and Prehearing Statement. The parties shall also jointly identify the 10 terms likely to be most significant to resolving the parties' dispute, including those terms for which construction may be case or claim dispositive.

4-2. Exchange of Preliminary Claim Constructions and Extrinsic Evidence.

(a) Not later than 20 days after the exchange of the lists pursuant to Patent L.R. 4-1, the parties shall simultaneously exchange proposed constructions of each term identified by either party for claim construction. Each such "Preliminary Claim Construction" shall also, for each term which any party contends is governed by 35 U.S.C. § 112(6), identify the structure(s), act(s), or material(s) corresponding to that term's function.

(b) At the same time the parties exchange their respective "Preliminary Claim Constructions," each party shall also identify all references from the specification or prosecution history that support its proposed construction and designate any supporting extrinsic evidence including, without limitation, dictionary definitions, citations to learned treatises and prior art, and testimony of percipient and expert witnesses. Extrinsic evidence shall be identified by production number or by producing a copy if not previously produced. With respect to any supporting witness, percipient or expert, the identifying party shall also provide a description of the substance of that witness' proposed testimony that includes a listing of any opinions to be rendered in connection with claim construction.

(c) The parties shall thereafter meet and confer for the purposes of narrowing the issues and finalizing preparation of a Joint Claim Construction and Prehearing Statement.

4-3. Joint Claim Construction and Prehearing Statement.

Not later than 60 days after service of the "Invalidity Contentions," the parties shall complete and file a Joint Claim Construction and Prehearing Statement, which shall contain the following information:

(a) The construction of those terms on which the parties agree;

(b) Each party's proposed construction of each disputed term, together with an identification of all references from the specification or prosecution history that support that construction, and an identification of any extrinsic evidence known to the party on which it intends to rely either to support its proposed construction or to oppose any other party's proposed construction, including, but not limited to, as permitted by law, dictionary definitions, citations to learned treatises and prior art, and testimony of percipient and expert witnesses;

(c) An identification of the terms whose construction will be most significant to the resolution of the case up to a maximum of 10. The parties shall also identify any term among the 10 whose construction will be case or claim dispositive. If the parties cannot agree on the 10 most significant terms, the parties shall identify the ones which they do agree are most significant and then they may evenly divide the remainder with each party identifying what it believes are the remaining most significant terms. However, the total terms identified by all parties as most significant cannot exceed 10. For example, in a case involving two parties, if the parties agree upon the identification of five terms as most significant, each may only identify two additional terms as most significant; if the parties agree upon eight such terms, each party may only identify only one additional term as most significant.

(d) The anticipated length of time necessary for the Claim Construction Hearing;

(e) Whether any party proposes to call one or more witnesses at the Claim Construction Hearing, the identity of each such witness, and for each witness, a summary of his or her testimony including, for any expert, each opinion to be offered related to claim construction.

4-4. Completion of Claim Construction Discovery.

Not later than 30 days after service and filing of the Joint Claim Construction and Prehearing Statement, the parties shall complete all discovery relating to claim construction, including any depositions with respect to claim construction of any witnesses, including experts, identified in the Preliminary Claim Construction statement (Patent L.R. 4-2) or Joint Claim Construction and Prehearing Statement (Patent L.R. 4-3).

4-5. Claim Construction Briefs.

(a) Not later than 45 days after serving and filing the Joint Claim Construction and Prehearing Statement, the party claiming patent infringement, or the party asserting invalidity if there is no infringement issue present in the case, shall serve and file an opening brief and any evidence supporting its claim construction.

(b) Not later than 14 days after service upon it of an opening brief, each opposing party shall serve and file its responsive brief and supporting evidence.

(c) Not later than 7 days after service upon it of a responsive brief, the party claiming patent infringement, or the party asserting invalidity if there is no infringement issue present in the case, shall serve and file any reply brief and any evidence directly rebutting the supporting evidence contained in an opposing party's response.

4-6. Claim Construction Hearing.

Subject to the convenience of the Court's calendar, two weeks following submission of the reply brief specified in Patent L.R. 4-5(c), the Court shall conduct a Claim Construction Hearing, to the extent the parties or the Court believe a hearing is necessary for construction of the claims at issue.

4-7. Good Faith Participation.

A failure to make a good faith effort to narrow the instances of disputed terms or otherwise participate in the meet and confer process of any of the provisions of section 4 may expose counsel to sanctions, including under 28 U.S.C. § 1927.

B. Procedures and Schedules

Phone or email messages without case name, number and a brief message will not be returned. Due to the high volume of calls and emails, not all e-mails/phone calls can be returned. Requests that can be answered by reviewing the local rules, orders issued by the Court, or the Court's website will not be returned.

Electronic Filing

- Counsel shall E-FILE all criminal and civil filings for Judge Fairbank pursuant to Fed. R. Civ. P. 5(d)(3), L.R. 5-4 and General Order **General Order 10-07**, as follows:
    - All proposed signature items, including applications and stipulations to extend time, shall be accompanied by a proposed order. After the application/stipulation and proposed order have been filed electronically, **counsel shall email the PDF version of the application/stipulation and a WordPerfect or Microsoft Word version of the proposed order to chambers at vbf_chambers@cacd.uscourts.gov.** The subject line of the email should include the case name and case number. DO NOT use this email address for communication with the Court or the clerk.
    - ***A MANDATORY CHAMBERS COPY of all e-filed documents shall be delivered to the courtesy bin outside the entrance to Judge Fairbank's chambers (chambers is located at the end of the hallway, to the right of the courtroom) by noon on the day following the filing. All mandatory chambers copies shall have the notice of e-filing attached.***
    - Failure to comply with this direction regarding MANDATORY CHAMBERS COPIES could result in a delay, i.e., in the consideration of your motion.
- For UNDER SEAL FILINGS, process documents the traditional way, but attach a Notice of Manual Filing to the paper copies delivered to the courtesy bin. DO NOT send these documents to the chamber's email. See below for additional information regarding under seal filings.

Criminal

- Criminal matters are heard on Monday at 10:00 am, unless otherwise specially set by the CRD at the Court or counsel's request.
- Motions shall be filed and served at least two weeks prior to the noticed hearing date and opposition papers shall then be filed and served at least one week prior to the hearing date. Less notice will be allowed only on a proper showing of urgency or necessity, i.e. 5 days notice per Fed. R. Crim. P. 47(c).
- Counsel shall deliver a **MANDATORY CHAMBERS COPY** of all documents filed to the bin outside Judge Fairbank's chambers by noon on the day following the filing.
- Except on a showing of good cause, **all** Motions should be heard on or before the pretrial conference, which is generally set by the Court at least two weeks before trial.
- Counsel for Government and counsel for the Defendant shall comply **promptly** with discovery and notice matters pursuant to Fed. R. Crim. P. 12, 12.1, 12.2, 12.3, 15 and 16. Counsel are reminded that failure to promptly comply with discovery obligations can result in a continuance of the trial, exclusion of evidence or other orders that are just under the circumstances. At the status conference re trial, the Court will inquire about the status of discovery and notice, particularly the status of the Government's

disclosure under Rule 16(a)(1)(A)-(G).
- For further information, see the Court's Criminal Motions and Trial Order.

Civil

- Civil motions are heard on Monday at 1:30 pm, unless otherwise specially set by the CRD. It is not necessary to clear a motion date with the court clerk prior to filing the motion. If Monday is a holiday, the next motion date is the next available Monday.
- Counsel shall deliver a **MANDATORY CHAMBERS COPY** of all documents filed to the bin outside Judge Fairbank's chambers by noon on the day following the filing.
- Discovery motions are to be calendared before the Magistrate Judge.
- **Continuances** are granted only upon a showing of good cause. Requests for continuances must be made by motion, stipulation, or application with a separate proposed order accompanied by a declaration setting forth the reasons for the requested continuance. The declaration should also include whether there have been any prior requests for continuances, and whether these requests were granted or denied by the Court. Stipulations extending dates set by this Court are not effective unless approved by the Court. Requests for continuance should be submitted well in advance of the requested relief.
- **Filing Civil Documents Under Seal:** The party seeking to seal documents must file a proper application with the Court, in which the applicant must demonstrate for each document or category of documents sufficient grounds to warrant placing the documents under seal. See L.R. 79-5; Schwarzer, et al., Cal. Prac. Guide: Fed. Civ. Pro. Before Trial, ch. 11(III)-C, §§ 11:1085-1087.7 (The Rutter Group 2006). For requirements regarding sealing dispositive motions, such as motions for summary judgment, see Kamakana v. City & County of Honolulu, 447 F.3d 1172 (9th Cir. 2006) (requiring applicant to show "compelling reasons" to seal the documents). Litigants should also refer to "Preparing Sealed Documents for Filing" located under Filing Procedures on the Court's website for other requirements.
- **Patent Cases:** With the exception of Rule 2-2 dealing with protective orders, the Court adopts the Northern District of California Patent Local Rules (version effective 3/1/2008) in all patent cases filed after April 21, 2008. A modified copy of the Rules is posted below. If the parties disagree in whole or in part with the Court's adoption of the Northern District Patent Local Rules, the parties may file a stipulation, noticed motion or, if appropriate, ex parte application setting forth their objections. Counsel shall set forth any objections promptly; ideally any objections should be made at or before the scheduling conference. Applications or stipulations for protective orders, as in all cases, may be made to the assigned magistrate judge.

General Information

- All filed documents must contain counsel's email address (pursuant to L.R. 11-3.8).
- The Court will permit **appearances by telephone** in civil cases for all status conferences, scheduling conferences and oral argument on motions. If counsel wishes to appear by telephone, you must:
  - Notify the clerk at least two days in advance of the scheduled appearance;
  - Provide the clerk with the telephone number at which the Court can reach you;
  - Agree to be available at the number (land lines only; no cellular phones) for up to one hour from the time of the scheduled hearing.

- **Ex parte applications** are for extraordinary relief. *See Mission Power Engineering Co. v. Continental Casualty Co., 883 F. Supp. 488 (C.D. Cal. 1995).* Ex parte applications are normally considered on the papers and are rarely set for hearing. If a hearing is necessary, the parties will be notified. Applications that fail to conform to L.R. 7-19 and L.R. 7-19.1, including a statement of opposing counsel's position, will not be considered except on a specific showing of good cause. In addition to the requirements of L.R. 7-19 and L.R. 7-19.1, the moving party shall notify the opposition that opposing papers must be filed no later than twenty-four (24) hours following service, except in cases where the opposing party has not previously appeared (i.e., responded to the Complaint). In those cases where the opposing party has not previously appeared, the moving party shall notify the opposition that opposing papers must be filed no later than forty-eight (48) hours following service. A mandatory chambers copy of the ex parte application, opposition or notice of non-opposition and reply are to be delivered to the courtesy bin outside the entrance to Judge Fairbank's chambers. Counsel will be notified by the clerk of the Court's ruling.
- For general information on how to order a transcript of any reported or digitally recorded proceeding, please contact 213-894-3015 or visit www.cacd.uscourts.gov > General Information > Court Reporter/Recorder Transcripts. If you require an estimate of cost for the preparation of a transcript, contact the court reporter/recorder for the desired proceeding.
  To determine the court reporter/recorder for a particular proceeding, go to the Court Reporter Schedule web page and click on View by Date. Once you've determined the correct court reporter/recorder for the desired session, click on Court Reporter Phone and Email List for contact information.
- All exhibits will be returned to counsel at the end of trial and will not be kept by the Court. Counsel shall keep the lodged and admitted exhibits in their possession pursuant to L.R. 79-3 and L.R. 79-4.
- It is the responsibility of counsel in a civil case to arrange for the services of an Interpreter. Interpreter's Office: (213) 894-4599.
- If counsel has received a "Notice to Parties of Alternate Dispute Resolution (ADR) Program" - forms ADR-08, ADR-10, or ADR-11 with an attached "ADR Program Questionnaire" form ADR-09, please see General Order 02-07, which is located in the "General Orders" section on the home page of the Court's website. The Attorney Settlement Officer information is located in the section "Attorney Information, ADR."
- Law clerk/extern positions: Submit resume by mail.

II. Judge Fairbank's Case Management Orders

A. *Criminal Motion and Trial Order*

IN THE UNITED STATES DISTICT COURT
FOR THE CENTRAL DISTRICT OF CALIFORNIA

UNITED STATES OF AMERICA, Plaintiff, v. Defendant(s).	)))))	Case No __________ **CRIMINAL MOTION AND TRIAL ORDER**

The above matter is set for trial before the Honorable Valerie Baker Fairbank, Courtroom 9, United States Courthouse, 312 N. Spring Street, Los Angeles, California 90012.

1. Mandatory Chambers Paper Copies of All Documents Filed Required:

Counsel shall deliver one mandatory chambers paper copy of all documents filed in this action to the bin outside the chambers of Judge Fairbank immediately after filing and no later than 10:00 a.m. the morning after filing.

2. Submission of Documents for Judge's Signature to Chambers via Email:

All proposed signature items, including applications and stipulations to extend time, shall be accompanied by a proposed order. After the application/stipulation and proposed order have been filed electronically, counsel shall email the PDF version of the application/stipulation and a WordPerfect or Microsoft Word version of the proposed order to chambers at vbf_chambers@cacd.uscourts.gov. The subject line of the e-mail should include the case name and case number.

3. Motions:

a. Motions in criminal matters are heard on Monday at 10:00 a.m., unless specially set by the Courtroom Deputy Clerk ("CRD") at the Court or counsel's request.

b. Motions shall be filed and served at least two weeks prior to the noticed hearing date. Opposition papers shall be filed and served at least one week prior to the hearing date. Less notice will be allowed only on a proper showing of urgency or necessity, *i.e.*, five days' notice per Fed. R. Crim. Pro. 47(c).

c. Except on a showing of good cause, all motions, including motions *in limine*, shall be heard on or before the pre-trial conference, which is generally set by the Court at least two weeks before trial. This is a motion deadline. *See* Fed. R. Crim. Pro. 12(c) and (e). Counsel are encouraged to notice motions for hearing much sooner, particularly motions pursuant to Fed. R. Crim. Pro. 12(b)(3).

4. Discovery and Notice:

Counsel for the Government and counsel for the Defendant shall comply promptly with discovery and notice matters pursuant to Fed. R. Crim. Pro. 12, 12.1, 12.2, 12.3, 15 and 16. Counsel are reminded that failure to promptly comply with discovery obligations can result in a continuance of the trial, exclusion of evidence or other orders that are just under the circumstances. *See* Fed. R. Crim. Pro. 16(d)(2). At the status conference regarding trial, the Court will inquire about the status of discovery and notice, particularly the status of the Government's disclosures under Fed. R. Crim. Pro. 16(a)(1)(A)-(G).

5. Pre-Trial Conference and Trial:

a. The Pre-Trial Conference is set for __________ at ______. This is the deadline for hearing motions, including motions in limine, absent a showing of good cause.

b. The trial is set for __________ at ______. The first day of trial will last from 8:30 a.m. to 4:30 p.m. Subsequent days of trial will commence at 8:30 a.m. and adjourn at 2:00 p.m. Counsel shall be present in court by 8:00 a.m. each day of trial. The Court reserves the time from 8:00 to 8:30 a.m. and 2:00- 2:30 p.m. to handle legal and administrative matters outside the presence of the jury.

6. Trial Preparation:

a. By 8:30 a.m. on the first day of trial, counsel for the Government shall present the CRD with the following:

i. Three copies of the Government's witness list;

ii. Three copies of the Government's exhibit list;

iii. All of the Government's exhibits. The exhibits must have official exhibit tags. Exhibits shall be sequentially numbered; however, if an exhibit is an enlargement of an existing exhibit, counsel shall designate the enlargement with the number of the original exhibit followed by an "A;" and

iv. A benchbook containing a copy of all exhibits, *i.e.*, a tabbed exhibit notebook. Government's counsel shall also provide a copy of the tabbed exhibit notebook to counsel for each Defendant.

b. Defendant's counsel need not deliver his/her exhibits to the CRD on the first day of trial; however, Defendant's counsel is responsible for affixing completed exhibit tags with the case name and number to their exhibits. Defendant's counsel shall provide the Court with a copy of the Defendant's exhibits as introduced.

7. Jury Instructions and Verdict Forms:

a. Jury instructions and verdict forms shall be submitted no later than the Wednesday of the week prior to trial.

b. The parties must submit joint jury instructions and verdict forms. The parties shall meet and confer with the goal of agreeing upon instructions and verdict forms. The jury instructions shall be submitted as follows: (1) joint jury instructions, (2) disputed jury instructions, and (3) a "clean" set of instructions. The party objecting to the disputed instructions shall file written objections, stating the reasons for the objection and providing a proposed alternative instruction with supporting authority. Each requested jury instruction shall be numbered and set forth on a separate page, citing the authority or source of the requested instruction except on the "clean" copy.

c. The Court prefers counsel to use the instructions from the Manual of Model Criminal Jury Instructions for the Ninth Circuit.

d. An index page shall accompany all jury instructions that are submitted to the Court. The index page shall indicate: The number of the instruction; a brief title of the instruction; the source of the instruction; and the page number of the instruction.

8. Instructions Governing Procedure During Trial:

a. Counsel shall not refer to their clients or witnesses by their first names during trial.

b. Counsel shall not discuss the law or argue the case in opening statements.

c. When objecting, counsel shall state only "objection" and the legal ground for the objection (*e.g.*, hearsay, irrelevant, etc.). Court permission is needed to argue an objection and the argument must be outside of the hearing of the jury.

d. Counsel shall rise when the jury enters or leaves the courtroom.

e. Counsel shall address all remarks to the Court. Counsel shall not directly address the CRD, the Court Reporter, or opposing counsel.

f. Counsel shall not make an offer of stipulation in front of the jury.

g. When a party has more than one lawyer, only one of the lawyers may conduct the examination of a given witness and/or objections during the testimony of that witness.

h. If a witness was on the stand before a recess or adjournment, counsel shall have the witness back on the stand and ready to proceed when the Court resumes.

i. If you run out of witnesses and there is more than a brief delay, the Court may deem that you have rested, absent a showing of good cause.

DATED: ____________________

____

VALERIE BAKER FAIRBANK
United States District Judge

B. ***Scheduling and Case Management Order***

IN THE UNITED STATES DISTICT COURT
FOR THE CENTRAL DISTRICT OF CALIFORNIA

)	Case No. ______________
Plaintiff(s),)	
v.)	**SCHEDULING AND CASE**
Defendant(s).)	**MANAGEMENT ORDER FOR**
______________________________)	**CASES ASSIGNED TO JUDGE**
	VALERIE BAKER FAIRBANK

This case has been assigned to the calendar of Judge Valerie Baker Fairbank. This Order is to advise the parties and counsel of the schedule that will govern this action. SEE THE LAST PAGE OF THIS ORDER FOR THE SPECIFIED DATES.

Because this Order modifies or adds to the Local Rules in some respects, counsel are advised to read it carefully. Counsel are advised to pay particular attention to the Court's requirements for motions for summary judgment and partial summary judgment. IT IS HEREBY ORDERED:

1. **ELECTRONIC FILING**

   As of January 1, 2008, all civil and criminal matters must be electronically filed ("e-filed") pursuant to Fed. R. Civ. P. 5(d)(3), L.R. 5-4, and General Order 10-07. Counsel e-filing documents with Judge Fairbank must adhere to the following additional requirements:

   a. **Mandatory Chambers Copy.** One paper mandatory chambers copy of all filed documents, including **all** e-filed documents, shall be delivered to the courtesy copy box outside the entrance to Judge Fairbank's chambers (chambers is located at the end of the hallway, to the right of the courtroom) by **noon** the **day following the filing**. All mandatory chambers copies shall have the notice of e-filing attached. It is preferred, though not required, that mandatory chambers copies include a blue backing.

   b. Failure to comply with this direction regarding mandatory chambers copies could result in a delay in the consideration of a party's motion.

   c. **Proposed Signature Items.** All proposed signature items shall also be **emailed** to the chambers email address: **vbf_chambers@cacd.uscourts.gov**. The proposed signature items shall be submitted in either Word or Word Perfect format. DO NOT email other associated documents and DO NOT use this e-mail address for communication with the Court or the clerk.

   d. Any documents requiring manual filing must be accompanied by a Notice of Manual Filing explaining the reason(s) therefore. Notwithstanding the requisite Notice, such documents remain subject to rejection by the Court for failure to e-file.

      For **under seal filings**, process documents manually with the Clerk's office. A Notice of Manual Filing should also accompany the paper mandatory chambers copies submitted to chambers. DO NOT send these documents to the chambers' email account. See Judge Fairbank's Procedures and Schedules page for additional information regarding under seal filings.

2. **GENERAL MATTERS.**
Counsel should refer to the Court's Standing Order and the Court's website for information regarding policies and procedures. In particular, Counsel shall review the sections of the Court's Standing Order pertaining to the presence of responsible attorneys, mandatory chambers copies, ex parte applications, and motion requirements. See www.cacd.uscourts.gov > Judges' Procedures and Schedules > Hon. Valerie Baker Fairbank.

3. **DISCOVERY CUT-OFF.**
All discovery shall be completed by the discovery cut-off date specified on the last page of this Order. This is the date by which all discovery is to be completed. Any motion challenging the adequacy of responses to discovery must be heard sufficiently in advance of the discovery cut-off date to permit the responses to be obtained before that date if the motion is granted. The Magistrate Judge assigned to this case will rule on discovery motions. Counsel should not deliver courtesy copies of discovery-related documents to this Court.

4. **MOTIONS.**
   a. **Motion Filing Cut-Off Date.** All law and motion matters, except for motions in limine, must be filed by the motion filing cut-off date set at the Scheduling Conference. The parties are advised to adhere to the requirements of the Local Rules. See Local Rules 7-1 et seq.; Standing Order.

   b. **Motions in Limine.** Before filing any motion in limine, counsel shall comply with Local Rule 7-3. Unless otherwise ordered, motions in limine will be heard at the Final Pre-Trial Conference and should be noticed and filed as any other motion.

5. **MOTIONS FOR SUMMARY JUDGMENT.**
   a. Parties should not wait until the motion cutoff to bring motions for summary judgment or partial summary judgment.

   b. **Separate Statement of Uncontroverted Facts and Statement of Genuine Issues of Material Fact.**

   The Separate Statement of Uncontroverted Facts is to be prepared in a two column format. The left-hand column should set forth the allegedly undisputed fact. The right-hand column should set forth the evidence that supports the factual statement. The factual statements should be set forth in sequentially numbered paragraphs. Each paragraph should contain a narrowly-focused statement of fact.

   The opposing party's Statement of Genuine Issues of Material Fact must be in two columns and track the movant's Separate Statement exactly. The left-hand column must restate the allegedly undisputed fact, and the right-hand column must indicate whether the statement is undisputed or disputed. If disputing only a portion of the statement, the opposing party must clearly indicate what portion is disputed. Where disputing the fact in whole or part, the opposing party must, in the right-hand column, label and restate the moving party's evidence in support of the fact, and then set forth the opposing party's evidence controverting the fact. Where the opposing party disputes the fact on the basis of an evidentiary objection, the party must cite the allegedly objectionable evidence and state the ground of the objection. No argument should be set forth in this document.

The opposing party may submit additional material facts. The additional material facts shall follow the format described above for the moving party's Separate Statement and shall follow the movant's facts, in sequentially numbered paragraphs. The moving party, in its reply, shall respond to the additional facts in the same manner and format that the opposing party is required to adhere to in responding to the Statement of Uncontroverted Facts, as described above.

c. **Supporting Evidence.** All evidence in support of or in opposition to a motion for summary judgment, including declarations and exhibits to declarations, shall be separated by a tab divider. If evidence in support of or in opposition to a motion for summary judgment exceeds fifty pages, the Court's mandatory chambers copy of the supporting evidence shall be placed in a binder with a Table of Contents and each item of evidence separated by a tab divider.

d. **Objections to Evidence.** If a party disputes a fact in whole or in part based on an evidentiary objection, the ground for the objection, as indicated above, should be stated in the Separate Statement, but not argued in that document. Evidentiary objections should be addressed in a separate memorandum to be filed with the opposition or reply brief. Blanket or boilerplate objections are improper and will be disregarded and/or overruled.

e. **Memorandum of Points and Authorities.** The movant's and respondent's memoranda of points and authorities should conform with Local Rule 7 and contain a narrative statement of facts as to those aspects of the case that are before the Court. All facts should be supported with citations to the evidence and to a paragraph number in the Separate Statement or Statement of Genuine Issues of Material Fact.

f. **Proposed Statement of Decision.** Each party shall file and serve a Proposed Statement of Decision, not to exceed five pages, which shall contain a statement of the relevant facts and applicable law with citations to case law and the record.

6. **FINAL PRE-TRIAL CONFERENCE AND PRE-TRIAL FILINGS.**

a. **General Provisions.** The parties must comply with Local Rule 16. At the Final Pre-Trial Conference ("FPTC"), the parties should be prepared to discuss means of streamlining the trial and settlement. Lead counsel who will actually try the case must attend the Final Pretrial Conference. A party who is not represented must attend all proceedings in person. If the Court waives a FPTC, the parties must follow Local Rule 16-11.2.

b. **Memoranda; Witness Lists; Exhibit Lists.** At least twenty-one days prior to the date of the FPTC, the parties shall file and serve Memoranda of Contentions of Fact and Law, Witness Lists, and Exhibit Lists in compliance with Local Rules 16-4, 16-5, and 16-6.

Witness Lists. Witness lists shall include a brief summary (one or two paragraphs) of each witness's expected testimony, an estimate of the length of time needed for direct examination, and whether the witness will testify by deposition or in person.

If a witness is to testify by deposition, counsel shall designate the portions of the deposition to be read at trial in lieu of live testimony in the Witness List. Then, by the first day of trial, counsel shall lodge copies of the deposition transcripts to be read with the following annotations in the margin: (1) portions designated to be read by each party, and (2) evidentiary objections. One week before the trial, counsel should meet and confer to arrange for the preparation of annotated deposition transcripts.

c. **Exhibit Stipulation.** The parties shall prepare a Final Pre-Trial Exhibit Stipulation that contains each party's numbered list of all trial exhibits, with objections, if any, to each exhibit including the basis of the objection and the offering party's response. This Exhibit Stipulation shall be clear as to which party seeks to introduce the exhibit. All exhibits to which there is no objection shall be deemed admitted where they are identified in trial. Parties shall stipulate to the authenticity of exhibits whenever possible.

   Though this Exhibit Stipulation should be filed separately, the parties should reference this Stipulation in the Proposed Final Pretrial Conference Order and file such Stipulation on the same date as the Proposed Final Pretrial Conference Order. This Exhibit Stipulation shall satisfy the requirement of Local Rule 16-6.3.

d. **Jury Instructions, Verdict Forms, Special Interrogatories.** The parties shall lodge proposed jury instructions, verdict forms and/or special interrogatories at least seven days prior to the date of the FPTC. Cf. Local Rule 51-1.

   (i) Format. Per Local Rules 51-1 - 51-5, if the parties cannot agree upon one complete set of instructions, verdict form and/or special interrogatories, they shall file two documents with the Court: A joint document reflecting the agreed upon instructions, verdict form and/or special interrogatories; and a second document in the form of a joint statement regarding the disputed jury instructions, verdict forms and/or special interrogatories, in the following format: (1) A page containing the text of the disputed language with an identification of the party proposing it; (2) a second page containing the opposing party's statement of objections to the disputed language (as well as proposed alternative language if appropriate) with citation to legal authority (not to exceed one page); and (3) a third page containing the proposing party's response to the objection with citation to supporting legal authority (not to exceed one page).

   The Court will send copies of the instructions into the jury room for the jury's use during deliberations. Therefore, in addition to the copies described above, counsel shall submit a "clean set" of Joint Proposed and/or Disputed Jury Instructions, containing only the text of each instruction set forth in full on each page, with the caption "Court's Instruction No. ___."

   (ii) Preferred Instructions. The Court directs counsel to use the instructions from the Manual of Model Jury Instructions for the Ninth Circuit where applicable. Where the above instructions are not applicable, the Court prefers counsel to use the Judicial Council of California Civil Jury Instructions ("CACI"). If neither of these sources is applicable, counsel are directed to use the instructions from O'Malley, Grenig and Lee, Federal Jury Practice and Instructions. Modifications of instructions from the foregoing sources (or any other form instructions) must be set forth with particularity (e.g. by underlining) as well as authority supporting the modification.

e. **Final Pre-Trial Conference Order ("FPTCO").** The proposed FPTCO shall be lodged at least seven days prior to the date of the FPTC. The form of the proposed FPTCO shall comply with Appendix A to the Local Rules. See also ¶6c of this Scheduling & Case Management Order. The parties must file a Status Report regarding settlement at the time they lodge the Proposed FPTCO. This Report shall not disclose the parties' settlement positions, but shall merely describe the efforts made by the parties to resolve the dispute.

f. **Joint Statement of the Case and Requests for Voir Dire.** At least seven days prior to the FPTC, the parties shall lodge their proposed voir dire questions and their joint statement of the case.

g. **Court Reporter.** At the FPTC, all parties shall provide to the court reporter a list of all words, terms, technical terminology, proper names, acronyms, and case citations that would not be found in a standard word-processing spell-check dictionary. The court reporter shall maintain the confidence of the parties submitting this information.

h. **Court Trial.** Counsel for each party shall lodge and serve initial proposed findings of fact and conclusions of law seven days before the FPTC.

i. **Day of Trial.** On the first day of trial the following shall be submitted to the Courtroom Deputy Clerk: (1) The original exhibits, identified and pre-marked as directed by the courtroom deputy clerk at the FPTC. (2) One bench book with a copy of each exhibit for the Court's use, with tabbed dividers between each exhibit. (3) A copy of the exhibit book for opposing counsel. (4) Three copies of exhibit lists and three copies of witness lists in the order in which the witnesses will be called to testify.

Dated: ____________________

____
VALERIE BAKER FAIRBANK
United States District Judge

Judge Valerie Baker Fairbank
Schedule of Trial and Pre-Trial Dates

1. Parties and Case Number:

a. __________ (PLAINTIFF), v. ____________ (DEFENDANT)

b. Case number: _______________ (CASE NUMBER)

2. Trial ____________________ at 8:30 AM

a. Jury _______________

b. Court _______________

c. Time Est. ________

3. FPTC and MIL ________________ at 2:30 PM

4. Motion Filing Cut-off ______________

5. Non-expert Discovery Cut-off _______________

6. Expert Discovery Cut-off ________________

____

____

7a. ADR - Settlement Procedure No. 1, 2 or 3

7b. Settlement Conference/Mediation to be held no later than _______________

7c. The Parties are expected to contact the neutral promptly and certainly no later than 4 months in advance of the Settlement Conference/Mediation deadline to arrange the date of the Conference/Mediation in light of the neutral's schedule. Failure to comply may lead to sanctions.

8. Motion for Leave to Amend the Pleadings and/or Add Parties: ____________________.

Later-filed motions must show good cause to amend the Court's Scheduling Order.

C. Standing Order

**IN THE UNITED STATES DISTICT COURT
FOR THE CENTRAL DISTRICT OF CALIFORNIA**

	)	Case No. _______________
Plaintiff(s),	)	
v.	)	**STANDING ORDER**
Defendant(s).	)	
____________________	)	

This case has been assigned to the calendar of Judge Valerie Baker Fairbank. Read this order carefully. It controls this case and adds to the Local Rules in some respects. IT IS SO ORDERED:

1. SERVICE.

Counsel for Plaintiff shall immediately serve this order on all parties. If this case was removed from state court, the defendant who removed the case shall immediately serve this order on all other parties.

2. GENERAL MATTERS.

a. Compliance with FRCP, Local Rules, and Standing Orders. At all stages of the proceedings, the parties and counsel are expected to comply with the Federal Rules of Civil Procedure ("FRCP"), Local Rules and this Court's orders. Counsel are referred to the Court's website for further information regarding procedures. *See* www.cacd.uscourts.gov > Judges' Procedures and Schedules > Hon. Valerie Baker Fairbank. Counsel are further advised to review and adhere to the Central District's Civility and Professionalism Guidelines.

b. Communications with Chambers. Counsel shall not attempt to contact the Court or chambers staff unless responding to an inquiry they initiated. Counsel may contact the courtroom deputy clerk with appropriate inquiries (213-894-0066). To facilitate communication with the courtroom deputy clerk, counsel should list their e-mail addresses, facsimile number, and telephone number on all papers. *See* L.R. 11-3.8.

c. Mandatory Chambers Copies. Conformed mandatory chambers copies of all papers filed with the Court, including those filed electronically, shall be delivered on the next day of filing, by 12 noon, to the drop box outside the Chambers of Judge Valerie Baker Fairbank. The Judge's Chambers are located at the end of the hallway, past the courtroom.

d. Presence of Responsible Counsel. The attorney attending any proceeding before this Court must be an attorney who is thoroughly knowledgeable about the case, responsible for the conduct of the litigation, and who has authority to enter into stipulations and to make admissions.

e. Telephonic Appearances. The Court believes it is productive for counsel to appear personally at motion hearings and Scheduling Conferences. An attorney requesting a telephonic appearance should file and serve a written notice of telephonic appearance at the earliest possible date, but no later than five days prior to the scheduled hearing or conference, absent an emergency.

3. PARTIES' 26(f) PLANNING MEETING.

Counsel shall adhere to FRCP 26. No later than 14 days before the date of the

Scheduling Conference, counsel for all appearing parties and/or all unrepresented appearing parties shall file a joint "Report of the Parties Planning Meeting." This report shall address the subjects in Rule 26(f)(1) – (4) and the following:

a. **Jurisdiction.** The basis for subject matter jurisdiction.

b. **Claims and Defenses.** The report shall include a concise statement of the factual and legal basis of the claims and defenses.

c. **Discovery Cut-Off.** The report shall propose a date by which all discovery shall be completed. If the parties anticipate calling expert witnesses, they shall propose a schedule for the completion of discovery directed at expert witnesses.

d. **Trial Matters.** The report shall propose dates for the Final Pre-Trial Conference and Trial; a realistic estimate of the number of court dates required to present each side's case-in-chief; and whether trial is to be by jury or the Court.

e. **Anticipated Problems.** The report shall address major procedural or evidentiary problems, if any.

f. **Settlement.** The report shall address prospects of settlement and propose a date and procedure for compliance with Local Rule 16-15.

4. DISCOVERY.

a. **Compliance with Rule 26(a) & (f).** The Court expects and orders that counsel participate in the meeting required by Rule 26(f) as soon as possible, and that initial disclosures be made promptly after that meeting and before the Scheduling Conference set by the Court. Rule 26(a)(1)(C). Counsel are also directed to commence discovery promptly after their Rule 26(f) meeting, and if possible, before the Scheduling Conference. Rule 26(d)(1). It is advisable for counsel to begin discovery and conduct it actively at the earliest possible time because they will have limited time to complete discovery after the Court's Rule 26(f) Scheduling Conference. Early meeting, disclosure and discovery is particularly important in certain cases such as class actions where Local Rule 23-3 requires that within 90 days after service of a pleading purporting to commence a class action, the proponent shall file a motion for certification, unless otherwise ordered by the Court.

b. **Discovery Motions.** All discovery disputes have been referred to the assigned magistrate judge. All discovery documents must include the words "DISCOVERY MATTER" in the caption to ensure proper routing. Counsel should contact the magistrate judge's courtroom deputy clerk to schedule hearings. Counsel should not deliver courtesy copies of discovery-related documents to this Court.

5. *EX PARTE* APPLICATIONS.

Ex parte applications are solely for extraordinary relief and are rarely justified. *See Mission Power Engineering Co. v. Continental Casualty Co.*, 883 F. Supp. 488 (C.D. Cal. 1995). Applications must be filed in the Clerk's office. *Ex parte* applications are normally considered on the papers. Applications that fail to conform to Local Rules 7-19 and 7-19.1, including a statement of opposing counsel's position, will not be considered except on a specific showing of good cause.

In addition to the requirements of Local Rules 7-19 and 7-19.1, the moving party shall, following service of the *ex parte* papers by facsimile transmission or personal service, notify the opposition that opposing papers must be filed no later than twenty-four hours (1 court day) following service, except in cases where the opposing party has not previously appeared (*i.e.*, responded to the Complaint). In those cases where the opposing party has not previously appeared, the moving party shall, following service of the *ex parte* papers by facsimile or personal service, notify the opposition that opposing papers must be filed no later than forty-eight hours (2 court days) following service.

6. **CASES REMOVED FROM STATE COURT.**

All documents filed in state court, including documents appended to the complaint, answers and motions, must be refiled in this Court as a supplement to the notice of removal, if not already included. *See* 28 U.S.C. § 1447(a) and (b). If, before the case was removed, a motion was pending in state court, it must be re-noticed in accordance with Local Rule 7. If an action removed to this Court contains a form pleading, *i.e.*, a pleading in which boxes are checked, the party or parties that filed the form pleading must file an appropriate pleading with this Court within 30 days of receipt of the notice of removal.

7. **PATENT CASES.**

With minor modifications, the Court follows the Northern District of California Patent Local Rules (version effective 3/1/2008) in all patent cases. Counsel are referred to the Court's website for more information and a modified copy of the Rules. *See* www.cacd.uscourts.gov > Judges' Procedures and Schedules > Hon. Valerie Baker Fairbank.

8. **FICTITIOUSLY NAMED DEFENDANTS.**

This Court adheres to the following procedures when a matter is removed to this Court on diversity grounds with fictitiously named defendants referred to in the complaint. *See* 28 U.S.C. §§ 1441(a) and 1447. Plaintiff shall ascertain the identity of and serve any fictitiously named defendants before the Scheduling Conference. Doe defendants not served by the date of the Scheduling Conference will be deemed dismissed.

9. **GENERAL MOTION REQUIREMENTS.**

a. **Time for Hearing Motions.** Motions shall be filed in accordance with Local Rule 7. Motion dates need not be reserved in advance. This Court hears motions on Mondays at 1:30 p.m.

b. **Pre-filing Requirement.** Counsel must comply with Local Rule 7-3, which requires counsel to engage in a pre-filing conference "to discuss thoroughly . . . the substance of the contemplated motion and any potential resolution."

c. **Length and Format of Motion Papers.** Memoranda of points and authorities in support of or in opposition to motions shall not exceed 25 pages. Replies shall not exceed 12 pages. Only in rare instances and for good cause will the Court grant an application to extend these page limitations. If documentary evidence in support of or in opposition to a motion exceeds 50 pages, the Court's mandatory chambers copy of all evidence shall be placed in a binder, including a Table of Contents, with each item of evidence separated by a tab divider. Typeface shall comply with Local Rule 11-3.1.1. Footnotes shall be in typeface no less than one size smaller than text size.

d. **Calendar Conflicts.** Counsel are to inform opposing counsel and the courtroom deputy clerk as soon as a potential calendar conflict is discovered. Counsel should attempt to agree on a proposed date to accommodate the calendar conflict and the schedules of the counsel and the Court.

e. **Requests to Take Matters Off-Calendar.** Requests to continue a motion or to take it off-calendar must be communicated to the courtroom deputy clerk as soon as possible. For example, if a case settles, the courtroom deputy clerk should be notified immediately so as to avoid the waste of judicial time and resources.

10. SPECIFIC MOTION REQUIREMENTS.

a. **Motions Pursuant to Rule 12.** Many motions to dismiss or to strike can be avoided if the parties confer in good faith, especially for perceived defects in a complaint, answer or counterclaim that could be corrected by amendment. Moreover, a party has the right to amend the complaint "once as a matter of course" before a responsive pleading is served. FRCP 15(a)(1). A Rule 12(b)(6) motion is not a responsive pleading and therefore plaintiff might have a right to amend. *See St. Michael's Convalescent Hospital v. California*, 643 F.2d 1369, 1374 (9th Cir. 1981). Even after a complaint has been amended or a responsive pleading has been served, the Federal Rules provide that leave to amend should be freely given "when justice so requires." FRCP 15(a)(2). These principles require that plaintiff's counsel should carefully evaluate defendant's contentions as to the deficiencies in the complaint and the moving party should agree to any amendment that would cure the defect.

b. **Applications and Stipulations to Extend Time.** Applications to extend the time to file any required document or to continue any hearing, Final Pre-Trial Conference or Trial must set forth: (1) the existing due date or hearing date, as well as the discovery cut-off date, the Final Pre-Trial Conference date, and the Trial date; (2) specific, concrete reasons showing good cause for the extension; and (3) whether there have been prior requests for extensions and whether these requests

were granted or denied by the Court.

c. **Submission of Documents for Judge's Signature to Chambers via Email.**

All applications and stipulations shall be accompanied by a proposed order. After the application/stipulation and proposed order have been filed electronically, counsel shall email the PDF version of the application/stipulation and a WordPerfect or Microsoft Word version of the proposed order to chambers at vbf_chambers@cacd.uscourts.gov. The subject line of the email should include the case name and case number.

DATED: August 14, 2009

VALERIE BAKER FAIRBANK
United States District Judge

Hon. Gary A. Feess

District Judge

Chambers Information

U.S. District Court, Central District of California
Courtroom 740
255 East Temple Street
Los Angeles, CA 90012

Scheduling Information

Courtroom Deputy: (213) 894-3480

Civil Law and Motion	Mondays at 9:30 a.m.
Criminal Law and Motion	Mondays at 1:30 p.m.

Biographical Information

Born 1948 in Alliance, OH

Federal Judicial Service:

-Judge, U. S. District Court, Central District of California
-Nominated by William J. Clinton on January 26, 1999, to a seat vacated by James M. Ideman; Confirmed by the Senate on June 30, 1999, and received commission on July 7, 1999.

Education:

-Ohio State University, B.A., 1970
-University of California at Los Angeles, J.D., 1974

Professional Career:

-Private Practice, Los Angeles, CA, 1974-1979
-Assistant U.S. Attorney, U.S. Attorney's Office, U.S. District Court, Central District of California, 1979-1987
-Private Practice, Los Angeles, CA, 1987-1988
-Chief Assistant U.S. Attorney, U.S. Attorney's Office, U.S. District Court, Central District of California, 1988-1989
-Private Practice, Los Angeles, CA, 1989-1996
-Judge, Los Angeles Superior Court, CA, 1996-1999

I. Judge Feess' Procedures and Practices

A. *Procedures and Schedules*

1. Civil motions are heard on Mondays at 9:30 a.m.

Criminal motions are heard on Mondays at 1:30 p.m.

(If Monday is a holiday, next motion date is the following Monday.)

It is not necessary to clear a motion date with the court clerk prior to filing a motion.

2. Discovery motions are to be calendared before the magistrate judge.

3. Written tentative rulings are not issued in most cases. The tentative will be stated from the bench at the hearing.

4. A mandatory chambers copy of ALL e-filed documents is to be delivered to chambers (Room 730) in the Roybal Courthouse and placed in the courtesy copy box located on the 7th floor outside the entry door to chambers not later than 12:00 noon the day following e-filing.

5. Procedures for filing an ex parte application: Follow Local Rule 7.19. An appearance is generally not required. Proof of service and declaration of notification are necessary for acceptance of papers.

6. A request to continue any scheduled civil court proceeding must be made in writing at least one week in advance.

7. A continuance of any criminal court proceedings will require the appearance of the parties and will not be granted on the papers, even if the parties stipulate to the continuance.

8. Counsel are not allowed to contact the judge's law clerk or secretary unless responding to a contact they initiated.

9. Inquiries regarding the status of a motion, stipulation or proposed order are not available by telephone. Follow Local Rule 11-4.5.

10. Calendar conflicts: (Procedures for attorneys to follow if they have a calendar conflict) Fax to the clerk at least 3 days in advance. Court will start on time and there will be **no second call**.

11. Procedures for bringing electronic equipment into the courtroom: Submit a written order with description (including serial number) at least one week in advance.

12. For general information on how to order a transcript of any reported or digitally recorded proceeding, please contact 213-894-3015 or visit www.cacd.uscourts.gov > General Information > Court Reporter/Recorder Transcripts. If you require an estimate of cost for the preparation of a transcript, contact the court reporter/recorder for the desired proceeding.

To determine the court reporter/recorder for a particular proceeding, go to the Court Reporter Schedule web page and click on View by Date. Once you've determined the correct court reporter/recorder for the desired session, click on Court Reporter Phone and Email List for contact information.

13. Questions regarding law clerk/extern positions shall be addressed to the judge's secretary.

14. Trial preparation:
    a. Court hours 8:30 a.m.-2:30 p.m. with two 20 minute breaks OR 9:00-5:00 with two breaks and a lunch hour.
    b. Exhibit preparation: Per Order given to counsel at the MSC or arraignment.
    c. Jury instructions: Per Scheduling Order.
    d. Verdict forms: Per Scheduling Order.
15. Procedures for obtaining the services of an interpreter on a civil case: Counsel are responsible for retaining the services of a certified interpreter through any appropriate source.

B. Standing Order Regarding Protective Orders and Treatment of Confidential Information

STANDING ORDER RE: PROTECTIVE ORDERS AND TREATMENT OF CONFIDENTIAL INFORMATION

The Court has adopted the following substantive and procedural guidelines for protective orders, whether stipulated or not:

I. Guidelines for Protective Order Provisions

A. Clear and Precise. A protective order must be sufficiently precise and clear, so that:

1. All parties and other persons who are bound by the order know precisely what they are required to do, permitted to do, and forbidden from doing.

2. In the event that any party seeks to have another party who supposedly violated the order held in contempt, it is necessary that the order contain no ambiguity concerning the parties' rights and responsibilities.

B. Narrowly Tailored. A protective order must be narrowly tailored and cannot be overbroad. Therefore,

1. The documents, information, items or materials that are subject to the protective order shall be described in a meaningful fashion. (For example, "blueprints," "customer lists," or "market surveys," *etc.*) It is not sufficient to use only the conclusory term "trade secrets."

2. In proposing or agreeing to the protection of "trade secrets," the definition for that term in California Civil Code § 3426.1 should be incorporated into the protective order, either by reference or by quotation.[1]

C. Burden of Proof. The party designating information, documents, materials or items as confidential bears the burden of establishing the confidentiality.

D. Procedures for Filing Confidential Information with the Court. All Court orders will be presumptively available to the public. Therefore, if a protective order provides that evidence may be filed under seal and if a party does file such evidence under seal, all papers that refer to or rely upon such evidence shall designate the particular aspects that are confidential. This will enable the Court, in drafting orders, to determine whether there is evidence which the Court should attempt not to disclose. Absent such advance notification, the Court will be free to incorporate all such evidence in its written and oral rulings.

E. Use of Confidential Information at Trial. In the event that the case proceeds to trial, all of the information that was designated as confidential and/or kept and maintained pursuant to the terms of a protective order becomes public and will be presumptively available to all members of the public, including the press, unless sufficient

[1] Cal. Civil Code § 3426.1 provides that trade secret "means information, including a formula, pattern, compilation, program, device, method, technique, or process, that: (1) Derives independent economic value, actual or potential, from not being generally known to the public or to other persons who can obtain economic value from its disclosure or use; and (2) Is the subject of efforts that are reasonable under the circumstances to maintain its secrecy.

cause is shown in advance of trial to proceed otherwise.

II. Procedure for Obtaining Protective Order

A. Stipulated Protective Orders. Any proposed stipulated protective order submitted to the Court shall reflect the guidelines set forth in this order. If satisfactory, the Court will sign the proposed protective order and cause it to be filed. If not satisfactory, the Court will return it to counsel, with reference to the provisions that have to be added or changed. Thereafter, any revised proposed stipulated protective order shall contain such modifications.

B. Motions for a Protective Order. In the event that the parties are unable to agree upon the terms of a protective order, the procedure for obtaining such an order is that set forth in the Local Rules concerning discovery motions. In civil cases, the motion will be addressed to and resolved by the magistrate judge. The party initiating the motion shall ensure that the proposed order is attached to the joint stipulation. When filing the motion, the party seeking the protective order shall lodge with the court *in camera* copies of the evidence for which it seeks a protective order.

The Court thanks counsel for their anticipated cooperation and compliance with this order.

Dated: ________________

____
GARY ALLEN FEESS
United States District Judge

II. Judge Fees' Case Management Orders

A. *Civil Trial Order*

IN THE UNITED STATES DISTICT COURT
FOR THE CENTRAL DISTRICT OF CALIFORNIA

)	Case No. ______________
Plaintiff(s),)	
v.)	**CIVIL TRIAL ORDER**
Defendant(s).)	
______________________________)	

This case has been set for trial on the date specified in the Court's "Case Management and Scheduling Order." The Court's procedures and requirements for civil trials are set forth below.

A. MOTIONS *IN LIMINE*

1. Motions *in limine* are not to be used as disguised motions for summary judgment or as discovery motions that were not timely filed before the discovery cut-off. Their purpose is limited to alerting the Court to significant evidentiary issues that can be addressed and resolved prior to trial.

2. The Court has found that many of the issues raised in motions *in limine* can be readily resolved by counsel if they prepare for trial in a spirit of professionalism and cooperation. Therefore, before filing any motion *in limine*, counsel are to meet and confer regarding the potential evidentiary dispute, and the Court is to be advised in the motion that such meeting has occurred. If either party refuses to participate in the meet and confer process, the Court will impose sanctions including a resolution of the issue against the party refusing to cooperate.

B. THE COMMENCEMENT OF THE TRIAL

1. Counsel shall arrive in the Courtroom at 8:30 a.m. on the first day of trial for the purpose of handling logistical and administrative matters pertaining to the trial, including the submission of exhibits as discussed below.

2. Counsel shall present the Courtroom Deputy with the following documents on the first day of trial:

a. THREE copies of the trial Witness List and Exhibit List.

b. ALL of the original exhibits, with official exhibit tags attached and bearing the same number shown on the exhibit list. The original, tagged exhibits are to be placed in a tabbed binder with the exhibit number displayed prominently on the tab corresponding to the exhibit. Exhibit tags can be obtained from the receptionist in the main Clerk's Office, located at 312 North Spring Street, Room G-8.

c. A bench book containing a copy of all exhibits that can be reproduced. Each exhibit shall be side-tabbed with the exhibit number for easy referral.

d. An exhibit list, proposed jury instructions, and the proposed special verdict in WordPerfect format on electronic media. A copy of the exhibit list with all **admitted exhibits** will be given to the jury during deliberations. Counsel shall review and approve the exhibit list with the Courtroom Deputy prior to it being given to the jury.

3. If counsel need to arrange for the installation of their own additional equipment, such as video monitors, overhead projectors, etc., notify the Court's Space & Facilities Department, 213-894-1400 no later than 4:30 p.m. the Thursday BEFORE trial so that the necessary arrangements can be made.

4. Trials commence on Tuesday at 8;30 a.m., with jury selection beginning at 9:30 a.m., or as soon thereafter as possible. Trials are conducted Tuesday through Friday on a schedule to be determined by the Court. Depending on the nature of the case and the anticipated length of the trial, the Court may conduct trial from: (1) 9:00 a.m. to 5:00 p.m., with two fifteen (15) minute breaks normally at 10:30 a.m. and 3:00 p.m., and a lunch recess from 12:00 p.m. to 1:30 p.m; or (2) 8:30 a.m. to approximately 2:30 p.m. with two 20 minute breaks.

5. Before trial commences, the Court will give counsel an opportunity to discuss administrative matters and anticipated procedural or legal issues. On the first day of trial, this will include a final discussion regarding voir dire questions and the content of the joint statement. During the trial, if there are any matters you wish to discuss, please inform the Courtroom Deputy.

6. During the trial, the Court reserves the time immediately prior to the daily commencement of testimony to handle legal and administrative matters outside of the presence of the jury. Counsel is urged to anticipate matters which may need discussion or hearing outside of the presence of the jury and to raise them during this period, during breaks or at the end of the day.

C. WITNESSES

1. The Court's Scheduling and Case Management Order provides for the service of witness lists two weeks prior to the Pre-trial Conference. *These lists are to include those witnesses who counsel anticipates calling at trial. These lists may be amended no later than one week before trial, at which time counsel are to give final notice of those witnesses whom they intend to call at trial. Modification of the witness list thereafter will be permitted only on motion to the court and a showing of good cause.*

2. During trial counsel are to give their opponent ***48 hour notice*** of the witnesses they intend to call to testify. Thus, for example, plaintiff must advise defendant, no later than Sunday of the witnesses plaintiff intends to call on the first Tuesday of trial. Failure to adhere to this provision of the Court's order may result in the Court precluding the witness from testifying at trial.

D. TIME LIMITS

1. The Court will, in every case, impose time limits on the amount of time each side will have for opening statements, witness examination and closing argument. The time limits will be established at, or shortly after, the pre-trial conference. The time allotted for the presentation of evidence by a party represents the amount of time given to that party to examine witnesses whether on direct or cross-examination.

2. **N.B.** At trial, the Court may cut witness examination time if it appears to the Court that the evidence being presented is cumulative. In other words, the Court may reduce the amount of time that it has initially allotted for the examination of witnesses if events occurring during the course of trial suggest that further limitation is appropriate.

E. *VOIR DIRE* AND JURY SELECTION

1. The Court will conduct *voir dire* after conferring with counsel regarding potential areas of questioning. A substantial portion of the *voir dire* will be based on written

questions given to the jurors when they arrive at Court.

2. In most cases, the Court will conduct its initial *voir dire* of 14 prospective jurors who will be seated in the jury box. Normally the Court selects a jury of eight.

3. Except in an unusual case, each side will have three peremptory challenges. Therefore, if 14 jurors are in the box and all six peremptories are exercised, the remaining eight jurors will constitute the jury panel. If fewer than six peremptories are exercised, the eight low-numbered jurors (by seat number in the jury box) will constitute the jury panel

F. COURT TRIALS

1. In Court trials, the Court may require the submission of direct testimony in the form of an affidavit, a declaration under penalty of perjury, or excerpts of deposition testimony. The witness must be present in Court for cross-examination on the proffered direct testimony.

2. The party proffering the witness may conduct a re-direct examination, but limited to new matter raised on cross which is not covered by the direct testimony of the witness.

G. INSTRUCTIONS GOVERNING PROCEDURE DURING TRIAL

1. Counsel are expected to cooperate with each other during trial to insure the efficient and expeditious use of the time of the Court and the jurors.

2. Counsel shall not refer to their clients or any witness over 14 years of age by their first names during trial.

3. Do not discuss the law or argue the case in opening statements.

4. When objecting, stand before speaking, state only that you are objecting and the legal ground of the objection, *e.g.*, hearsay, irrelevant, etc. Do not argue an objection before the jury.

5. Questions should not be preceded by editorial comment of any sort. Attorneys are not witnesses and should not behave as if they are.

6. The Court disfavors argumentative questions and will sustain its own objection to such questions.

7. In multi-party cases, counsel are expected to coordinate their cross-examination. The Court will not permit each party's counsel to repeat previous cross-examination questions.

8. Do not approach the Courtroom Deputy or the witness box without the Court's permission. Please return to the lectern when your purpose has been accomplished. Do not enter the well of the Court without the Court's permission.

9. Please rise when addressing the Court. In jury cases, please rise when the jury enters or leaves the courtroom.

10. Address all remarks to the Court. Do not directly address the Courtroom Deputy, the reporter or opposing counsel. If you wish to speak with opposing counsel, ask permission to talk to counsel off the record. All requests for the re-reading of questions or answers, or to have an exhibit placed in front of a witness, shall be addressed to the Court.

11. Although the Court encourages the parties to stipulate to facts that are not reasonably in dispute, do not offer a stipulation unless you have previously conferred with opposing counsel and reached an agreement.

12. While court is in session, do not leave the counsel table to confer with

investigators, secretaries, or witnesses unless permission is granted in advance.

13. When a party has more than one lawyer, only one may conduct the examination of a given witness and only that lawyer may handle objections during the testimony of that witness.

14. If a witness was on the stand at a recess or adjournment, have the witness back on the stand and ready to proceed when court resumes.

15. Do not run out of witnesses. If you are out of witnesses and there is more than a brief delay, the Court may deem that you have rested.

16. The Court attempts to cooperate with doctors and other professional witnesses and will, except in extraordinary circumstances, accommodate them by permitting them to be put on out of sequence. Anticipate any such possibility and discuss it with opposing counsel. If there is an objection, confer with the Court in advance.

17. Counsel are advised to be on time as the Court starts promptly.

18. During closing argument counsel should avoid the following:

a. Do not speak in the first person and offer opinions regarding the evidence. Argue the evidence and inferences that may be drawn from the evidence.

b. Do not discuss personal experiences and how they may reveal anything about the evidence.

c. Do not use contemporary news events or other lawsuits to make a point during argument, *e.g.*, the McDonald's spilled coffee case or anything involving O.J. Simpson. Stick to the evidence in this case. At the same time, counsel in argument may draw on matters that have become well established in the broader culture, e.g., the fable of the Good Samaritan, literary classics such as the works of Shakespeare, Dickens and Mark Twain, and the like.

d. Do not appeal to the personal interest of the members of the jury panel, such as arguing that a plaintiff's verdict would cause an increase in insurance premiums.

e. Do not present demonstrative materials without showing them to opposing counsel; insure that the information in the demonstrative finds support in the record or its use will be precluded.

IT IS SO ORDERED.

Dated: ____________________

____
GARY ALLEN FEESS
United States District Judge

B. *Criminal Trial Order*

IN THE UNITED STATES DISTICT COURT
FOR THE CENTRAL DISTRICT OF CALIFORNIA

UNITED STATES OF AMERICA,) Case No. ______________
Plaintiff,)
v.) **ORDER RE CRIMINAL TRIAL**
Defendant(s).)
______________________________)

The above matter is set for trial before the Honorable Gary Allen Feess, Courtroom 740, Roybal Federal Building.

PRE-TRIAL AND TRIAL DATES

1. **Status Conference/Hearing** is set for ____________ at __________.
Trial is set for **Tuesday at 8:30 A.M.** on______________________.

2. All pleadings shall be served personally on opposing counsel or faxed to opposing counsel no later than 4:30 p.m. on the day of filing.

3. **Counsel are ORDERED to serve conformed courtesy copies of all motions, oppositions and replies directly to Chambers at the Roybal Federal Building, 255 East Temple Street, Suite 730, Los Angeles, California 90012 in accordance with the Local Rules.**

4. Counsel are ORDERED to list their facsimile transmission numbers along with their address and telephone numbers on all papers submitted to the Court in order to facilitate communication by the Court.

DISCOVERY & NOTICE

5. Counsel for the government and counsel for defendant shall comply promptly with discovery and notice pursuant to Fed. R. Crim. P. 12, 12.1, 12.2, 12.3, 15, and 16. Upon government counsel's discovery of any evidence within the scope of *Brady v. Maryland*, 373 U.S. 83 (1963), such evidence shall be produced forthwith to counsel for the defendant. Counsel for the government shall also disclose to counsel for defendant the existence or non-existence of: (1) evidence obtained by electronic surveillance; (2) testimony by a government informer.

TRIAL

6. Counsel for the government shall file with the Court *in camera* (under seal) all statements of all witnesses to be called by the government in its case-in-chief. Such statements shall be filed at least five (5) calendar days before trial in a bench book tabbed with the witness(es)' name(s) for easy referral.

7. On the scheduled trial date, trial commences at 8:30 a.m. at which time the Court will conduct a final conference with counsel regarding voir dire, jury selection and related matters. Counsel are expected to arrive promptly and to be prepared to deal with these issues.

8. Counsel for the government shall present the Courtroom Deputy with the following documents on the first day of trial:

a. THREE copies of the government's witness list.

b. THREE copies of the government's exhibit list in the form specified in Local Rule 16-6 (Civil).

c. ALL of the government's exhibits, with official exhibit tags attached and bearing the same number shown on the exhibit list. The government should provide an original to be made a part of the trial record, and copies for all counsel and the Court. Exhibit tags can be obtained from the receptionist in the main Clerk's Office, located at 312 North Spring Street, Room G-8.

d. A bench book containing a copy of all exhibits that can be reproduced. Each exhibit shall be tabbed with the exhibit number for easy referral. Defendant's counsel shall provide the Court with a copy of their exhibits as they are introduced during trial.

e. An electronic disk containing the exhibit list. A copy of the exhibit list with all **admitted exhibits** will be given to the jury during deliberations. Government and defense counsel shall review and approve the exhibit list with the Courtroom Deputy prior to it being given to the jury.

9. Defendant's counsel does not have to deliver his or her exhibits to the Courtroom Deputy on the first day of trial; however, is expected to have exhibit tags affixed to all exhibits that it might use, including those that might be used to refresh recollection, and to have copies of each exhibit available for the Court and all counsel.

10. Counsel is responsible for providing copies in accordance with this order. COUNSEL MAY NOT IMPOSE ON THE COURT'S STAFF TO MAKE COPIES DURING THE COURSE OF TRIAL.

11. Counsel for the government should be aware that the Court will order that exhibits such as firearms, narcotics, etc., remain in the custody of the agents during the pendency of the trial. The agent will be required to sign the appropriate form in order to take custody of such exhibits. It shall be the responsibility of the agents to produce said items for court, secure them at night and guard them at all times while in the courtroom.

12. If counsel need to arrange for the installation of their own additional equipment, such as video monitors, overhead projectors, etc., notify the Court's Space and Facilities Department at 213-894-1400, no later than 4:30 p.m. two days BEFORE trial so that the necessary arrangements can be made.

13. Trials commence on Tuesday at 8:30 a.m., with jury selection beginning at 9:00 a.m., or as soon thereafter as possible. Trials are conducted Tuesday through Friday either from 9:00 a.m. to 5:00 p.m., with two fifteen (15) minute breaks normally at 10:00 a.m. and 3:00 p.m., and a lunch recess from 12:00 p.m. to 1:30 p.m; or, in the case of longer trials, from 8:30 a.m. to approximately 2:30 p.m. with two 20 minute breaks.

14. Before trial commences, the Court will give counsel an opportunity to discuss administrative matters and anticipated procedural or legal issues. During the trial, if there are any matters you wish to discuss, please inform my Courtroom Deputy. **The Court will rarely grant requests for sidebar while the jury is in session**.

15. The Court reserves the time immediately prior to the commencement of the trial day to handle legal and administrative matters outside of the presence of the jury. The trial before the jury will commence promptly at 9:00 a.m. Counsel is urged to anticipate matters which may need discussion or hearing outside of the presence of the jury and to raise them during this period, during breaks or at the end of the day.

JURY INSTRUCTIONS AND VERDICT FORMS

16. Jury instructions in the form described below are to be submitted not later than the Wednesday of the week prior to trial. Counsel need only submit proposed SUBSTANTIVE instructions, the Court will propound its own general instructions and will essentially follow the format set out in the *Manual of Model Criminal Jury Instructions for the Ninth Circuit* (West Publishing, latest edition). In those cases where a special verdict is desired, counsel shall submit a proposed verdict form with the jury instructions. Counsel shall submit an electronic disk containing the proposed joint and disputed instructions, and the proposed special verdict.

17. The parties must submit JOINT jury instructions and a JOINT proposed verdict form (if a special verdict is desired). In order to produce these joint instructions, the parties shall meet and confer sufficiently in advance of the required submission date with the goal of agreeing upon instructions and verdict forms. The jury instructions shall be submitted as follows: 1) JOINT jury instructions, those instructions which are agreed to by all parties; and 2) DISPUTED jury instructions,

those instructions propounded by a party to which another party objects. Objections to disputed instructions shall be filed no later than the Friday before the trial. Each requested jury instruction shall be numbered and set forth in full on a separate page, citing the authority or source of the requested instruction.

18. The Court prefers counsel to use the instructions from the *Manual of Model Criminal Jury Instructions for the Ninth Circuit*, West Publishing, latest edition. Another suggested source is Federal Jury Practice and Instructions, Devitt, Blackmar, Wolff and O'Malley, West Publishing Co., current edition.

19. An index page shall accompany all jury instructions that are submitted to the Court. The index page shall indicate the following:

a. The number of the instruction;
b. A brief title of the instruction;
c. The source of the instruction; and
d. The page number of the instruction.

EXAMPLE:

Number	Title	Source	Page Number
#1	Duty of the Jury	9th Cir. 1.01	1

INSTRUCTIONS GOVERNING PROCEDURE DURING TRIAL

20. Counsel are expected to cooperate with each other during trial to insure the efficient and expeditious use of the time of the Court and the jurors.

21. Counsel shall not refer to their clients or any witness over 14 years of age by their first names during trial.

22. Do not discuss the law or argue the case in opening statements.

23. When objecting, state only that you are objecting and the legal ground of the objection, *e.g.*, hearsay, irrelevant, etc. Do not argue an objection before the jury.

24. Questions should not be preceded by any editorial comment of any sort. Attorneys are not witnesses and should not behave as if they are. The Court will admonish counsel for any violation of this rule.

25. The Court disfavors argumentative questions and will sustain its own objection to any such questions.

26. In multi-defendant cases the Court encourages defense counsel to coordinate their cross-examination to avoid unnecessary duplication.

27. Do not approach the Courtroom Deputy or the witness box without the Court's permission. Please return to the lectern when your purpose has been accomplished. Do not enter the well of the Court without the Court's permission.

28. Please rise when addressing the Court. In jury cases, please rise when the jury enters or leaves the courtroom.

29. Address all remarks to the Court. Do not directly address the Courtroom Deputy, the reporter or opposing counsel. If you wish to speak with opposing counsel, ask permission to talk to counsel off the record. All requests for the rereading of questions or answers, or to have an exhibit placed in front of a witness, shall be addressed to the Court.

30. Do not make an offer of stipulation unless you have conferred with opposing counsel and reached an agreement. Any stipulation of fact will require the defendant's personal concurrence and shall be submitted to the Court in writing for approval. A proposed stipulation should be explained to him or her in advance. **The Court encourages the parties to stipulate to any facts that are not reasonably in dispute**.

31. While court is in session, do not leave the counsel table to confer with investigators, secretaries, or witnesses unless permission is granted in advance.

32. When a party has more than one lawyer, only one may conduct the examination of a given witness and only that same lawyer may handle objections during the testimony of that witness.

33. If a witness was on the stand at a recess or adjournment, have the witness back on the stand and ready to proceed when court resumes.

34. Do not run out of witnesses. If you are out of witnesses and there is more than a brief delay, the Court may deem that you have rested.

35. The Court attempts to cooperate with doctors and other professional witnesses and will, except in extraordinary circumstances, accommodate them by permitting them to be put on out of sequence. Anticipate any such possibility and discuss it with opposing counsel. If there is an objection, confer with the Court in advance.

36. Counsel are advised to be on time as the Court starts promptly.

37. Counsel may use exhibits in opening statement and demonstratives in opening statement, but only if adequate notice is given to opposing counsel and only if the Court concludes that the exhibit will be admitted into evidence and that the demonstrative either will be admitted or is based on admissible evidence and that the demonstrative is not unduly argumentative.

38. During closing argument, counsel should avoid the following:

a. Do not speak in the first person and offer opinions regarding the evidence. Argue only the evidence and inferences that may be drawn from the evidence. An expression of opinion regarding the state of the evidence is improper.

b. Do not discuss personal experiences and how those experiences may reveal anything about the evidence.

c. Counsel may not use contemporary news events or other cases to make a point during argument, but may illustrate points through the use of non-contemporary matters that have become well established in the broader culture.

d. Do not argue from the position of a juror (if I were a juror . . .) or appeal to the personal interests of members of the jury panel.

e. Do not use demonstrative materials without showing them to opposing counsel; insure that the information in the demonstrative materials finds support in the record or the Court will not permit its use.

DATED: ____________________

____
GARY ALLEN FEESS
United States District Judge

C. ***Order Regarding Rule 26(f) Conference and Joint Report***

IN THE UNITED STATES DISTICT COURT
FOR THE CENTRAL DISTRICT OF CALIFORNIA

Plaintiff(s),)	Case No. ______________
v.)	**ORDER REGARDING RULE 26(f) CONFERENCE AND JOINT REPORT**
Defendant(s).)	
______________________________)	Date: __________
	Time: **1:30 p.m.**

NOTICE TO COUNSEL: UNDER THE 2000 AMENDMENTS TO THE FEDERAL RULES OF CIVIL PROCEDURE, RULES 16(b), 26(a)(1), 26(a)(3), 26(a)(4), 26(d), AND 26(f) ARE NOW EFFECTIVE IN THIS DISTRICT. COUNSEL ARE EXPECTED TO BE FAMILIAR WITH THOSE RULES AND WITH THIS COURT'S ORDER REGARDING THE RULE 26(f) EARLY MEETING.

This action has been assigned to Judge Gary Allen Feess for all purposes.

The responsibility for the progress of litigation in the Federal Courts falls not only upon the attorneys in the action, but upon the Court as well. To secure the "just, speedy, and inexpensive determination of every action," Fed. R. Civ. P. 1, all counsel are hereby ordered to become familiar with the Federal Rules of Civil Procedure and the Local Rules of the Central District of California.

The Court further orders as follows:

1. **Rule 26(f) Meeting of Counsel and Commencement of Discovery.** The Court expects that counsel will participate in the meeting required by Rule 26(f) in a good faith manner, **with full disclosures and open (not grudging) exchanges of information as contemplated by Rules 26(a)**. It is advisable for counsel to begin discovery and conduct it actively at the earliest possible time because they will have limited time to complete discovery after this Court's Rule 26(f) Scheduling Conference.

2. **Joint Scheduling Conference Report.** Counsel shall jointly file a Joint Scheduling Conference Report (hereinafter "Joint Report") ***at least seven (7) calendar days before the date set for the Scheduling Conference***. It should be titled "Joint Scheduling Conference Report Pursuant to Rule 26(f)." A Joint Scheduling Conference Report which does not comply with this Order likely will result in a continuance of the Scheduling Conference and possible sanctions.

"Jointly" contemplates a single report, regardless of how many separately represented parties there are. The Joint Report **shall report shall include the following**:

a. a short synopsis (not to exceed two pages) of the main claims, counterclaims, and/or affirmative defenses.

b. a brief description of the key legal issues.

c. a list of percipient witness and key documents on the core issues of the case.

d. the realistic range of provable damages.

e. whether there is insurance coverage.

f. a statement of the likelihood of: motions seeking to add other parties or to file amended pleadings; motions to transfer venue.

g. a discussion of the present state of discovery, including a description of completed discovery and a schedule of all contemplated future discovery.

h. a detailed written discovery plan, as contemplated by Rule 26(f), including the identity of all anticipated depositions by each party, contemplated written discovery requests, including requests for admission, document requests, and written interrogatories, and a schedule for the completion of all items of discovery.

i. a proposed discovery cut-off date. THIS MEANS THE LAST DAY BY WHICH ALL DEPOSITIONS MUST BE COMPLETED AND RESPONSES TO ALL PREVIOUSLYSERVED WRITTEN DISCOVERY MUST BE PROVIDED ***AND ALL HEARINGS ON DISCOVERY MOTIONS CONCLUDED***.

j. a description of the issues or claims that any party believes may be determined by motion for summary judgment or motion *in limine*.

k. a schedule of contemplated law and motion matters and a proposed cut-off date for motions. THIS MEANS THE LAST DATE ON WHICH MOTIONS MAY BE HEARD, NOT NOTICED.

l. a statement of what settlement discussions and/or written communications have occurred (specifically excluding any statement of the terms discussed).

m. a realistic (not padded) estimate of the time required for trial and whether trial will be by jury or by court. Each side should specify (by number, not by name) how many witnesses it contemplates calling.

n. proposed dates (complete attached schedule on Exhibit A).

o. a statement of any other issues affecting the status or management of the case (*e.g.*, unusually complicated technical or technological issues, disputes over protective orders, discovery in foreign jurisdictions, *etc.*).

p. for conflict purposes, corporate parties must identify all subsidiaries, parents and affiliates.

The Joint Report should set forth the requested information under section headings corresponding to the above-enumerated topics.

3. Rule 26(f) Scheduling Conference. The Scheduling Conference will be held in Courtroom 740 of the Roybal Federal Courthouse at 255 East Temple Street. Counsel shall comply with the following:

a. Participation. The lead trial attorney must attend the Scheduling Conference. Unless excused for good cause shown in advance of the Conference, the Court reserves the right to designate the attorney attending the Conference as lead trial counsel. Counsel should be prepared to discuss not only the Joint Report but also what the case is really about at its core and whether there are ways to litigate it that will enhance the prospects for settlement (*e.g.*, limited trial on bifurcated issues). If the time estimate for trial given in the Joint Report exceeds ten court days, counsel shall be prepared to explain the trial estimate. In a realistic manner, they should disclose approximately how many witnesses and exhibits truly are necessary and whether there are unusual factors, such as non-English speaking witnesses, that are likely to extend the length of trial.

b. Continuance. A continuance of the Scheduling Conference will be granted only for good cause.

c. Use of Conference Telephone. If one or more of the lead counsel has his or her office outside of Los Angeles County, the Court is normally willing, at counsel's request, to conduct the status conference by conference telephone call. Please contact the court clerk at 213/894-3480 to get approval no later than the Wednesday before the Scheduling Conference. Opposing counsel who are outside of Los Angeles County may also participate by telephone The attorney requesting the telephonic status conference shall call 213/894-0779 at the time and date specified above for specific instructions. After the other participants are assembled, that attorney will be notified that he or she must promptly originate the conference call.

4. **Protective Orders.** If you seek a protective order, propose it to opposing counsel before the Scheduling Conference if at all possible. In a separate standing order, the Court has adopted precise requirements for protective orders and the treatment of confidential information. Please comply with that order, which is available on the Court's website (*www.cacd.uscourts.gov*), or upon request from the Courtroom Deputy Clerk.

5. **Settlement Procedures.** The Court will normally be guided by the parties' agreement as to what settlement procedure is appropriate and when the optimum time for that procedure is. If the parties cannot agree, they should so inform the Court in the Joint Report.

Not to the exclusion of other procedures, the following are available:

a. A settlement conference with this Court or the Magistrate Judge assigned to the case.

b. A settlement conference or other settlement procedure before an attorney appointed by the Court or retained by the parties or selected from the Attorney Settlement Panel.

c. Arbitration, mediation, mini-trial procedures or other alternative dispute resolutions, possibly in conjunction with a. or b. above.

d. A settlement conference before another District Judge or Magistrate Judge selected at random from the Court's Civil Settlement Panel.

6. **Pretrial of All Civil Actions.** Pursuant to Rule 16, Fed. R. Civ. P. and Local Rule 16, all civil actions or proceedings shall be pretried. The schedule for filing the required documents is set forth as part of Exhibit A attached hereto.

7. **Compliance With Local Rules and this Court's Standing Orders.** At all stages of the proceeding, the parties are expected to comply with the Local Rules of this District and this Court's Standing Orders. Before the Scheduling Conference, counsel shall review the Central District's Civility and Professionalism Guidelines, which shall be the standard of conduct to which they will be expected to adhere.

8. **Notice.** Plaintiff's counsel, or if plaintiff is appearing *pro se*, defendant's counsel, shall provide this Order to any parties who first appear after the date of this Order or who are known but have not yet entered appearances.

9. **Disclosures to Clients.** Counsel are ordered to deliver to their respective clients a copy of this Order and of the schedule that the Court imposes at the Scheduling Conference.

The Court thanks the parties and their counsel for their anticipated cooperation in carrying out these requirements.

IT IS SO ORDERED.

Dated: ________________

____

GARY ALLEN FEESS
United States District Judge

D. *Scheduling and Case Management Order*

IN THE UNITED STATES DISTICT COURT
FOR THE CENTRAL DISTRICT OF CALIFORNIA

Plaintiff(s),)	Case No. ______________
v.)	**SCHEDULING AND CASE MANAGEMENT ORDER**
Defendant(s).)	SEE LAST PAGE FOR PRETRIAL AND TRIAL DATES

The purpose of this Order is to enable the parties and their counsel to know well in advance the schedule to which they will be expected to adhere. SEE THE LAST PAGE OF THIS ORDER FOR THE SPECIFIED DATES. Ordinarily the dates set forth on the last page are determined after consultation with the parties at the Rule 26(f) Scheduling Conference, and this Order is distributed to them at that time. Accordingly, the dates and requirements are firm. The Court is very unlikely to grant continuances, even if stipulated by the parties, unless the parties establish good cause through a concrete showing. **Because this order, in some respects modifies the applicable Local Rule of Civil Procedure, counsel are advised to read it carefully to avoid default on the obligations established herein. Counsel are advised to pay particular attention to the requirements of the Court in respect to the filing of motions for summary judgment and documents to be submitted at the pre-trial conference and trial.**

I. DISCOVERY CUTOFF

All discovery shall be completed by the discovery cutoff on the last page. **THIS IS NOT THE DATE BY WHICH DISCOVERY REQUESTS MUST BE SERVED; IT IS THE DATE BY WHICH ALL DISCOVERY IS TO BE COMPLETED.**

Any motion challenging the adequacy of responses to discovery must be filed timely, served and calendared sufficiently in advance of the discovery cutoff date to permit the responses to be obtained before that date, if the motion is granted. The Court requires compliance with Local Rule 37-1 and 37-2 in the preparation and filing of discovery motions. Except in the case of an extreme emergency which was not created by the lawyer briefing the motion, discovery motions may not be heard on ex parte application.

In an effort to provide further guidance to the parties, the Court notes the following:

1. Depositions. All depositions shall be scheduled to commence sufficiently in advance of the discovery cutoff date to permit their completion and to permit the deposing party enough time to bring any discovery motions concerning the deposition prior to the cutoff date.

2. Written Discovery. All interrogatories, requests for production of documents, and requests for admissions shall be served sufficiently in advance of the discovery cutoff date to permit the discovering party enough time to challenge (via motion practice) responses deemed to be deficient.

3. Discovery Motions. Whenever possible, the Court expects the parties to resolve discovery problems among themselves in a courteous, reasonable and professional manner. If they do so, resort to the Court for guidance in discovery is seldom necessary. The Magistrate Judge assigned to this case will rule on discovery motions.

4. Expert Discovery. Expert discovery is to be concluded by the discovery cutoff date. Accordingly, the initial disclosure of expert witnesses in full compliance with the Federal Rules of Civil Procedure is ordered no later than seventy (70) days before the discovery cutoff. Counter-designations of rebuttal experts in full compliance with the Federal Rules of Civil procedure are to be made thirty (30) days after the other party's disclosure.

5. Rule 26(e)(1) Supplementation: The parties are under a continuing obligation to supplement their Rule 26(a) disclosures; the Court expects the parties to disclose such materials immediately upon identification.

II. MOTIONS AND MOTION CUTOFF DATE

A. GENERAL PROVISIONS

All law and motion matters, except for motions in limine, must be set for hearing (not filing) by the motion cutoff date specified on the last page.

The parties must adhere to the requirements of the Local Rules. See C. D. Cal. R. 7-1 et seq. If any party does not oppose a motion, that party shall submit a written statement in accordance with Local Rule 7-16 that it does not oppose the motion. The parties should note that failure to meet the time limits set forth in Local Rule 7 may be deemed consent to the granting of the motion. C. D. Cal. R. 7-12. The Court will not decide late-filed motions.

Motion should be filed:	28 days before hearing date
Opposition is due:	21 days before hearing date
Reply is due:	14 days before hearing date

To insure that the Court receives oppositions and replies in a timely fashion, chamber's copies ***conformed to reflect that they have been e-filed***, should be deposited in the drop box in the back entrance way to the chambers of Courtroom 740 in accordance with Local Rules.

Issues left undetermined after the passage of the motion cutoff date should be listed as issues for trial in the pre-trial conference order. As an exception to the above, motions in limine dealing with evidentiary matters may be heard pursuant to the schedule attached hereto; however, the Court will not hear or resolve summary judgment motions disguised as motions in limine. In addition, delay which interferes with preparation by the Court and its staff may cause imposition of sanctions under Local Rule 83-7.

Ex parte practice is strongly discouraged. See Mission Power Eng. Co. v. Continental Casualty Co., 883 F.Supp. 488 (C.D. Cal. 1995). The Court will require strict adherence to proper ex parte procedures for any ex parte application filed with the Court. Id. at 492; See C.D. Cal. R. 7-19

B. APPLICATIONS AND STIPULATIONS TO EXTEND TIME

Applications to extend the time to file any required document or to continue any pretrial or trial date must set forth:

(i) the existing due date or hearing date;

(ii) specific, concrete reasons supporting good cause for granting the extension. In this regard, a statement that an extension "will promote settlement" is insufficient. The requesting party or parties must indicate the status of ongoing negotiations: Have written proposals been exchanged? Is counsel in the process of reviewing a draft settlement agreement? Has a mediator been selected?

(iii) whether there have been prior requests for extensions, and whether these were granted or denied by the Court.

The parties requesting the extension must provide the Court with a proposed order setting forth the proposed new dates and/or proposed new schedule.

C. SUMMARY JUDGMENT MOTIONS

As caseloads increase, the Court is seeing a corresponding increase in the filing of motions for summary judgment. These motions frequently do not comply with the requirements of the Local Rules in one or more respects, and there are ambiguities in the Local Rules regarding the preparation of the Separate Statement of Undisputed Facts and related materials. As a result the Court is receiving documents in a wide variety of formats, some that are not in compliance and some that may technically comply with the literal language of the rule, but which are confusing, difficult to decipher and interfere with the Court's ability to address these motions in an efficient and expeditious manner. To increase the Court's efficiency, and to assist counsel in structuring and focusing these motions, the Court is issuing the following order regarding the filing motions for summary judgment in this Court. The Court will require strict adherence to these requirements.

1. Separate Statement Of Undisputed Facts and Statement of Genuine Issues

The Separate Statement of Undisputed Facts is to be prepared in a two column format. The left hand column should set forth the allegedly undisputed fact. The right hand column should set forth the evidence that supports the factual statement. The fact statements should be set forth in sequentially numbered paragraphs. Each paragraph should contain a narrowly focused statement of fact. The Court has observed cases where an allegedly undisputed fact was set forth in three pages of text. This is unacceptable. Each numbered paragraph should address a single subject in as concise a manner as possible.

The opposing party's statement of genuine issues must be in two columns and track the movant's separate statement exactly as prepared. The document must be in two columns; the left hand column must restate the allegedly undisputed fact, and the right hand column must indicate either undisputed, or disputed. The opposing party may dispute all or only a portion of the statement, but if disputing only a portion, must clearly indicate what part is being disputed. Where the opposing party is disputing the fact in whole or part, the opposing party must, in the right hand column, label and restate the moving party's evidence in support of the fact, followed by the opposing party's evidence controverting the fact. Where the opposing party is disputing the fact on the basis of an evidentiary objection, the party must cite to the evidence alleged to be objectionable and state the ground of the objection and nothing more. **No argument should be set forth in this document.**

The opposing party may submit additional material facts that bear on or relate to the issues raised by the movant, which shall follow the format described above for the moving party's separate statement. These additional facts shall follow the movant's facts, shall continue in sequentially numbered paragraphs (i.e., if movant's last statement of fact was set forth in paragraph 30, then the first new fact will be set forth in paragraph 31), and shall set forth in the right hand column the evidence that supports that statement.

The moving party, in its reply, shall respond to the additional facts in the same manner and format that the opposition party is required to adhere to in responding to the statement of undisputed facts, as described above.

2. Supporting Evidence

No party should submit any evidence other than the specific items of evidence or testimony necessary to support or controvert a proposed statement of undisputed fact. Thus, for example, the entire transcript of a deposition, entire sets of interrogatory responses, and documents that do not specifically support or controvert material in the separate statements, should not be submitted in support or opposition to a motion for summary judgment. Any such material will not be considered.

Evidence submitted in support or opposition to a motion should be submitted either by way of stipulation or as exhibits to declarations sufficient to authenticate the proffered evidence, and should not be attached to the Memorandum of Points and Authorities. The Court will accept counsel's authentication of deposition transcripts, of written discovery responses, and of the receipt of documents in discovery if the fact that the document was in the opponent's possession is of independent significance. Documentary evidence as to which there is no stipulation regarding foundation must be accompanied by the testimony, either by declaration or properly authenticated deposition transcript, of a witness who can establish its authenticity.

3. Objections to Evidence

If a party disputes a fact based in whole or in part on an evidentiary objection, the ground of the objection, as indicated above, should be stated in the separate statement but not argued in that document. Evidentiary objections are to be addressed in a separate memorandum to be filed with the opposition or reply brief of the party. This memorandum should be organized **to track the paragraph numbers of the separate statement in sequence**. It should identify the specific item of evidence to which objection is made, the ground of the objection, and a very brief argument with citation to authority as to why the objection is well taken. The following is an example of the format contemplated by the Court:

Separate Statement Paragraph 1: Objection to the supporting deposition transcript of Jane Smith at 60:1-10 on the grounds that the statement constitutes inadmissible hearsay and no exception is applicable. To the extent it is offered to prove her state of mind, it is irrelevant since her state of mind is not in issue. FED. R. EVID. 801, 802.

N.B: DO NOT SUBMIT BLANKET OR BOILERPLATE OBJECTIONS TO THE OPPONENT'S STATEMENTS OF UNDISPUTED FACT: THESE WILL BE DISREGARDED AND OVERRULED.

4. The Memorandum of Points and Authorities

The movant's memorandum of points and authorities should be in the usual form required under Local Rule 7 and should contain a narrative statement of facts as to those aspects of the case that are before the Court. All facts should be supported with citations to the paragraph number in the Separate Statement that supports the factual assertion and not to the underlying evidence.

Unless the case involves some unusual application of Rule 56, the motion need only contain a brief statement of the Rule 56 standard; the Court is familiar with the Rule and with its interpretation under Celotex and its progeny. If at all possible, the argument should be organized to focus on the pertinent elements of the cause(s) of action or defense(s) in issue, with the purpose of showing the existence or nonexistence of a genuine issue of material fact for trial on that element of the claim or defense.

Likewise, the opposition memorandum of points and authorities should be in the usual form required by Local Rule 7, and where the opposition memorandum sets forth facts, the memorandum should cite to paragraphs in the separate statement if they are not in dispute, to the evidence that contravenes the fact where the fact is in dispute, or, if the fact is contravened by an additional fact in the statement of genuine issues, the citation should be to such fact by paragraph number.

5. Timing

In virtually every case, the Court expects that the moving party will provide more than the minimum twenty-eight (28) day notice for such motions. The moving party should deliver to chambers a copy of a diskette, in WordPerfect format (9.0 or earlier versions), containing the Statement of Uncontroverted Facts and Conclusions of Law. [***NOTE: Parties need not wait until the motion cutoff to bring motions for summary judgment or partial summary judgment. Early completion of non-expert discovery and filing of motions for summary judgment may eliminate or reduce the need for expensive expert depositions which are normally conducted in the last stages of discovery.***]

D. ORAL ARGUMENT

If the Court concludes that a motion can be resolved without argument, the Court will notify the parties in advance.

E. MOTIONS IN LIMINE

The parties must file motions in limine addressing the admissibility of evidence in accordance with Local Rule 7-3 by the date specified on the last page. The parties shall file their opposing and reply papers in accordance with Local Rules 7-9 and 7-10 respectively.

III. PRE-TRIAL CONFERENCE AND LOCAL RULE 9 FILINGS

1. GENERAL PROVISIONS

The Pre-Trial Conference ("PTC") will be held at 3:30 P.M. on the date specified,unless the Court expressly waived a PTC at the Status Conference. (In the rare cases where the Court waives a PTC, the parties must follow Local Rule 16-11 – specifically 16-11.2.) If adjustments in the Court's calendar to accommodate congestion become necessary, the Court may re-calendar the PTC instead of the trial date. Therefore, the parties should assume that if the PTC goes forward, the trial will go forward without continuance, although some brief period of trailing may prove necessary.

The lead trial attorney on behalf of each party shall attend both the PTC and all meetings of the parties in preparation of the PTC, unless excused for good cause shown in advance of the PTC.

A continuance of the PTC at the parties' request or by stipulation is highly unlikely. Specifically, failure to complete discovery is not a ground for continuance. In the unlikely event that the Court agrees to continue the PTC, the trial date is likely to be delayed as a result. If a change in the trial date is necessitated or likely because of the Court's calendar or otherwise, modifications of that date will be discussed at the PTC.

At the PTC, the parties should be prepared to discuss means of streamlining the trial, including, but not limited to: bifurcation; presentation of foundational and noncritical testimony and direct testimony by deposition excerpts; narrative summaries and/or stipulations as to the content of testimony; presentation of testimony on direct examination by affidavit or by declaration subject to cross-examination; and qualification of experts by admitted resumes. The Court will also discuss settlement.

2. FORM OF PRE-TRIAL CONFERENCE ORDER ("PTCO")

The proposed PTCO shall be lodged fourteen (14) calendar days before the PTC. Adherence to this time requirement is necessary for in-chambers preparation of the matter. The form of the proposed PTCO shall comply with Appendix A to the Local Rules and the following:

1. Place in "ALL CAPS" and in bold the separately numbered headings for each category in the PTCO (e.g., "**1. THE PARTIES**" or "**7. CLAIMS AND DEFENSES OF THE** PARTIES.")
2. Include a Table of Contents at the beginning.
3. In specifying the surviving pleadings under Section 1, please state which claims or counterclaims have been dismissed or abandoned. *E.g.*, "Plaintiff's second cause of action for breach of fiduciary duty has been dismissed." Also, in multiple party cases where not all claims or counterclaims will be prosecuted against all remaining parties on the other side, please specify to which party each claim or counterclaim is directed.

4. In drafting Sections 5 and 6 of the PTCO, the Court expects that the parties will attempt to agree on and set forth as many non-contested facts as possible. The Court will usually read the uncontested facts to the jury at the start of the trial. A carefully drafted and comprehensively stated stipulation of facts will reduce the length of trial and increase jury understanding of the case.

5. *In specifying the parties' claims and defenses under Section 7, each party shall closely follow the examples set forth in Appendix A of the Local Rules.* As those examples demonstrate, the parties should attempt to state issues in terms of **the elements of the claims or defenses** (ultimate facts), not in the form of evidentiary fact issues, which outline the elements of the claims and defenses. The elements to most claims and defense can be found in the Ninth Circuit Model Jury Instructions, the California Book of Approved Jury Instructions (BAJI), and Devitt & Blackmar. Counsel are reminded that the purpose of this section is to focus and clarify the issues to be presented at trial. No argument is to be included in this section.

6. The Court may well submit fact issues to the jury in the form of findings on a special verdict. The issues of fact should track the elements of a claim or defense on which the jury will be required to make findings.

3. RULE 16 FILINGS; MEMORANDA; WITNESS LISTS; EXHIBIT LISTS

The parties must comply fully with the requirements of Local Rule 16. They shall file carefully prepared Memoranda of Contentions of Fact and Law (which may also serve as the trial brief), along with their respective Witness Lists and Exhibit Lists, all in accordance with Local Rules 16-3, 16-4, 16-5 and 16-6. See the last page for dates.

4. JURY INSTRUCTIONS, VERDICT FORMS, SPECIAL INTERROGATORIES

1. Fourteen (14) days before the Rule 16 meeting, the parties shall exchange proposed jury instructions, verdict forms and special interrogatories. Seven (7) days before the meeting, counsel shall exchange written objections, if any, to proposed jury instructions, verdicts and special interrogatories. At the Rule 16 meeting, the parties shall confer with the objective of submitting one set of agreed upon substantive instructions, verdict forms and, if necessary, special interrogatories. "Substantive jury instructions" means all instructions relating to the elements of all claims and defenses in the case. The Court would appreciate the parties delivering a chamber's copy of these filings in an electronic format compatible with WordPerfect at the time the documents are filed.

2. If the parties cannot agree upon one complete set of substantive instructions, verdict forms and/or special interrogatories, they shall file two documents with the Court: a joint document reflecting the agreed upon instructions, verdict forms, and a second document in the form of a joint statement regarding the disputed instructions, verdicts and interrogatories in the following format for each instruction, verdict or interrogatory in issue:

(a) A separate page containing the text of the disputed language with an identification of the party proposing it;

(b) Following the instruction, the opposing party's statement of objections to the instruction along with legal authority in support of the argument (not to exceed one page) and proposed alternative language where appropriate;

(c) The proposing party's response to the objection with legal authority supporting the proposed language, not to exceed one page.

Both the agreed upon set of instructions, and the joint statement re disputed instructions are to be filed with the Pre-Trial Conference Order and other Rule 16 documents fourteen (14) days before the Pre-Trial Conference.

3. All proposed jury instructions shall be in the format specified by Local Rule 51-2. The parties need not submit a separate copy of instructions without citations to authority.

4. A table of contents shall be included with all jury instructions submitted to the Court. The table of contents shall set forth the following:
(a) The number of the instruction;
(b) A brief title of the instruction;
(c) The source of the instruction; and
(d) The page number of the instruction.

For example:

Number	Title	Source	Page Number
1	Burden of Proof	9th Cir. 12.2	5

5. The Court directs counsel to use the instructions from the *Manual of Model Jury Instructions for the Ninth Circuit* (West 1997) where applicable. Where California law is to be applied and the above instructions are not applicable, the Court prefers counsel to use the CACI forms. If neither of these sources is applicable, counsel are directed to use the instructions in Devitt, Blackmar and Wolff, *Federal Jury Practice and Instructions.*

6. Modifications of instructions from the foregoing sources (or any other form instructions) must specifically state the modification made to the original form instruction and the authority supporting the modification.

5. JOINT STATEMENT OF THE CASE AND REQUESTS FOR VOIR DIRE

At the Pre-Trial Conference, the parties shall lodge their proposed voir dire questions and their joint statement of the case which the Court shall read to all prospective jurors prior to the commencement of voir dire. The statement should be not longer than two or three paragraphs.

The Court conducts voir dire of all prospective jurors. The parties need not submit requests for standard voir dire questions, such as education, current occupation, marital status, prior jury service, etc., but should include only proposed questions specifically tailored to the parties and issues of the case.

6. **FINDINGS OF FACT AND CONCLUSIONS OF LAW**

For a non-jury trial, the parties shall lodge their proposed findings of fact and conclusions of law in accordance with Local Rule 52-1 not later than one week before trial. The Court would appreciate the parties delivering to chambers a copy of these findings on disk in WordPerfect 9.0 format. Please see the Court's Civil Trial Order.

IV. SETTLEMENT

Local Rule 16-15.2 provides that the Settlement Conference shall be concluded not later than 45 days before the Pretrial Conference. **This Court requires a slightly different approach.** The Settlement Conference shall take place not later than three weeks before the Pre-Trial Conference, which is after discovery is closed and motions have been heard. The Court expects that completion of all discovery and dispositive motions will help the parties assess their positions before they complete the costly pretrial process under Local Rule 16. But sometimes parties find it more difficult to settle after they incurred the cost of all discovery and motion practice. The Court therefore strongly encourages counsel and the parties to pursue settlement earlier. In any event, as indicated in the Schedule of Pretrial Dates attached hereto, the parties must file a Status Report re Settlement at the time that they lodge the Proposed Pretrial Conference Order, indicating whether they have conducted the Local Rule 16 Settlement Conference and/or what additional steps are being taken to achieve settlement.

This Court will not conduct settlement conferences in non-jury cases which he is to try. In jury cases, the Court will conduct a settlement conference at the parties' joint request if three conditions exist:

1. The parties are satisfied that the fact issues in the case will be tried to a jury.
2. All significant pre-trial rulings which the Court must make have been made.
3. The parties desire the Court to conduct the conference, understanding that if settlement fails, the Court will preside over trial of the case.

   If the parties are inclined to select this Court to conduct a settlement conference, the parties should consult the Court's Standing Order re Settlement Conference so that they fully understand the Court's requirements for the settlement conference. That order will govern the settlement conference procedures before this Court, but may also serve as a useful reference for settlement conferences conducted pursuant to the other available procedures. Copies of that order and all other standard orders of this Court are available through the Courtroom Deputy Clerk or on the Central District of California website, at "www.cacd.uscourts.gov."

V. CONCLUSION

The Court thanks the parties and their counsel for their anticipated cooperation in carrying out these requirements.

IT IS SO ORDERED.

DATED: ______________

____
GARY ALLEN FEESS
United States District Judge

SCHEDULE OF TRIAL AND PRETRIAL DATES[1]

Matter	Time	Weeks before trial	Plaintiff(s) (Request)	Defendant(s) (Request)	Court Order
Trial (jury) (court) Estimated length: ____ days	8:30 am				
[Jury trial] Hearing on Motions in Limine; Hearing on Disputed Jury Instructions		-1			
[Court trial] File Findings of Fact and Conclusions of Law; Hearing on Motions in Limine		-1			
Pretrial Conference; Motions in Limine to be filed; Proposed Voir Dire Qs Lodged and Agreed-to Statement of Case	3:30 p.m.	-4			
Lodge Pretrial Conf. Order; File Memo of Contentions of Fact and Law; Exhibit & Witness Lists; File Status Report re Settlement; File Agreed Upon Set of Jury Instructions and Verdict Forms; File Joint Statement re Disputed Instructions, Verdicts, etc.		-6			
Last date to conduct Settlement Conference		-8			
Last day for hearing motions	9:30 a.m.	-9			
Discovery cut-off [Note: Expert disclosure no later than 70 days prior to this date.]		-10			
Last to Amend Pleadings or Add Parties					

[1] Review the Court's Order re "Rule 26(f) Scheduling Conference" to be sure of the meaning of these terms.

E. *Settlement Conference Order*

IN THE UNITED STATES DISTICT COURT
FOR THE CENTRAL DISTRICT OF CALIFORNIA

	)	Case No. ______________
Plaintiff(s),	)	
v.	)	**ORDER REGARDING**
Defendant(s).	)	**SETTLEMENT CONFERENCE**
______________________________	)	**BEFORE THIS COURT**

PLEASE READ THIS ORDER CAREFULLY

The Court has agreed to conduct the settlement conference in this matter. To facilitate the settlement conference, the Court hereby orders as follows:

1. **Settlement Conference Date.** [The parties should contact the Clerk of the Court to arrange a mutually agreeable date for the settlement conference to take place.] OR [The Court hereby schedules this case for a Scheduling Conference at __________________.]

2. **Confidentiality.** Pursuant to Local Rule 16-15.8, all settlement proceedings shall be confidential and no statement made therein shall be admissible in any proceeding in the case, unless the parties otherwise agree. No part of a settlement proceeding shall be reported or otherwise recorded without the consent of the parties.

3. **Consultation with Clients Before Settlement Conference.** In order to provide the parties with a starting point for their settlement discussions with the Court, plaintiff(s) shall advise defendant(s) of the terms upon which plaintiff(s) then is prepared to settle the case, in a letter delivered or faxed no later than seven (7) court days prior to the settlement conference. Within forty-eight (48) hours of receipt of plaintiff(s)'s settlement offer, defendant(s) shall respond to the same by letter delivered or faxed advising plaintiff(s) of the terms upon which they are prepared to settle the case.

5. **Settlement Conference Statements.**

(A) Statements That Are Exchanged.

No later than three (3) court days prior to the settlement conference, the parties shall deliver settlement conference statements in compliance with Local Rule 16-15.8 directly to the Court's chambers and shall fax or personally deliver the statement to opposing counsel. The statement shall include (1) a brief statement of the facts of the case, including claims and defenses remaining to be tried and the party's position on each issue; (2) an itemized statement of the damages claimed in non-conclusionary form; and (3) a summary of the history of past settlement discussions and offers and demands, including the most recent settlement offers exchanged pursuant to this Order. The statements shall also disclose the parties' positions about non-monetary terms that they may seek (or oppose), including (but not necessarily limited to): the form and scope of releases – *e.g.*, general and/or specific; waiver of California Civil Code § 1542; releases of and/or covenants not to sue third parties who either are not participants in the settlement conference or may not even be parties in the lawsuit, but whose interests could affect the negotiating parties' ability to settle; indemnifications against claims of other parties; whether there should be a confidentiality provision (strongly disfavored by the Court); whether there should be recitals of non-admission of fault or liability; whether each settling party is to pay his, her of its own costs and attorneys' fees; and any other provision which is likely to be the subject of negotiation. The statement shall be brief and to the point and shall not exceed 10 pages, double-spaced. Unless absolutely essential to inform the Court of key considerations, please do not attach exhibits or transcript excepts; the purpose of the statement is to enable the Court to become familiar with the issues, not to try the case.

(B) Confidential Statement

Each party shall also prepare a Confidential Addendum to the Settlement Conference Statement, which shall also be delivered to chambers but *shall not be served upon the other parties.* The Confidential Addendum shall contain a forthright evaluation of the party's likelihood of prevailing on its claims and/or defenses; the party's evaluation of the terms on which the case could *fairly* be settled; the approximate amount of fees and costs expended to date; an estimate of the fees and costs to be expended for future discovery, pretrial and trial; and any additional information the party wishes to impart to the judge confidentially.

(C) Exceptions

Sometimes the foregoing requirements maybe unnecessary – *e.g.*, if there is only one relatively narrow or discrete issue that divides the parties, after they have reached agreement on all, or virtually all, other material terms. In such case, the parties' settlement conference statements and addenda should focus on the "sticking point" issue and provide the Court the background or context necessary to help break the impasse.

Failure to timely deliver a Settlement Conference Statement and Confidential Addendum will likely result in sanctions being imposed.

6. **Persons to be Present at Settlement Conference.** All persons whose consent is necessary to conclude settlement shall be present personally. This means the individual with the authority to say "yes," not just "no." As an exception, out-of-district parties, or agents empowered to settle may be available by telephone, provided they are absolutely committed to remaining available at the telephone (regardless of the hour) until released by the Court and further provided that a written request for their participation by telephone is submitted to and approved by the Court in advance of the conference.

Counsel appearing without their clients and/or the person or persons whose presence is required to achieve settlement (such as insurance representatives) will cause the settlement conference to be canceled and rescheduled, *regardless of whether counsel purportedly has been given settlement authority.* (This will not result if the Court granted prior authorization for the client to participate telephonically.) The noncomplying party, attorney, or both, may be assessed the costs and expenses incurred by other parties as a result of such cancellation and rescheduling.

If a settlement proposal must be presented to a board or committee, the attendance of at least one sitting and knowledgeable member of the Board (preferably the Chairperson) is *absolutely required*, unless the entity commits absolutely to the discretionary authority of another representative.

In lawsuits involving the United States or any of its agencies, the Assistant United States Attorney in charge of the case must appear with the full measure of settlement authority provided by his or her superiors within the United States Attorney's Office.

In cases involving insurance, a representative with *unrestricted* settlement authority must appear on behalf of the insurance company or, if out of the district, must be available by telephone.

7. **Conduct of Settlement Conference.** The Court may, in its discretion, converse with the lawyers, the parties, the insurance representatives, or any one of them outside of the hearing of the others. The comments of the Court during such separate sessions are not to be used by counsel in settlement negotiations with opposing counsel. This is a necessary requirement in order to avoid intentional or unintentional misquotation of the Court's comments. Violation of this policy may mislead the adverse party and therefore hinder settlement.

At the commencement of the settlement conference, each party through counsel may be required to make an oral presentation (not to exceed 10 minutes) of the relevant facts *and* law, in the presence of all parties and counsel.

If settlement between any or all parties is reached as a result of the Settlement Conference, the Court will enter the settlement terms on the record at the end of the conference and the parties will be expected to assent to those terms, at which point the settlement will be final and binding.

All papers submitted for the Settlement Conference will either be returned to the parties or destroyed by the Court after the settlement proceedings are concluded, unless the parties otherwise agree.

The Court thanks the parties and their counsel for their anticipated cooperation in carrying out these requirements.

IT IS SO ORDERED.

DATED: ________________

____
GARY ALLEN FEESS
United States District Judge

Hon. Dale S. Fischer

District Judge

Chambers Information

U.S. District Court, Central District of California
Courtroom 840
255 East Temple Street
Los Angeles, CA 90012

Scheduling Information

Courtroom Deputy: (213) 894-0435

Civil Law and Motion	Mondays at 1:30 p.m.
Criminal Law and Motion	Mondays at 8:30 a.m.

Biographical Information

Born 1951 in Orange, NJ

Federal Judicial Service:

-Judge, U. S. District Court, Central District of California
-Nominated by George W. Bush on May 1, 2003, to a new seat created by 116 Stat. 1758; Confirmed by the Senate on October 27, 2003, and received commission on November 5, 2003.

Education:

-University of South Florida, B.A., 1977
-Harvard Law School, J.D., 1980

Professional Career:

-Private Practice, California, 1980-1997
-Judge, Los Angeles Judicial District, Municipal Court of California, 1997-2000
-Judge, County of Los Angeles, Superior Court of California, 2000-2003

I. Judge Fischer's Procedures and Practices

A. *Order Regarding Format of Time and Expense Records*

ORDER REGARDING FORMAT OF TIME AND EXPENSE RECORDS

In addition to any other requirements imposed by statute, case law, and rules of professional conduct, counsel who will be seeking an award of fees from this Court must maintain their records in a manner calculated to permit the Court to evaluate the lodestar amount and the reasonable expenses and costs efficiently and effectively, and must comply with the following:

1. All services rendered must be listed chronologically in a single document (presumably prepared monthly, but no less often than quarterly) so that the Court can readily determine what services were rendered by all timekeepers on each day. Counsel are not to submit separate billings by timekeeper or by firm.

2. The records shall state, for each entry: the name or initials of the timekeeper, the hourly rate sought for the timekeeper, a description of the services performed, the amount of time billed, and the dollar amount charged for that entry (i.e., the time spent multiplied by the hourly rate). These dollar amounts may not be "rounded up." While the Court will not mandate use of the litigation codes from the Uniform Task-Based Management System (UTBMS) if counsel do not already use that system, the Court will require that counsel provide, at the time a fee request is made, a summary of the total fees attributable to categories such as those described in the UTBMS.

3. The services rendered must be described in sufficient detail for the Court to determine the nature and reasonableness of the services. Generic or general activity descriptions are inappropriate. Entries such as "research and preparation of motion to dismiss," "conference with client," and other non-specific descriptions will generally not be considered adequate, especially if the amount of time billed is significant. (Time records ultimately filed publicly with a motion for fees may be redacted to preserve confidentiality. The Court will require an *in camera* unredacted submission.)

4. Time records must be maintained on a contemporaneous basis. Timekeepers should not attempt to reconstruct their time days after the services were rendered.

5. The minimum time increment will not be greater than one-tenth of an hour. See Welch v. Metropolitan Life Ins. Co., 480 F.3d 942, 949 (9th Cir. 2007).

6. "Block-billing," i.e., a line item with a single time charge for multiple activities is inappropriate. See id. at 948.

7. Time charged for intra or inter-office conferences, correspondence, e-mails, etc. should be kept to a minimum.

8. If more than one timekeeper charges for attending hearings, depositions, etc., the Court will ultimately require an explanation of why the second appearance was appropriate. (If counsel believe nonchargeable attendance by others is desirable in order for young lawyers or para-professionals to gain training or experience, and such time is normally recorded by the firm, the billing records should indicate

that the time is not being charged.)

9. Expenses and costs must be listed by reasonably narrow and specific category, preferably the applicable categories described in the UTBMS. Only expenses and costs normally billed to a client and otherwise permitted by statute or case law will be awarded. Only actual costs, without markup, will be permitted. Counsel should not seek reimbursement for items generally regarded as overhead. If a law firm maintains a flat-rate contract with an electronic legal database (e.g., Westlaw or Lexis), reimbursement is ordinarily inappropriate, unless the database was reasonably utilized for activity outside of the firm's flat-rate contract.

10. Reimbursement should not be sought for first class airfare, or meals and accommodations in amounts higher than a reasonable client would permit. Counsel shall exercise good judgment in selecting reasonably-priced transportation, accommodations, and meals.

If there is a contested motion for attorneys' fees in the future, the Court will issue a further order establishing the required format for such motion.

IT IS SO ORDERED.

Dated: ____________________

____
DALE S. FISCHER
United States District Judge

B. Procedures and Schedules

1. Civil motions are heard on **Mondays** at **1:30 p.m.**

   Criminal motions are heard on **Mondays** at **8:30 a.m.**

   (If Monday is a holiday, the next motion date is the following Monday.)

   It is not necessary to clear a motion date with the Courtroom Deputy Clerk ("CRD") before filing the motion.

   Motions will be heard two weeks after the deadline for filing the Reply. Therefore, Motion papers must be filed and served not later than 28 days before the hearing date. Opposition papers must be filed and served not later than 21 days before the hearing date. Reply papers must be filed and served not later than 14 days before the hearing date.

2. All discovery motions and stipulations, including those relating to protective orders, are to be calendared before the magistrate judge whose initials appear in parentheses after the case number.

   Documents may not be filed under seal in matters pending before the district judge based on a protective order signed by the magistrate judge. A separate and additional showing of good cause as to each category of document or information is required. Fed. R. Civ. P. 26(c); *Phillips ex rel. Estates of Byrd v. General Motors Corp., 307 F.3d 1206, 1212 (9th Cir. 2002).*

   The parties must also comply with Local Rule 79-5.

3. Tentative rulings are not issued.

4. All papers filed with the Court must conform to Local Rule 11-3.1.1, which generally requires typeface of 14 point or larger for Times New Roman and 12 point or larger for Courier.

5. Conformed mandatory chambers copies of all moving, opposition, and reply papers shall be hand-delivered to chambers and placed in the tray outside the door to chambers.

6. Ex parte applications are solely for extraordinary relief and are rarely granted. *See Mission Power Engineering Co. v. Continental Casualty Co., 883 F. Supp. 488 (C.D. Cal. 1995).* Applications must be efiled pursuant to the Local Rules. All ex parte applications shall be sent in pdf version to the chambers email at dsf_chambers@cacd.uscourts.gov (dsf_chambers@cacd.uscourts.gov) along with a word or word perfect version of the order. A mandatory chambers copy of moving, opposition, or notice of non-opposition papers must be delivered to the tray outside the door to chambers. Both the email to the Court, and the application, should advise whether opposing counsel will be filing opposition. Applications that fail to conform to Local Rule 7-19 and 7-19.1, including a statement of opposing counsel's position, will not be considered. In addition to the requirements of Local Rules 7-19 and 7-19.1, the moving party shall serve the opposing party by email, facsimile transmission, or personal service and shall notify the opposition that opposing papers must be filed no later than twenty-four hours (or one court day) following such service. The Court considers ex parte applications on the papers and usually does not set these matters for hearing. The CRD will notify counsel of a hearing date and time, if the Court determines a hearing

is necessary. Rulings on ex partes will be efiled by the Court. Sanctions may be imposed for misuse of ex parte applications.

7. Continuanccs are granted only on a showing of good cause. Requests for continuances must be by motion, stipulation, or application accompanied by a declaration setting forth the reasons for the requested continuance. The declaration should also include whether there have been any previous requests for continuances and whether these requests were granted or denied by the Court. Stipulations extending dates set by this Court are not effective unless approved by the Court. Requests for continuance should be submitted well in advance of the date to be continued. Continuances will not always be granted.

8. Counsel should not contact the judge's law clerks or secretary/judicial assistant unless responding to an inquiry they initiated.

9. Calls will not be returned regarding the status of submitted motions, stipulations, or proposed orders. Sufficient copies of any proposed order should be provided for conforming, along with a self-addressed, stamped envelope. Counsel may also determine the status of any submitted motion, stipulation, or proposed order by accessing the docket sheet through www.cacd.uscourts.gov > General Information > Pacer Access.

10. If counsel has a conflicting appearance in the court of a more senior district judge, counsel must email the CRD indicating the time of the appearance, the case name, and the name of the other judge. On the day of the appearance, if possible, request the other judge's CRD to update Judge Fischer's CRD as to when counsel will be appearing in Judge Fischer's courtroom.

    If counsel will be late, or cannot make a court appearance for any other reason, good cause must be shown. The Court must approve all continuances and special requests. Counsel must make such requests in pleading form by submitting a stipulation and a proposed order to the filing window (Clerk's Office, Room G-19). Refer to Local Rule 52.9 for the proper format.

    If a stipulation cannot be reached, counsel must submit an ex parte application and proposed order following the requirements of paragraph 6.

11. Counsel shall contact the CRD by telephone to request leave to bring electronic equipment into the courtroom. Counsel will be advised by the CRD that such a request shall be made by a letter addressed to the U.S. Marshal's Office, carbon copied to the Court Coordinator and prepared for the CRD's signature, along with the case name and case number. Counsel may fax the letter to the CRD for signature. On arrival at the courthouse, counsel shall present the letter to Court Security for approval.

12. For general information on how to order a transcript of any reported or digitally recorded proceeding, please contact 213-894-3015 or visit www.cacd.uscourts.gov > General Information > Court Reporter/Recorder Transcripts. If you require an estimate of cost for the preparation of a transcript, contact the court reporter/recorder for the desired proceeding.

    To determine the court reporter/recorder for a particular proceeding, go to the Court Reporter Schedule web page and click on View by Date. Once you've determined the correct court reporter/recorder for the desired session, click on Court Reporter

Phone and Email List for contact information.

13. Call 213-894-7115 if you have questions regarding law clerk or extern positions.

14. It is the responsibility of counsel in a civil case to arrange for the services of an interpreter. Interpreter's Office: 213-894-4599.

15. Pursuant to Local Rule 16-14, the parties in every case must elect a settlement procedure.

16. For Judge Fischer's case management, scheduling, and trial procedures, see the Orders below.

17. If counsel have received a "Notice to Parties of ADR Program" (form ADR-8, ADR-10 or ADR-11 with an attached "ADR Program Questionnaire" form ADR-9), please see the section on the Clerk's website entitled "ADR" > General Order 07-01, for further information. The ADR section also contains information regarding Attorney Settlement Officers.

18. All requests from the media should be directed to Theresa Doty at 213-894-3651 or 213-894-8248. The CRD will not return calls from the media or answer questions from the media. The media are directed to check the Court's electronic record at www.cacd.uscourts.gov > General Information > Pacer Access for current information.

19. If counsel has received a "Notice to Parties of Court-Directed ADR Program" (form ADR-08), the Court will presumptively refer the case to the Court Mediation Panel or to private mediation at the time of the initial scheduling conference. See General Order 11-10, § 5.1. Counsel are directed to furnish and discuss this Notice with their clients in preparation for the parties' Fed.R.Civ.P. 26(f) conference. Counsel should include their shared or separate views regarding a preference for the Court Mediation Panel or private mediation, and when the mediation should occur, in the written report required by Fed.R.Civ.P. 26(f) and Civil L.R. 26-1. A settlement conference with a magistrate judge is generally not available for cases in the Court-Directed ADR Program. See Civil L.R. 26-1(c). For information about the Court's ADR Program, please see General Order 11-10 which is located in the "General Orders" section on the home page and in the "ADR" page of the Court's website.

II. Judge Fischer's Case Management Orders

A. *Criminal Motion, Trial, and Sentencing Order*

IN THE UNITED STATES DISTICT COURT
FOR THE CENTRAL DISTRICT OF CALIFORNIA

UNITED STATES OF AMERICA, Plaintiff, v. Defendant(s).	)	Case No. __________ DSF **CRIMINAL MOTION, TRIAL, AND SENTENCING ORDER**

This matter has been assigned to the Honorable Dale S. Fischer, United States District Judge, Courtroom 840, Roybal Federal Building, 255 E. Temple St., Los Angeles, California, 90012.

A. GENERAL REQUIREMENTS

1. The captioned title of every pleading shall contain the name of the first-listed defendant as well as the name(s) and number(s) (in the order listed in the indictment) of the particular defendant(s) to whom the pleading applies, unless the document applies to all defendants. The individual defendant's registration number (if known) should be provided on any document pertaining to defendant's custody status (e.g., requests for transfer, medical requests). All parties shall docket items only as to the particular defendant(s) the item pertains to, not as to all defendants, unless the item pertains to all. With the exception of documents filed under seal, every pleading shall be electronically filed in such a way that it is clear from the docketing entry to which defendants it applies. The outer envelope containing any pleading filed under seal should identify only the case title with first-listed defendant and case number, and should state that the document is filed under seal.

2. Mandatory paper Chambers copies of all e-filed documents must be delivered to Judge Fischer's box across from the Clerk's office on the first floor of the Roybal Federal Building - by noon on the day after filing. Documents will not be considered until paper Chambers copies are submitted. Attach the NEF to the BACK of the Chambers copy. Chambers copies delivered by Federal Express should not require the signature of the recipient. The Court will not rule on stipulations, ex parte applications, etc. until the mandatory paper Chambers copies have been received.

B. EX PARTE APPLICATIONS AND MOTIONS

1. Ex parte applications are disfavored. The Court is unlikely to grant an ex parte application that recites that the moving party has been unable to obtain the position of the opposing party. Counsel should make serious efforts to obtain the agreement (or at least the position) of opposing counsel before filing an application.

2. Ex parte applications to allow defendant to travel should be made well in advance of the date of travel. Counsel should indicate whether the pretrial services officer has approved the travel. Applications by defendants with appointed counsel must indicate who will pay for the travel and related expenses. If these expenses are not to be paid by the defendant's employer, the Court may require declarations under

penalty of perjury from the persons paying the expenses.

3. Pretrial motions shall be filed on or before the Monday preceding four weeks before trial. Counsel must meet and confer with opposing counsel and attempt to resolve the issue before filing a motion. Motions expected to take more than one-half hour of court time must include a time estimate beneath the hearing date on the face page of the motion.

   Oppositions (or notices of non-opposition) shall be filed no more than one week after the filing of the motion.

   Replies (optional) shall be filed no more than one week after the filing of the opposition.

   Adherence to these timing requirements is essential to Chambers' preparation of motion matters. Counsel must follow the Central District's General Orders and Local Rules concerning electronic filing, unless superseded by this Order.

4. Memoranda of Points and Authorities in support of or in opposition to motions shall not exceed 25 pages. Replies shall not exceed 12 pages. Only in rare instances and for good cause shown will the Court grant an application to extend these page limitations. No supplemental brief shall be filed without prior leave of court. **Typeface shall comply with Local Rule 11-3.1.1. (Civil). NOTE: If Times Roman font is used, the size must be no less than 14; if Courier is used, the size must be no less than 12.** Footnotes shall be in typeface no less than one size smaller than text size and shall be used sparingly.

5. Filings that do not conform to the Local Rules and this Order may not be considered.

6. Before filing any motion for discovery, a party shall consult with opposing counsel to ascertain whether the requested discovery will be provided. All discovery motions shall state with particularity what is requested, the basis for the request, whether the discovery has been requested from opposing counsel, and whether the discovery has been declined, in whole or in part. Motions made without prior consultation with opposing counsel or that fail to include the above information may not be heard.

C. DISCOVERY & NOTICE

Counsel shall comply promptly with discovery and notice pursuant to Rules 12, 12.1, 12.2, 12.3, 12.4, 15, and 16 of the Federal Rules of Criminal Procedure. On government counsel's discovery of any evidence within the scope of Brady v. Maryland, 373 U.S. 83 (1963), and related cases, such evidence shall be produced forthwith to counsel for the defendant. Counsel for the government shall also disclose to counsel for defendant the existence or non-existence of: (1) evidence obtained by electronic surveillance; and (2) testimony by a government informant.

D. TRIAL REQUIREMENTS

1. **No later than one week before trial**, counsel for the government shall file with the Court:

   a. In camera (under seal) all statements of all witnesses to be called by the Government in its case-in-chief;

   b. A trial memorandum setting forth a factual summary of the government's case, a statement of the charges and the elements of each charge, an estimate of the length of the government's case in chief, including anticipated cross-examination, the names of witnesses the government intends to call, and a discussion of relevant legal and evidentiary issues as applied to the facts of the particular case. Counsel for the government shall attempt to obtain defense counsel's agreement to the factual summary, statement of the charges, time estimate for cross-examination of the government's witnesses, and legal and evidentiary issues.

2. Counsel shall arrive at the Courtroom no later than 8:30 a.m. on the first day of trial.

3. Counsel for the government shall present the courtroom deputy clerk (CRD) with the following:

a. The government's witness list, which shall be sent in Word or WordPerfect format to the Chambers email box no later than noon on the Monday before trial;

b. The government's exhibit list in the form specified in Local Rule 16-5 (Civil), which shall be sent in Word or WordPerfect format to the Chambers email box no later than noon on the Monday before trial;

c. All of the government's exhibits, with official exhibit tags attached and bearing the same number shown on the exhibit list. Exhibit tags may be obtained from the receptionist in the Public Intake Section, located on the Main Street level of the courthouse at 312 North Spring Street, Room G-19. Exhibits shall be numbered 1, 2, 3, etc., NOT 1.1, 1.2, etc. If a "blow-up" is an enlargement of an existing exhibit, it shall be designated with the number of the original exhibit followed by an "A." These items (and the items listed in d and e below) shall be provided on the first day of trial;

d. A three-ring binder containing a copy of the indictment/information, a copy of all exhibits that can be reproduced, and a copy of the witness list. Each exhibit shall be tabbed with the exhibit number for easy reference;

e. A three-ring binder containing a copy of all exhibits for use by witnesses.

4. Exhibits such as firearms, narcotics, etc., must remain in the custody of a law enforcement agent during the pendency of the trial. It shall be the responsibility of the agent to produce any such items for court, secure them at night and guard them at all times while in the courtroom. The United States Marshals Service shall be advised if weapons or contraband is to be brought into the courthouse.

5. The Court prefers that defense counsel email witness and exhibit lists to the Chambers email box by noon on the Monday before trial and provide defense exhibits to the CRD on the first day of trial, but counsel are not required to do so unless these witness names and exhibits have previously been provided to the government. Defense counsel are responsible for attaching completed exhibit tags with the case name and case number to all exhibits to be used in defendant's case. Defense counsel should be sure that defense exhibit numbers do not duplicate government exhibit numbers.

6. In trials where the defense expects to admit more than 20 exhibits, defense counsel shall provide two three-ring binders (one for the Court and one for witnesses), tabbed if possible with numbers to correspond to the exhibits counsel expects to introduce. Defense counsel shall provide the Court with a copy of defense exhibits as they are introduced during trial, if they have not previously been provided.

7. Defense counsel shall email to the Chambers email box and provide the CRD and the court reporter with the defense witness list and defense exhibit list at the start of the defense case, if they have not previously done so.

8. At least one week before trial, the parties must provide a case-specific glossary for the court reporter that includes applicable medical, scientific, or technical terms, gang terms, slang, the names and spellings of case names likely to be cited, street/city/country names, all parties/agents/departments/entities involved in the case, names of people interviewed/deposed, names of family members, friends, or others who might be mentioned, and other case-specific terminology.

9. A copy of the exhibit list with all **admitted exhibits** will be given to the jury during deliberations. Government and defense counsel shall review and approve the exhibit list with the CRD before the list is given to the jury.

10. Counsel should consider such devices as overhead projectors, jury notebooks for admitted exhibits, or enlargements of important exhibits. The Court has an Elmo and other equipment available for use during trial. Information concerning training on the use of electronic equipment is available. Details are posted on the Court's website. To make reservations for training, call 213-894-3061. The Court does not permit exhibits to be "published" by passing them up and down the jury box. Exhibits may be displayed briefly using the screens in the courtroom, unless the process becomes too time-consuming.

11. Counsel shall not attempt to display or use any charts or enlargements of exhibits unless all counsel have agreed to their use or objections have been heard and a ruling has been made.

12. On the day of jury selection, trial will begin at 9:00 a.m. Counsel will appear at 8:30 a.m. Thereafter, trial days are Tuesday through Friday, 8:00 a.m. To 2:00 p.m., with three fifteen-minute breaks during the session. When necessary, trials may continue beyond the normal schedule. If counsel contemplate that this schedule will be problematic due to the unavailability of witnesses, counsel should provide details to the Court at the Status Conference.

13. On the day of jury selection, the Court reserves the time from 8:30 a.m. to 9:00 a.m. to handle legal and administrative matters. Jury selection will commence promptly at 9:00 a.m. or as soon as jurors are available. Thereafter, legal and administrative matters shall be addressed between 7:45 a.m. And 8:00 a.m. All counsel are urged to anticipate matters that may need to be addressed outside of the presence of the jury and to raise them during this period, during breaks, or at the end of the day. The Court does not make jurors wait while counsel discuss matters that should have been addressed previously. Counsel are urged to consider any unusual substantive or evidentiary issues that may arise, and to advise the Court of such issues. Short briefs addressing such disputed issues are welcome.

14. Before trial begins, the Court will give counsel an opportunity to discuss administrative matters and anticipated procedural or legal issues. Before trial begins, and as soon as the information becomes available to counsel, counsel should advise the court of any concerns or accommodations that are requested for parties or witnesses. During trial, if there are any matters to be discussed

outside the presence of the jury, counsel shall advise the CRD of the request. The Court discourages sidebars during trial.

E. JURY INSTRUCTIONS, VERDICT FORMS & QUESTIONNAIRES

1. **No later than the Monday one week before trial**, counsel shall submit both general and substantive jury instructions in the form described below. If possible, all instructions should be taken from the *Manual of Model Criminal Jury Instructions for the Ninth Circuit* (West Publishing, current edition). Where no applicable Ninth Circuit model instruction is available, counsel should consult the instructions manuals from other circuits or O'Malley, Grenig & Lee (formerly Devitt, et al.), *Federal Jury Practice and Instructions* (West Publishing Co., current edition). When submitting other than Ninth Circuit instructions, counsel should be sure that the law on which the instruction is based is the same as Ninth Circuit law on the subject. Counsel may submit alternatives to the Ninth Circuit model jury instructions, other circuit manuals, or O'Malley, Grenig & Lee instructions only if counsel has a reasoned argument that those instructions do not properly state the law or they are incomplete.
2. The parties must submit JOINT jury instructions and a JOINT proposed verdict form. In order to produce these joint instructions, the parties shall meet and confer sufficiently in advance of the required submission date with the goal of agreeing on instructions and verdict forms. Where the parties cannot agree, disputed instructions shall be filed and submitted (electronically to the Chambers email box and in paper form) on the Monday one week before trial as follows: 1) JOINT jury instructions (those instructions agreed to by all parties), and 2) DISPUTED jury instructions (those instructions propounded by a party to which another party objects). On a separate page following each disputed jury instruction, the party opposing the instruction shall briefly state the basis for the objection, any authority in support thereof and, if applicable, an alternative instruction. On the following page, the party proposing the disputed instruction shall briefly state its response to the objection, and any authority in support of the instruction. Each requested jury instruction shall be numbered and set forth in full on a separate page, citing the authority or source of the requested instruction.
3. Jury instructions should be modified as necessary to fit the facts of the case (e.g., inserting names of defendant(s) or witness(es) to whom instruction applies). Where language appears in brackets in the model instruction, counsel shall select the appropriate text and eliminate the inapplicable bracketed text.
4. An index page shall accompany all jury instructions submitted to the Court. The index page shall indicate the following:
   a. The number of the instruction;
   b. A brief title of the instruction;
   c. The source of the instruction; and
   d. The page number of the instruction.

EXAMPLE:

Number	Title	Source	Page Number
#1	Conspiracy-Elements	9th Cir. 8.20	1

5. One or more copies of the instructions will be given to the jury during

deliberations. Counsel must submit to the Chambers email box a "clean" set of all instructions in Word or WordPerfect format, containing only the text of each instruction, set forth in full on each page, with the caption "Instruction No. ____" (eliminating titles, supporting authority, indication of party proposing, etc.). A paper Chambers copy must also be submitted.

6. Counsel shall submit a proposed verdict form with the jury instructions.
7. At least one week before trial, each counsel must file any proposed questions to be asked of prospective jurors.

F. INSTRUCTIONS GOVERNING PROCEDURE DURING TRIAL

1. Counsel shall not refer to any witness -- including a client – more than 14 years of age by his/her first name during trial.
2. Counsel shall not discuss the law or argue the case in opening statements.
3. Counsel shall not use objections for the purpose of making a speech, repeating testimony, or attempting to guide the witness. When objecting, counsel shall stand, state only the legal ground of the objection, e.g., hearsay, irrelevant, etc. Counsel shall not argue an objection before the jury. Requests to approach sidebar to further argue an objection should be made sparingly, and may not be granted.
4. Counsel shall not make facial expressions, nod, or shake their heads, comment, or otherwise exhibit in any way any agreement, disagreement, or other opinion or belief concerning the testimony of a witness. Counsel shall admonish their clients and witnesses not to engage in such conduct.
5. Counsel should not talk to jurors at all, and should not talk to co-counsel, opposing counsel, witnesses, or clients where the conversation can be overheard by jurors. Each counsel should admonish counsel's own clients and witnesses to avoid such conduct.
6. Counsel shall question witnesses from the lectern. Counsel shall not approach the witness box or enter the well without the Court's permission, and shall return to the lectern when counsel's purpose has been accomplished.
7. Counsel should speak clearly when questioning witnesses, making objections, etc.
8. No document shall be placed before a witness or shown to the jury unless a copy has been provided to the Court and opposing counsel.
9. Counsel shall rise when addressing the Court. In jury trials, counsel and the defendant shall rise when the jury enters or leaves the courtroom. Special procedures or exceptions may apply when the defendant is restrained or otherwise unable to rise.
10. In trial, all remarks shall be addressed to the Court. Counsel shall not directly address the CRD, the court reporter, or opposing counsel. All requests for re-reading of questions or answers, or to have an exhibit placed in front of a witness, shall be addressed to the Court
11. Counsel should not offer a stipulation without having conferred with opposing counsel and having reached an agreement. Any stipulation of fact will require defendant's personal concurrence and shall be submitted to the Court in writing for approval. A proposed stipulation should be explained to defendant in advance.

12. While court is in session, counsel shall not leave counsel table to confer with investigators, paralegals, secretaries, witnesses, etc. unless permission is granted in advance.
13. When a party has more than one lawyer, only one lawyer may conduct the examination of a given witness, and only that same lawyer may handle objections during the testimony of that witness.
14. If a witness was on the stand at a recess or adjournment, counsel who called the witness shall ensure the witness is back on the stand and ready to proceed when trial resumes.
15. Counsel are directed to have witnesses available throughout the court day. If no witnesses are available and there is more than a brief delay, the Court may deem counsel to have rested.
16. The Court attempts to cooperate with expert witnesses and other professionals, and will, except in extraordinary circumstances, accommodate them by permitting them to be called out of sequence. Counsel are urged to anticipate any such possibility and to discuss it with opposing counsel. If there is an objection, counsel shall confer with the Court in advance.
17. Counsel must notify the CRD in advance if any witness should be accommodated based on the Americans with Disabilities Act or for other reasons.
18. Counsel are ordered to be on time, as the Court makes every effort to start promptly.

G. SENTENCING

1. Sentencing positions should be filed in accordance with the Court's order. Requests for continuance are discouraged, as the order provides for sufficient time for counsel to prepare their position papers. That the parties have stipulated to a continuance will not ensure that it will be granted.
2. The Court discourages the use of sentencing videos. If counsel believes a video is necessary, it should not be longer than 10 minutes. Videos will not be considered unless a transcript is provided.
3. Sentencing is a matter of significant public interest and concern. Generally, the public has a right to know the basis on which the Court makes sentencing determinations. Therefore, the Court discourages under seal filings of entire sentencing documents. Sentencing documents may be filed under seal along with a redacted version that deletes *only* information that is properly filed under seal, and an explanation of the basis for each document or portion deleted, *e.g.*, medical information, private information relating to family members (which explanation may be filed under seal). If all or nearly all of the sentencing position contains such information, counsel may seek leave to file the entire document under seal.

IT IS SO ORDERED.

Dated: ______________

DALE S. FISCHER
United States District Judge

B. Order Regarding Court Trial

IN THE UNITED STATES DISTICT COURT
FOR THE CENTRAL DISTRICT OF CALIFORNIA

Plaintiff(s), v. Defendant(s).	Case No. ______________ **ORDER RE COURT TRIAL** **I. ORDER RE DEADLINES:** A. Adding Parties or Amending Pleadings: ________ B. Discovery Cut-off: ___________ C. Expert Witness Exchange Deadline: Initial _______; Rebuttal ______; Cut-off _______ D. Motion Hearing Cut-off:__________ E. Settlement Conference Cut-off:______ F. Final Pretrial Conference: __ at 3:00 p.m. G. Trial Date: __________ at 8:00 a.m. **II. ORDER RE TRIAL PREPARATION** **III. ORDER GOVERNING CONDUCT OF ATTORNEYS AND PARTIES**

I.
DEADLINES

A. PARTIES/PLEADINGS

The Court has established a cut-off date for adding parties or amending pleadings. All motions to add parties or to amend the pleadings must be noticed to be heard on or before the cut-off date. All unserved parties will be dismissed at the time of the pretrial conference pursuant to Local Rule 16-8.1.

B. DISCOVERY AND DISCOVERY CUT-OFF

1. Discovery Cut-off: The Court has established a cut-off date for discovery, including expert discovery, if applicable. This is not the date by which discovery requests must be served; it is the date by which all discovery, including all hearings on any related motions, is to be completed.

2. Discovery Disputes: Counsel are expected to comply with all Local Rules and the Federal Rules of Civil Procedure concerning discovery. Whenever possible, the Court expects counsel to resolve discovery problems among themselves in a courteous, reasonable, and professional manner. The Court expects that counsel will adhere strictly to the Civility and Professionalism Guidelines (which can be found on the Court's website under "Attorney Information> Attorney Admissions").

3. Discovery Motions: Any motion challenging the adequacy of discovery responses must be filed, served, and calendared sufficiently in advance of the discovery cut-off date to permit the responses to be obtained before that date, if the motion is granted.

4. Depositions: All depositions shall commence sufficiently in advance of the discovery cut-off date to permit their completion and to permit the deposing party enough

time to bring any discovery motions concerning the deposition before the cut-off date. Given the requirements to "meet and confer," and notice requirements, in most cases a planned motion to compel must be discussed with opposing counsel at least six weeks before the cut-off.

5. Written Discovery: All interrogatories, requests for production of documents, and requests for admissions must be served sufficiently in advance of the discovery cut-off date to permit the discovering party enough time to challenge (via motion practice) responses deemed to be deficient.

6. Expert Discovery: All disclosures must be made in writing. The parties should begin expert discovery shortly after the initial designation of experts. The final pretrial conference and trial dates will not be continued merely because expert discovery is not completed. Failure to comply with these or any other orders concerning expert discovery may result in the expert being excluded as a witness.

C. LAW AND MOTION

The Court has established a cut-off date for the hearing of motions. All motions must be noticed so that the hearing takes place on or before the motion cut-off date. Counsel are to provide chambers with conformed courtesy copies of all documents. Courtesy copies should not be put in envelopes. Counsel should consult the Court's Standing Order, previously provided, to determine the Court's requirements concerning motions. A copy of the Standing Order is also available on the Court's website at www.cacd.uscourts.gov>Judges' Procedures and Schedules>Hon. Dale S. Fischer.

D. FINAL PRETRIAL CONFERENCE

1. A final pretrial conference date has been set pursuant to Rule 16 of the Federal Rules of Civil Procedure and Local Rule 16-8. Unless excused for good cause, each party appearing in this action shall be represented at the final pretrial conference by the attorney who is to have charge of the conduct of the trial on behalf of such party. Counsel should be prepared to discuss streamlining the trial, including presentation of testimony by deposition excerpts or summaries, time limits, stipulations as to undisputed facts, and qualification of experts by admitted resumés. The Court encourages, but does not require, counsel to agree to submit direct testimony of witnesses by way of declaration or written statement confirmed under oath by the witness. *See* Local Rule 16-11.2(b).

E. SETTLEMENT PROCEDURES

A settlement procedure must be identified in every case pursuant to Local Rule 16-15, *et seq*. The Court will normally be guided by counsel's agreement as to what procedure is appropriate for the case and when the optimum time for that procedure is. Counsel must, however, complete a settlement conference no later than the date set by the Court at the scheduling conference. Not to the exclusion of other procedures, the following are available:

(1) a settlement conference before the magistrate judge assigned to the case;

(2) a settlement conference or mediation before an attorney selected from the Attorney Settlement Panel;

(3) the employment (at the parties' expense) of a private judge, mediator, or arbitrator.

If a case is selected for the Mandatory ADR Program, the parties may choose option (3) instead, but may not choose option (1). Judge Fischer will hold a settlement conference at the request of the parties in cases with a trial estimate of more than four days.

No case will proceed to trial unless all parties, including the principals of all corporate parties, have appeared personally at a settlement conference.

II.
ADDITIONAL TRIAL PREPARATION

A. MOTIONS *IN LIMINE*

All motions *in limine* must be filed at least three weeks before the final pretrial conference. Counsel are to meet and confer with opposing counsel to determine whether opposing counsel intends to introduce the disputed evidence, and to attempt to reach an agreement that would obviate the motion. Opposition must be filed ten days before the final pretrial conference. The Court will rule on motions in limine at the final pretrial conference. Motions *in limine* should address specific issues (*i.e.*, *not* "to exclude all hearsay," *etc.*). Motions *in limine* should not be disguised motions for summary adjudication of issues.

B. PROPOSED FINDINGS OF FACT AND CONCLUSIONS OF LAW

1. For any matter requiring findings of fact and conclusions of law, counsel for each party shall, no later than 21 days before trial, file with the Court and serve on opposing counsel that party's proposed findings of fact and conclusions of law in the format specified in Local Rule 52-3.

2. Seven days before the trial date, each counsel shall file with the Court and serve on opposing counsel a copy of the opposing party's proposed findings of fact and conclusions of law, marked as follows:

(a) Strike through those portions the party disputes;

(b) Bold those portions the party admits; and

(c) Underline those portions the party admits but considers irrelevant.

The parties may agree to and advise the Court of some other method of differentiating among these three categories, such as color coding.

3. Counsel need not make a uniform determination as to an entire proposed finding or conclusion. Counsel may agree with a portion, dispute another portion, and consider a portion irrelevant. Counsel are urged, however, to have only a single fact or conclusion of law contained in each paragraph.

4. The parties may submit supplemental proposed findings of fact and conclusions of law during the course of the trial. If more than five supplemental findings are proposed, the same designating procedure should be used.

6. Each party must submit its own unmarked proposed findings of fact and conclusions of law to the Chambers e-mail box in Word or WordPerfect format.

C. TRIAL EXHIBITS

1. Counsel are to prepare their exhibits for presentation at the trial by placing them in binders indexed by exhibit number with tabs or dividers on the right side. Counsel shall submit to the Court an original and one copy of the binders. The exhibits shall be in three-ring binders labeled on the spine portion of the binder as to the volume number and contain an index of each exhibit included in the volume. Exhibits must be numbered in accordance with Local Rule 16.6.

2. The Court requires that the following be submitted to the Courtroom Deputy Clerk ("CRD") on the first day of trial:

(a) The original exhibits with the Court's exhibit tags, yellow tags for plaintiff and blue tags for defendant, shall be stapled to the front of the exhibit on the upper right-hand corner with the case number, case name, and exhibit number placed on each tag.

(b) One bench book with a copy of each exhibit tabbed with numbers as described above for use by the Court. (Exhibit tags are not necessary on this copy.)

(c) Three copies of exhibit lists.

(d) Three copies of witness lists in the order in which the witnesses may be called to testify.

3. All counsel are to meet not later than ten days before trial and to stipulate, so far as is possible, to foundation, to waiver of the best evidence rule, and to those exhibits that may be received into evidence at the start of the trial. The exhibits to be so received will be noted on the extra copies of the exhibit lists.

D. TRIAL

Trial days are Tuesday through Friday from 8:00 a.m. to 1:45 p.m. With three fifteen-minute breaks. If the Court is engaged in a jury trial, this court trial may be conducted during the afternoons if the parties prefer that approach to a continuance.

III.
CONDUCT OF ATTORNEYS AND PARTIES

A. OPENING STATEMENTS, EXAMINING WITNESSES AND SUMMATION

1. Counsel must use the lectern for opening statements, examination of witnesses, and summation.

2. Counsel must not consume time by writing out words, drawing charts or diagrams, *etc.* Counsel may do so in advance.

3. The Court will honor (and may establish) reasonable time estimates for opening statements and closing arguments, examination of witnesses, *etc.*

B. OBJECTIONS TO QUESTIONS

1. Counsel must not use objections for the purpose of making a speech, recapitulating testimony, or attempting to guide the witness.

2. When objecting, counsel must rise to state the objection and state only that counsel objects and the legal ground of objection. If counsel wishes to argue an objection further, counsel must ask for permission to do so.

C. GENERAL DECORUM

1. Counsel should not approach the CRD or the witness box without specific permission. If permission is given, counsel should return to the lectern when their purpose has been accomplished. Counsel should not question a witness at the witness stand.

2. Counsel should rise when addressing the Court, and when the Court enters or leaves the courtroom.

3. Counsel should address all remarks to the Court. Counsel are not to address the CRD, the court reporter, persons in the audience, or opposing counsel. If counsel wish to speak with opposing counsel, counsel must ask permission to do so. Any request for the re-reading of questions or answers shall be addressed to the Court. Such requests should be limited. Repeated requests may not be granted.

4. Counsel should not address or refer to witnesses or parties by first names alone. Young witnesses (under 14) may, however, be addressed and referred to by first names.

5. Counsel must not offer a stipulation unless counsel has conferred with opposing counsel and has verified that the stipulation will be acceptable.

6. While Court is in session, counsel must not leave counsel table to confer with

any personnel or witnesses in the back of the courtroom unless permission has been granted in advance.

7. Counsel should not by facial expression, nodding, or other conduct exhibit any opinion, adverse or favorable, concerning any testimony being given by a witness. Counsel should admonish counsel's own clients and witnesses to avoid such conduct.

8. Where a party has more than one lawyer, only one may conduct the direct or cross-examination of a particular witness, or make objections as to that witness.

D. PROMPTNESS OF COUNSEL AND WITNESSES

1. The Court makes every effort to begin proceedings at the time set. Promptness is expected from counsel and witnesses. Once counsel are engaged in trial, this trial is counsel's first priority. The Court will not delay the trial except under extraordinary circumstances. The Court will advise other courts that counsel are engaged in trial in this Court on request.

2. If a witness was on the stand at a recess, counsel must have the witness back on the stand, ready to proceed, when the court session resumes.

3. If a witness was on the stand at adjournment, counsel must have the witness adjacent to, but not on the stand, ready to proceed when the court session resumes.

4. Counsel must notify the CRD in advance if any witness should be accommodated based on a disability or for other reasons.

5. No presenting party may be without witnesses. If counsel has no more witnesses to call and there is more than a brief delay, the Court may deem that party to have rested.

6. The Court attempts to cooperate with professional witnesses and will, except in extraordinary circumstances, accommodate them by permitting them to be called out of sequence. Counsel must anticipate any such possibility and discuss it with opposing counsel. If there is an objection, counsel must confer with the Court in advance.

E. EXHIBITS

1. Each counsel should keep counsel's own list of exhibits and should note when each has been admitted into evidence.

2. Each counsel is responsible for any exhibits that counsel secures from the CRD and must return them before leaving the courtroom at the end of the session.

3. An exhibit not previously marked should, at the time of its first mention, be accompanied by a request that the CRD mark it for identification. To save time, counsel must show a new exhibit to opposing counsel before it is mentioned in Court.

4. Whenever in counsel's opinion a particular exhibit is admissible, it should be moved into evidence, unless tactical or other considerations dictate otherwise.

5. Counsel are to advise the CRD of any agreements they have with respect to the proposed exhibits and as to those exhibits that may be received so that no further motion to admit need be made.

6. When referring to an exhibit, counsel should refer to its exhibit number whenever possible. Witnesses should be asked to do the same.

7. Counsel must not ask witnesses to draw charts or diagrams nor ask the Court's permission for a witness to do so. If counsel wishes to question a witness in connection with graphic aids, the material must be fully prepared before the court session starts.

F. DEPOSITIONS

1. All depositions to be used at trial, either as evidence or for impeachment, must be with the CRD on the first day of trial or such earlier date as the Court may order. Counsel should verify with the CRD that the relevant deposition is in the CRD's possession.

2. In using depositions of an adverse party for impeachment, either one of the following procedures may be adopted:

> **(a)** If counsel wishes to read the questions and answers as alleged impeachment and ask the witness no further questions on that subject, counsel shall first state the page and line where the reading begins and the page and line where the reading ends, and allow time for any objection. Counsel may then read the portions of the deposition into the record.
>
> **(b)** If counsel wishes to ask the witness further questions on the subject matter, the deposition is placed in front of the witness and the witness is told to read silently the pages and lines involved. Then counsel may either ask the witness further questions on the matter and thereafter read the quotations, or read the quotations and thereafter ask further questions. Counsel should have an extra copy of the deposition for this purpose.

3. Where a witness is absent and the witness's testimony is offered by deposition, counsel may (a) have a reader occupy the witness chair and read the testimony of the witness while the examining lawyer asks the questions, or (b) have counsel read both the questions and answers.

G. USING NUMEROUS ANSWERS TO INTERROGATORIES AND REQUESTS FOR ADMISSIONS

Whenever counsel expects to offer a group of answers to interrogatories or requests for admissions extracted from one or more lengthy documents, counsel should prepare a new document listing each question and answer, and identifying the document from which it has been extracted. Copies of this new document should be given to the Court and opposing counsel. This procedure is intended to save time.

H. ADVANCE NOTICE OF UNUSUAL OR DIFFICULT ISSUES

If any counsel has reason to anticipate that a difficult question of law or evidence will necessitate legal argument requiring research or briefing, counsel must give the Court advance notice. Counsel are directed to notify the CRD at the day's adjournment if an unexpected legal issue arises that could not have been foreseen and addressed by a motion *in limine*. *See* Fed. R. Evid. 103.

***N.B.* "COUNSEL," AS USED IN THIS ORDER, INCLUDES PARTIES APPEARING *IN PROPRIA PERSONA*.**

IT IS SO ORDERED.

DATED: ________________

____
DALE S. FISCHER
United States District Judge

C. Order Regarding Jury Trial

IN THE UNITED STATES DISTICT COURT
FOR THE CENTRAL DISTRICT OF CALIFORNIA

Plaintiff(s),	Case No. ____________
v.	**ORDER RE JURY TRIAL**
Defendant(s).	**I. E-FILING REQUIREMENTS** **II. DEADLINES:** A. Adding Parties or Amending Pleadings: ________; B. Discovery Cut-off: _________; C. Expert Witness Exchange Deadline: Initial __; Rebuttal ___; Cut-off _____; D. Motion Hearing Cut-off:_________; E. Settlement Conference Cut-off:_____; F. Final Pretrial Conference: _______; G. Trial Date: @ 8:30 a.m. (day estimate) **II. TRIAL PREPARATION** **III. CONDUCT OF ATTORNEYS AND PARTIES**

I.
E-FILING REQUIREMENTS

Mandatory paper Chambers copies of all e-filed documents must be delivered to Judge Fischer's box across from the Clerk's office on the first floor of the Roybal Federal Building - by noon on the day after filing. Documents will not be considered until paper Chambers copies are submitted. Attach the NEF to the BACK of the Chambers copy. Chambers copies delivered by Federal Express should not require the signature of the recipient. The Court will not rule on stipulations, ex parte applications, etc. until the mandatory paper Chambers copies have been received.

II.
DEADLINES

A. PARTIES/PLEADINGS

The Court has established a cut-off date for adding parties or amending pleadings. All motions to add parties or to amend the pleadings must be noticed to be heard on or before the cut-off date. All unserved parties will be dismissed at the time of the pretrial conference pursuant to Local Rule 16-8.1

B. DISCOVERY AND DISCOVERY CUT-OFF

1. Discovery Cut-off: The Court has established a cut-off date for discovery, including expert discovery, if applicable. This is not the date by which discovery requests must be served; it is the date by which all discovery, including all hearings on any related motions, is to be completed.

2. Discovery Disputes: Counsel are expected to comply with all Local Rules and the Federal Rules of Civil Procedure concerning discovery. Whenever possible, the Court expects counsel to resolve discovery problems among themselves in a

courteous, reasonable, and professional manner. The Court expects that counsel will adhere strictly to the Civility and Professionalism Guidelines, which can be found on the Court's website under "Attorney Information> Attorney Admissions."

3. Discovery Motions: Any motion challenging the adequacy of discovery responses must be filed, served, and calendared sufficiently in advance of the discovery cut-off date to permit the responses to be obtained before that date, if the motion is granted.

4. Depositions: All depositions must commence sufficiently in advance of the discovery cut-off date to permit their completion and to permit the deposing party enough time to bring any discovery motions concerning the deposition before the cut-off date. Given the requirements to "meet and confer," and notice requirements, in most cases a planned motion to compel must be discussed with opposing counsel at least six weeks before the cut-off.

5. Written Discovery: All interrogatories, requests for production of documents, and requests for admissions must be served sufficiently in advance of the discovery cut-off date to permit the discovering party enough time to challenge (via motion practice) responses deemed to be deficient.

6. Expert Discovery: All disclosures must be made in writing. The parties should begin expert discovery shortly after the initial designation of experts. The final pretrial conference and trial dates will not be continued merely because expert discovery is not completed. Failure to comply with these or any other orders concerning expert discovery may result in the expert being excluded as a witness.

C. LAW AND MOTION

The Court has established a cut-off date for the hearing of motions. All motions must be noticed so that the hearing takes place on or before the motion cut-off date. Counsel must provide Chambers with conformed Chambers copies of all documents. Chambers copies should not be put in envelopes. Counsel should consult the Court's Standing Order, previously provided, to determine the Court's requirements concerning motions. A copy of the Standing Order is also available on the Court's website at www.cacd.uscourts.gov>Judges' Procedures and Schedules>Hon. Dale S. Fischer.

D. FINAL PRETRIAL CONFERENCE

1. A final pretrial conference date has been set pursuant to Rule 16 of the Federal Rules of Civil Procedure and Local Rule 16-8. Unless excused for good cause, each party appearing in this action shall be represented at the final pretrial conference by the attorney who is to have charge of the conduct of the trial on behalf of such party. Counsel should be prepared to discuss streamlining the trial, including presentation of testimony by deposition excerpts or summaries, time limits, stipulations as to undisputed facts, and admission of exhibits.

2. STRICT COMPLIANCE WITH LOCAL RULE 16 IS REQUIRED. THIS ORDER SETS FORTH SOME DIFFERENT AND SOME ADDITIONAL REQUIREMENTS. THIS COURT DOES NOT EXEMPT *PRO PER* PARTIES FROM THE REQUIREMENTS OF RULE 16. Carefully prepared memoranda of contentions of fact and law, witness lists, a joint exhibit list, and a

proposed final pretrial conference order shall be submitted in accordance with the Rules, and the format of the proposed final pretrial conference order shall conform to the format set forth in Appendix A to the Local Rules. Failure of these documents to comply with these requirements may result in the final pretrial conference being taken off-calendar or continued, or in other sanctions.

3. The memoranda of contentions of fact and law, witness lists, and the joint exhibit list must be filed not later than 21 days before the final pretrial conference, and the proposed final pretrial conference order is to be lodged not later than 11 days before the final pretrial conference.

4. In addition to the requirements of Local Rule 16, the witness lists must include a brief (one or two paragraph) description of the testimony, and a time estimate for both direct and cross-examination (separately stated). A separate version of the witness list containing only the names of the witness and a separate column to insert the dates on which the witness testified, and the joint exhibit list, must be submitted to the Chambers email box in Word or Word Perfect format. Mandatory paper Chambers copies must also be submitted.

5. Other documents to be filed in preparation for, and issues to be addressed at, the final pretrial conference are discussed below.

E. SETTLEMENT PROCEDURES/NOTICE OF SETTLEMENT

1. A settlement procedure must be identified in every case pursuant to Local Rule 16-15, et seq. Counsel must complete a settlement conference no later than the date set by the Court at the scheduling conference. Not to the exclusion of other procedures, the following are available:

   (a) a settlement conference before the magistrate judge assigned to the case;

   (b) a settlement conference or mediation before an attorney selected from the Attorney Settlement Panel;

   (c) the employment (at the parties' expense) of a private judge, mediator, or arbitrator. If a case is selected for the Mandatory ADR Program, the parties may choose option (3) instead, but may not choose option (1).

2. No case will proceed to trial unless all parties, including the principals of all corporate parties, have appeared personally at a settlement conference.

3. If settlement is reached, it must be reported immediately to the CRD as required by Local Rule 16-15.7, regardless of the day or time settlement is reached. In addition, counsel must immediately send a notification to the Chambers email box if a motion or other hearing is set or if trial is scheduled to occur within 30 days.

4. In all cases set for jury trial, the parties must notify the Court no later than the Wednesday preceding the Tuesday trial date of any settlement so that the necessary arrangements can be made to schedule a different case for trial or notify the members of the public who would otherwise be reporting for jury duty that their services are not needed on that date.

5. Failure to comply with these notification requirements will cause counsel/parties to be charged for the costs related to processing jurors and may result in the

imposition of sanctions on counsel for one or more parties, their clients, or both.

III.
ADDITIONAL TRIAL PREPARATION

A. MOTIONS *IN LIMINE*

All motions *in limine* must be filed at least three weeks before the final pretrial conference, or at such other time ordered by the Court. Counsel are to meet and confer with opposing counsel to determine whether opposing counsel intends to introduce the disputed evidence, etc. and to attempt to reach an agreement that would obviate the motion. Opposition must be filed two weeks before the final pretrial conference, or at such other time ordered by the Court. The Court generally will rule on motions *in limine* at the final pretrial conference. Motions *in limine* should address specific issues (i.e., not "to exclude all hearsay," etc.). Motions *in limine* should not be disguised motions for summary adjudication of issues.

B. JURY INSTRUCTIONS, SPECIAL VERDICT FORMS, VOIR DIRE, JURY SELECTION

1. Fourteen days before the meeting of counsel required by Local Rule 16-2, plaintiff shall serve plaintiff's proposed jury instructions and verdict/special verdict forms, and defendant shall serve defendant's proposed jury instructions and verdict/special verdict forms. Within ten days each shall serve objections, if any, to the other's instructions and verdict forms. Before or at the Rule 16-2 meeting, counsel are ordered to meet and confer and attempt to come to agreement on the proposed jury instructions and verdict forms.

2. When the Manual of Model Jury Instructions for the Ninth Circuit provides an applicable jury instruction, the parties should submit the most recent version, modified and supplemented to fit the circumstances of this case. Where language appears in brackets, the appropriate language should be selected. All blanks should be completed. Where California law applies, counsel should use the current edition of California Jury Instructions -- Civil ("BAJI" or "CACI"). If neither is applicable, counsel should consult the instructions manuals from other circuits or O'Malley, Grenig & Lee (formerly Devitt, et al.), Federal Jury Practice and Instructions (West Publishing Co., current edition). When submitting other than Ninth Circuit instructions, counsel should be sure that the law on which the instruction is based is the same as Ninth Circuit law (or California law, if applicable) on the subject. Counsel may submit alternatives to the Ninth Circuit model jury instructions, other circuit manuals, or O'Malley, Grenig & Lee instructions only if counsel has a reasoned argument that those instructions do not properly state the law or they are incomplete. Each requested instruction shall (a) cite the authority or source of the instruction, (b) be set forth in full, (c) be on a separate page, (d) be numbered, (e) cover only one subject or principle of law, and (f) not repeat principles of law contained in any other requested instruction.

3. At the time of lodging the proposed final pretrial conference order, counsel shall file with the Court and submit (electronically to the Chambers email box and in paper form) a JOINT set of jury instructions on which there is agreement. All blanks in standard forms should be filled in. The Court expects counsel to agree on the substantial majority of jury instructions, particularly when pattern or model instructions provide a statement of applicable law. If one party fails to comply with the provisions of this section, the other party must file a unilateral set of jury instructions, unless that party wishes to waive jury trial.

4. At the same time, each party shall file with the Court and submit (electronically to the Chambers email box and in paper form) its proposed jury instructions that are objected to by any other party. Each disputed instruction must have attached a short (one or two paragraph) statement, including points and authorities in support of the instruction as well as a brief statement, including points and authorities, in support of any objections. A proposed alternative instruction must be provided, if applicable. If the Court believes that there are so many disputed instructions that the trial would be unnecessarily interrupted in order for the Court to resolve disputes, the Court may determine that the matter is not yet ready to be tried, and may order counsel to continue to meet and confer until most of the disputes are resolved.

5. Counsel must provide the documents described in paragraphs 3 and 4 to the Chambers email box in Word or WordPerfect 9 (or above) format at the time they file their proposed jury instructions.

6. The Court will send one or more copies of the instructions into the jury room for the jury's use during deliberations. Therefore, in addition to the copies described above, the Chambers email version must contain a "clean" set of jury instructions, containing only the text of the instruction (one per page) with the caption "Instruction No. __" at the top (eliminating titles, supporting authority, etc.).

7. Counsel must provide an index of all instructions submitted, which must include the following:
   - **a.** The number of the instruction;
   - **b.** The title of the instruction;
   - **c.** the source of the instruction and any relevant case citations;
   - **d.** The page number of the instruction.

   For example:

Number	Title	Source	Page
1	Preliminary Instruction Trademark	9th Cir. 15.0	7

8. **FAILURE TO FOLLOW THE PRECEDING PROVISIONS OF THIS SECTION WILL SUBJECT THE NON-COMPLYING PARTY AND/OR ATTORNEY TO SANCTIONS AND WILL BE DEEMED TO CONSTITUTE A WAIVER OF JURY TRIAL.**

9. During the trial and before argument, the Court will meet with counsel and settle the instructions, and counsel will have an opportunity to make a further record concerning their objections.

10. At the time of lodging the proposed final pretrial conference order, counsel should file a jointly prepared one or two page statement of the case to be read by the Court to the prospective panel of jurors before commencement of voir dire.

11. The Court will conduct the voir dire. The Court provides a list of basic questions, and may provide a list of additional questions to jurors before voir dire. (This is not a questionnaire to be completed by jurors.) Counsel may, but are not required to, file and submit (electronically to the Chambers email box and in paper form) a

list of proposed case-specific voir dire questions at the time they lodge the proposed final pretrial conference order.

12. In most cases the Court will conduct its initial voir dire of 14 prospective jurors who will be seated in the jury box. Generally the Court will select seven or eight jurors.

13. Each side will have three peremptory challenges. If fourteen jurors are seated in the box and all six peremptory challenges are exercised, the remaining eight jurors will constitute the jury panel. If fewer than six peremptory challenges are exercised, the eight jurors in the lowest numbered seats will be the jury. The Court will not necessarily accept a stipulation to a challenge for cause. If one or more challenges for cause are accepted, and all six peremptory challenges are exercised, the Court may decide to proceed with six or seven jurors.

C. TRIAL EXHIBITS, ETC.

1. At least one week before trial, the parties must provide a case-specific glossary for the court reporter that includes applicable medical, scientific, or technical terms, slang, the names and spellings of case names likely to be cited, street/city/country names, all parties/entities involved in the case, names of people interviewed/deposed, names of family members, friends, or others who might be mentioned, and other case-specific terminology.

2. Counsel shall provide the courtroom deputy clerk (CRD) with the following:

   a. The party's witness list, with a column to add the date on which the witness testified, which shall be sent in Word or WordPerfect format to the Chambers email box no later than noon on the Monday before trial;

   b. The joint exhibit list in the form specified in Local Rule 16-5 (Civil), which shall be sent in Word or WordPerfect format to the Chambers email box no later than noon on the Monday before trial;

   c. All of the exhibits (except those to be used for impeachment only), with official exhibit tags attached and bearing the same number shown on the exhibit list. Exhibit tags may be obtained from the receptionist in the Public Intake Section, located on the Main Street level of the courthouse at 312 North Spring Street, Room G-19. Exhibits shall be numbered 1, 2, 3, etc., NOT 1.1, 1.2, etc. The defense exhibit numbers shall not duplicate plaintiff's numbers. If a "blow-up" is an enlargement of an existing exhibit, it shall be designated with the number of the original exhibit followed by an "A." These items (and the items listed in d and e below) shall be provided on the first day of trial;

   d. A three-ring binder containing a copy of all exhibits that can be reproduced, and a copy of the witness list. Each exhibit shall be tabbed with the exhibit number for easy referral;

   e. A three-ring binder containing a copy of all exhibits for use by witnesses.

3. A copy of the exhibit list with all **admitted exhibits** will be given to the jury during deliberations. Counsel shall review and approve the exhibit list with the CRD before the list is given to the jury.

4. Where a significant number of exhibits will be admitted, the Court encourages

counsel, preferably by agreement, to consider ways in which testimony about exhibits may be made intelligible to the jury while it is being presented. Counsel should consider such devices as overhead projectors, jury notebooks for admitted exhibits, or enlargements of important exhibits. The Court has an Elmo and other equipment available for use during trial. Information concerning training on the use of electronic equipment is available. Details are posted on the Court's website. To make reservations for training, call 213-894-3061. The Court does not permit exhibits to be "published" by passing them up and down the jury box. Exhibits may be displayed briefly using the screens in the courtroom, unless the process becomes too time-consuming.

5. All counsel are to meet not later than ten days before trial and to stipulate, so far as is possible, to foundation, to waiver of the best evidence rule, and to those exhibits that may be received into evidence at the start of the trial. The exhibits to be so received will be noted on the Court's copy of the exhibit list.

6. Counsel shall not attempt to display or use any charts or enlargements of exhibits unless all counsel have agreed to their use or objections have been heard and a ruling has been made.

7. On the day of jury selection, trial will begin at 9:00 a.m. Counsel will appear at 8:30 a.m. Thereafter, trial days are Tuesday through Friday, 8:00 a.m. to 2:00 p.m., with three fifteen-minute breaks during the session. When necessary, trials may continue beyond the normal schedule. If counsel contemplate that this schedule will be problematic due to the unavailability of witnesses, counsel should provide details to the Court at the Status Conference.

8. On the day of jury selection, the Court reserves the time from 8:30 a.m. to 9:00 a.m. to handle legal and administrative matters. Jury selection will commence promptly at 9:00 a.m. or as soon as jurors are available. Thereafter, legal and administrative matters shall be addressed between 7:45 a.m. And 8:00 a.m. All counsel are urged to anticipate matters that may need to be addressed outside of the presence of the jury and to raise them during this period, during breaks, or at the end of the day. The Court does not make jurors wait while counsel discuss matters that should have been addressed previously. Counsel are urged to consider any unusual substantive or evidentiary issues that may arise, and to advise the Court of such issues. Short briefs addressing such disputed issues are welcome.

9. Before trial begins, the Court will give counsel an opportunity to discuss administrative matters and anticipated procedural or legal issues. Before trial begins, and as soon as the information becomes available to counsel, counsel should advise the court of any concerns or accommodations that are requested for parties or witnesses. During trial, if there are any matters to be discussed outside the presence of the jury, counsel shall advise the CRD of the request. The Court discourages sidebars during trial.

10. All orders for transcripts must be ordered through the court reporter, Pamela Batalo, who can be contacted through www.pamelabatalo.com.

IV.
CONDUCT OF ATTORNEYS AND PARTIES

A. OPENING STATEMENTS, EXAMINING WITNESSES, AND SUMMATION

1. Counsel must use the lectern for opening statements, examination of witnesses, and summation.

2. Counsel must not consume time by writing out words, drawing charts or diagrams, etc. Counsel may do so in advance and explain that the item was prepared earlier as ordered by the Court to save time.

3. The Court will honor (and may establish) reasonable time estimates for opening and closing arguments, examination of witnesses, etc.

B. OBJECTIONS TO QUESTIONS

1. Counsel must not use objections for the purpose of making a speech, recapitulating testimony, or attempting to guide the witness.

2. When objecting, counsel must rise to state the objection and state only that counsel objects and the legal ground of objection. If counsel wishes to argue an objection further, counsel must ask for permission to do so.

C. GENERAL DECORUM

1. Counsel should not approach the CRD or the witness box without specific permission. If permission is given, counsel should return to the lectern when the purpose has been accomplished. Counsel should not question a witness at the witness stand.

2. Counsel and parties should rise when addressing the Court, and when the Court or the jury enters or leaves the courtroom.

3. Counsel should address all remarks to the Court. Counsel are not to address the CRD, the court reporter, persons in the audience, or opposing counsel. If counsel wish to speak with opposing counsel, counsel must ask permission to do so. Any request for the re-reading of questions or answers shall be addressed to the Court. Such requests should be limited. Requests may not be granted.

4. Counsel should not address or refer to witnesses or parties by first names alone. Young witnesses (under 14) may, however, be addressed and referred to by first names.

5. Counsel must not offer a stipulation unless counsel has conferred with opposing counsel and has verified that the stipulation will be acceptable.

6. While Court is in session, counsel must not leave counsel table to confer with any personnel or witnesses in the back of the courtroom unless permission has been granted in advance.

7. Counsel should not by facial expression, nodding, or other conduct exhibit any opinion, adverse or favorable, concerning any testimony being given by a witness. Counsel should admonish counsel's own clients and witnesses to avoid such conduct.

8. Counsel should not talk to jurors at all, and should not talk to co-counsel, opposing counsel, witnesses or clients where the conversation can be overheard by jurors. Each counsel should admonish counsel's own clients and witnesses to

avoid such conduct.

9. Where a party has more than one lawyer, only one may conduct the direct or cross-examination of a particular witness, or make objections as to that witness.

D. PROMPTNESS OF COUNSEL AND WITNESSES

1. The Court makes every effort to begin proceedings at the time set. Promptness is expected from counsel and witnesses. Once counsel are engaged in trial, this trial is counsel's first priority. The Court will not delay the trial or inconvenience jurors except under extraordinary circumstances. The Court will advise other courts that counsel are engaged in trial in this Court on request.

2. If a witness was on the stand at a recess, counsel must have the witness back on the stand, ready to proceed, when the court session resumes.

3. If a witness was on the stand at adjournment, counsel must have the witness adjacent to, but not on the stand, ready to proceed when the court session resumes.

4. Counsel must notify the CRD in advance if any witness should be accommodated based on a disability or for other reasons.

5. No presenting party may be without witnesses. If counsel has no more witnesses to call and there is more than a brief delay, the Court may deem that party to have rested.

6. The Court attempts to cooperate with professional witnesses and will, except in extraordinary circumstances, accommodate them by permitting them to be called out of sequence. Counsel must anticipate any such possibility and discuss it with opposing counsel. If there is an objection, counsel must confer with the Court in advance.

E. EXHIBITS

1. Each counsel should keep counsel's own list of exhibits and should note when each has been admitted into evidence.

2. Each counsel is responsible for any exhibits that counsel secures from the CRD and must return them before leaving the courtroom at the end of the session.

3. An exhibit not previously marked should, at the time of its first mention, be accompanied by a request that the CRD mark it for identification. To save time, counsel must show a new exhibit to opposing counsel before it is mentioned in Court.

4. Counsel are to advise the CRD of any agreements they have with respect to the proposed exhibits and as to those exhibits that may be received so that no further motion to admit need be made.

5. When referring to an exhibit, counsel should refer to its exhibit number whenever possible. Witnesses should be asked to do the same.

6. Counsel must not ask witnesses to draw charts or diagrams nor ask the Court's permission for a witness to do so. If counsel wishes to question a witness in connection with graphic aids, the material must be fully prepared before the court session starts.

F. DEPOSITIONS

1. All depositions to be used at trial, either as evidence or for impeachment, must be lodged with the CRD on the first day of trial or such earlier date as the Court may order. Counsel should verify with the CRD that the relevant deposition is in the CRD's possession.

2. In using depositions of an adverse party for impeachment, either one of the following procedures may be adopted:

   a. If counsel wishes to read the questions and answers as alleged impeachment and ask the witness no further questions on that subject, counsel shall first state the page and line where the reading begins and the page and line where the reading ends, and allow time for any objection. Counsel may then read the portions of the deposition into the record.

   b. If counsel wishes to ask the witness further questions on the subject matter, the deposition is placed in front of the witness and the witness is told to read silently the pages and lines involved. Then counsel may either ask the witness further questions on the matter and thereafter read the quotations, or read the quotations and thereafter ask further questions. Counsel should have an extra copy of the deposition for this purpose.

3. Where a witness is absent and the witness's testimony is offered by deposition, counsel may (a) have a reader occupy the witness chair and read the testimony of the witness while the examining lawyer asks the questions, or (b) have counsel read both the questions and answers.

G. USING NUMEROUS ANSWERS TO INTERROGATORIES AND REQUESTS FOR ADMISSIONS

Whenever counsel expects to offer a group of answers to interrogatories or requests for admissions extracted from one or more lengthy documents, counsel should prepare a new document listing each question and answer, and identifying the document from which it has been extracted. Copies of this new document should be given to the Court and opposing counsel. This procedure is intended to save time.

H. ADVANCE NOTICE OF UNUSUAL OR DIFFICULT ISSUES

If any counsel has reason to anticipate that a difficult question of law or evidence will necessitate legal argument requiring research or briefing, counsel must give the Court advance notice. Counsel are directed to notify the CRD at the day's adjournment if an unexpected legal issue arises that could not have been foreseen and addressed by a motion *in limine*. See Fed. R. Evid. 103. Counsel must also advise the CRD at the end of each trial day of any issues that must be addressed outside the presence of the jury, so that there is no interruption of the trial. THE COURT WILL NOT KEEP JURORS WAITING.

N.B. "COUNSEL," AS USED IN THIS ORDER, INCLUDES PARTIES APPEARING *IN PROPRIA PERSONA*.

IT IS SO ORDERED.

DATED: ________________

DALE S. FISCHER
United States District Judge

D. Order Setting Scheduling Conference

IN THE UNITED STATES DISTICT COURT
FOR THE CENTRAL DISTRICT OF CALIFORNIA

	)	Case No. CV 10
Plaintiff(s),	)	
v.	)	**ORDER SETTING SCHEDULING**
Defendant(s).	)	**CONFERENCE**
	)	Date:
		Time: 11:00 a.m.

READ THIS ORDER CAREFULLY. IT DIFFERS IN SOME RESPECTS FROM THE LOCAL RULES.

This case has been assigned to Judge Dale S. Fischer. This matter is set for a scheduling conference on the above date. If plaintiff has not already served the operative complaint on all defendants, plaintiff shall promptly do so and shall file proofs of service within three days thereafter. Defendants also shall timely serve and file their responsive pleadings and file proofs of service within three days thereafter. For record-keeping purposes, the Court will dismiss all remaining fictitiously-named defendants (i.e., those who have not been named) at the scheduling conference. The Court will also set a date by which motions to amend the pleadings or add parties must be heard.

The conference will be held pursuant to Rule 16(b) of the Federal Rules of Civil Procedure (hereafter referred to as "Rule __"). The parties are reminded of their obligations under Rule 26(a)(1) to disclose information (without awaiting a discovery request), and under Rule 26(f) to confer on a discovery plan not later than 21 days before the scheduling conference and to file a "Joint Rule 26(f) Report" with the Court not later than 14 days after the conference. **Paper Chambers copies of the Joint Rule 26(f) Report and the ADR Program Questionnaire must be delivered to Judge Fischer's box across from the Clerk's office on the first floor of the Roybal Federal Building. Paper Chambers copies must be "blue-backed," with the title of the document on the lower right hand corner of the "blue-back," and must be "two-hole punched" at the top. Paper Chambers copies must be submitted no later than noon on the day after the e-filing. Failure to comply with the following requirements or to cooperate in the preparation of the Joint Rule 26(f) Report may lead to the imposition of sanctions.**

The Court encourages counsel to agree to begin to conduct discovery actively before the Scheduling Conference. At the very least, the parties shall comply fully with the letter and spirit of Rule 26(a) and thereby obtain and produce most of what would be produced in the early stage of discovery, because at the Scheduling Conference the Court will impose strict deadlines to complete discovery.

This Court does not exempt parties appearing *in propria persona* from compliance with any of the Local Rules, including Local Rule 16. "Counsel," as used in this order, includes parties appearing *in propria persona*.

1. Joint Rule 26(f) Report

The Joint Rule 26(f) Report, which shall be filed **not later than 7 days** before the scheduling conference, shall be drafted by plaintiff (unless the parties agree otherwise), but shall be submitted and signed jointly. "Jointly" contemplates a single report, regardless of how many separately-represented parties there are. The Joint Rule 26(f) Report shall specify the date of the scheduling conference on the caption page. It shall report on all matters described below, which include those required to be discussed by Rule 26(f) and Local Rule 26:

a. Statement of the case: a short synopsis (not to exceed two pages) of the main claims, counterclaims, and affirmative defenses.

b. Subject matter jurisdiction: a statement of the **specific** basis of federal jurisdiction, including supplemental jurisdiction.

c. Legal issues: a brief description of the **key legal issues**, including any unusual substantive, procedural, or evidentiary issues.

d. Parties, evidence, etc.: a list of parties, percipient witnesses, and key documents on the main issues in the case. For conflict purposes, corporate parties must identify all subsidiaries, parents, and affiliates.

e. Damages: the realistic range of provable damages.

f. Insurance: whether there is insurance coverage, the extent of coverage, and whether there is a reservation of rights.

g. Motions: a statement of the likelihood of motions seeking to add other parties or claims, file amended pleadings, transfer venue, etc.

h. Manual for Complex Litigation: whether all or part of the procedures of the Manual for Complex Litigation should be utilized.

i. Status of Discovery: a discussion of the present state of discovery, including a summary of completed discovery.

j. Discovery Plan: a detailed discovery plan, as contemplated by Rule 26(f), including the identity of all anticipated deponents and dates by which their depositions are to be completed (if possible), anticipated written discovery requests, including requests for admission, document requests, and interrogatories, and a schedule for completion of all discovery. State what, if any, changes in the disclosures under Rule 26(a) should be made, the subjects on which discovery may be needed and whether discovery should be conducted in phases or otherwise be limited, whether applicable limitations should be changed or other limitations imposed, and whether the Court should enter other orders. A statement that discovery will be conducted as to all claims and defenses, or other vague description, is not acceptable.

k. Discovery cut-off: a proposed discovery cut-off date. *N.B.* This means the final day for **completion of discovery**, including resolution of all discovery motions.

l. Expert discovery: proposed dates for expert witness disclosures (initial and rebuttal) and expert discovery cut-off under Rule 26(a)(2).

m. Dispositive motions: a description of the issues or claims that any party believes may be determined by motion for summary judgment or motion *in limine*.

n. Settlement: a statement of what settlement discussions or written communications have occurred (**excluding any statement of the terms discussed**) and a statement pursuant to Local Rule 16-15.4 selecting a settlement mechanism under that Rule. Note: If a case is selected for the ADR Pilot Program, the parties may choose private mediation (at their own expense) instead. The parties may **not** choose a settlement conference before the magistrate judge. No case will proceed to trial unless all parties, including an officer (with full authority to settle the case) of all corporate parties, have appeared personally at a settlement conference.

o. Trial estimate: a realistic estimate of the time required for trial and whether trial will be by jury or by court. Each side should specify (by number, not by name) how many witnesses it contemplates calling. If the time estimate for trial given in the Joint Rule 26(f) Report exceeds five court days, counsel shall be prepared to discuss in detail the estimate.

p. Trial counsel: the name(s) of the attorney(s) who will try the case.

q. Independent expert or Master: whether this is a case where the Court should consider appointing a master pursuant to Rule 53 or an independent scientific expert. (The appointment of a master may be especially appropriate if there are likely to be substantial discovery disputes, numerous claims to be construed in connection with a summary judgment motion, a lengthy Daubert hearing, a resolution of a difficult computation of damages, etc.)

r. Timetable: **complete the Schedule of Pretrial and Trial Dates form attached as Exhibit A to this Order and attach it to the Joint Rule 26(f) Report**. The entries in the "Weeks Before Trial" column reflect what the Court believes are appropriate for most cases and will allow the Court to rule on potentially dispositive motions sufficiently in advance of the pretrial conference. The form is designed to enable counsel to ask the Court to set different (earlier) last dates by which the key requirements must be completed. Each side should write in the month, day, and year it requests for each event. *E.g.*, for the expert discovery cut-off it might be "10/7/08" for plaintiff and "10/28/08" for defendant, if they cannot agree. At the conference, the Court will review this form with counsel. Each entry proposing Court dates shall fall on a Monday, except the trial date, which is a Tuesday. Counsel should insure that requested dates do not fall on a holiday. In appropriate cases the Court will order different dates after it hears from counsel. The discovery cut-off date is the last day by which all depositions must be completed, responses to previously-served written discovery must be provided, and motions concerning discovery disputes must be heard. The cut-off date for motions is the last date on which motions may be **heard**, not filed. The Court is not likely to continue this date, and will not do so unless the trial date is also continued.

s. Other issues: a statement of any other issues affecting the status or management of the case (*e.g.*, unusually complicated technical or technological issues, disputes over protective orders, extraordinarily voluminous document production, non-English speaking witnesses, ADA-related issues, discovery in foreign jurisdictions, etc.) and any proposals concerning severance, bifurcation, or other ordering of proof.

The Joint Rule 26(f) Report should set forth the above-described information under section headings corresponding to those in this Order.

2. Scheduling Conference

Scheduling conferences will be held in the Roybal Federal Building, Courtroom 840, 255 E. Temple Street. Counsel shall comply with the following:

a. Participation: The lead trial attorney **must** attend the scheduling conference, unless excused by the Court for good cause shown in advance of the scheduling conference. When seeking permission not to attend, lead counsel must identify the person who will appear by name and bar number, and specify that person's involvement in the case. The Court may choose to postpone the scheduling conference rather than to permit counsel other than lead counsel to attend. Local counsel may not appear at a scheduling conference in place of lead counsel. Counsel should not purport to be "co-lead" counsel as a means of avoiding this requirement.

b. Continuance: A continuance of the scheduling conference will be granted only for good cause.

3. **Notice to be Provided by Counsel**

Plaintiff's counsel or, if plaintiff is appearing *pro se*, defendant's counsel, shall provide this Order to any parties who first appear after the date of this Order and to parties who are known to exist but have not yet entered appearances.

4. **Disclosures to Clients**

Counsel are ordered to deliver to their respective clients a copy of this Order and of the Court's trial order, which will contain the schedule that the Court sets at the scheduling conference.

5. **Court's Website**

Copies of this and all other orders of this Court that may become applicable to this case are available on the Central District of California website, at www.cacd.uscourts.gov, under "Judge's Procedures and Schedules." Copies of the Local Rules are available on the website.[1]

The Court thanks the parties and their counsel for their anticipated cooperation in complying with these requirements.

Caveat: If counsel fail to file the required Joint Rule 26(f) Report, or the required pretrial documents, or if counsel fail to appear at the scheduling conference, the pretrial conference, or any other proceeding scheduled by the Court, and such failure is not satisfactorily explained to the Court: (a) the cause shall be dismissed for failure to prosecute, if such failure occurs on the part of the plaintiff; (b) default (and thereafter default judgment) shall be entered if such failure occurs on the part of the defendant; or (c) the Court may take such other action as it deems appropriate.

IT IS SO ORDERED.

Dated: ________________

____
DALE S. FISCHER
United States District Judge

---

[1] They may also be purchased from one of the following:

Los Angeles Daily Journal	West Publishing Company	Metropolitan News
915 East First Street	50 West Kellogg Blvd.	210 South Spring Street
Los Angeles, CA 90012	St. Paul, MN 55164-9979	Los Angeles, CA 90012

EXHIBIT A
SCHEDULE OF PRETRIAL AND TRIAL DATES

CASE NAME: ______________________

CASE NO: _________________________

Matter	Time	Weeks before trial	Plaintiff(s) Request	Defendant(s) Request	Court Order
Trial (jury)(court) (length ___days) (**Tuesday**)	8:00 a.m.				
For Court Trial Lodge Findings of Fact and Conclusions of Law, LR 52, and Summaries of Direct Testimony		3			
Pretrial Conference, LR 16; Hearing on Motions in Limine	3:00 p.m.	4			
For Jury Trial Lodge Pretrial Conference Order, LR 16-7; File Agreed Set of Jury Instructions and Verdict Forms; File Statement Regarding Disputed Instructions, Verdicts, etc.; File Oppositions to Motions in Limine		6			
For Jury Trial File Memo of Contentions of Fact and Law, LR 16-4; Exhibit & Witness Lists, LR 16-5, 6; File Status Report Regarding Settlement; File Motions in Limine		7			
Last date to conduct Settlement Conf., LR 16-15		12			
Last day for **hearing** motions, LR 7		14			
Non-expert Discovery Cut-off					
Expert Disclosure (initial)					
Expert Disclosure (rebuttal)					
Expert Discovery Cut-off					
Last Date to Amend Pleadings or Add Parties					

LR 16-15 Settlement Choice: □ 1. USMJ □ 2. Attorney Settlement Panel □ 3. Outside ADR

E. Standing Order for Cases Assigned to Judge Fischer

IN THE UNITED STATES DISTICT COURT
FOR THE CENTRAL DISTRICT OF CALIFORNIA

)	Case No. CV ______________
Plaintiff(s),)	
v.)	**STANDING ORDER FOR**
Defendant(s).)	**CASES ASSIGNED TO**
______________________________)	**JUDGE DALE S. FISCHER**

READ THIS ORDER CAREFULLY. IT CONTROLS THIS CASE AND DIFFERS IN SOME RESPECTS FROM THE LOCAL RULES.

COUNSEL FOR PLAINTIFF SHALL IMMEDIATELY SERVE THIS ORDER ON ALL PARTIES, INCLUDING ANY NEW PARTIES TO THE ACTION. IF THIS CASE WAS REMOVED FROM STATE COURT, THE DEFENDANT WHO REMOVED THE CASE SHALL SERVE THIS ORDER ON ALL OTHER PARTIES.

COUNSEL MUST ADVISE THE COURT IMMEDIATELY IF THE CASE OR ANY PENDING MATTER HAS BEEN RESOLVED.

Both the Court and counsel bear responsibility for the progress of litigation in federal court. To "secure the just, speedy, and inexpensive determination" of this case, Fed. R. Civ. P. 1, all counsel are ordered to become familiar with the Federal Rules of Civil Procedure ("Rule __") and the Local Rules of the Central District of California ("Local Rule __").

IT IS ORDERED:

1. **Service of the Complaint**
The plaintiff shall promptly serve the complaint in accordance with Rule 4 and file the proofs of service pursuant to Local Rule 5-3.1. Although Rule 4(m) does not require the summons and complaint to be served for 120 days, the Court expects service much sooner. The Court will require plaintiffs to show good cause to extend the service deadline beyond 120 days.

2. **Presence of Lead Counsel**
All lead trial counsel shall attend any proceeding set by this Court, including all scheduling, pretrial, and settlement conferences. Unless lead counsel's absence is excused by the Court for good cause in advance of the hearing, or is due to an emergency that prevented prior notice, the Court reserves the right to designate the attorney handling such proceeding as lead counsel for all purposes. The Court does not allow appearances by telephone. Failure of lead counsel to appear will be grounds for sanctions.

3. **Documents Filed With the Court**
Typeface shall comply with Local Rule 11-3.1.1. If Times New Roman font is used, the size must be no less than 14; if Courier is used, the size must be no less than 12. Footnotes shall be in typeface no less than one size smaller than text size and shall be used sparingly. Filings that do not conform to the Local Rules and this Order will not be considered.

4. **Discovery and Discovery Cut-off**

   a. Compliance with Rule 26(a): The Court encourages counsel to agree to begin to conduct discovery actively before the scheduling conference. The parties should comply fully with the letter and spirit of Rule 26(a) and obtain and produce most of what would otherwise be produced in the early stages of discovery. At the scheduling conference the Court will impose strict deadlines for completion of discovery. Inability to complete discovery within the deadlines set at the conference will not constitute grounds for a continuance in the absence of good cause.

   b. Discovery Motions: Counsel are expected to resolve discovery disputes among themselves in a courteous, reasonable, and professional manner. All discovery matters have been referred to the assigned magistrate judge, who will hear all discovery disputes. (The magistrate judge's initials follow the district judge's initials next to the case number.) All discovery documents must include the words "DISCOVERY MATTER" in the caption to ensure proper routing. Counsel are directed to contact the magistrate judge's courtroom deputy clerk to schedule matters for hearing. Counsel should not deliver Chambers copies of these documents to this Court. In accordance with 28 U.S.C. § 636(b)(1)(A), the Court will not reverse any order of the magistrate judge, including one imposing sanctions, unless it has been shown that the magistrate judge's order is clearly erroneous or contrary to law. Any party may file and serve a motion for review and reconsideration before this Court. The moving party must file and serve the motion within 14 days of service of a written ruling or within 14 days of an oral ruling that the magistrate judge states will not be followed by a written ruling. The motion must specify which portions of the ruling are clearly erroneous or contrary to law and support the contention with points and authorities. Counsel shall deliver a paper chambers copy of the moving papers and responses to the magistrate judge's courtroom deputy clerk no later than the day after filing.

5. **E-Filing Requirements**

   a. Applicable Rules: Counsel shall e-file all filings pursuant to Rule 5(d)(3), Local Rule 5-4, and General Order 10-07.

   b. Method of Filing: All items that do not require the Court's signature shall be e-filed in .pdf format. All proposed signature items shall be e-filed as an attachment to the main document in .pdf format.

   c. Use of Chambers E-Mail: All proposed signature items must be e-mailed to the Chambers e-mail address at dsf_chambers@cacd.uscourts.gov in WordPerfect (preferred) or Word format. A .pdf convertible to one of these formats is not acceptable. Parties seeking a proposed order based on a stipulation or an ex parte application should e-mail **both** the order and the stipulation or ex parte application. Parties should not e-mail the accompanying documents for other proposed signature items (such as a motion to dismiss) unless requested by the Court. Proposed orders must be on pleading paper and should not contain attorney names, addresses, etc. on the caption page, should not contain a footer with the document name or other information, and should not contain a watermark or designation of the firm name, etc. in the margin.

d. Mandatory Paper Chambers Copies: Paper Chambers copies of all e-filed documents must be delivered to Judge Fischer's box across from the Clerk's office on the first floor of the Roybal Federal Building. Paper Chambers copies must be "blue-backed," with the title of the document on the lower right hand corner of the "blue-back," and must be "two-hole punched" at the top. Paper Chambers copies must be submitted no later than noon on the day after the e-filing. **Documents will not be considered until paper Chambers copies are submitted, so paper Chambers copies of all documents for which priority processing is requested should be submitted on the same day as the filing.** For security reasons, documents should be removed from envelopes. **Attach the notice of e-filing to the BACK of the paper Chambers copy.** Paper Chambers copies delivered by Federal Express should **not** require the signature of the recipient. Paper Chambers copies are mandatory. Sanctions may be imposed for failure to provide paper Chambers copies.

6. Proposed Protective Orders and Filings Under Seal

Proposed protective orders pertaining to discovery must be submitted to the assigned magistrate judge. Proposed protective orders should not purport to allow, without further order of this Court, the filing under seal of pleadings or documents filed in connection with a dispositive motion (including a class certification motion) or trial before Judge Fischer. The existence of a protective order does not alone justify the filing of pleadings or other documents under seal, in whole or in part.

An application to file documents under seal must meet the requirements of Local Rule 79-5. Documents that are not confidential or privileged in their entirety should not be filed under seal if the confidential portions can be redacted and filed separately with a reasonable amount of effort. The parties should file both a complete version of the pleadings and documents under seal, and a redacted version for public viewing, omitting only such portions as the Court has ordered may be filed under seal.

There is a strong presumption of access in civil cases. *Foltz v. State Farm Mut. Auto. Ins. Co.*, 331 F.3d 1122, 1135 (9th Cir. 2003). For each document or other type of information sought to be filed under seal, the party seeking protection must identify and discuss the factual or legal justification for the Court to find "good cause" or "compelling reasons," as appropriate, that such document or type of information should be protected. *Kamakana v. City and County of Honolulu*, 447 F.3d 1172, 1179-80 (9th Cir. 2006).

Sealing must be justified for each individual item to be sealed or redacted; blanket claims of confidentiality are not allowed and will result in a denial of the application to seal. Counsel are strongly encouraged to consider carefully whether sealing or redaction is required for a given piece of evidence or argument. *The inclusion of clearly meritless requests to seal or redact documents may result in the complete rejection of an application to seal.*

Documents that are not confidential or privileged in their entirety will not be filed under seal if the confidential portions can be redacted and filed separately. The application to file documents under seal should include an explanation of why redaction is not feasible.

If a party wishes to file a document that has been designated confidential by another party, the submitting party must give any designating party five calendar days notice of intent to file. If the designating party objects, it should notify the submitting party and file an application to file documents under seal within two court days.

If the Court grants an application to file documents under seal, the Court's mandatory paper chambers copies must include a complete version of the documents with an appropriate notation identifying the document or the portion of the document that has been filed under seal.

7. **Motions - General Requirements**

a. Time for Filing and Hearing Motions: Except for summary judgment motions, which are governed by ¶ 8(c), motions will be heard no sooner than two weeks after the deadline for filing the reply. Therefore, motion papers must be filed and served not later than 28 days before the hearing date. Opposition papers must be filed and served not later than 21 days before the hearing date. Reply papers must be filed and served not later than 14 days before the hearing date. The remaining requirements of Local Rule 7 shall apply. This Court hears motions on Mondays, beginning at 1:30 p.m. If Monday is a court holiday, motions will be heard on the next Monday. If the motion date selected is not available, the Court will issue a minute order continuing the date. Opposition papers due on a Monday holiday may be filed the following Tuesday. In such cases, reply papers may be filed on the next Tuesday. Adherence to the timing requirements is mandatory for Chambers' preparation of motion matters. The parties may stipulate to a different briefing schedule, so long as the schedule provides at least two weeks between the filing of the reply and the hearing date.

If the parties are able to resolve the issue, or if a party intends to withdraw or declines to oppose a motion, the party(ies) must notify the court as soon as possible, but no later than seven days before the hearing date. Failure to oppose a motion will likely result in the motion being granted immediately after the opposition would have been due.

b. Pre-filing Requirement: Counsel **must** comply with Local Rule 7-3, which requires counsel to engage in a pre-filing conference "to discuss thoroughly . . . the substance of the contemplated motion and any potential resolution." Counsel should discuss the issues to a sufficient degree that if a motion is still necessary, the briefing may be directed to those substantive issues requiring resolution by the Court. **The *pro per* status of one or more parties does not eliminate this requirement. Failure to comply with this Rule will be grounds for sanctions. If fault is attributed to the moving party, the Court may decline to hear the motion.**

c. Length and Format of Motion Papers: Memoranda of points and authorities in support of or in opposition to motions shall not exceed 25 pages. Replies shall not exceed 12 pages. Only in rare instances and for good cause shown will the Court grant an application to extend these page limitations. All exhibits must be separated by a tab divider on the right or bottom of the document. If documentary evidence in support of or in opposition to a motion exceeds 50 pages, the evidence submitted to Chambers must be in a separately bound and tabbed pleading and include a Table of Contents. If such evidence exceeds 200 pages, the Chambers copy of such evidence shall be placed in a Slant D-Ring binder, including a Table of Contents, with each item of evidence separated by a tab divider on the right side or the bottom. All documents contained in the binder must be three-hole punched with the oversized 13/32' hole size, not the standard 9/32' hole size.

d. Citations to Case Law: Citations to case law must identify not only the case cited, but the specific page referenced. When citing to legal databases (which is not encouraged), whenever possible cite to Westlaw rather than Lexis.

e. Citations to Other Sources: Statutory references should identify with specificity the sections and subsections referenced (e.g., Jurisdiction over this cause of action may appropriately be found in 47 U.S.C. § 33, which grants the district courts jurisdiction over all offenses of the Submarine Cable Act, whether the infraction occurred within the territorial waters of the United States or on board a vessel of the United States outside said waters). Statutory references that do not specifically indicate the appropriate section and subsection (e.g., Plaintiffs allege conduct in violation of the Federal Electronic Communication Privacy Act, 18 U.S.C. § 2511, et seq.) are to be avoided. Citations to treatises, manuals, and other materials should include the volume, section, and pages being referenced. If these are not readily accessible, copies should be attached. This is especially important for historical materials, *e.g.*, older legislative history.

f. Oral Argument: If the Court deems a matter appropriate for decision without oral argument, the Court will notify the parties in advance.

g. Calendar Conflicts: Counsel are to inform opposing counsel and the courtroom deputy clerk (via Chambers e-mail) as soon as a potential calendar conflict is discovered. Counsel should attempt to agree on a proposed date to accommodate the calendar conflict and the schedules of the counsel and the Court.

h. Telephone Inquiries: Telephone inquiries regarding the status of a motion, stipulation, or proposed order will receive no response. Counsel may register for Pacer access to monitor the Court's database. See www.cacd.uscourts.gov>General Information>Pacer Access. Counsel are referred to the Court's website at www.cacd.uscourts.gov>Judges' Procedures and Schedules> Hon. Dale S. Fischer for further information regarding procedures and preferences.

8. Specific Motion Requirements

a. Motions Pursuant to Rule 12: Motions to dismiss are strongly discouraged. Many motions to dismiss or to strike can be avoided if the parties confer in good faith (as required under Local Rule 7-3), especially for perceived defects in a complaint, answer, or counterclaim that could be corrected by amendment. *See Chang v. Chen*, 80 F.3d 1293, 1296 (9th Cir. 1996) (where a motion to dismiss is granted, a district court should provide leave to amend unless it is clear that the complaint could not be saved by any amendment). Moreover, a party has the right to amend the complaint once before being served with a responsive pleading. Fed. R.Civ. P. 15(a). (Neither a stipulation nor the Court's permission is required.) A Rule 12(b)(6) motion is not a responsive pleading and therefore plaintiff might have a right to amend. *See St. Michael's Convalescent Hospital v. California*, 643 F.2d 1369, 1374 (9th Cir. 1981), *Nolen v. Fitzharris*, 450 F.2d 958, 958-59 (9th Cir. 1971). Even after a complaint has been amended or a responsive pleading has been served, the Federal Rules provide that the Court should "freely give leave [to amend] when justice so requires." Fed. R. Civ. P. 15(a)(2). The Ninth Circuit requires that this policy favoring amendment be applied with "extreme liberality." *Morongo Band of Mission Indians v. Rose*, 893 F.2d 1074, 1079 (9th Cir. 1990).

These principles require that plaintiff's counsel carefully evaluate defendant's contentions as to the deficiencies in the complaint. In most instances the parties should agree to any amendment (if agreement is required) that would cure the defect. These provisions apply as well to motions to dismiss a counterclaim, answer, or affirmative defense.

b. Amended Complaints: In addition to the requirements of Local Rule 15-1, all amended pleadings shall be serially numbered to differentiate the amendment from previous amendments. **All amended pleadings, whether filed by motion, stipulation, or right, shall include with them a paper: (1) stating the effect of the amendment; (2) stating the page and line number(s) and wording of any proposed change or addition of material; and (3) including a "redlined" version of the amended or proposed amended pleading indicating all additions and deletions of material.**

c. Motions for Summary Judgment: Parties should not wait until the motion cut-off to bring motions for summary judgment or partial summary judgment. Because summary judgment motions are fact-dependent, parties should prepare papers in a fashion that will assist the Court (*e.g.*, generous use of tabs, tables of contents, headings, indices, etc.). The parties are to comply precisely with Local Rule 56-1 through 56-3.

Multiple motions for summary adjudication by the same party are highly disfavored. Any party wishing to file more than one motion for summary adjudication must move for leave of court and explain why the issues cannot be addressed in a single motion. If multiple motions for summary adjudication are filed by the same party without leave of court, the first filed motion will be considered and the subsequent motions stricken.

1. Timing: Motions for summary judgment are to be filed at least 49 days prior to the noticed hearing date. Opposition papers are due 28 days prior to the hearing date. Reply papers are due 14 days prior to the hearing date.

2. Separate Statement of Uncontroverted Facts and Conclusions of Law: The separate statement shall be prepared in a two-column format. The left-hand column sets forth -- in sequentially-numbered paragraphs -- the allegedly undisputed fact. The right-hand column sets forth the evidence that supports that fact. Each paragraph should contain a narrowly-focused statement of fact addressing a single subject as concisely as possible. **The moving, opposing, and reply papers should refer to the numbered paragraphs in the separate statement, rather than the underlying evidence.**

3. Statement of Genuine Disputes: The opposing party's statement of genuine disputes must be in two columns. The left-hand column must restate the opposing party's allegedly undisputed fact and track the moving party's separate statement exactly as filed. The right-hand column must state whether the fact is undisputed or disputed. The opposing party may dispute all or only a portion of the statement of fact. If disputing only a portion, the statement of genuine disputes must clearly indicate what part is being

disputed, followed by the opposing party's evidence controverting the fact. The opposing party should not avoid admitting an undisputed fact by avoiding the issue. Only good faith disputes should be included. The Court will not wade through a document to determine whether a fact really is in dispute. To demonstrate that a fact is disputed, the opposing party must briefly state why it disputes the moving party's asserted fact, cite to the relevant exhibit or other evidence, and describe what in that exhibit or evidence refutes the asserted fact. No legal argument should be set forth in this document. The opposing papers should refer to the numbered paragraphs in the separate statement, rather than the underlying evidence.

The opposing party may also submit additional material facts that bear on or relate to the issues raised by the movant, which shall follow the format described above for the moving party's separate statement. These additional facts shall continue in sequentially-numbered paragraphs and shall set forth in the right-hand column the evidence that supports that statement.

4. Supporting Evidence: No party should submit evidence other than the specific items of evidence or testimony necessary to support or controvert a proposed statement of undisputed fact. For example, entire deposition transcripts, entire sets of interrogatory responses, and documents that do not specifically support or controvert material in the separate statements should not be submitted in support of or opposition to a motion for summary judgment. The Court will not consider such material. When submitting portions of deposition transcripts and other lengthy documents, however, the parties should be sure to provide all pages necessary to put the cited portion in context.

Evidence submitted in support of or in opposition to a motion should be submitted either by way of stipulation or as exhibits to declarations sufficient to authenticate the proffered evidence, and should not be attached to the memorandum of points and authorities. Documentary evidence as to which there is no stipulation regarding foundation must be accompanied by the testimony, either by declaration or properly authenticated deposition transcript, of a witness who can establish authenticity. The pleadings should refer to the exhibits by exhibit number only, or by exhibit number and title of document -- not merely by the title of the document. For example, if Exhibit 1 is the License Agreement, the papers should refer to "Exhibit 1," or "the License Agreement attached as Exhibit 1," not "the License Agreement."

5. Objections to Evidence: If a party disputes a fact based in whole or in part on an evidentiary objection, the ground of the objection, as indicated above, should be stated in the separate statement, but not argued in that document. Evidentiary objections are to be addressed in a separate memorandum to be filed with the opposition or reply brief. This memorandum should be organized to track the paragraph numbers of the separate statement and statement of genuine disputes in numerical sequence. It should identify the specific item of evidence to which objection is made, and a brief argument with citation to authority as to why the objection is well-taken. The following is the suggested format:

Separate Statement Paragraph 1: Objection to the supporting deposition transcript of Jane Doe at 1:1-10 on the grounds that the statement constitutes inadmissable hearsay for which no exception applies. To the extent it is offered to prove her state of mind, it is irrelevant because her state of mind is not in issue. Fed. R. Evid. 801, 802.

Do not submit blanket or boilerplate objections to the opponent's statements of undisputed fact. The objections will be overruled and disregarded.

d. Motions for Attorneys' Fees: In addition to any other requirements imposed by statute or case law, motions for attorneys' fees must comply with the following:

1. Conference of Counsel: Prior to filing any motion for attorneys' fees, the moving party ("Movant") shall contact opposing counsel ("Respondent") to discuss thoroughly the substance of the contemplated motion pursuant to Local Rule 7-3. This conference of counsel must occur at least 21 days prior to the filing of the motion. At least seven days prior to the conference of counsel:

(A) Movant shall provide Respondent with the billing records on which the motion will be based, and shall specify the hours for which compensation will and will not be sought. These records may be redacted to prevent disclosure of material protected by the attorney-client privilege or work product doctrine.

(B) Movant shall inform Respondent of the hourly rates that will be claimed for each lawyer, paralegal, or other person. If Movant's counsel or other billers have performed any legal work on an hourly basis during the period covered by the motion, Movant shall provide representative business records sufficient to show the types of litigation in which such hourly rates were paid and the rates that were paid in each type, including a properly redacted fee agreement under which they provided services in this action. If Movant's counsel has been paid on an hourly basis in the case in question or in litigation of the same type as the case in question, records showing the rates paid for those services must be provided. If Movant will rely on other evidence to establish appropriate hourly rates, such as evidence of rates charged by attorneys of comparable experience and qualifications or evidence of rates used in previous awards by courts or administrative agencies, Movant shall provide such other evidence.

(C) Movant shall furnish the evidence that will be used to support the related nontaxable expenses to be sought by the motion.

By providing the opposing party with information about the party's hours, billing rates, and related nontaxable expenses, no party shall be deemed to make any admission or waive any argument about the relevance or effect of such information in determining an appropriate award.

All information furnished by any party under this section shall be treated as strictly confidential by the party receiving the information. The information shall be used solely for purposes of the fee litigation, and shall be disclosed to other persons, if at all, only in court filings or hearings related to the fee litigation. A party receiving such information who proposes to disclose it in a court filing or hearing shall provide the party furnishing it with prior written notice and a reasonable opportunity to request an appropriate protective order.

2. Form of Motion: The parties are to produce a Joint Statement for submission. At least seven days prior to the conference of counsel, Movant shall provide to Respondent a draft of its portion of a Joint Statement that will eventually be submitted to the Court. The Joint Statement shall be formatted as a spreadsheet in Microsoft Excel, or a table in WordPerfect or Microsoft Word. The spreadsheet or table must include columns to identify: (1) the date of each time entry; (2) the biller for each time entry; (3) a brief description of the task; (4) the number of hours requested by the Movant for the task; (5) the number of hours, if any, Respondent believes should be awarded for the task; and for disputed items (6) a brief summary of Movant's position; and (7) a brief summary of Respondent's position. A separate spreadsheet or table shall be prepared for any nontaxable costs sought by Movant. The spreadsheet or table of nontaxable costs must include columns to identify: (1) the item; (2) the amount sought by Movant for the item; (3) the amount, if any, Respondent believes should be awarded for the item; and for disputed items (4) a brief summary of Movant's position; and (5) a brief summary of Respondent's position.

   Following the conference of counsel, and no more than 14 days prior to the filing of the Motion, Movant shall provide to Respondent the final version of its portion of the Joint Statement in an electronic format. Respondent shall then input its portion of the Joint Statement into the document and return the completed document to Movant at least seven days prior to the filing of the Motion. Movant shall then file the Joint Statement at the same time it files the Motion. In addition to filing the Joint Statement, Movant shall email an electronic version of the Joint Statement to this Court's chambers ECF email inbox.

   Attorneys who may be seeking an award of fees should maintain time, expense, and cost records in accordance with the order on the Court's website.

   N.B. PLEADINGS THAT FAIL TO COMPLY WITH THE ABOVE FORMAT MAY NOT BE CONSIDERED.

9. Proposed Orders

Each party filing or opposing a motion or seeking the determination of any matter shall serve and lodge a Proposed Order setting forth the relief or action sought and a brief statement of the rationale for the decision with appropriate citations. The proposed order must be in the form described in paragraph 5.c. 10.

10. Telephonic Hearings

The Court believes it is extremely useful for counsel to appear personally at motions, scheduling conferences, etc. Therefore, it is unlikely that the Court would agree to conduct such matters by telephone in the absence of an emergency, illness, etc. preventing counsel from appearing in person. If an emergency occurs, counsel shall attempt to contact all involved parties to advise of the situation. The attorney requesting the telephonic hearing must contact the courtroom deputy clerk at the earliest possible time before the date scheduled for the motion or conference to seek the Court's permission to appear by telephone and to make the necessary arrangements. The Court may choose instead to continue the hearing.

11. **Ex Parte Applications**

Ex parte applications are solely for extraordinary relief and are rarely justified. *See Mission Power Engineering Co. v. Continental Casualty Co.*, 883 F. Supp. 488 (C.D. Cal. 1995). Applications that fail to conform to Local Rules 7-19 and 7-19.1, including a statement under oath about service and opposing counsel's position, will not be considered. The moving party shall electronically serve the opposing party, if permitted, and shall also advise by telephone that such service has been made. If the opposing party has not agreed to electronic service, the moving papers must be faxed, if a facsimile number has been provided. Moving party shall also notify the opposition that opposing papers must be filed no later than 24 hours (or one court day) following such service. Failure of the opposing party to accept electronic service or to provide a facsimile number will not extend this time period. If opposing counsel does not intend to oppose the ex parte application, counsel must advise the courtroom deputy clerk by telephone and Chambers e-mail. A paper Chambers copy of moving, opposition, or notice of non-opposition papers must be hand-delivered to Judge Fischer's courtroom deputy clerk. The Court considers ex parte applications on the papers and usually does not set these matters for hearing. The application will not be considered until the paper Chambers copy has been provided. Sanctions may be imposed for misuse of ex parte applications.

12. **Applications or Stipulations to Extend the Time to File any Required Document or to Continue any Date**

No stipulation extending the time to file any required document or to continue any date is effective until and unless the Court approves it, or unless the Federal Rules of Civil Procedure provide for an automatic extension. Both applications and stipulations must set forth:

a. The existing due date or hearing date, the discovery cut-off date, the last day for hearing motions, the pretrial conference date and trial date;

b. Specific reasons (contained in a detailed declaration) supporting good cause for granting the extension or continuance. (A statement that an extension "will promote settlement" is insufficient. The requesting party or parties must indicate the status of ongoing settlement negotiations. The possibility of settlement ordinarily will not be grounds for continuance.);

c. Whether there have been prior requests for extensions, and whether these requests were granted or denied by the Court; and

d. A description of the diligence of the party seeking the continuance and any prejudice that may result if the continuance is denied.

The request must be made before the date to be continued. The Court grants continuances only on a showing of good cause. Failure to comply with the Local Rules and this Order will result in rejection of the request without further notice to the parties.

13. TROs and Injunctions

Parties seeking emergency or provisional relief shall comply with Rule 65 and Local Rule 65. The Court generally will not rule on any application for such relief for at least twenty-four hours after the party subject to the requested order has been served, unless service is excused. The opposing party may file position papers in the interim.

14. Cases Removed From State Court

All documents filed in state court, including documents appended to the complaint, answers, and motions, must be refiled in this Court as a supplement to the notice of removal. See 28 U.S.C. § 1447(a) and (b). If the defendant has not yet answered or moved, the answer, responsive pleading, or motion filed in this Court must comply with the Federal Rules of Civil Procedure and the Local Rules of the Central District. If, before the case was removed, a motion was pending in state court, it must be re-noticed in accordance with Local Rule 7.

If an action removed to this Court contains a "form pleading" i.e. a pleading in which boxes are checked, the party or parties that filed the form pleading must file an appropriate pleading with this Court within 30 days of receipt of the notice of removal. This pleading must comply with the requirements of Rules 7, 7.1, 8, 9, 10, and 11.

15. Status of Fictitiously Named Defendants

This Court adheres to the following procedures when a matter is removed to this Court on diversity grounds with fictitiously named defendants referred to in the complaint. *See* 28 U.S.C. §§ 1441(a) and 1447.

a. Plaintiff shall ascertain the identity of and serve any fictitiously named defendants before the date of the Rule 16(b) scheduling conference. The Court generally will dismiss Doe defendants on the date of the scheduling conference, as they prevent the Court from accurately tracking its cases.

b. If plaintiff believes (by reason of the necessity for discovery or otherwise) that fictitiously named defendants cannot be fully identified within that period, a request to extend the time must be made in the Joint Rule 26 Report. Counsel should be prepared to state the reasons why fictitiously named defendants have not been identified and served.

c. If a plaintiff wants to substitute a defendant for one of the fictitiously named defendants, plaintiff shall first seek the consent of counsel for all defendants (and counsel for the fictitiously named party, if that party has separate counsel). If consent is withheld or denied, plaintiff should file a motion on regular notice. The motion and opposition should address whether the matter should thereafter be remanded to the superior court if diversity of citizenship is destroyed by the addition of the newly substituted party. *See* 28 U.S.C. §1447(c) and (e).

16. ERISA Cases Concerning Benefit Claims

The Court will hear motions to determine the standard of review, whether discovery will be permitted, and the scope of the administrative record. There will be a court trial (usually confined to oral argument) on the administrative record. Counsel are discouraged from filing motions for summary judgment or partial summary judgment on any other issue. If they choose to do so, they must distinguish *Kearney v. Standard Insurance Co.*, 175 F.3d 1084, 1095 (9th Cir. 1999) in the moving papers and explain why summary judgment is not precluded.

17. **Bankruptcy Appeals**
Counsel shall comply with the NOTICE REGARDING APPEAL FROM BANKRUPTCY COURT issued at the time the appeal is filed in the District Court. The Court will determine whether oral argument will be held.

18. **Communications with Chambers**
Counsel shall not attempt to contact the Court or its Chambers staff by telephone or by any other ex parte means. Counsel may contact the **courtroom deputy clerk** with **appropriate** inquiries. To facilitate communication with the courtroom deputy clerk, counsel should list their e-mail addresses and facsimile transmission numbers along with their telephone numbers on all papers.

19. **Parties Appearing *in Propria Persona***
Pro per litigants are required to comply with all local rules, including Local Rule 16. In this Order, the term "counsel" includes parties appearing *in propria persona*. Only individuals may represent themselves.

20. **"Notice of Unavailability"**
While the Court expects that counsel will conduct themselves appropriately and will not deliberately schedule Court or other proceedings when opposing counsel are unavailable, a "Notice of Unavailability" has no force or effect in this Court. Such documents should not be filed.

21. **Compliance with Local Rules and Standing Orders**
At all stages of the proceedings, the parties and counsel are expected to comply with the Local Rules and this Court's standing orders. Before the scheduling conference counsel shall review the Central District's Civility and Professionalism Guidelines (which can be found on the Court's website under "Attorney Information> Attorney Admissions"). Counsel are expected to adhere to this standard of conduct. Counsel are required to advise their clients of the terms of this Order.

CAVEAT: IF COUNSEL FAIL TO FILE THE REQUIRED JOINT RULE 26(f) REPORT, OR THE REQUIRED PRETRIAL DOCUMENTS, OR IF COUNSEL FAIL TO APPEAR AT THE SCHEDULING CONFERENCE, THE PRETRIAL CONFERENCE, OR ANY OTHER PROCEEDING SCHEDULED BY THE COURT, AND SUCH FAILURE IS NOT SATISFACTORILY EXPLAINED TO THE COURT: (1) THE CAUSE SHALL BE DISMISSED FOR FAILURE TO PROSECUTE, IF SUCH FAILURE OCCURS ON THE PART OF THE PLAINTIFF, (2) DEFAULT (AND THEREAFTER DEFAULT JUDGMENT) SHALL BE ENTERED IF SUCH FAILURE OCCURS ON THE PART OF THE DEFENDANT, OR (3) THE COURT MAY TAKE SUCH ACTION AS IT DEEMS APPROPRIATE.

Dated: ____________________

____
DALE S. FISCHER
United States District Judge

III. Judge Fischer's Forms

A. Exhibit List

IN THE UNITED STATES DISTICT COURT
FOR THE CENTRAL DISTRICT OF CALIFORNIA

)	Case No. CV ________ DSF(__x)
Plaintiff(s),)	
v.)	**EXHIBIT LIST**
Defendant(s).)	
________________________________)	*SAMPLE FORMAT*

EX. No.	DESCRIPTION	IDENTIFIED	ADMITTED

B. Final Joint Trial Witness Estimate Form

FINAL JOINT TRIAL WITNESS ESTIMATE FORM

Case: _______________ Trial Date: ________________

	WITNESS NAME	PARTY CALLING WITNESS AND ESTIMATE	X-EXAMINER'S ESTIMATE	DESCRIPTION OF TESTIMONY	COMMENTS
1					
2					
3					
4					
	TOTAL ESTIMATES THIS PAGE:				

Instructions:

(1) List witnesses (last name first); (2) For description, be extremely brief, e.g., "eyewitness to accident" or "expert on standard of care;" (3) Use estimates within fractions of an hour, rounded off to closest quarter of an hour, e.g., if you estimate 20 minutes, make it .25. An estimate of one and one-half hours would be 1.5. An estimate of three-quarters of an hour would be .75; (4) Note special factors in "Comments" column, *e.g.*, "Needs interpreter;" (5) Entries may be in handwriting if very neat and legible.

Hon. Michael W. Fitzgerald
District Judge

Chambers Information
U.S. District Court, Central District of California
Courtroom 1600, 16th Floor
312 N. Spring Street
Los Angeles, CA 90012

Scheduling Information
Courtroom Deputy (213) 894-1527

Biographical Information
Born 1959 in Los Angeles, CA

Federal Judicial Service:
-Judge, U.S. District Court, Central District of California
-Nominated by Barack Obama on July 20, 2011, to a seat vacated by A. Howard Matz. Confirmed by the Senate on March 15, 2012, and received commission on March 15, 2012.

Education:
-Harvard University, A.B., 1981
-University of California, Berkeley, Boalt Hall School of Law, J.D., 1985

Professional Career:
-Law clerk, Hon. Irving R. Kaufman, U.S. Court of Appeals for the Second Circuit, 1985-1986
-Private practice, Los Angeles, California, 1986-1987, 1991-2012
-Assistant U.S. attorney, Criminal Division, Southern District of California, 1988-1991

Hon. Dolly M. Gee

District Judge

Chambers Information

U.S. District Court, Central District of California
Courtroom 7, 2nd Floor
312 N. Spring Street
Los Angeles, CA 90012

Scheduling Information

Courtroom Deputy: (213) 894-5452

Civil Law and Motion	Fridays at 9:30 a.m.
Criminal Law and Motion	Wednesdays at 2:00 p.m.

Biographical Information

Born 1959 in Hawthorne, CA

Federal Judicial Service:

-Judge, U. S. District Court, Central District of California
-Nominated by Barack Obama on August 6, 2009, to a seat vacated by George P. Schiavelli; Confirmed by the Senate on December 24, 2009, and received commission on January 4, 2010.

Education:

-University of California at Los Angeles, B.A., 1981
-University of California at Los Angeles School of Law, J.D., 1984

Professional Career:

-Law Clerk, Hon. Milton L. Schwartz, U.S. District Court for the Eastern District of California, 1984-1986
-Private Practice, Los Angeles, Calif., 1986-2009

I. Judge Gee's Procedures and Practices

A. Procedures and Schedules

1. **Calendar:**
   Civil Motions: **Friday at 9:30 a.m.**
   Criminal Motions: **Wednesday at 2:00 p.m.**

2. **Motions:** You must click on the link at the top of the page to view closed motion dates. It is not necessary to clear a hearing date with the court clerk prior to filing a motion, **except for motions for summary judgment or preliminary injunction**. Moving papers are to be filed and served at least twenty-eight (28) days before the hearing date. Opposition papers are to be filed and served no later than twenty-one (21) days before the hearing date, and any reply papers are to be filed and served at least fourteen (14) days before the hearing date. See Local Rules 6-1, 7-9, 7-10.

   Prior to filing a motion, Counsel shall comply with the requirement of conference of counsel under Local Rule 7-3.

3. **Telephonic Appearances:** The Court may permit appearances by telephone for status conferences, scheduling conferences, and for oral argument on motions upon a showing that a personal appearance will cause undue hardship. If you wish to appear by telephone, you must:
   - notify the court clerk and opposing counsel at least three (3) court days in advance of the scheduled appearance;
   - provide the court clerk with the telephone number (land lines only; no cellular phones) at which the Court can reach you;
   - be available at that number for at least one-half hour before the time of the scheduled hearing.

4. **Tentative Rulings:** The Court makes every effort to issue a tentative ruling on the day of the hearing.

5. **Mandatory Chambers Copies:** ***All original filings are to be filed electronically pursuant to Local Rule 5-4.*** **ONE** mandatory chambers copy of ALL electronically filed documents MUST be delivered to the courtroom deputy clerk (Room G-19) no later than 12:00 p.m. the following business day. See Local Rule 11-4.1 ONLY documents pertaining to ***ex parte* applications** should be delivered directly to the mandatory chambers copy box located next to the chambers (Room 218P, 312 N. Spring Street). Mandatory chambers copies **DO NOT** need to be blue-backed. All mandatory chambers copies of pretrial documents shall be two-hole punched at the top.

6. ***Ex Parte* Applications:** *Ex parte* applications are solely for extraordinary relief and should be used with discretion. (*See Mission Power Engineering Co. v. Continental Casualty Co., 883 F. Supp. 488 (C.D. Cal. 1995*). *Ex parte* applications are taken under submission on the papers and are rarely set for hearing. Counsel will be notified of the Court's ruling. If a hearing is necessary, the court clerk will notify counsel of the date and time of the hearing. The moving party shall immediately serve the *ex parte* application on the opposing party by fax, email, or hand delivery and shall notify the opposing party that any opposition must be filed not later than 24 hours (or one court day) after the service of the application. The moving party shall advise the Court in its application whether opposing counsel will be filing opposition and explain what

efforts, if any, have been made to confer with opposing counsel regarding the substance of the application and any potential resolution prior to the filing of the application. **The mandatory chambers copy of the *ex parte* application and any opposition must be delivered directly to the Chambers (courtesy box outside Chambers door) on the same day it is e-filed.** All *ex parte* applications should include a proposed order. See Local Rules 7-19 and 7-19.1.

7. **Continuances:** A stipulation to continue the date of any matter before this Court must be supported by a sufficient basis that demonstrates good cause why the change in the date is essential. Counsel requesting a continuance must electronically file a stipulation and lodge a proposed order including a detailed explanation of the grounds for the requested continuance or extension of time. **Counsel should avoid submitting requests for continuance or extension of time less than at least five (5) court days prior to the expiration of the scheduled date.**

8. **Conformed copies:** Sufficient copies of any proposed orders or face pages of papers should be provided for conforming along with a self-addressed, stamped envelope.

9. **Telephone contact:** Counsel may determine the status of any submitted motion, stipulation, proposed order, or hearing date by accessing the docket sheet through PACER. Parties shall first check the Local Rules or the docket sheet before calling the court clerk with inquiries in that regard. Counsel may not contact the Judge's law clerks unless responding to an inquiry they initiated.

10. **Electronic equipment:** The Local Rules prohibit the recording of federal proceedings, either by electronic recording means or by camera. Video cassette recorders, monitors, computers, overhead projectors, and silent copiers, and the like for presentation of evidence are permitted, only by approval. Counsel may contact the Help Desk at 213-894-3061 to arrange training on the Court's Audio Visual Equipment. Counsel shall contact the Courtroom Deputy Clerk by telephone to request leave to bring electronic equipment into the courtroom. Counsel will be advised by the Courtroom Deputy Clerk that such a request shall be made by a letter addressed to the U.S. Marshal's Office, carbon copied to Space and Facilities and prepared for the Courtroom Deputy Clerk's signature, along with the case name and case number, the purpose, and on what date or for what duration equipment is needed. Counsel may email the letter listing the equipment that he or she intends to utilize to the Courtroom Deputy Clerk for signature, in advance of the trial or hearing, for approval and authorization. Upon approval, counsel shall present the letter to Court Security on the day(s) of the hearing, for admission.

11. **Transcripts:** For general information on how to order a transcript of any reported or digitally recorded proceeding, please contact 213-894-3015 or visit www.cacd.uscourts.gov > General Information > Court Reporter/Recorder Transcripts. If you require an estimate of cost for the preparation of a transcript, contact the court reporter/recorder for the desired proceeding.

    To determine the court reporter/recorder for a particular proceeding, go to the Court Reporter Schedule web page and click on View by Date. Once you've determined the correct court reporter/recorder for the desired session, click on Court Reporter Phone and Email List for contact information.

12. **Discovery:** All discovery motions are to be calendared before the Magistrate Judge assigned to the case.

13. **Scheduling and Case Management Orders:** A Scheduling and Case Management Order will be issued after the Scheduling Conference has been held. The Order will set case management deadlines, pre-trial conference dates, and trial dates.

14. **Trial:**

    a. **Hours:** Trials are generally conducted Tuesday through Friday, from 8:30 a.m. to 4:00 p.m., with two 15-minute breaks, and a 75-minute lunch break, unless otherwise ordered by the Court.

    b. **Exhibits:** Counsel shall comply with Local Rule 16-6 with regard to exhibits. In addition, on the first day of trial, Counsel shall submit to the court clerk three copies of the Joint Exhibit List. The Joint Exhibit List shall be substantially in the format indicated by the following example.

Case Title: ____________________ Case No.: ____________________

No. of Exhibit	Description	Date Identified	Date Admitted
3	1/30/80 letter from Doe to Rose		
105	$500 check dated 2/3/82 drawn on Roe payable to Doe		
1002*	Handwritten notes dated 1/16/80		
[*An asterisk shall be placed next to the exhibits which a party may offer if the need arises.]			

Counsel are to prepare their exhibits for submission to the court clerk on the first day of trial by placing them in tabbed binders indexed by exhibit number with exhibit tags affixed. Counsel shall submit to the court clerk an original and one copy of the binder. The exhibits shall be in three-ring binders labeled on the spine portion of the binder as to the volume number and contain an index of each exhibit included in the volume. Plaintiffs shall use yellow tags; defendants shall use blue tags. Each tag shall be affixed consistently on the upper or lower right hand side of the front of the exhibit. Exhibit tags can be obtained from the Clerk's Office. All exhibits will be returned to Counsel at the end of trial and will not be kept by the Court. Counsel shall keep the lodged and admitted exhibits in their possession pursuant to Local Rules 79-3 and 79-4.

    c. **Witness Lists:** Counsel shall comply with Local Rule 16-5. In addition, on the first day of trial, Counsel shall submit to the court clerk three (3) copies of witness lists, with witnesses listed in the order in which they are expected to be called.

    d. **Jury Instructions:** At the time of filing the proposed final pretrial conference order, Counsel are to submit to the Court a joint set of agreed-upon jury instructions, along with a separate set of proposed instructions as to which there are objections. The disputed instructions, if any, shall have a section for each party's proffered instructions and all other parties' briefly stated objections and citation of authorities in support of such objections.

    e. **Verdict Forms:** The court clerk will prepare any verdict forms necessary in a criminal trial. In a civil matter, the parties shall prepare a proposed verdict form(s) and lodge it at the time designated in the Court's scheduling and case management order.

15. **Interpreters:** It is the responsibility of Counsel in a civil case to arrange for the services of an Interpreter. The Interpreter's Office may be reached at 213-894-4599.

16. **Settlement Conferences:** Counsel are required to comply with Local Rule 16 regarding Mandatory Settlement Procedures.

17. **Settlement:** Please notify the court clerk as soon as a settlement of your case has been reached.

18. **Electronic Filings:** Counsel shall e-file all criminal and civil filings pursuant to Federal Rules of Civil Procedure 5(d)(3), Local Rule 5-4, and General Order 10-07, as follows:

    Step 1: All non-signature items shall be E-FILED in pdf format. All proposed signature items shall be E-FILED as an attachment to the main document in pdf format.

    Step 2: All proposed signature items shall be E-MAILED to the chambers email address at dmg_chambers@cacd.uscourts.gov in Word or Word Perfect format. ONLY proposed signature items should be emailed to the chambers' email address. Please do NOT email other associated documents, and DO NOT use this email address for communication with the Court or the court clerk.

    Step 3: A MANDATORY CHAMBERS COPY of all e-filed documents shall be delivered to the Clerk's Office, Room G-19, Attention: Valencia Vallery, by no later than 12:00 noon the business day following any electronic filing or on the same day if priority processing is being requested. Only emergency matters or Ex Parte Applications must be delivered directly to the Chambers (box outside Chambers door). Each document must be prominently labeled, "CHAMBERS COPY" on the front page. All courtesy copies shall have the notice of E-filing attached at the end of the document.

19. **Filings Under Seal:** See Local Rule 79-5.

20. **Other Information:** Counsel are directed to comply with all Local Rules, except as modified herein. If Counsel have received a "Notice to Parties of Alternative Dispute Resolution (ADR) Program" with an attached "ADR Program Questionnaire" (form ADR-09), please see General Order 07-01, which is located in the "General Orders" section on the home page of the Central District's website, for further information. The "Attorney Information > ADR" section also contains Attorney Settlement Officer information.

II. Judge Gee's Case Management Orders

A. *Criminal Motion and Trial Order*

IN THE UNITED STATES DISTICT COURT
FOR THE CENTRAL DISTRICT OF CALIFORNIA

UNITED STATES OF AMERICA, Plaintiff, v. Defendant(s).	Case No. CR - ____ - DMG
	CRIMINAL MOTION AND TRIAL ORDER
	Final Pretrial Conference: __ **at 2:00 p.m.**
	Trial Date: ___ **at 8:30 a.m.**

A. MOTIONS

1. Counsel must meet and confer with opposing counsel and attempt to resolve the issue before filing a motion. Pretrial motions shall be filed on or before the Tuesday four weeks before trial. Opposition (or notice of non-opposition) shall be filed no later than one week after the filing of the motion. A reply, if any, shall be filed no later than one week after the filing of the opposition. Replies relating to motions in limine are not accepted absent leave of court. Counsel must follow the Central District's General Orders and Local Rules concerning electronic filing, unless superseded by this Order.

2. Hearings on motions are held on Wednesdays at 3:00 p.m., unless otherwise set by the Court.

3. All papers shall be served personally, electronically mailed, or faxed to opposing counsel no later than 4:30 p.m. on the day of filing, with conformed Chambers copies of documents delivered to the Court's courtroom deputy clerk ("CRD") at the Spring Street courthouse. Paper Chambers copies are mandatory.

4. Counsel shall meet and confer with opposing counsel to informally resolve discovery disputes prior to filing a motion for discovery. All discovery motions shall state with particularity what is requested, the basis for the request, whether discovery has been requested, and opposing counsel's response to such request. Motions made without prior consultation with opposing counsel may not be heard.

5. *Ex parte* applications are disfavored. Counsel should obtain the agreement (or at least the position) of opposing counsel before filing such an application.

B. DISCOVERY & NOTICE

Counsel shall comply promptly with discovery and notice pursuant to Rules 12, 12.1, 12.2, 12.3, 12.4, 15, and 16 of the Federal Rules of Criminal Procedure. On government counsel's discovery of any evidence within the scope of *Brady v. Maryland*, 373 U.S. 83 (1963), such evidence shall be produced forthwith to defense counsel. Government counsel shall also disclose to defense counsel the existence or non-existence of (1) evidence obtained by electronic surveillance and (2) testimony by a government informant.

C. TRIAL REQUIREMENTS

1. **No later than one week before trial**, government counsel shall file with the Court a trial memorandum setting forth a factual summary of the government's case, a statement of the charges and the elements of each charge, an estimate of the length of the government's case in chief, including anticipated cross-examination, the names of witnesses the government intends to call, and a discussion of relevant legal and evidentiary issues as applied to the facts of the particular case. Government counsel shall attempt to obtain defense counsel's agreement to the factual summary, statement of the charges, time estimate for cross-examination of the government's witnesses (using the attached sample "Joint Trial Witness Estimate" form), and legal and evidentiary issues.

2. Counsel shall arrive at the Courtroom no later than 8:30 a.m. on the first day of trial.

3. Government counsel shall present the CRD with the following documents on the first day of trial:

   a. Three copies of the government's witness list, which shall also be sent in Word or WordPerfect format to the Chambers e-mail box;

   b. Three copies of the government's exhibit list in the form specified in the attached sample, which shall also be sent in Word or WordPerfect format to the Chambers e-mail box;

   c. All of the government's exhibits, with official exhibit tags attached and bearing the same number shown on the exhibit list. Exhibit tags may be obtained from the receptionist in the Public Intake Section, located on the Main Street level of the courthouse at 312 North Spring Street, Room G-19. Exhibits shall be numbered 1, 2, 3, etc., <u>NOT</u> 1.1, 1.2, etc. If a "blow-up" is an enlargement of an existing exhibit, it shall be designated with the number of the original exhibit followed by an "A";

   d. A three-ring binder containing a copy of the indictment/information, a copy of all exhibits that can be reproduced, and a copy of the witness list. Each exhibit shall be tabbed with the exhibit number for easy referral;

   e. A three-ring binder containing a copy of all exhibits for use by witnesses.

4. Exhibits such as firearms, narcotics, etc., must remain in the custody of a law enforcement agent during the pendency of the trial. It shall be the responsibility of the agent to produce any such items for court, secure them at night, and guard them at all times while in the courtroom.

5. The Court prefers that defense counsel deliver defense exhibits to the CRD on the first day of trial, but counsel are not required to do so unless these exhibits have previously been provided to the government. Defense counsel are responsible for affixing completed exhibit tags with the case name and case number to all exhibits to be used in defendant's case.

6. In trials where the defense expects to admit more than 20 exhibits, defense counsel shall provide two three-ring binders (one for the Court and one for witnesses), tabbed if possible with numbers to correspond to the exhibits counsel expects to introduce. Defense counsel shall provide the Court with a copy of

defense exhibits as they are introduced during trial, if they have not previously been provided.

7. Defense counsel shall provide the CRD and the court reporter with the defense witness list and defense exhibit list.

8. A copy of the exhibit list with all **admitted exhibits** will be given to the jury during deliberations. Government and defense counsel shall review and approve the exhibit list with the CRD before the list is given to the jury.

9. If any counsel wishes to arrange for the use of additional equipment, such as video monitors, overhead projectors, etc., counsel shall notify the CRD no later than 4:00 p.m. at least one week before trial so that the necessary arrangements may be made in advance of trial.

10. Counsel shall not attempt to display or use any charts or enlargements of exhibits unless all counsel have agreed to their use or objections have been heard and a ruling has been made by the Court

11. On the day of jury selection, trial will begin at 9:00 a.m. Counsel will appear at 8:30 a.m. Thereafter, trial days are Tuesday through Friday, 9:00 a.m. To 4:00 p.m., with two fifteen-minute breaks and a one-hour lunch break, unless otherwise ordered by the Court. When necessary, trials may continue beyond the normal schedule.

12. On the day of jury selection, the Court reserves the time from 8:30 a.m. To 9:00 a.m. to handle legal and administrative matters. Jury selection will commence promptly at 9:00 a.m. or as soon as jurors are available. All counsel must anticipate matters that may need to be addressed outside of the presence of the jury and raise them during this period, during breaks, or at the end of the day. The Court does not make jurors wait while counsel discuss matters that should have been addressed previously. Counsel are urged to consider any unusual substantive or evidentiary issues that may arise and to advise the Court of such issues. Short briefs (no more than five pages) addressing such disputed issues are welcome. The Court discourages sidebars during trial.

13. Should government counsel wish to order transcripts, they shall provide agency authorization to the court reporter at the time the request is made.

14. Any party requesting special court reporter services for any hearing (e.g., real time transmission, daily transcripts) shall notify the reporter at least two weeks before the hearing date.

D. JURY INSTRUCTIONS, VERDICT FORMS & QUESTIONNAIRES

1. **No later than one week before trial**, counsel shall submit both general and substantive jury instructions in the form described below. If possible, all instructions should be taken from the *Manual of Model Criminal Jury Instructions for the Ninth Circuit* (West Publishing, current edition). Where no applicable Ninth Circuit model instruction is available, counsel should consult the instructions from O'Malley, Grenig & Lee (formerly Devitt, et al.), *Federal Jury Practice and Instructions* (West Publishing Co., current edition). Counsel may submit alternatives to the Ninth Circuit model jury instructions or O'Malley, Grenig & Lee instructions only if counsel has a reasoned argument that those instructions do not properly state

the law or they are incomplete.

2. The parties must submit JOINT jury instructions and a JOINT proposed verdict form. In order to produce these joint instructions, the parties shall meet and confer sufficiently in advance of the required submission date with the goal of agreeing on instructions and verdict forms. Where the parties cannot agree, disputed instructions shall be submitted at least one week before trial as follows: (1) JOINT jury instructions (those instructions agreed to by all parties), and (2) DISPUTED jury instructions (those instructions propounded by a party to which another party objects). On a separate page following each disputed jury instruction, the party opposing the instruction shall briefly state the basis for the objection, any authority in support thereof and, if applicable, an alternative instruction. On the following page, the party proposing the disputed instruction shall briefly state its response to the objection, and any authority in support of the instruction. Each requested jury instruction shall be numbered and set forth in full on a separate page, citing the authority or source of the requested instruction.

3. Jury instructions should be modified as necessary to fit the facts of the case (e.g., inserting names of defendant(s) or witness(es) to whom instruction applies). Where language appears in brackets in the model instruction, counsel shall select the appropriate text and eliminate the inapplicable bracketed text.

4. An index page shall accompany all jury instructions submitted to the Court. The index page shall indicate the following:
   - **a.** The number of the instruction;
   - **b.** A brief title of the instruction;
   - **c.** The source of the instruction; and
   - **d.** The page number of the instruction.

   EXAMPLE:

Number	Title	Source	Page Number
#1	Conspiracy-Elements	9th Cir. 8.5.1	1

5. One or more copies of the instructions will be given to the jury during deliberations. Accordingly, counsel must submit to the Chambers e-mail (dmg_chambers@cacd.uscourts.gov) a "clean" set of all instructions in Word or WordPerfect format, containing only the text of each instruction, set forth in full on each page, with the caption "Instruction No. ____" (eliminating titles, supporting authority, indication of party proposing, etc.). A paper Chambers copy must also be submitted.

6. Counsel shall submit a joint proposed verdict form with the jury instructions.

7. At least one week before trial, each counsel must file any proposed questions to be asked of prospective jurors.

8. The Court, in its discretion, may display certain *voir dire* questions and general jury instructions on the large screen inside the courtroom.

E. INSTRUCTIONS GOVERNING PROCEDURE DURING TRIAL

1. Counsel shall not refer to any witness – including a client – over 14 years of age by his/her first name during trial.

2. Counsel shall not discuss the law or argue the case in opening statements.

3. No "speaking objections" are allowed. Counsel shall not use objections for the purpose of making a speech, repeating testimony, or attempting to guide the witness. When objecting, counsel shall stand, state only the legal ground of the objection, e.g., hearsay, irrelevant, etc. Counsel shall not argue an objection before the jury. Requests to approach sidebar to further argue an objection should be made sparingly and may not be granted.

4. Counsel shall not make facial expressions, nod, or shake their heads, comment, or otherwise exhibit in any way any agreement, disagreement, or other opinion or belief concerning the testimony of a witness. Counsel shall admonish their clients and witnesses not to engage in such conduct.

5. Counsel should not talk to jurors at all, and should not talk to co-counsel, opposing counsel, witnesses, or clients where the conversation can be overheard by jurors. Each counsel should admonish counsel's own clients and witnesses to avoid such conduct.

6. Counsel shall question witnesses from the lectern. Counsel shall not approach the witness box or enter the well without the Court's permission, and shall return to the lectern when counsel's purpose has been accomplished.

7. Counsel should speak clearly when questioning witnesses, making objections, etc.

8. No document shall be placed before a witness unless a copy has been provided to the Court and opposing counsel. Counsel may consider such devices as overhead projectors, jury notebooks for admitted exhibits, or enlargements of important exhibits. The Court has an Elmo and other equipment available for use during trial. Counsel may call the CRD if they wish to visit when the Court is not in session to practice using the equipment. The Court does not permit exhibits to be "published" by passing them up and down the jury box. Exhibits may be displayed briefly using the screen in the courtroom, unless the process becomes too time-consuming.

9. Water is permitted in the courtroom. Food is not permitted in the courtroom.

10. Counsel shall rise when addressing the Court, including when objecting to opposing counsel's questions. In jury trials, counsel, designated case agents and the defendant shall rise when the jury enters or leaves the courtroom. Special procedures or exceptions may apply when the defendant is in custody or restrained.

11. In trial, all remarks shall be addressed to the Court. Counsel shall not directly address the CRD, the court reporter, or opposing counsel. All requests for rereading of questions or answers, or to have an exhibit placed in front of a witness, shall be addressed to the Court.

12. Counsel should not offer a stipulation without having conferred with opposing counsel and having reached an agreement. Any stipulation of fact will require defendant's personal concurrence and shall be submitted to the Court in writing for approval. A proposed stipulation should be explained to defendant in advance.

13. While court is in session, counsel shall not leave counsel table to confer with

investigators, paralegals, secretaries, witnesses, etc. unless permission is granted in advance.

14. When a party has more than one lawyer, only one lawyer may conduct the examination of a given witness, and only that same lawyer may handle objections during the testimony of that witness.

15. If a witness was on the stand at a recess or adjournment, counsel who called the witness shall ensure the witness is back on the stand and ready to proceed when trial resumes.

16. Counsel are directed to have witnesses available throughout the court day. If no witnesses are available and there is more than a brief delay, the Court may deem counsel to have rested.

17. The Court attempts to cooperate with expert witnesses and other professionals and will, except in extraordinary circumstances, accommodate them by permitting them to be called out of sequence. Counsel should anticipate any scheduling issues and discuss them with opposing counsel. If there is an objection, counsel shall confer with the Court in advance.

18. Counsel must notify the CRD in advance if any witness should be accommodated based on the Americans with Disabilities Act or for other reasons.

19. Counsel shall be on time, as the Court makes every effort to start promptly.

IT IS SO ORDERED.

DATED: _______________

____
DOLLY M. GEE
United States District Judge

B. Initial Standing Order for Cases Assigned to Judge Gee

IN THE UNITED STATES DISTICT COURT
FOR THE CENTRAL DISTRICT OF CALIFORNIA

)	Case No. _______________
Plaintiff(s),)	
v.)	**INITIAL STANDING ORDER**
Defendant(s).)	**FOR CASES ASSIGNED TO**
__________________________)	**JUDGE GEE**

PLEASE READ THIS ORDER CAREFULLY. IT GOVERNS THIS CASE AND DIFFERS IN SOME RESPECTS FROM THE LOCAL RULES.

COUNSEL FOR PLAINTIFFS SHALL SERVE THIS ORDER IMMEDIATELY ON ALL PARTIES AND/OR THEIR COUNSEL, INCLUDING ANY NEW PARTIES TO THE ACTION. IF THIS CASE WAS REMOVED FROM STATE COURT, DEFENDANT WHO REMOVED THE CASE SHALL SERVE THIS ORDER ON ALL OTHER PARTIES.

This case has been assigned to the calendar of Judge Dolly M. Gee.

Both the Court and counsel bear responsibility for the progress of this litigation in federal court. To "secure the just, speedy, and inexpensive determination" of this case, as called for in Fed.R.Civ.P. 1, all parties or their counsel are ordered to become familiar with the Federal Rules of Civil Procedure, the Local Rules of the Central District of California, and this Court's standing orders.

1. SERVICE OF THE COMPLAINT

Plaintiff shall promptly serve the complaint in accordance with Fed.R.Civ.P. 4 and file the proofs of service pursuant to Local Rule 5-3.1. Any defendant not timely served under Fed. R. Civ. P. 4(m) shall be dismissed from the action without prejudice.

2. ASSIGNMENT TO A MAGISTRATE JUDGE

Under 28 U.S.C. § 636, the parties may consent to have a Magistrate Judge preside over all proceedings, including trial. The Magistrate Judges who accept those designations are identified on the Central District's website, which also contains the consent form.

3. DISCOVERY

a. Discovery Matters Referred to Magistrate Judge

All discovery matters have been referred to the assigned United States Magistrate Judge, who will hear all discovery disputes. The Magistrate Judge's initials follow the District Judge's initials next to the case number. All discovery-related documents must include the words "DISCOVERY MATTER" in the caption to ensure proper routing. Counsel are directed to contact the Magistrate Judge's courtroom deputy clerk to schedule matters for hearing. Please comply with Local Rule 37 and deliver mandatory chambers copies of discovery-related papers to the Magistrate Judge assigned to this case rather than to this Court.

In accordance with 28 U.S.C. § 636(b)(1)(A), the Court will not reverse any order of the Magistrate Judge unless it has been shown that the Magistrate Judge's order is clearly erroneous or contrary to law.

Any party may file and serve a motion for review and reconsideration before this Court. See Local Rule 72-2. The moving party must file and serve the motion within fourteen (14) days of service of a written ruling or within fourteen (14) days of an oral ruling that the Magistrate Judge states will not be followed by a written ruling. The motion must specify which portions of the ruling are clearly erroneous or contrary to law and support the contention with points and authorities. Counsel shall deliver a conformed copy of the moving papers and responses to the Magistrate Judge's courtroom deputy clerk at the time of filing.

b. Compliance with Fed. R. Civ. P. 26(a)

Unless there is a likelihood that upon motion by a party the Court would order that any or all discovery is premature, it is advisable for counsel to begin to conduct discovery actively before the Scheduling Conference. At the very least, the parties shall comply fully with the letter and spirit of Fed. R. Civ. P. 26(a) and thereby obtain and produce most of what would be produced in the early stage of discovery, because at the Scheduling Conference the Court will impose firm deadlines to complete discovery.

4. MOTIONS - GENERAL REQUIREMENTS

a. Time for Filing and Hearing Motions

Motions shall be filed in accordance with Local Rule 7. This Court hears motions on Fridays, beginning at 9:30 a.m. If Friday is a national holiday, motions will be heard on the next Friday. It is not necessary to clear a hearing date with the court clerk before filing a motion, except for motions for summary judgment or preliminary injunction. If the motion date selected is not available, the Court will issue a minute order continuing the date.

b. Pre-Filing Requirement To Meet and Confer

Counsel must comply with Local Rule 7-3, which requires counsel to engage in a pre-filing conference "to discuss thoroughly . . . the substance of the contemplated motion and any potential resolution." Counsel should discuss the issues to a sufficient degree that if a motion is still necessary, the briefing may be directed to those substantive issues requiring resolution by the Court. Counsel should resolve minor procedural or other non-substantive matters during the conference. The *in propria persona* status of one or more parties does not negate this requirement.

c. Length and Format of Motion Papers

Memoranda of points and authorities shall not exceed 25 pages. See Local Rule 11-6. Only in rare instances and for good cause shown will the Court grant an application to extend these page limitations. **No supplemental brief shall be filed without prior leave of Court.**

If documentary evidence in support of or in opposition to a motion exceeds 50 pages, the evidence must be separately bound and tabbed and include an index. If such evidence exceeds 200 pages, the documents shall be placed in a Slant D-ring binder, with an index and with each item of evidence separated by a tab divider on the right side.

d. Citations to Case Law

Citations to case law must identify not only the case cited, but the specific page referenced.

e. Citations to Other Sources

Statutory references should identify with specificity the sections and subsections referenced. Citations to treatises, manuals, and other materials should include the volume, section, and pages being referenced.

f. Oral Argument

If the Court deems a matter appropriate for decision without oral argument, the Court will notify the parties in advance.

5. SPECIFIC MOTION REQUIREMENTS

a. Motions Pursuant to Rule 12

Many motions to dismiss or to strike can be avoided if the parties confer in good faith (as required by Local Rule 7-3), especially for perceived defects in a complaint, answer, or counterclaim that could be corrected by amendment. *See Chang v. Chen*, 80 F.3d 1293, 1296 (9th Cir. 1996) (where a motion to dismiss is granted, a district court should provide leave to amend unless it is clear that the complaint could not be saved by any amendment). Moreover, a party has the right to amend the complaint "once as a matter of course at any time before a responsive pleading is served." Fed. R. Civ. P. 15(a). A Rule 12(b)(6) motion is not a responsive pleading and therefore plaintiff might have a right to amend. *See, e.g., St. Michael's Convalescent Hospital v. California*, 643 F.2d 1369, 1374 (9th Cir. 1981); *Nolen v. Fitzharris*, 450 F.2d 958, 958-59 (9th Cir. 1971). Even after a complaint has been amended or a responsive pleading has been served, the Federal Rules provide that leave to amend should be "freely given when justice so requires." Fed. R. Civ. P. 15(a). The Ninth Circuit requires that this policy favoring amendment be applied with "extreme liberality." *Morongo Band of Mission Indians v. Rose*, 893 F.2d 1074, 1079 (9th Cir. 1990).

These principles require that plaintiff's counsel carefully evaluate defendant's contentions as to the deficiencies in the complaint. In most instances, the moving party should agree to any amendment that would cure the defect.

b. Motions to Amend

In addition to the requirements of Local Rule 15-1, all motions to amend pleadings shall: (1) state the effect of the amendment and (2) identify the page and line number(s) and wording of any proposed change or addition of material. The proposed amended pleading shall be serially numbered to differentiate it from previously amended pleadings.

In addition to Local Rule 15-1's requirement of electronic filing of the proposed amended pleading as a document separate from the motion, counsel shall attach as an appendix to the moving papers a "redlined" version of the proposed amended pleading indicating all additions and deletions of material.

c. Motions for Class Certification

Motions for class certification shall be filed in accordance with Local Rule 23-3. Parties seeking to extend the deadline to file a motion for class certification beyond 90 days after the filing of the class action complaint shall meet and confer with opposing counsel and endeavor to stipulate to an extension of time prior to seeking relief from the Court.

d. Summary Judgment Motions

Parties need not wait until the motion cutoff to bring motions for summary judgment or partial summary judgment. **Whenever possible, the party moving for summary judgment should provide more than the minimum twenty-eight (28) day notice for motions.** The parties should prepare papers in a fashion that will assist the Court in absorbing the mass of facts (e.g., generous use of tabs, tables of contents, headings, indices, etc.). The parties are to comply with Local Rule 56-1 through 56-2, taking into account the Court's additional requirements described below.

i. Statements of Uncontroverted Facts and Genuine Disputes

The separate Statement of Uncontroverted Facts required under Local Rule 56-1 shall be prepared in a two-column format. The left hand column sets forth the allegedly undisputed fact. The right hand column sets forth the evidence that supports the factual statement. The factual statements should be set forth in sequentially numbered paragraphs. Each paragraph should contain a narrowly focused statement of fact. Each numbered paragraph should address a single subject as concisely as possible. The "Conclusions of Law" portion of the Statement should be inserted after the Statement of Uncontroverted Facts.

The opposing party's Statement of Genuine Disputes of Material Fact must be in two columns and track the movant's separate statement exactly as prepared. The left hand column must restate the allegedly undisputed fact, and the right hand column must state either that it is undisputed or disputed. The opposing party may dispute all or only a portion of the statement, but if disputing only a portion, it must clearly indicate what part is being disputed, followed by the opposing party's evidence controverting the fact. To demonstrate that a fact is disputed, the opposing party must briefly state why it disputes the moving party's asserted fact, cite to the relevant exhibit or other piece of evidence, and describe what it is in that exhibit or evidence that refutes the asserted fact. No legal argument should be set forth in this document.

The opposing party may submit additional material facts that bear on or relate to the issues raised by the movant, which shall follow the format described above for the moving party's separate statement. These additional facts shall continue in sequentially numbered paragraphs and shall set forth in the right hand column the evidence that supports that statement.

ii. Supporting Evidence

No party shall submit evidence other than the specific items of evidence or testimony necessary to support or controvert a proposed statement of undisputed fact. For example, entire deposition transcripts, entire sets of interrogatory responses, and documents that do not specifically support or controvert material in the separate statement shall not be submitted in opposition to a motion for summary judgment.

Evidence submitted in support of or in opposition to a motion should be submitted either by way of stipulation or as exhibits to declarations sufficient to authenticate the proffered evidence, and should not be attached to the memorandum of points and authorities. Documentary evidence as to which there is no stipulation regarding foundation must be accompanied by the testimony, either by declaration or properly authenticated deposition transcript, of a witness who can establish authenticity.

iii. Objections to Evidence

If a party disputes a fact based in whole or in part on an evidentiary objection, the ground of the objection should be succinctly stated in a separate statement of evidentiary objections in a two-column format. The left column should identify the items objected to (including page and line number if applicable) and the right column should set forth a concise objection (e.g., hearsay, lacks foundation, etc.) with a citation to the Federal Rules of Evidence or, where applicable, a case citation.

6. PROPOSED ORDERS

Each party filing or opposing a motion or seeking the determination of any matter shall serve and electronically lodge a proposed order setting forth the relief or action sought and a brief statement of the rationale for the decision with appropriate citations. In addition, a copy of the Proposed Order in Word or WordPerfect format shall be emailed to chambers at dmg_chambers@cacd.uscourts.gov on the day the document is e-filed.

7. COURTESY COPIES

All original filings are to be filed electronically pursuant to Local Rule 5-4. Courtesy copies of ALL electronically filed documents MUST be delivered to the courtroom deputy clerk no later than 12:00 p.m. the following business day. Only documents pertaining to *ex parte* applications should be delivered directly to the courtesy copy box located next to the chambers (Room 218P, 312 N. Spring Street). Courtesy copies **DO NOT** need to be blue-backed. All courtesy copies of pretrial documents (e.g., witness lists, proposed pretrial conference orders, etc.) shall be two-hole punched at the top.

8. TELEPHONIC HEARINGS

The Court may permit appearances or arguments by way of telephone conference calls upon a showing that a personal appearance will cause undue hardship. If you wish to appear by telephone, you must (a) notify the courtroom deputy clerk and opposing counsel at least three (3) days in advance of the scheduled appearance; (b) provide the court clerk with the telephone number (land lines only; no cell phones) at which the Court can reach you; and (c) be available at that number for at least one-half hour before the time of the scheduled hearing.

9. *EX PARTE* APPLICATIONS

The Court considers *ex parte* applications on the papers and does not usually set these matters for hearing. If a hearing is necessary, the parties will be notified. *Ex parte* applications are solely for extraordinary relief and should be used with discretion. Sanctions may be imposed for misuse of *ex parte* applications. *See Mission Power Engineering Co. v. Continental Casualty Co.*, 883 F. Supp. 488 (C.D. Cal. 1995).

Counsel's attention is directed to the Local Rules. Ex parte applications that fail to conform to Local Rule 7-19 and 7-19.1, **including a statement of opposing counsel's position**, will not be considered except on a specific showing of good cause. The moving party shall electronically serve the opposing party, if possible. A party is considered served once the *ex parte* application has been e-filed (all parties set up for electronic service are sent a notification of ECF filing each time a document is e-filed with a link to the document for one free view). Parties set up for service by fax or mail must be served the *ex parte* application by fax or personal service.

Following service of the *ex parte* papers by electronic service, fax, or personal service, the moving party shall notify the opposition that opposing papers must be filed no later than twenty-four (24) hours (or one court day) following service, except in cases where the opposing party has not previously appeared (i.e., responded to the Complaint). In those cases where the opposing party has not previously appeared, the moving party shall, following service of the *ex parte* papers, notify the opposition that opposing papers must be filed no later than forty-eight (48) hours following service. **On the day the documents are e-filed**, a conformed courtesy copy of moving, opposition, or notice of non-opposition papers are to be hand-delivered to the courtesy box outside the entrance to Judge Gee's chambers at Room 218P, 312 North Spring Street. Counsel will be notified by the clerk of the Court's ruling. If counsel does not intend to oppose an *ex parte* application, he or she must inform the courtroom deputy clerk at (213) 894-5452.

10. CONTINUANCES

This Court has a strong interest in keeping scheduled dates certain. Changes in dates are disfavored. Trial dates set by the Court are firm and will rarely be changed. Therefore, a stipulation to continue or extend the date of any matter before this Court **must** be supported by a sufficient factual basis that demonstrates good cause why the change in the date is essential. Without such compelling factual support, stipulations continuing dates set by this Court will not be approved. Counsel requesting a continuance or extension of time must electronically file a stipulation and lodge a proposed order including a **detailed** declaration of the grounds for the requested continuance or extension of time. Failure to comply with the Local Rules and this Order will result in rejection of the request without further notice to the parties. Proposed stipulations extending scheduling dates do not become effective unless and until this Court so orders. Counsel wishing to know whether a stipulation has been signed shall comply with the applicable Local Rule. **Counsel should avoid submitting requests for continuance or extension of time less than at least five (5) court days prior to the expiration of the scheduled date.**

11. ORDER SETTING SCHEDULING CONFERENCE

Pursuant to Fed. R. Civ. P.16(b), the Court will issue an Order setting a Scheduling Conference as required by Fed. R. Civ. P. 26 and the Local Rules of this Court. Strict compliance with Fed. R. Civ. P. 16 and 26 is required.

IT IS SO ORDERED.

DATED: _______________

____
DOLLY M. GEE
United States District Judge

C. *Scheduling Conference Order*

IN THE UNITED STATES DISTICT COURT
FOR THE CENTRAL DISTRICT OF CALIFORNIA

Plaintiff(s),)	Case No. _______________
v.)	**SCHEDULING MEETING OF COUNSEL** [Fed. R. Civ. P. 16, 26(f)]
Defendant(s).)	
______________________________)	**SCHEDULING CONFERENCE** set for _____________, 2010 at 9:30 a.m. [Fed. R. Civ. P.16]

This case has been assigned to the calendar of United States District Judge Dolly M. Gee. The responsibility for the progress of litigation in the federal courts falls not only upon the attorneys in the action, but upon the court as well.

In order "to secure the just, speedy, and inexpensive determination of every action," (Fed. R. Civ. P. 1), all counsel are hereby ordered to familiarize themselves with the Federal Rules of Civil Procedure and the Local Rules of the Central District of California.

A Scheduling Conference is set for the date and time set forth in the caption.[1] Counsel shall meet at least twenty-one (21) days in advance of the Scheduling Conference to prepare a jointly signed report for the court to be submitted no less than fourteen (14) days before the Scheduling Conference. The report is to contain the items set forth below. Pursuant to Fed. R. Civ. P. 16(c), the parties shall be represented by counsel with authority to enter into stipulations regarding all matters pertaining to conduct of the case.

The joint report to be submitted shall contain the items listed in Fed. R. Civ. P. 26(f), the parties' recommendations and agreements, if any, about the final scheduling order as listed in Fed. R. Civ. P. 16(b)(1) through (6), and those items listed in Fed. R. Civ. P. 16(c) which counsel believe will be useful to discuss at the Scheduling Conference. Items which must be addressed are the following:

(1) initial disclosures, preservation of discoverable information, and a discovery plan, including a listing and proposed schedule of written discovery, depositions, and a proposed discovery cut-off date;

(2) a listing and proposed schedule of law and motion matters, and a proposed dispositive motion cut-off date;

(3) a statement of what efforts have been made to settle or resolve the case to date and what settlement procedure is recommended pursuant to Local Rule 16-15.4 (specifically excluding any statement of the terms discussed);

(4) an estimated length of trial and a proposed date for the final pretrial conference and for trial;

---

1 Unless there is a likelihood that upon motion by a party the Court would order that any or all discovery is premature, it is advisable for counsel to begin to conduct discovery actively before the Scheduling Conference required by Fed. R. Civ. P. 16(b). At the very least, the parties shall comply fully with the letter and spirit of Fed. R. Civ. P. 26(a) and thereby obtain and produce most of what would be produced in the early stage of discovery, because at the Scheduling Conference the Court will impose tight deadlines to complete discovery.

(5) a discussion of other parties likely to be added;

(6) whether trial will be by jury or to the court;

(7) any other issues affecting the status or management of the case; and

(8) proposals regarding severance, bifurcation or other ordering of proof.

In addition, the Scheduling Conference Report shall contain the following:

(1) a short synopsis of the principal issues in the case;

(2) a statement of whether pleadings are likely to be amended;

(3) a statement as to issues which any party believes may be determined by motion.

At the Scheduling Conference, the court will set a date for discovery cutoff,[2] a final date by which motions must be filed and served, a final pretrial conference date, and a trial date.

To facilitate the scheduling process, counsel **shall complete the Schedule of Pretrial and Trial Dates form attached as Exhibit A to this Order and attach it to the Joint Rule 26(f) Report**. The Court urges the parties to make every effort to agree upon joint dates and deadlines. The entries in the "Time Computation" column reflect what the Court believes are appropriate for most cases and will allow the Court to rule on potentially dispositive motions sufficiently in advance of the final pretrial conference. The form is designed to enable counsel to ask the Court to set different (earlier) last dates by which the key requirements must be completed.

A continuance of the Scheduling Conference will be granted only for good cause. **The failure to submit a joint report in advance of the Scheduling Conference or the failure to attend the Scheduling Conference may result in the dismissal of the action, striking the answer and entering a default, and/or the imposition of sanctions.**

A settlement procedure appropriate to the particular case will be used in every civil action pursuant to Local Rule 16-15.1. In the Scheduling Conference Report, counsel are to recommend a specific settlement procedure provided for in Local Rule 16-15 which will be utilized in this case. Available alternatives for consideration, not to the exclusion of others, include:

(1) a settlement conference before the magistrate or district judge assigned to this case (Local Rule 16-15.4(1));

(2) appearance before an attorney selected from the Attorney Settlement Officer Panel (Local Rule 16-15.4(2));

(3) appearance before a retired judicial officer or other private or non-profit dispute

resolution body for non-judicial settlement or mediation proceedings (Local Rule 16-15.4(3));

---

2 This is not the date by which discovery requests must be served; but the date by which all discovery is to be completed. Any motion challenging the adequacy of discovery responses must be filed timely, served and calendared sufficiently in advance of the discovery cut-off date to permit the responses to be obtained before that date, if the motion is granted. The Court requires compliance with Local Rule 37-1 and 37-2 in the preparation and filing of discovery motions. Except in the case of an extreme emergency which was not created by the lawyer bringing the motion, discovery motions may not be heard on an *ex parte* basis.

(4) such other settlement mechanism proposed by the parties and approved by the court.

The report to the court as to the above items should be preceded by a thorough and frank discussion among the attorneys for the parties. A Joint Scheduling Report which does not comply with Fed. R. Civ. P. 16, 26(f), and this Order may cause continuance of the Scheduling Conference and a possible award of sanctions under Rule 16(f) against the party or parties responsible. **A conformed courtesy copy** of the Joint Report shall be delivered to the Courtroom Deputy Clerk at the Clerk's Office, Room G-19, **by 12:00 p.m. on the business day following e-filing**.

Counsel for plaintiff shall immediately serve this Order on all parties, including any new parties to the action.

The Court appreciates Counsel's anticipated cooperation and compliance with this Order.

IT IS SO ORDERED.

DATED: ______________

____
DOLLY M. GEE
United States District Judge

EXHIBIT A

Judge Dolly M. Gee
SCHEDULE OF PRETRIAL & TRIAL DATES WORKSHEET

Case No. ____________________ Case Name: __________________________

MATTER	JOINT REQUESTED DATE or PLNTF/DEFT REQUESTED DATE	TIME
TRIAL [ ] Court [ ] Jury Duration Estimate: ________	(Tuesday)	8:30 a.m.
FINAL PRETRIAL CONFERENCE ("FPTC") – 4 wks before trial	(Tuesday)	2:00 p.m.

MATTER	TIME COMPUTATION	JOINT REQUESTED DATE or PLNTF/DEFT REQUESTED DATE
Amended Pleadings and Addition of Parties Cut-Off (includes hearing of motions to amend)	90 days after scheduling conf	
Non-Expert Discovery Cut-Off (includes hearing of discovery motions)	at least 14 wks before FPTC	
Motion Cut-Off (filing deadline)	at least 13 wks before FPTC	
Initial Expert Disclosure & Report Deadline	at least 9 wks before FPTC	
Rebuttal Expert Disclosure & Report Deadline	at least 5 wks before FPTC	
Expert Discovery Cut-Off (includes hearing of discovery motions)	at least 3 wks before FPTC	
Settlement Conference Completion Date	at least 4 wks before FPTC	
Motions in Limine Filing Deadline	at least 3 wks before FPTC	
Opposition to Motion in Limine Filing Deadline	at least 2 wks before FPTC	
Other Dates: (e.g., class cert motion cut-off)	at least 90 days after complaint served (unless longer time justified)	

Hon. Andrew J. Guilford
District Judge

Chambers Information
U.S. District Court, Central District of California
Courtroom 10D
411 West Fourth Street
Santa Ana, CA 9270

Scheduling Information
Courtroom Deputy: (714) 338-4757

Civil Law and Motion	Mondays at 10:00 a.m.
Criminal Law and Motion	Mondays at 2:00 p.m.

Biographical Information
Born 1950 in Santa Monica, CA

Federal Judicial Service:
-Judge, U. S. District Court, Central District of California
-Nominated by George W. Bush on January 25, 2006, to a seat vacated by Dickran M. Tevrizian; Confirmed by the Senate on June 22, 2006, and received commission on June 26, 2006.

Education:
-University of California, Los Angeles, A.B., 1972
-University of California, Los Angeles, School of Law, J.D., 1975

Professional Career:
-Private Practice, Costa Mesa, California, 1975-2006

I. Judge Guilford's Procedures and Practices

A. Procedures and Schedules

Frequently Asked Questions are answered here, and other information appears in the attachments. This Court keeps its special rules to a minimum, relying on the existing Federal Rules of Civil Procedure ("F.R.Civ.P.") and Local Rules of this District ("L.R."), which should be reviewed carefully. The standards for professionalism and civility for this community are attached, and a resume is attached to assist in identifying conflicts.

1. When are motions heard?
Except when specially set, motions are heard as follows:
Civil: **Monday at 10:00 a.m.**
Criminal: **Monday at 2:00 p.m.**

2. How are discovery motions handled?
Discovery motions are handled by the assigned Magistrate Judge, whose initials usually appear at the end of the case number.

3. Are tentative rulings issued?
This Court usually issues tentative rulings, either through the link on this page a few days before the hearing, or in the Courtroom the morning of the hearing.

4. Are mandatory chambers copies required?
Mandatory Chambers Copies of all e-filed documents shall be delivered to the mandatory chambers copy box on the 10th Floor. It is imperative that the mandatory chambers copies be delivered by noon following the date of filing as required by General Order 10-07.IV.D. Failure to deliver timely mandatory chambers copies may result in a delay in hearing a motion or ordering the matter off calendar.

5. How are ex parte matters handled?
This Court follows L.R. 7-19, L.R. 7-19.1, and L.R. 7-19.2. An ex parte application has due process implications and is for extraordinary situations only. Fuentes v. Shevin, 407 U.S. 67, 80-82 (1972) (due process requires that affected parties "are entitled to be heard" following "meaningful" notice, except in "extraordinary situations"); Sniadach v. Family Fin. Corp. of Bay View, 395 U.S. 337, 339-40 (1969) ("the right to be heard 'has little reality or worth unless one is informed that the matter is pending and can choose for himself whether to appear or default, acquiesce or contest'"). An ex parte application is usually considered on the papers only. If the application is opposed, opposition papers should be filed no later than noon on the first court day following service of the application. In most cases, the Court will wait until that time before ruling. If needed, the Court will schedule a hearing.

6. What is the policy on continuances?
Continuances are granted only on a showing of good cause. The supporting papers must state the following about the event to be continued, with dates preferably in the form of a chart.

- Whether all parties agree to the continuance.
- Whether there have been any prior requested continuances and the rulings on

any prior requested continuances.
- The requested date and the presently scheduled date for the event.
- The scheduled trial date.
- Any other dates that will be affected.

7. Who in chambers is best to contact concerning cases?
The Courtroom Deputy Clerk, who is at AG_chambers@cacd.uscourts.gov.

8. What rules apply to motions, stipulations and orders?
Motions and stipulations to seal documents require a showing of good cause, recognizing the public's right to access information.

MOTIONS. The following local rules apply, but NOTE that summary judgments require longer periods under F.R.Civ.P. 56(c) and these local rules.

- L.R. 6-1 NOTICE AND SERVICE OF MOTION (28/31 day rules)
- L.R. 7-9 OPPOSING PAPERS (21/10 day rules)
- L.R. 7-10 REPLY PAPERS (14 day rule)
- L.R. 11-6 POINTS AND AUTHORITIES -- TRIAL BRIEFS -- LENGTH (25 page rule -- NOTE that excessive length and footnotes usually reduce effectiveness)
- L.R. 83-2.9 WITHDRAWAL AND SUBSTITUTION OF ATTORNEYS (NOTE: this Court carefully reviews whether the client has received notice of the motion and its consequences)

STIPULATIONS AND ORDERS. Orders on stipulations will not be signed unless all parties to the case (or their counsel) have signed the stipulation, and stipulations should clearly state that all parties join in the stipulation. This Court is cautious about ordering broad stipulated injunctive relief against parties who have not signed the stipulation, and F.R.Civ.P. 65(d) should be reviewed carefully.

9. What should be done if there is a calendar conflict?
Immediately contact the Courtroom Deputy Clerk at her email address AG_chambers@cacd.uscourts.gov.

10. What is the best way to handle questions about electronic equipment?
Contact the Courtroom Deputy Clerk at her email address AG_chambers@cacd.uscourts.gov.

11. What is the best way to handle questions about transcripts?
For general information on how to order a transcript of any reported or digitally recorded proceeding, please contact 213-894-3015 or visit www.cacd.uscourts.gov > General Information > Court Reporter/Recorder Transcripts. If you require an estimate of cost for the preparation of a transcript, contact the court reporter/recorder for the desired proceeding.

To determine the court reporter/recorder for a particular proceeding, go to the Court Reporter Schedule web page and click on View by Date. Once you've determined the correct court reporter/recorder for the desired session, click on Court Reporter Phone and Email List for contact information.

12. What is the hiring process for regular law clerks?
    Regular law clerk applications should be submitted as provided by the Federal Law Clerk Hiring Plan.

13. What is the hiring process for externs?
    This Court welcomes applications for full-time extern positions lasting a sufficient length at any time during the year. Extern applicants should submit at least a cover letter and resume.

14. This Court supports the reduction of hard copies where possible through digital alternatives.

15. Because of economic difficulties, civil litigants in this Court sometimes ask that a lawyer be provided to them free, and some lawyers are underemployed. There is also a growing spirit of commendable volunteerism in the country, and a growing concern that all civil litigants should be represented by a lawyer. Some underemployed lawyers who seek opportunities to help people pro bono and represent deserving litigants in matters pending before this Court have been frustrated in finding the best way to do their good work. The Court therefore invites lawyers to state their willingness to volunteer their time to unrepresented litigants in this Court by simply sending your resume in an envelope addressed as follows:

    Pro Bono Volunteers
    Courtroom 10D
    411 West Fourth Street
    Santa Ana, CA 92701

    When, and only when, civil litigants appear at a regularly scheduled hearing, such as a Scheduling Conference, and ask that a lawyer be provided to them free, the name of a volunteer lawyer may then be provided if appropriate. When the Court provides a name of a volunteer lawyer, it is making no assurances about the skills or qualifications of the lawyer or about any malpractice coverage for the lawyer, and the volunteer lawyer is always permitted to decline the representation.

B. *Standards for Professionalism and Civility Among Attorneys*

Judge Guilford's court adopts the ***Orange County Bar Association Standards for Professionalism and Civility Among Attorneys***, which are available at the court's webpage, *http://www.cacd.uscourts.gov/CACD/JudgeReq.nsf/* and the Bar Association's webpage, *http://www.ocbar.org/About/Conduct.aspx*.

II. Judge Guilford's Case Management Orders

A. Order Regarding Early Meeting of Parties and Scheduling Conference

IN THE UNITED STATES DISTICT COURT
FOR THE CENTRAL DISTRICT OF CALIFORNIA

Plaintiff(s),	Case No. ________________
v.	**ORDER RE EARLY MEETING OF PARTIES AND SCHEDULING CONFERENCE**
Defendant(s).	Scheduling Conference: _____ at 9:00 a.m. (Fed. R. Civ. P. 16(b) and 26(f))

Welcome to the Court of Judge Andrew J. Guilford. The responsibility for the progress of Federal Court litigation is upon both the attorneys and the Court. Counsel are ordered to be completely familiar with the Federal Rules of Civil Procedure, the Local Rules of the Central District of California, and the FAQ's about Judges' Procedures and Schedules posted by these Chambers on the Central District website at http://www.cacd.uscourts.gov. Counsel are also ordered to keep the Court informed concerning the status of this case, "to secure the just, speedy, and inexpensive determination of every action" (F.R. Civ. P. 1).

1. Early Meeting of Parties. IT IS ORDERED that, as provided in Fed. R. Civ. P. 26(f), the parties shall meet at least 21 days before the Scheduling Conference, and report on the meeting in writing to the Court within 14 days after the meeting. In all cases, the report SHALL STATE THE PROPOSED DATE AND LENGTH OF THE TRIAL, and whether it will be a jury or non-jury trial. Failure to comply with this Order may result in sanctions.

2. Scheduling Conference. IT IS FURTHER ORDERED that this case is set for a Scheduling Conference under Fed. R. Civ. P. 16(b) on the date and time stated in the caption of this Order, in Courtroom 10D of the United States Courthouse, 411 West Fourth Street, Santa Ana, California. Counsel shall appear at the Scheduling Conference and at all pretrial meetings fully informed concerning the facts of the case and shall be the attorney who will be in charge of the trial, unless good cause is shown for the appearance of other counsel or for a telephonic appearance. If there is a first appearance by any party after the date of this Order, counsel for Plaintiff shall give a copy of this Order to that party.

IT IS SO ORDERED.

Dated: ________________

____
ANDREW J. GUILFORD
United States District Judge

B. Scheduling Order Specifying Procedures

IN THE UNITED STATES DISTICT COURT
FOR THE CENTRAL DISTRICT OF CALIFORNIA

Plaintiff(s),	) Case No. ______________
v.	)
Defendant(s).	) **SCHEDULING ORDER SPECIFYING PROCEDURES**
______________________________	)

1. Discovery Cut-Off: ___________
2. Final Pretrial Conference:__ at 8:30 a.m.
3. Trial:____________ at 9:00 a.m.

With this Scheduling Order Specifying Procedures, the Court orders the following concerning the dates and procedures in this case. Counsel are ordered to be completely familiar with the Federal Rules of Civil Procedure, the Local Rules of the Central District of California, and the FAQ's about Judges' Procedures and Schedules posted by these Chambers on the Central District website at http://www.cacd.uscourts.gov. If there is a first appearance by any party after the date of this Order, Plaintiff counsel shall give notice of this Order to that party.

1. Discovery. The Court sets a discovery cutoff on the date stated in the caption of this Order. The following discovery schedule shall apply.

1.1 Depositions. All depositions shall occur on or before the discovery cutoff date. A deposition which was started on or before the discovery cutoff date may continue beyond the cutoff date, if reasonably necessary for completion.

1.2 Other Discovery. All interrogatories, requests for admission, requests for production, or the like, shall be served at least forty-five days before the discovery cutoff date. The Court will not approve stipulations between counsel which permit discovery responses to be served after the cutoff date except in unusual circumstances and upon a showing of good cause.

1.3 Discovery Motions. The Magistrate Judge assigned to this case shall hear all discovery motions. Discovery motions shall be filed and served as soon as possible and never later than 30 days after the discovery cutoff date. **The parties are ordered to strictly comply with the requirements of all Local Rules at Local Rule 37 *et seq.* in preparing and filing Discovery Motions**. The Court expects counsel to resolve most discovery problems among themselves in a courteous, reasonable, and professional manner. Frequent resort to the Court for guidance in discovery is generally unnecessary.

1.4 Expert Discovery. The discovery cutoff provisions in this Order include expert discovery, unless otherwise ordered by the Court. Unless the parties otherwise stipulate in writing and obtain the Court's approval, the Court orders the sequence of disclosures as provided by Fed. R. Civ. P. 26(a)(2)(C), except that the initial disclosure shall occur at least 120 (not 90) days before trial, and if an expert is identified under Fed. R. Civ. P. 26(a)(2)(C)(ii), any deposition of such expert shall occur as soon as reasonably possible, but may occur after the discovery cutoff date.

2. Final Pretrial Conference. The Court sets a Final Pretrial Conference under Fed. R. Civ. P. 16 on the date stated in the caption of this Order. **The parties are ordered to strictly comply with the requirements of all Local Rules at Local Rule 16 *et seq.*** The proposed

Final Pretrial Conference Order shall be in the format set forth in Appendix A to the Local Rules, and state the settlement procedure that was followed.

3. Joinder and Amendment Motions. Absent exceptional circumstances, any motion to join another party or to amend a pleading shall be filed and served within 60 days after the date of this Order and noticed for a hearing occurring within 90 days after the date of this Order.

4. Summary Judgment or Partial Summary Judgment Motions. Such motions shall be noticed for a hearing occurring not less than 25 days before the Final Pretrial Conference, unless otherwise allowed by the Court.

5. Settlement. In every case, if the parties and attorneys are unable to resolve the matter on their own, the Court requires that there be a settlement conference before an independent settlement officer, to be conducted before the Final Pretrial Conference. Counsel may agree on an appropriate procedure, such as a settlement conference with a magistrate judge, retired judge, or attorney, or similar alternative devised by counsel.

6. Trials. The Court sets a trial date on the date stated in the caption of this Order. The following procedures shall apply.

6.1 In limine motions (jury trials). Any motion in limine shall be filed and served not later than ten court days before the Final Pretrial Conference, and any opposition shall be filed and served five court days before the Final Pretrial Conference. Motions in limine are most proper when directed to prevent even the improper mention of a highly sensitive issue, or to save expense by determining whether a witness will be allowed to testify, or to allow a thorough review of a significant and difficult evidentiary issue. Most motions in limine are best left for rulings in the context of the trial.

6.2 Voir dire questions (jury trials). The Court will question jurors concerning standard topics. Any special questions or topics requested to be put to prospective jurors by the Court on voir dire shall be filed and served at least seven days before trial.

6.3 Jury instructions (jury trials). The Court prefers to use instructions from the Manual of Model Jury Instructions for the Ninth Circuit, following all the Local Rules at Local Rule 51 *et seq*. The Court usually gives the following preliminary instructions to the jury before opening statement: 1.1B, 1.3, 1.6, 1.7, 1.8, 1.9, 1.10, 1.11, 1.12, 1.13, 1.14, 1.18, and 1.19. At least seven days before trial, counsel shall file with the Court the following:

6.3.1 A joint set of jury instructions on which there is agreement. (Plaintiff counsel has the burden of preparing the joint set of jury instructions.)

6.3.2 Each party's proposed jury instructions which are objected to by any other party, accompanied by points and authorities in support of those instructions.

6.3.3 Each party's points and authorities supporting their objections to another party's proposed jury instructions.

6.4 Special verdict in jury trials. If any special forms of verdict are requested, they shall be prepared, filed, and served under Local Rules 49-1 and 49-2.

6.5 Exhibits. Unless an electronic alternative is approved by the Court, counsel shall prepare an original set and a copy set of trial exhibits in 3-ring binders, each tabbed down the right side with the exhibit number, prefaced by an index of each exhibit, following Local Rule 26 3 in numbering exhibits. If voluminous exhibits will be delivered to the Court's loading dock, the delivery should be coordinated before trial with the Courtroom Deputy Clerk at AG_chambers@cacd.uscourts.gov.

6.6 Submission at trial. Counsel shall submit the following to the Courtroom Deputy Clerk on the first day of trial:

6.6.1 The original exhibits binder set with the Court's exhibit tags attached and filled out showing the case number, case name, and exhibit number. (Exhibit tags must be attached so as not to cover exhibit text.)

6.6.2 The copy exhibit binder set for use by the Judge.

6.6.3 Three copies of exhibit lists, showing which exhibits may be received into evidence without objection.

6.6.4 Three copies of witness lists with estimates of the total time on the stand for each witness..

6.6.5 A transcript or copy of any deposition or other discovery response to be read to the jury, following Local Rule 16-2.7.

6.6.6 (Jury trials) A very short description of the case approved by all parties to be read to the jury at the beginning of the trial. As an alternative, the Court may allow the parties to briefly describe the case to the jury.

6.7 Trial times. Trial times generally are 9:00 a.m. to 12:00 p.m. and 1:30 p.m. to 4:30 p.m. Tuesday through Thursday, and 8:00 a.m. to 1:30 p.m. on Friday.

6.8 Witnesses. If counsel runs out of witnesses, the Court may deem that counsel has rested. Counsel must keep opposing counsel informed about upcoming witnesses, always informing opposing counsel of the witness for the next court day before 5:00 p.m. of the previous court day. Only one attorney per party shall examine and defend a witness.

6.9 Admission of Exhibits. When counsel thinks an exhibit is admissible and should be admitted, counsel should move its admission.

6.10 Objections. Objections should be brief, stating only, "Objection" followed by the specific legal ground such as "Hearsay" or "403."

6.11 Decorum. Trials will be conducted in a dignified manner, following the traditional rules of trial decorum. Show respect for the trial process by being on time. Do not address witnesses over age 14 by their first names. Most examination and argument should be done at the lectern. The Court recognizes that at times it is necessary to enter the well in this courtroom.

IT IS SO ORDERED.

Dated: ________________

____

ANDREW J. GUILFORD
United States District Judge

Hon. Philip S. Gutierrez

District Judge

Chambers Information

U.S. District Court, Central District of California
Courtroom 880
255 East Temple Street
Los Angeles, CA 90012

Scheduling Information

Courtroom Deputy: (213) 894-8899

Civil Law and Motion	Mondays at 1:30 p.m.
Criminal Law and Motion	Mondays at 10:00 a.m.

Biographical Information

Born 1959 in Los Angeles, CA

Federal Judicial Service:

-Judge, U. S. District Court, Central District of California
-Nominated by George W. Bush on January 9, 2007, to a seat vacated by Terry J. Hatter, Jr.; Confirmed by the Senate on January 30, 2007, and received commission on February 16, 2007.

Education:

-University of Notre Dame, B.A., 1981
-UCLA School of Law, J.D., 1984

Professional Career:

-Private Practice, California, 1986-1997
-Judge, Los Angeles County Superior Court, California, 1997-2007

I. Judge Gutierrez's Procedures and Practices

A. *Procedures and Schedules*

1. Civil motions are heard on Mondays at 1:30 p.m.

   Criminal motions are heard on Mondays at 10:00 a.m.

   Motion dates are not reserved accordingly, parties are instructed to review the Closed Motion Dates Calendar (see above) before e-filing a motion.

   If Monday is a holiday, please select the next available **Monday**.

2. Discovery motions are to be calendared before the assigned magistrate judge. Discovery proposed stipulations and protective orders are to be properly referenced before the assigned magistrate judge.

3. Please see the attached Initial Standing Order for detailed procedures regarding cases assigned to Judge Gutierrez.

4. Civil and criminal trials are held Tuesday through Friday from 9:00 a.m. to 4:30 p.m. Motions In Limine are heard on the first day of trial at 9:00 a.m. Please review the attached orders regarding court or jury trials. These orders contain information regarding trial pleadings.

5. Pursuant to the General Order, **mandatory chambers copies** of all criminal and civil electronically filed documents should be delivered directly to Courtroom 880 no later than the **following business day before Noon**. The mandatory chamber copies shall be blue-backed and shall include the e-filing confirmation sheet and/or the e-filing header at the top of each document. Counsel are advised that failure to comply may result in the imposition of sanctions. In addition, all proposed orders should be electronically mailed in WordPerfect or Microsoft Word to the Judge's generic e-mail address at psg_chambers@cacd.uscourts.gov.

6. Inquiries regarding the status on a motion, stipulation, or proposed order are not handled telephonically. Counsel may review the Court's docket via PACER, in order to obtain updated case information. Parties may register for access to PACER by visiting the court's website.

7. Ex Parte applications are only for extraordinary relief. Sanctions may be imposed for misuse of Ex Parte applications. See Mission Power Engineering Co. v. Continental Casualty Co., 883 F. Supp. 488 (C.D. Cal. 1995). Ex Parte applications shall be electronically filed, along with a declaration indicating the necessity of the Ex Parte, stating that opposing counsel has been notified and/or whether there is an opposition to the application. Ex Parte applications are typically considered on the papers. Therefore, if the Court finds that a hearing is necessary, then the parties shall be notified by minute order. Opposition to an Ex Parte application shall be filed no later than 3:00 p.m. on the first business day following service of the application. Ex Parte applications and oppositions shall be served by personal delivery or facsimile. A mandatory chambers copy of the application or opposition shall be delivered directly to Courtroom 880. Counsel shall be notified by minute order of the Court's ruling.

8. Counsel shall not contact the Judge's chambers' staff for any reason. All inquiries shall be directed to the court clerk.

9. Calendar conflicts should be immediately brought to the attention of the court clerk

by telephone. Please include the name of the judge and the conflicting time.

10. Counsel shall electronically file a stipulation and order if they are seeking a hearing continuance or an extension of time. A mandatory chambers copy of the application shall be delivered directly to chambers no later than the following business day before Noon, and the proposed orders should be electronically mailed in WordPerfect or Microsoft Word to the Judge's generic e-mail address at psg_chambers@cacd.uscourts.gov.

11. Telephonic appearances and/or telephonic conferences are not permitted by the Court.

12. Electronic equipment is not allowed into the courtroom, without first obtaining the Court's approval by stipulation and proposed order.

13. To obtain a transcript of any reported proceeding, please contact the court reporter by reviewing the hearing date on the docket or by visiting the court's web site and clicking General Information > Court Reporter Schedule > by Date. Once you have determined the correct court reporter for the desired hearing, click on Phone List > Official Court Reporters or Contract Court Reporter Panel.

14. Law Clerk and Extern Applicants may submit applications to District Judge Philip S. Gutierrez, United States District Court, Room 870 at 255 East Temple Street, Los Angeles, California 90012. Please include a cover letter, resume, transcript, and writing sample. Letters of recommendation are to be directed to this address.

15. To obtain the services of a court-certified interpreter on a civil case, please visit the Court's website and click General Information > Interpreters.

16. If counsel has received a "Notice to Parties of Court-Directed ADR Program" (form ADR-08), the Court will presumptively refer the case to the Court Mediation Panel or to private mediation at the time of the initial scheduling conference. See General order 11-10, § 5.1. Counsel are directed to furnish and discuss this Notice with their clients in preparation for the parties' Fed.R.Civ.P. 26(f) conference. Counsel should include their shared or separate views regarding a preference for the Court Mediation Panel or private mediation, and when the mediation should occur, in the written report required by Fed.R.Civ.P. 26(f) and Civil L.R. 26-1. A settlement conference with a magistrate judge is generally not available for cases in the Court-Directed ADR Program. See Civil L.R.26-1(c). For information about the Court's ADR Program, please see General Order 11-10 which is located in the "General Orders" section on the home page and in the "ADR" page of the Court's website.

17. A copy of the Local Rules may be purchased at the following addresses:

- Los Angeles Daily Journal, 915 East First Street, Los Angeles, California 90012
- Metropolitan News, 210 South Spring Street, Los Angeles, California 90012
- West Publishing Company, 50 West Kellogg Boulevard, St. Paul, Minnesota 55164-9979

II. Judge Gutierrez's Case Management Orders

A. *Criminal Motion and Trial Order*

IN THE UNITED STATES DISTICT COURT
FOR THE CENTRAL DISTRICT OF CALIFORNIA

UNITED STATES OF AMERICA, Plaintiff, v. Defendant(s).	)))))	Case No. ______________ **CRIMINAL MOTION AND TRIAL ORDER**

This matter is set for trial before the Honorable Philip S. Gutierrez, United States District Judge, Courtroom 880, Roybal Federal Building, 255 E. Temple St., Los Angeles California, 90012.

A. PRETRIAL AND TRIAL DATES AND MOTIONS

1. Pretrial motions shall be filed on or before __________ (Monday preceding four weeks before status conference/motion hearing). Motions expected to take more than one hour of court time must include a time estimate beneath the hearing date on the face page of the motion.

Oppositions (or notices of non-opposition) shall be filed on ___________. (Monday preceding three weeks before status conference/motion hearing.)

Replies (optional) shall be filed on _____________. (Monday before status conference/motion hearing).

Local Rule 7-12 will apply to papers not timely filed by a party.

Adherence to these timing requirements is essential to chambers' preparation of motion matters.

2. Memoranda of Points and Authorities in support of or in opposition to motions shall not exceed 25 pages. Replies shall not exceed 12 pages. Only in rare instances and for good cause shown will the Court grant an application to extend these page limitations. No supplemental brief shall be filed without prior leave of court. **Typeface shall comply with Local Rule 11-3.1.1. (Civil). NOTE: If Times Roman font is used, the size must be no less than 14; if Courier is used, the size must be no less than 12.** Footnotes shall be in typeface no less than one size smaller than text size and shall be used sparingly.

3. Filings that do not conform to the Local Rules and this Order may not be considered.

4. Before filing any motion for discovery, a party shall consult with opposing counsel to ascertain whether the requested discovery will be provided. All discovery motions shall state with particularity what is requested, the basis for the request, whether the discovery has been requested from opposing counsel, and whether the discovery has been declined, in whole or in part. Motions made without prior consultation with opposing counsel or that fail to include the above information may not be heard.

5. **A Status Conference/Motions Hearing is set for _______ at 10:00 a.m.**

6. **Trial is set for Tuesday, ______________ at 9:00 a.m.**

7. All documents shall be e-filed and served on opposing counsel at approximately the same time.

8. Mandatory chambers copies of all filed motions, oppositions or notice of non-opposition, and replies must be delivered to Judge Gutierrez' chambers on the seventh floor not later than 12:00 noon the following business day. For security reasons, mandatory chambers copies should be removed from envelopes or folders before placing them on the table.

9. All Counsel are to list e-mail addresses, facsimile transmission numbers, along with street address (no Post Office box numbers) and telephone numbers, on all papers submitted to the Court.

B. DISCOVERY & NOTICE

Counsel shall comply promptly with discovery and notice pursuant to Rules 12, 12.1, 12.2, 12.3, 12.4, 15, and 16 of the Federal Rules of Criminal Procedure. On government counsel's discovery of any evidence within the scope of *Brady v. Maryland*, 373 U.S. 83 (1963), such evidence shall be produced forthwith to counsel for the defendant. Counsel for the government shall also disclose to counsel for defendant the existence or non-existence of: (1) evidence obtained by electronic surveillance; and (2) testimony by a government informer.

C. TRIAL REQUIREMENTS

1. **No later than one week before trial**, counsel for the government shall file with the Court:

a. *In camera* (under seal) all statements of all witnesses to be called by the Government in its case-in-chief;

b. A Trial Memorandum setting forth a factual summary of the government's case, a statement of the charges and the elements of each charge, an estimate of the length of the government's case in chief, including anticipated cross-examination, the names of witnesses the government intends to call, and a discussion of relevant legal and evidentiary issues as applied to the facts of the particular case. Counsel for the government shall attempt to obtain defense counsel's agreement to the factual summary, statement of the charges, time estimate for cross-examination of the government's witnesses, and legal and evidentiary issues.

2. Counsel shall arrive at the Courtroom no later than 8:30 a.m. on the first day of trial.

3. Counsel for the government shall present the courtroom deputy clerk (CRD) with the following documents on the first day of trial:

a. Three copies of the government's witness list;

b. Three copies of the government's exhibit list in the form specified in Local Rule 16-5 (Civil);

c. A bench book containing a copy of the indictment/ information, a copy of all exhibits that can be reproduced, and a copy of the witness list. Each exhibit shall be tabbed with the exhibit number for easy referral;

d. All of the government's exhibits, with official exhibit tags attached and bearing the same number shown on the exhibit list. Exhibit tags may be obtained from the receptionist in the Public Intake Section, located on the Main Street level of the courthouse at 312 North Spring Street, Room G-19. Exhibits shall be numbered 1, 2, 3, *etc.*, NOT 1.1, 1.2, *etc.* If a "blowup" is an enlargement of an existing exhibit, it shall be designated with the number of the original exhibit followed by an "A."

4. The Court orders that exhibits such as firearms, narcotics, etc., remain in the custody of a law enforcement agent during the pendency of the trial. It shall be the responsibility of the agent to produce any such items for court, secure them at night and guard them at all times while in the courtroom.

5. Defense counsel need not deliver defense exhibits to the CRD on the first day of trial; however, defense counsel is responsible for affixing completed exhibit tags with the case name and case number to all exhibits to be used in Defendant's case.

6. Defense counsel shall provide a three ring binder, if possible, tabbed with numbers to correspond to the exhibits counsel expects to introduce. Defense counsel shall provide the Court with a copy of defense exhibits as they are introduced during trial.

7. Defense counsel shall provide the CRD and the court reporter with the defense witness list and defense exhibit list.

8. A copy of the exhibit list with all **admitted exhibits** will be given to the jury during deliberations. Government and defense counsel shall review and approve the exhibit list with the CRD before the list is given to the jury.

9. If any counsel wishes to arrange for the use of additional equipment, such as video monitors, overhead projectors, etc., counsel shall notify the CRD no later than 4:00 p.m. at least one week before trial so that the necessary arrangements may be made.

10. Counsel shall not attempt to display or use any charts or enlargements of exhibits unless all counsel have agreed to their use or objections have been heard and a ruling has been made by the Court.

11. On the day of jury selection, trial will begin at 9:00 a.m. Counsel will appear at 8:30 a.m. Thereafter, trial days are Tuesday through Friday, 9:00 a.m. to 4:30 p.m., with two fifteen-minute breaks during the morning and afternoon sessions. If counsel contemplate that this schedule will be problematic due to the unavailability of witnesses, counsel should provide details to the Court at the Status Conference.

12. Before trial begins, the Court will give counsel an opportunity to discuss administrative matters and anticipated procedural or legal issues. Before trial begins, and as soon as the information becomes available to counsel, counsel should advise the court of any concerns or accommodations that are requested for parties or witnesses. During trial, if there are any matters to be discussed outside the presence of the jury, counsel shall advise the CRD of the request. The Court discourages sidebars during trial.

13. On the day of jury selection, the Court reserves the time from 8:30 a.m. to 9:00 a.m. to handle legal and administrative matters. Jury selection will commence promptly at 9:00 a.m. or as soon as jurors are available. Thereafter, legal and administrative matters shall be addressed between 8:30 a.m. and 9:00 a.m. All counsel are urged to anticipate matters that may need to be addressed outside of the presence of the jury and to raise them during this period, during breaks, or at the end of the day. The Court does not make jurors wait while counsel discuss matters that should have been addressed previously. Counsel are urged to consider any unusual substantive or evidentiary issues that may arise, and to advise the Court of such issues. Short briefs addressing such disputed issues are welcome.

14. Should counsel for the government wish to order transcripts, they shall provide agency authorization to the court reporter at the time the request is made.

D. JURY INSTRUCTIONS, VERDICT FORMS & QUESTIONNAIRES

1. **No later than one week before trial**, counsel shall submit both general and substantive jury instructions in the form described below. If possible, all instructions should be taken from the *Manual of Model Criminal Jury Instructions for the Ninth Circuit* (West Publishing, current edition). In those cases where a special verdict is requested, counsel shall submit a proposed verdict form with the jury instructions. Counsel shall submit a compact disc, compatible with Word Perfect 9.0 or 11.0, containing the proposed instructions and a "clean" set of such instructions, as set forth below.

2. The parties must submit JOINT jury instructions and a JOINT proposed verdict form (if a special verdict is requested). In order to produce these joint instructions, the parties shall meet and confer sufficiently in advance of the required submission date, with the goal of agreeing on instructions and verdict forms. Where the parties cannot agree, disputed instructions shall be submitted one week before trial as follows: 1) JOINT jury instructions (those instructions agreed to by all parties), and 2) DISPUTED jury instructions (those instructions propounded by a party to which another party objects). On a separate page following each disputed jury instruction, the party opposing the instruction shall briefly state the basis for the objection, any authority in support thereof and, if applicable, an alternative instruction. On the following page, the party proposing the disputed instruction shall briefly state its response to the objection, and any authority in support of the instruction. Each requested jury instruction shall be numbered and set forth in full on a separate page, citing the authority or source of the requested instruction.

3. Jury instructions should be modified as necessary to fit the facts of the case (*e.g.*, inserting names of defendant(s) to whom instruction applies). Where language appears in brackets in the model instruction, counsel shall select the appropriate text and eliminate the inapplicable bracketed text. Where no applicable Ninth Circuit model instruction is available, counsel are directed to use the instructions from O'Malley, Grenig & Lee (formerly Devitt, *et al.*), *Federal Jury Practice and Instructions* (West Publishing Co., current edition).

4. An index page shall accompany all jury instructions submitted to the Court. The index page shall indicate the following:

    a. The number of the instruction;
    b. A brief title of the instruction;
    c. The source of the instruction; and
    d. The page number of the instruction.

EXAMPLE:

Number	Title	Source	Page Number
#1	Conspiracy-Elements	9th Cir.8.5.1	1

5. One or more copies of the instructions will be given to the jury during deliberations. Accordingly, on the diskette submitted with jury instructions, counsel shall include a "clean" set of all instructions, containing only the text of each instruction, set forth in full on each page, with the caption "Court's Instruction No. ____" (eliminating titles, supporting authority, indication of party proposing, etc.)

6. If counsel wish to submit a written questionnaire to prospective jurors, a motion shall be made in writing, with the proposed questionnaire attached, no later than eight weeks before the trial date. The Court does not routinely use questionnaires. Counsel should attempt to discuss this issue and reach a proposed agreement before submitting the motion to the Court.

7. At least one week before trial, each counsel must file with the CRD and serve on opposing counsel any proposed questions to be asked of prospective jurors. Counsel shall also file a Joint Statement of the Case which the Court will read to prospective jurors prior to the commencement of voir dire. The statement shall not exceed one page.

E. <u>INSTRUCTIONS GOVERNING PROCEDURE DURING TRIAL</u>

1. Counsel shall not refer to any witness – including a client – over 14 years of age by his/her first name during trial.

2. Counsel shall not discuss the law or argue the case in opening statements.

3. Counsel shall not use objections for the purpose of making a speech, recapitulating testimony, or attempting to guide the witness. When objecting, counsel shall stand, state only the legal ground of the objection, *e.g.*, hearsay, irrelevant, *etc.* Counsel shall not argue an objection before the jury. Requests to approach sidebar to further argue an objection should be made sparingly, and may not be granted.

4. Counsel shall not make facial expressions, nod, or shake their heads, comment or otherwise exhibit in any way any agreement, disagreement or other opinion or belief concerning the testimony of a witness. Counsel shall admonish their clients and witnesses not to engage in such conduct.

5. Counsel should not talk to jurors at all, and should not talk to cocounsel, opposing counsel, witnesses or clients where the conversation can be overheard by jurors. Each counsel should admonish counsel's own clients and witnesses to avoid such conduct.

6. Counsel shall question witnesses from the lectern. Counsel shall not approach the witness box or enter the well without the Court's permission, and shall return to the lectern when counsel's purpose has been accomplished.

7. Counsel should speak clearly when questioning witnesses, making objections, etc.

8. No document shall be placed before a witness unless a copy has been provided to the Court. Counsel may consider such devices as overhead projectors, jury notebooks for admitted exhibits, or enlargements of important exhibits. The Court has an Elmo and other equipment available for use during trial. Call the CRD if you wish to visit when the Court is not in session to practice using the equipment. The Court does not permit exhibits to be "published" by passing them

up and down the jury box. Exhibits may be displayed using the screen in the courtroom.

9. Water will be provided at counsel table. Water cups are not to be brought to the lectern. No other beverages are permitted in the courtroom. Food is not permitted in the courtroom.

10. Counsel shall rise when addressing the Court. In jury trials, counsel and the defendant shall rise when the jury enters or leaves the courtroom. [Special procedures or exceptions may apply when the defendant is in custody or restrained.]

11. In trial, all remarks shall be addressed to the Court. Counsel shall not directly address the CRD, the court reporter or opposing counsel. All requests for re-reading of questions or answers, or to have an exhibit placed in front of a witness, shall be addressed to the Court.

12. Counsel should not offer a stipulation without having conferred with opposing counsel and having reached an agreement. Any stipulation of fact will require

defendant's personal concurrence and shall be submitted to the Court in writing for approval. A proposed stipulation should be explained to defendant in advance.

13. While court is in session, counsel shall not leave counsel table to confer with investigators, secretaries, or witnesses unless permission is granted in advance.

14. When a party has more than one lawyer, only one lawyer may conduct the examination of a given witness, and only that same lawyer may handle objections during the testimony of that witness.

15. If a witness was on the stand at a recess or adjournment, counsel who called the witness shall ensure the witness is back on the stand and ready to proceed when court resumes.

16. Counsel are directed to have witnesses available throughout the court day. If no witnesses are available and there is more than a brief delay, the Court may deem counsel to have rested.

17. The Court attempts to cooperate with expert witnesses and other professionals, and will, except in extraordinary circumstances, accommodate them by permitting them to be called out of sequence. Counsel are urged to anticipate any such possibility and to discuss it with opposing counsel. If there is an objection, counsel shall confer with the Court in advance.

18. Counsel must notify the CRD in advance if any witness should be accommodated based on the Americans with Disabilities Act or for other reasons.

19. Counsel are advised to be on time, as the Court makes every effort to start promptly.

IT IS SO ORDERED.

Dated: ________________

____
PHILIP S. GUTIERREZ
United States District Judge

B. Order for Court Trial

IN THE UNITED STATES DISTICT COURT
FOR THE CENTRAL DISTRICT OF CALIFORNIA

	) Case No. ______________
Plaintiff(s),	) **ORDER FOR COURT TRIAL**
v.	) Pretrial Conference: ________ at 2:30 p.m.
Defendant(s).	) Trial Date: ___________ at 9:00 a.m.
______________________________	)

UNLESS OTHERWISE ORDERED BY THE COURT, THE FOLLOWING RULES SHALL APPLY:

SCHEDULING

1. In General

All motions to join other parties or to amend the pleadings shall be filed and served by the cut-off date specified in the Scheduling Order.

2. Motions for Summary Judgment or Partial Summary Judgment

Motions for summary judgment or partial summary judgment shall be filed as soon as practical, however, in no event later than the motion cut-off date.

3. Discovery Cut-Off

The Court has established a cut-off date for discovery in this action. All discovery shall be complete by the discovery cut-off date specified in the Scheduling Order. **This is not the date by which discovery requests must be served; it is the date by which all discovery is to be completed.**

In an effort to provide further guidance to the parties, the Court notes the following:

a. Depositions

All depositions shall be scheduled to commence sufficiently in advance of the discovery cut-off date to permit their completion and to permit the deposing party enough time to bring any discovery motion concerning the deposition prior to the cut-off date.

b. Written Discovery

All interrogatories, requests for production of documents, and requests for admission shall be served sufficiently in advance of the discovery cut-off date to permit the discovering party enough time to challenge (via motion practice) responses deemed to be deficient.

c. Discovery Motions

Whenever possible, the Court expects the parties to resolve discovery problems among themselves in a courteous, reasonable, and professional manner. The Court expects that counsel will strictly adhere to the Civility and Professional Guidelines adopted by the United States District Court for the Central District of California in July 1995.

Discovery matters are referred to a United States Magistrate Judge. **Any motion challenging the adequacy of responses to discovery must be filed timely, and served and calendared sufficiently in advance of the discovery cut-off date to permit the responses to be obtained before that date, if the motion is granted.**

Consistent resort to the Court for guidance in discovery is unnecessary and will result in the appointment of a Special Master at the joint expense of the parties to resolve discovery disputes.

4. Mandatory Settlement Conference

Pursuant to Local Rule 16-15, the parties in every case must select a settlement procedure. The final meeting with the parties' settlement officer must take place no later than 45 days before the Final Pretrial Conference.

FINAL PRE-TRIAL CONFERENCE ("PTC")

This case has been placed on calendar for a Final Pre-Trial Conference pursuant to Fed. R. Civ. P. 16 and 26. Unless excused for good cause, each party appearing in this action shall be represented at the Final Pre-Trial Conference, and all pre-trial meetings of counsel, by the attorney who is to have charge of the conduct of the trial on behalf of such party.

STRICT COMPLIANCE WITH THE REQUIREMENT OF FED. R. CIV. P. 26 AND LOCAL RULES ARE REQUIRED BY THE COURT. Therefore, carefully prepared Memoranda of Contentions of Fact and Law, a Joint Witness List, and Joint Exhibit List shall be submitted to the Court. The Joint Witness List shall contain a brief statement of the testimony for each witness, **what makes the testimony unique** from any other witness testimony, and the time estimate for such testimony. The Joint Exhibit List shall contain any objections to authenticity and/or admissibility to the exhibit(s) and the reasons for the objections. The Memoranda of Contentions of Fact and Law, Witness List, and Exhibit List are due twenty-one (21) days before the Final Pre-Trial Conference.

FINAL PRETRIAL CONFERENCE ORDER ("PTCO")

The proposed PTCO shall be lodged seven calendar days before the PTC. Adherence to this time requirement is necessary for in-chambers preparation of the matter. The form of the proposed PTCO shall comply with Appendix A to the Local Rules and the following:

1. Place in "all caps" and in "bold" the separately numbered headings for each category in the PTCO (*e.g.*, **"1. THE PARTIES"** or **"7. CLAIMS AND DEFENSES OF THE PARTIES"**).

2. Include a table of contents at the beginning.

3. In specifying the surviving pleadings under section 1, state which claims or counterclaims have been dismissed or abandoned, e.g., "Plaintiff's second cause of action for breach of fiduciary duty has been dismissed." Also, in multiple party cases where not all claims or counterclaims will be prosecuted against all remaining parties on the opposing side, please specify to which party each claim or counterclaim is directed.

4. In specifying the parties' claims and defenses under section 7, each party shall closely follow the examples set forth in Appendix A of the Local Rules.

5. In drafting the PTCO, the court also expects that the parties will attempt to agree on and set forth as many non-contested facts as possible. The court will usually read the uncontested facts to the jury at the start of trial. A carefully drafted and comprehensively stated stipulation of facts will reduce the length of trial and increase jury understanding of the case.

6. In drafting the factual issues in dispute for the PTCO, the parties should attempt to state issues in ultimate fact form, not in the form of evidentiary fact issues. The issues of fact should track the elements of a claim or defense on which the jury will be required to make findings.

7. Issues of law should state legal issues on which the court will be required to rule during the trial and should not list ultimate fact issues to be submitted to the trier of fact.

TRIAL PREPARATION FOR COURT TRIAL – MOTIONS, FINDINGS OF FACT AND EXHIBITS

1. Motions *in Limine*

All motions *in limine* must be filed and served a minimum of forty-five (45) days prior to the scheduled trial date. Each motion should be separately filed and numbered. All opposition documents must be filed and served at least twenty-five (25) days prior to the scheduled trial date. All reply documents must be filed and served at least ten (10) days prior to the scheduled trial date.

All motions *in limine* will be ruled upon on or before the scheduled trial date.

2. Findings of Fact and Conclusion of Law

For a non-jury trial, the parties shall lodge their proposed findings of fact and conclusions of law not later than five (5) days before trial. The parties shall deliver to chambers a copy of these findings on disk in WordPerfect format. Refer to Local Rule 52-1.

3. Narrative Statements

The judge may order that the direct testimony of a witness be presented by written narrative statement subject to the witness's cross-examination at the trial.

Such written, direct testimony shall be adopted by the witness orally in open court, unless such requirement is waived. Refer to Local Rule 43-1.

4. Trial Exhibits

Counsel are to prepare their exhibits for presentation at the trial by placing them in binders which are indexed by exhibit number with tabs or dividers on the right side. Counsel shall submit to the Court an original and one copy of the binders. The exhibits shall be in a three-ring binder labeled on the spine portion of the binder as to the volume number and contain an index of each exhibit included in the volume. Exhibits must be numbered in accordance with Fed. R. Civ. P. 16, 26 and the Local Rules.

Exhibit list shall indicate which exhibits are objected to, the reason for the objection, and the reason it is admissible. Failure to object will result in a waiver of objection.

The Court requires that the following be submitted to the Courtroom Deputy Clerk on the first day of trial:

- The original exhibits with the Court's exhibit tags shall be stapled to the front of the exhibit on the upper right-hand corner with the case number, case name, and exhibit number placed on each tag. Exhibit tags can be obtained from the Clerk's Office, Room G-8, 312 North Spring Street, Los Angeles, CA 90012.
- One bench book with a copy of each exhibit for use by the Court, tabbed with numbers as described above. (Court's exhibit tags not necessary.)
- Three (3) copies of exhibit lists.
- Three (3) copies of witness lists in the order in which the witness may be called to testify.
- All counsel are to meet not later than ten (10) days before trial and to stipulate so far as is possible as to foundation, waiver of the best evidence rule, and to those exhibits which may be received into evidence at the start of trial. The exhibits to be so received will be noted on the copies of the exhibit lists.
- Any items that have not been admitted into evidence and are left in the courtroom overnight without prior approval will be discarded.

DATED: ________________

____
PHILIP S. GUTIERREZ
United States District Judge

C. Order for Jury Trial

IN THE UNITED STATES DISTICT COURT
FOR THE CENTRAL DISTRICT OF CALIFORNIA

Plaintiff(s),	Case No. ______________
v.	**ORDER FOR JURY TRIAL**
Defendant(s).	Final Pretrial Conference: ___ at 2:30 p.m. Trial Date: ___ at 9:00 a.m.

UNLESS OTHERWISE ORDERED BY THE COURT, THE FOLLOWING RULES SHALL APPLY:

SCHEDULING

1. In General

All motions to join other parties or to amend the pleadings shall be filed and served by the cut-off date specified in the Scheduling Order.

2. Motions for Summary Judgment or Partial Summary Judgment

Motions for summary judgment or partial summary judgment shall be filed as soon as practical, however, in no event later than the motion cut-off date.

3. Discovery Cut-Off

The Court has established a cut-off date for discovery in this action. All discovery shall be complete by the discovery cut-off date specified in the Scheduling Order. **This is not the date by which discovery requests must be served; it is the date by which all discovery is to be completed.**

In an effort to provide further guidance to the parties, the Court notes the following:

a. Depositions

All depositions shall be scheduled to commence sufficiently in advance of the discovery cut-off date to permit their completion and to permit the deposing party enough time to bring any discovery motion concerning the deposition prior to the cut-off date.

b. Written Discovery

All interrogatories, requests for production of documents, and requests for admission shall be served sufficiently in advance of the discovery cut-off date to permit the discovering party enough time to challenge (via motion practice) responses deemed to be deficient.

c. Discovery Motions

Whenever possible, the Court expects the parties to resolve discovery problems among themselves in a courteous, reasonable, and professional manner. The Court expects that counsel will strictly adhere to the Civility and Professional Guidelines adopted by the United States District Court for the Central District of California in July 1995.

Discovery matters are referred to a United States Magistrate Judge. **Any motion challenging the adequacy of responses to discovery must be filed timely, and served and calendared sufficiently in advance of the discovery cut off date to permit the**

responses to be obtained before that date, if the motion is granted.

Consistent resort to the Court for guidance in discovery is unnecessary and will result in the appointment of a Special Master at the joint expense of the parties to resolve discovery disputes.

4. Mandatory Settlement Conference

Pursuant to Local Rule 16-15, the parties in every case must select a settlement procedure. The final meeting with the parties' settlement officer must take place no later than 45 days before the Final Pretrial Conference.

FINAL PRE-TRIAL CONFERENCE ("PTC")

This case has been placed on calendar for a Final Pre-Trial Conference pursuant to Fed. R. Civ. P. 16 and 26. Unless excused for good cause, each party appearing in this action shall be represented at the Final Pre-Trial Conference, and all pre-trial meetings of counsel, by the attorney who is to have charge of the conduct of the trial on behalf of such party.

STRICT COMPLIANCE WITH THE REQUIREMENT OF FED. R. CIV. P. 16, 26 AND LOCAL RULES ARE REQUIRED BY THE COURT. Therefore, carefully prepared Memoranda of Contentions of Fact and Law, a Joint Witness List, and Joint Exhibit List shall be submitted to the Court. The Joint Witness List shall contain a brief statement of the testimony for each witness, **what makes the testimony unique** from any other witness testimony, and the time estimate for such testimony. The Joint Exhibit List shall contain any objections to authenticity and/or admissibility to the exhibit(s) and the reasons for the objections.

The Memoranda of Contentions of Fact and Law, Witness List, and Exhibit List are due twenty-one (21) days before the Final Pre-Trial Conference.

FINAL PRETRIAL CONFERENCE ORDER ("PTCO")

The proposed PTCO shall be lodged seven calendar days before the PTC. Adherence to this time requirement is necessary for in-chambers preparation of the matter. The form of the proposed PTCO shall comply with Appendix A to the Local Rules and the following:

1. Place in "all caps" and in "bold" the separately numbered headings for each category in the PTCO (*e.g.*, **"1. THE PARTIES"** or "**7. CLAIMS AND DEFENSES OF THE PARTIES"**).

2. Include a table of contents at the beginning.

3. In specifying the surviving pleadings under section 1, state which claims or counterclaims have been dismissed or abandoned, *e.g.*, "Plaintiff's second cause of action for breach of fiduciary duty has been dismissed." Also, in multiple party cases where not all claims or counterclaims will be prosecuted against all remaining parties on the opposing side, please specify to which party each claim or counterclaim is directed.

4. In specifying the parties' claims and defenses under section 7, each party shall closely follow the examples set forth in Appendix A of the Local Rules.

5. In drafting the PTCO, the court also expects that the parties will attempt to agree on and set forth as many non-contested facts as possible. The court will usually read the uncontested facts to the jury at the start of trial. A carefully drafted and comprehensively stated stipulation of facts will reduce the length of trial and increase jury understanding of the case.

6. In drafting the factual issues in dispute for the PTCO, the parties should attempt to state issues in ultimate fact form, not in the form of evidentiary fact issues. The issues of fact should track the elements of a claim or defense on which the jury will be required to make findings.

7. Issues of law should state legal issues on which the court will be required to rule during the trial and should not list ultimate fact issues to be submitted to the trier of fact.

TRIAL PREPARATION FOR JURY TRIAL – MOTIONS, INSTRUCTIONS AND EXHIBITS

1. MOTIONS *IN LIMINE*

All motions *in limine* must be filed and served a minimum of forty-five (45) days prior to the scheduled trial date. Each motion should be separately filed and numbered. All opposition documents must be filed and served at least twenty-five (25) days prior to the scheduled trial date. All reply documents must be filed and served at least ten (10) days prior to the scheduled trial date.

All motions *in limine* will be ruled upon on or before the scheduled trial date.

2. JURY INSTRUCTIONS/SPECIAL VERDICT FORMS

Thirty-five (35) days before trial, plaintiff shall serve plaintiff's proposed jury instructions and special verdict forms on defendant. Twenty-eight (28) days before trial, defendant shall serve on plaintiff defendant's objections to plaintiff's instructions together with any additional instructions defendant intends to offer. Twenty-one (21) days before trial, plaintiff shall serve on defendant plaintiff's objections to defendant's instructions. Twenty-one (21) days before trial, counsel are ordered to meet and confer to attempt to come to agreement on the proposed jury instructions. The parties shall make every attempt to agree upon the jury instructions before submitting them to the Court. It is expected that counsel will agree on the substantial majority of jury instructions.

Sixteen (16) days before trial, counsel shall file with the Court a JOINT set of jury instructions on which there is agreement. Defendant's counsel has the burden of preparing the joint set of jury instructions. At the same time, each party shall file its proposed jury instructions which are objected to by any other party, accompanied by points and authorities in support of those instructions.

When the parties disagree on an instruction, the party opposing the instruction must attach a short statement (one to two paragraphs) supporting the objection, and the party submitting the instruction must attach a short reply supporting the instruction. Each statement should be on a separate page and should follow directly after the disputed instruction.

The parties ultimately must submit one document, or if the parties disagree over any proposed jury instructions, three documents. The three documents shall consist of: (1) a set of Joint Proposed Jury Instructions; (2) Plaintiff's Disputed Jury Instructions; and (3) Defendant's Disputed Jury Instructions. Any disputed Jury Instructions shall include the reasons supporting and opposing each disputed instruction in the format set forth in the previous paragraph.

The Court directs counsel to use the instructions from the *Manual of Model Jury Instructions for the Ninth Circuit* where applicable. Where California law is to be applied and the above instructions are not applicable, the Court prefers counsel to use the California Jury Instructions in CACI. If none of these sources is applicable, counsel are directed to use the instructions in Devitt, Blackmar and Wolff, *Federal Jury Practice and Instructions.*

Modifications of instructions from the foregoing sources (or any other form instructions) must specifically state the modification made to the original form instruction and the authority supporting the modification.

Each requested instruction shall be set forth in full; be on a separate page; be numbered; cover only one subject or principle of law; not repeat principles of law contained in any other requested instructions; and cite the authority for a source of the requested instruction. In addition to the foregoing, each party shall file with the Courtroom Deputy on the first day of trial a "clean set" of the aforesaid requested duplicate jury instructions in the following form: Each requested instruction shall be set forth in full; be on a separate page with the caption "COURT'S INSTRUCTION NUMBER"; cover only one subject or principle of law; and not repeat principles of law contained in any other requested instruction. The "clean set" shall not cite the authority for a source of the requested instruction. Counsel shall also provide the Court with a CD in WordPerfect format containing the proposed jury instructions.

An index page shall accompany all jury instructions submitted to the Court. The index page shall indicate the following:

- the number of the instruction;
- a brief title of the instruction;
- the source of the instruction and any relevant case citation; and
- the page number of the instruction.

EXAMPLE:

NO.	TITLE	SOURCE	PAGE NO.
5	Evidence for Limited Purpose	9th Cir. 1.5	9

During the trial and before argument, the Court will meet with counsel and settle the instructions. Strict adherence to time requirements is necessary for the Court to examine the submissions in advance so that there will be no delay in starting the jury trial. **Failure of counsel to strictly follow the provisions of this section may subject the non-complying party and/or its attorney to sanctions and SHALL CONSTITUTE A WAIVER OF JURY TRIAL in all civil cases.**

3. TRIAL EXHIBITS

Counsel are to prepare their exhibits for presentation at the trial by placing them in binders which are indexed by exhibit number with tabs or dividers on the right side. Counsel shall submit to the Court an original and one copy of the binders. The exhibits shall be in a three-ring binder labeled on the spine portion of the binder as to the volume number and contain an index of each exhibit included in the volume. Exhibits must be numbered in accordance with Fed. R. Civ. P. 16, 26 and the Local Rules.

Exhibit list shall indicate which exhibits are objected to, the reason for the objection, and the reason it is admissible. Failure to object will result in a waiver of objection.

The Court requires that the following be submitted to the Courtroom Deputy Clerk on the first day of trial:

- The original exhibits with the Court's exhibit tags shall be stapled to the front of the exhibit on the upper right-hand corner with the case number, case name, and exhibit number placed on each tag. Exhibit tags can be obtained from the Clerk's Office, Room G-8, 312 North Spring Street, Los Angeles, CA 90012.

- One bench book with a copy of each exhibit for use by the Court, tabbed with numbers as described above. (Court's exhibit tags not necessary.)
- Three (3) copies of exhibit lists.
- Three (3) copies of witness lists in the order in which the witness may be called to testify.
- Counsel are ordered to submit a short joint statement of the case seven (7) days before trial that the Court may read to the prospective panel.
- All counsel are to meet no later than ten (10) days before trial and to stipulate so far as is possible as to foundation, waiver of the best evidence rule, and to those exhibits which may be received into evidence at the start of trial. The exhibits to be so received will be noted on the copies of the exhibit lists.
- Counsel may, but need not, submit brief proposed voir dire questions for the jury seven (7) calendar days before the Pretrial Conference. The Court will conduct its own voir dire after considering any proposed voir dire submitted by counsel.
- Any items that have not been admitted into evidence and are left in the courtroom overnight without prior approval will be discarded.

DATED: ________________

____
PHILIP S. GUTIERREZ
United States District Judge

D. Standing Order Regarding Newly Assigned Cases

IN THE UNITED STATES DISTICT COURT
FOR THE CENTRAL DISTRICT OF CALIFORNIA

	)	Case No. _______________
Plaintiff(s),	)	
v.	)	**STANDING ORDER REGARDING**
Defendant(s).	)	**NEWLY ASSIGNED CASES**
______________________________	)	

READ THIS ORDER CAREFULLY. IT CONTROLS THIS CASE.

This action has been assigned to the calendar of Judge Philip S. Gutierrez. The responsibility for the progress of litigation in the Federal Courts falls not only upon the attorneys in the action, but upon the Court as well. "To secure the just, speedy, and inexpensive determination of every action," Fed.R.Civ.P. 1, all counsel are hereby ordered to familiarize themselves with the Fed.R.Civ.P., particularly Fed.R.Civ.P. 16, 26, the Local Rules of the Central District of California, this Court's Order for Jury Trial, and this Court's Order for Court Trial.[1]

UNLESS OTHERWISE ORDERED BY THE COURT, THE FOLLOWING RULES SHALL APPLY:

1. **Service of the Complaint.** The Plaintiff(s) shall promptly serve the Complaint in accordance with Fed. R. Civ. P. 4 and file the proofs of service pursuant to Local Rule. Any Defendant(s) not timely served shall be dismissed from the action without prejudice. Any "DOE" or fictitiously-named Defendant(s) who is not identified and served within 120 days after the case is filed shall be dismissed pursuant to Fed. R. Civ. P. 4(m).

2. **Removed Actions.** Any answers filed in state court must be refiled in this Court as a supplement to the petition. Any pending motions must be re-noticed in accordance with Local Rule. If an action is removed to this Court that contains a form pleading, i.e., a pleading in which boxes are checked, the party or parties utilizing the form pleading must file an appropriate pleading with this Court within thirty (30) days of receipt of the Notice of Removal. The appropriate pleading referred to must comply with the requirements of Fed. R. Civ. P. 7, 7.1, 8, 9, 10 and 11.

3. **Presence of Lead Counsel.** The attorney attending any proceeding before this Court, including all status and settlement conferences, must be the lead trial counsel.

4. Discovery. All discovery matters have been referred to a United States Magistrate Judge to hear all discovery disputes. (The Magistrate Judge's initials follow the Judge's initials next to the case number.) All documents must include the words "DISCOVERY MATTER" in the caption to ensure proper routing. Counsel are

---

[1] Copies of the Local Rules are available on our website at "http:\\www.cacd.uscourts.gov" or they may be purchased from one of the following:

Los Angeles Daily Journal	West Group	Metropolitan News
915 East 1st Street	610 Opperman Drive	210 South Spring Street
Los Angeles, CA 90012	P.O. Box 64526	Los Angeles, CA 90012
		St. Paul, MN 55164-0526

directed to contact the Magistrate Judge's Courtroom Deputy Clerk to schedule matters for hearing. Please do not deliver mandatory chambers copies of these papers to this Court.

The decision of the Magistrate Judge shall be final, subject to modification by the District court only where it has been shown that the Magistrate Judge's order is clearly erroneous or contrary to law. Any party may file and serve a motion for review and reconsideration before this Court. The moving party must file and serve the motion within ten (10) days of service of a written ruling or within ten (10) days of an oral ruling that the Magistrate Judge states will not be followed by a written ruling. The motion must specify which portions of the text are clearly erroneous or contrary to law, and the claim must be supported by points and authorities. Counsel shall deliver a conformed copy of the moving papers and responses to the Magistrate Judge's clerk at the time of filing.

5. **Motions - General Requirements**

   a. Time for Filing and Hearing Motions: Motions shall be filed in accordance with Local Rules 6 and 7. This Court hears motions on Mondays, beginning at 1:30 p.m. If the motion date selected is not available, the Court will issue a minute order striking the motion. (Counsel are advised to check the availability of a selected date *immediately* prior to filing the motion.) Opposition or reply papers due on a holiday must be filed the preceding Friday–not the following Tuesday–and must be hand-delivered or faxed to opposing counsel on that Friday. Professional courtesy dictates that moving parties should, whenever possible, avoid filing motions for which opposition papers will be due the Friday preceding a holiday. Such a filing is likely to cause a requested continuance to be granted.

      Adherence to the timing requirements is mandatory for Chambers' preparation of motion matters.

   b. Pre-filing Requirement: Counsel must comply with Local Rule 7-3, which requires counsel to engage in a pre-filing conference "to discuss thoroughly . . . the substance of the contemplated motion and any potential resolution." Counsel should discuss the issues to a sufficient degree that if a motion is still necessary, the briefing may be directed to those substantive issues requiring resolution by the Court. Counsel should resolve minor procedural or other non-substantive matters during the conference. The pro per status of one or more parties does not negate this requirement.

   c. Length and Format of Motion Papers: Memoranda of points and authorities in support of or in opposition to motions shall not exceed 25 pages. Replies shall not exceed 12 pages. Only in rare instances and for good cause shown will the Court grant an application to extend these page limitations. Pursuant to Local Rule, either a proportionally spaced or monospaced face may be used. A proportionally spaced face must be 14-point or larger, or as the Court may otherwise order. A monospaced face may not contain more than 10½ characters per inch. These typeface requirements apply to footnoted material.

   d. Citations to Case Law: Citations to case law must identify not only the case cited, but the specific page referenced.

e. Citations to Other Sources: Statutory references should identify with specificity the sections and subsections referenced (*e.g.*, Jurisdiction over this cause of action may appropriately be found in 47 U.S.C. § 33, which grants the district courts jurisdiction over all offenses of the Submarine Cable Act, whether the infraction occurred within the territorial waters of the United States or on board a vessel of the United States outside said waters). Statutory references that do not specifically indicate the appropriate section and subsection (*e.g.*, Plaintiffs allege conduct in violation of the Federal Electronic Communication Privacy Act, 18 U.S.C. § 2511, et seq.) are to be avoided. Citations to treatises, manuals, and other materials should include the volume, section, and pages being referenced.

f. Oral Argument: If the Court deems a matter appropriate for decision without oral argument, the Court will notify the parties in advance.

6. **Specific Motion Requirements**

a. Motions Pursuant to Rule 12: Many motions to dismiss or to strike can be avoided if the parties confer in good faith (as required under Local Rule 7-3), especially for perceived defects in a complaint, answer, or counterclaim that could be corrected by amendment. *See Chang v. Chen*, 80 F.3d 1293, 1296 (9th Cir. 1996) (where a motion to dismiss is granted, a district court should provide leave to amend unless it is clear that the complaint could not be saved by any amendment). Moreover, a party has the right to amend the complaint once as a matter of course within twenty-one (21) days of serving it or "if the pleading is one to which a responsive pleading is required, 21 days after service of a responsive pleading or 21 days after service of a motion under Rule 12(b), (e), or (f), whichever is greater." Fed. R. Civ. P. 15(a)(1). Even after a complaint has been amended or the time for amending it as a matter of course has run, the Federal Rules provide that leave to amend should be "freely given when justice so requires." Fed. R. Civ. P. 15(a). The Ninth Circuit requires that this policy favoring amendment be applied with "extreme liberality." *Morongo Band of Mission Indians v. Rose*, 893 F.2d 1074, 1079 (9th Cir. 1990).

These principles require that plaintiff's counsel carefully evaluate defendant's contentions as to the deficiencies in the complaint. In most instances the moving party should agree to any amendment that would cure the defect.

b. Motions to Amend: In addition to the requirements of Local Rule 15-1, all motions to amend pleadings shall: (1) state the effect of the amendment; (2) be serially numbered to differentiate the amendment from previous amendments; and (3) state the page and line number(s) and wording of any proposed change or addition of material.

The parties shall deliver to Chambers a "redlined" version of the proposed amended pleading indicating all additions and deletions of material. \

c. Summary Judgment Motions: Parties need not wait until the motion cutoff to bring motions for summary judgment or partial summary judgment. Moreover, the court expects that the party moving for summary judgment will strictly observe the timing requirements of the Local Rules and this Standing Order. A motion under Rule 56 must be filed at least forty-nine (49) days prior to the date on which the motion is noticed for hearing. The opposition is due not later than twenty-one (21) days before the date designated for the hearing of the motion, and the reply not later than fourteen (14) days before the date designated for the hearing of the motion. Because summary judgment motions are fact-dependent, parties should prepare papers in a fashion that will assist the court in absorbing the mass of facts (*e.g.*, generous use of tabs, tables of contents, headings, indices, etc.). The parties are to comply precisely with Local Rule 56-1 through 56-4.

No party may file more than one motion pursuant to Fed. R. Civ. P. 56, regardless of whether such motion is denominated as a motion for summary judgment or summary adjudication, without leave from the Court.

1. Statement of Undisputed Facts and Statement of Genuine Issues: The separate statement of undisputed facts shall be prepared in a two-column format. The left hand column sets forth the allegedly undisputed fact. The right hand column sets forth the evidence that supports the factual statement. The factual statements should be set forth in sequentially numbered paragraphs. Each paragraph should contain a narrowly focused statement of fact. Each numbered paragraph should address a single subject as concisely as possible.

   The opposing party's statement of genuine issues must be in two columns and track the movant's separate statement exactly as prepared. The left hand column must restate the allegedly undisputed fact, and the right hand column must state either that it is undisputed or disputed. The opposing party may dispute all or only a portion of the statement, but if disputing only a portion, it must clearly indicate what part is being disputed, followed by the opposing party's evidence controverting the fact. The court will not wade through a document to determine whether a fact really is in dispute. To demonstrate that a fact is disputed, the opposing party must briefly state why it disputes the moving party's asserted fact, cite to the relevant exhibit or other piece of evidence, and describe what it is in that exhibit or evidence that refutes the asserted fact. No legal argument should be set forth in this document.

   The opposing party may submit additional material facts that bear on or relate to the issues raised by the movant, which shall follow the format described above for the moving party's separate statement. These additional facts shall continue in sequentially numbered paragraphs and shall set forth in the right hand column the evidence that supports that statement.

2. Supporting Evidence: No party shall submit evidence other than the specific items of evidence or testimony necessary to support or controvert a proposed statement of undisputed fact. For example, entire deposition transcripts, entire sets of interrogatory responses, and documents that do not specifically support or controvert material in the separate statement shall not be submitted in support of opposition to a motion for summary judgment. The court will not consider such material.

Evidence submitted in support of or in opposition to a motion should be submitted either by way of stipulation or as exhibits to declarations sufficient to authenticate the proffered evidence, and should not be attached to the memorandum of points and authorities. The court will accept counsel's authentication of deposition transcripts, written discovery responses and the receipt of documents in discovery if the fact that the document was in the opponent's possession is of independent significance. Documentary evidence as to which there is no stipulation regarding foundation must be accompanied by the testimony, either by declaration or properly authenticated deposition transcript, of a witness who can establish authenticity.

3. Objections to Evidence: If a party disputes a fact based in whole or in part on an evidentiary objection, the ground of the objection, as indicated above, should be stated in a separate statement but not argued in that document.

7. **Proposed Orders.** Each party filing or opposing a motion or seeking the determination of any matter shall serve and lodge a proposed order setting forth the relief or action sought and a brief statement of the rationale for the decision with appropriate citations.

8. **Mandatory Chambers Copies.** Mandatory chambers copies of all filed motions, oppositions or notice of non-opposition, and replies must be delivered to Judge Gutierrez' chambers on the eighth floor not later than 12:00 noon the following business day. For security reasons, mandatory chambers copies should be removed from envelopes or folders before placing them on the table.

9. **Telephonic Hearings.** The Court does not permit appearances or arguments by way of telephone conference calls.

10. **Ex Parte Applications.** The Court considers ex parte applications on the papers and does not usually set these matters for hearing. If a hearing is necessary, the parties will be notified. Ex parte applications are solely for extraordinary relief and should be used with discretion. Sanctions may be imposed for misuse of ex parte applications. *See Mission Power Engineering Co. v. Continental Casualty Co.*, 883 F. Supp. 488 (C.D. Cal. 1995).

    Counsel's attention is directed to Local Rules. The moving party shall serve the opposing party by facsimile transmission and shall notify the opposition that opposing papers must be filed not later than 3:00 p.m. on the first business day following such facsimile service. If counsel does not intend to oppose an ex parte application, he or she must inform the Courtroom Deputy Clerk at (213) 894-8899.

11. **TROs and Injunctions.** Parties seeking emergency or provisional relief shall comply with Rule 65 and Local Rule 65. The Court will not rule on any application for such relief for at least twenty-four hours after the party subject to the requested order has been served, unless service is excused. Such party may file opposing or responding papers in the interim.

12. **Continuances.** This Court has a strong interest in keeping scheduled dates

certain. Changes in dates are disfavored. Trial dates set by the Court are firm and will rarely be changed. Therefore, a stipulation to continue the date of any matter before this Court **must** be supported by a sufficient basis that demonstrates good cause why the change in the date is essential. Without such compelling factual support, stipulations continuing dates set by this Court will not be approved. Counsel requesting a continuance must lodge a proposed stipulation and order including a **detailed** declaration of the grounds for the requested continuance or extension of time. Failure to comply with the Local Rules and this Order will result in rejection of the request without further notice to the parties. Proposed stipulations extending scheduling dates do not become effective unless and until this Court so orders. Counsel wishing to know whether a stipulation has been signed shall comply with the applicable Local Rule.

13. **Communications with Chambers.** Counsel shall not attempt to contact the Court or its staff by telephone or by any other ex parte means. Counsel may contact the Courtroom Deputy Clerk with appropriate inquiries only. Counsel shall not contact the Courtroom Deputy regarding status of ex parte application/ruling or stipulation/ruling. If counsel desires a conformed copy of any proposed order submitted to the Court, counsel shall provide an extra copy of the document, along with a self-addressed, stamped envelope. Counsel should list their facsimile transmission numbers along with their telephone numbers on all papers to facilitate communication with the Courtroom Deputy.

14. **Order Setting Scheduling Conference.** Pursuant to Fed. R. Civ. P. 16(b), the Court will issue an Order setting a Scheduling Conference as required by Fed. R. Civ. P. 26 and the Local Rules of this Court. Strict compliance with Fed. R. Civ. P. 16 and 26 is required.

15. **Alternative Dispute Resolution (ADR).** This Court participates in the Court-Directed ADR Program. If counsel have received a Notice to Parties of Court-Directed ADR Program (ADR-08), the case will be presumptively referred to the Court Mediation Panel or to private mediation at the time of the initial scheduling conference. *See* General Order 11-10, § 5.1. Counsel should include their shared or separate views regarding a preference for the Court Mediation Panel or private mediation, and when the mediation should occur, in the written report required by Fed.R.Civ.P. 26(f) and Civil L.R. 26-1. This Court generally does not refer settlement conferences to magistrate judges. For information about the Court's ADR Program, the Mediation Panel, and mediator profiles, visit the "ADR" page of the Court website.

16. **Notice of this Order.** Counsel for plaintiff or plaintiff (if appearing on his or her own behalf) shall immediately serve this Order on all parties, including any new parties to the action. If this case came to the Court by a Petition for Removal, the removing defendant(s) shall serve this Order on all other parties.

DATED: ________________

____

PHILIP S. GUTIERREZ
United States District Judge

Hon. Terry J. Hatter, Jr.

District Judge

Chambers Information

U.S. District Court, Central District of California
Courtroom 17, Spring Street Floor
312 N. Spring Street
Los Angeles, CA 90012

Scheduling Information

Courtroom Deputy: (213) 894-5276

Civil Law and Motion	Mondays
Criminal Law and Motion	Mondays at 10:00 a.m.

Biographical Information

Born 1933 in Chicago, IL

Federal Judicial Service:

-Judge, U. S. District Court, Central District of California
-Nominated by Jimmy Carter on September 28, 1979, to a new seat created by 92 Stat. 1629; Confirmed by the Senate on December 19, 1979, and received commission on December 20, 1979. Served as chief judge, 1998-2001. Assumed senior status on April 22, 2005.

Education:

-Wesleyan University, B.A., 1954
-University of Chicago Law School, J.D., 1960

Professional Career:

-U.S. Air Force NCO-In-Charge, 1955-1956
-Adjudicator, U.S. Veterans Administration, Chicago, Illinois, 1960-1961
-Private Practice, Chicago, Illinois, 1961-1962
-Assistant Public Defender, Cook County, Illinois, 1961-1962
-Assistant U.S. Attorney, Northern District of California, 1962-1966
-Special Assistant U.S. Attorney, Eastern District of California, 1965-1966
-Chief Counsel, San Francisco Neighborhood Legal Assistance Foundation, 1966-1967
-Regional Legal Services Director, Office of Economic Opportunity, San Francisco, California, 1967-1970
-Executive Director, Western Center on Law and Poverty, Los Angeles, California, 1970-1973
-Associate Clinical Professor of Law, Univ. of Southern California Law Center, 1970-1974
-Professor of Law, Loyola University, Los Angeles, California, 1973-1975
-Special Assistant to the Mayor and Director of Criminal Justice Planning, Los Angeles, California, 1974-1975
-Special Assistant to the Mayor and Director of Urban Dev., Los Angeles, CA, 1975-1977
-Judge, Superior Court of California, Los Angeles County, 1977-1980

I. Judge Hatter's Procedures and Practices

A. Procedures and Schedules

1. Civil motions are noticed for Mondays, excluding holidays. If Monday is a holiday, skip to the following Monday. Indicate the date and for the time it should read "UNDER SUBMISSION," no appearance necessary, unless the court notifies parties. Judge Hatter takes all motions under submission as of the calendared date of the motion, (see Local Rule 83-9.2).

   Criminal motions are noticed for hearing on Mondays at 10:00 a.m., unless there has been a previously ordered date and time for hearing pre-trial motions.

   It is NOT NECESSARY to clear a motion date with the court clerk prior to filing the motion.

2. Discovery motions are to be calendared before the magistrate judge. Counsel should contact the magistrate judge's court clerk regarding these motions.

3. Tentative rulings are not issued.

4. Mandatory chambers copies on **all** electronic filed documents shall be delivered to the Courtroom Deputy in the CLERK'S OFFICE, Civil Intake Section (Room G-19) by **12 noon** the next business day.

5. Ex parte applications: Ex parte applications are for extraordinary relief only. Applications must be in accordance with Local Rule 7-19 and any applicable General Order except as to the date and time for a hearing. Ex parte applications for TROs or Under Seal filings shall be filed in the Clerk's Office filing window. Judge Hatter will determine whether a hearing is necessary after he reviews the application. Counsel will be notified if a hearing is required. Mandatory chambers copies must be delivered to the Courtroom Deputy in the CLERK'S OFFICE, Civil Intake Section (Room G-19), by 12:00 p.m. the next business day. Sanctions may be imposed for misuse of ex parte applications.

   When opposing counsel has been notified of an ex parte application and intends to submit a written objection, the court clerk is to be immediately notified.

6. To request a continuance of any scheduled court proceeding, telephone the courtroom deputy clerk or submit a stipulation or ex parte application and proposed order stating the reason for this continuance.

7. Counsel are not to contact the judge's law clerks.

8. Stipulations: When seeking approval of a stipulation, remit an extra copy or copies to be conformed and returned with self-addressed, stamped envelope(s). Once a stipulation has been approved and filed, the information may be obtained by checking the docket on PACER. Telephonic inquiries regarding the status of a stipulation, as well as a motion, may not be returned.

9. Calendar conflicts: Telephone the courtroom deputy clerk.

10. Procedures for bringing electronic equipment into the courtroom: None is allowed without prior approval of the Judge's Court Clerk.

    ELMO/Courtroom Technology & Equipment reservations and/or tutorials may be made by first referring to the court website at www.cacd.uscourts.gov , under

"Attorney Information," and then "Attorney Services." Alternatively, you can contact the Courtroom Technology Help Desk at 213-894-3061.

If approved by the Clerk, counsel may contact the Space & Facilities Help Desk at (213) 894-3061 to make arraignments with the U. S. Marshal's Office on how and when to bring the equipment into the building via the public entrances or loading dock if vehicle access is needed. Arrangements for bringing voluminous exhibits into the courtroom can also be made through the S&F Help Desk. (Please note that prior to calling Space & Facilities to se up an appointment, counsel shall contact the Court Clerk to arrange for a date and time for the delivery into the courtroom of the equipment or the voluminous exhibits.)

11. For general information on how to order a transcript of any reported or digitally recorded proceeding, please contact 213-894-3015 or visit www.cacd.uscourts.gov > General Information > Court Reporter/Recorder Transcripts. If you require an estimate of cost for the preparation of a transcript, contact the court reporter/recorder for the desired proceeding.

To determine the court reporter/recorder for a particular proceeding, go to the Court Reporter Schedule web page and click on View by Date. Once you've determined the correct court reporter/recorder for the desired session, click on Court Reporter Phone and Email List for contact information.

12. Questions regarding externships are to be made to the judge's law clerk at 213-894-2088.

13. Trial preparation:

Trial Hours:

Tuesday through Friday (except holidays)
Beginning at 9:00 a.m. (except the first day, begins at 10:00 a.m.)
Adjournment between 5:00 p.m. and 6:00 p.m.
Breaks: mid-morning and mid afternoon break.

Exhibits, Exhibit List, Witness List:

On the first day of trial, please provide to the court clerk the following items:

1. Three copies of the witness list.
2. Three copies of the exhibit list
3. A bench copy of the exhibits, in a binder with tabs as to the exhibit number at the right side of each exhibit.
4. All exhibits.
5. Each original exhibit shall have an exhibit tag stapled to the lower right corner of the exhibit, as not to obstruct the exhibit. Exhibit tags shall be properly filled out with the case number, case title and exhibit number.
6. Jury instructions are to be submitted on a PC Format disk, with a hard copy.
7. Verdict Form shall be provided to the court clerk on the first day of trial.

Depositions: Depositions are to be brought to court on the first day of trial. Do NOT lodge them prior to trial. Bring an original and one copy of each deposition intended to be used at trial. If a deposition will be used in lieu of live testimony for trial, indicate the designated portions by listing them as a separate document.

Jury Instructions: Refer to Judge Hatter's Order re Civil Jury Instructions. The order will be mailed to all counsel of record shortly after the trial date is set. Judge Hatter prefers instructions from Kevin F. O'Malley, et al, Federal Jury Practice and Instruction, due no later than 1 week prior to the trial. The disk is due Friday before the trial.

14. If an interpreter is required on a civil case, counsel is responsible for making the arrangements. Interpreters Office 213-894-4599.

15. If counsel has received a "Notice to Parties of Court-Directed ADR Program" (form ADR-08), the Court will presumptively refer the case to the Court Mediation Panel or to private mediation at the time of the initial scheduling conference. See General Order 11-10, § 5.1. Counsel are directed to furnish and discuss this Notice with their clients in preparation for the parties' Fed.R.Civ.P. 26(f) conference. Counsel should include their shared or separate views regarding a preference for the Court Mediation Panel or private mediation, and when the mediation should occur, in the written report required by Fed.R.Civ.P. 26(f) and Civil L.R. 26-1. A settlement conference with a magistrate judge is generally not available for cases in the Court-Directed ADR Program. See Civil L.R. 26-1(c). For information about the Court's ADR Program, please see General Order 11-10 which is located in the "General Orders" section on the home page and in the "ADR" page of the Court's website.

Hon. Robert J. Kelleher
District Judge

Chambers Information
U.S. District Court, Central District of California
Courtroom 1439
255 East Temple Street
Los Angeles, CA 90012

Scheduling Information
Courtroom Deputy: (213) 894-5285

Civil Law and Motion	Mondays at 1:30 p.m.
Criminal Law and Motion	Mondays at 1:30 p.m.

Biographical Information
Born 1913 in New York, NY

Federal Judicial Service:
-Judge, U. S. District Court, Central District of California
-Nominated by Richard M. Nixon on December 15, 1970, to a new seat created by 84 Stat. 294; Confirmed by the Senate on December 17, 1970, and received commission on December 21, 1970. Assumed senior status on March 5, 1983.

Education:
-Williams College, A.B., 1935
-Harvard Law School, J.D., 1938

Professional Career:
-Trial Attorney, U.S. Trucking Company, New York City, 1939-1940
-Associate Attorney, U.S. Department of the Army, Los Angeles, 1941-1942
-U.S. Naval Reserve, 1943-1945
-Private Practice, Santa Monica, California, 1945-1948
-Assistant U.S. Attorney, Southern District of California, 1948-1951
-Private Practice, Beverly Hills, California, 1951-1971

I. Judge Kelleher's Procedures and Practices

A. *Procedures and Schedules*

1. Civil motions are heard **Mondays** at **1:30 pm.** Criminal motions are heard **Mondays** at **1:30 pm.** If Monday is a holiday, the next motion hearing date is the following Monday. Counsel need not clear a motion date with the Court Clerk prior to filing a motion.

2. Discovery motions shall be calendared before Judge Kelleher, **not** before the assigned Magistrate Judge.

3. The Court does not issue tentative rulings.

4. All papers filed with the Court must conform to Local Rule 11-3.1.1, which requires all papers to use typeface 14-point or larger.

5. Mandatory chambers copies of all electronically filed documents shall be delivered directly to Room 1434 (Chambers), not later than 12:00 noon the day following the e-filing. The document should be marked "mandatory chambers copy, e-filed on (fill in the date)." Documents e-filed without a mandatory chambers copy delivered to chambers WILL SUBJECT COUNSEL TO SANCTIONS FOR FAILURE TO COMPLY WITH THE JUDGE'S POLICY AND PROCEDURES. The copy must conform to the standards set forth in the Local Rules.

   Mandatory chambers copies on all electronically filed documents shall be delivered to Room 1434 (Chambers), not later than 12:00 noon the day following the e-filing. Please mark the document "Mandatory Chambers Copy, e-filed on (fill in the date)." Documents e-filed without a mandatory chambers copy delivered to chambers WILL BE REJECTED AND WILL NOT BE CONSIDERED.

6. All ex parte applications and motions must conform to the standards set forth in Local Rule 7-9. Opposition papers are due within 48 hours. No hearing will be held unless the Court so notifies counsel.

7. Requests to continue any scheduled court proceeding shall be made in the form of a written stipulation, ex parte application or motion, along with a proposed order. Oral requests will not be considered. Counsel will not assume the request is granted without notification from the court.

8. Counsel may not contact the Judge's secretary or law clerks.

9. Please submit an extra copy of any stipulation or order with a self-addressed, stamped envelope pursuant to Local Rule 11-4.4. The Court Clerk will mail the copy back to counsel.

10. If counsel have a calendar conflict, counsel must notify the Court Clerk as soon as the conflict is known. Please inform the Court Clerk as to the name of the judge, the time of the conflict, the place of the court, etc.

11. If counsel need to bring electronic equipment into the courtroom, please notify the Court Clerk no later than five days prior to the scheduled appearance.

12. For general information on how to order a transcript of any reported or digitally recorded proceeding, please contact 213-894-3015 or visit www.cacd.uscourts.gov>General Information >Court Reporter/Recorder Transcripts.

If you require an estimate of cost for the preparation of a transcript, contact the court reporter/recorder for the desired proceeding.

To determine the court reporter/recorder for a particular proceeding, go to the Court Reporter Schedule web page and click on View by Date. Once you've determined the correct court reporter/recorder for the desired session, click on Court Reporter Phone and Email List for contact information.

13. Questions regarding law clerk positions may be submitted in writing to the attention of the Judge's secretary.

14. The moving party is responsible for hiring a qualified interpreter in a civil case. You may contact the Court Interpreter Coordinator at (213) 894 4599.

15. The Court will set cut off dates as well as the Pretrial Conference date after receipt of the parties' joint Rule 26(f) Report.

16. Applications for Substitution of Attorney must be accompanied by a declaration stating that there would be no delay in the progress of the case as a result of the substitution.

17. The direct testimony of expert witnesses shall consist entirely of a reading of the Rule 26(a)(2)(B) Report by the expert.

II. Judge Kelleher's Case Management Orders

A. *Order Regarding Trial Preparation for Bench Trials*

IN THE UNITED STATES DISTICT COURT
FOR THE CENTRAL DISTRICT OF CALIFORNIA

	)	Case No. ______________
Plaintiff(s),	)	
v.	)	**ORDER RE: TRIAL PREPARATION**
Defendant(s).	)	**FOR BENCH TRIALS**
______________________________	)	

The above-mentioned action is set for trial before United States District Judge Robert J. Kelleher. In order to guide counsel in preparing for trial, the Court makes the following Order:

Findings of Fact and Conclusions of Law

Counsel shall lodge **two copies** of proposed findings of fact and conclusions of law with the Court **twenty-one days before the trial date**. Counsel shall file a copy of the document on disk in Word Perfect 7 format as a courtesy to the Court. One additional copy shall be served on opposing counsel at that time.

Upon receipt of the proposed findings of fact and conclusions of law from opposing counsel, each party shall:

1. underline in ***red*** pencil those portions which it disputes;
2. underline in ***blue*** pencil those portions which it admits; and
3. underline in ***yellow*** pencil those portions which it does not dispute, but which it deems irrelevant.

Each counsel shall then file **two marked copies** of opposing counsel's proposed findings of fact and conclusions of law with the Court **seven days before the trial date**. One additional copy shall be served on opposing counsel at that time.

The parties shall be prepared to submit to the Court, and to exchange among themselves, supplemental findings of fact and conclusions of law during the course of the trial, with respect to which the same underlining procedure may be ordered.

Motions *in Limine*

Motions *in limine* shall concern ***only*** the admissibility of evidence at trial. Any such motion shall be noticed in accordance with the Local Rules. Such motions shall be filed no later than **seven days prior to the start of trial**. It is the Court's customary practice to defer ruling on motions concerning the admissibility of evidence until such issues arise during the course of trial.

Depositions Used During Trial

If you intend to use depositions during trial for any purpose, including impeachment, be prepared to lodge the original at any time during trial. If the original is not available, be prepared to lodge a copy with a stipulation that the copy may be used as if it were the original. The use of depositions at trial will not be permitted if the original or agreed copy has not been lodged.

Where witnesses testify by deposition, please do the following:

1. Mark with colored pencil, in the original and/or copy of the deposition, the proffered parts. Plaintiff will use ***blue***; defendant will use ***red***;

2. If there are objections to the underscored portions of the transcript, furnish a written list of objections by page and line. Make any such objections immediately prior to the use of the deposition at trial; and

3. In those instances when lengthy portions of deposition are to be read, please make arrangements with opposing counsel in advance as to the manner of presenting the testimony.

Expert Witnesses

Failure to include the name of an expert witness in the Pretrial Order precludes a party from calling that expert witness at trial. An expert witness' direct testimony shall consist exclusively of the expert's reading from his curriculum vitae and Rule 26 report.

Preparation for the First Day of Trial

On the first day of trial, report to the Courtroom at least fifteen minutes prior to the scheduled time for trial and present the Courtroom Deputy Clerk with the following:

1. Exhibit List: **Three copies** of the joint exhibit list in the form specified in the Local Rules. Each exhibit must be clearly described, and must denote any subparts that counsel may refer to individually (e.g., 3(a), 3(b), 3(c)). If any exhibits are objected to, such objections must be noted on the list. Counsel shall meet no later than **ten days prior to the trial date** to stipulate so far as is possible those exhibits that may be received into evidence at the start of trial;

2. Witness List: **Three copies** of your witness list. Indicate which, if any, witnesses will testify by deposition; and

3. Exhibits: **Three sets** of exhibits, with tabs and **official exhibit tags** attached, bearing the same numbers shown on our exhibit list. Official exhibit tags are available from the receptionist in the main clerk's office, Room G-8. Each bound set of exhibits shall include an index identifying the exhibits.

Instructions to Counsel Governing Trial in this Court

The Court shall be addressed as "Your Honor" at all times.

Opening statements, examination of witnesses, and closing arguments shall be made from the lectern only. Do not approach the Court Clerk or the witness without specific permission from the Court.

Do not run out of witnesses. If you are out of witnesses and there is more than a brief delay, the Court may deem that you have rested.

IT IS SO ORDERED.

DATED:_______________

____
ROBERT J. KELLEHER
United States District Judge

B. Order Regarding Trial Preparation for Jury Trials

IN THE UNITED STATES DISTICT COURT
FOR THE CENTRAL DISTRICT OF CALIFORNIA

)	Case No. ______________
Plaintiff(s),)	
v.)	**ORDER RE: TRIAL PREPARATION**
Defendant(s).)	**FOR JURY TRIALS**
______________________________)	

The above-mentioned action is set for trial before United States District Judge Robert J. Kelleher. In order to guide counsel in preparing for trial, the Court makes the following Order:

Jury Instructions and Verdict Form

No later than **seven days prior to trial**, the parties shall file proposed Joint Jury Instructions and a proposed Joint Verdict Form. In order to produce the joint instructions and verdict form, the parties shall meet and confer sufficiently in advance of the required submission date. Each proposed instruction must include a designation number, a descriptive phrase, and a recitation of authority supporting such an instruction.

If disagreements cannot be resolved, the parties shall submit, in addition to the agreed upon instructions and portions of the verdict form:

1. Those instructions and portions of the verdict form propounded by Plaintiff, opposed by Defendant; and

2. Those instructions and portions of the verdict form propounded by Defendant, opposed by Plaintiff.

For disputed instructions and portions of the verdict form, each party should note its objections and its reasons for putting forth its alternative.

The Court insists upon receiving lucid and accurate instructions and verdict forms, tailored to the facts of the case and setting forth the elements of each party's claims and defenses. Instructions and verdict forms shall be brief, clear, concise, written in plain English, free of argument and organized in a logical fashion so as to aid jury comprehension. Standard or form instructions, if used, must be revised to address the particular facts and issues of this case.

At the time the proposed Joint Jury Instructions and Joint Verdict Form are filed, counsel shall file an additional copy of the documents on diskette in Word Perfect 7 format as a courtesy to the Court.

Motions *in Limine*

Motions *in limine* shall concern ***only*** the admissibility of evidence at trial. Any such motion shall be noticed in accordance with the Local Rules. Such motions shall be filed no later than **seven days prior to the start of trial**. It is the Court's customary practice to defer ruling on motions concerning the admissibility of evidence until such issues arise during the course of trial.

Voir Dire

The parties shall submit proposed *voir dire* questions, if any, to the Court no later than **seven days prior to trial**. The Court does not utilize jury questionnaires in advance of *voir dire*.

Depositions Used During Trial

If you intend to use depositions during trial for any purpose, including impeachment, be prepared to lodge the original at any time during trial. If the original is not available, be prepared to lodge a copy with a stipulation that the copy may be used as if it were the original. The use of depositions at trial will not be permitted if the original or agreed copy has not been lodged.

Where witnesses testify by deposition, please do the following:

1. Mark with colored pencil, in the original and/or copy of the deposition, the proffered parts. Plaintiff will use ***blue***; defendant will use ***red***;

2. If there are objections to the underscored portions of the transcript, furnish a written list of objections by page and line. Make any such objections immediately prior to the use of the deposition at trial; and

3. In those instances when lengthy portions of deposition are to be read, please make arrangements with opposing counsel in advance as to the manner of presenting the testimony.

Expert Witnesses

Failure to include the name of an expert witness in the Pretrial Order precludes a party from calling that expert witness at trial. An expert witness' direct testimony shall consist exclusively of the expert's reading from his curriculum vitae and Rule 26 report. Preparation for the First Day of Trial On the first day of trial, report to the Courtroom at least fifteen minutes prior to the scheduled time for trial and present the Courtroom Deputy Clerk with the following:

1. Exhibit List: **Three copies** of the joint exhibit list in the form specified in Local Rule 16. Each exhibit must be clearly described, and must denote any subparts that counsel may refer to individually (*e.g.*, 3(a), 3(b), 3(c)). If any exhibits are objected to, such objections must be noted on the list. Counsel shall meet no later than **ten days prior to the trial date** to stipulate so far as is possible those exhibits that may be received into evidence at the start of trial;

2. Witness List: **Three copies** of your witness list. Indicate which, if any, witnesses will testify by deposition; and

3. Exhibits: **Three sets** of exhibits, with tabs and **official exhibit tags** attached, bearing the same numbers shown on our exhibit list. Official exhibit tags are available from the receptionist in the main clerk's office, Room G-8. Each bound set of exhibits shall include an index identifying the exhibits.

Instructions to Counsel Governing Trial in this Court

The Court shall be addressed as "Your Honor" at all times.

Opening statements, examination of witnesses, and closing arguments shall be made from the lectern only. Do not approach the Court Clerk or the witness without specific permission from the Court.

Do not run out of witnesses. If you are out of witnesses and there is more than a brief delay, the Court may deem that you have rested.

IT IS SO ORDERED.

DATED:____________________

____
ROBERT J. KELLEHER
United States District Judge

C. *Scheduling and Case Management Order*

IN THE UNITED STATES DISTICT COURT
FOR THE CENTRAL DISTRICT OF CALIFORNIA

	)	Case No. ______________
Plaintiff(s),	)	
v.	)	**SCHEDULING AND CASE**
Defendant(s).	)	**MANAGEMENT ORDER**
______________________________	)	

The Court issues this scheduling and case management order to govern the course of all pre-trial proceedings in this case. *See* Fed. R. Civ. P. 16(b). Unless otherwise ordered herein, the Court expects the parties and their counsel to follow the deadlines and procedures set forth in the Federal Rules of Civil Procedure, the Local Rules and this Court's standing orders.

1. JOINDER OF PARTIES AND AMENDMENT OF PLEADINGS

The deadline for joining parties and amending pleadings is ______________.

2. DISCOVERY CUTOFF

All discovery (expert and non-expert) shall be completed on or prior to _________.[1]

Disclosure of Expert Testimony. If disclosure of an expert report is required by Federal Rule of Civil Procedure 26(a)(2)(B), the disclosure shall be made at least forty (40) days before the discovery cutoff date. Disclosure of a counter-expert's report shall be made within thirty (30) days after the disclosure made by the other party.

3. MOTION CUTOFF

All law and motion matters, except for motions *in limine*, must be heard (not filed) by ______________.

4. REQUESTS FOR EXTENSION OF CUTOFF DATES

The Court expects the parties and their counsel to adhere to the above deadlines. Applications and stipulations to extend the cutoff dates must be supported by specific, concrete reasons establishing good cause for the extension. (For example, in this regard, a statement that an extension "will promote settlement" is insufficient. The application or stipulation should identify the status of ongoing negotiations, whether written proposals have been exchanged, whether a mediator has been selected, *etc.*) Additionally, the application or stipulation should identify what discovery has been accomplished since the case became at issue, what motions have been filed and determined, whether there have been prior requests for extensions of time and whether those prior requests were granted or denied by the Court.

5. MANDATORY SETTLEMENT CONFERENCE

The Court expects the parties to comply with settlement procedures and deadlines set forth in Local Rule 16-14.

6. FINAL PRETRIAL CONFERENCE

This case has been placed on this Court's calendar for Final Pretrial Conference at 10:00 a.m. on __________________. The parties and counsel are reminded that they must comply with the pre trial procedures and deadlines set forth in Local Rule 16. No requests for

[1] As a reminder, Judge Kelleher does not refer discovery motions to the Magistrate Judge.

a continuance of the pretrial conference, either by way of a motion or stipulation of the parties, will be granted unless the parties meet the standards set forth in Local Rule 16-8. Motions *in limine* must be heard (not filed) not later than the date of the Final Pretrial Conference.

IT IS SO ORDERED.

DATED: ______________

____

ROBERT J. KELLEHER
United States District Judge

Hon. William D. Keller

District Judge

Chambers Information

U.S. District Court, Central District of California
Courtroom N/A
312 N. Spring Street
Los Angeles, CA 90012

Scheduling Information

Courtroom Deputy: (213) 894-0539

Civil Law and Motion	As set by the Court.
Criminal Law and Motion	As set by the Court.

Biographical Information

Born 1934 in Los Angeles, CA

Federal Judicial Service:

-Judge, U. S. District Court, Central District of California
-Nominated by Ronald Reagan on September 11, 1984, to a new seat created by 98 Stat. 333; Confirmed by the Senate on October 3, 1984, and received commission on October 4, 1984.
-Assumed senior status on October 29, 1999.

Education:

-University of California, Berkeley, B.S., 1956
-University of California, Los Angeles, School of Law, LL.B., 1960

Professional Career:

-Assistant U.S. attorney, Southern District of California, 1961-1964
-Private Practice, California, 1964-1972
-U.S. Attorney for the Central District of California, 1972-1977
-Private Practice, California, 1977-1984

I. Judge Keller's Procedures and Practices

A. Procedures and Schedules

1. **Civil Motions:** Must be noticed pursuant to the local rules. It is not necessary to clear a motion date with the court clerk prior to filing the motion. If a hearing is necessary, the court clerk will notify counsel of the date and time of the hearing.

   Criminal Motions: Hearing to be set by the Court. The court clerk will notify the parties of the date and time of the hearing.

2. Discovery motions are to be scheduled before the Magistrate Judge.

3. Tentative rulings are not issued.

4. Mandatory Chambers Copies must be delivered to the Clerk's Office, Room G-19, Attention: Patricia Gomez. Chamber Copies must be delivered by 12:00 p.m. the court day following the e-filing date.

   All Chamber Copies must include the Notice of Electronic Filing.

5. Procedures for filing an Ex Parte Application: A party submits an Ex Parte Application, with a declaration of notification to the other parties and a separate proposed order and the matter then stands submitted. If a hearing is necessary, the court clerk will contact counsel of the date and time of the hearing.

6. To request a continuance of any scheduled court proceeding: The party(ies) must make the request in writing by either submitting a stipulation or ex parte application with a proposed order for the Court's signature; alternative dates should be cleared with the court clerk before submitting the document.

7. Are counsel allowed to contact the Judge's law clerks or secretary? No; all inquiries of any nature are to be directed to the court clerk, unless returning a phone call.

8. Inquiries regarding the status of a motion, stipulation or proposed order are to be made to the court clerk **ONLY IN EXTREME SITUATIONS**, otherwise the phone call will not be returned.

9. Calendar conflicts (procedures for attorneys to follow if they have a calendar conflict): If a date is set by the Judge in court, counsel must promptly advise the Judge at that time of any conflicts; if the conflict has arisen later, counsel must promptly advise the court clerk by telephone. (The Court will work with the parties to arrange priority at the hearing or have the matter put at the end of the calendar.)

10. Procedures for bringing electronic equipment into the courtroom: None is allowed without prior written approval of Court; contact the court clerk. If approved, the party bringing the equipment will have to make arrangements with the U.S. Marshal's Office to bring the equipment into the building (use of loading dock, etc.)

11. For general information on how to order a transcript of any reported or digitally recorded proceeding, please contact 213-894-3015 or visit www.cacd.uscourts.gov > General Information > Court Reporter/Recorder Transcripts. If you require an estimate of cost for the preparation of a transcript, contact the court reporter/recorder for the desired proceeding.

    To determine the court reporter/recorder for a particular proceeding, go to the Court Reporter Schedule web page and click on View by Date. Once you've determined the correct court reporter/recorder for the desired session, click on Court Reporter Phone and Email List for contact information.

12. Questions regarding law clerk/extern position shall be directed to the Judge's secretary.

13. Trial Preparation:

- **a.** Court hours: 9:00 A.M. to 12 noon; then 1:00 P.M. to 4:30 P.M., for the jury; the parties are normally ordered present at 8:00 A.M. and are excused sometime after the jury is excused for the day.

- **b.** Exhibit preparation: Pursuant to the local rules (the exhibits, except for physical exhibits, shall be in 3-ring binders, the original tagged set for the court clerk -- who will pass same to the witnesses -- and one set for the Judge.)

- **c.** Jury instructions: To be submitted in the form and time frames in accordance with the Federal Rules of Civil and Criminal Procedure and the local rules.

- **d.** Verdict forms: The court clerk prepares the verdict form in criminal cases; in civil cases the plaintiff submits the proposed verdict form in accordance with the Federal Rules of Civil Procedure and the local rules.

- **e.** Other: The parties shall come to court fully prepared, with the two sets of bound exhibits as described above; and also with three clean copies of their witness lists and three clean copies of their exhibit lists, all which shall be given to the court clerk before the start of court.

14. Procedures for obtaining the services of an interpreter on a civil case: The party must hire a certified Federal Court interpreter, whether it be done through the Court's Interpreter's Section, or from some outside source.

15. Other: If the parties want copies of documents returned after signature and filing, extra copies of the document and self-addressed stamped envelopes must be provided, in addition to the blue-backed original and copy, for the clerk to conform and mail. The court clerk will not make copies of any documents for mailing to the parties.

Hon. George H. King

District Judge

Chambers Information

U.S. District Court, Central District of California
Courtroom 650
255 East Temple Street
Los Angeles, CA 90012

Scheduling Information

Courtroom Deputy: (213) 894-6907

Civil Law and Motion	Mondays at 9:30 a.m.
Criminal Law and Motion	Mondays at 3:30 p.m.

Biographical Information

Born 1951 in Shanghai, China

Federal Judicial Service:

-Judge, U. S. District Court, Central District of California
-Nominated by William J. Clinton on April 27, 1995, to a new seat created by 104 Stat. 5089; Confirmed by the Senate on June 30, 1995, and received commission on June 30, 1995.
-U.S. Magistrate, U.S. District Court for the Central District of California, 1987-1995

Education:

-University of California, Los Angeles, A.B., 1971
-University of Southern California Law School, J.D., 1974

Professional Career:

-Private Practice, Los Angeles, California, 1974-1975
-Assistant U.S. Attorney, Central District of California, 1975-1979
-Private Practice, Los Angeles, California, 1979-1986
-Hearing Examiner, Los Angeles Police Commission, California,1980-1982

I. Judge King's Procedures and Practices

A. *Procedures and Schedules*

1. Civil Motion Hearings: **Mondays** only at **9:30 a.m.** No Tuesday motion days.

   Criminal Motion Hearings: Same as Civil except motion should be noticed for **3:30 p.m.**

2. All discovery motions shall be noticed before the assigned Magistrate Judge (see initials of Magistrate Judge in parentheses in the case number).

3. Tentative rulings are not issued in advance.

4. A mandatory chambers copy of all papers filed with the court SHALL be delivered to chambers at Room 660, Roybal Federal Building, no later than 12:00 noon the following business day. ALL mandatory chambers copies SHALL fully comply with the document formatting requirements of Local Rule 11-3, including the "backing" requirements of Local Rule 11-3.5. The filing party and their counsel MAY BE SUBJECT TO SANCTIONS for failure to deliver a mandatory chambers copy in full compliance with this Order and Local Rule 11-3.

5. *Ex parte* applications shall be electronically filed, and Local Rule 7-19 and 7-19.1 should be observed. Do not request or require opposing counsel to come to court at the time the application is being filed. Hearings are rarely held on ex parte applications. If a hearing is necessary, the parties will be notified. The judge allows only 24 hours for opposition papers to be filed. Service of all ex parte applications and oppositions shall be by personal delivery or electronic means and shall be effected at or before the time the document is filed.

6. It is best to leave a message for the court clerk at the above number as soon as you know a request for continuance is going to be made.

7. Counsel shall not contact the law clerks or secretary on any matters except if they are trying to locate the court clerk.

8. Calls will not be returned regarding the status of submitted motions, stipulations, or proposed orders. Counsel wishing to know whether or not a stipulation or proposed order has been approved shall comply with Local Rule 11-4.5.

9. If electronic equipment must be brought into the courtroom for trial, make prior arrangements with the Building Manager, (213)894-3483, as soon as possible. Notice should also be given to the court clerk

10. For general information on how to order a transcript of any reported or digitally recorded proceeding, please contact 213-894-3015 or visit www.cacd.uscourts.gov > General Information > Court Reporter/Recorder Transcripts. If you require an estimate of cost for the preparation of a transcript, contact the court reporter/recorder for the desired proceeding.

    To determine the court reporter/recorder for a particular proceeding, go to the Court Reporter Schedule web page and click on View by Date. Once you've determined the correct court reporter/recorder for the desired session, click on Court Reporter Phone and Email List for contact information.

11. Questions regarding law clerk/extern applications should be presented to the judge's

current law clerks at 213-894-5766.

12. Civil trial exhibits should be placed in binders with the exhibit number tabbed on the right hand side. The outside of the binder should clearly indicate what exhibit numbers are inside that binder. There should be two sets of binders - one set for the judge and a second set for the witness stand. The set for the witness stand should have the court exhibit tag placed consistently on the upper or lower right hand side of the front page. Never place an exhibit tag on the back side of a page. Do not block any part of the exhibit by using the exhibit tag. If necessary to preserve the exhibit, staple the tag onto the document. See Judge King's separate Order Re: Criminal Trial Preparation, linked below.

13. On the morning of civil trials counsel should be prepared to turn over to the court clerk the two sets of exhibits, the witness list in triplicate, and the exhibit list in triplicate. See Judge King's separate Order Re: Criminal Trial Preparation, linked below.

14. In civil trials, counsel shall submit a joint set of instructions. If counsel are unable to agree upon all the instructions to be given, then counsel shall have one set of joint/agreed to instructions, and a separate set of disputed instructions. The disputed instructions shall have a section for each party's proffered instructions, and all other parties' objections and citation of authorities in support of such objections. These instructions should be presented to the court no later than the commencement of trial. Generally, the court expects that counsel will have no more than a few disputed instructions. See Judge King's separate Order Re: Criminal Trial Preparation.

15. The clerk will prepare any verdict forms necessary in a criminal trial. In a civil matter the parties shall prepare proposed forms of verdict and present them at the commencement of trial.

16. If the assistance of an interpreter is necessary in a civil action, it is counsel's responsibility to contact the Court Interpreter Coordinator, 213-894-4599, to arrange for such services.

II. Judge King's Case Management Orders

A. *Order Regarding Criminal Trial Preparation*

IN THE UNITED STATES DISTICT COURT
FOR THE CENTRAL DISTRICT OF CALIFORNIA

UNITED STATES OF AMERICA, Plaintiff, v. Defendant(s).	)))))	Case No. ______________ **ORDER RE: CRIMINAL TRIAL PREPARATION**

The above-mentioned cause of action is set for trial before Judge George H. King on Tuesday, ___________ , 200_, at 9:30 a.m.

1. Arrive at courtroom not later than 8:30 a.m. on the first day of trial.

2. Counsel for the Government shall present the Courtroom Deputy Clerk (CRD) with the following documents:

(a) THREE copies of the Government's witness list.

(b) THREE copies of the Government's exhibit list in the form specified in Local Rule 9.9 (Civil).

(c) ALL of the Government's exhibits, with official exhibit tags attached, bearing the same number shown on the exhibit list, must be delivered to the CRD not later than 8:30 a.m. on the first day of trial. (Defense counsel need not deliver their exhibits to the Clerk on the first day of trial; however, counsel are responsible for affixing exhibit tags to exhibits they intend to use in their case.) Exhibits shall be numbered 1, 2, 3, 4, *etc.*, NOT 1.1, 1.50, *etc.* If a blowup is an enlargement of an existing exhibit, it shall be designated with the number of the original exhibit followed by an appropriate alphabetical design. Government counsel should be aware that the court will order exhibits such as firearms, narcotics, etc., remain in the custody of the agents during the pendency of the trial. It shall be the agents' responsibility to produce said items for court, secure them at night and guard them at all times while in the courtroom. Exhibit tags may be obtained from the receptionist in the main Clerk's Office, Room G-8.

(d) If counsel need additional equipment, such as a shadow box, overhead projector, *etc.*, call the CRD as soon as possible, but no later than 4:30 p.m. two court days BEFORE trial, so that necessary arrangements may be made.

3. The court finds it helpful to follow the testimony closely. Accordingly, counsel must have the following available:

(a) A bench book containing a copy of all exhibits which can, as a practical matter, be reproduced. Each exhibit shall be tabbed with the exhibit number for easy referral.

4. Usual "trial days" are Tuesdays through Fridays, 9:30 a.m. to 5:00 p.m. Lunch recess is normally 12:00 noon to 1:30 p.m.

5. Before trial commences, the court will give counsel an opportunity to discuss, in advance, housekeeping matters and anticipated problems of procedure or law.

6. TRANSCRIPTS: Counsel for the government shall obtain authorization from their agencies. A copy of said authorization shall be given to the court reporter when requesting transcripts.

7. JURY INSTRUCTIONS

Jury instructions are to be submitted not later than the Wednesday of the week prior to trial.

(a) Form of Jury Instructions

The parties must submit joint jury instructions and a joint proposed verdict form (if a special verdict). In order to produce these joint instructions, counsel shall meet and confer sufficiently in advance of the required submission date. The instructions shall be submitted in the order in which the parties wish to have the instructions read. This order should reflect a single organized sequence agreed to by all of the parties.

The joint jury instructions shall be submitted in three sets as follows: (1) those instructions which are agreed to by all parties; (2) those instructions which are propounded by the Government to which the defendant[s] object; and (3) those instructions which are propounded by the defendant[s] to which the Government objects.

Instructions upon which agreement cannot be reached should reflect the basic disagreements among the parties.

Attribution and case citation for each instruction should be placed on pages following a proposed instruction. For disputed instructions, a party shall note the objections to a proposed instruction and the reasons therefor.

INSTRUCTIONS SHALL BE BRIEF, CLEAR, CONCISE, WRITTEN IN PLAIN ENGLISH, FREE OF ARGUMENT, AND SHALL BE ORGANIZED IN LOGICAL FASHION AS TO AID JURY COMPREHENSION. Standard or form instructions, if used, must be revised to address the particular facts and issues of this case. The following list contains some suggested sources for jury instructions:

(1) Ninth Circuit Manual of Model Jury Instructions-Criminal (West Group (Online Edition));

(2) Federal Jury Practice and Instructions (O'Malley, Grenig and Lee (5th Edition))

8. INSTRUCTIONS TO COUNSEL GOVERNING TRIALS IN THIS COURT

(a) During trial counsel shall not refer to their clients by their first names.

(b) Opening statements, examination of witnesses, and closing arguments shall be made from the lectern only.

(c) Avoid discussing the law or arguing the case in opening statements.

(d) Do not use objections for the purpose of making a speech, recapitulating testimony, or attempting to guide the witness. When objecting, state only that you are objecting and the specific legal ground of the objection, *e.g.*, hearsay, irrelevant, *etc.* If you wish to argue an objection further, ask permission to do so at side bar. The court may or may not grant such requests.

(e) Speak up when making an objection. The acoustics in most courtrooms make it difficult for all to hear an objection when it is being made. Counsel must speak audibly and clearly when questioning witnesses or arguing to the court or jury. Counsel should instruct their witnesses to speak audibly and clearly.

(f) Do not approach the clerk or the witness box without specific permission. Please return to the lectern when the purpose of the approach is finished.

(g) Please <u>rise</u> when addressing the court.

(h) Address all remarks to the court. Do not address the clerk, the reporter, or opposing counsel. If counsel desire to confer off the record, ask permission to do so. All requests for the re-reading of questions or answers, or to have an exhibit placed in front of a witness, shall be addressed to the court.

(i) Do not make an offer of stipulation unless you have conferred with opposing counsel and have reason to believe the stipulation will be accepted. Any stipulation of fact will require the defendant's personal concurrence. A proposed stipulation should be explained to him or her in advance.

(j) While court is in session, do not leave counsel table to confer with investigators, secretaries, or witnesses in the back of the courtroom unless permission is granted in advance.

(k) Counsel shall not, by facial expression, nodding, or other conduct, exhibit any opinions, adverse or favorable, concerning any testimony which is being given by a witness. Counsel shall admonish their own clients and witnesses similarly to avoid such conduct.

(l) When a party has more than one lawyer, only one may conduct the direct or cross-examination of a given witness.

(m) If a witness was on the stand at a recess or adjournment, have the witness back on the stand, ready to proceed when court resumes.

(n) Do not run out of witnesses. If you are out of witnesses and there is more than a brief delay, the court may deem that you have rested.

(o) The court attempts to cooperate with doctors and other professional witnesses and will, except in extraordinary circumstances, accommodate them by permitting them to be called out of sequence. Anticipate any such possibility and discuss it with opposing counsel. If there is objection, confer with the court in advance.

(p) Counsel are advised to be on time as the court starts promptly. Morning and afternoon breaks are approximately fifteen minutes in length.

(q) Do not attempt to use or display any enlargements of exhibits or charts unless all counsel agree to such use, or the court has ruled on any objections in advance.

(r) Never enter the well of the court. Counsel shall ensure that his/her client(s) and witness(es) are admonished to never enter the well of the court.

(s) Counsel shall not bring any water cups to the lectern, and, while the court is in session, shall not speak while holding any water cup in his/her hand.

DATED: ____________________

____
GEORGE H. KING
United States District Judge

Hon. R. Gary Klausner

District Judge

Chambers Information

U.S. District Court, Central District of California
Courtroom 850
255 East Temple Street
Los Angeles, CA 90012

Scheduling Information

Courtroom Deputy: (213) 894-2649

Civil Law and Motion	Mondays at 9:00 a.m.
Criminal Law and Motion	Mondays at 1:30 p.m.

Biographical Information

Born 1941 in Los Angeles, CA

Federal Judicial Service:

-Judge, U. S. District Court, Central District of California
-Nominated by George W. Bush on July 18, 2002, to a seat vacated by William D. Keller; Confirmed by the Senate on November 14, 2002, and received commission on November 15, 2002.

Education:

-University of Notre Dame, B.A., 1963
-University of Notre Dame, B.S., 1964
-Loyola Law School, J.D., 1967

Professional Career:

-U.S. Army, 1967-1969
-Deputy District Attorney, District Attorney's Office of Los Angeles County, California, 1969-1974
-Court Commissioner, Pasadena Municipal Court, California, 1974-1980
-Judge, Pasadena Municipal Court, California, 1980-1985
-Judge, Los Angeles Superior Court, California, 1985-2002

I. Judge Klausner's Procedures and Practices

A. *Procedures and Schedules*

1. Mandatory chambers copies of ALL e-filed documents are to be delivered to Judge Klausner's Courtesy Box (located outside of the Clerk's Office, Room 181-L) not later than 12:00 noon the day following e-filing. Please mark the document "Mandatory Chambers Copy," E-filed on (fill in the date). Failure to comply may result in the document being stricken from the record.

2. Counsel shall not contact the clerk with procedural questions regarding e-filing. Counsel shall contact the e-filing help desk at (213) 894-0242.

3. Civil motions are heard on: **Mondays**: 9:00 a.m.

   Criminal motions are heard on: **Mondays**: 1:30 p.m.

   If Monday is a holiday, the next motion date is Tuesday following the Monday holiday. Opposition or reply papers due on a holiday Monday shall be filed the **preceding** Friday.

   MOTION DATES ARE NOT RESERVED.

4. Discovery motions are to be calendared before the Magistrate Judge assigned.

5. Tentative rulings on motions are not issued. Telephonic appearances are NOT permitted.

6. *Ex parte* applications are **ONLY** for extraordinary relief. Sanctions may be imposed for misuse of ex parte applications. *See Mission Power Engineering Co. v. Continental Casualty Co., 883 F. Supp. 488 (C.D. Cal. 1995). Ex Parte* applications are normally considered on the papers and are rarely set for hearing. If the Court finds that a hearing is necessary, the parties will be notified. Opposition papers are to be filed no later than 3:00 p.m. on the first business day following service of the application. Counsel will be notified by minute order of the Court's ruling. Counsel shall **NOT** contact the Courtroom Deputy Clerk regarding status.

7. Continuances are granted only upon a strong showing of good cause. Requests for continuances must be by motion, stipulation or application accompanied by a declaration setting forth detailed reasons for the requested continuance. The declaration **shall** also include whether there have been any prior requests for continuances and whether these requests were granted or denied by the Court. Stipulations extending dates set by this Court are not effective unless approved by the Court. Requests for continuance should be submitted well in advance of the requested relief. Requests for continuance not in compliance with this Order or the Local Rules of Practice for the Central District of California will be denied.

8. Counsel shall not contact the Judge's law clerks or secretary. All appropriate inquiries shall be directed to the Courtroom Deputy Clerk.

9. Telephone calls will **NOT** be returned regarding the status of submitted motions, stipulations or proposed orders. Counsel may determine the status of any submitted motion, stipulation or proposed order by accessing the docket sheet via the internet through the PACER program. Telephone calls with **NOT** be returned if the information sought is available on the Court's website, www.cacd.uscourts.gov.

10. If a calendar conflict exists, counsel shall immediately notify the Courtroom Deputy Clerk by telephone.

11. Procedures for reserving electronic equipment are available on the Court's web site under "Services." If the equipment is not available from the Court, counsel shall request leave to bring electronic equipment into the courtroom. The request shall be made by a letter addressed to the Judge with 2 additional copies, referencing the case name and number, equipment, and vehicles transporting such equipment. Upon delivery of equipment to the Courthouse, the letter shall be provided to Court Security for approval.

12. For general information on how to order a transcript of any reported or digitally recorded proceeding, please contact 213-894-3015 or visit www.cacd.uscourts.gov > General Information > Court Reporter/Recorder Transcripts. If you require an estimate of cost for the preparation of a transcript, contact the court reporter/recorder for the desired proceeding.

To determine the court reporter/recorder for a particular proceeding, go to the Court Reporter Schedule web page and click on View by Date. Once you've determined the correct court reporter/recorder for the desired session, click on Court Reporter Phone and Email List for contact information.

13. Requests for daily trial transcripts should be made through the Court Reporter. The request should be made at least 3 weeks before trial.

14. Law clerk applicants should consult the Federal Law Clerk Information System website for future openings, deadlines, and application requirements (available at https://lawclerks.ao.uscourts.gov/). Fall, Spring and Summer full-time externships are available to qualified law students. Extern applicants should mail the Court a cover letter, resume, 10-page writing sample, and a copy of law school transcripts. Please call (213) 894-3938 for any law clerk or extern position questions.

15. Please see the Judge's order regarding court or jury trials. These orders contain information regarding exhibit preparation, jury instructions, and verdict forms.

16. To obtain the services of a court certified interpreter on a civil case, please call the Interpreter's Section at (213) 894-4370.

II. Judge Klausner's Case Management Orders

A. *Order for Court Trial*

IN THE UNITED STATES DISTICT COURT
FOR THE CENTRAL DISTRICT OF CALIFORNIA

Plaintiff(s),	Case No. ______________
v.	**ORDER FOR COURT TRIAL**
Defendant(s).	

UNLESS OTHERWISE ORDERED BY THE COURT, THE FOLLOWING RULES SHALL APPLY:

SCHEDULING

1. **In General**

All motions to join other parties or to amend the pleadings shall be filed and served within fifteen (15) days of the date of this order.

2. **Motions for Summary Judgment or Partial Summary Judgment**

Motions for summary judgment or partial summary judgment shall be filed as soon as practical, however, in no event later than the motion cut-off date.

3. **Discovery Cut-Off**

The Court has established a cut-off date for discovery in this action. All discovery shall be complete by the discovery cut-off date specified in the Scheduling Order. **This is not the date by which discovery requests must be served; it is the date by which all discovery is to be completed.**

In an effort to provide further guidance to the parties, the Court notes the following:

a. **Depositions**

All depositions shall be scheduled to commence sufficiently in advance of the discovery cut-off date to permit their completion and to permit the deposing party enough time to bring any discovery motion concerning the deposition prior to the cut-off date.

b. **Written Discovery**

All interrogatories, requests for production of documents, and requests for admission shall be served sufficiently in advance of the discovery cut-off date to permit the discovering party enough time to challenge (via motion practice) responses deemed to be deficient.

c. **Discovery Motions**

Whenever possible, the Court expects the parties to resolve discovery problems among themselves in a courteous, reasonable and professional manner. The Court expects that counsel will strictly adhere to the Civility and Professional Guidelines adopted by the United States District Court for the Central District of California in July, 1995.

Discovery matters are referred to a United States Magistrate Judge. **Any motion challenging the adequacy of responses to discovery must be filed timely, and served and calendared sufficiently in advance of the discovery cut-off date to permit the responses to be obtained before that date, if the motion is granted.**

Consistent resort to the Court for guidance in discovery is unnecessary and will result in the appointment of a Special Master at the joint expense of the parties to resolve discovery disputes.

4. **Mandatory Settlement Conference**

Pursuant to Local Rule 16-14, the parties in every case must select a settlement procedure. The final meeting with the parties' settlement officer must take place no later than 45 days before the Final Pretrial Conference.

FINAL PRE-TRIAL CONFERENCE

This case has been placed on calendar for a Final Pre-Trial Conference pursuant to Fed.R.Civ.P. 16 and 26. Unless excused for good cause, each party appearing in this action shall be represented at the Final Pre-Trial Conference, and all pre-trial meetings of counsel, by the attorney who is to have charge of the conduct of the trial on behalf of such party.

STRICT COMPLIANCE WITH THE REQUIREMENT OF FED.R.CIV.P. 26 AND LOCAL RULES ARE REQUIRED BY THE COURT. Therefore, carefully prepared Memoranda of Contentions of Fact and Law, a Joint Witness List, and Joint Exhibit List shall be submitted to the Court. The Joint Witness List shall contain a brief statement of the testimony for each witness, **what makes the testimony unique** from any other witness testimony, and the time estimate for such testimony. The Joint Exhibit List shall contain any objections to authenticity and/or admissibility to the exhibit(s) and the reasons for the objections.

The Memoranda of Contentions of Fact and Law, Witness List and Exhibit List are due twenty-one (21) days before the Final Pre-Trial Conference.

If expert witnesses are to be called at trial, each party shall list and identify their respective expert witnesses. Failure of a party to list and identify an expert witness may preclude a party from calling an expert witness at trial. If expert witnesses are to be called at trial, the parties shall exchange at the Final Pre-Trial Conference short narrative statements of the qualifications of the expert and the testimony expected to be elicited at trial. If reports of experts to be called at trial have been prepared, they shall be exchanged at the Final Pre-Trial Conference but shall not substitute for the narrative statements required.

TRIAL PREPARATION FOR COURT TRIAL –
MOTIONS, FINDINGS OF FACT AND EXHIBITS

1. **Motions in Limine**

All motions in limine must be filed and served a minimum of forty-five (45) days prior to the scheduled trial date. Each motion should be separately filed and numbered. All opposition documents must be filed and served at least twenty-five (25) days prior to the scheduled trial date. All reply documents must be filed and served at least ten (10) days prior to the scheduled trial date.

All motions in limine will be ruled upon on or before the scheduled trial date.

2. **Findings of Fact and Conclusion of Law**

Twenty-one (21) days before the trial date, all counsel are to have prepared proposed findings of fact and conclusions of law. Three copies are to be served on opposing counsel, and the original and one copy are to be lodged with the Court.

Upon receiving these proposed findings of fact and conclusions of law from opposing counsel, each party shall:

(1) Underline with red pencil those portions which it disputes;
(2) Underline with blue pencil those portions which it admits; and
(3) Underline in yellow pencil those portions which it does not dispute, but deems irrelevant.

In this connection, counsel are to note that they need not come to a uniform conclusion as to an entire proposed finding, or, indeed an entire sentence within a proposed finding. They may agree with part of it, disagree with part of it, and/or consider a portion of it irrelevant.

Seven (7) days before the trial date, each counsel shall file two marked copies of opposing counsel's proposed findings of fact and conclusions of law with the Court, and return one marked copy to the opposing counsel.

The parties shall be prepared to submit to the Court, and to exchange among themselves, supplemental findings of fact and conclusions of law during the course of the trial, with respect to which the same underlining procedure may be ordered.

3. **Trial Exhibits**

Counsel are to prepare their exhibits for presentation at the trial by placing them in binders which are indexed by exhibit number with tabs or dividers on the right side. Counsel shall submit to the Court an original and one copy of the binders. The exhibits shall be in a three-ring binder labeled on the spine portion of the binder as to the volume number and contain an index of each exhibit included in the volume. Exhibits must be numbered in accordance with Fed.R.Civ.P. 16, 26 and the Local Rules.

Exhibit list shall indicate which exhibits are objected to, the reason for the objection, and the reason it is admissible. Failure to object will result in a waiver of objection.

The Court requires that the following be submitted to the Courtroom Deputy Clerk on the first day of trial:

- The original exhibits with the Court's exhibit tags shall be stapled to the front of the exhibit on the upper right-hand corner with the case number, case name, and exhibit number placed on each tag. Exhibit tags can be obtained from the Clerk's Office, Room G-8, 312 North Spring Street, Los Angeles, CA 90012.
- One bench book with a copy of each exhibit for use by the Court, tabbed with numbers as described above. (Court's exhibit tags not necessary.)
- Three (3) copies of exhibit lists.
- Three (3) copies of witness lists in the order in which the witness may be called to testify.
- All counsel are to meet not later than ten (10) days before trial and to stipulate so far as is possible as to foundation, waiver of the best evidence rule, and to those exhibits which may be received into evidence at the start of trial. The exhibits to be so received will be noted on the copies of the exhibit lists.
- Any items that have not been admitted into evidence and are left in the courtroom overnight without prior approval, will be discarded.

TRIAL ON THE BRIEFS

1. **Briefing Schedule**

The parties shall timely file Opening Briefs, Oppositions and Replies based on the briefing schedule set by the Court.

2. **Joint Separate Statement**

On the date Oppositions are due, the parties shall file a Joint Separate Statement of Undisputed and Disputed Facts. The statement shall contain the following: (1) a list of undisputed facts, including citations to the portion(s) of the administrative record that support those facts, and (2) a list of disputed fact, which also include citations to the administrative record that support each parties' disputed assertions of fact.

B. Order for Jury Trial

IN THE UNITED STATES DISTICT COURT
FOR THE CENTRAL DISTRICT OF CALIFORNIA

Plaintiff(s),)	Case No. ________________
v.)	**ORDER FOR JURY TRIAL**
Defendant(s).)	

UNLESS OTHERWISE ORDERED BY THE COURT, THE FOLLOWING RULES SHALL APPLY:

SCHEDULING

1. In General

All motions to join other parties or to amend the pleadings shall be filed and served within fifteen (15) days of the date of this order.

2. Motions for Summary Judgment or Partial Summary Judgment

Motions for summary judgment or partial summary judgment shall be filed as soon as practical, however, in no event later than the motion cut-off date.

3. Discovery Cut-Off

The Court has established a cut-off date for discovery in this action. All discovery shall be complete by the discovery cut-off date specified in the Scheduling Order. **This is not the date by which discovery requests must be served; it is the date by which all discovery is to be completed.**

In an effort to provide further guidance to the parties, the Court notes the following:

a. Depositions

All depositions shall be scheduled to commence sufficiently in advance of the discovery cut-off date to permit their completion and to permit the deposing party enough time to bring any discovery motion concerning the deposition prior to the cut-off date.

b. Written Discovery

All interrogatories, requests for production of documents, and requests for admission shall be served sufficiently in advance of the discovery cut-off date to permit the discovering party enough time to challenge (via motion practice) responses deemed to be deficient.

c. Discovery Motions

Whenever possible, the Court expects the parties to resolve discovery problems among themselves in a courteous, reasonable and professional manner. The Court expects that counsel will strictly adhere to the Civility and Professional Guidelines adopted by the United States District Court for the Central District of California in July, 1995.

Discovery matters are referred to a United States Magistrate Judge. **Any motion challenging the adequacy of responses to discovery must be filed timely, and served and calendared sufficiently in advance of the discovery cut-off date to permit the responses to be obtained before that date, if the motion is granted.**

Consistent resort to the Court for guidance in discovery is unnecessary and will result in the appointment of a Special Master at the joint expense of the parties to resolve discovery disputes.

4. **Mandatory Settlement Conference**

Pursuant to Local Rule 16-14, the parties in every case must select a settlement procedure. The final meeting with the parties' settlement officer must take place no later than 45 days before the Final Pretrial Conference.

FINAL PRE-TRIAL CONFERENCE

This case has been placed on calendar for a Final Pre-Trial Conference pursuant to Fed.R.Civ.P. 16 and 26. Unless excused for good cause, each party appearing in this action shall be represented at the Final Pre-Trial Conference, and all pre-trial meetings of counsel, by the attorney who is to have charge of the conduct of the trial on behalf of such party.

STRICT COMPLIANCE WITH THE REQUIREMENT OF FED.R.CIV.P. 26 AND LOCAL RULES ARE REQUIRED BY THE COURT. Therefore, carefully prepared Memoranda of Contentions of Fact and Law, a Joint Witness List, and Joint Exhibit List shall be submitted to the Court. The Joint Witness List shall contain a brief statement of the testimony for each witness, **what makes the testimony unique** from any other witness testimony, and the time estimate for such testimony. The Joint Exhibit List shall contain any objections to authenticity and/or admissibility to the exhibit(s) and the reasons for the objections.

The Memoranda of Contentions of Fact and Law, Witness List and Exhibit List are due twenty-one (21) days before the Final Pre-Trial Conference.

As for the disclosure of expert witnesses and exchange of written reports, the parties must follow Rule 26. In addition, if the parties intend to call expert witnesses at trial, they shall file within five (5) days before the Final Pre-Trial Conference short narrative statements of the qualifications of each expert and the testimony expected to be elicited at trial.

**TRIAL PREPARATION FOR JURY TRIAL –
MOTIONS, INSTRUCTIONS AND EXHIBITS**

THE COURT ORDERS that all counsel comply with the following in their preparation for trial:

1. **MOTIONS IN LIMINE**

All motions in limine must be filed and served a minimum of forty-five (45) days prior to the scheduled trial date. Each motion should be separately filed and numbered. All opposition documents must be filed and served at least twenty-five (25) days prior to the scheduled trial date. All reply documents must be filed and served at least ten (10) days prior to the scheduled trial date.

All motions in limine will be ruled upon on or before the scheduled trial date and should not be noticed for motion on any date other than the assigned trial date.

2. **JURY INSTRUCTIONS/SPECIAL VERDICT FORMS**

Thirty-five (35) days before trial, plaintiff shall serve plaintiff's proposed jury instructions and special verdict forms on defendant. Twenty-eight (28) days before trial, defendant shall serve on plaintiff defendant's objections to plaintiff's instructions together with any additional instructions defendant intends to offer. Twenty-one (21) days before trial, plaintiff shall serve on defendant plaintiff's objections to defendant's instructions. Twenty-one (21) days before trial, counsel are ordered to meet and confer to attempt to come to agreement on the proposed jury instructions. The parties shall make every attempt to agree upon the jury instructions before submitting them to the Court. It is expected that counsel will agree on the substantial majority of jury instructions, particularly where patent instructions are involved.

Sixteen (16) days before trial, counsel shall file with the Court a JOINT set of jury instructions on which there is agreement. Defendant's counsel has the burden of preparing the joint set of jury instructions. At the same time each party shall file its proposed jury instructions which are objected to by any other party, accompanied by points and authorities in support of those instructions.

When the parties disagree on an instruction, the party opposing the instruction must attach a short statement (one to two paragraphs) supporting the objection, and the party submitting the instruction must attach a short reply supporting the instruction. Each statement should be on a separate page and should follow directly after the disputed instruction.

The parties ultimately must submit one document, or if the parties disagree over any proposed jury instructions, three documents. The three documents shall consist of: (1) a set of Joint Proposed Jury Instructions; (2) Plaintiff's Disputed Jury Instructions; and (3) Defendant's Disputed Jury Instructions. Any disputed Jury Instructions shall include the reasons supporting and opposing each disputed instruction in the format set forth in the previous paragraph.

The Court directs counsel to use the instructions from the *Manual of Model Jury Instructions for the Ninth Circuit* where applicable. Where California law is to be applied and the above instructions are not applicable, the Court prefers counsel to use the California Jury Instructions in either BAJI or CACI. If none of these sources is applicable, counsel are directed to use the instructions in Devitt, Blackmar and Wolff, *Federal Jury Practice and Instructions.*

Modifications of instructions from the foregoing sources (or any other form instructions) must specifically state the modification made to the original form instruction and the authority supporting the modification.

Each requested instruction shall be set forth in full; be on a separate page; be numbered; cover only one subject or principle of law; not repeat principles of law contained in any other requested instructions; and cite the authority for a source of the requested instruction. In addition to the foregoing, each party shall file with the Courtroom Deputy on the first day of trial a "clean set" of the aforesaid requested duplicate jury instructions in the following form: Each requested instruction shall be set forth in full; be on a separate page with the caption "COURT'S INSTRUCTION NUMBER __"; cover only one subject or principle of law; and not repeat principles of law contained in any other requested instruction. The "clean set" shall <u>not</u> cite the authority for a source of the requested instruction. Counsel shall also provide the Court with a CD in WordPerfect format containing the proposed jury instructions.

An index page shall accompany all jury instructions submitted to the Court. The index page shall indicate the following:

- the number of the instruction;
- a brief title of the instruction;
- the source of the instruction and any relevant case citation; and
- the page number of the instruction.

<u>EXAMPLE:</u>

NO.	TITLE	SOURCE	PAGE NO.
5	Evidence for Limited Purpose	9th Cir. 1.5	9

During the trial and before argument, the Court will meet with counsel and settle the instructions. Strict adherence to time requirements is necessary for the Court to examine the submissions in advance so that there will be no delay in starting the jury trial. **Failure of counsel to strictly follow the provisions of this section may subject the non-complying party and/or its attorney to sanctions and SHALL CONSTITUTE A WAIVER OF JURY TRIAL in all civil cases.**

3. TRIAL EXHIBITS

Counsel are to prepare their exhibits for presentation at the trial by placing them in binders which are indexed by exhibit number with tabs or dividers on the right side. Counsel shall submit to the Court an original and one copy of the binders. The exhibits shall be in a three-ring binder labeled on the spine portion of the binder as to the volume number and contain an index of each exhibit included in the volume. Exhibits must be numbered in accordance with Fed.R.Civ.P. 16, 26 and the Local Rules.

Exhibit list shall indicate which exhibits are objected to, the reason for the objection, and the reason it is admissible. Failure to object will result in a waiver of objection.

The Court requires that the following be submitted to the Courtroom Deputy Clerk on the first day of trial:

- The original exhibits with the Court's exhibit tags shall be stapled to the front of the exhibit on the upper right-hand corner with the case number, case name, and exhibit number placed on each tag. Exhibit tags can be obtained from the Clerk's Office, Room G-8, 312 North Spring Street, Los Angeles, CA 90012.
- One bench book with a copy of each exhibit for use by the Court, tabbed with numbers as described above. (Court's exhibit tags not necessary.)
- Three (3) copies of exhibit lists.
- Three (3) copies of witness lists in the order in which the witness may be called to testify.
- Counsel are ordered to submit a short joint statement of the case seven (7) days before trial that the Court may read to the prospective panel.
- All counsel are to meet not later than ten (10) days before trial and to stipulate so far as is possible as to foundation, waiver of the best evidence rule, and to those exhibits which may be received into evidence at the start of trial. The exhibits to be so received will be noted on the copies of the exhibit lists.
- Counsel may, but need not, submit brief proposed voir dire questions for the jury seven (7) calendar days before the Pretrial Conference. The Court will conduct its own voir dire after considering any proposed voir dire submitted by counsel.
- Any items that have not been admitted into evidence and are left in the courtroom overnight without prior approval, will be discarded.

DATED: ______________

____
R. GARY KLAUSNER
United States District Court

C. Standing Order Regarding Newly Assigned Cases

IN THE UNITED STATES DISTICT COURT
FOR THE CENTRAL DISTRICT OF CALIFORNIA

Plaintiff(s),	Case No. ____________
v.	**STANDING ORDER REGARDING NEWLY ASSIGNED CASES**
Defendant(s).	

READ THIS ORDER CAREFULLY. IT CONTROLS THIS CASE.

This action has been assigned to the calendar of Judge R. Gary Klausner. The responsibility for the progress of litigation in the Federal Courts falls not only upon the attorneys in the action, but upon the Court as well. "To secure the just, speedy, and inexpensive determination of every action," Federal Rule of Civil Procedure 1, all counsel are hereby ordered to familiarize themselves with the Federal Rules of Civil Procedure, particularly Federal Rules of Civil Procedure 16, 26, the Local Rules of the Central District of California, this Court's Order for Jury Trial, and this Court's Order for Court Trial.[1]

UNLESS OTHERWISE ORDERED BY THE COURT, THE FOLLOWING RULES SHALL APPLY:

1. Service of the Complaint. The Plaintiff(s) shall promptly serve the Complaint in accordance with Fed. R. Civ. P. 4 and file the proofs of service pursuant to Local Rule. Any Defendant(s) not timely served shall be dismissed from the action without prejudice. Any "DOE" or fictitiously-named Defendant(s) who is not identified and served within 120 days after the case is filed shall be dismissed pursuant to Federal Rule of Civil Procedure 4(m).

2. Removed Actions. Any answers filed in state court must be refiled in this Court as a supplement to the petition. Any pending motions must be re-noticed in accordance with Local Rule. If an action is removed to this Court that contains a form pleading, i.e., a pleading in which boxes are checked, the party or parties utilizing the form pleading must file an appropriate pleading with this Court within thirty (30) days of receipt of the Notice of Removal. The appropriate pleading referred to must comply with the requirements of Federal Rules of Civil Procedure, Rules 7, 7.1, 8, 9, 10 and 11.

3. Petitions under 18 U.S.C. Section 983(f). Petitioner(s) shall file and serve within 3 days of the date of this order an ex parte application requesting a hearing on the Petition to ensure prompt resolution of the Petition in compliance with section 983(f)'s deadlines.

4. Presence of Lead Counsel. The attorney attending any proceeding before this Court, including all status and settlement conferences, must be the lead trial counsel.

5. Discovery. All discovery matters have been referred to a United States

---

[1] Copies of the Local Rules are available on our website at "http:\\www.cacd.uscourts.gov" or they may be purchased from one of the following:

Los Angeles Daily Journal	West Group	Metropolitan News
915 East 1st Street	610 Opperman Drive	210 South Spring Street
Los Angeles, CA 90012	P.O. Box 64526	Los Angeles, CA 90012
	St. Paul, MN 55164-0526	

Magistrate Judge to hear all discovery disputes. (The Magistrate Judge's initials follow the Judge's initials next to the case number.) All documents must include the words "DISCOVERY MATTER" in the caption to ensure proper routing. Counsel are directed to contact the Magistrate Judge's Courtroom Deputy Clerk to schedule matters for hearing. Please do not deliver courtesy copies of these papers to this Court.

The decision of the Magistrate Judge shall be final, subject to modification by the District court only where it has been shown that the Magistrate Judge's order is clearly erroneous or contrary to law. Any party may file and serve a motion for review and reconsideration before this Court. The moving party must file and serve the motion within ten (10) days of service of a written ruling or within ten (10) days of an oral ruling that the Magistrate Judge states will not be followed by a written ruling. The motion must specify which portions of the text are clearly erroneous or contrary to law, and the claim must be supported by points and authorities. Counsel shall deliver a conformed copy of the moving papers and responses to the Magistrate Judge's clerk at the time of filing.

6. **Motions.** Motions shall be filed and set for hearing in accordance with Local Rule 6-1, except that this Court hears motions on Mondays commencing at 9:00 a.m. If Monday is a national holiday, this Court will hear motions on the succeeding Tuesday. If the date the motion was noticed for hearing is not available, the Court will issue a minute order resetting the date. Any opposition or reply papers due on a holiday are due the **preceding** Friday, not the following Tuesday. **Memoranda of Points and Authorities in support of or in opposition to motions shall not exceed 20 pages. Replies shall not exceed 10 pages.** Only in rare instances and for good cause shown will the Court agree to extend these page limitations. Pursuant to Local Rule, either a proportionally spaced or monospaced face may be used. A proportionally spaced face must be 14-point or larger, or as the Court may otherwise order. A monospaced face may not contain more than 10½ characters per inch.

Without prior permission from the Court, no party may file more than one motion pursuant to Fed.R.Civ. P. 56 regardless of whether such motion is denominated as a motion for summary judgment or summary adjudication.

7. **Proposed Orders.** Each party filing or opposing a motion or seeking the determination of any matter shall serve and lodge a proposed order setting forth the relief or action sought and a brief statement of the rationale for the decision with appropriate citations.

8. **Telephonic Hearings.** The Court does not permit appearances or arguments by way of telephone conference calls.

9. **Ex Parte Applications.** The Court considers ex parte applications on the papers and does not usually set these matters for hearing. If a hearing is necessary, the parties will be notified. Ex parte applications are solely for extraordinary relief and should be used with discretion. Sanctions may be imposed for misuse of ex parte applications. See Mission Power Engineering Co. v. Continental Casualty Co., 883 F.Supp. 488 (C.D. Cal. 1995).

Counsel's attention is directed to the Local Rules. The moving party shall serve the opposing party by facsimile transmission and shall notify the opposition that opposing papers must be filed not later than 3:00 p.m. on the first business day following such facsimile service. If counsel does not intend to oppose an ex parte application, he or she must inform the Courtroom Deputy Clerk at (213) 894-2649.

10. **Continuances.** This Court has a strong interest in keeping scheduled dates certain. Changes in dates are disfavored. Trial dates set by the Court are firm and will rarely be changed. Therefore, a stipulation to continue the date of any matter before this Court **must** be supported by a sufficient basis that demonstrates good cause why the change in the date is essential. Without such compelling factual support, stipulations continuing dates set by this Court will not be approved. Counsel requesting a continuance must lodge a proposed stipulation and order including a **detailed** declaration of the grounds for the requested continuance or extension of time. See Local Rules. Failure to comply with the Local Rules and this Order will result in rejection of the request without further notice to the parties. Proposed stipulations extending scheduling dates do not become effective unless and until this Court so orders. Counsel wishing to know whether a stipulation has been signed shall comply with the applicable Local Rule.

11. **Communications with Chambers.** Counsel shall not attempt to contact the Court or its staff by telephone or by any other ex parte means. Counsel may contact the Courtroom Deputy Clerk with appropriate inquiries only. Counsel shall not contact the Courtroom Deputy regarding status of ex parte application/ruling or stipulation/ruling..

12. **Order Setting Scheduling Conference.** Pursuant to Federal Rule of Civil Procedure 16(b), the Court will issue an Order setting a Scheduling Conference as required by Federal Rule of Civil Procedure 26 and the Local Rules of this Court. Strict compliance with Federal Rules of Civil Procedure 16 and 26 is required.

13. **Notice of this Order.** Counsel for plaintiff or plaintiff (if appearing on his or her own behalf) shall immediately serve this Order on all parties, including any new parties to the action. If this case came to the Court by a Petition for Removal, the removing defendant(s) shall serve this Order on all other parties.

14. **Courtesy Copies:** Courtesy copies are not required with documents filed traditionally over the intake counter. Courtesy copies are required for documents filed electronically and shall be delivered to the judge's courtesy copy drop box located outside of the Clerk's Office, Room 181L, no later than the following business day.

DATED: ________________

R. GARY KLAUSNER
United States District Judge

Hon. John A. Kronstadt

District Judge

Chambers Information

U.S. District Court, Central District of California
Courtroom 750, 7th Floor
255 East Temple Street
Los Angeles, CA 90012

Scheduling Information

Courtroom Deputy: (213) 894-2156

Civil Law and Motion	Mondays at 8:30 a.m.
Criminal Law and Motion	Thursdays at 8:30 a.m.

Biographical Information

Born 1951 in Washington, D.C.

Federal Judicial Service:

-Judge, U. S. District Court, Central District of California
-Nominated by Barack Obama on January 5, 2011, to a seat vacated by Florence-Marie Cooper; Confirmed by the Senate on April 12, 2011, and received commission on April 14, 2011.

Education:

-Cornell University, B.A., 1973
-Yale Law School, J.D., 1976

Professional Career:

-Law clerk, Hon. William P. Gray, U.S. District Court, Central District of California, 1976-1977
-Private practice, Washington, D.C., 1978-1985
-Private practice, Los Angeles, California, 1985-2002
-Judge, Superior Court of California, Los Angeles County, 2002-2011

I. Judge Kronstadt's Procedures and Practices

A. *Procedures and Schedules*

Some information regarding procedures and schedules is provided below. Counsel should review and strictly comply with all provisions of the Local Rules (unless specifically superseded by an order of this Court) and the Federal Rules of Civil Procedure. Copies of the Local Rules can be found at www.cacd.uscourts.gov/CACD/LocRules or purchased from one of the following:

Los Angeles Daily Journal	Metropolitan News	West Group
915 East 1st Street	210 South Spring Street	610 Opperman Drive
Los Angeles, CA 90012	Los Angeles, CA 90012	Eagan, Minnesota 55123

1. **Scheduling Motions.**
   Civil motions are heard on Mondays at 8:30 a.m.

   Criminal motions are heard on Thursdays at 8:30 a.m.

   When Monday is a holiday, the next motion date is the following Monday.

   It is not necessary to reserve a motion date with the court clerk prior to filing the motion, but counsel must comply with all Local and Federal Rules regarding service and must review the Court's Closed Motion Dates. If the Court does not believe that oral argument will be helpful, the Court will advise the parties in advance.

2. **Telephone Appearances.** The Court does not entertain telephone appearances for hearings except in exceptional and unanticipated circumstances. Any request for a telephonic appearance due to such circumstances must be e-filed at least five (5) court days before the scheduled hearing and shall include a declaration from counsel setting forth the basis for the request.

3. **Discovery Motions.** All discovery motions are to be calendared before the Magistrate Judge.

4. **Tentative Rulings.** Written tentative rulings may be issued. If issued, they will be available in the courtroom on the morning of the hearing. If a written tentative ruling is not issued, the Court will provide an oral tentative ruling at the outset of the hearing on the motion.

5. **Mandatory Chambers Copies.** Mandatory Chambers' Copies of all e-filed documents shall be delivered to the courtesy copy box located outside the Clerk's Office (Suite 181-L). It is imperative that mandatory Chambers' Copies be delivered by noon following the date of filing as required by General Order 10-07. Failure to deliver timely mandatory Chambers' Copies may result in a delay in hearing a motion or order taking the matter off calendar. The Court does not require Chambers' Copies of stipulations, proposed orders, notices of appearance or change of counsel unless any of these documents includes exhibits of more than 20 pages. *Bluebacks are not required. All Notices of Electronic Filing ("NEF") shall be stapled to the last page of the pleading.*

   The Court does not accept mandatory Chambers' Copies of documents sought to be filed under seal pursuant to Local Rule 79-5.1.

6. **Ex Parte Applications.** Ex parte applications are for extraordinary relief only. Ex

parte applications are considered on the papers and ordinarily are not set for hearings. (If the Court decides to conduct a hearing, the Courtroom Deputy Clerk will notify the moving party of its time and date and will direct the moving party to provide immediate notice to the non-moving party.) The moving party shall serve the opposing party by facsimile or personal service and shall notify the opposing party that any opposition must be filed no later than 24 hours after such facsimile or personal service. If counsel do not intend to oppose the ex parte application, counsel must inform the Courtroom Deputy Clerk by telephone as soon as possible.

7. **Status Inquiries.** Please do not inquire by phone regarding the status of a motion, stipulation, or proposed order. Please follow Local Rule 11-4.5.

8. **Contact with Chambers.** Counsel shall not initiate telephone calls to Judge Kronstadt's chambers, law clerks, or judicial assistant.

9. **Calendar Conflicts.** Counsel shall notify the Courtroom Deputy Clerk for each judge prior to the date of the conflict. Counsel should appear before the most senior judge and request priority.

10. **Continuances.** Continuances are granted only upon a showing of good cause, particularly focusing upon evidence of diligent work by the party seeking delay and of prejudice that may result from the denial of the continuance. The Court sets firm trial dates and will not change them without good cause having been shown. Requests should be submitted well in advance of the relief requested. Counsel requesting a continuance, whether by application or stipulation, must submit a detailed declaration as to the reason(s). Such declaration shall include in its opening paragraph: the date the action was filed; the present trial date (if any); the date of the event whose continuance is sought; the date on which that date was set; and the date(s) and nature of any prior continuances of any proceeding in the action. The Court will not consider any request that does not comply with the Local Rules. Counsel should not assume the request is granted unless approved by the Court. See Local Rule 40-1. Any request shall be accompanied by a separate proposed order.

11. **Electronic Equipment.** ELMO reservations/tutorials may be made by referring to the Court website at www.cacd.uscourts.gov/CACD/Services.nsf. Counsel may also contact the Courtroom Technology Help Desk ((213) 894-3061) about such matters. Counsel should contact the Courtroom Deputy Clerk at the earliest possible date concerning procedures for bringing electronic equipment into the courtroom.

12. **Transcripts.** For general information on how to order a transcript of any reported or digitally recorded proceeding, please contact 213-894-3015 or visit www.cacd.uscourts.gov > General Information > Court Reporter/Recorder Transcripts. If you require an estimate of cost for the preparation of a transcript, contact the court reporter/recorder for the desired proceeding.

    To determine the court reporter/recorder for a particular proceeding, go to the Court Reporter Schedule web page and click on View by Date. Once you've determined the correct court reporter/recorder for the desired session, click on Court Reporter Phone and Email List for contact information.

13. **Law Clerk/Extern Positions.** Questions regarding law clerk/extern positions should be directed to Judge Kronstadt's chambers by letter.

14. **Trial.**

Hours: Trials are generally conducted Tuesday through Friday. The Court will adopt a particular time schedule on a case-by-case basis. In general, the schedule will be either: (i) from 8:30 a.m. to 2:30 p.m. with two or three 20-minute breaks; or (ii) from 9:00 a.m. to 4:00 p.m., with a 15-minute break in both the morning and the afternoon, and a one-hour lunch break.

The Court requires the following to be submitted to the Courtroom Deputy Clerk on the first day of trial:

Exhibit Binders: One original binder with tagged exhibits. Each volume is to be clearly labeled. One bench copy of the exhibit binder with tagged exhibits. Each volume is to be clearly labeled.

Exhibit and Witness Lists: Three copies of exhibit lists whose format complies with Local Rule 16-6. Lead trial counsel shall meet and confer at least fourteen (14) calendar days before the trial to discuss and seek to agree, to the extent possible, on issues including foundation, and admissibility of proposed exhibits. Three copies of witness lists in the order in which the witnesses will be called to testify. Three copies of witness lists in alphabetical order. A time estimate shall be provided for the direct and cross-examination of each witness.

Jury Instructions and Verdict Forms: The parties shall make every attempt to agree upon jury instructions and verdict forms before submitting proposals to the Court. The Court prefers Ninth Circuit model instructions. Counsel shall exchange proposed jury instructions (general and special) and special verdict forms (if applicable) twenty-one (21) calendar days prior to the Rule 16-2 Final Pre-Trial Conference. Counsel shall exchange any objections to the instructions and special verdict forms fourteen (14) calendar days prior to the Rule 16-2 Final Pre-Trial Conference. Counsel shall meet and confer with the goal of reaching an agreement on one set of joint jury instructions and one special verdict form prior to the Rule 16-2 conference.

The parties shall file proposed jury instructions and verdict form seven (7) calendar days before the Final Pre-Trial Conference. The parties shall present these documents in printed form along with a version in Word or Word Perfect stored on a CD or other media. If the parties disagree over any proposed jury instruction(s) or any aspects of the verdict form, the parties must submit: (a) a set of joint agreed upon proposed jury instructions and any agreed upon joint verdict form; (b) a set of disputed jury instructions; (c) their respective proposed verdict forms where there is not agreement as to the entire form. As to any disputed instruction(s) or verdict form, the parties are to submit a joint statement in which each sets forth the factual and legal basis for its position as to each disputed instruction and their respective positions on their alternative verdict forms. The joint statement shall be presented in the following format:

1. Set forth each disputed instruction followed by each party's position as to such instruction.
2. Where appropriate, organize the presentation of disputed instructions by subject, so that instructions that address the same or similar issues are presented sequentially.
3. The proposed verdict form of each side, with a red-line version showing

the differences between the two. Counsel shall also provide to the Court a CD containing the joint proposed and/or disputed jury instructions and any verdict form as filed and a "clean version" of each instruction and verdict form which includes only the text of each instruction (eliminating titles, supporting authority, indiction of party proposing, etc.).

Voir Dire: Counsel may submit proposed voir dire questions that are unique to the particular trial. Any such submission shall be made seven (7) calendar days prior to the Pre-Trial Conference.

Joint Statement of the Case; Mini-Opening Statements: Counsel shall meet and confer prior to the Final Pre-Trial Conference to determine if, in lieu of a Joint Statement of the Case, they will stipulate to having each side make a brief (less than five minute), mini-opening statement to the panel of prospective jurors prior to the commencement of voir dire. Such mini-opening statements are not to be arguments. If all parties do not stipulate to the use of mini-opening statements, they shall meet and confer and seek to reach agreement on a Joint Statement of the Case to be read by the Court to the panel of prospective jurors prior to the commencement of voir dire. If the parties cannot agree to such a Joint Statement, they shall submit to the Court a copy of the proposed statement of one side, together with a red-line showing the proposed changes of the other side(s). The parties shall present these documents in printed form along with a version in Word or Word Perfect stored on a CD or other media. All such materials are to be presented to the Court seven (7) calendar days prior to the Final Pre-Trial Conference.

All exhibits will be returned to counsel at the conclusion of the trial; copies will not be maintained by the Court. Counsel shall maintain the originals of all admitted and lodged exhibits as required by Local Rules 79-3 and 79-4.

Motions in limine in civil cases will be heard at the time of the Final Pre-Trial Conference.

15. **Settlement Procedure.** Pursuant to Local Rule 16-15, in every civil case, the parties shall select a settlement procedure. The Court will discuss the proposed procedure with the parties at the time of the Scheduling Conference.

II. Judge Kronstadt's Case Management Orders

A. *Initial Standing Order for Cases Assigned to Judge John A. Kronstadt*

IN THE UNITED STATES DISTICT COURT
FOR THE CENTRAL DISTRICT OF CALIFORNIA

Plaintiff(s),	) Case No. ________ -JAK (__x)
v.	)
Defendant(s).	) **INITIAL STANDING ORDER FOR CASES ASSIGNED TO JUDGE JOHN A. KRONSTADT**

PLEASE READ THIS ORDER CAREFULLY. IT GOVERNS THIS CASE AND DIFFERS IN SOME RESPECTS FROM THE LOCAL RULES.

This case has been assigned to the calendar of Judge John A. Kronstadt. Both the Court and counsel bear responsibility for the progress of this litigation in federal court. To "secure the just, speedy, and inexpensive determination" of this case, as called for in Fed. R. Civ. P. 1, all parties or their counsel are ordered to become familiar with the Federal Rules of Civil Procedure, the Local Rules of the Central District of California, and this Court's standing orders.

THE COURT ORDERS AS FOLLOWS:

1. **Service of the Complaint**
   The plaintiff shall promptly serve the complaint in accordance with Fed. R.Civ.P. 4 and file the proofs of service pursuant to Local Rule 5-3.1. Although Fed.R.Civ.P. 4(m) does not require the summons and complaint to be served for 120 days, the Court expects service as soon as service can reasonably be accomplished. The Court will require plaintiffs to show good cause to extend the service deadline beyond 120 days.

2. **Presence of Lead Counsel**
   Lead trial counsel shall attend any scheduling, pretrial, or settlement conference set by the Court unless engaged in trial. Should that occur, counsel are to contact the Courtroom Deputy Clerk in advance of the conference to determine whether the Court will proceed with alternate counsel. The Court does not permit special appearances; only counsel of record may appear at any proceeding.

3. **Ex Parte Applications**
   Ex parte applications are solely for extraordinary relief and should be used with discretion. *See Mission Power Engineering Co. v. Continental Casualty Co.*, 883 F.Supp. 488 (C.D. Cal. 1995). Ex parte applications that fail to conform to Local Rule 7-19 and 7-19.1, including a statement of opposing counsel's position, will not be considered, except on a specific showing of good cause. Concurrently with service of the ex parte papers by electronic service, facsimile, or personal service, the moving party shall notify the opposition that opposing papers must be filed no later than twenty-four (24) hours (or one court day) following service. On the day the documents are e-filed, a conformed courtesy copy of moving, opposition, or notice of non-opposition papers are to be hand-delivered to the Courtroom Deputy Clerk in Room 181-L of the Clerk's Office. If counsel do not intend to oppose the ex parte application, counsel must inform the Courtroom Deputy Clerk by telephone as soon as possible.

4. **Continuances or Extensions of Time**
This Court is very committed to adhering to all scheduled dates. In general, this makes the judicial process more efficient and less costly. Changes in dates are disfavored. Trial dates set by the Court are firm and will rarely be changed. Therefore, any request, whether by application or stipulation, to continue the date of any matter before this Court must be supported by a sufficient basis that demonstrates good cause why the change in the date is essential. Without such compelling factual support, requests to continue dates set by this Court will not be approved. Counsel requesting a continuance must electronically file any application or stipulation and lodge a proposed order including a detailed declaration of the grounds for the requested continuance or extension of time. The Court will not consider any request that does not comply with the Local Rules and this Order. Proposed stipulations extending scheduling dates become effective only if, and when, this Court approves the stipulation as presented to, or modified by, the Court, and an associated order is entered. Counsel should avoid submitting requests for a continuance less than at least five (5) court days prior to the scheduled date that is the subject of the request.

5. **TROs and Injunctions**
Parties seeking emergency or provisional relief shall comply with Fed. R. Civ. P. 65 and Local Rule 65. The Court will not rule on any application for such relief for at least 24 hours after the party subject to the requested order has been served, unless service is excused. Such party may file opposing or responding papers in the interim.

6. **Cases Removed from State Court**
All documents filed in state court, including documents appended to the complaint, answers, and motions, must be re-filed in this Court as a supplement to the notice of removal. *See* 28 U.S.C. § 1447(a) and (b). If the defendant has not yet answered or filed a motion in response to the complaint, the answer or responsive pleading filed in this Court must comply with the Federal Rules of Civil Procedure and the Local Rules. If, before the case was removed, a motion or demurrer in response to the complaint was pending in state court, it must be re-noticed in this Court in accordance with Local Rule 7. Counsel shall file with their first appearance an original and two copies of a Notice of Interested Parties in accordance with Local Rule 7.1.

If an action is removed to this Court that contains a form pleading, i.e., a pleading in which boxes are checked, the party or parties utilizing the form pleading must file an appropriate pleading with this Court within thirty (30) days of receipt of the Notice of Removal. The appropriate pleading referred to must comply with the requirements of Fed. R. Civ. P. 7, 7.1, 8, 9, 10 and 11.

7. **Status of Fictitiously Named Defendants**
This Court intends to adhere to the following procedures where a matter is removed to this Court on diversity grounds with fictitiously named defendants. *See* 28 U.S.C. §§ 1441(a) and 1447.

   a. Plaintiff is expected to ascertain the identity of, and serve, any fictitiously named defendant, within 120 days of the removal of the action to this Court.

   b. If plaintiff believes (by reason of the necessity for discovery or otherwise) that fictitiously named defendants cannot be fully identified within the 120-day period, an ex parte application requesting permission to extend that period to effectuate service may be filed with this Court. Such application shall state the specific reasons for the requested extension of time, including a description of all efforts made up to that time to identify and serve such person(s). The ex parte application shall be served upon all appearing parties, and shall state that appearing parties may file written comments within seven (7) days of the filing of the ex parte application.

c. If plaintiff wants to substitute a defendant for one of the fictitiously named defendants, plaintiff shall first seek the consent of counsel for all defendants (and counsel for the fictitiously named party, if that party has separate counsel). If consent is withheld or denied, plaintiff should file a motion on regular notice. The motion and opposition should address whether the matter should thereafter be remanded to the Superior Court if complete diversity of citizenship would no longer be present as a result of the addition of the new party. *See* U.S.C. § 1447(c), (d).

8. Discovery

a. Discovery Matters Referred to Magistrate Judge

All discovery matters, including all discovery motions, are referred to the assigned United States Magistrate Judge. The Magistrate Judge's initials follow the District Judge's initials next to the case number on this Order. All discovery-related documents must include the words "DISCOVERY MATTER" in the caption to ensure proper routing. Counsel are directed to contact the Magistrate Judge's Courtroom Deputy Clerk to schedule matters for hearing. Please deliver mandatory chambers copies of discovery-related papers to the Magistrate Judge assigned to this case rather than to this Court.

In accordance with 28 U.S.C. § 636(b)(1)(A), the Court will not reverse any order of the Magistrate Judge unless it has been shown that the Magistrate Judge's order is clearly erroneous or contrary to law.

Any party may file and serve a motion for review and reconsideration before this Court. *See* Local Rule 72-2. The moving party must file and serve the motion within 14 days of service of a written ruling or within 14 days of an oral ruling that the Magistrate Judge states will not be followed by a written ruling. The motion must specify which portions of the ruling are clearly erroneous or contrary to law and support the contention with points and authorities. Counsel shall deliver a conformed copy of the moving papers and responses to the Magistrate Judge's Courtroom Deputy Clerk at the time of filing.

b. Compliance with Fed. R. Civ. P. 26(a)

Unless there is a likelihood that, upon motion by a party, the Court would order that any or all discovery is premature, counsel should begin to conduct discovery actively before the Scheduling Conference. At the very least, the parties shall comply fully with the letter and spirit of Fed. R. Civ. P. 26(a) and thereby obtain and produce most of what would be produced in the early stage of discovery, because at the Scheduling Conference the Court will impose firm deadlines to complete discovery.

9. Motions

a. Time for Filing and Hearing Motions

Motions shall be filed in accordance with Local Rule 7. In general, this Court hears motions on Mondays, beginning at 8:30 a.m. If Monday is a national holiday, motions will be heard on the next Monday. It is not necessary to clear a hearing date with the Court Clerk before filing a motion. If the motion date selected is not available, the Court will issue a minute order continuing the date. Counsel should check the Court's website for Closed Motion Dates.

b. Pre-Filing Requirement To Meet and Confer

Counsel must comply with Local Rule 7-3, which requires counsel to engage in a pre-filing conference "to discuss thoroughly . . . the substance of the contemplated motion and any potential resolution." Counsel should discuss the issues to a sufficient degree that if a motion is still necessary, the briefing may be directed to those substantive issues requiring resolution by the Court. Counsel should resolve minor procedural or other non-substantive matters during the conference. The *in propria persona* status of one or more parties does not alter this requirement.

c. Length and Format of Motion Papers

Memoranda of points and authorities shall not exceed 25 pages and all footnotes shall be in the same type size as text. *See* Local Rules 11-6 and 11-3.1.1. Any reply shall not exceed 10 pages. Only in rare instances and for good cause shown will the Court grant an application to extend these page limitations. No supplemental brief shall be filed without prior leave of Court. If documentary evidence in support of or in opposition to a motion exceeds 50 pages, the evidence must be separately bound and tabbed and include an index. If such evidence exceeds 200 pages, the documents shall be placed in a Slant D-Ring binder, with an index and with each item of evidence separated by a tab divider on the right side.

d. Citations to Case Law

Citations to case law must identify not only the case cited, but the specific page referenced. For example, if a quotation is presented, the associated page citation shall be provided. Similarly, if a case is cited in support of a proposition based on language in the opinion, the page(s) on which such language appears shall be provided.

e. Citations to Other Sources

Statutory references should identify with specificity the sections and subsections referenced. Citations to treatises, manuals, and other materials should include the volume, section, and pages that are referenced.

f. Oral Argument

If the Court deems a matter appropriate for decision without oral argument, the Court will notify the parties in advance. Local Rule 7-15.

10. Specific Motions

a. Motions Pursuant to Rule 12

Many motions to dismiss or to strike can be avoided if the parties confer in good faith (as required by Local Rule 7-3), especially where perceived defects in a complaint, answer, or counterclaim that could be corrected by amendment. *See Chang v. Chen*, 80 F.3d 1293, 1296 (9th Cir. 1996) (where a motion to dismiss is granted, a district court should provide leave to amend unless it is clear that the complaint could not be saved by any amendment). Moreover, a party has the right to amend the complaint "once as a matter of course at any time before a responsive pleading is served." Fed. R. Civ. P. 15(a). A Rule 12(b)(6) motion is not a responsive pleading and therefore plaintiff might have a right to amend. *See, e.g.*, *St. Michael's Convalescent Hospital v. California*, 643 F.2d 1369, 1374 (9th Cir. 1981). Even after a complaint has been amended or a responsive pleading has been served, the Federal Rules provide that leave to amend should be "freely given when justice so requires." Fed. R. Civ. P. 15(a). The Ninth Circuit requires that this policy favoring amendment be applied with "extreme liberality." Morongo Band of Mission Indians v. Rose, 893 F.2d 1074, 1079 (9th Cir. 1990).

These principles require that plaintiff's counsel carefully evaluate defendant's contentions as to the deficiencies in the complaint. In most instances, the moving party should agree to any amendment that would cure the defect.

b. Motions to Amend

All motions to amend pleadings shall: (1) state the effect of the amendment and (2) identify the page and line number(s) and wording of any proposed change or addition of material. The proposed amended pleading shall be serially numbered to differentiate it from previously amended pleadings.

In addition to the requirements of Local Rule 15-1, counsel shall attach as an appendix to the moving papers a "redlined" version of the proposed amended pleading showing all additions and deletions of material.

c. Summary Judgment Motions

Parties need not wait until the motion cutoff date to bring motions for summary judgment or partial summary judgment. Whenever possible, the party moving for summary judgment should provide more than the minimum twenty-eight (28) day notice for motions. See Local Rule 6-1. The parties should prepare papers in a fashion that will assist the Court in locating the evidence with respect to the facts (e.g., generous use of tabs, tables of contents, headings, indices, etc.). The parties are to comply precisely with Local Rules 56-1 through 56-4.

i. Statements of Uncontroverted Facts and Genuine Issues

The Statement of Uncontroverted Facts and Conclusions of Law ("Statement of Uncontroverted Facts"), as required by Local Rule 56-1 shall separately identify each claim for relief on which the moving party seeks summary judgment and the legal grounds for summary judgment. In a two-column format beneath the identified claim for relief, the left-hand column shall set forth, sequentially numbered, each allegedly uncontroverted material fact as to that claim for relief, and the right-hand column shall set forth the evidence that supports the factual statement. Citation to the supporting evidence shall be specific, including reference to the exhibit, page, and line number. The Statement of Uncontroverted Facts shall be formatted based on the following examples:

Plaintiff's Claim for Relief for _________ is Barred by the Applicable Statute of Limitations. (Cite)

1. (Moving party's first undisputed fact)	(Supporting evidence citation)
2. (Moving party's second undisputed fact)	(Supporting evidence citation)

The opposing party's statement of genuine issues must be in two columns and track the movant's separate statement exactly as prepared. The left-hand column must restate the allegedly undisputed fact and the alleged supporting evidence, and the right-hand column must state either that it is undisputed or disputed. The opposing party may dispute all or only a portion of the statement, but if disputing only a portion, such party must clearly indicate what part is being disputed, followed by the opposing party's evidence controverting the fact. To demonstrate that a fact is disputed, the opposing party must briefly state why it disputes the moving party's asserted fact, cite to the relevant exhibit or other evidence, and describe what it is in that exhibit or evidence that refutes the asserted fact. No legal argument should be set forth in this document.

The opposing party may submit additional material facts that bear on, or relate to, the issues raised by the movant, which shall follow the format described above for the moving party's separate statement. These additional facts shall continue in sequentially numbered paragraphs and shall set forth in the right-hand column the evidence that supports that statement.

ii. Supporting Evidence

No party shall submit evidence other than the specific items of evidence or testimony necessary to support or controvert a proposed statement of undisputed fact. For example, entire deposition transcripts, entire sets of interrogatory responses, and documents that do not specifically support or controvert material in the separate statement shall not be submitted in opposition to a motion for summary judgment.

Evidence submitted in support of or in opposition to a motion should be submitted either by way of stipulation or as exhibits to declarations sufficient to authenticate the proffered evidence, and should not be attached to the memorandum of points and authorities. Documentary evidence as to which there is no stipulation regarding foundation must be accompanied by the testimony, either by declaration or properly authenticated deposition transcript, of a witness who can establish authenticity.

iii. Objections to Evidence

If a party disputes a fact based in whole or in part on an evidentiary objection, the ground of the objection should be succinctly stated in a separate statement of evidentiary objections in a three-column format. The left column should identify the items objected to (including page and line number if applicable). The middle column should set forth a concise objection (e.g., hearsay, lacks foundation, etc.) with a citation to the Federal Rules of Evidence or, where applicable, a case citation. The right column should provide space for the Court's entry of its ruling on the objection.

11. Notice of This Order

Plaintiff's counsel or plaintiff (if appearing on his or her own behalf) shall immediately serve this Order on all parties, including any new parties to the action. If this case came to the Court by a Petition for Removal, the removing defendant(s) shall serve this Order on all other parties.

IT IS SO ORDERED.

Dated: ______________________

JOHN A. KRONSTADT
United States District Judge

B. Order on Jury/Court Trial

IN THE UNITED STATES DISTICT COURT
FOR THE CENTRAL DISTRICT OF CALIFORNIA

Plaintiff(s),)	Case No. __________ -JAK (__x)
v.)	**ORDER ON JURY/COURT TRIAL**
Defendant(s).)	Final Pretrial Conference: ___ at 1:30 p.m.
)	Status Conference re Exhibits:__at 3:00p.m.
	Trial: ___ at 9:00 a.m.

A. SCHEDULING:

1. **In General:** The last day for hearing on any motion to join other parties or to amend the pleadings shall be specified in the Scheduling Order. All unserved parties shall be dismissed no later than the date set for the Final Pretrial Conference.

2. **Motions for Summary Judgment or Partial Summary Judgment:** Motions for Summary Judgment or Partial Summary Judgment shall be heard no later than the last day for hearing motions, as set forth in the Scheduling Order.

3. **Settlement Procedures:** It is the policy of the Court to encourage disposition of civil litigation by settlement when such is in the best interest of the parties. The Court favors any reasonable means to accomplish this goal. All settlement discussions shall be conducted in compliance with Local Rule 16-15. Consistent with Local Rule 16-15.2, the Scheduling Order establishes a deadline for participation in settlement proceedings. The parties must elect one of the settlement procedures outlined in Local Rule 16-15.4. If the parties do not timely file a Notice of Settlement Procedure Selection, the Court may order the parties to participate in any of the settlement procedures set forth in the Local Rule.

4. **Discovery Cut-Off:** The Scheduling Order establishes a cut-off date for discovery in this action. This is not the date by which discovery requests must be served; it is the date by which all discovery is to be completed. The Court will not approve stipulations between counsel that permit responses to be served after the cut-off date, except in extraordinary circumstances.

5. **Discovery Motions:** Any motion respecting the inadequacy of responses to discovery must be filed and served not later than ten days after the discovery cut-off date. Whenever possible, the Court expects counsel to resolve discovery issues among themselves in a courteous, reasonable, and professional manner. Thus, the Court expects that counsel will strictly adhere to the Civility and Professional Guidelines adopted by the United States District Court for the Central District of California.

B. FINAL PRETRIAL CONFERENCE:

This case has been placed on calendar for a Final Pretrial Conference pursuant to Fed. R. Civ. P. 16. Strict compliance with the requirements of the Federal Rules of Civil Procedure and the Local Rules is mandatory. Counsel shall lodge carefully prepared Memoranda of Contentions of Fact and Law (which may also serve as the parties' respective trial briefs) and a Final Pretrial Conference Order in accordance with the provisions of *Local Rules 16-4 and 16-7*. The Memoranda of Contentions of Fact and Law will be served no later than 21 calendar days before the Pretrial Conference. The Final Pretrial Conference Order will be lodged no later than 11 calendar days before the Final Pretrial Conference. The form of the Final Pretrial

Conference Order will be in the form set forth in Appendix A to the Local Rules.

C. PREPARATION FOR TRIAL AND SCHEDULING EXHIBIT CONFERENCE THE FRIDAY BEFORE TRIAL

The Court ORDERS that all counsel comply with the following rules in their preparation for trial:

1. **Motions *In Limine*:** All motions *in limine* will be heard at the Final Pretrial Conference. The purpose of these motions is to alert the Court to significant evidentiary issues that can be addressed and resolved prior to trial. All motions *in limine* must be filed and served in compliance with Local Rule 6-1. Opposition papers must be filed and served in compliance with Local Rule 7-9. Reply papers must be filed and served in compliance with Local Rule 7-10.

2. **Statement of the Case (Jury Trials):** Counsel will prepare a joint statement of the case that may be read by the Court to the prospective panel of jurors prior to the commencement of voir dire. The statement should not be more than two or three paragraphs. The statement will be filed with the Court five court days before the Final Pretrial Conference. If counsel cannot agree on a statement, each shall submit a proposed statement along with a red-line showing how each proposes to modify the other's proposed statement. In addition, both the proposed statements and the red-lines of such statements shall also be sent in Word or Word Perfect to the Court at the following email address: JAK_Chambers@cacd.uscourts.gov. At the time of the Final Pretrial Conference, the Court will confer with counsel with respect to the use of a Statement of the Case prior to the commencement of voir dire and/or the use at that time of a "mini opening" statement by counsel for each party. Each mini-opening statement will be for three to five minutes and will summarize the evidence that each side intends to present.

3. **Voir Dire (Jury Trials):** At least five court days before the Final Pretrial Conference, each counsel shall file with the Court any special questions requested to be posed by the Court to prospective jurors during voir dire.

4. **Witness Lists:** A witness list will be prepared in compliance with Local Rule 16-5. The witness list will be filed no later than five court days prior to the Final Pretrial Conference. Counsel will submit the names of the witnesses in the order that they are expected to testify, and will provide, to the extent possible, an accurate estimate of the time needed for each witness for direct, cross, redirect and re-cross. Counsel will also provide a brief summary of each witness' testimony. If more than one witness is offered on the same subject, the summary should be sufficiently detailed to allow the Court to determine if the testimony is cumulative.

Counsel shall set forth the information about the amount of time that is expected for the testimony of each witness on a jointly-prepared document with five columns: (i) the name of the witness; (ii) estimated time for direct examination (in hours, with portions thereof stated in decimal form, *e.g.*, "1.5 hours," if the estimate is for one hour and 30 minutes) ; (iii) estimated time for cross-examination; (iv) estimated time for re-direct examination; and (v) total time for the witness. At the bottom of each page the total time for all witnesses on that page shall be stated, with the grand total of all time stated on the final page of the chart.

5. **Jury Instructions:** In a jury trial, jury instructions are to be filed no later than five court days prior to the Final Pretrial Conference. The parties must submit joint jury instructions. The parties shall meet and confer sufficiently far in advance of the required submission date as part of a good faith effort to agree upon, and prepare, the joint jury instructions. The instructions should be submitted in the order in which the parties wish to

have the instructions read. This order should reflect a single organized sequence agreed to by all of the parties.

In the event that agreement on all instructions cannot be reached, counsel will submit four sets of instructions in the following format: (i) the agreed upon instructions; and (ii) the instructions proposed by any party and opposed by any other party. In addition, counsel must submit electronic versions (in Word Perfect of Word) to the Court at the following email address: JAK_Chambers@cacd.uscourts.gov. Instructions upon which agreement cannot be reached should reflect the basic disagreements among the parties as to the law. For disputed instructions, a party should note its objections to a proposed instruction and its reasons for putting forth its alternative on pages placed after its own alternative instruction.

6. <u>**Verdict Form(s) in Jury Trials:**</u> In a jury trial, proposed verdict form(s) are to be filed no later than five court days prior to the Final Pretrial Conference. The parties shall meet and confer sufficiently in advance of the required submission date as part of a good faith effort to agree upon, and prepare, any proposed verdict form(s). In the event that the parties cannot reach an agreement as to verdict form(s), each shall submit its proposed form(s) no later than five court days prior to the Final Pretrial Conference. At that same time, each shall also submit a red-line showing how each proposes to modify the other's proposed verdict form(s). In addition, both the proposed form(s) and the red-lines of such form(s) shall also be sent in Word or Word Perfect to the Court at the following email address: JAK_Chambers@cacd.uscourts.gov

7. <u>**Exhibits and Exhibit Conference:**</u>

a. Exhibit List: A joint exhibit list will be prepared in compliance with the example below and <u>Local Rule 16-6</u>.

<u>**JOINT EXHIBIT LIST**</u>					
Case Name:					
Case Number:					
No. of Exhibit	Description	Stip. to Authen.	Stip. to Admiss.	Date Identified	Date Admitted

The joint exhibit list will contain the information required by F.R.Civ.P. 26(a)(3)(A). The joint exhibit list will be filed no later than five court days prior to the Final Pretrial Conference. In order to produce the joint exhibit list, the parties will meet and confer sufficiently in advance of the required submission date. As part of the meet and confer process, counsel will stipulate so far as is possible as to foundation, waiver of the best evidence rule, and to those exhibits which may be received into evidence at the start of trial. The exhibits to be so received will be noted on the extra copies of the exhibit lists.

b. Exhibit Preparation: All exhibits will be placed in loose leaf binders that are tabbed on the right side with exhibit numbers. The spine of the notebook is to be marked with the case name and number and the numbers of the exhibits contained therein. The notebooks are to be prepared with an original for the Courtroom Deputy Clerk (which will be tagged with the appropriate exhibit tags in the upper right-hand corner of the first page of each exhibit) and one copy for the Court. Each notebook will contain a list of the included exhibits. The exhibits are to be numbered in accordance with <u>Local Rule 26-3</u>.

c. Exhibit Conference: AN EXHIBIT CONFERENCE REQUIRING

THE ATTENDANCE OF TRIAL COUNSEL WILL BE HELD AT 3:00 P.M. ON THE FRIDAY BEFORE THE SCHEDULED TRIAL DATE IN COURTROOM 750, UNLESS THE COURT ORDERS OTHERWISE. Exhibits are to be submitted to the Courtroom Deputy Clerk at the time of the exhibit conference.

8. **(Court Trials): Findings of Fact and Conclusions of Law; Declarations:** For any matter requiring findings of fact and conclusions of law, counsel for each party shall lodge and serve proposed findings of fact and conclusions of law as promptly as possible in compliance with Local Rule 52. In addition, counsel must submit electronic versions (in Word or Word Perfect) to the Court at the following email address: JAK_Chambers@cacd.uscourts.gov. When ordered by the Court in a particular case, each party shall, at least five court days prior to the trial, file declarations containing the direct testimony of each witness whom that party intends to call at trial. If such declarations are filed, each party shall file any evidentiary objections to the declaration(s) submitted by any other party at least two court days prior to the trial. If any party submits such objections, they shall be submitted in the following three-column format: (I) the left column should contain a verbatim quote of each statement objected to (including page and line number); (ii) the middle column should set forth a concise objection (e.g., hearsay, lacks foundation, etc.) with a citation to the Federal Rules of Evidence or, where applicable, a case citation; and (iii) the right column should provide space for the Court's entry of its ruling on the objection.

D. <u>ATTORNEY AND PARTY CONDUCT AT TRIAL:</u>

1. **<u>Trial Schedule:</u>** Unless otherwise ordered, trials will be held on Tuesdays through Fridays from 9:00 a.m. to 12:00 p.m. and 1:00 p.m. to 4:00 p.m. with a 15-minute break during each session. This schedule may be changed for each trial and during each trial depending on the Court's determination based on the scheduling needs of jurors, witnesses, counsel or the Court.

2. **<u>Trial Conduct:</u>**

a. **Jury Selection**

1. The Court will seat as prospective jurors the same number of jurors who will serve at trial. The Court will conduct voir dire of this panel, which may include questions proposed by counsel. The Court may permit limited voir dire by counsel where it is shown to the Court that it is necessary. After any potential juror is excused for cause, a replacement juror will be placed in the vacant seat and will respond to voir dire. Once a panel is in place to which there are no remaining or unadjudicated "for cause" challenges, counsel for each side will be permitted to exercise their respective peremptory challenge(s) through the Court. Upon the exercise of a peremptory challenge, a replacement juror will be seated, will respond to voir dire and will be subject to a "for cause" challenge before any remaining peremptory challenge is exercised.

b. **Opening Statements, Examining Witnesses, and Summation**

1. At the end of each day, counsel presenting his or her case shall advise opposing counsel of the witnesses expected to testify the following day with an estimate of the length of direct examination for each witness. Opposing counsel shall provide an estimate of the length of cross-examination for each witness. Cooperation of counsel will ensure a smooth flow of witnesses. It is the responsibility of all counsel to arrange the appearance of witnesses in order to avoid delay.

2. Opening statements, examination of witnesses, and summation will be from the lectern only. Counsel must not consume time by writing out words or drawing charts or diagrams. Counsel may do so in advance and explain that the item was prepared earlier to save time as ordered by the Court.
3. The Court will honor reasonable time estimates for opening and closing presentations to the jury.
4. In jury trials, where a party has more than one lawyer, only one may conduct the direct or cross-examination of a given witness.
5. If a witness is on the stand when a recess is taken, it is counsel's duty to have the witness back on the stand, ready to proceed, when the court session resumes.
6. If a witness was on the stand at adjournment, it is counsel's duty to have the witness adjacent to, but not on, the stand, ready to proceed when the court session resumes.
7. It is counsel's duty to notify the Courtroom Deputy Clerk in advance if any witness should be accommodated in an appropriate manner due to any disability or other physical need.
8. The Court attempts to accommodate physicians, scientists, and all other professional witnesses and will, except in extraordinary circumstances, permit them to testify out of order. The Court may do the same with respect to non-party witnesses who have work commitments. Counsel must anticipate any such possibility and discuss it with opposing counsel. If there is objection to having a particular witness called out of order, counsel shall confer with the Court in advance.

c. **Objections and General Decorum**

1. When objecting, counsel must rise to state the objection and state only that counsel objects and the legal ground of objection. If counsel wishes to argue an objection further, counsel must ask for permission to do so; the Court may or may not grant a request for conference at sidebar. The Court strongly discourages sidebars because they cause an inefficient use of jury time. Instead, evidentiary issues should be anticipated in advance of trial and should be addressed through motions in limine and/or in connection with the rulings on exhibits.
2. Counsel must not approach the Courtroom Deputy Clerk or the witness stand without specific permission. When permission is given, counsel shall return to the lectern when the purpose of the permission is finished. Counsel must not engage in questioning a witness at the witness stand absent specific

approval by the Court.

3. Counsel must address all remarks to the Court. Counsel are not to address the Courtroom Deputy Clerk, the Reporter, persons in the audience, or opposing counsel. If counsel wishes to speak with opposing counsel, counsel must ask permission to talk off the record. Any request for the re-reading of questions or answers shall be addressed to the Court, not to the court reporter.
4. Counsel must not make an offer of stipulation unless counsel already has conferred with opposing counsel and has reason to believe the stipulation will be acceptable.
5. On the first day of trial counsel shall advise the Court of any commitments that may result in counsel's absence or late arrival on any day of the trial.

d. **Exhibits**

1. Each counsel should keep counsel's own list of exhibits and should keep track when each has been admitted in evidence.
2. Each counsel is responsible for any exhibits that counsel secures from the Courtroom Deputy Clerk and, during all recesses and noontime and afternoon adjournments, counsel must return all exhibits in counsel's possession to the Courtroom Deputy Clerk.
3. An exhibit not previously marked should, at the time of its first mention, be accompanied by a request that the Courtroom Deputy Clerk mark it for identification. To save time, counsel must show a new exhibit to opposing counsel before it is mentioned in Court.
4. Counsel should move exhibits into evidence as soon as admissibility is established, while they are freshly in the minds of all participants. If there is an objection, the motion to admit will be dealt with at the next available recess. In jury trials, no exhibit shall be read or displayed to the jury until admitted absent a pre-trial stipulation by counsel or a ruling by the Court at the Exhibit Conference.
5. Absent unusual circumstances, counsel must not ask witnesses to draw charts or diagrams nor ask the Court's permission for a witness to do so. If counsel wishes to question a witness in connection with graphic aids, the material must be fully prepared before the court session starts.

e. **Depositions:**

1. All depositions that will be used in the trial, either as evidence or for impeachment, must be signed and lodged with the Courtroom Deputy Clerk on the first day of trial or such earlier date as the Court may order. For any deposition in which counsel is interested, counsel should check with the Courtroom Deputy Clerk to confirm that the Courtroom Deputy Clerk has

the transcript and that the transcript is properly signed.

2. In using depositions for impeachment, counsel shall first announce both the beginning and ending page and line references of the passage desired to be read, and allow opposing counsel an opportunity to state any objection. If an objection is made, counsel shall await a ruling before proceeding. In addition, counsel who has not requested the reading, shall advise the Court whether counsel requests a ruling as to any objection(s) made on the record or reserved during the deposition testimony at issue. In reading deposition testimony, counsel shall use one of the following procedures:
   - **a.** If counsel wishes to read the questions and answers as alleged impeachment and ask the witness no further questions on that subject, counsel may merely read the relevant portions of the deposition into the record.
   - **b.** If counsel wishes to ask the witness further questions on the subject matter (this does not include a question whether the witness's testimony has changed between deposition and trial) the deposition is placed in front of the witness and the witness is told to read silently the pages and lines involved. Then counsel may either ask the witness further questions on the matter and thereafter read the quotations or read the quotations and thereafter ask further questions. Counsel should have an extra copy of the deposition for this purpose.
3. Where a witness is absent and the witness' testimony is offered by deposition, please observe the following procedure. A reader should occupy the witness chair and read the testimony of the witness while the examining lawyer asks the questions.

f. **Advance Notice of Evidentiary or Difficult Questions**

If during trial counsel has reason to anticipate that a difficult and unexpected question of law or evidence will raise legal argument, requiring research and/or briefing, counsel must give the Court advance notice. Counsel are directed to notify the Courtroom Deputy Clerk at the day's adjournment if an unexpected legal issue arises that could not have been foreseen and addressed by a motion in limine (see Fed. R. Evid. 103). To the maximum extent possible such matters shall be taken outside normal trial hours (e.g., recess, before or after the trial day).

The Courtroom Deputy Clerk is ordered to serve a copy of this Order on counsel/parties in this action.

IT IS SO ORDERED.

Dated: ___________________

JOHN A. KRONSTADT
United States District Judge

C. *Order Setting Rule 16(b) Scheduling Conference*

IN THE UNITED STATES DISTICT COURT
FOR THE CENTRAL DISTRICT OF CALIFORNIA

Plaintiff(s),

v.

Defendant(s).

Case No. __________ -JAK (__x)

ORDER SETTING RULE 16(b) SCHEDULING CONFERENCE

Date: *
Time: 1:30 p.m.
Joint Report Due: [10 days before the date of the conference]

This case has been assigned to Judge John A. Kronstadt. This Order applies to all parties in this action, whether or not they are represented by counsel. "Counsel" as used in this Order, also refers to parties who are representing themselves. If plaintiff has not already served the complaint (or any amendment thereto) on each defendant, plaintiff shall promptly do so and shall file proofs of service within three days thereafter. Defendant(s) also shall timely serve and file their responsive pleadings and file proofs of service within three days thereafter.

This matter is set for a scheduling conference on the above date. The conference will be held pursuant to Fed.R.Civ.P. 16(b). The parties are reminded of their obligations under Fed.R.Civ.P. 26(a)(1) to disclose information (without awaiting a discovery request) and under R. 26(f) to confer on a discovery plan not later than twenty-one (21) days prior to the scheduling conference and to file a report with the Court entitled "Joint Rule 16(b) Report" not later than fourteen (14) days after they confer. Please comply with these requirements; it will simplify the Scheduling Conference.

The Court encourages counsel to begin to conduct discovery actively before the Scheduling Conference. The Court encourages prompt, early discovery because at the Scheduling Conference the Court will set firm deadlines to complete discovery. Even if there is no agreement to conduct discovery prior to the Scheduling Conference, the parties shall comply fully with the letter and spirit of Fed.R.Civ.P. 26(a) and thereby obtain and produce most of what would be produced in the early stage of discovery.

1. **Joint Rule 16(b) Report.**
The Joint Rule 16(b) Report, which shall be filed not later than one week before the scheduling conference, shall be drafted by plaintiff's counsel (unless the parties agree otherwise or unless plaintiff is self-represented, in which case defendant's counsel), but shall be submitted and signed jointly. "Jointly" contemplates a single report, regardless of how many separately-represented parties there are. The Joint Rule 16(b) Report shall report on all matters enumerated below, which include those required to be discussed by Rule 26(f) and Local Rule 26. The Joint Rule 26(f) Report should set forth the following information under section headings corresponding to those in this Order:

a. Statement of the case: A short synopsis (not to exceed two pages) of the main claims, counterclaims, and affirmative defenses.

b. Subject matter jurisdiction: A statement of the specific basis of federal jurisdiction, including supplemental jurisdiction.

c. Legal issues: A brief description of the key legal issues, including any unusual substantive, procedural or evidentiary issues.

d. Parties, and Non-Party Witnesses: A list of parties and percipient witnesses on the main issues in the case. For conflict purposes, corporate parties must identify all subsidiaries, parents, and affiliates.

e. Damages: The realistic range of provable damages.

f. Insurance: Whether there is insurance coverage.

g. Motions: A statement of the likelihood of motions seeking to add other parties or claims, file amended pleadings or transfer venue.

h. Manual for Complex Litigation: Whether all or part of the procedures of the Manual for Complex Litigation should be utilized.

i. Status of Discovery: A discussion of the present state of discovery, including a summary of completed discovery.

j. Discovery Plan: A detailed discovery plan, as contemplated by Rule 26(f), including the identity of all anticipated deponents and dates by which their depositions are to be completed (if possible), anticipated written discovery requests, including requests for admission, document requests, and interrogatories, and a schedule for completion of all discovery. State what, if any, changes in the disclosures under Rule 26(a) should be made, the subjects on which discovery may be needed and whether discovery should be conducted in phases or limited in some manner, whether applicable limitations should be changed or other limitations imposed, and whether the Court should enter other orders. Please note that a statement to the effect that discovery will be conducted as to all claims and defenses, will not satisfy this requirement.

k. Discovery cut-off: A proposed discovery cut-off date. This means the final day for completion of non-expert discovery, including resolution of all discovery motions.

l. Expert discovery: Proposed dates for expert witness disclosures (initial and rebuttal) and expert discovery cut-off under Rule 26(a)(2).

m. Dispositive motions: A description of the issues or claims that any party believes may be determined by motion for summary judgment or motion *in limine*.

n. Settlement: A statement of what settlement discussions or written communications have occurred (excluding any disclosure or discussion of the substantive matters or terms discussed) and a statement pursuant to Local Rule 16-15.4 about selecting a settlement mechanism under that Rule. If a case is selected for the ADR Program, the parties may choose private mediation at their own expense. No case will proceed to trial unless all parties with full authority to settle the case – including, as to each corporate party, an officer who has such authority – have appeared personally at a settlement conference.

o. Trial estimate: A realistic estimate of the time required for trial and whether trial will be by jury or by the Court. Each side should specify (by number, not by name) how many witnesses it contemplates calling. If the time estimate for trial given in the Joint Rule 26(f) Report exceeds five court days, counsel shall be prepared to discuss in detail the estimate.

p. Trial counsel: The name(s) of the attorney(s) who will try the case, including those will be lead trial counsel.

q. Independent Expert or Master: Whether this is a case in which the Court should consider appointing a Master pursuant to Rule 53 or an independent scientific expert.

r. Timetable: Please complete the Schedule of Pretrial and Trial Dates form attached as Exhibit A to this Order and attach it to the Joint Rule 26(f) Report. The entries in the "Weeks Before Trial" column reflect what the Court believes are appropriate for most cases and will allow the Court to rule on potentially dispositive motions sufficiently far in advance of the pretrial conference. The form is designed to enable counsel to ask the Court to set different last dates by which the key requirements must be completed. Each side should fill in the month, day, and year it requests for each event. *E.g.*, for the expert discovery cut-off it might be "10/7/12" for plaintiff and "10/28/12" for defendant, if they cannot agree. Each entry proposing a Court date shall be on a Monday, except the trial date, which will be a Tuesday. Counsel should ensure that requested dates do not fall on a court holiday. At the conference, the Court will review this form with counsel in determining the dates that will be set in the case. The cut-off date for motions is the last date on which motions may be heard, not filed. The Court is not likely to continue this date, and will not do so unless the trial date is also continued. Following the Scheduling Conference, the Court will issue an "Order on Court/Jury Trial." This Order will set forth all pre-trial and trial obligations of counsel, and, where applicable, the deadlines for each.

s. Other issues: A statement of any other issues affecting the status or management of the case (*e.g.*, unusually complicated technical or technological issues, disputes over protective orders, extraordinarily voluminous document production, non-English speaking witnesses, ADA-related issues, discovery in foreign jurisdictions) and any proposals concerning severance, bifurcation, or other ordering of proof.

t. Patent Cases: Propose dates and methodology for claim construction and *Markman* hearings.

u. **Do the parties wish to have a Magistrate Judge preside?** Under 28 U.S.C. § 636, the parties may consent to have a Magistrate Judge preside over all the proceedings, not just discovery. They may select any Magistrate Judge (not just the one assigned to this case) from among those Magistrate Judges who accept these designations. (They are identified on the Central District's website, which also contains the consent form.)

2. **Scheduling Conference.** The Scheduling Conference will be held in Courtroom 750 of the Roybal Federal Courthouse at 255 East Temple Street. Counsel shall comply with the following with respect to the Scheduling Conference:

a. Participation. The lead trial attorney for each party shall attend the Scheduling Conference unless such counsel is engaged in trial, on vacation, or excused for good cause following a written request addressed to the Clerk in advance of the Scheduling Conference.

b. Continuance. A continuance of the Scheduling Conference will be granted only for good cause, following a written request addressed to the Clerk in advance of the Scheduling Conference.

c. Use of Conference Telephone. In general , the Court prefers in- person appearances. However, if one or more of the lead counsel has his or her office outside of Los Angeles County, or under other appropriate circumstances, the Court may, upon the request of one or more counsel, conduct the status conference by conference telephone call. Please contact the court clerk at (213) 894-2156 to request approval of, and to receive details about, a call-in appearance.

3. **Protective Orders.** If you seek a protective order, please use your best efforts to propose it to opposing counsel before the Scheduling Conference.

4. **Notice to be Provided by Counsel.** Plaintiff's counsel or, if plaintiff is self-represented, defendant's counsel, shall serve this Order on any parties who first appear after the date of this Order and to parties who are known to exist but have not yet entered appearances.

5. **Disclosures to Clients.** Counsel are ordered to deliver to their respective clients a copy of this Order and of the Court's Scheduling and Case Management Order, which will set forth the schedule that the Court establishes at the Scheduling Conference.

6. **Court's Website.** A copy of this order is available on the Central District of California website, at "www.cacd.uscourts.gov," under "Judge's Requirements."
The Court thanks the parties and their counsel for their anticipated cooperation in carrying out these requirements.

IT IS SO ORDERED.

Dated:

____
JOHN A. KRONSTADT
United States District Judge

Copies to: All Counsel of Record

SCHEDULE OF PRETRIAL AND TRIAL DATES

Case No.:	
Case Name:	

Matter	Plaintiff(s) Request	Defendant(s) Request	Court Order
[ ] Jury Trial [ ] Court Trial: **(Tuesday at 9:00 a.m.)** Duration Estimate: _____ Days / _____Weeks			
Status Conference re Exhibits: **(Friday at 3:00 p.m.)** Friday before the trial date			
Final Pretrial Conference: **(Monday at 3:00 p.m.)** 2 weeks before the trial			
Post Mediation Status Conference: **(Monday at 1:30 p.m.)** 30 days before the cut-off date			

Matter	Weeks Before Trial	Plaintiff(s) Request	Defendant(s) Request	Court Order
Last Date to Amend Pleadings/Add Parties				
Non-Expert Discovery Cut-Off	16			
Expert Disclosure (initial)	15			
Expert Disclosure (rebuttal)	11			
Last Date to Conduct Settlement Conference	10			
Expert Discovery Cut-Off	8			
Last Date to Hear Motions	8			

Settlement Procedure Selection (ADR-12 Form will be completed by Court): 1. Magistrate Judge 2. Attorney Settlement Officer Panel 3. Outside ADR/Non-Judicial			

Hon. J. Spencer Letts
District Judge

Chambers Information
U.S. District Court, Central District of California
Courtroom 4, 2nd Floor
312 N. Spring Street
Los Angeles, CA 90012

Scheduling Information
Courtroom Deputy: (213) 894-2600

Civil Law and Motion	Every other Monday at 1:00 p.m.
Criminal Law and Motion	Mondays at 11:00 a.m.

Biographical Information
Born 1934 in St. Louis, MO

Federal Judicial Service:
-Judge, U. S. District Court, Central District of California
-Nominated by Ronald Reagan on November 7, 1985, to a new seat created by 98 Stat. 333; Confirmed by the Senate on December 16, 1985, and received commission on December 17, 1985. Assumed senior status on December 19, 2000.

Education:
-Yale University, B.A., 1956
-Harvard Law School, LL.B., 1960

Professional Career:
-U.S. Army Reserve Captain, 1956-1965
-Private Practice, Houston, Texas, 1960-1966
-Vice President and General Counsel, Teledyne, Inc., Los Angeles, California, 1966-1973
-Private Practice, Los Angeles, California, 1973-1975
-Vice President and General Counsel, Teledyne, Inc., Los Angeles, California, 1975-1978
-Private Practice, Los Angeles, California, 1978-1985

I. <u>Judge Letts' Procedures and Practices</u>

A. *<u>Procedures and Schedules</u>*

1. Civil motions are heard **every other Monday** at **1:00 p.m.**

   Criminal motions are heard on **Mondays** at **11:00 a.m.**

   (If Monday is a holiday, the next motion date is the Tuesday following the holiday.)

   It is not necessary to clear a motion date with the court clerk prior to filing the motion.

2. Discovery disputes are to be scheduled by conference call before the district judge by contacting the judge's secretary at 213-894-2600. No discovery motions are to be filed.

3. Tentative rulings are **NOT** issued.

4. Mandatory chambers copies are discouraged unless the hearing is set for the next day following the date the document is filed, in which case a Mandatory chambers copy is to be delivered to chambers.

   Mandatory chambers copies of e-filed documents shall be delivered to chambers.

5. Procedures for filing an ex parte application: Ex parte applications are to be filed in the Clerk's Office. You will be contacted either of the court's ruling or of a hearing set by the Court.

6. To request a continuance of any scheduled court proceeding: Submit a written Stipulation (with a reason for the continuance) and a Proposed Order, or submit an Ex Parte Application if the continuance is not stipulated to.

7. Counsel are allowed to contact the judge's law clerk or secretary for procedural matters and conference calls only.

8. Inquiries regarding the status of a motion, stipulation or proposed order: Leave a telephone message for the court clerk. If an extra conforming copy of a stipulation or proposed order has not been submitted, please check the docket sheet.

9. Calendar conflicts: Contact the court clerk.

10. Procedures for bringing electronic equipment into the courtroom: Must get prior approval by the judge.

11. Questions regarding law clerk/extern positions are to be made to the judge's chambers staff.

12. Trial preparation:
    a. **Court hours:** Tuesday - Friday, 9:00 a.m. - 3:00 or 4:00 p.m.
    b. **Exhibit preparation:** See the judge's written rules
    c. **Jury instructions:** Ninth Circuit

13. Procedures for obtaining the services of an interpreter on a civil case Contact the Interpreters Section.

14. For general information on how to order a transcript of any reported or digitally recorded proceeding, please contact 213-894-3015 or visit www.cacd.uscourts.gov > General Information > Court Reporter/Recorder Transcripts. If you require an estimate of cost for the preparation of a transcript, contact the court

reporter/recorder for the desired proceeding.

To determine the court reporter/recorder for a particular proceeding, go to the Court Reporter Schedule web page and click on View by Date. Once you've determined the correct court reporter/recorder for the desired session, click on Court Reporter Phone and Email List for contact information.

Hon. Ronald S. W. Lew

District Judge

Chambers Information

U.S. District Court, Central District of California
Courtroom 21, 5th Floor
312 N. Spring Street
Los Angeles, CA 90012

Scheduling Information

Courtroom Deputy: (213) 894-2682

Civil Law and Motion	Tuesdays or Wednesdays at 10:00 a.m.
Criminal Law and Motion	Tuesdays or Wednesdays at 10:00 a.m.

Biographical Information

Born 1941 in Los Angeles, CA

Federal Judicial Service:

-Judge, U. S. District Court, Central District of California
-Nominated by Ronald Reagan on February 2, 1987, to a seat vacated by Laughlin E. Waters; Confirmed by the Senate on May 7, 1987, and received commission on May 7, 1987. Assumed senior status on September 19, 2006.

Education:

-Loyola University, Los Angeles, CA, B.A., 1964
-Southwestern University School of Law, J.D., 1971

Professional Career:

-U.S. Army, 1967-1969
-Deputy City Attorney, Criminal and Civil Liability Divisions, Los Angeles City Attorney's Office, California, 1972-1974
-Private Practice, Los Angeles, California, 1974-1981
-Los Angeles Fire and Police Pension Commissioner, California, 1976-1982
-Judge, Los Angeles Municipal Court, California, 1982-1984
-Judge, Los Angeles Superior Court, California, 1984-1987

I. Judge Lew's Procedures and Practices

A. *Instruction Regarding Jury's Duties*

COURT'S INSTRUCTION NO. ___
DUTIES OF JURY TO FIND FACTS AND FOLLOW LAW

Members of the jury, now that you have heard all the evidence and the arguments of the attorneys, it is my duty to instruct you on the law which applies to this case. A copy of these instructions will be available in the jury room for you to consult if you find it necessary.

It is your duty to find the facts from all the evidence in the case. To those facts you will apply the law as I give it to you. You must follow the law as I give it to you whether you agree with it or not. You must not be influenced by any personal likes or dislikes, opinions, prejudices, or sympathy. That means that you must decide the case solely on the evidence before you. You will recall that you took an oath promising to do so at the beginning of the case.

In following my instructions, you must follow all of them and not single out some and ignore others; they are all equally important. You must not read into these instructions or into anything the court may have said or done any suggestion as to what verdict you should return —that is a matter entirely up to you.

Authority for Instruction: Ninth Circuit Model Civil Jury Instruction 1.1

B. Procedures and Schedules

Judge Lew requires paper copies (courtesy copies) of all filings. Mandatory courtesy copies are to be delivered to chambers located on the 5th floor of the 312 N. Spring Street courthouse. Documents should be: 1) properly e-filed or manually filed, 2) courtesy copies delivered no later than noon the next day, and, 3) emailed to the Judge's generic email address at rswl_chambers@cacd.uscourts.gov. Any questions, please call the Courtroom Deputy Clerk for further assistance.

(Motion dates are not reserved by the Court. Counsel shall file a properly noticed motion.)

1. **CIVIL MOTIONS are heard on Tuesdays or Wednesdays at 10:00 A.M.

   CRIMINAL MOTIONS are heard on Tuesdays or Wednesdays at 10:00 A.M. (Judge Lew does not ordinarily hold criminal status conferences/pretrial conferences). Counsel may file a request for such a hearing in writing.

   ****FINAL PRETRIAL CONFERENCES** are held on Tuesdays or Wednesdays at 10:00 A.M.

2. DISCOVERY MOTIONS are to be scheduled before the assigned Magistrate Judge.
3. Judge Lew **DOES NOT** issue tentative rulings.
4. To request a continuance of any scheduled court proceedings, the parties should properly file a Stipulation and properly file a Notice of Lodging of the proposed Order. Counsel should then email to rswl_chambers@cacd.uscourts.gov the following items: the pdf version of the Stipulation and a proposed order in word or word perfect format. Do **NOT** assume that your stipulation will be granted. All requests for continuances should be submitted at least **FIVE (5)** calendar days prior to the scheduled court proceeding.
5. Procedures for filing an Ex Parte Application: Papers are to be properly filed (whether that is manual filing or electronic filing.) Counsel should refer to Local Rules 7-19 and 7-20. As a general policy, all oppositions are due within 24 hours from the filing of the Ex Parte. Also, opposing counsel shall contact the Courtroom Deputy Clerk within 24 hours as to their position. Opposing party is to be notified that they have **24 hours** to file an opposition. Judge Lew will rule on the pleadings that are submitted to the Court. Ex Parte Applications should not include a hearing date. Judge Lew **DOES NOT** hold hearings on Ex Parte Applications. Counsel will be notified by telephone of Judge Lew's ruling.
6. Counsel shall not contact, via telephone or mail, the Judge or his chambers, including but not limited to his law clerks or secretary. All inquiries are to be made directly through the Courtroom Deputy Clerk.
7. Counsel shall contact the Courtroom Deputy Clerk, via email or telephone, at least **THREE (3)** calendar days prior to a hearing date if a calendar conflict is pending so that alternate arrangements can be made. Counsel are to make appearances based upon the Seniority List as established by the Chief Judge.
8. For general information on how to order a transcript of any reported or digitally recorded proceeding, please contact 213-894-3015 or visit www.cacd.uscourts.gov > General Information > Court Reporter/Recorder Transcripts. If you require an

estimate of cost for the preparation of a transcript, contact the court reporter/recorder for the desired proceeding.

To determine the court reporter/recorder for a particular proceeding, go to the Court Reporter Schedule web page and click on View by Date. Once you've determined the correct court reporter/recorder for the desired session, click on Court Reporter Phone and Email List for contact information.

9. ADR PROGRAM

If counsel has received a "Notice to Parties of Alternate Dispute Resolution (ADR) Program" - forms ADR-08, ADR-10, or ADR-11, with an attached "ADR Program Questionnaire" - form ADR-09, please see General Order 07-01, which is located in the "General Orders" section on the home page of the Court's website. The Attorney Settlement Officer information is located in the section "Attorney Information, ADR." (upper left hand side of the home page.)

10. TRIAL PREPARATION INSTRUCTIONS

MOTIONS IN LIMINE: All motions in limine shall be properly filed no later than the date of the Final Pretrial Conference. Oppositions shall be properly filed no later than **7** days after the Final Pretrial Conference; replies, if any, shall be properly filed no later than **14** days after the Final Pretrial Conference.

EXHIBITS: Counsel are to prepare their exhibits for presentation at trial by placing them in volumes which are tabbed down the front, right side with the exhibit numbers. These volumes are to be prepared in an original and one (1) copy for the Court. Each volume of exhibits shall be contained in a three-ring notebook. Exhibits must be numbered in accordance with Local Rules 11-5.2 and 11.5.3.

THE COURT REQUIRES THAT THE FOLLOWING BE SUBMITTED TO THE COURTROOM DEPUTY CLERK ON THE FIRST DAY OF TRIAL:

- **a.** **TWO** separate books of exhibits . The first book shall contain the original exhibits which shall be used by the witness. The second book shall be used by the Judge.
- **b.** **THREE** *copies of your EXHIBIT LIST (*no file stamp on these copies)
- **c.** **THREE** *copies of your WITNESS LIST (*no file stamp on these copies)

On first day of trial, counsel are to arrive no later than 8:45 a.m. Trial hours are 9:00 a.m. to 5:00 p.m, with a 90 minute lunch break.

11. To obtain the services of an interpreter in a civil case contact the Interpreters Department at 213-894-4599.

12. Counsel shall contact the Courtroom Deputy Clerk, via email or telephone, to request leave to bring electronic equipment into the courtroom. Counsel are advised that such a request shall be made by a letter addressed to the U.S. Marshal's Office and forwarded to the Courtroom Deputy Clerk for signature (please include case name and case number) Upon request, counsel may fax the letter to the Courtroom Deputy Clerk. Upon arrival at the courthouse, counsel shall present the letter to the Court Security Officer for entrance.

13. All exhibits will be returned to counsel at the end of trial and will not be kept by the

Court. Counsel are to keep the lodged and admitted exhibits in their possession pursuant to Local Rules 79-37 and 79-4.

14. For information regarding law clerk or extern positions, please call (213)894-3508.

15. Judge Lew follows the Local Rules and does not have any other special rules.

16. Judge Lew **DOES NOT** allow telephonic appearances.

17. In addition to hard copy submissions, parties must submit a copy of the proposed jury instructions in conformance with Local Rules 51-1 through 51-5.1 on disc in WordPerfect format. Please see the attached jury instruction for guidance.

Hon. Consuelo B. Marshall

District Judge

Chambers Information

U.S. District Court, Central District of California
Courtroom 2, 2nd Floor
312 N. Spring Street
Los Angeles, CA 90012

Scheduling Information

Courtroom Deputy: (213) 894-5288

Civil Law and Motion	Mondays at 11:00 a.m.
Criminal Law and Motion	Mondays at 1:30 p.m.

Biographical Information

Born 1936 in Knoxville, TN

Federal Judicial Service:

-Judge, U. S. District Court, Central District of California
-Nominated by Jimmy Carter on June 20, 1980, to a seat vacated by Robert Firth; Confirmed by the Senate on September 29, 1980, and received commission on September 30, 1980.
-Served as chief judge, 2001-2005. Assumed senior status on October 24, 2005.

Education:

-Los Angeles City College, A.A., 1956
-Howard University, B.A., 1958
-Howard University, LL.B., 1961

Professional Career:

-Deputy City Attorney, Los Angeles City Attorney's Office, California, 1962-1967
-Private Practice, Los Angeles, California, 1968-1970
-Commissioner, Juvenile Court, Los Angeles Superior Court, California, 1971-1976
-Judge, Civil and Criminal Division, Inglewood Municipal Court, Inglewood, California, 1976-1977
-Judge, Criminal Division, Los Angles Superior Court, California, 1977-1980

I. Judge Marshall's Procedures and Practices

A. *Procedures and Schedules*

1. Civil motions are heard: **Every Monday**; call Civil Intake at 213-894-3535 to check for dates. Time: **11:00 A.M.**

   Pre-Trial Conferences are heard on: **Mondays** as set by the Court. Time: **2:30 P.M.**

   Criminal motions are heard on: **Mondays**. Time: **1:30 P.M.**

   (If Monday is a holiday, motion date is: Next available motion day)

2. Discovery motions are to be noticed with the Magistrate Judge.

3. Are tentative rulings issued? Not prior to the hearing.

4. Are Mandatory Chambers Copies accepted by Court? Yes, to be placed in a tray outside chambers entrance.

   Mandatory chambers copies of e-filed documents shall be delivered to chambers.

5. Procedures for filing an Ex Parte Application: Counsel shall comply with Local Rule 7-19 and 7-19.1. Ex Parte Application shall stand submitted until further order of Court.

6. To request a continuance of any scheduled court proceeding: The party(ies) must make the request in writing by either submitting a stipulation or ex parte application with a proposed order for the Court's signature; alternative dates should be cleared with the court clerk before submitting the document.

7. Are counsel allowed to contact the Judge's law clerks or secretary? No; all inquiries of any nature are to be directed to the court clerk.

8. Inquiries regarding the status of a motion, stipulation or proposed order: Are to be made to the court clerk.

9. Calendar conflicts (procedures for attorneys to follow if they have a calendar conflict): If a date is set by the Judge in court, counsel must advise the Judge at that time of any conflicts. If the conflict arises later, for instance, just prior to a hearing, counsel must advise the court clerk by telephone. (Priority at the hearing can be arranged or the matter put at the end of the calendar, but without a written stipulation/ex parte application and an order signed by the Judge, counsel must appear or risk being held in contempt.)

10. Procedures for bringing electronic equipment into the courtroom: None is allowed without prior approval of Court; contact the court clerk.

11. For general information on how to order a transcript of any reported or digitally recorded proceeding, please contact 213-894-3015 or visit www.cacd.uscourts.gov > General Information > Court Reporter/Recorder Transcripts. If you require an estimate of cost for the preparation of a transcript, contact the court reporter/recorder for the desired proceeding.

    To determine the court reporter/recorder for a particular proceeding, go to the Court Reporter Schedule web page and click on View by Date. Once you've determined the correct court reporter/recorder for the desired session, click on Court Reporter Phone and Email List for contact information.

12. Questions regarding law clerk/extern positions shall be directed to the Judge's Judicial Assistant, Amy Emi, at 213-894-6314.

13. Trial Preparation:

   a. **Court hours:** 8:00 A.M. to 1:30 p.m., without lunch; or 9:00 to 12:00 p.m.; 1:30 p.m. to 5:00 p.m., unless otherwise indicated at the Pre-Trial Conference

   Exhibit preparation: Each paper exhibit shall be placed in a folder marked pursuant to the local rules, the original tagged set for the court clerk -- who will pass same to the witness -- and one set for the Judge.

   b. **Jury instructions:** To be submitted in the form and time frames in accordance with the Federal Rules of Civil and Criminal Procedure and the local rules; counsel need submit substantive instructions only.

   c. **Verdict forms:** The court clerk prepares the verdict form in criminal cases; in civil cases the plaintiff submits the proposed verdict form in accordance with the Federal Rules of Civil Procedure and the local rules.

   d. **Other:** The parties shall come to Court fully prepared, with the two sets of exhibits as described above; and also with three clean copies of their witness lists and three clean copies of their exhibit lists, all which shall be given to the court clerk before the commencement of trial.

14. Procedures for obtaining the services of an interpreter on a civil case: The party must hire a certified Federal Court interpreter, whether it be done through the Court's Interpreter's Section, or from some outside source

Hon. A. Howard Matz

District Judge

Chambers Information

U.S. District Court, Central District of California
Courtroom 14, Spring Street Floor
312 N. Spring Street
Los Angeles, CA 90012

Scheduling Information

Courtroom Deputy: (213) 894-5283

Civil Law and Motion	Mondays at 10:00 a.m.
Criminal Law and Motion	Mondays at 4:00 p.m.

Biographical Information

Born 1943 in Brooklyn, NY

Federal Judicial Service:

-Judge, U. S. District Court, Central District of California
-Nominated by William J. Clinton on October 20, 1997, to a seat vacated by Harry L. Hupp; Confirmed by the Senate on June 26, 1998, and received commission on June 29, 1998.
-Assumed senior status on July 11, 2011.

Education:

-Columbia University, A.B., 1965
-Harvard Law School, J.D., 1968

Professional Career:

-Law Clerk, Hon. Morris E. Lasker, U.S. District Court, Southern District of New York, 1969-1970
-Private Practice, New York City, 1970-1972
-Private Practice, Los Angeles, CA, 1972-1974
-Assistant U.S. Attorney, Central District of California, 1974-1978
-Chief, Special Prosecutions Unit, 1977-1978
-Private Practice, Los Angeles, CA, 1979-1998

I. Judge Matz's Procedures and Practices

A. *Amended Order Regarding Electronic Filing for Civil Cases*

AMENDED ORDER RE ELECTRONIC FILING

Effective January 1, 2008, electronic filing has been mandatory for most new and pending civil cases in the United States District Court for the Central District of California. Self-represented litigants and attorneys who take appropriate steps to opt out of the system need not comply with the following requirements.

All documents which are required to be filed in an electronic format pursuant to General Order No. 08-03 must be filed electronically no later than midnight on the date due, unless otherwise ordered by the Court. Documents filed late may be stricken by the Court. The Court will not accept documents which were filed electronically, but which otherwise fail to comply with filing requirements.

A. First step: Electronically Filed Proposed Documents. When a proposed order or other proposed document accompanies a filing, the proposed order or other proposed document shall be in PDF format and included, as an attachment, to the main electronically filed document (*e.g.*, stipulations, applications, motions). Proposed orders or other proposed documents that are not filed with a main document, such as a proposed judgment or proposed findings of fact, shall be electronically filed as an attachment to a Notice of Lodging and shall be electronically linked to the order or minute order directing the preparation of the proposed document.

B. Second step: WordPerfect or Microsoft Word Copy of Proposed Documents. After the document in paragraph A has been electronically filed, a WordPerfect or Microsoft Word version of the document, along with a copy of the PDF electronically filed main document, shall be e-mailed to Judge Matz's generic email address which is: ***ahm_chambers@cacd.uscourts.gov.*** The subject line of the e-mail shall be in the following format: court's divisional office, year, case type, case number, document control number assigned to the main document at the time of filing, judge's initials and filer (party) name.

C. Third step: Chambers Paper Copies. Unless otherwise ordered, chambers paper copies of all electronically filed documents must be delivered to the courtesy box outside chambers no later than 12:00 noon the following business day. The chambers paper copies must comply with Local Rule 11-3, *i.e.*, blue backed, font size, page numbering, tabbed exhibits, etc., unless otherwise directed. IF A DOCUMENT CONTAINS EXHIBITS THAT ARE NOT TABBED, THE COURT MAY DECLINE TO READ THE EXHIBITS. The chambers paper copy must be prominently labeled "CHAMBERS COPY" on the face page. The chambers paper copy must include the Notice of Electronic Filing, which should be the last page of the document. The court's CM/ECF website contains additional instructions for delivery of what are sometimes called "courtesy" copies.

Counsel seeking any kind of expedited relief, such as by an *Ex Parte* Application or an application for a Temporary Restraining Order, shall deliver the chambers paper copies to chambers *immediately* after the applicable filed document(s) have been filed.

If counsel cannot deliver chambers copies, but instead must send them by next day mail, the chambers copy should be mailed directly to chambers at the address below. Do not address the item to the Court or the Clerk of Court. Always mail chambers copies in a separate envelope than documents mailed to the intake department for filing.

U.S. District Court
Chambers of Judge A. Howard Matz
312 North Spring Street, Room 170
Los Angeles, CA 90012

Date: November 19, 2008

B. Order Regarding Electronic Filing for Criminal Cases

ORDER RE ELECTRONIC FILING

Effective January 1, 2007, electronic filing has been mandatory for most new and pending criminal cases in the United States District Court for the Central District of California. Self-represented litigants and attorneys who take appropriate steps to opt out of the system need not comply with the following requirements.

All documents which are required to be filed in an electronic format pursuant to General Order No. 08-03 must be filed electronically no later than midnight on the date due, unless otherwise ordered by the Court. Documents filed late may be stricken by the Court. The Court will not accept documents which were filed electronically, but which otherwise fail to comply with filing requirements.

A. First step: Electronically Filed Proposed Documents. When a proposed order or other proposed document accompanies a filing, the proposed order or other proposed document shall be in PDF format and included, as an attachment, to the main electronically filed document (*e.g.*, stipulations, applications, motions). Proposed orders or other proposed documents that are not filed with a main document, such as a proposed judgment or proposed findings of fact, shall be electronically filed as an attachment to a Notice of Lodging and shall be electronically linked to the order or minute order directing the preparation of the proposed document.

B. Second step: WordPerfect or Microsoft Word Copy of Proposed Documents. After the document in paragraph A has been electronically filed, a WordPerfect or Microsoft Word version of the document, along with a copy of the PDF electronically filed main document, shall be e-mailed to Judge Matz's generic email address which is: ***ahm_chambers@cacd.uscourts.gov.*** The subject line of the email shall be in the following format: court's divisional office, year, case type, case number, document control number assigned to the main document at the time of filing, judge's initials and filer (party) name.

C. Third step: Chambers Paper Copies. Unless otherwise ordered, chambers paper copies of all electronically filed documents must be delivered to the courtesy box outside chambers no later than 12:00 noon the following business day. The chambers paper copies must comply with Local Rule 11-3, *i.e.*, blue backed, font size, page numbering, tabbed exhibits, etc., unless otherwise directed. IF A DOCUMENT CONTAINS EXHIBITS THAT ARE NOT TABBED, THE COURT MAY DECLINE TO READ THE EXHIBITS. The chambers paper copy must be prominently labeled "CHAMBERS COPY" on the face page. The chambers paper copy must include the Notice of Electronic Filing, which should be the last page of the document. The court's CM/ECF website contains additional instructions for delivery of what are sometimes called "courtesy" copies.

Counsel seeking any kind of expedited relief, such as by an *Ex Parte* Application or an application for a Temporary Restraining Order, shall deliver the chambers paper copies to chambers immediately after the applicable filed document(s) have been filed.

If counsel cannot deliver chambers copies, but instead must send them by next day mail, the chambers copy should be mailed directly to chambers at the address below. Do not address the item to the Court or the Clerk of Court. Always mail chambers copies in a separate envelope than documents mailed to the intake department for filing.

U.S. District Court
Chambers of Judge A. Howard Matz
312 North Spring Street, Room 170
Los Angeles, CA 90012

Date: November 19, 2008

C. Order Regarding Protective Orders and Treatment of Confidential Information

ORDER RE: PROTECTIVE ORDERS AND TREATMENT OF CONFIDENTIAL INFORMATION

Please read and comply with Fed. R. Civ. P. 26(c). Make sure you show "good cause." *See also Foltz v. State Farm Mutual Automobile Ins. Co.*, 33, F.3d 1122 (9th Cir. 2003). The Court has adopted the following additional guidelines for protective orders, whether stipulated or not:

I. Guidelines for Protective Order Provisions.

A. Clear and Precise. A protective order must be sufficiently precise and clear, so that:

1. All parties and other persons who are bound by the order know precisely what they are required to do, permitted to do, and forbidden from doing.

2. In the event that any party seeks to have another party who supposedly violated the order held in contempt, it is necessary that the order contain no ambiguity concerning the parties' rights and responsibilities.

B. Narrowly Tailored. A protective order must be narrowly tailored and cannot be overbroad. Therefore,

1. The documents, information, items or materials that are subject to the protective order shall be described in a meaningful fashion. (For example, "blueprints," "customer lists," or "market surveys," *etc.*) It is not sufficient to use only the conclusory term "trade secrets."

2. In proposing or agreeing to the protection of "trade secrets," the definition for that term in California Civil Code § 3426.1 should be incorporated into the protective order, either by reference or by quotation.[1]

C. Burden of Proof. The party designating information, documents, materials or items as confidential bears the burden of establishing the confidentiality.

D. Procedures for Filing Confidential Information with the Court. One cannot file a document under seal automatically; moreover, under seal filings must comply with Local Rule 79-5. All Court orders will be presumptively available to the public. Therefore, if a protective order provides that evidence may be filed under seal and if a party does file such evidence under seal, all papers that refer to or rely upon such evidence shall designate the particular aspects that are confidential. This will enable the Court, in drafting orders, to determine whether there is evidence which the Court should attempt not to disclose. Absent such advance notification, the Court will be free to incorporate all such evidence in its written and oral rulings.

E. Use of Confidential Information at Trial. In the event that the case proceeds to trial, all of the information that was designated as confidential and/or kept and

---

1 Cal. Civil Code § 3426.1 provides that trade secret "means information, including a formula, pattern, compilation, program, device, method, technique, or process, that: (1) Derives independent economic value, actual or potential, from not being generally known to the public or to other persons who can obtain economic value from its disclosure or use; and (2) Is the subject of efforts that are reasonable under the circumstances to maintain its secrecy."

maintained pursuant to the terms of a protective order becomes public and will be presumptively available to all members of the public, including the press, unless sufficient cause is shown in advance of trial to proceed otherwise.

F. **Disputes.** Do not incorporate procedures for resolving disputes that conflict with Local Rule 37 or other Local Rules.

II. Procedure for Obtaining Protective Order.

A. Stipulated Protective Orders. Any proposed stipulated protective order submitted to the Court shall reflect the guidelines set forth in this order. If satisfactory, the Court will sign the proposed protective order and cause it to be filed. If not satisfactory, the Court will return it to counsel, with reference to the provisions that have to be added or changed. Thereafter, any revised proposed stipulated protective order shall contain such modifications.

B. Motions for a Protective Order. In the event that the parties are unable to agree upon the terms of a protective order, the procedure for obtaining such an order is that set forth in Local Rule 37-1 through 37-4, concerning discovery motions. In civil cases, the motion will be addressed to and resolved by the magistrate judge. The party initiating the motion shall ensure that this order is attached to the joint stipulation. When filing the motion, the party seeking the protective order shall lodge with the court *in camera* copies of the evidence for which it seeks a protective order.

The Court thanks counsel for their anticipated cooperation and compliance with this order.

Dated: April 22, 2008

A. HOWARD MATZ
United States District Judge

D. Procedures and Schedules

1. Civil motions are to be heard on **Mondays**, at **10:00 A.M.**

   Criminal motions are to be heard on **Mondays**, at **4:00 P.M.**

   Be aware that the Court is likely upon many occasions to shift the date of the hearing to days other than a Monday, if a hearing is deemed necessary. If so, the Court will provide sufficient notice to counsel.

   If Monday is a holiday, the motion date must be calendared for the following Monday. It is not necessary to clear a motion date with the court clerk prior to filing the motion.

2. Discovery motions are to be calendared before the Magistrate Judge assigned to the case.

3. Tentative rulings may be issued. If issued, they will be available in the courtroom around 9:30 A.M. on the date the motion is set.

4. Chambers copies are required for all e-filed documents and must be delivered to the drop box in the entrance way to chambers, to the left of Courtroom 14, located at 312 N. Spring Street, Spring Street level, no later than noon the following business day. **BE SURE TO TAB ALL EXHIBITS AND DECLARATIONS.** In addition, chambers copies of manually filed documents are required when: (1) reply papers are filed late; or (2) emergency circumstances make them essential -- e.g., for TROs, ex parte applications or papers filed during trial or within two days of a scheduled hearing, pre-trial conference or trial. When the Court requires an electronic version of any document be submitted (e.g., with summary judgment papers or proposed jury instructions), that Word/WordPerfect formatted document should be emailed to the court clerk at ahm_chambers@cacd.uscourts.gov. Counsel should avoid leaving extra copies of voluminous documents with chambers when they are not necessary to comply with this paragraph.

5. *Ex parte* applications are considered on the papers and may not be set for hearing. If a party has not consented to e-service or is not eligible for e-service, the moving party shall serve that party by FAX or hand service and shall notify the opposing party that any opposition must be filed not later than 24 hours after such FAX or hand service. If counsel do not intend to oppose the *ex parte* application, counsel must inform the court clerk.

6. To request a continuance of a scheduled court proceeding, counsel must request such continuance by a stipulation of the parties or ex parte application.

7. Counsel are not to initiate telephone calls to Judge Matz's chambers, law clerks or secretary.

8. Telephone inquiries regarding the status of a motion, stipulation or proposed order are not returned. Please refer to the docket for such information.

9. If there is a calendar conflict, counsel are to inform the court clerk prior to the date of the conflict.

10. Counsel are to request, through the court clerk, bringing in or using audio, video or electronic equipment into the courtroom. If counsel have technical questions or

require training on our electronic equipment (i.e, ELMO/DAR), please contact our Courtroom IT Department at (213) 894-3061.

11. To obtain a transcript of any reported or digitally recorded proceeding, please contact the assigned court reporter/recorder. To determine the court reporter/recorder for a particular proceeding, go to the Court Reporter Schedule web page and click on View by Date. Once you've determined the correct court reporter/recorder for the desired session, click on Court Reporter Phone and Email List for contact information.

12. Questions regarding law clerk/extern positions should be directed to chambers.

13. Trial preparation:

Court hours - Trial days usually are Tuesday through Friday, 9:00 a.m. to 4:00 p.m., with various breaks and a lunch break. On each day after the first, the Court reserves the time from 8:30 - 9:00 a.m. to handle legal and administrative issues outside of the presence of the jury. This schedule is subject to change.

Exhibit preparation - Original and one copy, in 3-ring binders, tabbed at the side; the original also must have the original Court exhibit tags. Please see Judge Matz's Civil Jury Trial Order for further explanations.

Jury instructions - Judge Matz prefers 9th Circuit model instructions. Counsel are to submit instructions by email to ahm_chambers@cacd.uscourts.gov.

On first day of trial, counsel shall provide the court with three (3) additional copies of the joint witness/exhibit lists.

Verdict Forms - See Civil Jury Trial Order.

Other - Review the court's standing orders attached below.

14. Counsel in civil cases are to obtain the services of an interpreter, if one is needed.

15. Other information: Judge Matz requires compliance with Local Rule 7-3, particularly with respect to motions to dismiss pleadings and other motions under Federal Rule 12.

E. Standing Order Regarding Sentencing Letters

STANDING ORDER RE: SENTENCING LETTERS

The Court welcomes receiving, and does read, letters about individuals facing sentences. But on occasion the Court has been inundated with literally scores of letters; at times there have been as many as 75. Frequently, these are single spaced, typed, multi-page missives which sometimes are almost as much about the writer as about the defendant. The Court has too many complicated and demanding responsibilities to read all such communications, especially since at a certain point they become redundant and predictable. Accordingly, the Court will not commit to reading more than fifteen (15) letters from any given sentence (and would prefer fewer).

IT IS SO ORDERED.

DATED: ____________, 2005.

____

A. HOWARD MATZ
United States District Judge

II. Judge Matz's Case Management Orders

A. Civil Jury Trial Order

IN THE UNITED STATES DISTICT COURT
FOR THE CENTRAL DISTRICT OF CALIFORNIA

Plaintiff(s),	Case No. CV 10-00000-AHM (__x)
v.	**CIVIL JURY TRIAL ORDER**
Defendant(s).	

This matter is set for trial before the Honorable A. Howard Matz, Courtroom 14 (1st Floor, Spring Street level), United States Courthouse, 312 North Spring Street, Los Angeles, California. To facilitate the efficient conduct of the pretrial conference and trial in this matter, all parties shall review carefully the following order and instructions re civil trials, as well as the Court's Scheduling and Case Management Order.

I. Rule 16 Filings.

The parties must comply fully with the requirements of Local Rule 16. At the times set at the Scheduling Conference, they shall file carefully prepared Memoranda of Contentions of Fact and Law (which may also serve as the trial brief), along with their respective Witness Lists and Exhibit Lists, all in accordance with Local Rules 16-4, 16-5 and 16-6.

The parties shall complete the Trial Witness Time Estimate Form attached to this Order and discussed at the Pre-Trial Conference, and deliver it to the Clerk on the first morning of trial. Be realistic in each of your estimates; do not pad your estimates or provide unreasonably short estimates. At the Pretrial Conference, the opposing party will be expected to disclose to the Court an estimate for his or her cross-examination of each witness identified by the other side.

II. Jury Instructions, Verdict Form and/or Special Interrogatories.

Specifications and requirements for form and content of jury instructions are set forth in the Scheduling and Case Management Order which the parties received at the Scheduling Conference.

Unless all counsel agree to have the Court instruct the jury after closing argument, the Court will instruct the jury before closing argument.

The Court will send copies of the jury instructions and verdict forms into the jury room for use by the jury during deliberations.

III. Agreed Statement of the Case.

The parties shall jointly prepare a statement of the case which the Court shall read to all prospective jurors at the beginning of voir dire. The statement usually should not be longer than two or three paragraphs. The parties shall file their joint statement with the Court at the PTC.

IV. Trial Times.

On the first day of trial, all counsel are to be present in the Courtroom and ready to begin at 8:30 a.m. At 9:00 a.m., the Court will meet with counsel to ensure that all matters necessary for resolution prior to trial are resolved. Trial days usually are Tuesday through Friday, 9:00 a.m. to 4:00 p.m., with various breaks and a lunch break. On each day after the first, the Court reserves the time from 8:30 - 9:00 a.m. to handle legal and administrative matters outside of the presence of the jury. Counsel are urged to anticipate matters which may need discussion or hearing outside of the presence of the jury and to raise them during this period.

V. Jury Selection.

The Court conducts voir dire of all prospective jurors. As specified in the Scheduling and Case Management Order, the Court will consider each party's timely filed proposed voir dire questions.

In selecting a jury, the clerk will initially seat the entire group of prospective jurors in the benches toward the rear of the Courtroom. The Court will then read the agreed-to statement of the case and determine whether any prospective jurors should be excused for cause because, for example, they know a lawyer, party or prospective witness. The Court will also determine whether the length of the trial requires that prospective jurors be excused due to work constraints or other issues. From the remaining pool of jurors, the Court Clerk will select at random the names of 14 jurors who will be seated in the jury box . Each of these prospective jurors will then answer a pre-printed form containing general questions, including their name, occupation etc. The Court will then ask more specific voir dire questions that have been individually tailored for the case.

Following the questioning of each of the 14 prospective jurors, each party will be permitted three (3) peremptory challenges. Peremptory challenges should be addressed to prospective jurors seated at seats 1-8 only. If any such prospective juror is stricken, the remaining jurors who have been "voir dire'd" will not move into the vacant seats. To avoid the potential embarrassment of a disallowed peremptory challenge on the grounds set forth in *Batson v. Kentucky*, 476 U.S. 79, 106 S.Ct. 1712, 90 L.Ed.2d 69 (1986), before openly exercising a peremptory, counsel should inform opposing counsel, and if opposing counsel believes a *Batson* objection is in order s/he should request a side bar. At side bar, the party with the *Batson* objection is expected to show reasonable grounds to support the claim of bias before the party exercising the peremptory will be called upon for an explanation. If there is no *Batson* objection, however, counsel may openly exercise a peremptory challenge.

Following the resolution of all challenges, eight (8) of the jurors placed in the box will be chosen as the jury panel. There will be no alternates.

In complex or lengthy cases, the Court will consider the use of jointly-proposed jury questionnaires. Because use of questionnaires requires the active, time-consuming participation of the Jury Department, counsel desiring to use such questionnaires shall contact the Court's Deputy Clerk, Stephen Montes (213-894-5283), at least sixty (60) calendar days in advance of the trial date to inform him that such a questionnaire will be proposed. He will then explain the necessary procedures.

VI. Exhibits.

A. **Format.** The parties shall prepare their exhibits for presentation at the trial by placing them in 3-ring binders in the following manner:

   1. There shall be no separate exhibit books for plaintiff[s] and defendant[s]. Instead, there shall be a single set of exhibit books with the exhibits arranged in numerical order, regardless of who is the proponent. This set of books shall be provided to the Courtroom Deputy Clerk, but during presentation of evidence it shall be for the use of the lawyers and shall be kept at or near the lectern. Two additional, identical copies of these books shall be lodged: one for the Court and one for the witness.

2. Each binder shall be divided by tabs down the side with corresponding exhibit numbers.

3. In the original set of exhibits to be filed with the Court and maintained by the Courtroom Deputy during trial, each exhibit shall be tagged with the appropriate exhibit tags in the lower or upper right hand corner of the first page of each exhibit.

4. The exhibits shall be numbered in accordance with Local Rule 16-6.

5. The front pages of each notebook shall contain a list of each exhibit included. A label should be placed on the spine specifying which exhibit numbers are in that particular volume.

B. **Extra Copies of Exhibit and Witness Lists.** In addition to the exhibit binders, the parties shall bring with them to the first day of trial three (3) copies of their exhibit list and three (3) copies of their witness list in the order in which the witnesses may be called to testify.

C. **Presentation to Jury.** In jury cases where a significant number of exhibits are to be admitted, the Court encourages counsel, preferably by prior agreement, to consider ways in which testimony about exhibits may be clarified for the jury while it is being presented. Counsel may consider such devices as overhead or ELMO projectors, jury notebooks for admitted exhibits, or blow-ups of important exhibits. Counsel should take advantage of Federal Rule of Evidence 1006 ("Summaries") to present voluminous evidence. Only in rare circumstances will the Court permit counsel to pass exhibits up and down the jury box.

D. **Stipulation to Admissibility.** Not later than four (4) calendar days before trial, the parties shall meet to stipulate as far as possible to foundation, waiver of the best evidence rule and exhibits may be received into evidence at the start of trial. The parties shall note the exhibits to which admissibility has been stipulated on the exhibit list included in the front of the exhibit binder.

VII. Courtroom Conduct.

A. During trial, counsel shall not refer to their clients by their first name.

B. Opening statements, examination of witnesses, and closing arguments shall be made from the lectern only. Counsel should feel free to turn the lectern if they wish to address the jury directly.

C. Counsel should keep in mind that the purpose of an opening statement is to inform the jurors of the nature of the case, the facts they expect to be proved in the trial and the issues in the case. An opening statement is *not* an argument to the jury, and it is *not* permissible to attempt to argue to the jury about the application of the law to the facts at this stage of the case.

D. Do not use objections for purposes of making a speech, recapitulating testimony, or attempting to guide the witness. When objecting, please rise and state only that you are objecting and the specific legal ground of the objection, e.g., hearsay, irrelevant, etc. Only rarely will the Court permit side-bar conferences about evidentiary issues during a jury trial. Most unusual or complex evidentiary issues can be foreseen and disposed of in advance, those that cannot ordinarily will be disposed of at the next recess, with the witness retained until the issue is resolved.

E. Counsel shall speak audibly and clearly -- and not too rapidly -- when questioning a witness or making an objection. Counsel should instruct their witnesses to speak audibly and clearly as well. The microphone at the lectern is powerful; you need not lean directly into it.

F. Obtain the Court's permission to approach a witness for the limited purpose of placing a document (shown first to opposing counsel) before the witness. If necessary to direct the witness's attention to something in the document, counsel may remain adjacent to the witness box for that limited purpose. Otherwise, counsel shall return to the lectern when the purpose of the approach is finished.

G. Counsel shall not, by facial expression, nodding, or other conduct, exhibit any opinions, adverse or favorable, concerning any testimony which is being given by a witness. Counsel shall admonish their own clients and witnesses similarly to avoid such conduct.

H. When a party has more than one lawyer, only one may conduct the direct or cross-examination of a given witness.

I. If a witness was on the stand at a recess or adjournment, have the witness back on the stand and ready to proceed when court resumes.

J. Do not run out of witnesses. If you are out of witnesses and there is more than a brief delay, the Court may well deem that you have rested.

K. The Court attempts to cooperate with doctors and other witnesses with restricted schedules and will, except in extraordinary circumstances, accommodate them by permitting them to be called out of sequence. Anticipate any such possibility and discuss it with opposing counsel. If there is an objection, confer with the Court in advance.

L. Be on time, as the Court intends to start promptly.

M. Do not attempt to emphasize contents of exhibits or charts by highlighting or enlarging selective portions of them if doing so would be misleading, unless opposing counsel agree in advance to your proposed use or the Court has ruled on any objections in advance.

N. The maintenance of personal dignity requires care in the pronunciation of a witness's name. If necessary, counsel should inquire privately, in advance of the first reference to the name in court, how a person pronounces his or her name and how he or she prefers to be called (e.g., whether Marcos Lopez Garcia prefers to be referred to as Mr. Garcia or Mr. Lopez Garcia).

O. During recesses, counsel shall not congregate near the door that jurors use to gain access to the jury room.

VIII. MISCELLANEOUS.

Counsel shall notify the Courtroom Deputy in advance if any witness or member of the litigation team requires an accommodation for a disability.

The Court thanks counsel in advance for their anticipated compliance with this Order.

IT IS SO ORDERED.

DATED: ____________, 2011

____
A. HOWARD MATZ
United States District Judge

B. Initial Order Following Filing of Complaint

IN THE UNITED STATES DISTICT COURT
FOR THE CENTRAL DISTRICT OF CALIFORNIA

)	Case No. CV 10-*-AHM (*x)
Plaintiff(s),)	
v.)	**INITIAL ORDER FOLLOWING**
Defendant(s).)	**FILING OF COMPLAINT**
______________________________)	**ASSIGNED TO JUDGE MATZ**

COUNSEL FOR PLAINTIFF SHALL SERVE THIS ORDER ON ALL DEFENDANTS AND/OR THEIR COUNSEL ALONG WITH THE SUMMONS AND COMPLAINT, OR IF THAT IS NOT PRACTICABLE AS SOON AS POSSIBLE THEREAFTER. IF THIS CASE WAS ASSIGNED TO THIS COURT AFTER BEING REMOVED FROM STATE COURT, THE DEFENDANT WHO REMOVED THE CASE SHALL SERVE THIS ORDER ON ALL OTHER PARTIES.

This case has been assigned to the calendar of Judge A. Howard Matz. Judge Matz is intent on assuring that, as called for in Fed.R.Civ. P. 1, this case will proceed so as "to secure [a] just, speedy and inexpensive determination . . ." The parties are hereby informed of how they are expected to proceed.

A. THE COURT'S ORDERS

Copies of Judge Matz's orders that may have specific application to this case are available on the Central District of California website. See ¶ J. Those orders include the following (this is not necessarily a complete list):

(1) Order Setting Rule 16(b) Scheduling Conference
(2) Scheduling and Case Management Order
(3) Order re Protective Orders and Treatment of Confidential Information
(4) Orders (separate) re Civil Jury Trials and Court Trials
(5) Order re Settlement Conference Before This Court

B. SERVICE OF PLEADINGS

Although Fed.R.Civ.P. 4(m) does not require the summons and complaint to be served for as much as 120 days, the Court expects that they will be served much sooner than that, and will require plaintiff to show cause before then if it appears that there is undue delay.

C. ASSIGNMENT TO A MAGISTRATE JUDGE

Under 28 U.S.C. § 636, the parties may consent to have a Magistrate Judge preside over all proceedings, including trial. The Magistrate Judges who accept those designations are identified on the Central District's website, which also contains the consent form. See ¶ K.

D. APPLICATIONS AND STIPULATIONS FOR EXTENSIONS OF TIME

A. Applications or Stipulations to Extend the Time to File any Required Document or to Continue any Pretrial or Trial Date.

No stipulations extending scheduling requirements or modifying applicable rules are effective until and unless the Court approves them. Both applications and stipulations must set forth:

1. the existing due date or hearing date;

2. specific, concrete reasons supporting good cause for granting the extension.

In this regard, a statement that an extension "will promote settlement" is insufficient. The requesting party or parties must indicate the status of ongoing negotiations: have written proposals been exchanged? Is counsel in the process of reviewing a draft settlement agreement? Has a mediator been selected?

3. whether there have been prior requests for extensions, and whether these were granted or denied by the Court.

E. TRO'S AND INJUNCTIONS

Parties seeking emergency or provisional relief shall comply with F.R.Civ.P. 65 and Local Rule 65. The Court will not rule on any application for such relief for at least 24 hours after the party subject to the requested order has been served; such party may file opposing or responding papers in the interim. The parties shall lodge a courtesy copy, conformed to reflect that it has been filed, of all papers relating to TROs and injunctions. The courtesy copy shall be placed in the drop box in the entrance way to chambers, to the left of Courtroom 14. All such papers shall be filed "loose" – *i.e.*, not inside envelopes.

F. CASES REMOVED FROM STATE COURT

All documents filed in state court, including documents appended to the complaint, answers and motions, must be refiled in this Court as a supplement to the Notice of Renewal, if not already included. *See* 28 U.S.C. § 1447(a)(b). If the defendant has not yet answered or moved, the answer or responsive pleading filed in this Court must comply with the Federal Rules of Civil Procedure and the Local Rules of the Central District. If before the case was removed a motion was pending in state court, it must be re-noticed in accordance with Local Rule 7.

G. STATUS OF FICTITIOUSLY NAMED DEFENDANTS

This Court intends to adhere to the following procedures where a matter is removed to this Court on diversity grounds with fictitiously named defendants referred to in the complaint. (*See* 28 U.S.C. ¶¶ 1441(a) and 1447.)

1. Plaintiff is normally expected to ascertain the identity of and serve any fictitiously named defendants within 120 days of the removal of the action to this Court.

2. If plaintiff believes (by reason of the necessity for discovery or otherwise) that fictitiously named defendants cannot be fully identified within the 120-day period, an *ex parte* application requesting permission to extend that period to effectuate service may be filed with this Court. Such application shall state the reasons therefor, and may be granted upon a showing of good cause. The *ex parte* application shall be served upon all appearing parties, and shall state that appearing parties may comment within seven (7) days of the filing of the *ex parte* application.

3. If plaintiff desires to substitute a named defendant for one of the fictitiously named parties, plaintiff first shall seek to obtain consent from counsel for the previously-identified defendants (and counsel for the fictitiously named party, if that party has separate counsel). If consent is withheld or denied, plaintiff may apply *ex parte* requesting such amendment, with notice to all appearing parties. Each party shall have seven calendar days to respond. The *ex parte* application and any response should comment not only on the substitution of the named party for a fictitiously named defendant, but on the question of whether the matter should thereafter be remanded to the Superior Court if diversity of citizenship is destroyed by the addition of the new substituted party. *See* U.S.C. § 1447(c)(d).

H. BANKRUPTCY APPEALS

Counsel shall comply with the Notice Regarding Appeal From Bankruptcy Court issued at the time the appeal is filed in the District Court. The matter is considered submitted upon the filing of the appellant's reply brief. No oral argument is held unless otherwise ordered by this Court.

I. MOTIONS UNDER FED.R.CIV.P. 12

Many motions to dismiss or to strike could be avoided if the parties confer in good faith (as they are required to do under L.R. 7-3), especially for perceived defects in a complaint, answer or counterclaim which could be corrected by amendment. *See Chang v. Chen*, 80 F.3d 1293, 1296 (9th Cir. 1996) (where a motion to dismiss is granted, a district court should provide leave to amend unless it is clear that the complaint could not be saved by *any* amendment). Moreover, a party has the right to amend his complaint "once as a matter of course at any time before a responsive pleading is served." Fed.R.Civ.P. 15(a). A 12(b)(6) motion is not a responsive pleading and therefore plaintiff might have a right to amend. *See Nolen v. Fitzharris*, 450 F.2d 958, 958-59 (9th Cir. 1971); *St. Michael's Convalescent Hospital v. California*, 643 F.2d 1369, 1374 (9th Cir. 1981). And even where a party has amended his Complaint once or a responsive pleading has been served, the Federal Rules provide that leave to amend should be "freely given when justice so requires." F.R.Civ.P. 15(a). The Ninth Circuit requires that this policy favoring amendment be applied with "extreme liberality." *Morongo Band of Mission Indians v. Rose*, 893 F.2d 1074, 1079 (9th Cir. 1990). These principles require that counsel for the plaintiff should carefully evaluate the defendant's contentions as to the deficiencies in the complaint and that in many instances the defendant (or moving party) should agree to any amendment that would cure a curable defect.

In the unlikely event that motions under Fed.R.Civ.P. 12 challenging pleadings are filed after the Rule 16(b) Scheduling Conference, the moving party shall attach a copy of the challenged pleading to the Memorandum of Points and Authorities in support of the motion.

The foregoing provisions apply as well to motions to dismiss a counterclaim, answer or affirmative defense, which a plaintiff might contemplate bringing.

J. ELECTRONIC FILING AND CHAMBERS COPIES

All documents which are required to be filed in an electronic format pursuant to General Order No. 10-07[1] must be filed electronically no later than midnight on the date due, unless otherwise ordered by the Court. Documents filed late may be stricken by the Court. The Court will not accept documents which were filed electronically, but which otherwise fail to comply with filing requirements.

A. First step: Electronically Filed *Proposed* Documents. When a proposed order or other proposed document accompanies a filing, the proposed order or other proposed document shall be in PDF format and included, as an attachment, to the main electronically filed document (e.g., stipulations, applications, motions). Proposed orders or other proposed documents that are not filed with a main document, such as a proposed judgment or proposed findings of fact, shall be electronically filed as an attachment to a Notice of Lodging and shall be electronically linked to the order or minute order directing the preparation of the proposed document.

---

1 In the Matter of: Order Authorizing Electronic Filing – General Order No. 10-07 (Supersedes General Order Nos. 08-02 and 08-11)

B. Second step: WordPerfect or Microsoft Word Copy of Proposed Documents. After the document in paragraph A has been electronically filed, a WordPerfect or Microsoft Word version of the document, along with a copy of the PDF electronically filed main document, shall be e-mailed to Judge Matz's generic email address which is: ahm_chambers@cacd.uscourts.gov. The subject line of the e-mail shall be in the following format: court's divisional office, year, case type, case number, document control number assigned to the main document at the time of filing, judge's initials and filer (party) name (example, 2:10-cv-00000-AHM (_ _ _x): Mr. Smith, *Smith v. Jones*).

C. Third step: Chambers Paper Copies. Unless otherwise ordered, chambers paper copies of all electronically filed documents must be delivered to the courtesy box outside chambers no later than 12:00 noon the following business day. The chambers paper copies must comply with Local Rule 11-3, i.e., blue backed, font size, page numbering, tabbed exhibits, etc., unless otherwise directed. IF A DOCUMENT CONTAINS EXHIBITS THAT ARE NOT TABBED, THE COURT MAY DECLINE TO READ THE EXHIBITS. The chambers paper copy must be prominently labeled "CHAMBERS COPY" on the face page. The chambers paper copy must include the Notice of Electronic Filing, which should be the last page of the document. The court's CM/ECF website contains additional instructions for delivery of what are sometimes called "courtesy" copies.

Counsel seeking any kind of expedited relief, such as by an Ex Parte Application or an application for a Temporary Restraining Order, shall deliver the chambers paper copies to chambers immediately after the applicable filed document(s) have been filed.

If counsel cannot deliver chambers copies, but instead must send them by next day mail, the chambers copy should be mailed directly to chambers at the address below. Use the following address only:

U.S. District Court
Chambers of Judge A. Howard Matz
312 North Spring Street, Room 170
Los Angeles, CA 90012

Always place documents to be mailed to chambers in a separate envelope than documents mailed to the intake department for filing.

K. NOTICE TO UNREPRESENTED ("PRO SE") LITIGANTS

The Court may not provide advice to any party, including persons who are not represented by a lawyer. Such unrepresented persons are known as "pro se litigants." However, this District does have a "Pro Se Clinic" that can provide information and assistance about many aspects of civil litigation in this Court. The Clinic is administered by Public Counsel, a public interest law firm, and it is staffed by lawyers and a paralegal. The Clinic is not operated by the Court and its services are not to be viewed as being provided by the Court. In order to benefit from the guidance the Clinic may be in a position to provide, you have to go there directly. The Pro Se Clinic is open to members of the public on Mondays, Wednesdays, and Fridays from 10:00 am - 12:00 p.m. and from 2:00 p.m. to 4:00 p.m. It is located in Room 525 on the 5th Floor of the U.S. Courthouse at 312 N. Spring Street, Los Angeles, California.

Although the Clinic does not provide information telephonically, for further information about it you may call (213) 385-2997, ext. 270. In addition, the Court has information of importance to unrepresented or pro se litigants at the "Pro Se" link on its website: http://www.cacd.uscourts.gov/ProSe.

L. WEBSITE

Copies of this Order and other orders of this Court are available on the Central District of California's website, at "www.cacd.uscourts.gov," under "FAQs about Judges' Procedures and Schedules." The Court thanks counsel and the parties for their anticipated cooperation.

The Court thanks counsel and the parties for their anticipated cooperation.

IT IS SO ORDERED.

Dated: June 2, 2011

A. HOWARD MATZ
United States District Judge

C. Order Regarding Markman Hearing

IN THE UNITED STATES DISTICT COURT
FOR THE CENTRAL DISTRICT OF CALIFORNIA

Plaintiff(s),	Case No. ______________
v.	**ORDER RE MARKMAN HEARING**
Defendant(s).	

The Court will schedule or has scheduled a *Markman* Hearing. THE COURT WILL NOT CONSTRUE MORE THAN SIX TERMS, UNLESS A PARTY DEMONSTRATES A COMPELLING CAUSE TO DO SO.

By not later than three weeks before the *Markman* hearing, the parties shall file the following:

1. A Joint Statement of Disputed and Undisputed Terms for each patent at issue. This statement shall list in chart form each disputed and undisputed term (and each column and line where the term appears), Plaintiff's interpretation and Defendant's interpretation. (Only undisputed terms that are important for the Court's construction of the disputed terms need be included.) The Statement shall be brief and shall not contain argument; however, Plaintiff and Defendant shall reference, by page number, the section of their brief supporting their interpretation. Attached to this Order is a sample joint statement.

2. An Electronic Copy of the Joint Statement of Disputed and Undisputed Terms

3. A List of Exhibits and of All Witnesses (identified by status or function) upon whose testimony the parties will rely at the hearing.

4. Declarations containing the direct testimony of each party's witnesses.

5. A Brief not to exceed 25 pages. The brief shall include a description of both the patented product or process and the allegedly infringing product or process.[1]

By not later than one week before the *Markman* hearing, each party may file a Reply. Reply briefs shall not exceed 10 pages.

IT IS SO ORDERED.

DATE: ___________

____
A. HOWARD MATZ
United States District Judge

---

[1] "While a trial court should certainly not prejudge the ultimate infringement analysis by construing claims with an aim to include or exclude an accused product or process, knowledge of that product or process provides meaningful context for the first step of the infringement analysis, claim construction." *Wilson Sporting Goods Co. v. Hillerich & Bradsby Co.*, 442 F.3d 1322, 1326-27 (Fed. Cir. 2006).

IDENTIFICATION OF PATENT CLAIM PHRASES FOR U.S. PATENT NO. _________

<table>
<tr><th>CLAIM TEXT AND COLUMN/LINE REFERENCE</th><th>PLAINTIFF'S INTERPRETATION AND AUTHORITY</th><th>DEFENDANT'S INTERPRETATION AND AUTHORITY</th></tr>
<tr><td>1. "In a switched power supply" (Col. 6, Lns 41-42; Col. 9, Lns 36-54)</td><td colspan="2">AGREED TERM
switched power supply: A circuit that delivers power to a load by using an electronic switch (e.g., power switch).</td></tr>
<tr><td rowspan="2">2. "a rectifier adapted to be connected to the alternating current line" (Col. 10, Lns 13-15)</td><td colspan="2">AGREED TERM
rectifier: A circuit or device that converts an alternating polarity signal to a single polarity signal (i.e., typically a full-wave diode bridge).</td></tr>
<tr><td>DISPUTED TERM
alternating current line: Electrical conductors capable of carrying a current whose direction changes at recurring intervals of time.
Authority: Plaintiff's Brief at 9-10.</td><td>DISPUTED TERM
alternating current line: Two or more physical conductors that carry a voltage waveform that varies in amplitude and polarity in a sinusoidal fashion (e.g., the wires leading up to a typical wall outlet).
Authority: Defendant's Brief at 14-19.</td></tr>
</table>

D. *Order Regarding Markman Hearing in a Design Patent Case*

IN THE UNITED STATES DISTICT COURT
FOR THE CENTRAL DISTRICT OF CALIFORNIA

Plaintiff(s),	Case No. ________________
v.	**ORDER RE MARKMAN HEARING**
Defendant(s).	**IN A DESIGN PATENT CASE**

The Court will schedule or has scheduled a *Markman* Hearing. THE COURT WILL NOT CONSTRUE MORE THAN SIX TERMS, UNLESS A PARTY DEMONSTRATES A COMPELLING CAUSE TO DO SO.

By not later than three weeks before the *Markman* hearing, the parties shall file the following:

1. A Joint Statement of Disputed and Undisputed Terms for each patent at issue. This statement shall list in chart form each disputed and undisputed term (and each column and line where the term appears), Plaintiff's interpretation and Defendant's interpretation. (Only undisputed terms that are important for the Court's construction of the disputed terms need be included.) The Statement shall be brief and shall not contain argument; however, Plaintiff and Defendant shall reference, by page number, the section of their brief supporting their interpretation. Attached to this Order is a sample joint statement.

Because in a design patent dispute the Joint Statement of Disputed and Undisputed Terms ordinarily cannot, and need not, address or deal with the meaning of words, the parties shall instead entitle the left column "ORNAMENTAL FEATURES and POINTS OF NOVELTY." Their entries in the Joint Statement shall identify what it is about the overall design that is (or is not, as the defendant would urge) substantially similar (or, as defendant would urge, different) to the ordinary purchaser or observer. They also should identify the specific features and points of novelty in the original patent and shall summarize their contentions as to the presence or absence of those features and points in the allegedly infringing item. They should, if possible, incorporate pictures, diagrams and schema in their submission.

2. An Electronic Copy of the Joint Statement of Disputed and Undisputed Terms
3. A List of Exhibits and of All Witnesses (identified by status or function) upon whose testimony the parties will rely at the hearing.
4. Declarations containing the direct testimony of each party's witnesses.
5. A Brief not to exceed 25 pages.

By not later than one week before the *Markman* hearing, each party may file a Reply. Reply briefs shall not exceed 10 pages.

IT IS SO ORDERED.

DATE: ________________

____
A. HOWARD MATZ
United States District Judge

IDENTIFICATION OF PATENT CLAIM PHRASES FOR U.S. PATENT NO. _________

<table>
<tr><th>CLAIM TEXT AND COLUMN/LINE REFERENCE</th><th>PLAINTIFF'S INTERPRETATION AND AUTHORITY</th><th>DEFENDANT'S INTERPRETATION AND AUTHORITY</th></tr>
<tr><td>1. "In a switched power supply" (Col. 6, Lns 41-42; Col. 9, Lns 36-54)</td><td colspan="2">AGREED TERM
switched power supply: A circuit that delivers power to a load by using an electronic switch (e.g., power switch).</td></tr>
<tr><td rowspan="2">2. "a rectifier adapted to be connected to the alternating current line" (Col. 10, Lns 13-15)</td><td colspan="2">AGREED TERM
rectifier: A circuit or device that converts an alternating polarity signal to a single polarity signal (i.e., typically a full-wave diode bridge).</td></tr>
<tr><td>DISPUTED TERM
alternating current line: Electrical conductors capable of carrying a current whose direction changes at recurring intervals of time.
Authority: Plaintiff's Brief at 9-10.</td><td>DISPUTED TERM
alternating current line: Two or more physical conductors that carry a voltage waveform that varies in amplitude and polarity in a sinusoidal fashion (e.g., the wires leading up to a typical wall outlet).
Authority: Defendant's Brief at 14-19.</td></tr>
</table>

E. Order Regarding RICO Case Statement

IN THE UNITED STATES DISTICT COURT
FOR THE CENTRAL DISTRICT OF CALIFORNIA

	)	Case No. ________________
Plaintiff(s),	)	
v.	)	**ORDER RE RICO CASE**
Defendant(s).	)	**STATEMENT**
____________________________________	)	

In this action, claims arising out of alleged acts of mail fraud and/or wire fraud have been asserted under the Racketeer Influenced and Corrupt Organizations provisions of the Organized Crime Control Act of 1970 ("RICO"), 18 U.S.C. § 1961 *et seq*. Accordingly,

IT IS HEREBY ORDERED as follows:

Plaintiff[1] shall file, within twenty (20) days hereof, a RICO case statement. The statement shall include the facts relied upon to initiate this RICO complaint as a result of the reasonable inquiry required by Rule 11 of the Federal Rules of Civil Procedure. It shall use the caption numbers and letters set forth below, and shall state in detail and with specificity the following information.

1. **RICO Provision.** State whether the alleged unlawful conduct is in violation of 18 U.S.C. §§ 1962(a), (b) (c), and/or (d).

2. **Defendants.** List each RICO defendant and state the alleged misconduct and basis of liability of each defendant.

3. **Other RICO Violators.** List all alleged RICO violators, other than the defendants listed above, and state the alleged misconduct of each wrongdoer.

4. **Victims.** List the alleged victims and state how each victim was allegedly injured.

5. **Pattern of Racketeering Activity.** Describe in detail the pattern of racketeering activity or collection of unlawful debts alleged for each RICO claim. A description of the pattern of racketeering shall include the following information:

a. List the alleged predicate acts and the specific statutes which were allegedly violated;

b. Provide the dates of the predicate acts, the participants in the predicate acts, and a description of the facts surrounding the predicate acts;

c. Since the RICO claim is based on the predicate offenses of mail fraud, wire fraud or fraud in the sale of securities, the "circumstances constituting fraud or mistake shall be stated with particularity." Fed. R. Civ. P. 9(b). Identify the time, place and contents of the alleged failures to disclose and/or misrepresentations, and the identity of persons to whom and by whom the alleged misrepresentations and/or failures to disclose were made;

d. State whether there has been a criminal conviction for violation of the predicate acts and if so, provide particulars;

e. State whether civil litigation has resulted in a judgment with respect to the predicate acts and if so, provide particulars;

f. Describe how the predicate acts are both "related" and "continuous" within

---

1 If the party asserting a RICO violation is not the plaintiff, such as a counter-claimant defendant, this requirement applies to that party.

the meaning of *H.J. Inc. v. Northwestern Bell Telephone Co.*, 492 U.S. 229, 239, 109 S.Ct. 2893, 2900 (1989) and its progeny, including *Allwaste, Inc. v. Hecht*, 65 F.3d 1523, 1527 (9th Cir. 1995).

6. **Enterprise.** Describe in detail the alleged enterprise for each RICO claim and specify just what structure it had. A description of the enterprise shall include the following information:

a. The names of the individuals, partnerships, corporations, associations or other legal entities that allegedly constitute the enterprise;

b. The purpose, function and course of conduct of the enterprise, and whether its usual and daily activities were part of or separate from the pattern of racketeering activity. *See Chang v. Chen*, 80 F.3d 1293, 1298 (9th Cir. 1996.)

c. Whether any named defendants are or were employees, officers or directors of the alleged enterprise;

d. Whether you are alleging that the defendants are or were separate from the alleged enterprise, collectively constitute the enterprise itself, or are or were members of the enterprise; and

e. Whether (and if so how) the enterprise was affected by or benefited from the pattern of racketeering activity.

7. **Interstate or Foreign Commerce.** Describe the effect of the activities of the enterprise on interstate or foreign commerce.

8. **Section 1962(a).** If the complaint alleges a violation of 18 U.S.C. § 1962(a), provide the following information:

a. State who received the income derived from the pattern of racketeering activity or through the collection of an unlawful debt; and

b. Describe the use or investment of such income.

9. **Section 1962(b).** If the complaint alleges a violation of 18 U.S.C. § 1962(b), describe in detail the acquisition or maintenance of any interest in or control of the alleged enterprise.

10. **Section 1962(c).** If the complaint alleges a violation of 18 U.S.C. § 1962(c), provide the following information:

a. State who is employed by or associated with the enterprise; and

b. State whether the same entity is both the liable "person" and the "enterprise" under § 1962(c).

11. **Section 1962(d).** If the complaint alleges a violation of 18 U.S.C. § 1962(d), describe in detail the alleged conspiracy.

12. **Injury to Business or Property.**

a. Describe the alleged injury to business or property.

b. Describe the direct causal relationship between the alleged injury and the violation of the RICO statute.

13. **Damages.** List the damages sustained for which each defendant is allegedly liable.

14. **State Claims.** List all supplemental state claims, if any.

Dated: ________________

____
A. HOWARD MATZ
United States District Judge

F. *Order Regarding Settlement Conference*

IN THE UNITED STATES DISTICT COURT
FOR THE CENTRAL DISTRICT OF CALIFORNIA

Plaintiff(s),	Case No. ______________
v.	**ORDER REGARDING SETTLEMENT CONFERENCE BEFORE THIS COURT**
Defendant(s).	Settlement Conference Date:__________
	Time: _____ p.m.

PLEASE READ THIS ORDER AND LOCAL RULE 16-15 CAREFULLY

The Court has agreed to conduct the settlement conference in this matter. The Court has a keen interest in helping the parties achieve settlement. To facilitate the settlement conference, the Court hereby orders as follows:

1. **Settlement Conference Date.** [The parties should contact the Clerk of the Court to arrange a mutually agreeable date for the settlement conference to take place.] OR [The Court hereby schedules this case for a Mandatory Settlement Conference at ________.]

2. **Confidentiality.** Pursuant to Local Rule 16-15, all settlement proceedings shall be confidential and no statement made therein shall be admissible in any proceeding in the case, unless the parties otherwise agree. No part of a settlement proceeding shall be reported or otherwise recorded without the consent of the parties except for any memorialization of a settlement.

3. **Consultation with Clients Before Settlement Conference.** Before the settlement conference, the attorneys are directed to explore the parameters of possible settlement with their respective clients and insurance representatives. Counsel should disclose in writing, although not necessarily in formal, itemized budget form, the amount it will realistically cost to continue the case through trial and appeal. At the conference itself, counsel will be required to confirm that they have done so, and each party will be expected to discuss all economic and non-economic factors relevant to reaching a full and final settlement.

4. **Exchanging Settlement Offers Before Settlement Conference.** In order to provide the parties with a starting point for their settlement discussions with the Court, Plaintiff(s) shall advise Defendant(s) of the terms upon which Plaintiff(s) then is prepared to settle the case, in a letter delivered or faxed no later than seven (7) calendar days prior to the settlement conference. Within forty-eight (48) hours of receipt of Plaintiff(s')'s settlement offer, Defendant(s) shall respond to the same by letter delivered or faxed advising Plaintiff(s) of the terms upon which they are prepared to settle the case. Counsel shall bring copies of those letters to the settlement conference.

5. **Settlement Conference Statements.**

(a) Statements That Are Exchanged.

No later than three (3) court days prior to the settlement conference, the parties shall deliver directly to the Court's chambers their separate settlement conference statements and shall fax or personally deliver their statement to opposing counsel. The statement, which shall be brief and to the point and may not exceed 10 double-spaced pages, shall include (1) a succinct statement of the facts of the case, including claims and defenses remaining to be tried and the party's position on each issue; (2) an itemized statement of the damages claimed, in non-conclusory form; and (3) a summary of the history of past settlement discussions and offers and demands, including the most recent settlement offers exchanged pursuant to paragraph 4 of this Order. The statements shall also disclose the parties' positions about non-monetary terms that they may seek (or oppose). Depending on the case, such statements should include (but are not necessarily limited to): the form and scope of releases – *e.g.*, general and/or specific; waiver of California Civil Code § 1542; releases of and/or covenants not to sue third parties who either are not participants in the settlement conference or are not even parties in the lawsuit, but whose interests could affect the negotiating parties' ability to settle; indemnifications against claims of other parties; whether there should be a confidentiality provision; whether there should be recitals of non-admission of fault or liability; whether each settling party is to pay his, her or its own costs and attorneys' fees; and any other provision which is likely to be the subject of negotiation. Each side should cite reported decisions that they think support their position as to the amount (if any) of damages (including punitive damages), and each side may attach a copy of published summaries of comparable cases taken from publications that contain the terms and amounts of settlements or verdicts. Unless absolutely essential to inform the Court of key considerations, please do not attach other items, such as exhibits or transcript excerpts; the purpose of the statement is to enable the Court to become familiar with the issues, not to try the case. Accordingly, do not include discussions of the legal principles affecting the substantive claims and defenses.

(b) Confidential Statement.

Pursuant to Local Rule 16-15, each party shall also prepare a Confidential Addendum to the Settlement Conference Statement, which shall also be delivered to chambers but *shall not be served upon the other parties.* The Confidential Addendum shall contain a forthright, honest statement of the terms on which the case realistically can be settled; the approximate amount of fees and costs expended to date; an estimate of the fees and costs to be expended for future discovery, pretrial and trial; and any additional information the party wishes to impart to the judge confidentially. The Court relies on the Confidential Statement to ascertain the terms that the parties are really prepared to accept.

(c) Exceptions.

Sometimes the foregoing requirements may be unnecessary – *e.g.*, if there is only one relatively narrow or discrete issue that divides the parties, after they have reached agreement on all, or virtually all, other material terms. In such case, the parties' settlement conference statements and addenda should focus on the "sticking point" issue and provide the Court the background or context necessary to help break the impasse.

(d) Consequences of Non-Compliance

Failure to timely deliver a Settlement Conference Statement and Confidential Addendum will likely result in sanctions being imposed.

6. **Persons to be Present at Settlement Conference.** All persons whose consent is necessary to conclude settlement shall be present personally. This means the individual with the authority to say "yes," not just "no." As an exception, out-of-district parties, or agents empowered to settle may be available by telephone, provided they are absolutely committed to remaining available at the telephone (regardless of the hour) until released by the Court and further provided that a written request for their participation by telephone is submitted to and approved by the Court in advance of the conference. (WARNING: The Court is not always inclined to routinely permit such telephonic participation.)

The plaintiff's representative must have full and final authority, in the representative's sole discretion, to authorize dismissal of the case with prejudice, or to accept a settlement amount recommended by the settlement judge down to the defendant's last offer made prior to the settlement conference. The defendant's representative must have final settlement authority to commit the defendant to pay, in the representative's sole discretion, a settlement amount recommended by the settlement judge up to the plaintiff's prayer (excluding punitive damage prayers), or up to the plaintiff's last demand made prior to the settlement conference, whichever is lower.

Counsel appearing without their clients and/or the person or persons whose presence is required to achieve settlement (such as insurance representatives) will cause the settlement conference to be canceled and rescheduled, regardless of whether counsel purportedly has been given settlement authority. (This will not result if the Court granted prior authorization for the client to participate telephonically.) The noncomplying party, attorney, or both, may be assessed the costs and expenses incurred by other parties as a result of such cancellation and rescheduling.

If a settlement proposal must be presented to a board or committee, the attendance of at least one sitting and knowledgeable member of the Board (preferably the Chairperson) is *absolutely required*, unless the entity commits absolutely to the discretionary authority of another representative.

In lawsuits involving the United States or any of its agencies, the Assistant U.S. Attorney in charge of the case must appear with the full measure of settlement authority provided by his or her superiors within the United States Attorneys' Office.

Any insurance company that is a party to the case or is contractually required to defend or to pay damages assessed within policy limits, must have a settlement representative present at the conference. Such representative must have final settlement authority to commit the company to pay, in the representative's sole discretion, an amount recommended by the settlement judge within the policy limits. The purpose of this requirement is to have an insurance representative present who can settle the outstanding claim or claims during the course of the conference without consulting a superior. An insurance representative authorized to pay, in his or her sole discretion, up to the plaintiff's last demand made prior to the settlement conference will also satisfy this requirement. Counsel of record will be responsible for timely advising any involved nonparty insurance company of the requirements of this Order.

7. **Conduct of Settlement Conference.** The Court may, in its discretion, converse with the lawyers, the parties, the insurance representatives, or any one of them outside of the hearing of the others. The comments of the Court during such separate sessions are not to be used by counsel in settlement negotiations with opposing counsel. This is a necessary requirement in order to avoid intentional or unintentional misquotation of the Court's comments. Violation of this policy may mislead the adverse party and therefore hinder settlement.

At the commencement of the settlement conference, each party through counsel may be required to make an oral presentation (not to exceed 10 minutes) of the relevant facts *and* law, in the presence of all parties and counsel.

If settlement between any or all parties is reached as a result of the Settlement Conference, the Court will enter the settlement terms on the record at the end of the conference and the parties will be expected to assent to those terms, at which point the settlement will be final and binding.

All papers submitted for the Settlement Conference will either be returned to the parties or destroyed by the Court after the settlement proceedings are concluded, unless the parties otherwise agree.

The Court thanks the parties and their counsel for their anticipated cooperation in carrying out these requirements.

IT IS SO ORDERED.

Dated: ___________

____
A. HOWARD MATZ
United States District Judge

G. *Order Setting Rule 16(b) Scheduling Conference*

IN THE UNITED STATES DISTICT COURT
FOR THE CENTRAL DISTRICT OF CALIFORNIA

Plaintiff(s),)	Case No. ______________
v.)	**ORDER SETTING RULE 16(b) SCHEDULING CONFERENCE**
Defendant(s).)	Date: ______
______________________)	Time: 1:30 p.m.

This case has been assigned to Judge A. Howard Matz. If plaintiff has not already served the complaint (or any amendment thereto) on all defendants, plaintiff shall promptly do so and shall file proofs of service within three days thereafter. Defendants also shall timely serve and file their responsive pleadings and file proofs of service within three days thereafter.

This matter is set for a scheduling conference on the above date. The conference will be held pursuant to Fed.R.Civ.P. 16(b). The parties are reminded of their obligations under Fed.R.Civ.P. 26(a)(1) to disclose information (without awaiting a discovery request) and under R. 26(f) to confer on a discovery plan not later than twenty-one (21) days prior to the scheduling conference and to file a report with the Court entitled "Joint Rule 16(b) Report" not later than fourteen (14) days after they confer. Failure to comply with the following requirements or to cooperate in the preparation of the Joint Rule 16(b) Report may lead to the imposition of sanctions.

Unless there is a likelihood that upon motion by a party the Court would order that any or all discovery is premature, it is advisable for counsel to begin to conduct discovery actively before the Scheduling Conference. At the very least, the parties shall comply fully with the letter and spirit of Fed.R.Civ.P. 26(a) and thereby obtain and produce most of what would be produced in the early stage of discovery, because at the Scheduling Conference the Court will impose tight deadlines to complete discovery.

1. Joint Rule 16(b) Report. The Joint Rule 16(b) Report, which shall be filed not later than one week before the scheduling conference, shall be drafted by plaintiff (unless the parties agree otherwise), but shall be submitted and signed jointly. "Jointly" contemplates a single report, regardless of how many separately-represented parties there are. The Joint Rule 16(b) Report shall report on all matters enumerated below, which include those required to be discussed by Rule 26(f) and Local Rule 26:

a. **a short synopsis** (not to exceed two pages) of the main claims, counterclaims, and/or affirmative defenses.

b. a brief description of the **key legal issues**.

c. the realistic range of **provable damages**.

d. whether there is **insurance coverage**.

e. a statement of the **likelihood of motions** seeking to (I) add other parties or claims or (ii) file amended pleadings or (iii) transfer venue.

f. **Discovery and Experts.** Pursuant to Rule 26(f), state what, if any, changes in the disclosures under R. 26(a) should be made; the subjects on which discovery may be needed and whether discovery should be conducted in phases or otherwise be limited; what issues exist or are likely to arise, and what agreements (if any) have been reached concerning the identification maintenance and production of electronically stored information; what discovery has been conducted thus far; whether applicable limitations should be changed or other limitations imposed; and whether the Court should enter other orders. Please state how many depositions each side will conduct. Also discuss the proposed time of **expert witness disclosures** under F.R.Civ.P. 26(a)(2).

g. a description of the issues or claims that any party believes may be determined by motion for **summary judgment or motion *in limine***.

h. a statement of what **settlement** discussions and/or written communications have occurred (specifically excluding any statement of the terms discussed) and a statement pursuant to the Local Rule 16-14.4 selecting a settlement mechanism under that rule.

i. a realistic (not padded) **estimate of the time required for trial** and whether trial will be by jury or by court. Each side should specify (by number, not by name) how many witnesses it contemplates calling. If the time estimate for trial given in the Rule 16(b) Joint Report exceeds eight court days, counsel shall be prepared at the Scheduling Conference to explain why a lengthier trial is estimated.

j. **Presumptive Schedule of Pretrial Dates.** The parties should fill in the form attached as Exhibit A to this Order and attach it to the Rule 16(b) report. *The pre-printed entries in the "Weeks Before Trial" column merely reflect what the Court believes are appropriate for many, if not most, cases; those entries are not necessarily applicable to this case. (Thus, in most cases there will be 14 weeks between the non-expert discovery cutoff and trial.) You should use the form to request the Court to set different last dates by which the key requirements must be completed.* Each side should write in the month, day and year it requests for each event. *E.g.*, for the expert discovery cut-off, it might be "10/7/06" for plaintiff and "10/28/06" for defendant, if they cannot agree. At the conference, the Court will review this form with counsel. Each entry proposing dates shall fall on a Monday, except the trial date which is a Tuesday. In appropriate cases the Court will order different dates after it hears from Counsel. ***The proposed non-expert and expert discovery cut-off date means:*** The last day by which all depositions must be completed and responses to all previously-served written discovery must be provided. **It does not mean** the last day to initiate discovery or to file a motion with the magistrate judge seeking to compel discovery. **The proposed cut-off date for motions means:** The last date on which motions may be heard, not noticed.

k. a statement of any **other issues affecting the status or management** of the case (*e.g.*, unusually complicated technical or technological issues, disputes over protective orders, extraordinarily voluminous document production, non-English speaking witnesses, discovery in foreign jurisdictions, *etc.*).

l. **for conflict purposes**, corporate parties must identify all subsidiaries, parents and affiliates.

m. **Patent Cases:** Propose dates and methodology for claim construction and *Markman* hearings.

n. **Do the parties wish to have a Magistrate Judge preside?** Under 28 U.S.C. § 636, the parties may consent to have a Magistrate Judge preside over all the proceedings, not just discovery. They may pick *any* Magistrate Judge (not just the one assigned to this case) from among those Magistrate Judges who accept these designations. (They are identified on the Central District's website, which also contains the consent form.)

The Joint Rule 16(b) Report should set forth the above enumerated information under section headings corresponding to this Order.

2. **Scheduling Conference.** The Scheduling Conference will be held in Courtroom 14 of the Federal Courthouse at 312 N. Spring Street. Counsel shall comply with the following:

a. Participation. The lead trial attorney must attend the Scheduling Conference, unless excused for good cause shown in advance of the Scheduling Conference.

b. Continuance. A continuance of the Scheduling Conference will be granted only for good cause

c. Use of Conference Telephone. If one or more of the lead counsel has his or her office outside of Los Angeles County, the Court is normally willing, at counsel's request, to conduct the status conference by conference telephone call. Please contact the court clerk at (213) 894-5283 to get approval. Opposing counsel who are outside of Los Angeles County may also participate by telephone. The attorney who has received approval to participate by telephone shall call (213) 894-5290 at the time and date specified above for specific instructions, which might include being required to remain available on the telephone until the case is called. After the other participants are assembled, that attorney will be notified that he or she must promptly originate the conference call.

3. **Protective Orders.** If you seek a protective order, propose it to opposing counsel before the Scheduling Conference, if at all possible. In a separate order, the Court has enumerated precise requirements for protective orders and the treatment of confidential information. In proposing a protective order for this case, please comply with that order, which is available on the Court's website.

4. **Notice to be Provided by Counsel.** Plaintiff's counsel or, if plaintiff is appearing *pro se*, defendant's counsel, shall provide this Order to any parties who first appear after the date of this Order and to parties who are known to exist but have not yet entered appearances.

5. **Disclosures to Clients.** Counsel are ordered to deliver to their respective clients a copy of this Order and of the Court's Scheduling and Case Management Order, which contains the schedule that the Court imposes at the Scheduling Conference.

6. **Court's Website.** Copies of this and all other orders of this Court that may become applicable to this case are available on the Central District of California website, at "www.cacd.uscourts.gov," under "Judge's Requirements." Copies of the Local Rules are available on the website.[1]

The Court thanks the parties and their counsel for their anticipated cooperation in carrying out these requirements.

IT IS SO ORDERED.

Dated: March 14, 2007

____
A. HOWARD MATZ
United States District Judge

---

[1] They may also be purchased from one of the following:

Los Angeles Daily Journal	West Publishing Company	Metropolitan News
915 East First Street	50 West Kellogg Blvd.	210 South Spring Street
Los Angeles, CA 90012	St. Paul, MN 55164-9979	Los Angeles, CA 90012

H. *Scheduling and Case Management Order*

IN THE UNITED STATES DISTICT COURT
FOR THE CENTRAL DISTRICT OF CALIFORNIA

Plaintiff(s),	Case No. CV *-AHM (x)
v.	**SCHEDULING AND CASE MANAGEMENT ORDER**
Defendant(s).	**SEE LAST PAGE FOR PRETRIAL AND TRIAL DATES**

I. APPLICABLE SCHEDULE

This case shall be litigated according to the schedule on the last page. Ordinarily, those dates are determined after consultation with the parties at the Rule 16(b) Scheduling Conference, and this Order is distributed to them at that time. Accordingly, the dates and requirements are firm. The Court is very unlikely to grant continuances, even if stipulated by the parties, unless the parties establish good cause through a strong, concrete showing.

The following provisions sometimes refer to the Local Rules. **PLEASE NOTE THAT UNDER RULE 83-7, THE VIOLATION OR FAILURE TO CONFORM TO THE LOCAL RULES MAY SUBJECT THE OFFENDING PARTY OR COUNSEL TO A VARIETY OF SANCTIONS.**

II. DISCOVERY AND DISCOVERY CUTOFF

A. Non-Expert Discovery

All non-expert discovery shall be completed by the non-expert discovery cutoff on the last page. **THIS IS NOT THE DATE BY WHICH DISCOVERY REQUESTS MUST BE SERVED; IT IS THE DATE BY WHICH ALL DISCOVERY IS TO BE COMPLETED.** Any motion challenging the adequacy of responses to discovery must be filed, served and calendared sufficiently in advance of the discovery cutoff date to permit the responses to be obtained before that date, if the motion is granted.

In an effort to provide further guidance to the parties, the Court notes the following:

1. Depositions. All depositions shall be scheduled to commence sufficiently in advance of the discovery cutoff date to permit their completion and to permit the deposing party enough time to bring any discovery motions concerning the deposition prior to the cutoff date. Given the requirements of notice and "meet and confer," that means that in most cases a planned motion to compel would have to be discussed with opposing counsel approximately six weeks before the cutoff.

2. Written Discovery. All interrogatories, requests for production of documents, and requests for admissions shall be served sufficiently in advance of the discovery cutoff date to permit the discovering party enough time to challenge (via motion practice) responses deemed to be deficient.

3. Discovery Motions. Whenever possible, the Court expects the parties to resolve discovery problems among themselves in a courteous, reasonable and

professional manner. If they do so, resort to the Court for guidance in discovery is seldom necessary.

The Magistrate Judge assigned to this case will rule on discovery motions. The Court requires compliance with Local Rules 37-1 through 37-4 in the preparation and filing of discovery motions. Any review of a Magistrate Judge's discovery order must proceed by way of noticed motion under Local Rule 7-3. In accordance with 28 U.S.C. § 636(b)(1)(A), the Court will not reverse any such order, *including one imposing sanctions*, unless the moving party demonstrates that the Magistrate Judge's order "is clearly erroneous or contrary to law." If this Court overrules a Magistrate Judge's order denying discovery, the Discovery Cutoff will, upon application, be extended.

4. Exceptions to Discovery Cutoff. The Court establishes a discovery cutoff date to facilitate the timely, efficient and just resolution of this case. So long as that objective is in no way impeded, and provided that the parties meet the other conditions in this paragraph, the parties are permitted to conduct discovery beyond the cutoff date. These conditions are: (a) they all agree to do so; (b) no discovery motions resulting from post-cutoff discovery disputes may be brought; and (c) the fact that discovery is being conducted after the cutoff will not be cause for continuing the trial date or for not complying with the other deadlines and requirements in this order. Thus, parties conducting discovery after the cutoff accept the risk that they will not be able to enforce their rights in the event of a dispute.

B. Expert Discovery

If expert discovery necessitates motion practice which cannot be resolved until after the deadlines set forth below for motion practice, then those deadlines shall not apply. But because Local Rules 7-3 and 37-1 require ample time to meet and confer as well as brief the matters, the parties should commence expert discovery shortly after the initial designations of experts, because in no event will the Final Pre-Trial Conference and trial dates be continued merely because expert discovery is still underway.

III. MOTIONS AND MOTION CUTOFF DATE

A. General Provisions.

Motions are heard on Mondays at 10:00 a.m., unless the Court orders otherwise. If Monday is a national holiday, the motion will not be heard the next day (Tuesday) but instead automatically set for the next succeeding Monday.

All law and motion matters, except for motions in limine, must be set for hearing (not filing) by the motion cutoff date specified on the last page. Issues left undetermined after the passage of the motion cutoff date should be listed as issues for trial in the final pre-trial conference order. As an exception to the above, motions in limine dealing with evidentiary matters may be heard at the Final Pre-Trial Conference or (at the Court's discretion) at the start of trial; however, the Court will not hear or resolve summary judgment motions disguised as motions in limine.

The applicable Local Rules are Rules 7-1, *et seq.* If any party does not oppose a motion, that party shall submit a written statement that it does not oppose the motion, in accordance with Local Rule 7-16. Failure to meet the time limits set forth in Local Rule 7 may be deemed consent to the granting of the motion. Local Rule 7-12. The Court will not decide late-filed motions, and a party or counsel who files such late papers may be subject to sanctions under Local Rule 7-13.

Reply papers shall be limited to argument and/or authorities responsive to the opposition papers. The Court will ignore new matter that was improperly introduced.

To assure that the Court receives oppositions and replies in a timely fashion, courtesy copies of all oppositions and replies, conformed to reflect that they have been filed, shall be deposited in the drop box in the entrance way to chambers, to the left of Courtroom 14. All such papers shall be filed "loose" -- i.e., not inside envelopes.

B. Motions under Fed.R.Civ.P 12.
See the Court's "Initial Case-Specific Order Following Filing of Complaint Assigned to Judge Matz."

C. Summary Judgment Motions.
Parties need not, and in many cases they should not, wait until the motion cutoff to bring motions for summary judgment or partial summary judgment. However, in virtually every case, the Court expects that the party moving for summary judgment will provide more than the minimum twenty-eight (28) day notice for motions. Summary judgment motions are, of course, very fact-dependent. All parties should prepare their papers in a fashion that will assist the Court in absorbing the mass of facts. (*E.g.*, generous use of tabs, tables of contents, headings, indices, etc.) The parties are directed to comply precisely with Local Rules 56-1 through 56-4. The Court will place a great deal of importance on these respective statements and ***the parties shall deliver to chambers an electronic copy of the respective "Statement of Uncontroverted Facts and Conclusions of Law" and "Statement of Genuine Issues."***

1. Statement of Undisputed Facts and Statement of Genuine Issues
The Separate Statement of Undisputed Facts shall be prepared in a two column format. The left hand column sets forth the allegedly undisputed fact. The right hand column sets forth the evidence that supports the factual statement. The fact statements should be set forth in sequentially numbered paragraphs. Each paragraph should contain a narrowly focused statement of fact. Each numbered paragraph should address a single subject in as concise a manner as possible.

The opposing party's Statement of Genuine Issues must be in two columns and track the movant's separate statement exactly as prepared. The left hand column must restate the allegedly undisputed fact, and the right hand column must state either that it is undisputed or disputed. The opposing party may dispute all or only a portion of the statement, but if disputing only a portion, it must clearly indicate what part is being disputed, followed by the opposing party's evidence controverting the fact. The Court will not wade through a document to determine whether a fact really is in dispute. To demonstrate that a fact is disputed, the opposing party must briefly state why it disputes the moving party's asserted fact, cite to the relevant exhibit or other piece of evidence, and describe what it is in that exhibit or evidence that refutes the asserted fact. No legal argument should be set forth in this document.

The opposing party may submit additional material facts that bear on or relate to the issues raised by the movant, which shall follow the format described above for the moving party's separate statement. These additional facts shall continue in sequentially numbered paragraphs (*i.e.*, if movant's last statement of fact was set forth in paragraph 30, then the first new fact will be set forth in paragraph 31), and shall set forth in the right hand column the evidence that supports that statement.

2. Supporting Evidence

No party should submit any evidence other than the specific items of evidence or testimony necessary to support or controvert a proposed statement of undisputed fact. Thus, for example, the entire transcript of a deposition, entire sets of interrogatory responses, and documents that do not specifically support or controvert material in the separate statements should not be submitted in support of opposition to a motion for summary judgment. The Court will not consider such material.

Evidence submitted in support of or opposition to a motion should be submitted either by way of stipulation or as exhibits to declarations sufficient to authenticate the proffered evidence, and should not be attached to the Memorandum of Points and Authorities. The Court will accept counsel's authentication of deposition transcripts, of written discovery responses and of the receipt of documents in discovery if the fact that the document was in the opponent's possession is of independent significance. Documentary evidence as to which there is no stipulation regarding foundation must be accompanied by the testimony, either by declaration or properly authenticated deposition transcript, of a witness who can establish authenticity. The parties should use colored markers to highlight the testimony or portions of exhibits that they are relying on.

3. Objections to Evidence

If a party disputes a fact based in whole or in part on an evidentiary objection, the ground of the objection, as indicated above, should be stated in a separate statement but not argued in that document.

4. Evidence Not Properly Cited

When a party relies on deposition testimony in a summary judgment motion without citing to page and line numbers, the Court in its discretion may exclude or disregard the supposed "evidence." *See Orr v. Bank of America*, 285 F.3d 764, 775 (9th Cir. 2002).

5. Cross-Motions on Identical Issues of Law

The parties shall avoid filing cross-motions for summary judgment on identical issues of law, such that the papers would be unnecessarily cumulative. (*E.g.*, a party's moving and reply papers on its own motion would advance the same arguments as its opposition papers to the other party's cross-motion). The parties shall discuss in advance which party should be designated as the moving party. The moving party's reply papers shall be limited to responding to the non-moving party's opposition papers. The non-moving party may not file a sur-reply unless the Court first grants leave to do so.

D. Motions in Limine.

Parties often do not focus on evidentiary and related issues until the last stages of trial preparation. This is a mistake. Such motions can be very helpful in narrowing issues, limiting or allowing evidence and promoting settlement. With these benefits in mind, the Court encourages the parties carefully to consider filing such motions <u>before</u> the last stages of trial preparation. In any event, the parties must file and respond to motions in limine in accordance with Local Rule 7 by the date specified on the last page of this order. The Court will make every effort to rule upon motions in limine at or before the Final Pre-Trial Conference.

E. Oral Argument.

Sometimes the Court will not hear oral argument. When that is the case, the Court will notify the parties in advance. If there is a hearing, tentative rulings will often be available in the courtroom approximately one-half hour before the call of the calendar. The parties are expected to be familiar with the tentative ruling at the time of argument.

IV. APPLICATIONS AND STIPULATIONS FOR EXTENSIONS OF TIME

A. Applications or Stipulations to Extend the Time to File Any Required Document or to Continue Any Pretrial or Trial Date.

No stipulations extending scheduling requirements or modifying applicable rules are effective until and unless the Court approves them. Both applications and stipulations must set forth:

1. the existing due date or hearing date;
2. specific, concrete reasons supporting good cause for granting the extension. In this regard, a statement that an extension "will promote settlement" is insufficient. The requesting party or parties must indicate the status of ongoing negotiations: have written proposals been exchanged? Is counsel in the process of reviewing a draft settlement agreement? Has a mediator been selected?
3. whether there have been prior requests for extensions, and whether these were granted or denied by the Court.

B. Ex Parte Applications.

Think twice! The Court strongly discourages ex parte applications. *See Mission Power Eng. Co. v. Continental Casualty Co.*, 883 F.Supp. 488 (C.D. Calif.1995). Strict adherence to Local Rule 7-19 is necessary.

V. PRE-TRIAL CONFERENCE AND LOCAL RULE 16 FILINGS

A. General Provisions.

The Final Pre-Trial Conference ("PTC") will be held at 11:00 a.m. on the date specified, unless the Court expressly waived a PTC at the Scheduling Conference. (In the rare cases where the Court waives a PTC, the parties must follow Local Rule 16-11.) If adjustments in the Court's calendar to accommodate congestion become necessary, the Court may re-calendar the PTC instead of the trial date. Therefore, the parties should assume that if the PTC goes forward, the trial <u>will</u> go forward without continuance, although some brief period of trailing may prove necessary.

The lead trial attorney on behalf of every party shall attend both the PTC and all meetings of the parties in preparation for the PTC. Unless counsel has been excused for good cause shown in advance of the PTC, the Court reserves the right to designate the attorney attending the PTC as lead trial counsel.

A continuance of the PTC at the parties' request or by stipulation is highly unlikely. Specifically, failure to complete discovery is not a ground for continuance. In the unlikely event that the Court agrees to continuing the PTC, the trial date is likely to be delayed as a result, possibly for a few months. If a change in the trial date is necessitated or likely because of the Court's calendar or otherwise, modifications of that date will be discussed at the PTC.

At the PTC, the parties should be prepared to discuss means of streamlining the trial, including, but not limited to: bifurcation; presentation of foundational and non-critical testimony and direct testimony by deposition excerpts, narrative summaries and/or stipulations as to the content of testimony; presentation of testimony on direct examination or by declaration subject to cross-examination; and qualification of experts by admitted resumes. The Court will attempt to rule upon previously-filed motions in limine at the PTC. The Court will also discuss settlement.

B. Form of Final Pre-Trial Conference Order ("PTCO").

The proposed PTCO shall be lodged seven calendar days before the PTC. Adherence to this time requirement is necessary for in-chambers preparation of the matter. The form of the proposed PTCO shall comply with Appendix A to the Local Rules and the following:

1. Please place in "ALL CAPS" and in bold the separately numbered headings for each category in the PTCO (e.g., "**1. THE PARTIES**" or "**7. CLAIMS AND DEFENSES OF THE PARTIES**.")

2. Please include a Table of Contents at the beginning.

3. In specifying the surviving pleadings under Section 1, please state which claims or counterclaims have been dismissed or abandoned. *E.g.*, "Plaintiff's second cause of action for breach of fiduciary duty has been dismissed." Also, in multiple party cases where not all claims or counterclaims will be prosecuted against all remaining parties on the other side, please specify to which party each claim or counterclaim is directed.

4. *In specifying the parties' claims and defenses under Section 7, each party shall closely follow the examples set forth in Appendix A of the Local Rules.*

5. In drafting the PTCO, the Court also expects that the parties will attempt to agree on and set forth as many non-contested facts as possible. The Court will usually read the uncontested facts to the jury at the start of the trial. A carefully drafted and comprehensively stated stipulation of facts will reduce the length of trial and increase jury understanding of the case.

6. In drafting the factual issues in dispute for the PTCO, the parties should attempt to state issues in ultimate fact form, not in the form of evidentiary fact issues (*e.g.*, "Was the defendant negligent? Was such negligence the

proximate cause of injury to the plaintiff? Was the plaintiff negligent?" etc. Not "Was the plaintiff standing on the corner of 5th and Spring at 10 a.m. on May 3?" etc.). The parties may, if they so desire, list sub-issues under the headings of ultimate fact issues, but should not use this as a device to list disputes over evidentiary matters. In general, the issues of fact should set forth the disputed elements of the claim or affirmative defenses.

7. The Court may well submit fact issues to the jury in the form of findings on a special verdict. The issues of fact should track the elements of a claim or defense on which the jury will be required to make findings.

8. Issues of law should state legal issues on which the Court will be required to rule at or after the PTC, or during the trial, and should not list ultimate fact issues to be submitted to the trier of fact.

C. Rule 16 Filings; Memoranda; Witness Lists (Including Experts); Exhibit Lists.

1. Generally. The parties must comply fully with the requirements of Local Rule 16. They shall file carefully prepared Memoranda of Contentions of Fact and Law (which may also serve as the trial brief), along with their respective Witness Lists and Exhibit Lists, all in accordance with Local Rule 16. See the last page for dates. Failure to include the name of an expert witness precludes a party from calling that expert witness. An expert witness's direct testimony shall consist of a non-exhaustive description of his background and the contents of his Rule 26 report.

2. Pre-Trial Exhibit Stipulation. The parties shall prepare a Pre-Trial Exhibit Stipulation which shall contain each party's numbered list of all trial exhibits, with objections, if any, to each exhibit including the basis of the objection and the offering party's response. All exhibits to which there is no objection shall be deemed admitted. All parties shall stipulate to the authenticity of exhibits whenever possible, and the Pre-Trial Exhibit Stipulation shall identify any exhibits whose authenticity has not been stipulated to and the specific reasons for the party's failure to stipulate.

   The Stipulation shall be substantially in the following form:

Pre-Trial Exhibit Stipulation

Plaintiff(s)' Exhibits

Number	Description	If Objection, State Grounds	Response to Objection

Defendant(s)' Exhibits

Number	Description	If Objection, State Grounds	Response to Objection

   The Pre-Trial Exhibit Stipulation shall be filed at the same time counsel lodge the PTCO. Failure to comply with this paragraph shall constitute a waiver of all objections.

3. **Consequences of Non-Compliance. If counsel fail to file the required Pre-Trial documents or fail to appear at the Pre-Trial Conference and such failure is not otherwise satisfactorily explained to the Court, (a) the cause shall stand dismissed for failure to prosecute, if such failure occurs on the part of the plaintiff, (b) default judgment shall be**

entered if such failure occurs on the part of the defendant; or (c) the Court may take such action as it deems appropriate.

D. Trial Witness Estimate Form

At the pre-trial conference the parties will be given a Joint Trial Witness Time Estimate Form, which they will be required to fill in and give to the Court on the first day of trial.

E. Real Time Court Reporting Requirement

Each party must email the court reporter at cindycsr@gmail.com. prior to the PTC a prepared typed list of proper names, unusual or scientific terms, or any other uncommon words that are likely to be used during trial. This list will enable the court reporter to prepare accurate transcripts in real time.

F. Jury Instructions, Verdict Forms and Special Interrogatories.

1. On the dates specified on the attached "Schedule of Pretrial Dates," the parties are required jointly to submit one set of agreed upon substantive instructions, a verdict form and, if necessary, special interrogatories. "Substantive jury instructions" means all instructions relating to the elements of all claims and defenses in the case. The parties need not submit general instructions. The parties shall deliver to chambers an electronic copy of these filings at the time the documents are filed.

2. If the parties cannot agree upon one complete set of substantive instructions, special or general verdict form and/or special interrogatories, they shall file two documents with the Court: first, the agreed upon instructions and verdict forms, and second a joint statement regarding the disputed instructions, verdicts and interrogatories. In the second document (the joint statement) the parties shall place the text of the disputed instruction (or verdict or interrogatory) with an identification of the party proposing it and following that text they shall place the opposing party's statement of objections, along with legal authority in support of the objections (not to exceed one page) and proposed alternative language where appropriate. The entirety of the objection shall be typed in capital letters.

   Each party shall provide an electronic copy when it serves its proposed instructions on opposing parties to simplify the preparation of the joint statement regarding the disputed instructions.

   Both the agreed on set, and the joint statement re disputed instructions are to be filed at the Final Pre-Trial Conference.

3. A table of contents shall be included with all jury instructions submitted to the Court. The table of contents shall set forth the following:
   a. The number of the instruction;
   b. A brief title of the instruction;
   c. The source of the instruction; and
   d. The page number of the instruction.

   For example:

Number	Title	Source	Page Number
1	Burden of Proof	9th Cir. 12.2	5

The parties need not submit a separate copy of instructions without citations to authority.

4. The Court prefers counsel to use the instructions from the *Manual of Model Jury Instructions for the Ninth Circuit* (West 2007 (to be published around June 2007)) where applicable. Those instructions are "on-line" in the Ninth Circuit's website. Where California law is to be applied and the above instructions are not applicable, the Court prefers counsel to use *California Jury Instructions - Civil* (CACI). If neither of these sources is applicable, counsel are directed to use the instructions in O'Malley, Grenig & Lee, *Federal Jury Practice and Instructions (Fifth).*

5. Modifications of instructions from the foregoing sources (or any other form instructions) must specifically state the modification made to the original form instruction and the authority supporting the modification.

G. Joint Statement of the Case and Requests for Voir Dire.

On the same date the parties file their joint and separate proposed jury instructions, the parties shall also file their joint statement of the case which the Court shall read to all prospective jurors prior to the commencement of voir dire. Ordinarily, the statement should be not longer than two or three paragraphs.

The Court conducts voir dire of all prospective jurors. On the same date that the parties file their Joint Statement of the Case, each party shall file its separate proposed voir dire questions. The parties need not submit requests for standard voir dire questions, such as education, current occupation, marital status, prior jury service, etc., but should include only proposed questions specifically tailored to the parties and issues of the case.

H. Findings of Fact and Conclusions of Law.

For a non-jury trial, the parties shall lodge their proposed findings of fact and conclusions of law not later than one week before trial. The parties shall deliver to chambers an electronic copy of these findings in Word or WordPerfect 11 compatible format. Please see the Court's Civil Trial Order.

VI. SETTLEMENT

Local Rule 16-15 provides that the Settlement Conference shall be concluded not later than 45 days before the Pretrial Conference. The Court believes that in most cases completion of all discovery and dispositive motions will help the parties assess their positions before they embark on the costly pretrial process. But sometimes parties find it more difficult to settle after they incurred the cost of all discovery and motion practice. The Court therefore strongly encourages counsel and the parties to pursue settlement earlier.

The Court has a keen interest in helping the parties achieve settlement. If the parties believe that it would be more likely that a settlement would be reached if they conduct the settlement conference at a different time than that in the attached schedule, they should conduct it at that time. In any event, as indicated in the Schedule of Pretrial Dates attached hereto, the parties must file a Status Report re Settlement at the time that they file their respective memorandum of fact and law, witness lists and exhibit lists.

This Court will not conduct settlement conferences in non jury cases which he is to try. In jury cases, the Court will conduct a settlement conference at the parties' joint request if three conditions exist:

1. The parties are satisfied that the fact issues in the case will be tried to a jury.
2. All significant pre-trial rulings which the Court must make have been made.
3. The parties desire the Court to conduct the conference, understanding that if settlement fails, the Court will try the case.

   If the parties are inclined to select this Court to conduct the Mandatory Settlement Conference, the parties should consult the Court's Standing Order re Settlement Conference so that they fully understand the Court's requirements for the settlement conference. That order will govern the settlement conference procedures before this Court, but may also serve as a useful reference for settlement conferences conducted pursuant to the other available procedures.

VII. WEBSITE

Copies of this Order and all other orders of this Court that may apply specifically to this case are available on the Central District of California website, at "www.cacd.uscourts.gov," under "Judge's Requirements."

VIII. TRIAL DATE

This case has been set for trial on the date specified on Exhibit "A" below at 9:00 A.M. Please review the Court's separately-issued Civil Trial Order for the procedures and requirements for civil trials.

IX. CONCLUSION

The Court thanks the parties and their counsel for their anticipated cooperation in carrying out these requirements.

IT IS SO ORDERED.

DATED: October 20, 2011

____
A. HOWARD MATZ
United States District Judge

I. Standing Civil Bench Trial Order

IN THE UNITED STATES DISTICT COURT
FOR THE CENTRAL DISTRICT OF CALIFORNIA

)	Case No. CV __-_________-AHM (__x)
Plaintiff(s),)	
v.)	**STANDING ORDER RE**
Defendant(s).)	**BENCH TRIAL**
_______________________)	

This matter is currently scheduled for a ____ day court trial beginning on ___________ at 9:00 a.m. Good cause appearing therefor, the Court hereby orders as follows:

1. **Stipulated Facts.** The parties shall submit a detailed stipulation of those facts to which they agree. *E.g.*, "Plaintiff was hired on [date] to be the Manager of Human Relations. Her duties consisted of ______________.

   She reported to ___________________. Six employees reported to her."

2. **Opening Statements and Proposed Findings of Fact and Conclusions of Law.** If they have not already done so, each party shall file his, her or its Proposed Findings of Fact and Conclusions of Law not later than eight days before trial - - *i.e.*, ordinarily the Monday of the week preceding trial. These shall incorporate the agreed-to facts as well as facts not stipulated. If possible, each party shall provide the Court with an electronic copy of its proposed findings and conclusions in Word or WordPerfect format prior to the first day of trial. Opening statements shall be brief and shall summarize how the attorney expects to prove the key components of his/her proposed fact findings.

3. **Joint Trial Witness Time Estimate Form.** Not later than eight days before trial, the parties shall complete and file the Joint Trial Witness Time Estimate Form (see attached).

4. **Joint Exhibit List.** Not later than eight days before trial, the parties shall file a final Joint Exhibit List. *See* Local Rule 16-5. They shall specifically designate by asterisk those exhibits to which there is an objection.

5. **Witness Declarations and Narrative Summaries.**

   (a) Not later than eight days before trial, for each witness a party intends to call at trial, counsel for that party shall either (1) file an executed declaration in lieu of direct testimony, or (2) if the testimony of the witness is contained in the transcript of a deposition, convert the questions and answers that were given at the deposition into a coherent, substantive narrative that can serve as that witness's direct testimony. If option (2) is exercised, the proponent shall seek from the other side a stipulation that the narrative is a fair and accurate distillation of the deposition testimony. At trial, the Court will permit "live" questioning only for cross-examination and re-direct of each such witness.

   (b) This paragraph does not apply to adverse or hostile witnesses; *i.e.*, counsel may call such witnesses to the stand for live examination in their case-inchief.

6. **Objections to Declarations and Narrative Summaries.** Not later than four days before trial -- *i.e.*, ordinarily the Friday before trial -- each party shall file a copy of its written objections to the testimony contained in the opposing party's declarations and/or narrative summaries and file a chambers copy with the Court. Failure to file such written objections will be deemed a waiver of any such evidentiary objections. The Court will read the declarations, narrative summaries and objections in chambers. The Court will rule on such objections before the declaration or summary is received.

7. **Depositions in Lieu of Narrative Summaries.**
In certain cases, such as where numerous objections were asserted at a deposition and a fair and accurate distillation of the witness's deposition testimony cannot be prepared because the deposition testimony was fragmented, incomplete or ambiguous, the proponent may mark and lodge the proffered portions of the deposition transcript in accordance with the Local Rules. In those circumstances, which the Court expects will *not* be the norm, the Court will read the lodged portions, rule (if necessary) on the objections in court and treat the admitted portions of the transcript as the witness's direct testimony.

8. **Closing Statements and Post-Trial Briefs.** For an overview and review of the evidence, the Court will rely exclusively on closing statements. It will not accept or read post-trial briefs, unless specifically authorized. In delivering closings, counsel shall use their respective proposed findings of fact and conclusions of law as a "checklist" and should identify the evidence that supports the proposals. At trial, therefore, counsel shall be prepared to be specific, meticulous and complete in pointing to such evidence.

The Court thanks counsel in advance for their anticipated cooperation and compliance with this order.

IT IS SO ORDERED.

DATE: December 8, 2011

____
A. HOWARD MATZ
United States District Judge

J. Standing Order Regarding Criminal Trials

IN THE UNITED STATES DISTICT COURT
FOR THE CENTRAL DISTRICT OF CALIFORNIA

UNITED STATES OF AMERICA,	)	Case No. CR ____________ AHM
Plaintiff,	)	
v.	)	**STANDING ORDER RE:**
Defendant(s).	)	**CRIMINAL TRIALS**
______________________________	)	

THE GOVERNMENT SHALL SERVE A COPY OF THIS ORDER ON ALL DEFENSE COUNSEL PROMPTLY AFTER THE FIRST APPEARANCE OF COUNSEL AT THE POST-INDICTMENT ARRAIGNMENT.

The above mentioned cause of action is set for trial before the Honorable A. Howard Matz.

COURTROOM PREPARATION AND LAST CONFERENCE

1. Please arrive at the Courtroom not later than 8:30 a.m. on the first day of trial. At 9:00 a.m. counsel will meet with the Court for the "last conference" (see below). As is disclosed in the ensuing provisions, please use the preceding quarter-hour to set up audio equipment, distribute exhibits, and discuss logistical and other matters with the Courtroom Deputy Clerk. If counsel need to arrange for the installation of their own equipment, such as video monitors or an overhead projector, etc., they should call the Courtroom Clerk no later than 4:30 p.m. 2 COURT DAYS BEFORE trial, so that the necessary arrangements may be made.

2. Upon arriving for trial, Counsel for the Government shall present the Courtroom Deputy Clerk with the following documents:

   (a) Three copies of the Government's witness list.

   (b) Three copies of the Government's exhibit list.

   (c) In addition to the original exhibits, two sets of all of the Government's exhibits (except those that cannot be reproduced, such as weapons) with official exhibit tags attached, bearing the same number shown on the exhibit list. Exhibit tags can be obtained from the Clerk's Office – Records Department.

   (d) An agreed statement (accepted by defense counsel) that briefly describes the charges, in clear, simple paraphrased fashion. Each separate alleged crime shall be mentioned. *E.g.*, "Defendant is accused of defrauding Bank of America by kiting checks drawn on accounts that lacked the necessary funds. He also is accused of conspiring with John Smith to defraud that bank. He denies the charges."

3. The Court and witness' copies of the Government's exhibits shall be placed in three-ring binders tabbed with the exhibit number for easy reference. Defense counsel shall use the same method, if practical, in providing the Court with a copy of their exhibits as introduced. That is, defense counsel should provide a pre-tabbed binder and 3-hole punch the exhibit(s) before handing them to the Clerk. (Defense counsel do not have to deliver their exhibits to the Clerk on the first day of trial; however, they are responsible for affixing tags to these exhibits which they intend to use in the Defendant's case.) (Also, defense counsel must provide both the courtroom Deputy

Clerk and the Court Reporter with the defense witness list and defense exhibit list.) Exhibits shall be numbered 1, 2, 3, 4, etc., NOT 1.1, 1.50, etc. Counsel for both (all) sides should agree on the range of numbers to be assigned. (*E.g.*, Government exhibits to be 1-99, Defendant One to be 100-199; Defendant Two 200-299, etc.) If a blow up is an enlargement of an existing exhibit, it shall be designated with the number of the original exhibit followed by an "A."

4. Counsel for the government should be aware that the Court will order that exhibits such as firearms, narcotics, etc., remain in the custody of the agents during the pendency of the trial. It shall be the responsibility of the agents, in coordination with Courthouse Security Officers, to produce such items for court, secure them at night and guard them while in the courtroom. All exhibits will be returned to counsel at the conclusion of the trial.

5. Last Conference. Before trial commences, at the 9:00 a.m. Last Conference, the Court will give counsel an opportunity to discuss administrative matters and anticipated procedural or legal problems. At that time we will discuss *voir dire* procedures, *Batson* objections, and any unusual factors. Counsel for the Government shall bring to the meeting the attached Trial Witness Estimate Form which all counsel should have filled in. In the event defense counsel has not provided estimates for cross-examination, she or he will have to do so at the Last Conference.

JURY INSTRUCTIONS AND VERDICT FORMS

6. Jury instructions in the form described below shall be submitted no later than the Wednesday of the week prior to trial. Counsel need only submit proposed substantive instructions. The Court will formulate general instructions based primarily on the format set out by the Committee on Model Jury Instructions for the Ninth Circuit, *Manual of Model Criminal Jury Instructions for the Ninth Circuit.*

7. The parties must submit joint jury instructions, and shall email a Word/WordPerfect version of the instructions to ahm_chambers@cacd.uscourts.gov. (See ¶ 11.) In order to do so, the parties shall meet and confer sufficiently in advance of the required submission date with the goal of agreeing upon instructions and any proposed special verdict forms. (The Courtroom Deputy will prepare general verdict forms.) The Court prefers counsel to use the instructions recommended by the Committee on Model Criminal Jury Instructions for the Ninth Circuit, *Manual of Model Criminal Jury Instructions for the Ninth Circuit.* Another suggested source is Edward J. Devitt, et al., *Federal Jury Practice and Instruction.* The jury instructions shall be submitted as follows: (1) joint jury instructions, i.e ., those instructions to which all parties agree; and (2) disputed jury instructions, i.e., those instructions propounded by a party to which another party objects. The party objecting to the disputed instructions shall file its objections no later than the Friday before the trial. The party must state the reasons for the objection, provide a proposed alternative instruction with supporting authority, and provide copies of all authorities. Each requested jury instruction shall be numbered and set forth in full on a separate page, citing the authority or source of the requested instruction except on the "jury copy" described below in paragraph 8. Please be brief, clear and concise. Write in plain English. Do not slip argument into the proposals, and please organize them in logical sequence.

8. The Court will send several copies of the jury instructions into the jury room for use by the jury during deliberations. Accordingly, in addition to the filed copies, an extra set of the proposed instructions (the "jury copy,") shall be submitted to the Court with only the text of an instruction on each page (i.e., no titles, supporting authority, indication of party proposing, etc). This will be referred to as the "jury copy" of the instructions. (Duplicates will be made by the Court.)

9. An index page shall accompany all jury instructions that are submitted to the Court. The index page shall indicate the following:
(a) The number of the instruction;
(b) A brief title of the instruction;
(c) The source of the instruction; and
(d) The page number of the instruction.

EXAMPLE:

Number	Title	Source	Page Number
1	Duty of the Jury	9th Cir. 1.01	1

10. If counsel seek a special verdict, counsel shall follow the procedure set forth in paragraph 7 in order to formulate a joint proposed verdict form. Counsel shall submit the proposed verdict form with the proposed jury instructions.

11. If counsel prepared the jury instructions or the proposed special verdict, counsel shall provide the Court with an electronic version of the proposed instructions in either Word or WordPerfect, along with the hard copy. Counsel should email these documents to ahm_chambers@cacd.uscourts.gov.

TRIAL PROCEEDINGS

12. Trial days usually are Tuesday through Friday, 9:00 a.m. to 4:00 p.m., with various breaks and a lunch break. On each day after the first, the Court reserves the time from 8:30 - 9:00 a.m. to handle legal and administrative matters outside of the presence of the jury. Counsel are urged to anticipate matters which may need discussion or hearing outside of the presence of the jury and to raise them during this period.

13. Counsel shall not refer to their clients by their first names during trial.

14. Counsel shall not discuss the law or argue the case in opening statements.

15. When objecting, counsel shall state only "objection" and the legal ground for the objection (*e.g.*, hearsay, irrelevant, etc.). Court permission is needed to argue an objection, and the argument must be outside of the hearing of the jury. No counsel shall respond directly to any other lawyer's statements or objections; there shall be no colloquy between the lawyers.

16. Counsel shall not approach the clerk or the witness box without the Court's permission.

17. Counsel shall rise when addressing the Court. In jury cases, counsel and the defendants shall rise when the jury enters or leaves the courtroom. [Special procedures or exceptions may apply to defendants who are restrained.]

18. Counsel shall address all remarks to the Court. Counsel shall not directly address the Courtroom Deputy Clerk, the Court Reporter, or opposing counsel, unless it is to propose a stipulation or other procedure, in which case it shall be out of the hearing range of jurors. Counsel shall address to the Court all requests to have an exhibit placed in front of a witness.

19. Counsel shall not make an offer of stipulation unless he/she has conferred with opposing counsel and believes that the stipulation will be accepted. Any stipulation of fact will require the defendant's personal concurrence and shall be submitted to the Court in writing for approval. Defense counsel should explain any proposed stipulation to him/her in advance.

20. While Court is in session, counsel may not leave the counsel table to confer with investigators, secretaries, or witnesses in the back of the courtroom unless the Court grants permission to do so in advance.

21. When a party has more than one lawyer, only one of the lawyers may conduct the examination of a given witness and only that lawyer may handle objections during the testimony of that witness.

22. If a witness was on the stand before a recess or adjournment, counsel shall have the witness back on the stand and ready to proceed when Court resumes. If there is more than a brief delay between witnesses, the Court may deem that the party has rested.

23. The Court attempts to cooperate with physicians and other professional witnesses and, except in extraordinary circumstances, will accommodate them by permitting them to be examined out of sequence. Counsel should discuss this issue with opposing counsel. If there is an objection, please inform the Court in advance.

QUESTIONNAIRES

24. If any counsel wishes to submit a written questionnaire to each prospective juror, s/he shall move in writing for leave to do so, and shall include the proposed questionnaire with the motion. Because the Jury Department needs ample time to arrange for pre-selected jurors to be available to complete a questionnaire, such motion shall be filed not later than nine weeks before the trial date, to be heard not later than five weeks before the trial date.

MISCELLANEOUS

25. Please read the Court's Civil Jury Trial Order for guidance as to other matters that may have bearing in a criminal case.

26. Counsel shall inform the Courtroom Deputy in advance if any witness or member of the trial team requires an accommodation for a physical disability.

The Court thanks counsel for their anticipated cooperation.

Dated: ________________

A. HOWARD MATZ
United States District Judge

III. Judge Matz's Forms

A. *Joint Trial Witness Time Estimate Form*

JOINT TRIAL WITNESS TIME ESTIMATE FORM

CASE: ____________________ TRIAL DATE: ______________________

	WITNESS NAME	PARTY CALLING WITNESS AND ESTIMATE	X-EXAMINER'S ESTIMATE	DESCRIPTION OF TESTIMONY	COMMENTS
1					
2					
3					
4					
5					
6					
7					
8					
9					
10					
	TOTAL ESTIMATE S THIS PAGE:				

Instructions: (1) List witnesses (last name first); (2) For description, be extremely brief, *e.g.*, "eyewitness to accident." Or "expert on standard of care." (3) Use estimates within fractions of an hour, rounded off to closest quarter of an hour. *E.g.*, if you estimate 20 minutes, make it .25. An estimate of one and one-half hours would be 1.5. An estimate of three-quarters of an hour would be 75; (4) Note special factors in "Comments" column. *E.g.*, "Needs interpreter." (5) Entries may be in handwriting if very neat and legible.

B. Presumptive Schedule of Pretrial Dates

PRESUMPTIVE SCHEDULE OF PRETRIAL DATES

Matter	Time	Weeks before trial	Plaintiff's Request	Defendant's Request	Court Order
Trial date (jury) (court) Estimated length: _____ days	9:00 a.m.				
[Court trial:] File Findings of Fact and Conclusions of Law and Summaries of Direct Testimony		-1			
Final Pretrial Conference; Hearing on Motions *in Limine*; File Agreed Upon Set of Jury Instructions and Verdict Forms and Joint Statement re Disputed Instructions and Verdict Forms; File Proposed *Voir Dire* Qs and Agreed-to Statement of Case	11:00 a.m.	-2			
Lodge Pretrial Conf. Order File Memo of Contentions of Fact and Law; Exhibit List; Witness List; Status Report re Settlement		-4			
Last day for hand-serving Motions *in Limine*		-6			
Last Day to Meet Before Final Pretrial Conference (L.R. 16-2)		-8			
Last day for hearing motions	10:00 a.m.	-8			
Last day for hand-serving motions and filing (other than Motions *in Limine*)		-12			
Non-expert Discovery cut-off		-14			

ADDITIONAL MATTERS TO BE DETERMINED AT SCHEDULING CONFERENCE

L.R. 16-15 Settlement Choice: (1) CT/USMJ (2) Atty (3) Outside ADR

Expert discovery cut-off		-6			
Rebuttal Expert Witness Disclosure		-9			
Opening Expert Witness Disclosure [*See* F.R.Civ.P. 26(a)(2)]		-13			
Last day to conduct Settlement Conference					
Last Day to Amend Pleadings or Add Parties					

Hon. Margaret M. Morrow

District Judge

Chambers Information

U.S. District Court, Central District of California
Courtroom 780
255 East Temple Street
Los Angeles, CA 90012

Scheduling Information

Courtroom Deputy: (213) 894-7857

Civil Law and Motion	Mondays at 10:00 a.m.
Criminal Law and Motion	Mondays at 1:15 p.m

Biographical Information

Born 1950 in Columbus, NE

Federal Judicial Service:

-Judge, U. S. District Court, Central District of California
-Nominated by William J. Clinton on January 7, 1997, to a seat vacated by Richard A. Gadbois, Jr.; Confirmed by the Senate on February 11, 1998, and received commission on February 24, 1998.

Education:

-Bryn Mawr College, A.B., 1971
-Harvard Law School, J.D., 1974

Professional Career:

-Private Practice, Los Angeles, California, 1974-1998

I. Judge Morrow's Procedures and Practices

A. *Procedures and Schedules*

The best way to contact the judge's courtroom deputy clerk is by calling (213) 894-7857; if the clerk does not answer the phone, be sure to leave a voice-mail message. Phone messages without case name, number and a brief message will not be returned. Due to the high volume of calls, not all phone calls can be returned. Requests that can be answered by reviewing the Local Rules, G.O. 10-07, or the Court's website will not be returned. Do not leave multiple messages regarding the same issue.

Counsel shall not contact the clerk with procedural questions regarding electronic filing. Counsel shall refer to G.O. 10-07 and/or contact the electronic filing help desk at (213) 894-0242.

1. Civil motions are heard on: **Mondays**, Time: **10:00 a.m.**

   It **is not** necessary to clear a motion date with the court clerk prior to filing a motion. Available date for motions can be obtained on the court's website www.cacd.uscourts.gov. Go to Court Calendars, Motion Calendar then Hon. Margaret M. Morrow for closed dates.

   All documents which are required to be filed in an electronic format pursuant to General Order No. 10-07 shall be filed electronically no later than 5:00 p.m. on the date due unless otherwise ordered by the Court. Any documents filed electronically after 5:00 p.m. on the date due will be considered late and may be stricken by the Court.

   CIVIL MOTIONS IN LIMINE: All motions in limine will be heard at the time of the Final Pretrial Conference and must be filed according to the Local Rules and G.O. 10-07.

2. **CRIMINAL MOTIONS: Mondays**, Time: **1:15 p.m.**

   CRIMINAL E-FILING: All documents which are required to be filed in an electronic format pursuant to General Order No. 10-07 shall be filed electronically no later than 5:00 p.m. on the date due unless otherwise ordered by the Court. Any documents filed electronically after 4:00 p.m. on the date due will be considered late and may be stricken by the Court. Any documents which counsel attempt to file electronically which are improperly filed will not be accepted by the Court.

3. **Mandatory Chambers Copies**
   SEE G.O. 10-07: VI. Electronic Filing C. Courtesy Paper Copies

4. Discovery motions: Are to be calendared before the magistrate judge.

5. Are tentative rulings issued? In most cases, tentative rulings are available from the court clerk in the courtroom from 8:45 am - 9:45 am on the day the motion is scheduled to be heard. Tentative orders are NOT faxed to counsel nor are they available for pickup prior to the date motion is set for (see above).

6. **PROCEDURES FOR FILING AN EX PARTE APPLICATION:** Refer to L.R. 7-19 and G.O. 10-07. A hearing is not required unless notified by the court. As a general policy, all oppositions are due within 24-hours from service of the ex parte.

Also, opposing counsel shall contact the clerk within 24-hours as to their position. Counsel shall be notified by order of the Court's ruling. DO NOT CONTACT THE CLERK INQUIRING THE STATUS OF THE EX PARTE APPLICATION.

7. STIPULATIONS AND PROPOSED ORDERS
SEE G.O. 10-07: VIII. Orders. A. Proposed Orders, Judgments or Other Proposed Documents Which Require a Judge's Signature.

8. To Request a Continuance of Any Scheduled Court Proceeding: A proposed stipulation and order must be submitted at least one week in advance. Counsel must comply with L.R. 11-4.5 for conformed copies.

9. Are Counsel Allowed to Contact the Judge's Law Clerk or Secretary? NO.

10. Inquiries Regarding the Status of a Motion, Stipulation or Proposed Order: Information regarding the status of motions, ex parte applications, stipulations or proposed orders are not available. Counsel shall follow L.R. 11-4.5. DO NOT CONTACT THE CLERK. It's the court's policy not to return such calls.

11. Calendar Conflicts: (Procedures for attorneys to follow if they have a calendar conflict): Counsel shall contact the court clerk at least 3 calendar days prior to a hearing date if counsel has an appearance with another district judge. Counsel shall indicate the time of the appearance and the name of the judge.

12. Procedures for Bringing Electronic Equipment into the Courtroom: Counsel shall contact the Courtroom Deputy Clerk by telephone to request leave to bring electronic equipment into the courtroom. Counsel will be advised by the Courtroom Deputy Clerk that such a request shall be made by a letter addressed to the U.S. Marshal's Office, with a copy to the Court Coordinator and prepared for the Courtroom Deputy Clerk's signature, along with the case name and case number. Counsel may fax the letter to the Courtroom Deputy Clerk for signature at (213) 894-1815. Upon arrival to the courthouse, counsel shall present the letter to Court Security for approval.

13. To order an audio tape or transcript: For general information on how to order a transcript of any reported or digitally recorded proceeding, please contact 213-894-3015 or visit www.cacd.uscourts.gov > General Information > Court Reporter/Recorder Transcripts. If you require an estimate of cost for the preparation of a transcript, contact the court reporter/recorder for the desired proceeding.

To determine the court reporter/recorder for a particular proceeding, go to the Court Reporter Schedule web page and click on View by Date. Once you've determined the correct court reporter/recorder for the desired session, click on Court Reporter Phone and Email List for contact information.

14. Trial preparation:

- **a.** Court hours: 8:30 a.m. - 5:00 p.m.
- **b.** Exhibit preparation: L.R. 16-5.1.
- **c.** Jury instructions (form, when they're to be submitted, whether counsel need to submit general or substantiative instructions or both). The Court will instruct counsel at the time of the Pretrial Conference.
- **d.** Verdict forms:

  Criminal: Court clerk

Special verdict form: Government

Civil: Counsel

Special verdict form: Counsel

e. Other: Three copies of witness list and exhibit list shall be provided to the court clerk the morning of trial.

15. Procedures for obtaining the services of an interpreter on a civil case. It is the responsibility of counsel in a civil case to arrange for the services of an Interpreter. Interpreter's Office: (213) 894-4599.

16. Other information: Counsel are directed to comply with all Local rules. If counsel have received a "Notice to Parties of ADR Program" (from ADR-08, ADR-10, or ADR-11 with attached "ADR Program Questionnaire" form ADR-09), please see the section on the Court's website entitled "ADR" General Order 02-07, for further information. The ADR section also contains Attorney Settlement Officer information.

COURT'S WEBSITE: www.cacd.uscourts.gov

JUDGE'S GENERIC E-MAIL ADDRESS FOR ELECTRONIC FILING ONLY: MMM_Chambers@cacd.uscourts.gov

Hon. Jacqueline H. Nguyen

District Judge

Chambers Information

U.S. District Court, Central District of California
Courtroom 790
255 East Temple Street
Los Angeles, CA 90012

Scheduling Information

Courtroom Deputy: (213) 894-2554

Civil Law and Motion	Mondays at 2:00 p.m.
Criminal Law and Motion	Mondays at 9:00 a.m.

Biographical Information

Born 1965 in Dalat, Vietnam

Federal Judicial Service:

-Judge, U. S. District Court, Central District of California
-Nominated by Barack Obama on July 31, 2009, to a seat vacated by Nora Margaret Manella; Confirmed by the Senate on December 1, 2009, and received commission on December 4, 2009.

Education:

-Occidental College, A.B., 1987
-University of California, Los Angeles, School of Law, J.D., 1991

Professional Career:

-Private practice of law, Los Angeles, California, 1991-1994
-Assistant U.S. Attorney, U.S. Attorney's Office, Central District of California, 1995-2000
-Deputy Chief, General Crimes Division, U.S. Attorney's Office, Central District of California, 2000-2002
-Judge, Los Angeles County Superior Court, Alhambra, California, 2002-2009

I. Judge Nguyen's Procedures and Practices

A. *Procedures and Schedules*

1. Calendar:
   Civil Motions: **Mondays at 2:00 p.m.** or as otherwise set by the Court

   Criminal Motions: **Mondays at 9:00 a.m.** or as otherwise set by the Court

2. Holidays: If Monday is a holiday, motions will be heard the following Monday. Motions will not be set on Tuesday following a Monday holiday.

3. Motions: Please include your e-mail address on all documents.

   a. Filing: It is not necessary to clear a date with the court clerk prior to filing a motion. However, you must first click on the link at the top of the page to view closed motion dates. It is not necessary to lodge depositions in support of motions for summary judgment.

   b. Motion Briefing Schedule: Motions will be heard two weeks after the deadline for filing Reply documents. Motion papers are to be filed and served no later than 28 days before the hearing date; Opposition papers are to be filed and served not later than 21 days before the hearing date, and any Reply papers are to be filed and served not later than 14 days before the hearing date.

   c. In its trial order for each case, the Court establishes a cut-off date for the hearing of motions. All motions must be noticed so that the **hearing** takes place on or before the motion cut-off date. Counsel are advised that the Court may close a hearing date once the number of motions filed exceeds the maximum number of motions that can reasonably be heard on that date. Counsel should anticipate that a preferred hearing date may be unavailable. Therefore, to avoid being unable to file a motion to be heard by the cut-off date, counsel **should file motions sufficiently in advance of the hearing cut-off date to ensure that a hearing date is available**.

4. Discovery: All discovery motions are to be calendared before the Magistrate Judge.

5. Tentatives: The Court makes every effort to issue a tentative ruling one or two court days prior to oral argument. Tentatives, if any, will be e-mailed to counsel. If you wish to waive oral argument and submit on the tentative decision, please so advise opposing counsel and then notify the court clerk, Alicia Mamer, at 213-894-2554.

6. Ex Partes: *Ex Parte* applications are ONLY for extraordinary relief. Sanctions may be imposed for misuse of ex parte applications. *See Mission Power Engineering Co. v. Continental Casualty Co., 883 F. Supp. 488 (C.D. Cal. 1995).* These applications are taken UNDER SUBMISSION on the papers. If oral argument is necessary, the court clerk will notify counsel of the date and time of hearing. If the application is opposed, opposing counsel must notify the court clerk and e-file its opposition within two days.

7. Continuances: If both sides are seeking a continuance of any scheduled court proceeding, counsel must file a stipulation and proposed order and notify the clerk telephonically.

8. Telephone contact: Parties shall first check the case docket and/or Master Calendar before calling the court clerk, Alicia Mamer, to inquire about the status of a motion, stipulation, proposed order, or hearing date. If the clerk does not answer the phone,

be sure to leave a voice mail message (always include case name and number). Counsel are NOT to telephone either the judge's chambers/office or the judge's law clerks.

9. Electronic Equipment: ELMO reservations/tutorials may be made by first referring to the court website at www.cacd.uscourts.gov, under "Attorney Information," and then "Attorney Services." Alternatively, you can contact the Courtroom Technology Help Desk at 213-894-3061. If counsel would like to arrange to bring in their own electronic equipment, they should submit a proposed order for the Judge's signature to the chambers mailbox and call Alicia Mamer to advise of the request.

10. Court Reporter Services: Any party requesting special court reporter services for any hearing (i.e., real time transmission, daily transcripts) shall notify the court reporter at least 2 weeks before the hearing date.

11. Transcripts: For general information on how to order a transcript of any reported or digitally recorded proceeding, please contact 213-894-3015 or visit www.cacd.uscourts.gov > General Information > Court Reporter/Recorder Transcripts. If you require an estimate of cost for the preparation of a transcript, contact the court reporter/recorder for the desired proceeding.

To determine the court reporter/recorder for a particular proceeding, go to the Court Reporter Schedule web page and click on View by Date. Once you've determined the correct court reporter/recorder for the desired session, click on Court Reporter Phone and Email List for contact information.

12. Law Clerks/Externs: Regular law clerk applications should be submitted as provided by the Federal Law Clerk Hiring Plan. The Court welcomes applications for full-time extern positions lasting a sufficient length at any time during the year. Extern applicants should submit a cover letter and resume to the Hon. Jacqueline H. Nguyen, Courtroom 790, Roybal Federal Building, 255 East Temple Street, Los Angeles, CA 90012, attn: Externship application.

13. Trial Orders: Trial orders are issued after the parties submit a Joint Scheduling Report and ADR Questionnaire. The Court will review the submitted report and questionnaire and issue a trial order setting case management deadlines, pre-trial conference dates, and trial dates. The Court will hold a scheduling conference with counsel if the Court deems it necessary. Counsel will be notified if the scheduling conference is removed from the Court's calendar. Examples of court orders setting court and jury trials are appended to this webpage.

14. Trial:

a. Hours: Trials are generally conducted Tuesday through Friday each week, from 9:00 a.m. to 4:00 p.m., with two 15-minute breaks, and a one hour lunch break.

b. Exhibits: Two copies of tabbed exhibit binders are to be submitted to the Court on the first day of trial (one set for the witness and one set for the Court). Each volume shall be clearly labeled. Three copies of the Joint Exhibit List must be submitted to the Court on the first day of trial.

c. Witness Lists: Three copies of witness lists, in the order in which witnesses are expected to be called, must be submitted to the court on the first day of trial.

d. Jury Instructions: Follow the schedule and deadlines in the trial order. Failure to timely submit jury instructions will be deemed a waiver of jury trial.

15. Interpreters: It is the responsibility of counsel in a civil case to arrange for the services of an Interpreter. The Interpreter's office may be reached at 213-894-4599.

16. Settlement Conferences: Counsel are required to comply with Local Rule 16, concerning Mandatory Settlement Procedures.

17. Settlement: Please notify the court clerk as soon as a settlement of your case has been reached.

18. Other Information: Counsel are directed to comply with all Local Rules. If counsel have received a Notice to Parties of ADR Program (form ADR-08 or ADR-11) with attached ADR Program Questionnaire (ADR-09), please see the section on the Central District Court's website entitled ADR for further information. The ADR section also contains Attorney Settlement Officer Information.

19. Electronic Filings: Counsel shall e-file all criminal and civil filings for JUDGE NGUYEN pursuant to Federal Rules of Civil Procedure 5(d)(3), Local Rule 5.4, and General Order 10-07, as follows:

Step 1: All non-signature items shall be E-FILED in pdf format. All proposed signature items shall be E-FILED as an attachment to the main document in pdf format.

Step 2: All proposed signature items shall be EMAILED to the chambers email address at jhn_chambers@cacd.uscourts.gov [jhn (underscore)chambers@cacd.uscourts.gov] in Word or Word Perfect format. **ONLY proposed orders signature items should be emailed to the chambers' email address. Please do NOT email other associated documents, and do NOT use this email address for communication with the Court or the Clerk.**

Step 3: A chambers copy of stipulations, proposed orders, and ex parte applications is not required unless exhibits are attached. A MANDATORY CHAMBERS COPY is required for all other filings. The chambers copy shall be delivered to the DROP BOX OUTSIDE the Clerk's Office located at Suite 181-L, 255 East Temple Street, no later than 12:00 noon the business day following any electronic filing or on the same day, if priority processing is being requested. The documents must comply with Local Rule 11-3 and be blue-backed, proper font size, page numbering,etc. ALL EXHIBITS TO CHAMBERS COPIES MUST BE TABBED. Each document must be prominently labeled "CHAMBERS COPY" on the front page. All copies delivered to the courtesy bin shall have the notice of E-filing attached to the back of the document. DO NOT PLACE THESE COPIES IN ENVELOPES.

DO NOT OMIT ANY OF THE ABOVE STEPS.

20. **FOR UNDER SEAL FILINGS:** An application for Under Seal filing and proposed order thereon shall be submitted to Civil or Criminal intake for manual processing of every item requested to be filed under seal. An original and copy of each item (and an envelope for each) shall be submitted; the envelopes shall be presented **unsealed**. The Notice of Manual filing shall have been electronically filed, prior to presentation at intake. The Notice of Manual filing shall accompany the documents delivered to intake. DO NOT DELIVER ADDITIONAL CHAMBERS COPIES OF THESE DOCUMENTS and DO NOT SEND THESE DOCUMENTS TO THE CHAMBERS EMAIL ADDRESS.

For additional questions, please refer to the General Orders or call the help line at 213-894-0242.

II. Judge Nguyen's Case Management Orders

A. *Criminal Motion and Trial Order*

IN THE UNITED STATES DISTICT COURT
FOR THE CENTRAL DISTRICT OF CALIFORNIA

UNITED STATES OF AMERICA, Plaintiff, v. Defendant(s).	Case No. _______________ **CRIMINAL MOTION AND TRIAL ORDER** STATUS CONFERENCE: ____, 2010 at 9:00 a.m. TRIAL DATE: _______, 2010 at 8:30 a.m.

A. MOTIONS

1. Counsel must meet and confer with opposing counsel and attempt to resolve the issue before filing a motion. Pretrial motions shall be filed on or before the Monday four weeks prior to trial. Oppositions (or notice of non-oppositions) shall be filed no later than one week after the filing of the motion. Replies, if any, shall be filed no later than one week after the filing of the opposition. Counsel must follow the Central District's General Orders and Local Rules concerning electronic filing, unless superseded by this Order.

2. Hearings on motions and Status Conferences are held on Mondays, at 9:00 a.m., unless otherwise set by the Court.

3. All papers shall be served personally or faxed to opposing counsel no later than 4:30 p.m. on the day of filing, with conformed courtesy copies of documents delivered to Judge Nguyen's drop box outside of the Roybal clerk's office: Suite L-181. Paper chambers copies are mandatory.

4. Counsel shall meet and confer with opposing counsel to resolve informally discovery disputes prior to filing a motion for discovery. All discovery motions shall state with particularity what is requested, the basis for the request, whether discovery has been requested and opposing counsel's response to such request. Motions made without prior consultation with opposing counsel may not be heard.

B. DISCOVERY & NOTICE

Counsel shall comply promptly with discovery and notice pursuant to Rules 12, 12.1, 12.2, 12.3, 12.4, 15 and 16 of the Federal Rules of Criminal Procedure.

C. TRIAL REQUIREMENTS

1. **No later than Wednesday before trial**, counsel for the government shall file with the Court a trial memorandum setting forth a factual summary of the government's case, a statement of the charges and the elements of each charge, an estimate of the length of the government's case in chief, including anticipated cross-examination, the names of witnesses the government intends to call, and a discussion of relevant legal and evidentiary issues as applied to the facts of the particular case. Counsel for the government shall attempt to obtain defense counsel's agreement to the factual summary, statement of the charges, time estimate for cross-examination of the government's witnesses, and legal and evidentiary issues.

2. Counsel shall arrive at the Courtroom no later than 8:30 a.m. on the first day of trial.

3. Counsel for the government shall present the courtroom deputy clerk (CRD)

with the following documents on the first day of trial:

- **a.** Three copies of the government's witness list, which shall also be sent in Word or WordPerfect format to the Chamber's e-mail box;
- **b.** Three copies of the government's exhibit list in the form specified in Local Rule 16-5 (Civil), which shall also be sent in Word or WordPerfect format to the Chamber's e-mail box;
- **c.** All of the government's exhibits, with official exhibit tags attached and bearing the same number shown on the exhibit list. Exhibit tags may be obtained from the receptionist in the Public Intake Section, located on the Main Street level of the Courthouse at 312 North Spring Street, Room G-19. Exhibits shall be numbered 1, 2, 3, etc., NOT 1.1, 1.2, etc. If a "blow-up" is an enlargement of an existing exhibit, it shall be designated with the number of the original exhibit followed by an "A";
- **d.** A three-ring binder containing a copy of the indictment/information, a copy of all exhibits that can be reproduced, and a copy of the witness list. Each exhibit shall be tabbed with the exhibit number for easy referral;
- **e.** A three-ring binder containing a copy of all exhibits for use by witnesses.

4. Exhibits such as firearms, narcotics, etc., must remain in the custody of a law enforcement agent during the pendency of the trial. It shall be the responsibility of the agent to produce any such items for court, secure them at night, and guard them at all times while in the courtroom.

5. The Court prefers that defense counsel deliver defense exhibits to the CRD on the first day of trial, but counsel are not required to do so unless these exhibits have previously been provided to the government. Defense counsel are responsible for affixing completed exhibit tags with the case name and case number to all exhibits to be used in defendant's case.

6. In trials where the defense expects to admit more than 20 exhibits, defense counsel shall provide two three-ring binders (one for the Court and one for witnesses), tabbed if possible with numbers to correspond to the exhibits counsel expects to introduce. Defense counsel shall provide the Court with a copy of defense exhibits as they are introduced during trial, if they have not previously been provided.

7. Defense counsel shall provide the CRD and the court reporter with the defense witness list and defense exhibit list.

8. A copy of the exhibit list with all **admitted exhibits** will be given to the jury during deliberations. Government and defense counsel shall review and approve the exhibit list with the CRD before the list is given to the jury.

9. If any counsel wishes to arrange for the use of additional equipment, such as video monitors, overhead projectors, etc., counsel shall notify the CRD no later than 4:00 p.m. at least one week before trial so that the necessary arrangements may be made.

10. Counsel shall not attempt to display or use any charts or enlargements of exhibits unless all counsel have agreed to their use or objections have been heard and a ruling has been made by the Court.

11. On the day of jury selection, trial will begin at 9:00 a.m. Counsel will appear at 8:30 a.m. Thereafter, trial days are Tuesday through Friday, 9:00 a.m. to 4:00 p.m., with two

fifteen-minute breaks and a one hour lunch break. When necessary, trials may continue beyond the normal schedule.

12. On the day of jury selection, the Court reserves the time from 8:30 a.m. to 9:00 a.m. to handle legal and administrative matters. Jury selection will commence promptly at 9:00 a.m. or as soon as jurors are available. All counsel must anticipate matters that may need to be addressed outside of the presence of the jury and raise them at the end of the day or during breaks. The Court does not make jurors wait while counsel discuss matters that should have been addressed previously. Short briefs addressing disputed issues are welcome. The Court strongly discourages sidebars during trial.

13. Any party requesting special court reporter services for any hearing (i.e., real time transmission, daily transcripts) shall notify the reporter as least 2 weeks before the hearing date.

D. JURY INSTRUCTIONS, VERDICT FORMS & QUESTIONNAIRES

1. **No later than Wednesday before trial**, counsel shall submit both general and substantive jury instructions in the form described below. If possible, all instructions should be taken from the *Manual of Model Criminal Jury Instructions for the Ninth Circuit* (West Publishing, current edition). Where no applicable Ninth Circuit model instruction is available, counsel should consult the instructions from O'Malley, Grenig & Lee (formerly Devitt, *et al.*), *Federal Jury Practice and Instructions* (West Publishing Co., current edition). Counsel may submit alternatives to the Ninth Circuit model jury instructions or O'Malley, Grenig & Lee instructions only if counsel has a reasoned argument that those instructions do not properly state the law or they are incomplete.

2. The parties must submit JOINT jury instructions and a JOINT proposed verdict form. In order to produce these joint instructions, the parties shall meet and confer sufficiently in advance of the required submission date with the goal of agreeing on instructions and verdict forms. Where the parties cannot agree, disputed instructions shall be submitted Wednesday before trial as follows: 1) JOINT jury instructions (those instructions agreed to by all parties), and 2) DISPUTED jury instructions (those instructions propounded by a party to which another party objects). On a separate page following each disputed jury instruction, the party opposing the instruction shall briefly state the basis for the objection, any authority in support thereof and, if applicable, an alternative instruction. On the following page, the party proposing the disputed instruction shall briefly state its response to the objection, and any authority in support of the instruction. Each requested jury instruction shall be numbered and set forth in full on a separate page, citing the authority or source of the requested instruction.

3. Jury instructions should be modified as necessary to fit the facts of the case (e.g., inserting names of defendant(s) or witness(es) to whom instruction applies). Where language appears in brackets in the model instruction, counsel shall select the appropriate text and eliminate the inapplicable bracketed text.

4. An index page shall accompany all jury instructions submitted to the Court. The index page shall indicate the following:

a. The number of the instruction;

b. A brief title of the instruction;

c. The source of the instruction; and

d. The page number of the instruction.

EXAMPLE:

Number	**Title**	**Source**	**Page Number**
#1	Conspiracy-Elements	9th Cir. 8.5.1	1

5. One or more copies of the instructions will be given to the jury during deliberations. Accordingly, counsel must submit to the Chambers e-mail a "clean" set of all instructions in Word or WordPerfect format, containing only the text of each instruction, set forth in full on each page, with the caption "Instruction No. ____" (eliminating titles, supporting authority, indication of party proposing, etc.). A paper Chambers copy must also be submitted.

6. Counsel shall submit a proposed verdict form with the jury instructions.

7. At least by Wednesday before trial, each counsel must file any proposed questions to be asked of prospective jurors.

E. INSTRUCTIONS GOVERNING PROCEDURE DURING TRIAL

1. Counsel shall not refer to any witness – including a client – over 14 years of age by his/her first name during trial.

2. Counsel shall not discuss the law or argue the case in opening statements.

3. No "speaking objections" are allowed. When objecting, counsel shall stand, state only the legal ground of the objection, e.g., hearsay, irrelevant, etc.

4. Counsel shall not make facial expressions, nod, or shake their heads, comment, or otherwise exhibit in any way any agreement, disagreement, or other opinion or belief concerning the testimony of a witness. Counsel shall admonish their clients and witnesses not to engage in such conduct.

5. Counsel should not talk to jurors at all, and should not talk to co-counsel, opposing counsel, witnesses, or clients where the conversation can be overheard by jurors. Each counsel should admonish counsel's own clients and witnesses to avoid such conduct.

6. Counsel shall question witnesses from the lectern. Counsel shall not approach the witness box or enter the well without the Court's permission, and shall return to the lectern when counsel's purpose has been accomplished.

7. No document shall be placed before a witness unless a copy has been provided to the Court and opposing counsel. Counsel may consider such devices as overhead projectors, jury notebooks for admitted exhibits, or enlargements of important exhibits. The Court has an Elmo and other equipment available for use during trial. Counsel may call the CRD if they wish to visit when the Court is not in session to practice using the equipment. The Court does not permit exhibits to be "published" by passing them up and down the jury box. Exhibits may be displayed briefly using the screen in the courtroom, unless the process becomes too time-consuming.

8. Water is permitted in the courtroom. Food is not permitted in the courtroom.

9. Counsel shall rise when addressing the Court. In jury trials, counsel and the defendant shall rise when the jury enters or leaves the courtroom. Special procedures or exceptions may apply when the defendant is in custody or restrained.

10. In trial, all remarks shall be addressed to the Court. Counsel shall not directly address the CRD, the court reporter, or opposing counsel. All requests for re-reading of questions or answers, or to have an exhibit placed in front of a witness, shall be addressed to the Court.

11. Counsel should not offer a stipulation without having conferred with opposing counsel and having reached an agreement. Any stipulation of fact will require defendant's personal concurrence and shall be submitted to the Court in writing for approval. A proposed stipulation should be explained to defendant in advance.

12. While court is in session, counsel shall not leave counsel table to confer with investigators, paralegals, secretaries, witnesses, etc. unless permission is granted in advance.

13. When a party has more than one lawyer, only one lawyer may conduct the examination of a given witness, and only that same lawyer may handle objections during the testimony of that witness.

14. If a witness was on the stand at a recess or adjournment, counsel who called the witness shall ensure the witness is back on the stand and ready to proceed when trial resumes.

15. Counsel are directed to have witnesses available throughout the court day. If no witnesses are available and there is more than a brief delay, the Court may deem counsel to have rested.

16. The Court attempts to cooperate with expert witnesses and other professionals, and will, except in extraordinary circumstances, accommodate them by permitting them to be called out of sequence. Counsel are urged to anticipate any such possibility and to discuss it with opposing counsel. If there is an objection, counsel shall confer with the Court in advance.

17. Counsel must notify the CRD in advance if any witness should be accommodated based on the Americans with Disabilities Act or for other reasons.

18. Each counsel should keep counsel's own list of exhibits and should note when each has been admitted into evidence.

19. Each counsel is responsible for any exhibits that counsel secures from the CRD and must return them before leaving the courtroom at the end of the session.

20. An exhibit not previously marked should, at the time of its first mention, be accompanied by a request that the CRD mark it for identification. To save time, counsel must show a new exhibit to opposing counsel before it is mentioned in Court.

IT IS SO ORDERED.

DATED: April 27, 2010

____

JACQUELINE H. NGUYEN
United States District Judge

B. *Order for Rule 26 Joint Scheduling Report*

IN THE UNITED STATES DISTICT COURT
FOR THE CENTRAL DISTRICT OF CALIFORNIA

	)	Case No. ________________
Plaintiff(s),	)	
v.	)	**ORDER FOR RULE 26 JOINT**
Defendant(s).	)	**SCHEDULING REPORT**
______________________________	)	
		Deadline to File Joint Report: _________

READ THIS ORDER CAREFULLY. IT DIFFERS IN SOME RESPECTS FROM THE LOCAL RULES.

This case has been assigned to Judge Jacqueline H. Nguyen. For initial case management in accordance with Rule 16(b) and Rule 26 of the Federal Rules of Civil Procedure, Judge Nguyen will review the Joint Report filed by counsel in accordance with Rule 26(f) and will issue a Trial Order thereafter. Generally, no scheduling conference hearing is set, but counsel will be notified if the Court deems a scheduling conference hearing necessary.

If plaintiff has not already served the operative complaint on all defendants, plaintiff shall promptly do so and shall file proofs of service within three days thereafter. Defendants also shall timely serve and file their responsive pleadings and file proofs of service within three days thereafter.

The parties are reminded of their obligations under Rule 26(a)(1) to disclose information (without awaiting a discovery request), and under Rule 26(f) to confer on a discovery plan and to file a "Joint Rule 26(f) Report" by the deadline set by the Court. Failure to comply with the following requirements or to cooperate in the preparation of the Joint Rule 26(f) Report may result in the imposition of sanctions.

Counsel should begin to conduct discovery actively prior to the due date for the Report, and at the very least, the parties shall comply fully with the letter and spirit of Rule 26(a) and thereby obtain and produce most of what would be produced in the early stage of discovery, because with its Trial Order, the Court will impose deadlines to complete discovery.

The Court does not exempt parties appearing *in propria persona* from compliance with any of the Local Rules, including Local Rule 16. "Counsel," as used in this order, includes parties appearing *in propria persona.*

1. **Joint Rule 26(f) Report**
   The Joint Rule 26(f) Report shall be drafted by plaintiff (unless the parties agree otherwise), but shall be submitted and signed jointly. "Jointly" contemplates a single report, regardless of the number of separately represented parties. The Joint Rule 26(f) Report shall report on all matters described below, which include those required to be discussed by Rule 26(f) and Local Rule 26:

   a. Statement of the case: a short synopsis (not to exceed two pages) of the main claims, counterclaims, and affirmative defenses.

   b. Subject matter jurisdiction: a statement of the **specific** basis of federal jurisdiction, including supplemental jurisdiction.

c. Legal issues: a brief description of the **key legal issues**, including any unusual substantive, procedural, or evidentiary issues.

d. Parties, evidence, etc.: a list of parties, percipient witnesses, and key documents on the main issues in the case. For conflict purposes, corporate parties must identify all subsidiaries, parents, and affiliates.

e. Damages: the realistic range of provable damages.

f. Insurance: whether there is insurance coverage, the extent of coverage, and whether there is a reservation of rights.

g. Motions: a statement of the likelihood of motions seeking to add other parties or claims, file amended pleadings, transfer venue, etc.

h. Manual for Complex Litigation: whether all or part of the procedures of the Manual for Complex Litigation should be utilized.

i. Status of discovery: a discussion of the present state of discovery, including a summary of completed discovery.

j. Discovery plan: a detailed discovery plan, as contemplated by Rule 26(f), including the identity of all anticipated deponents and dates by which their depositions are to be completed (if possible), anticipated written discovery requests, including requests for admission, document requests, and interrogatories, and a schedule for completion of all discovery. State what, if any, changes in the disclosures under Rule 26(a) should be made, the subjects on which discovery may be needed and whether discovery should be conducted in phases or otherwise be limited, whether applicable limitations should be changed or other limitations imposed, and whether the Court should enter other orders. A statement that discovery will be conducted as to all claims and defenses, or other vague description, is not acceptable.

k. Dispositive motions: a description of the issues or claims that any party believes may be determined by motion for summary judgment or motion *in limine*.

l. Settlement: a statement of what settlement discussions or written communications have occurred (**excluding any statement of the terms discussed**) and a statement pursuant to Local Rule 16-15.4 selecting a settlement mechanism under that Rule. Note: If a case is selected for the ADR Pilot Program, the parties may choose private mediation (at their own expense) instead, but the parties may **not** choose a settlement conference before the magistrate judge. No case will proceed to trial unless all parties, including the principals of all corporate parties, have appeared personally at a settlement conference.

m. Trial estimate: a realistic estimate of the time required for trial and whether trial will be by jury or by the Court. Each side should specify (by number, not by name) how many witnesses it contemplates calling. If the time estimate for trial given in the Joint Rule 26(f) Report exceeds four court days, details regarding the estimate shall be provided.

n. Trial counsel: the name(s) of the attorney(s) who will try the case.

o. Independent expert or master: whether this is a case where the Court should consider appointing a master pursuant to Rule 53 or an independent scientific expert. (The appointment of a master may be especially appropriate if there are likely to be substantial discovery disputes, numerous claims to be construed in connection with a summary judgment motion, a lengthy Daubert hearing, a resolution of a difficult computation of damages, etc.)

p. Proposed trial date: the preferred date for trial to commence. The proposed date must fall on a Tuesday. The parties should agree on a proposed trial date if possible. Otherwise, counsel should provide the date preferred by each party. Based on the parties' proposed dates, the Court will determine the trial date and set pretrial dates accordingly. The parties may, if they wish, also indicate proposed pretrial dates, including proposed discovery cut-off and motion cut-off dates.

q. Other issues: a statement of any other issues affecting the status or management of the case (e.g., unusually complicated technical or technological issues, disputes over protective orders, extraordinarily voluminous document production, non-English-speaking witnesses, ADA-related issues, discovery in foreign jurisdictions, etc.) and any proposals concerning severance, bifurcation, or other ordering of proof.

2. Notice to be Provided by Counsel

a. Plaintiff's counsel, or if plaintiff is appearing *pro se*, defendant's counsel, shall provide this Order to any parties who appear after the date of this Order and to parties who are known to exist but have not yet entered appearances.

3. Disclosures to Clients

Counsel are ordered to deliver to their respective clients a copy of this Order and of the Court's trial order, which will contain the schedule that the Court sets after reviewing the Rule 26(f) Report.

4. Court's Website

Copies of this and all other orders of this Court that may become applicable to this case are available on the Central District of California website, at www.cacd.uscourts.gov, under "Judges' Procedures and Schedules." Copies of the Local Rules are available on the website.

The Court thanks the parties and their counsel for their anticipated cooperation in complying with these requirements.

IT IS SO ORDERED.

Dated: July 22, 2011

JACQUELINE H. NGUYEN
United States District Judge

C. Order Regarding Court Trial

IN THE UNITED STATES DISTICT COURT
FOR THE CENTRAL DISTRICT OF CALIFORNIA

Plaintiff(s),	) Case No. ________________
	)
v.	) **ORDER RE COURT TRIAL**
	) **I. ORDER RE DEADLINES:** (SEE PAGE TWO)
Defendant(s).	) **II. ORDER RE TRIAL PREPARATION**
________________________________	) **III. ORDER GOVERNING CONDUCT OF ATTORNEYS AND PARTIES**

I.
DEADLINES

A. Adding Parties or Amending Pleadings: ______________
B. Discovery Cut-off: ________________
C. Expert Witness Exchange Deadline:
Initial: ____________;
Rebuttal: ________________;
Cut-off: ________________;
D. Motion Hearing Cut-off: ______________
E. Settlement Conference Cut-off: ______________
F. Final Pretrial Conference (and hearing on Motions in Limine): _______ at 10:30 a.m.;
G. Trial Date: ____________ at 8:30 a.m.

A. PARTIES/PLEADINGS

The Court has established a cut-off date for adding parties or amending pleadings. All motions to add parties or to amend the pleadings must be noticed to be heard on or before the cut-off date. All unserved parties will be dismissed at the time of the pretrial conference pursuant to Local Rule 16-8.1.

B. DISCOVERY AND DISCOVERY CUT-OFF

1. Discovery Cut-off: The Court has established a cut-off date for discovery, including expert discovery, if applicable. This is not the date by which discovery requests must be served; it is the date by which all discovery, including all hearings on any related motions, is to be completed.

2. Discovery Disputes: Counsel are expected to comply with all Local Rules and the Federal Rules of Civil Procedure concerning discovery. Whenever possible, the Court expects counsel to resolve discovery problems among themselves in a courteous, reasonable, and professional manner. The Court expects that counsel will adhere strictly to the Civility and Professionalism Guidelines (which can be found on the Court's website under Attorney Information>Attorney Admissions).

3. Discovery Motions: Any motion challenging the adequacy of discovery responses must be filed, served, and calendared sufficiently in advance of the discovery cut-

off date to permit the responses to be obtained before that date if the motion is granted.

4. Depositions: All depositions shall commence sufficiently in advance of the discovery cut-off date to permit their completion and to permit the deposing party enough time to bring any discovery motions concerning the deposition before the cut-off date. Given the requirements to "meet and confer" and to give notice, in most cases a planned motion to compel must be discussed with opposing counsel at least six weeks before the cut-off.
5. Written Discovery: All interrogatories, requests for production of documents, and requests for admissions must be served sufficiently in advance of the discovery cut-off date to permit the discovering party enough time to challenge (via motion practice) responses deemed to be deficient.
6. Expert Discovery: All disclosures must be made in writing. The parties should begin expert discovery shortly after the initial designation of experts. The final pretrial conference and trial dates will not be continued merely because expert discovery is not completed. Failure to comply with these or any other orders concerning expert discovery may result in the expert being excluded as a witness.

C. LAW AND MOTION

1. The Court has established a cut-off date for the hearing of motions. All motions must be noticed so that the hearing takes place on or before the motion cut-off date. Counsel are advised that the Court may close a hearing date once the number of motions filed exceeds the maximum number of motions that can reasonably be heard on that date. Counsel should anticipate that a preferred hearing date may be unavailable. Therefore, to avoid being unable to file a motion to be heard by the cut-off date, counsel *should file motions sufficiently in advance of the hearing cut-off date to ensure that a hearing date is available.*
2. Counsel must provide Chambers with conformed Chambers copies of all documents. Chambers copies should not be put in envelopes. Counsel should consult the Court's website at www.cacd.uscourts.gov>Judges' Procedures and Schedules>Hon. Jacqueline H. Nguyen for further information regarding Chambers copies and motion procedures.

D. SETTLEMENT PROCEDURES

A settlement procedure must be identified in every case pursuant to Local Rule 16-15, et seq. Counsel must complete a settlement conference no later than the date set by the Court. Not to the exclusion of other procedures, the following are available:

(1) a settlement conference before the magistrate judge assigned to the case;

(2) a settlement conference or mediation before an attorney selected from the Attorney Settlement Panel;

(3) the employment (at the parties' expense) of a private judge, mediator, or arbitrator.

If a case is selected for the Mandatory ADR Program, the parties may choose option (3) instead, but may not choose option (1). Judge Nguyen may hold a settlement conference at the request of the parties in jury trial cases with a trial estimate of more than four days.

No case will proceed to trial unless all parties, including the principals of all corporate parties, have appeared personally at a settlement conference.

E. FINAL PRETRIAL CONFERENCE

1. A final pretrial conference date has been set pursuant to Rule 16 of the Federal Rules of Civil Procedure and Local Rule 16-8. Unless excused for good cause, each party appearing in this action shall be represented at the final pretrial conference by the lead trial counsel for that party. Counsel should be prepared to discuss streamlining the trial, including presentation of testimony by deposition excerpts or summaries, time limits, stipulations as to undisputed facts, and qualification of experts by admitted resumes.
2. The Court encourages, but does not require, counsel to agree to submit direct testimony of witnesses by way of declaration or written statement confirmed under oath by the witness. *See* Local Rule 16-11.2(b).

II.
ADDITIONAL TRIAL PREPARATION

A. PRETRIAL DOCUMENTS

1. ALL PRETRIAL DOCUMENT COPIES DELIVERED TO THE COURT SHALL BE "BINDER-READY" (three-hole punched on the left side, without blue-backs, and stapled only in the top left corner).
2. STRICT COMPLIANCE WITH LOCAL RULE 16 IS REQUIRED. THIS ORDER SETS FORTH SOME DIFFERENT AND SOME ADDITIONAL REQUIREMENTS. THIS COURT DOES NOT EXEMPT *PRO PER* PARTIES FROM THE REQUIREMENTS OF RULE 16. Carefully prepared memoranda of contentions of fact and law, witness lists, a joint exhibit list, and a proposed final pretrial conference order shall be submitted in accordance with the Rules, and the format of the proposed final pretrial conference order shall conform to the format set forth in Appendix A to the Local Rules. Failure to comply with these requirements may result in the final pretrial conference being taken off-calendar or continued, or in other sanctions.
3. The filing schedule for pretrial documents is as follows.
   a. At least 21 days before final pretrial conference:
      - Memoranda of contentions of fact and law
      - Witness lists
      - Joint exhibit list
      - Motions *in limine*
   b. At least 14 days before final pretrial conference:
      - Proposed final pretrial conference order lodged
      - Proposed jury instructions
      - Statement of the case
      - Proposed additional voir dire questions, if desired
      - Oppositions to motions *in limine*
   c. At least 21 days before trial:
      - Proposed findings of fact and contentions of law, if the matter requires them
   d. At least 7 days before trial:
      - Trial briefs, if desired

- Opposing parties' proposed findings of fact and conclusions of law, marked as described in this Order.

4. In addition to the requirements of Local Rule 16, the witness lists must include a brief description (one or two paragraphs) of the testimony and a time estimate for both direct and cross-examination (separately stated). See attached samples.

B. MOTIONS *IN LIMINE*

All motions *in limine* must be filed *at least three weeks before the final pretrial conference.* Counsel are to meet and confer with opposing counsel to determine whether opposing counsel intend to introduce the disputed evidence and to attempt to reach an agreement that would obviate the motion. Oppositions must be filed *two weeks before the final pretrial conference.* The Court will rule on motions *in limine* at the final pretrial conference. Motions *in limine* should address specific issues (e.g., *not* "to exclude all hearsay"). Motions *in limine* should not be disguised motions for summary adjudication of issues.

C. PROPOSED FINDINGS OF FACT AND CONCLUSIONS OF LAW

1. For any matter requiring findings of fact and conclusions of law, counsel for each party shall, no later than 21 days before trial, file with the Court and serve on opposing counsel that party's proposed findings of fact and conclusions of law in the format specified in Local Rule 52-3.
2. Seven days before the trial date, each counsel shall file with the Court and serve on opposing counsel a copy of the opposing party's proposed findings of fact and conclusions of law, marked as follows:
   - **(a)** Strike through those portions the party disputes;
   - **(b)** Bold those portions the party admits; and
   - **(c)** Underline those portions the party admits but considers irrelevant.

   The parties may agree to and advise the Court of some other method of differentiating among these three categories, such as color coding.
3. Counsel need not make a uniform determination as to an entire proposed finding or conclusion, and may agree with a portion, dispute another portion, and consider a portion irrelevant. Counsel should, however, have only a single fact or conclusion of law contained in each paragraph.
4. The parties may submit supplemental proposed findings of fact and conclusions of law during the course of the trial. If more than five supplemental findings are proposed, the same designating procedures should be used.
5. At the time of filing, each party must also submit its own unmarked proposed findings of fact and conclusions of law to the Chambers e-mail box in Microsoft Word format.

D. TRIAL EXHIBITS

1. Exhibits must be placed in three-ring binders indexed by exhibit number with tabs or dividers on the right side. Counsel shall submit to the Court an original and two copies of the binders. The spine portion of the binder shall indicate the volume number and contain an index of each exhibit included in the volume.
2. The Court requires that the following be submitted to the Courtroom Deputy Clerk ("CRD") on the first day of trial:

   a. The binder of original exhibits with the Court's exhibit tags, yellow tags for plaintiff and blue tags for defendant, stapled to the front of the exhibit on the upper right-hand corner with the case number, case name, and exhibit number placed on each tag.

b. Two binders with a copy of each exhibit tabbed with numbers as described above for use by the Court. (Exhibit tags are not necessary on these copies.)

c. Three copies of exhibit lists.

d. Three copies of witness lists in the order in which the witnesses may be called to testify.

E. TRIAL

Trial days are Tuesday through Friday from 9:00 a.m. to approximately 4:00 p.m. with two fifteen-minute breaks and a one-hour lunch break.

F. COURT REPORTER

Any party requesting special court reporter services for any hearing (i.e., real time transmission, daily transcripts) shall notify the reporter *at least 2 weeks before the hearing date.*

III.
CONDUCT OF ATTORNEYS AND PARTIES

A. OPENING STATEMENTS, EXAMINING WITNESSES, AND SUMMATION

1. Counsel must use the lectern.
2. Counsel must not consume time by writing out words, drawing charts or diagrams, etc. Counsel may prepare such materials in advance.

B. OBJECTIONS TO QUESTIONS

1. Counsel must not use objections for the purpose of making a speech, recapitulating testimony, or attempting to guide the witness.
2. When objecting, counsel must rise to state the objection and state only that counsel objects and the legal ground of objection. If counsel wishes to argue an objection further, counsel must ask for permission to do so.

C. GENERAL DECORUM

1. Counsel should not approach the CRD or the witness box without specific permission and must return to the lectern when the purpose for approaching has been accomplished.
2. Counsel should rise when addressing the Court, and when the Court enters or leaves the courtroom.
3. Counsel should address all remarks to the Court. Counsel are not to address the CRD, the court reporter, persons in the audience, or opposing counsel. If counsel wish to speak with opposing counsel, counsel must ask permission to do so. Any request for the re-reading of questions or answers shall be addressed to the Court. Requests may not be granted.
4. Counsel should not address or refer to witnesses or parties by first names alone, with the exception of witnesses under 14 years old.
5. Counsel must not offer a stipulation unless counsel have conferred with opposing counsel and have verified that the stipulation will be acceptable.
6. While Court is in session, counsel must not leave counsel table to confer with any

person in the back of the courtroom unless permission has been granted in advance.

7. Counsel should not by nonverbal conduct exhibit any opinion concerning testimony being given by a witness. Counsel should admonish counsel's own clients and witnesses to avoid such conduct.

8. Where a party has more than one lawyer, only one may conduct the direct or cross-examination of a particular witness, or make objections as to that witness.

D. PROMPTNESS OF COUNSEL AND WITNESSES

1. Promptness is expected from counsel and witnesses. Once counsel are engaged in trial, this trial is counsel's first priority. The Court will not delay the trial.

2. If a witness was on the stand at a recess or adjournment, counsel who called the witness shall ensure the witness is back on the stand and ready to proceed when trial resumes.

3. Counsel must notify the CRD in advance if any witness should be accommodated based on a disability or for other reasons.

4. No presenting party may be without witnesses. If a party's remaining witnesses are not immediately available and there is more than a brief delay, the Court may deem that party to have rested.

5. The Court attempts to cooperate with professional witnesses and will, except in extraordinary circumstances, accommodate them by permitting them to be called out of sequence. Counsel must anticipate any such possibility and discuss it with opposing counsel. If there is an objection, counsel must confer with the Court in advance.

E. EXHIBITS

1. Each counsel should keep counsel's own list of exhibits and should note when each has been admitted into evidence.

2. Each counsel is responsible for any exhibits that counsel secures from the CRD and must return them before leaving the courtroom at the end of the session.

3. An exhibit not previously marked should, at the time of its first mention, be accompanied by a request that it be marked for identification. Counsel must show a new exhibit to opposing counsel before the court session in which it is mentioned.

4. Counsel are to advise the CRD of any agreements with respect to the proposed exhibits and as to those exhibits that may be received without further motion to admit.

5. When referring to an exhibit, counsel should refer to its exhibit number. Witnesses should be asked to do the same.

6. Counsel must not ask witnesses to draw charts or diagrams nor ask the Court's permission for a witness to do so. Any graphic aids must be fully prepared before the court session starts.

F. DEPOSITIONS

1. All depositions to be used at trial, either as evidence or for impeachment, must be lodged with the CRD *on the first day of trial or such earlier date as the Court may order.* Counsel should verify with the CRD that the relevant deposition is in the CRD's

possession.

2. In using depositions of an adverse party for impeachment, either one of the following procedures may be adopted:
   - **(a)** If counsel wishes to read the questions and answers as alleged impeachment and ask the witness no further questions on that subject, counsel shall first state the page and line where the reading begins and the page and line where the reading ends, and allow time for any objection. Counsel may then read the portions of the deposition into the record.
   - **(b)** If counsel wishes to ask the witness further questions on the subject matter, the deposition shall be placed in front of the witness and the witness told to read the relevant pages and lines silently. Then counsel may either ask the witness further questions on the matter and thereafter read the quotations, or read the quotations and thereafter ask further questions. Counsel should have an extra copy of the deposition for this purpose.
3. Where a witness is absent and the witness's testimony is offered by deposition, counsel may (a) have a reader occupy the witness chair and read the testimony of the witness while the examining lawyer asks the questions, or (b) have counsel read both the questions and answers.

G. USING NUMEROUS ANSWERS TO INTERROGATORIES AND REQUESTS FOR ADMISSIONS

Whenever counsel expects to offer a group of answers to interrogatories or requests for admissions extracted from one or more lengthy documents, counsel should prepare a new document listing each question and answer and identifying the document from which it has been extracted. Copies of this new document should be given to the Court and opposing counsel.

H. ADVANCE NOTICE OF UNUSUAL OR DIFFICULT ISSUES

If any counsel have reason to anticipate that a difficult question of law or evidence will necessitate legal argument requiring research or briefing, counsel must give the Court advance notice. Counsel are directed to notify the CRD at the day's adjournment if an unexpected legal issue arises that could not have been foreseen and addressed by a motion in limine. See Fed. R. Evid. 103.

IT IS SO ORDERED.

DATED: July 22, 2011

JACQUELINE H. NGUYEN
United States District Judge

D. *Order Regarding Jury Trial*

IN THE UNITED STATES DISTICT COURT
FOR THE CENTRAL DISTRICT OF CALIFORNIA

Plaintiff(s),	Case No. ______________
v.	**ORDER RE JURY TRIAL**
	I. ORDER RE DEADLINES: (SEE PAGE TWO)
Defendant(s).	**II. ORDER RE TRIAL PREPARATION**
	III. ORDER GOVERNING CONDUCT OF ATTORNEYS AND PARTIES

I.
DEADLINES

A. Adding Parties or Amending Pleadings: ______________
B. Discovery Cut-off: ______________
C. Expert Witness Exchange Deadline:
Initial: ______________
Rebuttal: ______________
Cut-off: ______________
D. Motion Hearing Cut-off: ______________
E. Settlement Conference Cut-off: ______________
F. Final Pretrial Conference (and hearing on Motions in Limine): _______ at 10:30 a.m.
G. Trial Date: ____________ at 8:30 a.m.

A. PARTIES/PLEADINGS

The Court has established a cut-off date for adding parties or amending pleadings. All motions to add parties or to amend the pleadings must be noticed to be heard on or before the cut-off date. All unserved parties will be dismissed at the time of the pretrial conference pursuant to Local Rule 16-8.1.

B. DISCOVERY AND DISCOVERY CUT-OFF

1. Discovery Cut-off: The Court has established a cut-off date for discovery, including expert discovery, if applicable. This is not the date by which discovery requests must be served; it is the date by which all discovery, including all hearings on any related motions, is to be completed.

2. Discovery Disputes: Counsel are expected to comply with all Local Rules and the Federal Rules of Civil Procedure concerning discovery. Whenever possible, the Court expects counsel to resolve discovery problems among themselves in a courteous, reasonable, and professional manner. The Court expects that counsel will adhere strictly to the Civility and Professionalism Guidelines (which can be found on the Court's website under Attorney Information>Attorney Admissions).

3. Discovery Motions: Any motion challenging the adequacy of discovery responses must be filed, served, and calendared sufficiently in advance of the discovery cut-off date to permit the responses to be obtained before that date if the motion is granted.

4. Depositions: All depositions shall commence sufficiently in advance of the discovery cut-off date to permit their completion and to permit the deposing party enough time to bring any discovery motions concerning the deposition before the cut-off date. Given the requirements to "meet and confer" and to give notice, in most cases a planned motion to compel must be discussed with opposing counsel at least six weeks before the cut-off.

5. Written Discovery: All interrogatories, requests for production of documents, and requests for admissions must be served sufficiently in advance of the discovery cut-off date to permit the discovering party enough time to challenge (via motion practice) responses deemed to be deficient.

6. Expert Discovery: All disclosures must be made in writing. The parties should begin expert discovery shortly after the initial designation of experts. The final pretrial conference and trial dates will not be continued merely because expert discovery is not completed. Failure to comply with these or any other orders concerning expert discovery may result in the expert being excluded as a witness.

C. LAW AND MOTION

1. The Court has established a cut-off date for the hearing of motions. All motions must be noticed so that the hearing takes place on or before the motion cut-off date. Counsel are advised that the Court may close a hearing date once the number of motions filed exceeds the maximum number of motions that can reasonably be heard on that date. Counsel should anticipate that a preferred hearing date may be unavailable. Therefore, to avoid being unable to file a motion to be heard by the cut-off date, counsel *should file motions sufficiently in advance of the hearing cut-off date to ensure that a hearing date is available.*

2. Counsel must provide Chambers with conformed Chambers copies of all documents. Chambers copies should not be put in envelopes. Counsel should consult the Court's website at www.cacd.uscourts.gov>Judges' Procedures and Schedules>Hon. Jacqueline H. Nguyen for further information regarding Chambers copies and motion procedures.

D. SETTLEMENT PROCEDURES

A settlement procedure must be identified in every case pursuant to Local Rule 16-15, et seq. Counsel must complete a settlement conference no later than the date set by the Court. Not to the exclusion of other procedures, the following are available:

(1) a settlement conference before the magistrate judge assigned to the case;

(2) a settlement conference or mediation before an attorney selected from the Attorney Settlement Panel;

(3) the employment (at the parties' expense) of a private judge, mediator, or arbitrator.

If a case is selected for the Mandatory ADR Program, the parties may choose option (3) instead, but may not choose option (1). Judge Nguyen may hold a settlement conference at the request of the parties in jury trial cases with a trial estimate of more than four days.

No case will proceed to trial unless all parties, including the principals of all corporate parties, have appeared personally at a settlement conference.

E. FINAL PRETRIAL CONFERENCE

A final pretrial conference date has been set pursuant to Rule 16 of the Federal Rules of Civil Procedure and Local Rule 16-8. Unless excused for good cause, each party appearing in this action shall be represented at the final pretrial conference by the lead trial counsel for that party. Counsel should be prepared to discuss streamlining the trial, including presentation of testimony by deposition excerpts or summaries, time limits, stipulations as to undisputed facts, and qualification of experts by admitted resumes.

II.
ADDITIONAL TRIAL PREPARATION

A. PRETRIAL DOCUMENTS

1. ALL PRETRIAL DOCUMENT COPIES DELIVERED TO THE COURT SHALL BE "BINDER-READY" (three-hole punched on the left side, without blue-backs, and stapled only in the top left corner).

2. STRICT COMPLIANCE WITH LOCAL RULE 16 IS REQUIRED. THIS ORDER SETS FORTH SOME DIFFERENT AND SOME ADDITIONAL REQUIREMENTS. THIS COURT DOES NOT EXEMPT *PRO PER* PARTIES FROM THE REQUIREMENTS OF RULE 16. Carefully prepared memoranda of contentions of fact and law, witness lists, a joint exhibit list, and a proposed final pretrial conference order shall be submitted in accordance with the Rules, and the format of the proposed final pretrial conference order shall conform to the format set forth in Appendix A to the Local Rules. Failure to comply with these requirements may result in the final pretrial conference being taken off-calendar or continued, or in other sanctions.

3. The filing schedule for pretrial documents is as follows.
   a. At least 21 days before final pretrial conference:
      - Memoranda of contentions of fact and law
      - Witness lists
      - Joint exhibit list
      - Motions *in limine*
   b. At least 14 days before final pretrial conference:
      - Proposed final pretrial conference order lodged
      - Proposed jury instructions
      - Statement of the case
      - Proposed additional voir dire questions, if desired
      - Oppositions to motions *in limine*
   c. At least 7 days before trial:
      - Trial briefs, if desired

4. In addition to the requirements of Local Rule 16, the witness lists must include a

brief description (one or two paragraphs) of the testimony and a time estimate for both direct and cross-examination (separately stated). See attached samples.

B. MOTIONS *IN LIMINE*

All motions *in limine* must be filed *at least three weeks before the final pretrial conference.* Counsel are to meet and confer with opposing counsel to determine whether opposing counsel intend to introduce the disputed evidence and to attempt to reach an agreement that would obviate the motion. Oppositions must be filed *two weeks before the final pretrial conference.* The Court will rule on motions in limine at the final pretrial conference. Motions *in limine* should address specific issues (e.g., *not* "to exclude all hearsay"). Motions *in limine* should not be disguised motions for summary adjudication of issues.

C. JURY INSTRUCTIONS, STATEMENT OF THE CASE, AND VOIR DIRE

1. Pursuant to Local Rule 16-2, lead trial counsel for each party are required to meet and confer in person. The Court expects strict compliance with Local Rule 16-2. Fourteen days before the Local Rule 16-2 meeting, the parties shall exchange their respective proposed jury instructions and special verdict forms. Ten days prior to the Local Rule 16-2 meeting, each shall serve objections to the other's instructions and verdict forms. Before or at the Rule 16-2 meeting, counsel are ordered to meet and confer and attempt to come to agreement on the proposed jury instructions and verdict forms.

2. At the time of filing the proposed final pretrial conference order, counsel shall file with the Court a JOINT set of jury instructions on which there is agreement. All blanks in standard forms should be filled in. The Court expects counsel to agree on the substantial majority of jury instructions, particularly when pattern or model instructions provide a statement of applicable law. If one party fails to comply with the provisions of this section, the other party must file a unilateral set of jury instructions.

3. At the same time, each party shall file its proposed jury instructions that are objected to by any other party. Each disputed instruction must have attached a short statement (one or two paragraphs), including points and authorities, in support of the instruction and a brief statement, including points and authorities, in support of any objections. If applicable, a proposed alternative instruction must be provided.

4. When the *Manual of Model Jury Instructions for the Ninth Circuit* provides an applicable jury instruction, the parties should submit the most recent version, modified and supplemented to fit the circumstances of this case. Where California law applies, counsel should use the current edition of *California Jury Instructions—Civil* ("BAJI" or "CACI"). If neither is applicable, counsel should consult the current edition of O'Malley, et al., *Federal Jury Practice and Instructions.* Each requested instruction shall (a) cite the authority or source of the instruction, (b) be set forth in full, (c) be on a separate page, (d) be numbered, (e) cover only one subject or principle of law, and (f) not repeat principles of law contained in any other requested instruction.

   Counsel may submit alternatives to these instructions only if counsel has a reasoned argument that they do not properly state the law or they are incomplete.

5. Counsel must provide the documents described in paragraphs 2 and 3 on a flash drive in Microsoft Word 2003 (or above) format *at the time they file their proposed jury instructions.*

6. The Court will send one or more copies of the instructions into the jury room for the jury's use during deliberations. Therefore, in addition to the copies described above, the flash drive must contain a "clean" set of jury instructions, containing only the text of the instruction (one per page) with the caption "Instruction No. __" at the top (eliminating titles, supporting authority, etc.).

7. Counsel must provide an index of all instructions submitted, which must include the following:
   a. the number of the instruction;
   b. the title of the instruction;
   c. the source of the instruction and any relevant case citations; and
   d. the page number of the instruction.

   For example:

Number	Title	Source	Page
1	Trademark – Defined (15 U.S.C. § 1127)	9th Cir. 15.3.2	7

8. During the trial and before argument, the Court will meet with counsel and settle the instructions, and counsel will have an opportunity to make a further record concerning their objections.

9. At the time of filing the proposed final pretrial conference order, counsel should file a jointly prepared one- or two-page statement of the case to be read by the Court to the prospective panel of jurors before commencement of voir dire.

10. The Court will conduct the voir dire. *At the time they file the proposed final pretrial conference order, counsel for each party may*, but are not required to, submit a list of proposed case-specific voir dire questions.

D. TRIAL EXHIBITS

1. Exhibits must be placed in three-ring binders indexed by exhibit number with tabs or dividers on the right side. Counsel shall submit to the Court an original and one copy of the binders. The spine portion of the binder shall indicate the volume number and contain an index of each exhibit included in the volume.

2. The Court requires that the following be submitted to the Courtroom Deputy Clerk ("CRD") on the first day of trial:

   a. The binder of original exhibits with the Court's exhibit tags, yellow tags for plaintiff and blue tags for defendant, stapled to the front of the exhibit at the upper right-hand corner with the case number, case name, and exhibit number placed on each tag.

   b. One binder with a copy of each exhibit tabbed with numbers as described above for use by the Court. (Exhibit tags are not necessary on these copies.)

   c. Three copies of exhibit lists.

   d. Three copies of witness lists in the order in which the witnesses may be called to testify.

3. Where a significant number of exhibits will be admitted, the Court encourages counsel to consider ways in which testimony about exhibits may be made intelligible to the jury. The Court has an Elmo and other equipment available for use during trial. Call the CRD if you wish to visit when the Court is not in session to practice using the equipment. The Court does not permit exhibits to be "published" by passing them up and down the jury box.

E. COURT REPORTER

Any party requesting special court reporter services for any hearing (i.e., real time transmission, daily transcripts) shall notify the reporter *at least 2 weeks before the hearing date.*

F. JURY TRIAL

1. On the first day of trial, court will commence at 9:00 a.m. and conclude at approximately 4:30 p.m. with a one-hour lunch break. On the first day of trial, counsel must appear at 8:30 a.m. to discuss preliminary matters with the Court. After the first day of trial, trial days are Tuesday through Friday from 9:00 a.m. To approximately 4:00 p.m. with two fifteen-minute breaks and a one-hour lunch break.

2. On the first day of trial, the jury panel will be called when the Court is satisfied that the matter is ready for trial. Jury selection usually takes only a few hours. Counsel should be prepared to proceed with opening statements and witness examination immediately after jury selection.

3. In most cases the Court will conduct its initial voir dire of 14 prospective jurors who will be seated in the jury box. Generally the Court will select seven or eight jurors.

4. Each side will have three peremptory challenges. If 14 jurors are seated in the box and all six peremptories are exercised, the remaining eight jurors will constitute the jury panel. If fewer than six peremptories are exercised, the eight jurors in the lowest-numbered seats will be the jury. The Court will not necessarily accept a stipulation to a challenge for cause. If one or more challenges for cause are accepted and all six peremptories are exercised, the Court may decide to proceed with six or seven jurors.

III.
CONDUCT OF ATTORNEYS AND PARTIES

A. OPENING STATEMENTS, EXAMINING WITNESSES, AND SUMMATION

1. Counsel must use the lectern.

2. Counsel must not consume time by writing out words, drawing charts or diagrams, etc. Counsel may prepare such materials in advance.

B. OBJECTIONS TO QUESTIONS

1. Counsel must not use objections for the purpose of making a speech, recapitulating testimony, or attempting to guide the witness.

2. When objecting, counsel must rise to state the objection and state only that counsel objects and the legal ground of objection. If counsel wishes to argue an objection further, counsel must ask for permission to do so.

C. GENERAL DECORUM

1. Counsel should not approach the CRD or the witness box without specific permission and must return to the lectern when the purpose for approaching has been accomplished.

2. Counsel should rise when addressing the Court, and when the Court or the jury enters or leaves the courtroom.

3. Counsel should address all remarks to the Court. Counsel are not to address the CRD, the court reporter, persons in the audience, or opposing counsel. If counsel wish to speak with opposing counsel, counsel must ask permission to do so. Any request for the re-reading of questions or answers shall be addressed to the Court. Requests may not be granted.

4. Counsel should not address or refer to witnesses or parties by first names alone, with the exception of witnesses under 14 years old.

5. Counsel must not offer a stipulation unless counsel have conferred with opposing counsel and have verified that the stipulation will be acceptable.

6. While Court is in session, counsel must not leave counsel table to confer with any person in the back of the courtroom unless permission has been granted in advance.

7. Counsel should not by nonverbal conduct exhibit any opinion concerning testimony being given by a witness. Counsel should admonish counsel's own clients and witnesses to avoid such conduct.

8. Counsel should not talk to jurors at all, and should not talk to co-counsel, opposing counsel, witnesses, or clients where the conversation can be overheard by jurors. Each counsel should admonish counsel's own clients and witnesses to avoid such conduct.

9. Where a party has more than one lawyer, only one may conduct the direct or cross-examination of a particular witness, or make objections as to that witness.

D. PROMPTNESS OF COUNSEL AND WITNESSES

1. Promptness is expected from counsel and witnesses. Once counsel are engaged in trial, this trial is counsel's first priority. The Court will not delay the trial or inconvenience jurors.

2. If a witness was on the stand at a recess or adjournment, counsel who called the witness shall ensure the witness is back on the stand and ready to proceed when trial resumes.

3. Counsel must notify the CRD in advance if any witness should be accommodated based on a disability or for other reasons.

4. No presenting party may be without witnesses. If a party's remaining witnesses are not immediately available and there is more than a brief delay, the Court may deem that party to have rested.

5. The Court attempts to cooperate with professional witnesses and will, except in extraordinary circumstances, accommodate them by permitting them to be called out of sequence. Counsel must anticipate any such possibility and discuss it with

opposing counsel. If there is an objection, counsel must confer with the Court in advance.

E. EXHIBITS

1. Each counsel should keep counsel's own list of exhibits and should note when each has been admitted into evidence.

2. Each counsel is responsible for any exhibits that counsel secures from the CRD and must return them before leaving the courtroom at the end of the session.

3. An exhibit not previously marked should, at the time of its first mention, be accompanied by a request that it be marked for identification. Counsel must show a new exhibit to opposing counsel before the court session in which it is mentioned.

4. Counsel are to advise the CRD of any agreements with respect to the proposed exhibits and as to those exhibits that may be received without further motion to admit.

5. When referring to an exhibit, counsel should refer to its exhibit number. Witnesses should be asked to do the same.

6. Counsel must not ask witnesses to draw charts or diagrams nor ask the Court's permission for a witness to do so. Any graphic aids must be fully prepared before the court session starts.

F. DEPOSITIONS

1. All depositions to be used at trial, either as evidence or for impeachment, must be lodged with the CRD *on the first day of trial or such earlier date as the Court may order.* Counsel should verify with the CRD that the relevant deposition is in the CRD's possession.

2. In using depositions of an adverse party for impeachment, either one of the following procedures may be adopted:

   (a) If counsel wishes to read the questions and answers as alleged impeachment and ask the witness no further questions on that subject, counsel shall first state the page and line where the reading begins and the page and line where the reading ends, and allow time for any objection. Counsel may then read the portions of the deposition into the record.

   (b) If counsel wishes to ask the witness further questions on the subject matter, the deposition shall be placed in front of the witness and the witness told to read the relevant pages and lines silently. Then counsel may either ask the witness further questions on the matter and thereafter read the quotations, or read the quotations and thereafter ask further questions. Counsel should have an extra copy of the deposition for this purpose.

3. Where a witness is absent and the witness's testimony is offered by deposition, counsel may (a) have a reader occupy the witness chair and read the testimony of the witness while the examining lawyer asks the questions, or (b) have counsel read both the questions and answers.

G. USING NUMEROUS ANSWERS TO INTERROGATORIES AND REQUESTS FOR ADMISSIONS

Whenever counsel expects to offer a group of answers to interrogatories or requests for admissions extracted from one or more lengthy documents, counsel should prepare a new document listing each question and answer and identifying the document from which it has been extracted. Copies of this new document should be given to the Court and opposing counsel.

H. ADVANCE NOTICE OF UNUSUAL OR DIFFICULT ISSUES

If any counsel have reason to anticipate that a difficult question of law or evidence will necessitate legal argument requiring research or briefing, counsel must give the Court advance notice. Counsel are directed to notify the CRD at the day's adjournment if an unexpected legal issue arises that could not have been foreseen and addressed by a motion *in limine. See* Fed. R. Evid. 103. Counsel must also advise the CRD at the end of each trial day of any issues that must be addressed outside the presence of the jury, so that there is no interruption of the trial. THE COURT WILL NOT KEEP JURORS WAITING.

IT IS SO ORDERED.

DATED: July 22, 2011

____

JACQUELINE H. NGUYEN
United States District Judge

III. Judge Nguyen's Forms

A. *Exhibit List*

IN THE UNITED STATES DISTICT COURT
FOR THE CENTRAL DISTRICT OF CALIFORNIA

)	Case No. ________________
Plaintiff(s),)	
v.)	**EXHIBIT LIST**
Defendant(s).)	***SAMPLE FORMAT***
____)	

EX. No.	DESCRIPTION	IDENTIFIED	ADMITTED

B. *Final Joint Trial Witness Estimate Form*

FINAL JOINT TRIAL WITNESS ESTIMATE FORM

CASE: ______________________ TRIAL DATE: ___________________________

	WITNESS NAME	PARTY CALLING WITNESS AND ESTIMATE	X-EXAMINER'S ESTIMATE	DESCRIPTION OF TESTIMONY	COMMENTS
1					
2					
3					
4					
5					
	TOTAL ESTIMATE S THIS PAGE:				

Instructions:

(1) List witnesses (last name first); (2) For description, be extremely brief, *e.g.*, "eyewitness to accident." Or "expert on standard of care." (3) Use estimates within fractions of an hour, rounded off to closest quarter of an hour. *E.g.*, if you estimate 20 minutes, make it .25. An estimate of one and one half hours would be 1.5. An estimate of three-quarters of an hour would be .75; (4) Note special factors in "Comments" column. *E.g.*, "Needs interpreter." (5) Entries may be in handwriting if very neat and legible.

C. Witness List

IN THE UNITED STATES DISTICT COURT
FOR THE CENTRAL DISTRICT OF CALIFORNIA

Plaintiff(s),	)	Case No. ___________-JHN-x
v.	)	**WITNESS LIST**
Defendant(s).	)	***SAMPLE FORMAT***

WITNESSES FOR PLAINTIFF	DATES OF TESTIMONY
	(to be filled in during trial)
WITNESSES FOR DEFENDANT	

Hon. S. James Otero
District Judge

Chambers Information
U.S. District Court, Central District of California
Courtroom 1, 2nd Floor
312 N. Spring Street
Los Angeles, CA 90012

Scheduling Information
Courtroom Deputy: (213) 894-1796

Civil Law and Motion	Mondays at 10:00 a.m.
Criminal Law and Motion	Mondays at 10:00 a.m.

Judge's Biography
Born 1951 in Los Angeles, CA

Federal Judicial Service:
-Judge, U. S. District Court, Central District of California
-Nominated by George W. Bush on January 7, 2003, to a seat vacated by Richard A. Paez; Confirmed by the Senate on February 10, 2003, and received commission on February 12, 2003.

Education:
-California State University, B.A., 1973
-Stanford Law School, J.D., 1976

Professional Career:
-Law Clerk/Attorney, Office of the City Attorney, Los Angeles, California, 1976-1987
-General Counsel & Vice President, Regional Counsel Southern Pacific Transportation, 1987-1988
-Judge, Municipal Court of Los Angeles, California, 1988-1990
-Judge, Superior Court of the State of California, 1990-2003

I. Judge Otero's Procedures and Practices

A. *Procedures and Schedules*

1. Civil and criminal motions are heard on Monday at 10:00 a.m. If Monday is a holiday, the next motion date is Tuesday following the Monday holiday. It is not necessary to clear a motion date.
2. Discovery motions are to be calendared before the Magistrate Judge.
3. Civil and criminal trials are held Monday through Friday from 8:30 a.m. to 11:30 a.m. and from 1:00 p.m. to 4:00 p.m. Motions in Limine are heard at the beginning of trial. See the attached Initial Standing Order for further procedures.
4. Tentative rulings are not issued.
5. *Ex Parte* Applications are not noticed for any date or time certain. If a hearing is necessary, the courtroom deputy clerk will contact counsel.
6. One mandatory chambers copy, blue-backed and two-hole punched, is required for each e-filing, with the date and time of the e-filing indicated on the face page. The chambers copy box is located at the door of courtroom 1, second floor.
7. Request for Continuance of a scheduled court proceeding is not automatically granted. Refer to Local Rule 52.9 for proper format.
8. Counsel are not to initiate telephone calls to chambers unless first contacted by a law clerk or Judge Otero's assistant.
9. Inquiries regarding the status of a motion, stipulation, or proposed order are not handled telephonically. Counsel may sign-up for Pacer access to monitor the clerk's database. See www.cacd.uscourts.gov > General Information > Pacer Access.
10. For general information on how to order a transcript of any reported or digitally recorded proceeding, please contact 213-894-3015 or visit www.cacd.uscourts.gov > General Information > Court Reporter/Recorder Transcripts. If you require an estimate of cost for the preparation of a transcript, contact the court reporter/recorder for the desired proceeding.

    To determine the court reporter/recorder for a particular proceeding, go to the Court Reporter Schedule web page and click on View by Date. Once you've determined the correct court reporter/recorder for the desired session, click on Court Reporter Phone and Email List for contact information.
11. Law Clerk and Extern Applicants may submit applications to District Judge S. James Otero, United States District Court, *Suite 244P, 312 North Spring Street, Los Angeles, California 90012*. Include a cover letter, resume, transcript, and writing sample. Letters of recommendation are to be directed to this address.
12. Interpreter: Obtaining the services of a certified interpreter on a civil case is the responsibility of counsel. For information, dial (213) 894-4599 or check the court's website at www.cacd.uscourts.gov > General Information > Interpreters.
13. Please see the attached Civil and Criminal Initial Standing Orders for detailed procedures regarding cases assigned to Judge Otero. Counsel are advised to **regularly** check for updates.

14. Counsel are directed to comply with all Local Rules. If counsel have received a "Notice to Parties of ADR Program" (form ADR-08, ADR-10, or ADR-11 with attached "ADR Program Questionnaire" form ADR-09), please see the section on the Court's website entitled "ADR," General Order 02-07, for further information. The ADR section also contains Attorney Settlement Officer information.

15. Arrangements for bringing voluminous exhibits into the courtroom may be made through the Space and Facilities Help Desk, at (213) 894-1400.

16. ELMO reservations/tutorials may be made by first referring to the court website at www.cacd.uscourts.gov under "Attorney Information" and then "Attorney Services."

II. Judge Otero's Case Management Orders

A. *Discovery and Trial Order in Criminal Cases*

IN THE UNITED STATES DISTICT COURT
FOR THE CENTRAL DISTRICT OF CALIFORNIA

UNITED STATES OF AMERICA,)	Case No. CR ______________
Plaintiff,)	
v.)	**DISCOVERY AND TRIAL ORDER**
Defendant(s).)	**IN CRIMINAL CASES BEFORE**
______________________________)	**JUDGE S. JAMES OTERO**

READ THIS ORDER CAREFULLY. IT CONTROLS THIS CASE AND DIFFERS IN SOME RESPECTS FROM THE LOCAL RULES.

This case has been assigned to the calendar of The Honorable S. James Otero. To obviate unnecessary motions for discovery in criminal actions, proceedings, matters, or cases assigned to the undersigned Court for trial, the Court notes the following:

1. Court Hours: Criminal motions are heard on MONDAY at 10:00 a.m., unless the Court orders otherwise. (If Monday is a holiday, the next motion date is Tuesday following the Monday holiday.) It is not necessary to clear a motion date. Motions *in limine* are heard on Tuesday, on the FIRST DAY OF TRIAL, at 9:00 a.m.

2. Location: Judge Otero's courtroom is located in Courtroom 1, United States District Court, 312 North Spring Street, 2nd Floor, Los Angeles, California 90012.

3. Telephone Inquiries: Telephone inquiries regarding the status of a motion, stipulation or proposed order are NOT returned.

a. Counsel may, however, sign-up for Pacer access to monitor the clerk's database. *See* www.cacd.uscourts.gov > General Information > Pacer Access.

b. Counsel are referred to the clerk's website at www.cacd.uscourts.gov > Judges' Procedures and Schedules > Hon. S. James Otero for further information regarding the Court's preferences.

4. Communication with Chambers: If counsel is requesting information that can be obtained from the Court's 24-hour automated calling system or internet website at www.cacd.uscourts.gov, such call will not be returned.

a. For the 24-hour automated calling system, please call the appropriate number below:

i. Western Division at Los Angeles (213) 894-1565;
ii. Eastern Division at Riverside (909) 328-4450; or
iii. Southern Division at Santa Ana (714) 338-4750.

b. Counsel may access the Court's website for local rules, filing procedures, judges' procedures and schedules, calendars, forms, and other information. Counsel are not to initiate telephone calls to Judge Otero's chambers, law clerks or secretary. However, if counsel need to contact the Courtroom Deputy Clerk, Victor Cruz, Mr. Cruz may be reached at (213) 894-1796 or via e-mail at victor_cruz@cacd.uscourts.gov.

c. Counsel are ordered to list their facsimile transmission number along with their address, telephone number, and e-mail address on all papers submitted to the Court in order to facilitate communication by the Court.

5. Calendar Conflicts: If there is a calendar conflict, counsel are to inform the Courtroom Deputy Clerk prior to the date of the conflict and are to follow the Local Rules ("L.R.") and Federal Rules of Criminal Procedure ("Fed. R. Crim. P.").

6. Transcripts: To order a transcript, counsel are to call the Court Reporter's Office at (213) 894-3015. The Court uses a court recorder, Margarita Lopez, who can be reached at (213) 894-2717.

7. Mandatory Chambers Copies: Counsel are ordered to provide conformed mandatory chambers copies without envelopes of all motions, oppositions, and replies. Documents are to be placed in the chambers copy box outside of Courtroom 1 on the second floor of the Spring Street Courthouse, United States District Court, 312 North Spring Street, Los Angeles, California 90012 by 5:00 p.m. (PST) on the day of the filing. Further, counsel are ordered to e-mail courtesy copies of all trial documents to the Courtroom Deputy Clerk, Victor Cruz.

8. Discovery and Discovery Cut-Off:

a. Counsel for the government and counsel for defendant shall comply promptly with discovery and notice pursuant to Fed. R. Crim. P. 12, 12.1, 12.2, 12.3, 15, and 16.

b. Discovery by Defendant: Within seven (7) days of the trial setting of any criminal action, proceeding, matter or case, the United States Attorney, or an Assistant United States Attorney, and the defendant's attorney shall meet and confer, and upon request of the attorney for the defendant, the government shall provide defendant's attorney with:

i. Statement of Defendant: The government shall disclose to defendant's attorney its intent to use any statements or confessions made by the defendant. If defendant questions the admissibility of such statement or confession, the hearing required by *Jackson v. Denno*, 378 U.S. 368 (1964), shall be held on the day of trial prior to the opening statements of counsel. The government shall permit defendant's attorney to inspect and copy or photograph any relevant written or recorded statements or confessions made by the defendant, or copies thereof, within the possession, custody or control of the government, the existence of which is known, or may become known, to the attorney for the government. The government shall advise defendant's attorney of the substance of an oral statement available to the government in response to any interrogation by an employee or agent of any governmental agency, local, state, or federal, or private source involved in the investigation or reporting of the offense(s) charged in the information/indictment.

ii. Reports or Examinations and Tests: The government shall permit defendant's attorney to inspect and copy or photograph any relevant results or reports of physical or mental examinations, and of specific tests or experiments made in connection with the case, or copies thereof, within the possession, custody or control of the government, the existence of which is known, or may become known, to the attorney for the government and which are material to the defendant's case.

iii. Testimony Before the Grand Jury: The government shall permit defendant's attorney to inspect and copy or photograph any relevant recorded testimony of the defendant before a grand jury.

iv. **Documents and Tangible Objects:** The government shall permit defendant's attorney to inspect and copy or photograph books, papers, documents, tangible objects, buildings or places which are the property of the defendant and which are within the possession, custody or control of the government.

v. **Prior Record:** The government shall make known to defendant's attorney the defendant's prior criminal record in the possession of the attorney for the government.

vi. **Evidence Favorable to the Defendant:** The government shall permit defendant's attorney to inspect, copy or photograph any evidence favorable to the defendant.

vii. **Electronic Surveillance:** The government shall advise defendant's attorney of the existence or non-existence of any evidence in the possession of the government obtained as the result of any electronic surveillance or wiretap.

viii. **Informers:** The government shall advise defendant's attorney of the contemplated use of informer testimony (fact of informer only, not name or testimony).

ix. ***Brady* Material:** The government shall permit defendant's attorney to inspect and copy or photograph all material within the purview of *Brady v. Maryland*, 373 U.S. 83 (1963) and *Giglio v. United States*, 405 U.S. 150 (1972).

x. **Expert Witnesses:** The government shall permit defendant's attorney to inspect and copy or photograph a written resume of the qualifications of any expert witness which the United States Attorney intends to call in the case in chief together with a statement of the substance of such expert's expected testimony.

c. If, in the judgment of the United States Attorney, it would not be in the interest of justice to make any one or more disclosures set forth in paragraph (b) and requested by defendant's counsel, disclosure may be declined, and defense counsel is advised to immediately bring a formal noticed motion to the Court.

d. **Discovery by Government:**

i. **Expert Witnesses:** The defendant's attorney shall at the conference disclose to the United States Attorney a written resume of the qualifications of any expert witness which the defendant intends to call in his case in chief together with a statement of the substance of such expert's expected testimony.

ii. **Scientific or Medical Reports:** The defendant's attorney shall at the conference disclose to the United States Attorney the results (original or a copy) of any scientific or medical report which defendant intends to use in the presentation of his case in chief.

iii. **Defense of Alibi:** The United States Attorney shall at the conference notify defendant in writing of the specific time, date and place at which the offense/offenses charged in the information/indictment is/are alleged to have been committed.

(1) Defendant shall in writing, within three (3) days thereafter, notify the United States Attorney of the specific place at which he claims to have been at the time of the alleged offense/offenses to which a defense of alibi will be addressed and the names and addresses of the witnesses upon whom he intends to establish such alibi.

(2) Within five (5) days thereafter or such other time as the Court may direct, the United States Attorney shall inform the defendant of the names and addresses of the witnesses upon whom the government intends to establish defendant's presence at the scene of the alleged offense/offenses.

(3) Failure to comply with the time limits set forth herein shall invoke the sanction provided in Federal Rules of Criminal Procedure Rule 12.1(d).

iv. **Defense Based on Mental Condition:** The defendant's attorney shall at the conference disclose to the United States Attorney in writing that the defendant will rely upon the defense of insanity at the time of the alleged crime, or of mental disease, defect or other condition bearing upon whether he had the mental state required for the offense/offenses charged.

(1) Notice of such claimed defense shall also be filed with the Clerk.

(2) Failure to give such notification in writing shall involve the sanctions set forth in Federal Rules of Criminal Procedure Rule 12.2(d).

v. **Entrapment:** The defendant's attorney shall at the conference disclose to the United States Attorney that defendant will rely on the defense of the procurement of government employees or agents to commit the offense/offenses charged in the information/indictment.

e. **Report of Conference:** Within five (5) days of the completion of the conference required herein, the parties shall file a Joint Statement:

i. That the prescribed conference was held;

ii. The date of the said conference;

iii. The name of the Assistant United States Attorney with whom the conference was held;

iv. The contested matters of discovery and inspection and any additional discovery or inspection desired by the defendant;

v. The fact of disclosure of all material favorable to the defendant or the absence thereof within the meaning of *Brady v. Maryland*, 373 U.S. 83 (1963) and related cases;

vi. The resolution of foundational objections to documentary evidence proposed to be used by both parties (except for the purposes of impeachment);

vii. The resolution of chain of custody (where in issue); and

viii. The resolution of the admissibility of scientific analysis without need of calling the expert at the trial.

f. **Continuing Duty of Counsel:** Any duty of disclosure and discovery set forth herein is a continuing one.

g. **Objections to Evidence:** Unless specific objection to the evidentiary foundation of any document, photograph, book, paper, or other tangible object disclosed by the required conference of counsel is made in the report to the Court hereafter required to be filed, it shall be deemed that the requirement of foundation (including chain of custody) for the introduction of such evidence at trial is waived.

i. If a report produced at the required conference of counsel contains the result of a scientific test, performed by a competent expert witness (as shown by a resume) is not objected to in the report to the Court hereafter required to be filed, an objection to the admissibility of said report in lieu of the testimony of the expert performing such scientific test shall be deemed to have been waived.

h. This order is not intended to preclude discovery by the government pursuant to Fed. R. Crim. P. 16(c).

i. It shall be the joint duty of counsel for the defendant and the United States Attorney to schedule and hold the conference contemplated herein.

i. The United States Attorney shall assure time and availability for such conference within the time herein provided unless the discovery conference is waived in writing by defendant and his counsel and such waiver is filed with the Court.

ii. Counsel for defendant shall (1) have reviewed all the disclosures made and received, and (2) had sufficient discussion with his/her client and the United States attorney by the time of the first status conference with the Court to enable counsel to meaningfully discuss with the Court at said status conference the disposition and likelihood of trial of this case.

iii. The government shall be represented at all status conferences with the Court by the Assistant United States Attorney who is assigned to the trial of the case, and who is most knowledgeable about the aforesaid matters, as well as any other matters scheduled for discussion with the Court at the status conferences.

j. The Clerk is ordered to serve a copy of this Order personally or by mail on all counsel for parties to this action.

9. Trial

a. **Last Conference Prior to Trial:** Before trial commences, the Court will give counsel an opportunity to discuss administrative matters and anticipated procedural or legal problems. At that time, we will discuss *voir dire* procedures, *Batson* objections, and any unusual factors. Counsel for the government shall bring to the meeting the Attached Trial Witness Estimate Form which all counsel should have filled in. In the event defendant's counsel has not provided estimates for cross-examination, she or he will have to do so at the Last Conference.

b. Counsel shall arrive at the courtroom thirty (30) minutes before the scheduled trial time on the first day of trial.

c. Defense counsel MUST present appropriate number of copies of exhibits for all parties to the action.

d. Counsel for the government shall present the Courtroom Deputy Clerk with the following documents on the first day of trial:

i. **Three (3) copies** of the government's witness list.

ii. **Three (3) copies** of the government's exhibit list in the form specified in Local Rule 9.9 (Civil).

iii. **All of the government's exhibits**, with official exhibit tags attached and bearing the same number shown on the exhibit list.

(1) Defendant's counsel does not have to deliver his or her exhibits to the Courtroom Deputy Clerk on the first day of trial; however, defendant's counsel is responsible for affixing completed exhibit tags with the case name and case number to his or her exhibits which are intended to be used in the defendant's case.

(2) Exhibit tags can be obtained from the receptionist in the main Clerk's Office, located at 312 North Spring Street, Room G-8.

(3) Exhibits shall be numbered 1, 2, 3, 4, etc., NOT 1.1, 1.50, etc. Counsel for both (all) sides should agree on the range of numbers to be assigned (e.g., Government exhibits to be 1-99, Defendant One to be 100-199; Defendant Two 200-299, etc.) If a blow up is an enlargement of an existing exhibit, it shall be designated with the number of the original exhibit followed by an "A."

(4) Counsel for the government should be aware that the Court will order that exhibits such as firearms, narcotics, etc., remain in the custody of the agent(s) during the pendency of the trial. The agent(s) will be required to sign the appropriate form in order to take custody of such exhibits. It shall be the responsibility of the agent(s) to produce said items for the Court, secure them at night and guard them at all times while in the courtroom.

iv. **A Bench Book** containing a copy of all exhibits that can be reproduced.

(1) Each exhibit shall be tabbed with the exhibit number for easy referral. Defendant's counsel shall provide the Court with a copy of their exhibits as they are introduced during trial.

v. **Exhibit List:** The exhibit list shall be e-mailed to the Courtroom Deputy Clerk. A copy of the exhibit list with all admitted exhibits will be given to the jury during deliberations. Government and defense counsel shall review and approve the exhibit list with the Courtroom Deputy Clerk prior to it being given to the jury.

vi. **Witness List:** Counsel shall submit a joint witness list listing each witness. Counsel shall identify witnesses who will actually testify at trial.

(1) **Trial Witness Estimate:** The witness list and summary must give accurate time estimates for each witness to conduct direct, cross, redirect and re-cross. Counsel shall include a summary of the testimony of each witness. If more than one witness is offered on the same subject matter, the witness summary should be sufficiently detailed to allow the Court to determine if the testimony is cumulative.

(2) The list shall be substantially in the form indicated by the following example:

CASE:__________ TRIAL DATE:__________

Witness Name	Party Calling Witness and Estimate	Cross- Examiner's Estimate	Description of Testimony	Comments

vii. **Witness Statement:** The United States Attorney shall file with the Court *in camera* a list of the statements of all witnesses to be called by the government in its case in chief.

(1) Such statement shall be filed at least ten (10) days before trial.

(2) Such statement shall include the name of the person taking the statement.

(3) Failure to file such statement with the Court may, at the discretion of the Court, preclude the presentation testimony of any witness whose statement has been previously taken and available to the government.

e. If counsel need to arrange for the installation of their own additional equipment, such as a video monitor, overhead projector, etc., refer to the Court website at www.cacd.uscourts.gov under "Services" in order to reserve this equipment so that necessary arrangements can be made.

f. Before trial commences, the Court will give counsel an opportunity to discuss administrative matters and anticipated procedural or legal issues. During the trial, if there are any matters counsel wish to discuss, counsel shall inform the Courtroom Deputy Clerk.

g. The trial before the jury shall commence promptly at 8:30 a.m. or earlier at the direction of the Court. Counsel are urged to anticipate matters which may need discussion or hearing outside of the presence of the jury and to raise them during this period, during breaks, or at the end of the day.

10. **Joint Statement:** Counsel shall file their Joint Statement of the Case which the Court shall read to all prospective jurors prior to the commencement of *voir dire*. The statement shall not exceed one page. The Joint Statement is to be submitted no later than THE WEDNESDAY OF THE WEEK PRIOR TO TRIAL.

11. Jury Instructions and Verdict Forms

a. **Jury Instructions:** Counsel must submit proposed SUBSTANTIVE and GENERAL instructions.

i. In those cases where a special verdict is desired, counsel shall submit a proposed verdict form with the jury instructions.

b. The parties must submit **joint jury instructions** and a **joint proposed verdict form** (if a special verdict is desired). In order to produce these joint instructions, the parties shall meet and confer sufficiently in advance of the required submission date with the goal of agreeing upon instructions and verdict forms. The jury instructions shall be submitted as follows:

i. JOINT JURY INSTRUCTIONS, those instructions which are agreed to by all parties; and

ii. DISPUTED JURY INSTRUCTIONS, those instructions propounded by a party to which another party objects.

iii. Objections to disputed INSTRUCTIONS shall be filed no later than the FRIDAY BEFORE the trial. Each requested jury instruction shall be numbered and set forth in full on a separate page, citing the authority or source of the requested instruction.

c. The Court prefers counsel to use the instructions from the MANUAL OF MODEL CRIMINAL JURY INSTRUCTIONS FOR THE NINTH CIRCUIT, West Publishing, latest edition. Another suggested source is FEDERAL JURY PRACTICE AND INSTRUCTIONS, Devitt, Blackmar, Wolff and O'Malley, West Publishing Co., current edition.

d. The Court will send several copies of the jury instructions into the jury room for use by the jury during deliberations. Accordingly, in addition to the filed copies, an extra set of the proposed instructions (the "Jury Copy") shall be submitted to the Court with only the text of an instruction on each page (i.e., no titles, supporting authority, indication of party proposing, etc.). This will be referred to as the "Jury Copy" of the instructions. (Duplicates will be made by the Court.)

e. **Special Verdict:** If counsel seek a special verdict, counsel shall follow the procedure set forth in paragraphs b and c in order to formulate a Joint Proposed Verdict Form. Counsel shall submit the proposed verdict form with the proposed jury instructions.

f. An **Index Page** shall accompany all jury instructions that are submitted to the Court. The index shall indicate the following:

i. The number of the instruction;
ii. A brief title of the instruction;
iii. The source of the instruction; and
iv. The page number of the instruction.

For example:

Number	Title	Source	Page Number
1	Duty of the Jury	9th Cir. 1.01	5

12. Instructions Governing Procedure During Trial

a. Criminal trials are held Monday through Friday from 8:30 a.m. to 11:30 a.m. and from 1:00 p.m. to 4:00 p.m.

b. Opening statements, examination of witnesses, and closing arguments should be made from the lectern only.

c. Counsel shall not refer to their clients or any witness by their first names during trial.

d. Counsel shall not discuss the law or argue the case in opening statements.

e. When objecting, counsel shall state only that counsel is objecting and the legal ground of the objection, e.g., hearsay, irrelevant, etc. Counsel shall *not* argue an objection before the jury.

f. Counsel shall *not* approach the Courtroom Deputy Clerk or the witness box without the Court's permission.

g. Counsel shall return to the lectern when his or her purpose has been accomplished.

h. Counsel shall not enter the well of the Court without the Court's permission.

i. Counsel shall rise when addressing the Court. In jury cases, please rise when the jury enters or leaves the courtroom.

j. Counsel shall address all remarks to the Court.

k. Counsel shall not directly address the Courtroom Deputy Clerk, the reporter, or opposing counsel.

l. If counsel wish to speak with opposing counsel, counsel shall ask permission to talk to counsel OFF THE RECORD.

m. All requests for the re-reading of questions or answers or to have an exhibit placed in front of a witness shall be addressed to the Court.

n. Counsel shall not make an offer of stipulation unless counsel has conferred with opposing counsel and reached an agreement.

o. Any stipulation of fact will require the defendant's personal concurrence and shall be submitted to the Court in writing for approval.

p. A proposed stipulation shall be explained to him or her in advance.

q. While the Court is in session, counsel shall not leave the counsel table to confer with investigators, secretaries, or witnesses unless permission is granted in advance.

r. When a party has more than one lawyer, only one may conduct the examination of a given witness and only that same lawyer may handle objections during the testimony of that witness.

s. If a witness was on the stand at a recess or adjournment, counsel shall have the witness back on the stand and ready to proceed when Court resumes.

t. Counsel shall not run out of witnesses. If counsel is out of witnesses and there is more than a brief delay, the Court may deem that counsel has rested.

u. The Court attempts to cooperate with doctors and other professional witnesses and will, except in extraordinary circumstances, accommodate them by permitting them to be out of sequence. Counsel should anticipate any such possibility and discuss it with opposing counsel. If there is an objection, counsel shall confer with the Court in advance.

v. Counsel are advised to be on time as the Court starts promptly.

w. Counsel should not by facial expression, nodding, or other conduct exhibit any opinions, adverse or favorable, concerning any testimony which is being given by a witness. Counsel should similarly admonish their own clients and witnesses to avoid such conduct.

x. SPEAK UP when making an objection, the acoustics in the courtroom make it difficult for all to hear an objection when it is being made.

y. **Questionnaires:** If any counsel wishes to submit a written questionnaire to each prospective juror, s/he shall move in writing for leave to do so, and shall include the proposed questionnaire with the motion. Because the Jury Department needs ample time to arrange for pre-selected jurors to be available to complete a questionnaire, such motion shall be filed not later than nine (9) weeks before the trial date, to be heard not later than five (5) weeks before the trial date.

z. ***Voir Dire*:** At least four (4) court days prior to trial, each counsel shall file with the Clerk and served on opposing counsel any special question requested to be put to prospective jurors on *voir dire*. The parties need not submit requests for standard *voir dire* questions, such as education, current occupation, marital status, prior jury service, etc., but should include only proposed questions specifically tailored to the parties and issues of the case.

13. Motions and Motion Cut-Off Date: Unless the Local Rules prescribe a different time for filing a particular motion, all pretrial motions and motions in limine, except motions governed by Local Criminal Rule 9, shall be filed and served not later than twenty-one (21) days before the trial and set for hearing not later than the Monday eight (8) days prior to trial at 9:00 a.m., or otherwise allowed by the Court. Counsel's estimate of the time required for presentation of the motion must be set forth adjacent to the caption.

a. The party opposing the motion shall file a response not later than fourteen (14) days before trial or not later than seven (7) days after service of the motion, whichever is earlier, or as otherwise allowed by the Court. Responding counsel's estimate of the time required for presentation of opposition of the motion must be set forth in the caption of the responding papers.

b. All criminal law and motion matters shall be filed on the electronic filing system.

c. Memoranda of points and authorities in support of or in opposition to motions shall not exceed twenty-five (25) pages. Replies shall not exceed twelve (12) pages. Only in rare instances and for good cause shown will the Court grant an application to extend page limitations. No supplemental brief shall be filed without proof of leave of Court. Typeface shall comply with Local Rule 11-3.1.1. (Civil). **NOTE:** If the Times Roman font is used, the size must be no less than 14; if Courier is used, the size must be no less than 12. Footnotes shall be in typeface no less than one size smaller than text size and shall be used sparingly. Filings which do not conform to the Local Rules and this Order will not be considered.

14. Motions to Suppress: Motions to Suppress must be filed thirty-five (35) days prior to the trial date and set for hearing two (2) weeks prior to the trial date at 8:30 a.m.

15. Sentencing Proceedings: Sentencing proceedings are conducted pursuant to Fed. R. Crim. P. 32(a) of the Federal Rules of Criminal Procedure and the Local Rules. If any party wishes to present material to the Court related to the sentencing, such party must file, or otherwise make available to, and serve opposing counsel/parties and the assigned United States Probation Officer, such information or evidence no later than **two (2) weeks** before the scheduled sentencing hearing. The foregoing notwithstanding, a statement of each party's position concerning sentencing shall be filed, or otherwise made available, and served no later than two (2) weeks before the sentencing hearing and the proof of service shall reflect service on the Probation Officer. The Probation Officer must be able to prepare and disclose any addendum that may be required in response to new information and/or evidence and/or a party's sentencing position. Failure to timely file or present and serve such information or evidence or statement of position may result in such information not being considered by the Court in imposing a defendant's sentence.

If any item regarding pretrial or trial is not specifically addressed in this Order, the Local Rules and Federal Rules of Criminal Procedure shall be observed.

The Court thanks counsel and the parties for their anticipated cooperation.

DATED: ______________

____

S. JAMES OTERO
United States District Judge

B. Initial Standing Order for Cases Assigned to Judge Otero

IN THE UNITED STATES DISTICT COURT
FOR THE CENTRAL DISTRICT OF CALIFORNIA

Plaintiff(s),
v.
Defendant(s).

Case No. ______________

INITIAL STANDING ORDER FOR CASES ASSIGNED TO JUDGE S. JAMES OTERO

READ THIS ORDER CAREFULLY.
IT CONTROLS THIS CASE AND DIFFERS
IN SOME RESPECTS FROM THE LOCAL RULES.

- Plaintiff(s) must immediately serve this Order on all Defendant(s) along with the Summons and Complaint.
- If this case was assigned to this Court after being removed from state court, the Defendant(s) who removed the case must serve this Order on all other parties. This case has been assigned to the calendar of Judge S. James Otero. To secure the just, speedy and inexpensive determination of this action, counsel are ordered to familiarize themselves with the Federal Rules of Civil Procedure ("Fed. R. Civ. P.") and the Local Rules ("L.R.") of the Central District of California.

In an effort to provide further guidance to the parties, the Court notes the following:

1. **Court Hours:** Civil motions are heard on Monday at 10:00 a.m., unless the Court orders otherwise. (If Monday is a holiday, the next motion date is Tuesday following the holiday.) It is not necessary to clear a motion date. Do not call the clerk to reserve a hearing date; comply with Local Rules.

2. **Location:** Judge Otero's courtroom is: Courtroom 1, United States District Court, 312 North Spring Street, 2nd Floor, Los Angeles, California 90012.

3. **E-Filing of Civil Cases:** E-filing is **mandatory** for all new and pending civil cases. The Court adheres to the e-filing practices of the Central District of California (see http://support.cacd.uscourts.gov) **with two important exceptions**:

   a. The deadline to e-file a document is 4:00 p.m.; any document e-filed after 4:00 p.m. will be deemed filed on the next court day.

   b. For every e-filed motion and ex parte application, the moving party must e-mail the Court at **Judge Otero's generice - mail address (SJO_Chambers@cacd.uscourts.gov)** a Word or WordPerfect version of the proposed order, pursuant to the e-filing rules in General Order 08-02.

4. **Mandatory Chambers Copies:** Mandatory chambers copies are required only for e-filed documents. One mandatory chambers copy must be delivered to the chambers copy box located at the door of Courtroom 1, by <u>12 noon the day after the document was e-filed</u>. This mandatory chambers copy must be blue-backed and two-hole punched as if it were a manual filing, and the caption page must indicate the date and time the document was e-filed (place date and time of filing below title of filing on the caption page). *All original filings not subject to the e-filing requirements are to be filed at the*

filing window (Clerk's Office, Room G-19, Spring Street Courthouse), NOT in chambers and NOT in the courtroom.

5. **Telephone Inquiries:** Telephone inquiries regarding the status of a motion, stipulation, or proposed order are not returned. Do not call the clerk to check the docket.

6. **Communications with Chambers:** Counsel are not to initiate telephone calls to Judge Otero's chambers, law clerks or assistant. Counsel may access the Court's website (www.cacd.uscourts.gov) for Local Rules, filing procedures, **judges' procedures** and schedules, calendars, forms and Pacer access. Additional questions can be resolved by accessing the Western Division 24-hour automated calling system ((213) 894-1565) or the case docket. Only in the event that counsel cannot find the desired information through all available resources, counsel may contact the Courtroom Deputy Clerk, Victor Cruz, by telephone at (213) 894-1796 or by e-mail at victor_cruz@cacd.uscourts.gov.

7. **Service of Pleadings:** Plaintiff must promptly serve the Complaint in accordance with Fed. R. Civ. P. 4 and file proof of service pursuant to L.R. 5-3.1. Any defendant not timely served will be dismissed from the action. Any "DOE" or fictitiously named defendant who is not identified and served within 120 days after the case is filed will be dismissed pursuant to Fed. R. Civ. P. 4(m).

8. **Assignment to a Magistrate Judge:** Under 28 U.S.C. § 636, the parties may consent to have a magistrate judge preside over all proceedings, including trial. Magistrate judges who accept those designations are identified on the Central District's website, which also contains the consent form.

9. **Temporary Restraining Orders and Injunctions:** Parties seeking emergency or provisional relief must comply with Fed. R. Civ. P. 65 and L.R. 65.

10. **Calendar Conflicts:** If there is a calendar conflict, counsel are to inform the Courtroom Deputy Clerk as soon as possible prior to the date of the conflict and are to follow the Local Rules and Federal Rules of Procedure.

11. **Transcripts:** To order a transcript, e-mail the Court Recording Department at courtrecording_cacd@cacd.uscourts.gov. The Court uses a court recorder, Margarita Lopez. Margarita Lopez may be reached at (213) 894-2717.

12. **Motions to Reconsider:** L.R. 7-18 is strictly enforced.

13. **Actions Invoking Subject Matter Jurisdiction Based on Diversity:** The burden of persuasion for establishing diversity jurisdiction rests on the party asserting it and must be supported by competent proof.

    To determine a corporation's "principal place of business" for the purposes of diversity jurisdiction, the Court will apply the "nerve center" test, which was adopted by the U.S. Supreme Court in *Hertz Corp. v. Friend*, 130 S.Ct. 1181 (2010). The "nerve center" test looks to the single location where the "corporation's high level officers direct, control, and coordinate the corporation's activities." *Hertz Corp. v. Friend*, 130 S.Ct. 1181 (2010). The "nerve center" will typically be the corporation's headquarters, provided that the headquarters is the actual center of direction, control, and coordination, and not simply an office where the corporation holds its board meetings. *Id.* For the purposes of simplicity and clarity in jurisdictional matters, the

Court has abandoned previous Circuit tests that required complex balancing factors and whose outcomes were difficult to predict. *Id.*

If a party seeks to remove an action to this Court on the basis of diversity in a case where it is not clear from the Complaint that more than $75,000 is in controversy, the removing party must prove by a preponderance of the evidence that the amount in controversy meets the jurisdictional threshold. *Matheson v. Progressive Specialty Ins. Co.*, 319 F.3d 1089, 1090 (9th Cir. 2003). The Court will consider facts presented in the removal petition as well as any summary-judgment-type evidence relevant to the amount in controversy at time of removal. *Id.* Conclusory allegations as to the amount in controversy are insufficient. *Id.*

Parties must file an Amended Complaint or Notice of Removal within **fifteen days from the date the action is assigned to Judge Otero** if there is a doubt as to whether they have met the test outlined in *Hertz*, whether they have otherwise established the citizenship of the parties, or whether they have established the amount in controversy. Failure to comply may result in dismissal or remand.

14. **Timing of Motions:** Parties must strictly comply with L.R. 6-1, 7-9 and 7-10.

15. **Scheduling Conference:** Scheduling conferences are held as soon as practicable and not later than 180 days from the filing of the Complaint. Trial counsel must be present.

    Counsel must timely comply with Fed. R. Civ. P. 26(f) and file a Joint Rule 26(f) Report within ten days after they meet and confer. The Report must, in addition to addressing the matters specified in Rule 26(f), set forth the parties' views regarding:

    a. A cut-off date for the completion of discovery and the hearing of motions, a final pretrial conference date, and a trial date;

    b. Whether discovery should be conducted in phases or otherwise ordered or limited;

    c. An estimate of the length of trial;

    d. Efforts made to settle or resolve the case to date, and the parties' plans for maximizing settlement prospects;

    e. Whether the case is complex or requires a reference to the procedures set forth in the Manual on Complex Litigation;

    f. The likelihood of the appearance of additional parties;

    g. Dispositive or partially dispositive motions the parties are likely to file;

    h. Any unusual legal issues presented by the case; and

    i. Proposals regarding severance, bifurcation or other ordering of proof.

    The Court does not hold telephonic conferences.

16. **Patent Cases - Scheduling Conference and Adoption of Local Rules:**

    a. Applicability of the Northern District of California Patent Local Rules: The parties are encouraged to use the Northern District of California Patent Local Rules ("P.L.R.") only in complex cases such as those involving computer technology, pharmaceuticals or cases involving Ph.D.-level skill. Parties must state in the Joint Rule 26(f) Report whether the parties have agreed to abide by the P.L.R. If the parties do not agree to use the P.L.R. or disagree only to the time line included therein, they must state their positions for disagreement in the Joint Rule 26(f) Report. In any case, the ultimate decision regarding all scheduling matters, including whether to apply the P.L.R., lies with the Court. The Court will take into consideration several factors, such as: number of patents at issue; number of claims asserted; number of likely disputed claims and the ease with which the parties can identify the claim language that will resolve their dispute; and complexity of the technology.

b. Claim Construction Hearings: The Court may hold claim construction hearings and hear argument from counsel. However, the Court generally does not hear expert testimony at claim construction hearings.

c. Joint Claim Construction Chart: The joint claim construction chart must be in a three-column format.

d. Time Line for Patent Cases Not Using Patent Local Rules: For cases in which the Court has elected not to use the P.L.R., the parties must include proposed deadlines in the Rule 26(f) Report, including expert report dates, discovery cut-off dates and a date for the claim construction hearing.

e. Time Line for Patent Cases Using Patent Local Rules: For cases in which the Court has elected to use the P.L.R., parties must include proposed deadlines in the Rule 26(f) Report. Parties may find the following list of suggested deadlines and dates helpful in writing their Rule 26(f) Report:

(1) One month after the Complaint is filed, the "Disclosure of Asserted Claims and Preliminary Infringement Contentions" under P.L.R. 3-1 is to be served on all parties.

(2) Three months after the Complaint is filed is the deadline to amend the pleadings to add and serve new parties, to bring third-party claims or to bring cross-claims.

(3) Four months after the Complaint is filed, the "Preliminary Invalidity Contentions" under P.L.R. 3-3 is due.

(4) Six months after the Complaint is filed, the "Joint Claim Construction Chart and Prehearing Statement" under P.L.R. 4-3 is due.

(5) Seven months after the Complaint is filed, claim construction discovery, both fact and expert, is to be completed.

(6) Discovery with regard to damages begins the day after the fact and expert discovery for the claim construction is due.

(7) Eight months after the Complaint is filed, the plaintiff's claim construction opening brief is due. Defendant's claim construction opposition is due two weeks after the opening brief is due and the plaintiff's claim construction reply is due two weeks after the opposition is due.

(8) Nine months after the Complaint is filed, a claim construction hearing is held.

(9) No sooner than one day after the Court's ruling on claim construction but no later than ten months after the filing of the Complaint, the "Final Infringement Contentions" are due, along with any motion for summary judgment regarding infringement.

(10) No sooner than after the "Final Infringement Contentions" are filed but no later than eleven months after the filing of the Complaint, the "Final Invalidity Contentions" are due, along with any motion for summary judgment regarding invalidity or unenforceability or non-infringement.

(11) Eleven months after the filing of the Complaint is the motion cut-off date for all motions other than motions for summary judgment on infringement.

(12) Eleven months after the Complaint is filed all discovery must be completed.

(13) One week before the trial, the pretrial conference will be held.

(14) Fourteen months after the filing of the Complaint, the trial will commence.

17. Discovery: Discovery motions and applications for discovery protective orders must be scheduled before the magistrate judge assigned to the case.

a. Non-Expert Discovery: All expert / non-expert discovery must be completed by the discovery cut-off set by the Court. Any motion challenging the adequacy of discovery responses must be calendared sufficiently in advance of the cut-off date to permit any compelled responses to be obtained before that date.

b. Non-Expert Depositions: All depositions must commence sufficiently in advance of the discovery cut-off date to permit their completion and to permit the deposing party enough time to bring any discovery motions concerning the deposition prior to the cut-off date. Given the requirements of notice and "meet and confer," this means that in most cases a planned motion to compel must be discussed with opposing counsel approximately six weeks before the cut-off.

c. Written Discovery: All interrogatories, requests for production of documents, and requests for admissions must be served sufficiently in advance of the discovery cutoff to enable the discovering party to challenge (via motion) deficient responses.

d. Discovery Motions: Parties are expected to resolve discovery disputes among themselves in a courteous, reasonable, and professional manner. Absent resolution, the magistrate judge assigned to the case will rule on discovery motions. The Court requires compliance with L.R. 37-1 through 37-4 in the preparation and filing of discovery motions. Any review of a magistrate judge's discovery order must proceed by way of noticed motion under L.R. 7-3. The decision of the magistrate judge is final. The Court will not reverse any such order, including one imposing sanctions, unless the moving party demonstrates that the magistrate judge's order "is clearly erroneous or contrary to law." A motion for review and reconsideration must be filed and served within ten days of a written ruling or within ten days of an oral ruling that the magistrate judge states will not be followed by a written ruling.

e. Expert Discovery: The parties must meet and confer and agree upon expert disclosure dates as required by Fed. R. Civ. P. 26(2). All disclosures must be made in writing. The parties should commence expert discovery shortly after the initial designation of experts, because the final pretrial conference and trial dates will not be continued merely because expert discovery is still underway.

18. Motions and Motion Cut-Off Date:

a. Meet and Confer Requirement: For all cases not exempt under L.R. 16-12, and except in connection with discovery motions, applications for temporary restraining orders or preliminary injunctions, counsel contemplating filing of any motion, shall first contact opposing counsel to "discuss *thoroughly*, preferably in person, the *substance* of the contemplated motion *and any potential resolution*." L.R. 7-3. The Court construes this requirement strictly. Half-hearted attempts at compliance with this rule will not satisfy counsel's obligation. The parties must discuss the substantive grounds for the motion and attempt to reach an accord that would eliminate the need for the motion. The Court strongly emphasizes that under L.R. 7-3, discussions of the substance of contemplated motions are to take place, if at all possible, in person. Only in exceptional cases will a telephonic conference be allowed. All motions must include a declaration by counsel briefly describing the parties' discussion and attempt to eliminate the need for the motion and the date of such discussion. Filings not in compliance with L.R. 7-3 will be denied.

b. Unless required to be filed electronically as referenced in Paragraph 7 of this Order, all motions, oppositions and replies must be filed at the filing window (Clerk's Office, Room G-19, Spring Street Courthouse). If mailing a civil filing, direct documents to: Filing Window, Civil Section, Clerk's Office, Room G-19, 312 North Spring Street, Los Angeles, California 90012.

c. All law and motion matters, except for motions in limine, must be set for hearing (not filing) by the motion hearing cut-off date. Issues left undetermined after passage of the cut-off date should be listed as issues for trial in the final pretrial conference order. As an exception, motions in limine dealing with evidentiary matters will be heard (at the Court's discretion) at the start of trial; however, the Court will not hear or resolve summary judgment motions disguised as motions in limine.

d. **Local Rule 7 governs the form of motions.** *See generally* L.R. 7. If a party does not oppose a motion, that party must file a statement of non-opposition. L.R. 7-16. Failure to meet the time limits set forth in L.R. 7 may be deemed consent to the granting of the motion. L.R. 7-12. The Court will not decide late-filed motions, and a party or counsel who files such late papers may be subject to sanctions under L.R. 7-13. Reply papers are limited to argument and authorities responsive to the opposition papers. The Court will not address new matter that was improperly introduced.

19. Motions - Form and Length: All pleadings must comply with L.R. 11, except that no memorandum or points and authorities or opposition may exceed twenty pages, excluding indices and exhibits, unless permitted by the Court. No reply may exceed five pages.

a. Summary Judgment Motions: Parties need not wait until the motion cut-off to bring motions for summary judgment or partial summary judgment. The moving party is expected to provide more than the minimum twenty-eight day notice. Because these motions are fact-dependent, parties should prepare papers in a fashion that will assist the Court in absorbing the mass of facts (e.g., tables of contents, headings, indices). The parties are to comply precisely with L.R. 56-1 through 56-4.

b. Without prior permission of the Court, no party may file more than one motion pursuant to Fed. R. Civ. P. 56 regardless of whether such motion is denominated as a motion for summary judgment or summary adjudication.

c. Statement of Undisputed Facts and Statement of Genuine Issues: The separate statement of undisputed facts must be prepared in a two-column format. The left-hand column sets forth the allegedly undisputed fact. The right-hand column sets forth the evidence that supports the factual statement. The opposing party's statement of genuine issues must be in two columns and track the movant's separate statement exactly as prepared. The opposing party may submit additional material facts that bear on or relate to the issues raised by the movant, which must follow the format described above for the moving party's separate statement.

d. Supporting Evidence: Supporting evidence should be submitted either by way of stipulation or as exhibits to declarations sufficient to authenticate the proffered evidence, and should not be attached to the memorandum of points and authorities. Documentary evidence as to which there is no stipulation regarding foundation must be accompanied by the testimony of a witness who can establish authenticity.

e. Objections to Evidence: If a party disputes a fact based in whole or in part on an evidentiary objection, the ground of the objection, as indicated above, should be stated in a separate statement but not argued in that document.

f. Oral Argument: If the Court deems a matter appropriate for decision without oral argument, the Court will notify the parties in advance.

g. Amici Status: The Court has broad discretion to appoint amicus curiae. Interested parties must request leave of the Court before filing an amicus brief, by showing:

- **(1)** That they have a "special interest" in the case;
- **(2)** That this interest is not represented competently or at all;
- **(3)** That they present information that is both timely and useful; and
- **(4)** That they are not partial to a particular outcome of the case.

20. Requests for Extensions of Time to File Documents or Continue Dates: The deadlines and requirements set by the Court are firm. No stipulations extending scheduling requirements or modifying applicable rules are effective unless and until approved by the Court. Applications and stipulations must set forth:

a. The existing due date or hearing date;

b. Specific, concrete reasons supporting good cause for granting the extension. A statement that an extension "will promote settlement" is insufficient. The requesting party or parties must indicate the status of ongoing negotiations (i.e.,

Have written proposals been exchanged? Is counsel reviewing a draft settlement agreement? Has a mediator been selected?); and

c. Whether there have been prior requests for extensions, and whether these were granted or denied by the Court.

The pretrial conference and trial dates <u>will not be continued</u> solely because the parties are in the process of settling or have "settled." If the parties wish to avoid the pretrial conference or trial, a valid stipulated dismissal under Fed. R. Civ. P. 41 must be filed at least one court day in advance.

21. Ex Parte Applications: Ex parte applications are discouraged. *Mission Power Eng'g Co. v. Cont'l Casualty Co.*, 883 F. Supp. 488 (C.D. Cal. 1995). Strictly comply with L.R. 7-19.

22. Settlement: L.R. 16-15 requires the parties to participate in one of the settlement procedures set forth in the Rule. The settlement conference must be concluded not later than thirty days before the pretrial conference. The Court may hold and preside over the settlement conference in certain cases. The Court on its own motion may set a settlement conference at any time following the scheduling conference. If the settlement conference is set before this Court, the parties must comply with L.R. 16-15.5.

23. Procedures for Settlement Conferences Held Before Judge Otero:

a. <u>Settlement Conference Briefs:</u> The parties must submit confidential settlement conference briefs to chambers in accordance with L.R. 16-15 **five days** before the conference, and must exchange non-confidential letters with all other parties of record. Each confidential settlement conference brief must contain:

(1) A summary of the important issues and the party's position on each issue;

(2) A summary regarding damages in a non-conclusory form; and

(3) A summary on the course of any prior settlement negotiations.

The brief must be concise, and large numbers of exhibits may not be appended. Proposals for settlement and counsel's evaluation of the case not yet communicated to opposing counsel must be included in the confidential settlement letter.

b. <u>Persons Present:</u> All persons whose consent is necessary to conclude settlement must be present at the settlement conference. Counsel are responsible for ensuring that all persons and parties are present.

c. <u>The Conference:</u> The Court will confer with the attorneys and representatives jointly and separately. Each party must be prepared to negotiate for as long as prospects of settlement are not foreclosed. The Court may confer with the parties in the presence of their attorneys. If settlement is reached, it will be placed on the record at the conclusion of the conference.

24. Trial Preparation:

a. <u>Pretrial Conference and L.R. 16 Filings</u>

The final pretrial conference ("PTC") will be held at 9:00 a.m. on the date set by the Court, unless expressly waived by the Court at the scheduling conference. The lead trial attorney on behalf of each party must attend the PTC and all meetings in preparation thereof. A continuance of the PTC at the parties' request or by stipulation is unlikely. Failure to complete discovery is not a ground for continuance.

At the PTC, parties should be prepared to discuss means of streamlining the trial, including: bifurcation; presentation of foundational and non-critical testimony by deposition excerpts, narrative summaries and stipulations as to the content of testimony; and qualification of experts by admitted resumes. The Court will also discuss settlement.

If counsel fail to file the required pretrial documents or fail to appear at the PTC and such failure is not otherwise satisfactorily explained to the Court: (a) the case will be dismissed for failure to prosecute, if such failure occurs on the part of the plaintiff; (b) default judgment will be entered, if such failure occurs on the part of the defendant; or (c) the Court may take such action as it deems appropriate. Failure of counsel to strictly follow the provisions of this Order may subject the non-complying party and its attorney to sanctions and may constitute a waiver of jury trial.

b. Pretrial Documents Must Comply with the Local Rules

(1) Pretrial Conference Order ("PTCO"): The [Proposed] PTCO must be lodged seven calendar days before the PTC. Parties are to consult Appendix A to the Local Rules in preparing the PTCO. In addition, parties must heed the following:

(a) Include a table of contents at the beginning of the PTCO.

(b) Place in "all caps" and in "bold" the separately numbered headings for each category in the PTCO (e.g., "1. **THE PARTIES**").

(c) In specifying the surviving pleadings under section 1 of Appendix A, state which claims or counterclaims have been dismissed or abandoned (e.g., "Plaintiff's first cause of action for fraud has been dismissed.") In multiple party cases where not all claims will be prosecuted against all remaining parties on the opposing side, specify to which party each claim is directed.

(d) In drafting the PTCO, the parties must attempt to agree on and set forth as many uncontested facts as possible. These facts are usually read to the jury at the start of trial. A carefully drafted stipulation of facts will reduce the length of trial and increase jury understanding of the case.

(e) In drafting the factual issues in dispute for the PTCO, the parties must state issues in ultimate fact form, not in the form of evidentiary fact issues. The issues of fact should track the elements of a claim or defense on which the jury will be required to make findings.

(f) Issues of law should state legal issues on which the Court will be required to rule during the trial, and should not list ultimate fact issues to be submitted to the trier of fact.

(2) Memoranda of Contentions of Fact and Law: Not later than twenty-one days in advance of the PTC, each party must serve and file a memorandum of contentions of fact and law containing a summary of the parties' basic factual contentions supported by legal authority in the form of a legal brief. L.R. 16-4.

(3) Joint Witness List: Not later than twenty-one days in advance of the PTC, the parties must submit a joint witness list in accordance with L.R. 16-5, except that the parties need not submit separate witness lists. The joint witness list must identify:

(a) All witnesses who will actually testify at trial. Failure to include the name of a witness may preclude a party from calling that witness.

(b) Trial Witness Estimate: The witness list and summary must give accurate time estimates for each witness to conduct direct, cross, re-direct, and re-cross. Counsel must include a summary of the testimony of each witness. If more than one witness is offered on the same subject matter, each summary must enable the Court to determine if the testimony is cumulative.

(c) Expert Witnesses: An expert witness's direct testimony must consist of a description of the expert's background and contents of her Rule 26 Report.

(4) Joint Exhibit List: Not later than twenty-one days in advance of the PTC, the parties must submit a joint exhibit list in accordance with L.R. 16-6.1 and Fed. R. Civ. P. 26(a)(3)(A)(iii). The list must also include an appropriate identification of each document or exhibit which the party expects to offer for impeachment purposes and those which the party may offer if the need arises. The list must be substantially in the form indicated by the following example:

Case Title: ____________________ *Case No.:* ____________________

Exhibit No.	*Description*	*Date Identified*	*Date Admitted*

Counsel must meet and confer and stipulate to authenticity and other foundational objections. Place exhibits in binders with each exhibit properly marked and tabbed.

(5) Pretrial Exhibit Stipulation: The parties must prepare a pretrial exhibit stipulation containing each party's numbered list of all trial exhibits, with objections to each exhibit and the offering party's response. All exhibits to which there is no objection will be admitted. All parties must stipulate to the authenticity of exhibits whenever possible. Identify any exhibits whose authenticity has not been stipulated to and the specific reasons for the parties' failure to stipulate. The stipulation must be in the following form:

Plaintiff's Exhibits

Exhibit No.	*Description*	*If Objection, State Grounds*	*Response to Objection*

Defendant's Exhibits

Exhibit No.	*Description*	*If Objection, State Grounds*	*Response to Objection*

The pretrial exhibit stipulation must be filed at the same time counsel lodge the PTCO. Failure to so comply may constitute a waiver of all objections.

(6) Motions in Limine Are Heard the First Day of Trial and Must Conform to the Local Rules and the Following Format:

(a) The parties must file any motions in limine thirty-five days before the trial date. Any opposition must be filed seven days thereafter. Any reply must be filed seven days thereafter. In addition, five court days before the PTC, each party must deliver to chambers a three-ring binder of its motions in limine, together with the objections and replies.

(b) If any of the issues addressed in said motions were raised in prior proceedings, counsel are to identify the proceedings and relevant pleadings.

(c) The binders must be clearly marked as to their content (e.g., Plaintiff's Motions in Limine Nos. 1-9) and each motion must be separated by marked dividers, identifying the particular motion. The spine of each binder must include the case name and number as well as the content of the binder.

(d) Binders should only contain the points of law, no declarations.

(e) Points and authorities, including motions in limine, may not exceed ten pages. Opposition to points and authorities may not exceed ten pages. Replies to points and authorities may not exceed five pages.

(f) In lodging deposition transcripts, counsel must stipulate to their authenticity.

(7) Jury Instructions and Verdict Forms: At the PTC, counsel must submit the text of each jury instruction in two sets.

(a) Set one consists of instructions that all parties agree should be submitted to the jury, and includes general and substantive instructions, a verdict form, and, if necessary, special interrogatories. "Substantive jury instructions" means all instructions relating to the elements of all claims and defenses in the case. Parties should also submit standard and general instructions.

(b) Set two consists of instructions that are objected to. Proposed special verdict forms are to be included. This second set must include a joint statement regarding the disputed instructions, verdicts and interrogatories. In the joint statement, place the text of the disputed instruction (or verdict or interrogatory) with an identification of the party proposing it. Following that text, place the opposing party's statement of objections with legal authority in support thereof (one page or less) and proposed alternative language if appropriate. The entirety of the objection must be typed in capital letters.

(c) A table of contents must be included with all jury instructions submitted to the Court. The table of contents must set forth: (i) the number of the instruction; (ii) a brief title of the instruction; (iii) the source of the instruction; and (iv) the page number of the instruction.

For example:

Number	*Title*	*Source*	*Page Number*
[1]	*[Burden of Proof]*	*[cite]*	*[5]*

(d) The Court prefers counsel to use instructions from the Manual of Model Jury Instructions for the Ninth Circuit where applicable. Where California law is to be applied, the Court requires counsel to use the State of California Judicial Council Approved Civil Jury Instructions.

(e) Modifications of instructions from the foregoing sources (or any other form instructions) must specifically state the modification made to the original form instruction and the authority supporting the modification.

(8) Joint Statement of the Case and Voir Dire: The Court conducts voir dire. At the PTC, the parties must submit separate proposed voir dire questions and a one page joint statement of the case, which is read to the jury pool. The parties need not submit requests for standard voir dire questions, but should include only proposed questions specifically tailored to the parties and issues of the case.

(9) Real-Time Reporting Requirement: At the PTC, each party must submit to the Deputy Clerk a typed list of proper names, unusual or scientific terms, or any other uncommon words that are likely to be used during the trial.

c. Bench Trial:

(1) Findings of Fact and Conclusions of Law: The parties must lodge their proposed findings of fact and conclusions of law no later than seven days before trial and deliver to chambers a digital copy of these findings in WordPerfect format. L.R. 52-1.

(2) Narrative Statements: The judge requires that the direct testimony of a witness be presented by written narrative statement subject to cross-examination at trial, to be adopted by the witness orally in open court, unless such requirement is waived. L.R. 43-1.

d. Installation of equipment: If counsel need to arrange for the installation of their own additional equipment, such as a video monitor, overhead projector, etc., refer to the Court website at www.cacd.uscourts.gov under "Services" in order to reserve this equipment so that necessary arrangements can be made. ELMO reservations/tutorials may be made through the Space and Facilities Help Desk, (213) 894-1400.

e. Voluminous exhibits: Arrangements for bringing voluminous exhibits into the courtroom may be made through Space and Facilities Help Desk.

25. Instructions Governing Procedure During Trial

a. Civil trials are held Monday through Friday from 8:30 a.m. to 11:30 a.m. and from 1:00 p.m. to 4:00 p.m.

b. Opening statements, examination of witnesses, and closing arguments should be made from the lectern only.

c. Counsel shall not refer to their clients or any witness by their first names during trial.

d. When objecting, counsel shall state only that counsel is objecting and the legal ground of the objection, e.g., hearsay, irrelevant, etc. Counsel shall not argue an objection before the jury.

e. Counsel shall not approach the Courtroom Deputy Clerk or the wintess box without the Court's permission.

f. Counsel shall return to the lectern when his or her purpose has been accomplished.

g. Counsel shall not enter the well of the Court without the Court's permission.

h. Counsel shall rise when addressing the Court. In jury cases, please rise when the jury enters or leaves the courtroom.

i. Counsel shall address all remarks to the Court.

j. Counsel shall not directly address the Courtroom Deputy Clerk, the reporter, or opposing counsel.

k. If counsel wish to speak with opposing counsel, counsel shall ask permission to talk to counsel OFF THE RECORD.

l. All requests for the re-reading of questions or answers or to have an exhibit placed in front of a witness shall be addressed to the Court.

m. Counsel shall not make an offer of stipulation unless counsel has conferred with opposing counsel and reached an agreement.

n. While the court is in session, counsel shall not leave the counsel table to confer with investigators, secretaries, or witnesses unless permission is granted in advance.

o. When a party has more than one lawyer, only one may conduct the examination of any given witness and only that same lawyer may handle objections during the testimony of that witness.

p. If a witness was on the stand at a recess or adjournment, counsel shall have the witness back on the stand and ready to proceed when Court resumes.

q. Counsel shall not run out of witnesses. If counsel is out of witnesses and there is more than a brief delay, the Court may deem that counsel has rested.

r. The Court attempts to cooperate with doctors and other professional witnesses and will, except in extraordinary circumstances, accommodate them by permitting them to be out of sequence. Counsel should anticipate any such possibility and discuss it with opposing counsel. If there is an objection, counsel shall confer with the Court in advance.

s. Counsel are advised to be on time as the Court starts promptly.

t. Counsel should not by facial expression, nodding, or other conduct exhibit any opinions, adverse or favorable, concerning any testimony which is being given by a witness. Counsel should similarly admonish their own clients and witnesses to avoid such conduct.

u. SPEAK UP when making an objection, the acoustics in the courtroom make it difficult for all to hear an objection when it is being made.

26. Protective Orders and Motions to Seal Documents

a. Protective Orders. The parties are permitted to enter into stipulated protective orders that govern how the parties are required to handle confidential material produced in discovery.

b. Sealing Determinations. It is the Court, not the parties, that determines whether a document can be filed under seal. Protective orders cannot pre-authorize a party to file documents under seal. The Court will only permit filings under seal if the party seeking to seal the information demonstrates why the public's traditional right of access to court documents and the public policies favoring disclosure are outweighed by good cause (if the motion is not case-dispositive) or compelling reasons (if the motion is case-dispositive) that support keeping the information under seal. The fact that a party has designated a particular document "Confidential" pursuant to a protective order is not sufficient to convince the Court that good cause or compelling reasons exist to seal that document. If a protective order attempts to authorize the filing of materials under seal without an independent showing of good cause or compelling reasons, the protective order will be rejected or that provision will be ignored.

c. Noticed Motions in Cases with Protective Orders. **In any case where the parties have entered into a stipulated protective order, noticed motions must be noticed at least 35 days before the hearing date.**

d. Filing One's Own Confidential Documents with the Court. Any party who wishes to file its own confidential material with the Court and have that information sealed must submit an application to seal concurrently with the filing of the document containing the confidential information.

e. Filing Another Party's Confidential Documents with the Court.

1. Meet-and-Confer Requirement. If a party wishes to file in Court a document containing information another party has designated "Confidential" pursuant to a protective order, the party filing the document (the "Filing Party") must give the party that designated the material "Confidential" (the "Designating Party") at least seven calendar days' notice, informing the Designating Party which specific documents or information the Filing Party intends to file with the Court and the date of the anticipated filing. No fewer than four calendar days prior to the anticipated filing, the Designating Party must inform the Filing Party which of the identified material it intends to move to seal. This subsection applies to any noticed motion or opposition to a noticed motion.

2. Filing Documents. If the Designating Party informs the Filing Party that it intends to move to seal certain information, the Filing Party must submit a public version of the document that redacts only the specific information the Designating Party seeks to seal. The Filing Party must also lodge conditionally under seal unredacted versions of the document with the Court. This subsection applies to any noticed motion or opposition to a noticed motion.

3. Timing of Applications to Seal. If the Designating Party wishes to seal certain information, it must file an application to seal on or before the date the Filing Party files the document containing the confidential information. This subsection applies to any noticed motion or opposition to a noticed motion.

4. Filings Other Than Noticed Motions or Oppositions to Noticed Motions. A party filing any document other than a noticed motion or opposition to a noticed motion need not inform the Designating Party which material it intends to file with the Court. If a Filing Party files a document other than a noticed motion or opposition to a noticed motion that includes information another party has designated "Confidential," the Filing Party must redact all of the other party's confidential information from the publicly-available version and lodge conditionally under seal unredacted copies with the Court. If the Designating Party seeks to have any of the information sealed, it must file an application to seal within four calendar days. If no application to seal is received, the Court will reject the filing and give the Filing Party two days to re-file unredacted versions of the documents.

f. Applications to File Under Seal. For each individual document or piece of information a party wishes to seal, the application to seal must explain why good cause (in the case of a non-case-dispositive motion) or compelling reasons (in the case of a case-dispositive motion) exist to seal that particular document or piece of information. Conclusory statements - such as that the information contains "confidential, sensitive financial information" - are insufficient to establish good cause or compelling reasons. For each individual document, the party applying to seal the document must explain what adverse consequences would occur if the document were made public. If the Court denies the application to seal, the Court will instruct the party that filed the document to file an unredacted copy of the document within two days of the Court's order.

Failure to conform with this Order may be deemed a waiver of trial by jury and may result in sanctions. The Local Rules and Federal Rules of Civil Procedure control any issue not specifically addressed in this Order. For further information regarding the Court's preferences, refer to www.cacd.uscourts.gov > Judges' Procedures and Schedules > Hon. S. James Otero.

The Court thanks counsel and the parties for their anticipated cooperation. Counsel are advised to check the Court's procedures regularly, as they are subject to change.

DATED: ________________

____

S. JAMES OTERO
United States District Judge

Hon. Mariana R. Pfaelzer
District Judge

Chambers Information
U.S. District Court, Central District of California
Courtroom 12, Spring Street Floor
312 N. Spring Street
Los Angeles, CA 90012

Scheduling Information
Courtroom Deputy: (213) 894-5286

Civil Law and Motion	Mondays at 11:00 a.m.
Pre-Trial Conferences	Mondays at 1:30 p.m.

Judge's Biography
Born 1926 in Los Angeles, CA

Federal Judicial Service:
-Judge, U. S. District Court, Central District of California
-Nominated by Jimmy Carter on August 8, 1978, to a seat vacated by Francis C. Whelan; Confirmed by the Senate on September 22, 1978, and received commission on September 23, 1978. Assumed senior status on December 31, 1997.

Education:
-University of California, Santa Barbara, A.B., 1949
-University of California, Los Angeles, School of Law, J.D., 1957

Professional Career:
-Private Practice, Los Angeles, California, 1957-1978

I. Judge Pfaelzer's Procedures and Practices

A. *Procedures and Schedules*

1. Civil motions are heard on: **Only Mondays**, time: **11:00 A.M.**

   Pre-Trial Conferences are heard on: **Mondays**, time: **1:30 P.M.**

   (If Monday is a holiday, motion date is: The **Next Monday**)

   It is not necessary to clear a motion date with the court clerk prior to filing a motion.
2. Discovery motions are to be scheduled before the District Judge. (Judge Pfaelzer will have the court clerk refer each motion to the Magistrate Judge)
3. Are tentative rulings issued? No.
4. Please submit three (3) conformed mandatory chambers copies to Chambers. **Three (3) mandatory chambers copies of e-filed documents shall be delivered to chambers.** Each of the 3 mandatory chambers copies must be clearly marked MANDATORY CHAMBERS COPY.
5. Procedures for filing an Ex Parte Application: A party submits an Ex Parte Application, with a declaration of notification to the other parties, and a separate proposed order. The Court will either grant, deny or have the party set the matter for a notice of motion.
6. To request a continuance of any scheduled court proceeding: The party(ies) must make the request in writing by either submitting a stipulation or ex parte application with a proposed order for the Court's signature.
7. Are counsel allowed to contact the Judge's law clerks or secretary? No; all inquiries of any nature are to be directed to the court clerk.
8. Inquiries regarding the status of a motion, stipulation or proposed order: Are to be made to the court clerk.
9. Calendar conflicts (procedures for attorneys to follow if they have a calendar conflict): If date is set by the Judge in court, counsel must advise the Judge at the time of any conflicts; if the conflict has arisen later, for instance just prior to a hearing, counsel must advise the court clerk by telephone (however, be advised: priority at the hearing can be arranged, but without a written stipulation/ex parte application and an order signed by the Judge, counsel must appear or risk being held in contempt).
10. Procedures for bringing electronic equipment into the courtroom: None is allowed without prior approval of the Judge's Court Clerk.

    ELMO/Courtroom Technology & Equipment reservations and/or tutorials may be made by first referring to the court website at www.cacd.uscourts.gov , under "Attorney Information," and then "Attorney Services." Alternatively, you can contact the Courtroom Technology Help Desk at 213-894-3061.

    If approved by the Clerk, counsel may contact the Space & Facilities Help Desk at (213) 894-1400 to make arrangements with the U. S. Marshal's Office on how and when to bring the equipment into the building via the public entrances or loading dock if vehicle access is needed. Arrangements for bringing voluminous exhibits into the courtroom can also be made through the S&F Help Desk. (Please note that prior to calling Space & Facilities to set up an appointment, counsel shall contact the court clerk to arrange for a date and time for the delivery into the courtroom of the equipment or the voluminous exhibits.)

11. For general information on how to order a transcript of any reported or digitally recorded proceeding, please contact 213-894-3015 or visit www.cacd.uscourts.gov > General Information > Court Reporter/Recorder Transcripts. If you require an estimate of cost for the preparation of a transcript, contact the court reporter/recorder for the desired proceeding.

To determine the court reporter/recorder for a particular proceeding, go to the Court Reporter Schedule web page and click on View by Date. Once you've determined the correct court reporter/recorder for the desired session, click on Court Reporter Phone and Email List for contact information.

12. Questions regarding law clerk positions: Shall be directed to the Judge's secretary Pat Patino at 213-894-7284. Judge Pfaelzer does not utilize the services of externs.

13. Trial Preparation:

a. **Court hours:** As determined by the Court

b. **Exhibit preparation:** Pursuant to the local rules (the exhibits, except for physical exhibits, shall be in 3-ring binders, the original tagged set for the court clerk -- one set for the Judge and a third set for the witnesses if possible).

c. **Jury instructions:** To be submitted in the form and time frames in accordance with the Federal Rules of Civil and Criminal Procedure and the local rules;

d. **Verdict forms:** The court clerk prepares the verdict form in criminal cases; in civil cases the plaintiff submits the proposed verdict form in accordance with the Federal Rules of Civil Procedure and the local rules.

e. **Other:** The parties shall come to court fully prepared, with the three sets of bound exhibits as described above; and also with two clean copies of their witness lists and two clean copies of their exhibit lists, all which shall be given to the court clerk before the start of court.

14. Procedures for obtaining the services of an interpreter on a civil case: The party must hire a certified Federal Court interpreter, whether it be done through the Court Interpreter's Section, or from some outside source. (Court Interpreter's telephone number: 213-894-4599).

Hon. Virginia A. Phillips
District Judge

Chambers Information
U.S. District Court, Central District of California
Courtroom 2
3470 Twelfth Street
Riverside, CA 92501

Scheduling Information
Courtroom Deputy: (951) 328-4461

Civil Law and Motion	Mondays at 2:00 p.m.
Criminal Law and Motion	Mondays at 9:00 a.m.

Judge's Biography
Born 1957 in Orange, CA

Federal Judicial Service:
-Judge, U. S. District Court, Central District of California
-Nominated by William J. Clinton on January 26, 1999, to a seat vacated by William M. Byrne, Jr.; Confirmed by the Senate on November 10, 1999, and received commission on November 15, 1999.
-U.S. Magistrate Judge, U.S. District Court for the Central District of California, 1995-1999

Education:
-University of California, Riverside, B.A., 1979
-University of California, Berkeley, Boalt Hall School of Law, J.D., 1982

Professional Career:
-Private Practice, Riverside, CA, 1982-1991
-Commissioner, Riverside Superior Court, CA, 1991-1995

I. Judge Phillips' Procedures and Practices

A. *Procedures and Schedules*

1. Civil motions are heard on: **Mondays**. Time: **2:00 PM**

   Criminal motions are heard on: **Mondays**. Time: **9:00 AM**

   (If Monday is a holiday, next motion date is the following Monday

   It is not necessary to clear a motion date with the court clerk prior to filing the motion.

2. Discovery motions are to be calendared before the Magistrate Judge.

3. Are tentative rulings issued? No.

4. Mandatory chambers copies: Counsel shall provide conformed mandatory chambers copies of all motions, responses, and replies in motion matters to Judge Phillips' courtesy box, located outside of Courtroom 2 , 3470 Twelfth Street, Riverside , CA 92501.

   Mandatory chambers copies of e-filed documents shall be delivered to the courtesy tray outside of the Courtroom.

5. Procedures for filing an ex parte application: Ex parte applications are considered on the papers and are not usually set for hearing. Counsel's attention is directed to Local Rule 7-19. The moving party shall serve the opposing party by FAX or hand service and shall notify the opposing party that any opposition must be filed not later than 24 hours after such FAX or hand service. If counsel do not intend to oppose the ex parte application, counsel must inform the court clerk by telephone.

6. To request a continuance of any scheduled court proceeding: Continuations and special requests must be approved by the Court. Good cause must be shown. Counsel must make such requests in pleading form by submitting a stipulation and a proposed order to the filing window, clerk's office, at least one week in advance. Refer to Local Rules 7-1 and 7-11 for proper format.

7. Are counsel allowed to contact the judge's law clerk or secretary? Counsel shall not attempt to contact the Court or its staff by telephone or by any other ex parte means.

8. Inquiries regarding the status of a motion, stipulation or proposed order are not available by telephone. Follow Local Rule 11.4.5.

9. Calendar conflicts: (Procedures for attorneys to follow if they have a calendar conflict). If there is a calendar conflict, counsel are to inform the court clerk prior to the date of the conflict.

10. Procedures for bringing electronic equipment into the courtroom: Counsel are to request, through the court clerk, bringing in or using audio, video or electronic equipment into the courtroom.

11. To order an audio tape or transcript: For general information on how to order a transcript of any reported or digitally recorded proceeding, please contact 213-894-3015 or visit www.cacd.uscourts.gov > General Information > Court Reporter/Recorder Transcripts. If you require an estimate of cost for the preparation of a transcript, contact the court reporter/recorder for the desired proceeding.

To determine the court reporter/recorder for a particular proceeding, go to the Court Reporter Schedule web page and click on View by Date. Once you've determined the correct court reporter/recorder for the desired session, click on Court Reporter Phone and Email List for contact information.

12. Questions regarding law clerk/extern positions should be directed to chambers.

13. Trial preparation: See also the Court's "Civil Trial Order" for details. A copy of this order was provided to counsel at the time of the mandatory status conference.

Trial Court hours - Tuesday through Friday, 8:30 a.m. to 4:00 p.m. on the first day of trial, and 9:00 a.m. to 4:00 p.m. on the remaining days, with a 15 minute break in the morning and afternoon, and a lunch break from 12:00 to 1:00 p.m.

14. Procedures for obtaining the services of an interpreter on a civil case: Counsel in civil cases are to obtain the services of an interpreter, if one is needed.

II. Judge Phillips' Case Management Orders

A. *Civil Trial Scheduling Order*

IN THE UNITED STATES DISTICT COURT
FOR THE CENTRAL DISTRICT OF CALIFORNIA

Plaintiff(s), v. Defendant(s).	Case No. ______________ **CIVIL TRIAL SCHEDULING ORDER** Deadline for Initial Designation of Expert Witnesses: __________ Deadline for Designation of Rebuttal Expert Witnesses: ______________ Discovery Cut-Off: ___________ Summary Judgment Motion Hearing Cut-Off:__________ Last day to conduct mediation:________ Pretrial Conference: ________ at 2:30 p.m Trial: ___________ at 8:30 a.m. Trial Estimate: _____ Day(s)

This case is set for trial before the Honorable Virginia A. Phillips, Courtroom 2, United States District Court, 3470 Twelfth Street, 2nd Floor, Riverside, California.

Motions

Judge Phillips hears motions in civil cases on Mondays at 10:00 a.m. The cut-off date for hearing motions is the last day on which motions will be heard, *i.e.*, the motion must be filed and served at least 24 days before the deadline, if served by mail, in accordance with the requirements of Local Civil Rule 6-1. **A copy of every document filed must be delivered to the chambers drop box outside Courtroom 2 ("the mandatory chambers copy").** The cut-off date applies to all non-discovery motions except motions directly related to the conduct of trial, *e.g.*, motions *in limine* and motions to sever parties or bifurcate issues for trial. If a cut-off date for hearing motions has not been set by the Court, the cut-off date shall be at least twenty-one (21) days before the Pretrial Conference. All motions *in limine* and other trial-related motions must be properly noticed for hearing no later than the date of the Pretrial Conference.

All parties and counsel must comply with Local Rule 7-16, which provides as follows:

> **Any moving party who does not intend to press the motion or who intends to withdraw it before the hearing date, any opposing party who does not intend to oppose the motion, and any party who intends to move for a continuance of the hearing of a motion, shall, not later than noon on the Tuesday preceding the hearing date, notify opposing counsel and the court clerk.**

Failure to comply with this notification requirement may result in the imposition of sanctions on the offending counsel and party.

Discovery

Counsel shall initiate all discovery other than depositions at least forty-five (45) days prior to the cut-off date. The Court will not approve stipulations between counsel which permit responses to be served after the cut-off date except in unusual circumstances and for good cause shown.

All depositions must be completed by the discovery cut-off deadline. Counsel shall lodge all original depositions that will be used in trial with the Courtroom Deputy Clerk on the first day of trial.

Discovery should be kept to a minimum and should focus only on issues genuinely in dispute. Counsel are expected to resolve discovery problems without the assistance of the Court. Discovery disputes have been referred to the United States Magistrate Judge assigned to this case. The **discovery cut-off** is the last date to complete discovery, including expert discovery. It is also the last day for hearing any discovery motion.

If not separately set forth above, the required expert disclosures shall be made seventy (70) days before the discovery cut-off date.

Settlement Procedures

Local Rule 16-2.9 requires the parties in every case to participate in a formal settlement proceeding. Counsel must complete the settlement conference or mediation by the date listed above and shall include in the proposed Pretrial Conference Order a status report detailing what procedure has been followed, and the status of settlement efforts. The following procedures are available:

Settlement Procedure No. 1 – Unless an alternative settlement procedure has been selected by the parties, and with the concurrence of the Court, the parties shall appear before the Court or before the Magistrate Judge assigned to the case for such settlement proceedings as the Court may conduct or direct.

Settlement Procedure No. 2 – The parties shall appear before an attorney selected from the Attorney Settlement Officer Panel, or before an attorney appointed by the Court for settlement proceedings.

Settlement Procedure No. 3 – The parties shall appear before a retired judicial officer or other private dispute resolution body for settlement proceedings.

Unless otherwise ordered by the Judge or the Magistrate Judge conducting a settlement conference (whose procedures will apply if different from those set forth here), the parties shall follow the "Requirements for Settlement Procedures" set forth in Local Rule 16-15.5.

If a settlement is reached, it shall be reported immediately to this Court as required by Local Rule 16-15.7. **In all cases set for jury trial, the parties must notify the Court, no later than the Wednesday preceding the Tuesday trial date, of any settlement, so that the necessary arrangements can be made to bring in a different case for trial or notify the members of the public who would otherwise be reporting for jury duty that their services are not needed that date.**

Failure to comply with this notification requirement may result in the imposition of sanctions on counsel for one or more parties, or their clients, or both.

Pretrial Conference

The Court will conduct a Pretrial Conference in this case pursuant to Federal Rule of Civil Procedure 16 and Local Rule 16-1 on the date and time listed above. Each party appearing in this action shall be represented at the Pretrial Conference and at all pretrial meetings by the lead trial counsel. Counsel should be prepared to discuss streamlining the trial, including presentation of testimony by deposition excerpts, time limits, stipulations as to undisputed facts, and qualification of experts by admitted resumes. In rare cases where the Pretrial Conference is waived by the Court, counsel must follow Local Rule 16-11.2.

Pretrial Filings

Counsel shall submit carefully prepared Memoranda of Contentions of Fact and Law (which may also serve as the trial briefs) and proposed Pretrial Conference Orders in accordance with the provisions of Local Rules 16-4 through 16-7. The form of the proposed Pretrial Conference Order shall be in conformity with the form set forth in Appendix A to the Local Rules.

The Memoranda of Contentions of Fact and Law shall be served not later than twenty-one (21) calendar days before the Pretrial Conference. The proposed Pretrial Conference Order shall be lodged seven (7) calendar days before the Pretrial Conference.

In drafting the proposed Pretrial Conference Order, counsel shall make a good faith effort to agree on and set forth as many uncontested facts as possible. The Court may read the uncontested facts to the jury at the start of the trial. Carefully drafted and comprehensively stated stipulations of facts will reduce the length of trial and increase the jury's understanding of the case.

In drafting the factual issues in dispute for the proposed Pretrial Conference Order, the issues of fact should track the elements of a claim or defense upon which the jury would be required to make findings. Counsel should attempt to state issues in ultimate fact form, not in the form of evidentiary fact issues (*i.e.*, "was the defendant negligent," "was such negligence the proximate cause of injury to the plaintiff," "was the plaintiff negligent;" not, "was the plaintiff standing on the corner of 5th and Spring at 10:00 a.m. on May 3"). Counsel may list sub-issues under the headings of ultimate fact issues, but should not use this as a device to list disputes over evidentiary matters. In general, the issues of fact should set forth the disputed elements of the claims or affirmative defenses.

Issues of law should state legal issues upon which the Court will be required to rule after the Pretrial Conference, including during the trial, and should not list ultimate fact issues to be submitted to the trier of fact.

If expert witnesses are to be called at trial, each party shall list and identify its respective expert witnesses. Failure of a party to list and identify an expert witness in the proposed Pretrial Conference Order shall preclude a party from calling that expert witness at trial.

Exhibit and Witness Lists

Counsel are to prepare their exhibits by placing them in 3-hole notebooks which are tabbed down the right side with exhibit numbers. The notebooks are to be prepared with an original for the Courtroom Deputy Clerk, which shall be tagged with the appropriate exhibit tags in the upper right hand corner of the first page of each exhibit, and one copy for the Court. Each notebook shall contain a list of the included exhibits. The exhibits are to be numbered in accordance with Local Rule 26-3. Counsel can obtain exhibit tags at the Clerk's Office, Room 134, 1st Floor, 3470 Twelfth Street, Riverside.

The Court requires the following to be submitted to the Courtroom Deputy Clerk on the first day of trial:

- The original exhibits with the Court's exhibit tags. The parties shall use yellow tags for plaintiff and blue tags for defendant, which shall be stapled to the front of the exhibit on the upper right corner with the case number, case name, and exhibit number placed on each tag.

- One bench book with a copy of each exhibit for use by the Court, tabbed with numbers as described above. (Court's exhibit tags not necessary.)
- Three (3) copies of exhibit lists.

The exhibit lists shall be in the form indicated by the following example:

Case Title: ______________ ***Case No.*** ______________

No. of Exhibit	Description	Date Identified	Date Admitted
3	1/30/80 letter from Doe to Roe	----	----

- Three (3) copies of witness lists in the order in which the witnesses may be called to testify.

The witness lists shall be in the form indicated by the following example:

Case Title: ______________ ***Case No.*** ______________

Name of Witness	Date called to testify
1. John Doe	
2. Jane Roe	

All counsel are to meet no later than ten (10) calendar days before trial and to stipulate to the extent possible to foundation, waiver of the best evidence rule, and which exhibits may be received into evidence at the start of trial. The exhibits to be received will be noted on the extra copies of the exhibit lists.

Jury Instructions

Fourteen (14) calendar days prior to the Rule 16-2 Meeting of Counsel, counsel shall exchange proposed jury instructions and special verdict forms (if applicable). Seven (7) calendar days prior to the Rule 16-2 meeting, counsel shall exchange any objections to the instructions and special verdict forms. Prior to, or at the time of the Rule 16-2 meeting, counsel shall meet and confer with the goal of reaching agreement to one set of joint, undisputed jury instructions and one special verdict form.

The parties must file proposed jury instructions seven (7) calendar days before the Pretrial Conference. As always, the parties must submit courtesy copies directly to the Court. In addition, the parties must submit electronic versions (either Word or WordPerfect format) to the Court at the following electronic mail address: VAP_Chambers@cacd.uscourts.gov.

As noted above, the parties must act jointly to submit proposed jury instructions. The parties must submit one set of agreed upon jury instructions. The parties must submit another set of jury instructions containing the instructions upon which the parties disagree and the objections to those instructions.

Where the parties disagree on an instruction, the party opposing the instruction must attach a short (*i.e.*, one to two paragraphs) statement supporting the objection and the party submitting the instruction must attach a short statement supporting the instruction. Each statement should be on a separate page and should follow directly after the disputed instruction.

Accordingly, the parties ultimately will submit one document or, if the parties disagree over any proposed jury instructions, two documents. If the parties submit two documents, those documents should consist of: (1) a set of agreed upon jury instructions and (2) a set of disputed jury instructions along with reasons supporting and opposing each disputed instruction.

The parties should make every attempt to agree upon the jury instructions before submitting them to the Court. In addition, where the Manual of Model Civil Jury Instructions for the Ninth Circuit (2001 edition) provides a version of a requested instruction, the parties should submit the Model instruction. Where California law applies, the Court prefers counsel to use *Judicial Council of California, Civil Instructions* - ("CACI"). If neither of the above sources has an instruction on the subject, counsel are directed to Edward J. Devitt, *et al.*, *Federal Jury Practice and Instructions* (4th ed. 1987 & Supp. 1995). Each requested jury instruction shall cover only one subject or principle of law and shall be numbered and set forth in full on a separate page, citing the authority or source of the requested instruction (except for the jury copy discussed *infra* at ¶ 26).

The Court will send a copy of the jury instructions into the jury room for use by the jury during deliberations. Accordingly, in addition to the file copies described above, the parties shall file with the Courtroom Deputy Clerk on the first day of the trial a "clean set" of joint and/or proposed jury instructions which contain only the text of each instruction set forth in full on each page, with the caption "Court's Instruction Number" (eliminating titles, supporting authority, indication of party proposing, *etc.*). This will be referred to as the "Jury Copy" of the jury instructions.

Counsel shall provide the Court with a CD-ROM containing the proposed jury instructions, in WordPerfect or Word, along with the hard copy, no later than the first day of trial.

An index page shall accompany all jury instructions submitted to the Court. The index page shall indicate the following:

- The number of the instruction;
- A brief title of the instruction;
- The source of the instruction and any relevant case citations; and
- The page number of the instruction.

EXAMPLE:

Number	Title	Source	Page
1	Burden of Proof	9th Cir. 12.02	7

Joint Statement of the Case

Counsel shall prepare a joint statement of the case which will be read by the Court to the prospective panel of jurors prior to the commencement of *voir dire*. The statement should not be longer than two or three paragraphs. The statement shall be filed with the Court seven (7) calendar days before the Pretrial Conference.

Matters to be Discussed at the Pretrial Conference

Counsel shall be prepared to discuss the following matters with the Court at the Pretrial Conference:

- the witnesses all parties intend to call during their respective cases, and the amount of time necessary for direct and cross examination of each witness;
- any anticipated problems in scheduling witnesses;
- any evidentiary issues, including anticipated objections under Rule 403, and objections to exhibits;
- jury selection procedures;
- all pretrial motions, including motions in limine, to bifurcate and to sever;
- any disputed jury instructions, and the form of the instructions which will be given to the jury at the outset of the case, i.e., before opening statements and

presentation of evidence;

- whether any counsel intends to use any evidence or demonstrative aid in opening statement; and
- motions to exclude witnesses from the courtroom during trial testimony.

If counsel for any party need to arrange for the installation of its own equipment, such as video monitors, tape or compact disk players, notebooks or overhead projectors, counsel shall notify the Courtroom Deputy Clerk no later than 4:00 p.m. two (2) days before trial so that the necessary arrangements can be made.

Trial

The Court sets firm trial dates. Counsel shall arrive at the Courtroom not later than 8:30 a.m. each day of trial. The Court reserves the time from 8:30 to 9:00 a.m. to handle legal and administrative matters outside the presence of the jury. The trial will commence promptly at 9:00 a.m. Counsel shall anticipate matters which may need discussion or hearing outside the presence of the jury and to raise them during this period.

The Court is in session with the jury on Tuesdays through Fridays, 9:00 a.m. to 4:30 p.m., with a morning and an afternoon break and a lunch recess from approximately 12:00 to 1:15 p.m. In most cases, jury selection is completed on the first morning of trial, and counsel should be prepared to give opening statements and begin presentation of evidence immediately thereafter.

All counsel are asked to observe the following practices during trial:

- All counsel, defendants, and parties shall rise when the jury enters and leaves the courtroom.
- Counsel shall stand when addressing the Court, including when objecting to opposing counsel's questions.
- When objecting, counsel should state only "objection," and the legal ground for the objection (*e.g.*, hearsay, irrelevant, etc.). Counsel should refrain from arguing the legal basis for the objection unless permission is granted to do so.
- Counsel must seek leave to approach the Courtroom Deputy Clerk or the witness, and should question witnesses while standing at the lectern.
- Counsel must address all witnesses, including their clients, by the witness's surname. Young witnesses, *i.e.*, children younger than age 15, may be addressed by first names, however.
- Counsel shall not discuss the law or argue the case in opening statements.
- Counsel shall address all remarks to the Court, and should not directly address the Courtroom Deputy Clerk, the Court Reporter, opposing counsel or the jury (except in opening statement and closing argument). Counsel must ask the Court for permission to talk off the record in order to speak with opposing counsel.
- Counsel shall not make an offer of stipulation unless he or she has conferred with opposing counsel and believes that the stipulation will be accepted. Any stipulation of fact will require the defendant's personal concurrence and shall be submitted to the Court in writing for approval.
- While Court is in session, counsel may not leave the counsel table to confer with witnesses, colleagues or assistants in the back of the courtroom unless the Court grants permission to do so in advance.
- When a party has more than one lawyer, only one of the lawyers may conduct the examination of a given witness and only that same lawyer may handle objections

during the testimony of that witness.

- If a witness was on the stand before a recess or adjournment, counsel shall have the witness back on the stand and ready to proceed when Court resumes.
- If there is more than a brief delay between witnesses, the Court may deem that the party has rested.
- The Court attempts to cooperate with witnesses and will, except in extraordinary circumstances, accommodate them by permitting them to be examined out of sequence. Counsel should discuss any scheduling issues with opposing counsel. If there is an objection, confer with the Court in advance.

Trial Preparation for Court Trials

Fourteen (14) calendar days before the trial date, each party shall prepare and serve on opposing counsel copies of the proposed Findings of Fact and Conclusions of Law. Each party shall review the other party's proposed Findings and Conclusions and make such changes in the party's own proposed Findings and Conclusions as necessary following such review. Seven (7) calendar days before the trial date, each party shall lodge two copies of its proposed Findings of Fact and Conclusions of Law with the Court, also serving other parties if changes have been made. The parties shall be prepared to submit to the Court, and to exchange among themselves, supplemental Findings of Fact and Conclusions of Law during the course of the trial.

Internet Site

Counsel are encouraged to review the Central District's website for additional information. The address is "***http://www.cacd.uscourts.gov***."

The Courtroom Deputy Clerk is ordered to serve a copy of this Order personally or by mail on counsel for all parties to this action.

IT IS SO ORDERED.

Dated: ________________

____
VIRGINIA A. PHILLIPS
United States District Judge

B. Criminal Motion and Trial Order

IN THE UNITED STATES DISTICT COURT
FOR THE CENTRAL DISTRICT OF CALIFORNIA

UNITED STATES OF AMERICA,	)	Case No. ______________
Plaintiff,	)	
v.	)	**CRIMINAL MOTION AND TRIAL**
Defendant(s).	)	**ORDER**
______________________________	)	

This case is set for trial before the Honorable Virginia A. Phillips, Courtroom 2, United States District Court, 3470 Twelfth Street, Riverside, CA 92501.

Motions

1. Judge Phillips hears motions in criminal cases on Mondays at 9:00 a.m. All pretrial motions, including motions to suppress evidence, motions to bifurcate or sever, motions challenging introduction of Fed. R. Evid. 404(b) evidence, and motions *in limine*, shall be filed and served on all other counsel in accordance with the requirements of Local Civil R. 6-1, *i.e.*, at least 21 days before the date set for hearing, if the motion is personally served on opposing counsel, and served at least 24 days before the scheduled hearing date if not personally served. Opposition and reply memoranda shall be filed and served in compliance with the requirements of Local Civil R. 7-9, *i.e.*, no later than 14 and seven days before the hearing date, respectively. **A chambers copy of every document filed must be delivered to the chambers drop box outside Courtroom 2 no later than noon the day after filing. The chambers copy must comply with all local rules, including Local R. 11-5.3 regarding formatting.**

2. The Pretrial Conference will be conducted at 9:00 a.m. on the Monday eight days before the trial date, ______________. (If that Monday is a court holiday, the Pretrial Conference will be conducted at 9:00 a.m. on ______________, the Monday fifteen days before the trial date.) All pretrial motions, including any motions *in limine*, must be timely filed and noticed for hearing no later than the date of the Pretrial Conference.

3. Trial is set for ________________________ at 8:30 a.m.

Discovery and Notice

5. Counsel for the Government and counsel for the Defendant(s) shall comply promptly with discovery and notice matters pursuant to Fed. R. Crim. P. 12, 12.1, 12.2, 12.3, 15, and 16.

Pretrial Deadlines

6. Counsel for the Government shall file with the Court *in camera* (under seal) all statements of all witnesses to be called by the Government in its case-in-chief. **The statements shall be filed at least ten (10) calendar days before trial and shall comply with local rules regarding text size and tabbing.**

7. The parties must submit joint jury instructions. In order to produce the instructions, the parties shall meet and confer sufficiently in advance of the required submission date with the goal of agreeing upon instructions and verdict forms. The jury instructions shall be submitted as follows: (1) joint jury instructions, i.e., those instructions to which all parties agree; and (2) disputed jury instructions, *i.e.*, those instructions propounded by a party to which another party objects. The party objecting to the disputed instructions must state the reasons for the objection and, if appropriate, provide a proposed alternative instruction with

supporting authority, or explain why no instruction on that point is needed. Each requested jury instruction shall be numbered and set forth in full on a separate page, citing the authority or source of the requested instruction except on the "jury copy" described below.

8. An index page shall accompany all jury instructions that are submitted to the Court. The index page shall indicate the following:

a. The number of the instruction;
b. A brief title of the instruction;
c. The source of the instruction; and
d. The page number of the instruction.

EXAMPLE:

Number	Title	Source	Page Number
1	Duty of the Jury	9th Cir. 1.01	1

9. **Jury instructions in the form described in paragraph 7 shall be lodged no later than the Wednesday of the week prior to the Pretrial Conference.** Counsel need only submit proposed substantive instructions. The Court will formulate general instructions based primarily on the format set out in Committee on Model Jury Instructions for the Ninth Circuit, *Manual of Model Criminal Jury Instructions for the Ninth Circuit* (2007 edition).

10. If either side seeks a special verdict, counsel shall follow the procedure set forth in paragraph 7 in order to formulate a joint proposed verdict form. Counsel shall submit the proposed verdict form with the proposed jury instructions.

11. Counsel shall submit electronic versions of the proposed jury instructions and the proposed special verdict (either Word or WordPerfect format) to the Court at the following electronic mail address: VAP_Chambers@cacd.uscourts.gov, along with a chambers copy.

12. The Court will send a copy of the jury instructions into the jury room for use by the jury during deliberations (the "jury copy"). Accordingly, in addition to the file copies, an extra set of the proposed instructions shall be submitted to the Court with only the text of an instruction on each page (*i.e.*, no titles, supporting authority, indication of party proposing, *etc.*).

13. The Court strongly prefers counsel use the instructions from Committee on Model Jury Instructions for the Ninth Circuit, *Manual of Model Criminal Jury Instructions for the Ninth Circuit* (2007 edition).

The Pretrial Conference

14. Counsel shall be prepared to discuss the following matters with the Court at the Pretrial Conference:

- the witnesses the Government expects to call in its case in chief, and the amount of time necessary for direct and cross examination of each witness;
- any anticipated problems in scheduling the witnesses;
- any evidentiary issues, including problems related to Fed. R. Evid. 404(b) evidence, anticipated objections under Rule 403, and objections to exhibits;
- jury selections procedures;
- all pretrial motions not previously heard and decided;
- any disputed jury instructions, and the form of the instructions which will be given to the jury at the outset of the case, *i.e.*, before opening statements and presentation of evidence;

- whether any counsel intends to use any evidence or demonstrative aid in opening statement; and
- motions to exclude witnesses from the courtroom during trial testimony.

15. If counsel for any party need to arrange for the installation of its own equipment, such as video monitors, tape or compact disk players, notebooks or overhead projectors, counsel shall notify the Courtroom Deputy Clerk no later than 4:00 p.m. Two days before trial so that the necessary arrangements can be made.

Requirements for Trial

16. On the first day of trial, counsel for the Government shall deliver to the Courtroom Deputy Clerk the following documents:

a. Three copies of the Government's witness list;

b. Three copies of the Government's exhibit list in the form specified by Local Civil R. 9.9;

c. All of the Government's exhibits, with official exhibit tags affixed, bearing the same number as that shown on the exhibit list. Defense counsel need not deliver his/her exhibits to the Courtroom Deputy Clerk on the first day of trial; however, defense counsel is responsible for affixing exhibit tags, complete with the case name and case number, to each exhibit to be used in the defense case. Exhibits shall be numbered 1, 2, 3, 4, *etc.* If an enlargement of an existing exhibit is to be used, counsel shall designate it with the number of the original exhibit followed by an "A." Counsel for the Government is notified that the Court will order exhibits such as firearms, narcotics, etc., to remain in the custody of the agent during the pendency of the trial. The agent will be required to sign the appropriate form to take custody of the exhibits. It shall be the responsibility of the agent to produce the items for court, secure them at night, and guard them while in the courtroom. Exhibit tags are available at the filing window in the Clerk's Office, Room 134; and

d. A bench book containing a copy of all exhibits that can be reproduced.

Counsel for the Government shall mark each exhibit with tabs indicating the exhibit number. Defense counsel shall provide the Court and Government counsel with a copy of the defense exhibits as introduced.

Courtroom Procedures

17. Counsel shall arrive at the Courtroom not later than 8:30 a.m. each day of trial. The Court reserves the time from 8:30 to 9:00 a.m. to handle legal and administrative matters outside the presence of the jury. The trial will commence promptly at 9:00 a.m.

Counsel shall anticipate matters which may need discussion or hearing outside the presence of the jury and to raise them during this period.

18. The Court is in session with the jury on Tuesdays through Fridays, 9:00 a.m. to 4:30 p.m., with a morning and an afternoon break and a lunch recess from approximately 12:00 to 1:15 p.m.

19. All counsel are asked to observe the following practices:

- All counsel, defendants, and designated case agents shall rise when the jury enters and leaves the courtroom.
- Counsel shall stand when addressing the Court, including when objecting to opposing counsel's questions.
- When objecting, counsel should state only "objection," and the legal ground for

the objection (*e.g.*, hearsay, irrelevant, *etc.*). Counsel should refrain from arguing the legal basis for the objection unless permission is granted to do so.

- Counsel must seek leave to approach the Courtroom Deputy Clerk or the witness, and should question witnesses while standing at the lectern.
- Counsel must address and refer to all witnesses, including their clients, by the witness's surname. Young witnesses, *i.e.*, children younger than age 15, may be addressed by first names, however.
- Counsel shall not discuss the law or argue the case in opening statements.
- Counsel shall address all remarks to the Court, and should not directly address the Courtroom Deputy Clerk, the Court Reporter, or opposing counsel. Counsel must ask the Court for permission to talk off the record in order to speak with opposing counsel.
- Counsel shall not make an offer of stipulation unless he or she has conferred with opposing counsel and believes that the stipulation will be accepted. Any stipulation of fact will require the defendant's personal concurrence and shall be submitted to the Court in writing for approval. A proposed stipulation should be explained to the defendant(s) in advance.
- While Court is in session, counsel may not leave the counsel table to confer with investigators, assistants, or witnesses in the back of the courtroom unless the Court grants permission to do so in advance.
- When a party has more than one lawyer, only one of the lawyers may conduct the examination of a given witness and only that same lawyer may handle objections during the testimony of that witness.
- If a witness was on the stand before a recess or adjournment, counsel shall have the witness back on the stand and ready to proceed when Court resumes.
- If there is more than a brief delay between witnesses, the Court may deem that the party has rested.

20. The Court attempts to cooperate with witnesses and will, except in extraordinary circumstances, accommodate them by permitting them to be examined out of sequence. Counsel should discuss any scheduling issues with opposing counsel. If there is an objection, confer with the Court in advance.

IT IS SO ORDERED.

Dated: June 12, 2009

____

VIRGINIA A. PHILLIPS
United States District Judge

C. *Standing Order*

IN THE UNITED STATES DISTICT COURT
FOR THE CENTRAL DISTRICT OF CALIFORNIA

Plaintiff(s),	Case No. ______________
v.	**STANDING ORDER**
Defendant(s).	

READ THIS ORDER CAREFULLY. IT CONTROLS THIS CASE AND DIFFERS IN SOME RESPECTS FROM THE LOCAL RULES.

This action has been assigned to the calendar of Judge Virginia A. Phillips.

The responsibility for the progress of litigation in the Federal Courts falls not only upon the attorneys in the action, but upon the Court as well. To secure the just, speedy, and inexpensive determination of every action, (Fed. R. Civ. P. 1), all counsel are hereby ordered to become familiar with the Federal Rules of Civil Procedure and the Local Rules of the Central District of California.*

The Court further orders as follows:

1. **Service of the Complaint.** The Plaintiff shall serve the Complaint promptly in accordance with Fed. R. Civ. P. 4 and filethe proofs of service pursuant to Local Rule 5-3.

2. **Proposed Orders.** Each party filing or opposing a motion or seeking the determination of any matter shall serve and file a proposed order which sets forth the relief or action sought and a brief statement of the rationale for the decision, including citation of authorities, that the party requests the Court to adopt.

3. **Presence of Lead Counsel. All** lead trial counsel must attend any scheduling and pretrial conferences set by the Court. Failure of lead trial counsel to appear for those proceedings is a basis for sanctions.

4. **Motions.** Motions shall be filed and set for hearing in accordance with Local Rule 6-1. Motions will be heard on Mondays commencing at 2:00 p.m. If Monday is a national holiday, this Court does not hear motions on the succeeding Tuesday. Any motion noticed for a holiday shall automatically be set to the next Monday without further notice to the parties. Any opposition or reply papers due on a holiday are due the preceding Friday, not the following Tuesday. Memoranda of Points and Authorities in support of or in opposition to motions shall not exceed 25 pages. Replies shall not exceed 12 pages. Only in rare instances, and for good cause shown, will the Court agree to extend these page limitations. When citing to

* Copies of the Local Rules are available on our website at "http://www.cacd.uscourts.gov" or they may be purchased from one of the following:

Los Angeles Daily Journal 915 East 1st Street Los Angeles, California 90012	West Publishing Company 610 Opperman Drive Post Office Box 64526 St. Paul, Minnesota 55164-0526	Metropolitan News 210 South Spring Street Los Angeles, California 90012

legal databases, wherever possible cite to Westlaw rather than Lexis.

Unless clearly justified under the circumstances of the case, "motions to dismiss or in the alternative for summary adjudication" are discouraged. These composite motions tend to blur the legitimate distinction[s] between the two motions, which have different purposes. Frequently, the composite motions introduce evidence that is extrinsic to the pleadings. On the one hand, such evidence is improper for consideration in a Fed. R. Civ. P. 12(b)(6) motion, while on the other hand, treatment of the motion as a Rule 56 motion frequently results in reasonable invocation of Rule 56(f) by the non moving party.

Moreover, Rule 12(b)(6) motions are discouraged unless counsel has a good faith belief that such motion will likely result in dismissal, without leave to amend, of all or at least some of the claims under applicable law.

Motions for Summary Judgment or Partial Summary Judgment: No party may file more than one motion pursuant to Fed. R. Civ. P. 56 regardless of whether such motion is denominated as a motion for summary judgment or summary adjudication. Parties offering evidence in support of, or in opposition to, a Rule 56 motion must cite to specific page and line numbers in depositions and paragraph numbers in affidavits. Furthermore, such evidence must be authenticated properly. The Court directs the parties to become familiar with Orr v. Bank of America, NT & SA, 285 F.3d 764 (9th Cir. 2002).

The moving party's brief shall also be accompanied by an statement of undisputed facts ("SUF"). The SUF shall be presented in a table format and include the following columns:

a. The first column shall contain the number of the fact alleged to be undisputed.

b. The second column shall contain a plain statement of the fact. **Facts shall not be compound.** If, for instance, the required response is that the fact is disputed in part, the fact is compound. Further, neither legal arguments nor conclusions constitute facts.

c. The third column shall contain a citation to admissible evidence the party believes supports the proffered fact.
For example:

Pl.'s SUF No.	Fact	Supporting Evidence
1	Plaintiff was driving her car when she went through the intersection.	Decl. of Plaintiff ¶ 2.
2	The light was green when Plaintiff went through the intersection.	Decl. of Plaintiff ¶ 4.
3	Plaintiff was driving at 35 miles per hour when she traveled through the intersection.	Decl. of Plaintiff ¶ 7; Decl. of Plaintiff's Expert ¶ 14.
. . .	. . .	. . .

The party opposing the summary judgment motion shall include with its opposition a statement of genuine issues that includes the moving party's table; but the opposing party shall add a fourth column to the moving table identifying those facts that are in dispute, briefly explaining the dispute, and citing the evidence supporting the dispute. The opposing party shall not set forth legal objections in the statement of genuine issues. For example:

Pl.'s SUF No.	Fact	Supporting Evidence	Def.'s Response
1	Plaintiff was driving her car when she went through the intersection.	Decl. of Plaintiff ¶ 2.	Undisputed.
2	The light was green when Plaintiff went through the intersection.	Decl. of Plaintiff ¶ 4.	Disputed. The light was red when Plaintiff traveled through the intersection. (Decl. of Defendant ¶ 6.)
3	Plaintiff was driving at 35 miles per hour when she traveled through the intersection.	Decl. of Plaintiff ¶ 7; Dec. of Plaintiff's Expert ¶ 14.	Disputed. Plaintiff was driving 52 miles per hour when she went through the intersection. (Decl. of Defendant's Expert ¶ 9.)
. . .. . .	. . .	. . .	. . .

If a party fails to dispute a fact properly by offering evidence that does not contradict the proffered fact, the Court will deem the fact undisputed for purposes of the motion. See Fed. R. Civ. P. 56(e)(2), L.R. 56-3.

If the party opposing the summary judgment motion wishes to include its own set of undisputed facts, it may include them in a second table at the end of its statement of genuine issues. The opposing party's undisputed facts shall be set forth in the same manner as the moving party's SUF. For example:

Def.'s SUF No.	Fact	Supporting Evidence
1	The tires on Plaintiff's car had only 1 millimeter of tread remaining at the time of the accident.	Decl. of Mechanic ¶ 5.
. . .. . .	. . .	. . .

If either party fails to provide a pincite to the supporting evidence, the Court will deem the proffered fact (or dispute) unsupported. See generally Christian Legal Soc. v. Wu, 626 F.3d 483, 488 (9th Cir. 2010) ("Judges are not like pigs, hunting for truffles buried in briefs." (quoting Greenwood v. FAA, 28 F.3d 971, 977 (9th Cir. 1994) (quoting United States v. Dunkel, 927 F.2d 955, 956 (7th Cir. 1991) (per curiam)) (alteration omitted)))).

Additionally, parties shall file any legal objections to the other party's proffered evidence under separate cover.

5. **Withdrawal or Non-Opposition of Motions: In the event that the parties are able to resolve a pending motion, *they must notify the Court* approximately one week before the hearing date.** Sanctions may issue for failure to comply with this requirement, or the broader requirement in Local Rule 7-16 that any party who intends either to withdraw a motion, to not oppose a motion, or to seek a continuance of the hearing date for a motion, **must notify**

the court by noon on the Tuesday preceding the hearing date.

6. **Electronic filing.** As of January 1, 2008, the United States District Court for the Central District of California implemented mandatory electronic filing ("e-filing") of documents in all new and pending civil cases. Information about the Court's Electronic Case Filing system, is available on the Court's website at www.cacd.uscourts.gov/cmecf.

   The "e-filing" of all documents required to be "e-filed" in this matter pursuant to General Order No. 10-07 shall be completed by **4:00 p.m. on the date due**. Any documents "e-filed" after 4:00 p.m. on the date due will be considered **untimely**.

7. **Mandatory chambers copies. Counsel shall provide one conformed chambers copy of any "e-filed" document.** Such chambers copies shall be delivered to the "Courtesy Box," located outside of Courtroom 2 on the 2nd floor at the United States District Court, 3470 Twelfth Street, Riverside, California 92501, no later than 5:00 p.m. on the day following "e-filing." All chambers copies shall comply fully with the document formatting requirements of Local Rule 11-3, including the "backing" and "tabbing" requirements of Local Rules 11-3.5 and 11-5.3, respectively. If the filing party and their counsel fail to deliver a mandatory chambers copy in full compliance with this Order and Local Rule 11-3, the Court may, on its own motion, reschedule any related hearing, as well as imposing sanctions.

8. **Discovery.** All discovery matters have been referred to a United States Magistrate Judge (see initial designation following the case number) to hear all discovery disputes. The words "DISCOVERY MATTER" shall appear in the caption of all documents relating to discovery to insure proper routing. Counsel are directed to contact the Magistrate Judge Courtroom Deputy Clerk for the assigned Magistrate Judge to schedule matters for hearing.

   The decision of the Magistrate Judge shall be final, subject to modification by the District Court only where it has been shown that the Magistrate Judge's order is clearly erroneous or contrary to law.

   Any party may file and serve a motion for review and reconsideration before this court. The party seeking review must do so within ten (10) days of service upon the party of a written ruling or within ten (10) days of an oral ruling that the Magistrate Judge states will not be followed by a written ruling. The motion must specify which portions of the text are clearly erroneous or contrary to law and the claim must be supported by points and authorities. A copy of the moving papers and responses shall be delivered to the Magistrate Judge's clerk for review upon the filing of the required documents.

9. ***Ex Parte* Applications.** *Ex parte* applications are considered on the papers and are not usually set for hearing. Counsel are advised that this Court allows *ex parte* applications solely for extraordinary relief -- sanctions may be imposed for misuse of *ex parte* applications. See In re Intermagnetics Am., Inc., 101 B.R. 191 (Bankr. C.D. Cal. 1989). Counsel also should become familiar with Mission Power Engineering Co. v. Continental Casualty Co., 883 F. Supp. 488 (C.D. Cal. 1995), regarding *ex parte* applications.

   Counsel's attention is directed to Local Rule 7-19. The moving party shall serve the opposing party by facsimile transmission and shall notify the opposition that opposing papers must be filed not later than twenty-four hours following such facsimile service. The moving party's declaration in support of an ex parte application shall show compliance with Local Rule 7-19 and this Order, failing which the application shall be DENIED. If counsel does not intend to oppose an ex parte application, they must so inform the Courtroom Deputy Clerk, (951) 328-4461. As with all motion papers, counsel must deliver a conformed courtesy copy of the papers to the "Courtesy Box," located outside of Courtroom 2 on the 2nd floor at United States District Court, 3470 Twelfth Street, Riverside, California 92501. Counsel will be notified by the Courtroom Deputy Clerk of the Court's ruling or of a hearing time and date should the Court determine that a hearing is necessary.

10. **Stipulations.** Stipulations extending scheduling dates set by this Court are not effective unless approved by the Court. Counsel requesting a continuance must submit a stipulation, with a detailed declaration of the basis for the requested continuance or extension of time, and a proposed order. Continuances will be granted only upon a showing of good cause, focusing on the diligence of the party seeking the continuance and any prejudice that may result if the continuance is denied. Any continuances that are requested without an accompanying declaration will be rejected without notice to the parties. The Court sets **firm** trial dates and will not change them without a showing of good cause.

11. **Applications to File Under Seal.** Parties are reminded that court proceedings are presumptively public, and no document shall be filed under seal without request for a court order that is narrowly tailored to cover only the document, the particular portion of the document, or category of documents for which good cause exists for filing under seal. To that end, if a party wishes to file a document under seal, that party shall first file a written request for a sealing order setting forth the good cause and accompanied by a proposed order that is narrowly tailored as specified above.

    If the sole ground for the sealing order is that the opposing party (or non-party) has designated the document as confidential, the opposing party (or non-party) shall file a declaration establishing good cause for the sealing along with a proposed order, or shall withdraw the designation. The declaration shall be filed within five days of service on the opposing party (or nonparty) of the request for a sealing order. If the declaration is not filed as required, the Court may order that the document be filed in the public record.

    Use of Sealed Documents in Motion Papers: The Court cautions parties that documents designated as confidential that are attached as exhibits to case-dispositive motions, or redacted portions of case-dispositive briefs that contain confidential information, must meet the high "compelling reasons" threshold. See Kamakana v. City of Honolulu, 447 F.3d 1172 (9th Cir. 2006). A good cause showing, without more, will not satisfy a compelling reasons test, but will only suffice to maintain the confidentiality of documents attached to *non-dispositive* motions. Documents designated as confidential in conjunction with case-dispositive motions or briefs that do not satisfy the compelling reasons test may accordingly be re-designated as public information upon proper request.

See Foltz v. State Farm Mut. Auto. Ins. Co., 331 F.3d 1122 (9th Cir. 2003).

Use of Sealed or Confidential Documents at Trial: Notwithstanding any provision of a protective order to the contrary, any document, whether previously designated confidential or previously sealed, will be unsealed and will lose its confidential status if offered as an exhibit at trial, absent a showing of the "most compelling" reasons. See Manual for Complex Litigation § 21.432; Foltz, 331 F.3d at 1135–36. Any party believing that a document, portions thereof, or witness testimony should remain confidential or sealed during trial must request in advance of trial that the court take extraordinary measures, such as closing the courtroom to the public or sealing the trial transcript, to protect the confidentiality of that information. The request must be made in writing and filed no later than the date on which pretrial papers are due.

If previously sealed documents are ordered unsealed for use at trial, counsel for the party offering the document as evidence shall, within two business days of the conclusion of the trial, identify which entries on the docket represent the exhibits actually received. Counsel are required to cooperate with the deputy clerk in order to complete the unsealing process in cases involving voluminous sealed documents.

12. **Removed Actions.** Any answers filed in state court must be re-filed in this Court (separately) as a supplement to the petition. Any pending motions must be re-noticed in accordance with Local Rule 6-1.

13. **Communications with Chambers.** Counsel shall not attempt to contact the Court or its staff by telephone or by any other *ex parte* means. Counsel must list their facsimile transmission numbers along with their telephone numbers on their papers.

14. **Notice of this Order.** Counsel for plaintiff, or plaintiff, if appearing on his or her own behalf, shall immediately serve this Order on all parties, including any new parties to the action. If this case came to the Court by noticed removal, the removing defendant shall serve this Order on all other parties.

15. **Internet Site.** Counsel are directed to review the Central District's website for additional information. The address is "http://www.cacd.uscourts.gov."

Dated: ________________

____
VIRGINIA A. PHILLIPS
United States District Judge

Hon. Dean D. Pregerson

District Judge

Chambers Information

U.S. District Court, Central District of California
Courtroom 3, 2nd Floor
312 N. Spring Street
Los Angeles, CA 90012

Scheduling Information

Courtroom Deputy: (213) 894-3913

Civil Law and Motion	Mondays at 10:00 a.m.
Criminal Law and Motion	Mondays at 3:00 p.m.

Judge's Biography

Born 1951 in Los Angeles, CA

Federal Judicial Service:

-Judge, U. S. District Court, Central District of California
-Nominated by William J. Clinton on January 26, 1996, to a seat vacated by A. Wallace Tashima; Confirmed by the Senate on July 24, 1996, and received commission on August 1, 1996.

Education:

-University of California, Los Angeles, B.A., 1972
-University of California, Davis, King Hall School of Law, J.D., 1976

Professional Career:

-Parole Hearing Officer, Department of Corrections, State of California, 1977
-Private Practice, Ventura, California, 1978
-Assistant Public Defender, Public Defender Service Corporation, Agana, Guam, 1978-1981
-Private Practice, Agana, Guam, 1982
-Private Practice, Napa, California, 1982
-Private Practice, Los Angeles, California, 1983-1985
-Vice President and General Counsel, The Torrance Company, California, 1985
-Private Practice, Los Angeles, California, 1986-1996

I. Judge Pregerson's Procedures and Practices

A. Procedures and Schedules

I. **COURT HOURS:**

A. **Trials** -- Generally 9:00 a.m. to 5:00 p.m. with a lunch break and short breaks in the morning and afternoon.

B. **Civil Motions** -- Mondays at 10:00 a.m. Only.

C. **Criminal Motions** -- Mondays at 3:00 p.m. Only.

D. **Civil Pre-Trial Conferences** -- Mondays at 11:00 a.m.

E. **Criminal Pre-Trial Conferences** -- Mondays at 9:00 a.m.

F. **Scheduling Conferences** -- Mondays at 3:30 p.m.

II. **CONTACT WITH CHAMBERS:** Counsel are not to communicate with chambers unless first contacted by a law clerk or Judge Pregerson's assistant.

III. **CALENDAR CONFLICTS:** If counsel has an appearance with another district judge, please leave a voice mail message with the Court Clerk at 213-894-3913 indicating the time of the appearance and the name of the other judge. On the day of the appearance, if possible, request the other judge's Court Clerk to update Judge Pregerson's Court Clerk as to when counsel will be appearing in Judge Pregerson's courtroom.

If counsel cannot make a court appearance, good cause must be shown. The Court must approve all continuances and special requests. Counsel must make such requests in pleading form by submitting a stipulation and proposed order in accordance with General Order 10-07(VI).

If a stipulation cannot be reached, counsel must submit an ex parte application and proposed order in accordance with General Order 10-07(VI). Please notify the Court Clerk at 213-894-3913 if there is any opposition to the ex parte application. The written opposition to the ex parte application must be submitted within 24 hours for consideration by the Court.

IV. **CONTINUANCES:** Continuances and special requests must be approved by the Court. Good cause must be shown.

If a stipulation cannot be reached, counsel must submit an ex parte application and proposed order in accordance with General Order 10-07(VI). (See Section X, infra.) Please notify the Court Clerk at 213-894-3913 if there is any opposition to the ex parte application. The written opposition to the ex parte application must be submitted within 24 hours for consideration by the Court.

Time does not permit the Court Clerk to respond to questions regarding whether the Court has approved requests, or to confirm a message left for counsel.

V. **MANDATORY CHAMBERS COPIES:** The Court requires delivery of two non-blue backed Mandatory Chambers Copies* of only the following manual and electronically filed documents to Room 244-J:

1. All noticed motions and related documents;
2. All ex parte applications and related documents; and

3. All exhibits and attachments must be separately tabbed.

*[Refer to the Court's General Order No. 10-07 regarding ECF Courtesy Paper Copies.]

VI. FILINGS: Follow the local rules and federal rules of procedure.

It is not necessary to clear a motion date with the Court Clerk prior to filing the motion. The Court hears motions only on Mondays (civil at 10:00 a.m. and criminal at 3:00 p.m.).

Motions in limine are to be noticed for hearing no later than the Monday eight days prior to the trial date. If the hearing date falls on a legal holiday, notice the motion-in-limine hearing fifteen days prior to the trial date.

Discovery motions are to be scheduled before the magistrate judge assigned to the case (the magistrate judge's initials, followed by a small "x," are in the parenthetical in the case number). All discovery motion papers must include "DISCOVERY MATTER" in the caption.

VII. TELEPHONIC HEARINGS: At least one week prior to the scheduled hearing, counsel located outside the Central District may arrange to appear telephonically. Contact the Court Clerk at 213-894-3913 for the Court's permission. The requesting attorney is responsible for informing all parties of the telephonic appearance, which parties are to appear in person or telephonically, as well as any change in the hearing time. The requesting attorney is responsible for coordinating and initiating the telephone call. No cellular or speaker telephones may be used. All participants are to be on the telephone line before connecting the Court.

VIII. DISCOVERY MOTIONS: All discovery motions must be heard prior to the discovery cut-off date.

IX. TRIAL EXHIBITS: Three non-blue backed copies each of exhibit lists and witness lists (in the order they are to be called) are to be delivered to the Court Clerk on the morning of the first day of trial.

Two exhibit notebooks (an original and the Judge's copy) are required to be delivered to the Court Clerk on the morning of the first day of trial. No additional notebook is needed for witnesses. Counsel are to prepare their exhibits by placing them in 3-hole notebooks. The notebooks are to be tabbed down the right side with numeric tabs separating each exhibit. The exhibits are to be numbered in accordance with Local Rule 26.4. Each exhibit must have an exhibit tag stapled to the upper right-hand corner of its first page. The spine on the exhibit notebook must reflect the exhibit numbers contained within. For example: Trial Exhibit Notebook 1, Exh. Nos. 1-25.

A. Exhibit Tags: The Court requires the large exhibit tags, which may be obtained from the Clerk's Office, Room G-19, 312 North Spring Street, Los Angeles.

Each exhibit should have an exhibit tag stapled to the upper right-hand corner of its first page. The plaintiff's exhibits shall be tagged with yellow tags; and the defendant's exhibits shall be tagged with blue tags. The tags shall indicate the case number, case name, and exhibit number.

X. JURY INSTRUCTIONS:

A. Civil Jury Trials – Local Rule 16.2 requires that counsel meet at least forty (40) days in advance of the date set for the final Pre-Trial Conference for the purpose of accomplishing various tasks in preparation for trial. In addition to the tasks set forth in Local Rule 16.2, the parties shall meet with the goal of reaching agreement to one set of joint jury instructions and one verdict form. The set of joint jury instructions must be filed at least five (5) court days before the final Pre-Trial Conference. The parties may submit another set of jury instructions containing the instructions upon which the parties disagree and the objections to those instructions.

Where the parties disagree on an instruction, the party opposing the instruction must attach a short (i.e., one to two paragraphs) statement supporting the objection and the party submitting the instruction must attach a short statement supporting the instruction. Each statement should be on a separate page and should follow directly after the disputed instruction.

Accordingly, the parties ultimately will submit one document or, if the parties disagree over any proposed jury instructions, two documents. If the parties submit two documents, those documents should consist of: (1) a set of agreed upon jury instructions and (2) a set of disputed jury instructions along with reasons supporting and opposing each disputed instruction.

The Court orders the parties to make every attempt to agree upon the jury instructions before submitting them to the Court. In addition, where the Manual of Model Civil Jury Instructions for the Ninth Circuit (2007 edition) provides a version of a requested instruction, the parties shall submit the Model instruction. Where California law applies, the Court prefers counsel to use *California Jury Instructions -- Civil* ("BAJI"). If neither of the above sources is applicable, counsel are directed to use the instructions from O'Malley-Grenig-Lee, et al., *Federal Jury Practice* and Instructions (Fifth Edition). Each requested jury instruction shall cover only one subject or principle of law and shall be numbered and set forth in full on a separate page, citing the authority or source of the requested instruction (except for the jury copy discussed below).

The Court will send a copy of the jury instructions into the jury room for use by the jury during deliberations. Accordingly, in addition to the file copies described above, the parties shall file with the Courtroom Deputy Clerk on the first day of the trial a "clean set" of joint and/or proposed jury instructions which contain only the text of each instruction set forth in full on each page, with the caption "Court's Instruction Number" (eliminating titles, supporting authority, indication of party proposing, etc.). This will be referred to as the "Jury Copy" of the jury instructions.

If counsel prepared the jury instructions using WordPerfect, counsel shall provide the Court with a compact disk (CD) containing the proposed jury instructions along with the hard copy.

An index page shall accompany all jury instructions submitted to the Court. The index page shall indicate the following:

a. The number of the instruction;
b. A brief title of the instruction;

c. The source of the instruction and any relevant case citations; and
d. The page number of the instruction.

EXAMPLE:

Number	Title	Source	Page
1	Burden of Proof	9th Cir. 12.02	7

Counsel shall also prepare a joint statement of the case which will be read by the Court to the prospective panel of jurors prior to the commencement of voir dire. The statement should not be longer than two or three paragraphs. The statement shall be filed with the Court five (5) court days before the Pre-Trial Conference.

B. Criminal Jury Trials – At least five (5) court days prior to the final Pre-Trial Conference, the parties shall meet with the goal of reaching agreement to one set of joint jury instructions.

Where the parties disagree on an instruction, the party opposing the instruction must attach a short (i.e., one to two paragraphs) statement supporting the objection and the party submitting the instruction must attach a short statement supporting the instruction. Each statement should be on a separate page and should follow directly after the disputed instruction.

Accordingly, the parties ultimately will submit one document or, if the parties disagree over any proposed jury instructions, two documents. If the parties submit two documents, those documents should consist of: (1) a set of agreed upon jury instructions and (2) a set of disputed jury instructions along with reasons supporting and opposing each disputed instruction.

The Court orders the parties to make every attempt to agree upon the jury instructions before submitting them to the Court. In addition, where the Manual of Model Criminal Jury Instructions for the Ninth Circuit provides a version of a requested instruction, the parties shall submit the Model instruction. The only exception to the above is that the Court prefers the instruction from Edward J. Devitt, et al., *Federal Jury Practice* and Instructions on the burden of proof. If a Model instruction does not exist for a particular subject, counsel may submit an instruction from Devitt (*supra*). Each requested jury instruction shall cover only one subject or principle of law and shall be numbered and set forth in full on a separate page, citing the authority or source of the requested instruction (except for the jury copy discussed below).

The Court will send a copy of the jury instructions into the jury room for use by the jury during deliberations. Accordingly, in addition to the file copies described above, the parties shall file with the Courtroom Deputy Clerk on the first day of the trial a "clean set" of joint and/or proposed jury instructions which contain only the text of each instruction set forth in full on each page, with the caption "Court's Instruction Number" (eliminating titles, supporting authority, indication of party proposing, etc.). This will be referred to as the "Jury Copy" of the jury instructions.

If counsel prepared the jury instructions using WordPerfect, counsel shall provide the Court with a three and one-half inch floppy disk containing the proposed jury instructions along with the hard copy.

An index page shall accompany all jury instructions submitted to the Court. The index page shall indicate the following:

a. The number of the instruction;
b. A brief title of the instruction;
c. The source of the instruction and any relevant case citations; and
d. The page number of the instruction.

EXAMPLE:

Number	Title	Source	Page
1	Burden of Proof	9th Cir. 12.02	7

Counsel shall also prepare a joint statement of the case which will be read by the Court to the prospective panel of jurors prior to the commencement of voir dire. The statement should not be longer than two or three paragraphs. The statement shall be filed with the Court five (5) court days before the Pre-Trial Conference.

XI. EX PARTE APPLICATIONS AND TEMPORARY RESTRAINING ORDERS: Do not attempt to schedule a hearing date and time for ex parte applications and temporary restraining orders. Follow the local rules and federal rules of procedure. Judge Pregerson will review your papers. If a hearing is necessary, counsel will be notified as soon as possible.

XII. TRANSCRIPT ORDERS: For general information on how to order a transcript of any reported or digitally recorded proceeding, please contact 213-894-3015 or visit www.cacd.uscourts.gov > General Information > Court Reporter/Recorder Transcripts. If you require an estimate of cost for the preparation of a transcript, contact the court reporter/recorder for the desired proceeding.

To determine the court reporter/recorder for a particular proceeding, go to the Court Reporter Schedule web page and click on View by Date. Once you've determined the correct court reporter/recorder for the desired session, click on Court Reporter Phone and Email List for contact information.

XIII. INTERPRETERS: Procedures for obtaining the services of an interpreter on a civil case are the responsibility of counsel. Interpreters must be certified. For information, dial 213-894-4599.

XIV. OTHER INFORMATION: General information: 213-894-3535 or 213-894-1565 (recording).

XV. LAW CLERK and EXTERN APPLICANTS: Applicants may submit applications to Judge Dean D. Pregerson, Room #244-J, 312 North Spring Street, Los Angeles, California 90012. Applications are to include a cover letter, resume, transcript, and writing sample. Letters of recommendation are to be directed to this address. **Please note: All law clerk positions for the 2009-10 term have been filled.**

XVI. PURCHASING COPIES OF LOCAL RULES:

Los Angeles Daily Journal, 915 East First Street, Los Angeles, California 90012;
Metropolitan News, 210 South Spring Street, Los Angeles, California 90012;
West Publishing Company, 50 West Kellogg Boulevard, St. Paul, Minnesota 55164-9979.

Hon. Manuel L. Real
District Judge

Chambers Information
U.S. District Court, Central District of California
Courtroom 8, 2nd Floor
312 N. Spring Street
Los Angeles, CA 90012

Scheduling Information
Courtroom Deputy: (213) 894-5696

Civil Law and Motion	First and third Mondays of each month at 10:00 a.m.
Criminal Law and Motion	Mondays at 1:30 p.m.

Biographical Information
Born 1924 in San Pedro, CA

Federal Judicial Service:
-Judge, U. S. District Court, Central District of California
-Nominated by Lyndon B. Johnson on September 26, 1966, to a new seat created by 80 Stat. 75; Confirmed by the Senate on October 20, 1966, and received commission on November 3, 1966.
-Served as chief judge, 1982-1993.

Education:
-University of Southern California, B.S., 1944
-Loyola Law School, Los Angeles, CA, LL.B., 1951

Professional Career:
-U.S. Naval Reserve, 1943-1945
-Assistant U.S. Attorney, Southern District of California, 1952-1955
-Private practice, San Pedro, California, 1955-1964
-U.S. Attorney for the Southern District of California, 1964-1966

I. Judge Real's Procedures and Practices

A. *Procedures and Schedules*

1. **Civil motions are heard on:** 1st and 3rd Mondays of each month, **Time:** 10:00A.M.

   Pre-Trial Conferences are heard on: Mondays as set by Court, **Time:** 11:00 A.M.

   Criminal motions are heard on: Mondays, **Time:** 1:30 P.M

   (If Monday is a holiday, motion date is: Next day (Tuesday). **It is not necessary to clear a motion date with the court clerk prior to filing a motion.**

2. **Discovery motions are to be scheduled before the District Judge.** (Judge Real handles all his own discovery, does not refer to a Magistrate Judge)

3. **Are tentative rulings issued?** No

4. **Are Mandatory Chambers Copies accepted by Court?** Mandatory chambers copies of e-filed documents shall be delivered to the Clerk's Office care of civil or criminal intake, placed in the courtesy copy in-box outside of chambers or sent to the Court via overnight mail, ***within 12 court business hours of the time the document was e-filed***. The courtesy copy shall be blue-backed and double-hole punched.

5. **Procedures for filing an Ex Parte Application:** A party submits an Ex Parte Application, with a declaration of notification to the other parties (which includes notice that they have 24 hours from actual receipt of the papers to file any opposition), and a separate proposed order; the other parties have 24 hours to file their responses, and the matter then stands submitted. If the Court wishes a hearing, the court clerk will contact all counsel with the date and time of the hearing.

6. **To request a continuance of any scheduled court proceeding:** The party(ies) must make the request in writing by either submitting a stipulation or ex parte application with a proposed order for the Court's signature; alternative dates should be cleared with the court clerk before submitting the document.

7. Are counsel allowed to contact the Judge's law clerks or secretary? No; all inquiries of any nature are to be directed to the court clerk.

8. **Inquiries regarding the status of a motion, stipulation or proposed order:** Are to be made to the court clerk.

9. **Calendar conflicts (procedures for attorneys to follow if they have a calendar conflict):** If a date is set by the Judge in court, counsel must advise the Judge at that time of any conflicts; if the conflict has arisen later, for instance just prior to a hearing, counsel must advise the court clerk by telephone (however, be advised: priority at the hearing can be arranged, or the matter put at the end of the calendar, but without a written stipulation/ex parte application and an order signed by the Judge, counsel must appear or risk being held in contempt).

10. **Procedures for bringing electronic equipment into the courtroom:**

    - Arrangements for bringing voluminous exhibits into the courtroom may be made through the Space and Facilities Help Desk, at (213) 894-1400.

    - ELMO reservations/tutorials may be made by first referring to the court website at www.cacd.uscourts.gov, under "Attorney Information," and then "Attorney Services." Alternatively, you can contact the Courtroom Technology Help Desk at 213-894-3061.

11. **To order a transcript of a proceeding:** For general information on how to order a transcript of any reported or digitally recorded proceeding, please contact 213-894-3015 or visit www.cacd.uscourts.gov > General Information > Court Reporter/Recorder Transcripts. If you require an estimate of cost for the preparation of a transcript, contact the court reporter/recorder for the desired proceeding.

    To determine the court reporter/recorder for a particular proceeding, go to the Court Reporter Schedule web page and click on View by Date. Once you've determined the correct court reporter/recorder for the desired session, click on Court Reporter Phone and Email List for contact information.

12. **Questions regarding law clerk/extern positions:** Shall be directed to the Judge's secretary.

13. **Trial Preparation:**
    a. **Court hours:** 9:00 A.M. to 12 noon; then 1:30 P.M. to whenever the Judge adjourns court for the evening.

    b. **Exhibition preparation:** Pursuant to the local rules (the exhibits, except for physical exhibits, shall be in 3-ring binders, the original tagged set for the court clerk -- who will pass same to the witnesses -- one set for the Judge, and a third set for the court reporter).

    c. **Jury instructions:** To be submitted in the form and time frames in accordance with the Federal Rules of Civil and Criminal Procedure and the local rules; counsel need submit substantive instructions only.

    d. **Verdict forms:** The court clerk prepares the verdict form in criminal cases; in civil cases the plaintiff submits the proposed verdict form in accordance with the Federal Rules of Civil Procedure and the local rules.

    e. **Other:** The parties shall come to court fully prepared, with the three sets of bound exhibits as described above; and also with three clean copies of their witness lists and three clean copies of their exhibit lists, all which shall be given to the court clerk before the start of court.

14. **Procedures for obtaining the services of an interpreter on a civil case:** The party must hire a certified Federal Court interpreter, whether it be done through the Court's Interpreter's Section, or from some outside source.

15. **Proposed Orders, Judgments or any other Signature Items:** Pursuant to General Order 10-07, a Microsoft Word or WordPerfect copy of any proposed document requiring a signature shall and must be e-mailed to the generic chambers e-mail address (r_chambers@cacd.uscourts.gov). The subject line of the e-mail shall be in the following format: court's divisional office, year, case type, case number, judge's initials and filer (party) name [e.g., *2:09 CV 09876* R *(Plaintiff or Defendant's name)*].

II. Judge Real's Case Management Orders

A. Notice of Pretrial Conference

IN THE UNITED STATES DISTICT COURT
FOR THE CENTRAL DISTRICT OF CALIFORNIA

	)	Case No. ______________
Plaintiff(s),	)	
v.	)	**NOTICE OF PRE-TRIAL**
Defendant(s).	)	**CONFERENCE**
______________________________	)	

TO: Counsel of Record

This case has been placed on calendar for Pre-Trial Conference in Courtroom 8 of this Court at ________ A.M. on _________ pursuant to F.R.Civ.P. 16 and Local Rule 16 *et seq.* Unless excused for good cause each party appearing in this action shall be represented at the Pre-Trial Conference and all pre-trial meetings of counsel by the attorney who is to have charge of the conduct of the trial on behalf of such party. A party appearing *pro se* shall be obligated to the same attendance required of an attorney for a party.

STRICT COMPLIANCE IS REQUIRED BY THE COURT WITH THE REQUIREMENTS OF LOCAL RULE 16 AND ALL DOCUMENTS REQUIRED THEREIN AND THE FEDERAL RULES OF CIVIL PROCEDURE. FAILURE TO COMPLY WITH THESE RULES MAY LEAD TO DISMISSAL OF THE ACTION.

Memoranda of contentions of fact and law, Exhibit Lists and Witness Lists shall be filed and served on or before _______________, which date also serves as the Discovery Cut-Off Date in this action. There is no Motion Cut-Off Date set.

Pre-Trial Conference Order shall be lodged with the Court on or before _________.

Trial date is set as _____________ at __________ a.m.

Dated: ________________

____
MANUEL L. REAL
United States District Judge

B. Order Regarding Notice to Counsel

IN THE UNITED STATES DISTICT COURT
FOR THE CENTRAL DISTRICT OF CALIFORNIA

)	Case No. ________________
Plaintiff(s),)	
v.)	**ORDER RE: NOTICE TO**
Defendant(s).)	**COUNSEL**
___________________________________)	

READ CAREFULLY: FAILURE TO COMPLY MAY LEAD TO SANCTIONS

This case has been assigned to the calendar of Judge Manuel L. Real. Counsel are advised that the Court expects strict compliance with the provisions of the Local Rules and the Federal Rules of Civil Procedure. **NONCOMPLIANCE MAY LEAD TO THE IMPOSITION OF SANCTIONS WHICH MAY INCLUDE THE STRIKING OF PLEADINGS AND ENTRY OF JUDGMENT OR DISMISSAL OF THE ACTION.**

The attention of counsel is particularly directed to Local Rule 16. Counsel should also be guided by the following special requirements when litigating cases assigned to Judge Real:

1. **INTERROGATORIES:** *See* Local Rules.

2. **MOTIONS:** Motions shall be heard on the first and third Monday of each month at 10:00 A.M., unless otherwise ordered by the Court. If the Monday is a national holiday, the succeeding Tuesday shall be the motion day. Counsel do not need to contact the Court in this regard, as there is no need to reserve dates.

3. ***EX PARTE* APPLICATIONS:** No hearing will be held unless deemed necessary by the Court; if the Court requires a hearing, the clerk will contact the parties and inform them of the date and time. In the moving papers' declaration of notification, the declarant shall state whether or not the

application is opposed; if opposed, the declarant shall state that the opposing party was informed that it has twenty-four (24) hours from receipt of the papers to file its opposition. The matter will then stand submitted.

4. **CONTINUANCES:** Counsel requesting a continuance must submit a stipulation with a detailed declaration as to the reason for the requested continuance or extension of time, together with a proposed order. Stipulations, including those for second and subsequent extensions of time to respond to the complaint, are effective ONLY when approved by this Court. Any stipulation not in compliance with this order or the Local Rules will automatically be denied without further notice to the parties.

5. **CONFORMED COPIES:** Parties will receive conformed copies through the Court's CM/ECF e-filing system; or by mail, if applicable.

6. **REMOVED ACTIONS:** Any answers filed in state court must be refiled in this Court as a supplement to the petition. Any pending motions must be renoticed in accordance with Local Rule 7.

7. **WAIVED LOCAL RULES:** (Local Rule 16-14.1). Settlement conferences are NOT mandatory; if the parties mutually agree to the holding of a settlement conference, they shall contact the clerk. (Local Rule 7-3): parties are NOT obligated to meet and confer, or file a

declaration in connection thereto, for the purposes of preparing and filing dispositive motions (to dismiss, summary judgment, etc).

8. **FEDERAL RULE 26(f):** This Court requires the following, and counsel are ORDERED to follow this outline: 30 days after the first answering defendant files a response to the complaint, the parties shall hold an early meeting, in person, for the purpose of making initial disclosures. Plaintiff's counsel shall have the duty of scheduling the meeting. The parties shall then file a Joint Report of Early Meeting within 14 days of the holding of the Early Meeting of Counsel. Counsel are informed that approximately 30 days after receipt of the Joint Report, this Court shall issue an Order setting the dates of the Final Pre-Trial Conference, and the Trial of the action. This Court shall not set a "scheduling conference" or issue a "scheduling order" other than as set out previously in this section.

9. **COURTESY COPIES OF E-FILED DOCUMENTS:** Courtesy copies are not accepted directly in chambers. Copies of all e-filed documents shall be delivered either to the civil intake section clearly marked as a courtesy copy, placed in the courtesy copy in-box outside of chambers or sent to the Court via overnight mail, within twelve (12) court business hours of the time the document was e-filed. The courtesy copy shall be blue-backed and double-hole punched.

10. **WORD/WORDPERFECT PROPOSED ORDERS, JUDGMENTS OR ANY OTHER SIGNATURE ITEMS:**

Pursuant to General Order 08-02, a Microsoft Word or WordPerfect copy of any proposed document requiring a signature shall and must be e-mailed to the generic chambers e-mail address (***r_chambers@cacd.uscourts.gov***). The subject line of the e-mail shall be in the following format: court's divisional office, year, case type, case number, judge's initials and filer (party) name [*e.g.*, 2:09 CV 09876 R (Plaintiff's or Defendant's name)].

11. **NOTICE OF THIS ORDER:** Counsel for plaintiff, or plaintiff, if appearing on his or her own behalf, is responsible for promptly serving this notice on defendant's counsel, and filing a proof of service with the notice attached as an exhibit with the Court. If this case came to the Court via a Noticed Removal, this burden falls to the removing defendant.

Date: ______________

____
MANUEL L. REAL
United States District Judge

Hon. James V. Selna

District Judge

Chambers Information

U.S. District Court, Central District of California
Courtroom 10C
411 West Fourth Street
Santa Ana, CA 92701

Scheduling Information

Courtroom Deputy: (714) 338-2848

Civil Law and Motion	Mondays at 1:30 p.m.
Criminal Law and Motion	Mondays at 9:00 a.m.

Biographical Information

Born 1945 in San Jose, CA

Federal Judicial Service:

-Judge, U. S. District Court, Central District of California
-Nominated by George W. Bush on January 29, 2003, to a seat vacated by J. Spencer Letts; Confirmed by the Senate on March 27, 2003, and received commission on March 27, 2003.

Education:

-Stanford University, A.B., 1967
-Stanford Law School, J.D., 1970

Professional Career:

-Captain, U.S. Army Reserve, 1967-1978
-Private Practice, California, 1970-1998
-Judge, Superior Court, Orange County, California, 1998-2003

I. Judge Selna's Procedures and Practices

A. *Procedures and Schedules*

1. Civil motions are heard on: **Mondays**, Time: **1:30 p.m.**

   Criminal motions are heard on: **Mondays**, Time: **9:00 a.m.**

   (If Monday is a holiday, next motion date is ***the following Monday.***)

   It **is not** necessary to clear a motion date with the court clerk prior to filing the motion. **Counsel MUST comply with the Federal and Local Rules regarding service when selecting a date for the hearing on their motion.** If the Court does not believe that oral argument will be helpful, the Court will advise the parties no later than the Friday before the hearing.
2. The Court does not entertain telephone appearances for hearings except in exceptional circumstances.
3. All discovery motions are to be calendared before the magistrate judge.
4. Tentative rulings may be issued. If issued, they will be available by clicking on the "Tentative Rulings" link above after Noon on the business day before the hearing and/or approximately 1/2 hour prior to the hearing in the courtroom. If all parties submit on the tentative ruling, please advise the Courtroom Deputy, and no appearance will be required.
5. Mandatory Chambers Copies of all e-filed documents shall be delivered to the mandatory chambers copy box on the 10th Floor. It is imperative that the mandatory chambers copies be delivered by noon following the date of filing as required by General Order 10-07.IV.D. Failure to deliver timely mandatory chambers copies may result in a delay in hearing a motion or ordering the matter off calendar.

   The Court does not accept mandatory chambers copies of Sealed Documents.
6. Ex Parte applications are for extraordinary relief only. Ex parte applications are considered on the papers and are rarely set for hearings. The moving party shall serve the opposing party by FAX or hand service and shall notify the opposing party that any opposition must be filed not later than 24 hours after such FAX or hand service. If counsel do not intend to oppose the ex parte application, counsel must inform the courtroom deputy by telephone as soon as possible.
7. To request a continuance of any scheduled court proceeding, counsel must make such request at least five days prior to the hearing date with a statement of good cause included in the request.
8. Counsel are not to initiate telephone calls to Judge Selna's chambers, law clerk or secretary.
9. Inquiries regarding the status of a motion, stipulation or proposed order are not available by phone. Please follow Local Rule 11-4.5.
10. If there is a calendar conflict, counsel are to inform the courtroom deputy prior to the date of the conflict.
11. Counsel should contact the courtroom deputy concerning procedures for bringing electronic equipment or extraordinary exhibits into the courtroom.
12. For general information on how to order a transcript of any reported or digitally recorded proceeding, please contact 213-894-3015 or visit www.cacd.uscourts.gov > General Information > Court Reporter/Recorder Transcripts. If you require an

estimate of cost for the preparation of a transcript, contact the court reporter/recorder for the desired proceeding.

To determine the court reporter/recorder for a particular proceeding, go to the Court Reporter Schedule web page and click on View by Date. Once you've determined the correct court reporter/recorder for the desired session, click on Court Reporter Phone and Email List for contact information.

13. Questions regarding law clerk/extern positions should be directed to the secretary.

14. Trial preparation:

   a. **Court hours:** The Court will, generally, try short cases (less than 10 days) from 9:00 a.m. to 12:00 noon and 1:30 p.m. to 4:30 p.m. Longer cases will be tried from 8:00 a.m. to 2:00 p.m. with no lunch break. The final determination of trial hours will be made at the final pretrial conference.

   b. **Exhibit preparation:**
   Under 10 Total Volumes of Exhibits - Counsel are to prepare exhibits for trial by placing them in three ring binders that are indexed by exhibit number with tabs or dividers on the right side and indicating on the spine of the binder the exhibit numbers contained and the volume number. The exhibits must be numbered in accordance with Fed. R. Civ. P. 16, 26 and the Local Rules. Counsel shall have the original set (with the exhibit tags affixed to the upper or lower right hand corner) and a bench copy on the exhibits, three (3) copies of the exhibit list and three (3) copies of the witness list to the Courtroom Deputy Clerk on the first day of trial.

   10 or More Total Volumes of Exhibits - Counsel are to prepare one (1) full set of the exhibits in three ring binders that are indexed by exhibit number with tabs or dividers on the right side and indicating on the spine of the binder the exhibit numbers contained and the volume number. Each exhibit shall have an exhibit tag placed in the upper or lower right hand corner of the first page of the exhibit. (These are the exhibits that will go to the jury during deliberations). Exhibits for the Judge & Witnesses: There should be a book for each witness that contains only the exhibits needed for that specific witness with dividers on the right side. This book should be presented to the witness when the witness is called. A copy of this book should be provided to the Judge at the time the witness is called. The Court requires counsel to submit the full set of exhibits, three (3) copies of the exhibit list and three (3) copies of the witness list to the Courtroom Deputy Clerk on the first day of trial.

   c. **Jury instructions:** Counsel shall submit all instructions on the first day of trial, to be supplemented to the extent that the evidence requires additional or modified instructions.

   d. **Verdict forms:** The plaintiff shall submit the verdict form prior to the close of the plaintiff's case in chief.

15. Counsel in civil cases are to obtain the services of an interpreter, if one is needed. Counsel may contact the Interpreter's Office for references.

16. The Court does not permit special appearances. Counsel of record shall appear at all court proceedings.

17. Judge Selna's AO-10, Financial Disclosure Report, may be reviewed at the Judicial Watch website. The reports for 2003 through 2010 are presently online .

II. Judge Selna's Case Management Orders

A. *Initial Order Following Filing of Complaint*

**IN THE UNITED STATES DISTICT COURT
FOR THE CENTRAL DISTRICT OF CALIFORNIA**

	)	Case No ________
Plaintiff(s),	)	
v.	)	**INITIAL ORDER FOLLOWING**
Defendant(s).	)	**FILING OF COMPLAINT**
________________________	)	**ASSIGNED TO JUDGE SELNA**

Important Notice: The Court posts tentative law and motions rulings to the internet. Please *see* Section P, below.

COUNSEL FOR PLAINTIFF SHALL SERVE THIS ORDER ON ALL DEFENDANTS AND/OR THEIR COUNSEL ALONG WITH THE SUMMONS AND COMPLAINT, OR IF THAT IS NOT PRACTICABLE AS SOON AS POSSIBLE THEREAFTER. IF THIS CASE WAS ASSIGNED TO THIS COURT AFTER BEING REMOVED FROM STATE COURT, THE DEFENDANT WHO REMOVED THE CASE SHALL SERVE THIS ORDER ON ALL OTHER PARTIES.

This case has been assigned to the calendar of Judge James V. Selna. The intent of this Order is to ensure that this case will proceed so as "to secure [a] just, speedy and inexpensive determination." (Fed.R.Civ. P., Rule 1.)

A. THE COURT'S ORDERS

Copies of Judge Selna's orders that may have specific application to this case are available on the Central District of California website. *See* ¶ N.

Those orders include the following:

(1) Order Setting Rule 26(f) Scheduling Conference
(2) Order re Civil Jury Trials
(3) Order re Civil Court Trials
(4) Order re RICO Case Statement

B. SERVICE OF PLEADINGS

Although Fed.R.Civ.P., Rule 4(m) does not require the summons and complaint to be served for as much as 120 days, the Court expects that the initial pleadings will be served much sooner than that, and will require plaintiff to show cause before then if it appears that there is undue delay.

C. ASSIGNMENT TO A MAGISTRATE JUDGE

Under 28 U.S.C. § 636, the parties may consent to have a Magistrate Judge preside over all proceedings, including trial. The Magistrate Judges who accept those designations are identified on the Central District's website, which also contains the consent form. *See* ¶ N.

D. *EX PARTE* PRACTICE

Ex parte applications are solely for extraordinary relief and should be used with discretion. *See Mission Power Engineering Company v. Continental Casualty Co.*, 883 F. Supp. 488 (C. D. Cal. 1995). The Court will generally decide *ex parte* matters on the papers. Opposition to an *ex parte* application, if any, should be submitted within 24 hours.

E. **APPLICATIONS AND STIPULATIONS FOR EXTENSIONS OF TIME**

No stipulations extending scheduling requirements or modifying applicable rules are effective until and unless the Court approves them. Both applications and stipulations must set forth:

1. The existing due date or hearing date;

2. Specific, concrete reasons supporting good cause for granting the extension. In this regard, a statement that an extension "will promote settlement" is insufficient. The requesting party or parties must indicate the status of ongoing negotiations: Have written proposals been exchanged? Is counsel in the process of reviewing a draft settlement agreement? Has a mediator been selected?

3. Whether there have been prior requests for extensions, and whether these were granted or denied by the Court.

F. **TRO'S AND INJUNCTIONS**

Parties seeking emergency or provisional relief shall comply with F.R.Civ.P., Rule 65 and Local Rule 65. The Court will not rule on any application for such relief for at least 24 hours after the party subject to the requested order has been served; such party may file opposing or responding papers in the interim.

G. **CASES REMOVED FROM STATE COURT**

All documents filed in state court, including documents appended to the complaint, answers and motions, must be refiled in this Court as a supplement to the Notice of Renewal, if not already included. *See* 28 U.S.C. § 1447(a),(b). If the defendant has not yet answered or moved, the answer or responsive pleading filed in this Court must comply with the Federal Rules of Civil Procedure and the Local Rules of the Central District. If before the case was removed a motion was pending in state court, it must be re-noticed in accordance with Local Rule 7.

H. **STATUS OF FICTITIOUSLY NAMED DEFENDANTS**

This Court intends to adhere to the following procedures where a matter is removed to this Court on diversity grounds with fictitiously named defendants. (*See* 28 U.S.C. §§ 1441(a) and 1447.)

1. Plaintiff is normally expected to ascertain the identity of and serve any fictitiously named defendants within 120 days of the removal of the action to this Court.

2. If plaintiff believes (by reason of the necessity for discovery or otherwise) that fictitiously named defendants cannot be fully identified within the 120-day period, an *ex parte* application requesting permission to extend that period to effectuate service may be filed with this Court. Such application shall state the reasons therefor, and may be granted upon a showing of good cause. The *ex parte* application shall be served upon all appearing parties, and shall state that appearing parties may comment within seven (7) days of the filing of the *ex parte* application.

3. If plaintiff desires to substitute a named defendant for one of the fictitiously named parties, plaintiff first shall seek to obtain consent from counsel for the previously-identified defendants (and counsel for the fictitiously named party, if that party has separate counsel). If consent is withheld or denied, plaintiff may apply *ex parte* requesting such amendment, with notice to all appearing parties. Each party shall have seven calendar days to respond. The *ex parte* application and any response should comment not only on the

substitution of the named party for a fictitiously named defendant, but on the question of whether the matter should thereafter be remanded to the Superior Court if diversity of citizenship is destroyed by the addition of the new substituted party. *See* U.S.C. § 1447(c), (d).

I. BANKRUPTCY APPEALS

Counsel shall comply with the ORDER RE PROCEDURE TO BE FOLLOWED IN APPEAL FROM BANKRUPTCY COURT issued at the time the appeal is filed in the District Court.

J. MOTIONS UNDER FED.R.CIV.P., Rule 12

Many motions to dismiss or to strike could be avoided if the parties confer in good faith (as they are required to do under L.R. 7-3), especially for perceived defects in a complaint, answer or counterclaim which could be corrected by amendment. *See Chang v. Chen*, 80 F.3d 1293, 1296 (9th Cir. 1996) (where a motion to dismiss is granted, a district court should provide leave to amend unless it is clear that the complaint could not be saved by any amendment). Moreover, a party has the right to amend his complaint "once as a matter of course at any time before a responsive pleading is served." Fed.R.Civ.P., Rule 15(a). A 12(b)(6) motion is not a responsive pleading and therefore plaintiff might have a right to amend. *See Nolen v. Fitzharris*, 450 F.2d 958, 958-59 (9th Cir. 1971); *St. Michael's Convalescent Hospital v. California*, 643 F.2d 1369, 1374 (9th Cir. 1981). And even where a party has amended his Complaint once or a responsive pleading has been served, the Federal Rules provide that leave to amend should be "freely given when justice so requires." F.R.Civ.P., Rule 15(a). The Ninth Circuit requires that this policy favoring amendment be applied with "extreme liberality." *Morongo Band of Mission Indians v. Rose*, 893 F.2d 1074, 1079 (9th Cir. 1990).

These principles require that counsel for the plaintiff should carefully evaluate the defendant's contentions as to the deficiencies in the complaint, and that in many instances the moving party should agree to any amendment that would cure a curable defect.

The moving party shall attach a copy of the challenged pleading to the Memorandum of Points and Authorities in support of the motion.

The foregoing provisions apply as well to motions to dismiss a counterclaim, answer or affirmative defense, which a plaintiff might contemplate bringing.

K. REQUIREMENTS FOR BRIEFS

In addition to the requirements in Local Rule 11, the Court requires the following for all briefs:

1. No footnote shall exceed 5 lines. The Court strongly discourages the use of extensive footnotes as a subterfuge to avoid page limitations in the Local Rules.

2. All footnotes shall be in the same type size as text. See Local Rule 11-3.1.1.

3. Each case cited shall include a jump cite to the page or pages where the relevant authority appears (*e.g.*, *United States v. Doe*, 500 U. S. 1, 14, 17 (1997)).

Failure to follow these requirements may result in rejection of a brief for correction.

L. LEAD COUNSEL

Lead counsel shall appear on all dispositive motions, scheduling conferences, and settlement conferences. **The Court does not entertain special appearances; only counsel of record may appear.**

M. COURTESY COPIES

A courtesy copy of all electronically filed pleadings shall be delivered to Judge Selna's courtesy copy drop on the tenth floor at the rear of the elevator lobby by noon the day following filing. **Failure to make timely delivery of the courtesy copies may result in a delay in hearing a motion or ordering the matter off calendar.**

N. ELECTRONIC COPIES

When the Court requires an electronic copy of a document (*e.g.*, with proposed jury instructions), a copy shall be submitted at time of filing in one the following manners: providing a copy on a disk, CD, or thumb drive in a labeled envelope and lodged with the clerk; or by e-mailing a copy to the Court Room Deputy (***JVS_Chambers@cacd.uscourts.gov***). Regardless of media, the document should be formatted in WordPerfect9 or higher.

O. WEBSITE

Copies of this Order and other orders of this Court are available on the Central District of California's website, at "www.cacd.uscourts.gov" at Judge Selna's home page located under "Judge's Procedures and Schedules."

P. TENTATIVES–DAY OF HEARING AND WEB POSTING

The Court attempts to issue tentative rulings on each motion. Tentatives will be posted on the Court's website: www.cacd.uscourts.gov/. From the home page, click on "Judges' Procedures and Schedules" in the left column. From the list, click on "Hon. James V. Selna," which will take you to Judge Selna's page. Click on the red notice in the upper left: "Click here to view Tentative Rulings." Then click on the desired ruling which comes up in a .pdf file which can be read with an Adobe Acrobat reader. Judge Selna attempts to post tentatives by late Friday afternoon preceding the hearing date. Hard copies of tentatives will also be available from the clerk approximately 15 minutes before the hearing.

The Court thanks counsel and the parties for their anticipated cooperation.

IT IS SO ORDERED.

Dated: January 6, 2010

____

JAMES V. SELNA
United States District Judge

B. Order Regarding Court Trial

IN THE UNITED STATES DISTICT COURT
FOR THE CENTRAL DISTRICT OF CALIFORNIA

Plaintiff(s), v. Defendant(s).	Case No. ________________ **I. ORDER FOR COURT TRIAL SETTING DATES FOR:** Discovery Cut-Off: ______________ Pre-Trial Conference: ______at 11:00 A.M. Trial: ________ at 9:00 A.M. **II. Order for Preparation for COURT TRIAL, Proposed Findings of Fact & Conclusions of Law, and Scheduling** **III. Order Governing Attorney and Party Conduct at Trial**

I.
ORDER FOR COURT TRIAL – SETTING DATES
Scheduling

1. **In General:** All motions to join other parties or to amend the pleadings shall be filed and served within sixty (60) days of the date of this order and noticed for hearing within ninety (90) days hereof. All unserved parties shall be dismissed no later than the date set for the Final Pre-Trial Conference.

2. **Motions for Summary Judgment or Partial Summary Judgment:** Motions for summary judgment or partial summary judgment shall be heard no later than the last day for hearing motions, as set forth in the accompanying minute order. Please note the extended notice requirements under F. R. Civ. P. 56(c) which are longer than provided in the Local Rules.

3. **Discovery Cut-Off:** The Court has established a cut-off date for discovery in this action. All discovery is to be completed on, or prior to, the cutoff date. Accordingly, the following discovery schedule shall apply to this case:

A. Depositions: All depositions shall be scheduled to commence at least five (5) working days prior to the discovery cut-off date. All original depositions to be used in trial shall be lodged with the Courtroom Deputy on the day of trial.

B. Interrogatories: All interrogatories must be served at least forty-five (45) days prior to the discovery cut-off date. The Court will not approve stipulations between counsel that permit responses to be served after the cut-off date except in extraordinary circumstances.

C. Production of Documents, *etc.*: All requests for production, etc., shall be served at least forty-five (45) days prior to the discovery cut-off date. The Court will not approve stipulations between counsel that permit responses to be served after the cut-off date except in extraordinary circumstances.

D. Request for Admissions: All requests for admissions shall be served at least forty-five (45) days prior to the discovery cut-off date. The Court will not approve stipulations between counsel that permit responses to be served after the cut-off date except in extraordinary circumstances.

E. Discovery Motions: Any motion respecting the inadequacy of responses to discovery must be filed and served not later than ten (10) days after the discovery cut-off date. Whenever possible, the Court expects counsel to resolve discovery problems among themselves in a courteous, reasonable, and professional manner. Repeated resort to the Court for guidance in discovery is unnecessary and will result in the Court appointing a Special Master at the joint expense of the parties to resolve discovery disputes. The Court expects that counsel will strictly adhere to the Civility and Professional Guidelines adopted by the United States District Court for the Central District of California.

F. Disclosure of Expert Testimony: The above discovery cutoff date includes expert discovery, unless the Court otherwise orders, and the Court orders the sequence of disclosures provided by Fed. R. Civ. Proc. 26(a)(2)(C), unless the parties otherwise stipulate in writing and obtain the Court's approval.

Final Pre-Trial Conference

This case has been placed on calendar for a Final Pre-Trial Conference pursuant to Fed. R. Civ. P. 16. Strict compliance with the requirements of the Fed. R. Civ. P. and Local Rules are required by the Court.

II.
ORDER FOR PREPARATION FOR COURT TRIAL, PROPOSED FINDINGS OF FACT AND CONCLUSIONS OF LAW, AND SCHEDULING EXHIBIT CONFERENCE FRIDAY BEFORE TRIAL: MOTIONS AND EXHIBITS

The Court ORDERS that all counsel comply with the following in their preparation for trial:

1. MOTIONS *IN LIMINE*: Because the matter will be tried to the Court, the Court believes that there should be a much reduced need for motions *in limine*.

All motions *in limine* must be filed and served a minimum of four (4) weeks prior to the scheduled pretrial date. Each motion should be separately filed and numbered. All opposition documents must be filed and served at least three (3) weeks prior to the scheduled pretrial date. All reply documents must be filed and served at least two (2) weeks prior to the scheduled pretrial date. All motions *in limine* will be heard on the scheduled pretrial date, unless the Court otherwise orders.

The Court limits the number of *in limine* motions which a party or group of affiliated parties may file to four, not including (1) any *in limine* motion which seeks an exclusionary sanction under Rule 37(c)(1) of the Federal Rules of Civil Procedure and (2) any *in limine* motion which invokes the Court's power under Rule 702 of the Federal Rules of Evidence and *Daubert v. Merrell Dow Pharmaceuticals*, 509 U.S. 579, 597 (1993), to exclude or limit expert testimony. Motions made on the latter two grounds shall prominently state the basis for the motion in the title of the motion on the caption page. Any party desiring to tender any other *in limine* motions shall file an *ex parte* application no later than seven days prior to the due date for such motions, attaching the proposed motion and making a showing why it is imperative that the issue be dealt with by a motion *in limine*.

The Court deems the following motions to have been made and granted:

- Exclusion of evidence of settlement talks, offers of compromise and similar evidence excludable under Federal Rule of Evidence 408 without an offer of proof first made outside the presence of the jury.
- Exclusion of expert opinions not disclosed under Rule 26(a)(2) of the Federal Rule of Civil Procedure or otherwise subjected to examination at the expert's

deposition.

All motions *in limine* will be heard on the scheduled pretrial date, unless the Court otherwise orders.

2. FINDINGS OF FACT AND CONCLUSION OF LAW: Findings of facts and Conclusions of Law shall be prepared, lodged, and served in accordance with the Local Rules, unless otherwise ordered by the Court.

3. TRIAL EXHIBITS: Counsel are to prepare their exhibits for presentation at the trial by placing them in binders that are indexed by exhibit number with tabs or dividers on the right side. Counsel shall submit to the Court an original and one copy of the binders. The exhibits shall be in a three-ring binder labeled on the spine portion of the binder showing both the volume number and the exhibit numbers and contain an index of each exhibit included in the volume. Exhibits must be numbered in accordance with Fed. R. Civ. P. 16, 26, and the Local Rules.

The Court requires that the following be submitted to the Courtroom Deputy Clerk on the first day of trial:

A. The original exhibits with the Court's exhibit tags shall be stapled to the front of the exhibit on the upper right-hand corner with the case number, case name, and exhibit number placed on each tag.

B. One bench book with a copy of each exhibit for use by the Court, tabbed with numbers as described above. (Court's exhibit tags not necessary.)

C. Three (3) copies of exhibit lists.

D. Three (3) copies of witness lists.

All counsel are to meet not later than ten (10) days before trial and to stipulate so far as is possible as to foundation, waiver of the best evidence rule, and to those exhibits which may be received into evidence at the start of trial. The exhibits to be so received will be noted on the extra copies of the exhibit lists.

III.
ORDER GOVERNING ATTORNEY AND PARTY CONDUCT AT TRIAL
Opening Statements, Examining Witnesses, and Summation

A. Opening statements, examination of witnesses, and summation will be from the lectern only.

B. Counsel must not consume time by writing out words or drawing charts or diagrams. Counsel may do so in advance and explain that the item was prepared earlier as ordered by the Court to save time.

C. In criminal cases, defense counsel should avoid asking their client self-serving questions such as whether the client is married, has children, has a war record or has ever been arrested. Such questions are almost always irrelevant. Where such information would be relevant, in counsel's opinion, counsel must obtain advance permission from the Court prior to making such inquiries.

D. Never strike the lectern for emphasis.

E. The Court will honor reasonable time estimates for opening and closing arguments.

Direct Examination by Declaration

The Court will receive all direct examination by way of declaration as outlined below.

A. Twenty days prior to trial, each party asserting a claim (*e.g.*, plaintiff, cross-claimant) shall file and personally deliver to all other parties a declaration for each witness who will testify in the party's case in chief setting forth the witness' direct testimony. The declaration should be in the usual

narrative fashion, but at a party's election, may be set out in question-and-answer format. Each declaration shall attach and authenticate each document intended to be offered through the witness.

B. Thirteen days prior to trial, each party defending a claim (*e.g.*, defendant, cross-defendant) shall personally deliver to all other parties a declaration for each witness who will testify in the party's case in chief setting forth the witness' direct testimony. The declaration should be in the usual narrative fashion, but at a party's election, may be set out in question-and-answer format. Each declaration shall attach and authenticate each document intended to be offered through the witness.

C. In the case of a witness not under a party's control, the offering party shall use its best efforts to secure the declaration required by paragraph A or B. However, inability to secure the required declaration will not preclude a party from calling such a witness.

D. Any evidentiary objections to a declaration shall be filed and served no later than five days before trial. Evidentiary objections should be made with the same thoughtfulness and care as if they were being made in open court. The Court is unlikely to give consideration to blanket or rote objections.

E. At trial, a party calling a witness who has submitted a declaration shall have the witness authenticate his or her declaration and make any additions or corrections. The witness shall then be tendered for cross-examination. In the normal course, the Court will then allow re-direct and re-cross.

Objections to Questions

A. Counsel must not use objections for the purpose of making a speech, recapitulating testimony, or attempting to guide the witness.

B. When objecting, counsel must rise to state the objection and state only that counsel objects and the legal ground of objection. If counsel wishes to argue an objection further, counsel must ask for permission to do so.

General Decorum

A. Please keep the trial low-key. It is not a contest of dramatic ability or an oratorical contest. It is to be a dignified search for the truth.

B. Counsel must not approach the Clerk or the witness box without specific permission. When permission is given, please return to the lectern when the purpose of the permission is finished. Counsel must not engage in questioning a witness at the witness stand.

C. Please rise when addressing the Court.

D. Counsel must address all remarks to the Court. Counsel are not to address the Clerk, the Reporter, persons in the audience, or opposing counsel. If counsel wishes to speak with opposing counsel, counsel must ask permission to talk off the record. Any request for the re-reading of questions or answers shall be addressed to the Court.

E. Counsel must not address or refer to witnesses or parties by first names alone. Young witnesses (under 14) may, however, be addressed and referred to by their first name.

F. Counsel must not make an offer of stipulation unless counsel has conferred with opposing counsel and has reason to believe the stipulation will be acceptable.

G. While Court is in session, counsel must not leave counsel table to confer with any personnel or witnesses in the back of the courtroom unless permission has been granted in advance.

H. Counsel should not by facial expression, nodding or other conduct exhibit any opinion, adverse or favorable, concerning any testimony being given by a witness. Counsel should admonish counsel's own client(s) and witnesses to avoid such conduct.

I. Where a party has more than one lawyer, only one may conduct the direct or cross-examination of a given witness.

Promptness of Counsel and Witnesses

A. The Court makes every effort to commence proceedings at the time set. Promptness is expected from counsel and witnesses. It is counsel's duty of the first day of trial to advise the Court on the first day of any commitments that may result in counsel's absence or late arrival.

B. If a witness is on the stand when a recess is taken, it is counsel's duty to have the witness back on the stand, ready to proceed, when the court session resumes.

> **(1)** If a witness was on the stand at adjournment, it is counsel's duty to have the witness adjacent to, but not on, the stand, ready to proceed when the court session resumes.
>
> **(2)** It is counsel's duty to notify the courtroom deputy clerk in advance if any witness should be accommodated by use of the witness stand's automated platform which lowers and raises to accommodate witnesses who are unable to otherwise take the witness stand.

C. No presenting party may be without witnesses. If counsel has no more witnesses to call and there is more than a brief delay, the Court may deem that the party has rested.

D. The Court attempts to cooperate with physicians, scientists, and all other professional witnesses and will, except in extraordinary circumstances, accommodate them by permitting them to be put on out of sequence. Counsel must anticipate any such possibility and discuss it with opposing counsel. If there is objection, confer with the Court in advance.

Exhibits

A. Each counsel should keep counsel's own list of exhibits and should keep track when each has been admitted in evidence.

B. Each counsel is responsible for any exhibits that counsel secures from the Clerk and, during all recesses and at noontime and afternoon adjournments, counsel must return all exhibits in counsel's possession to the Clerk.

C. An exhibit not previously marked should, at the time of its first mention, be accompanied by a request that the Clerk mark it for identification. To save time, counsel must show a new exhibit to opposing counsel before it is mentioned in Court.

D. Whenever in counsel's opinion a particular exhibit is admissible, it should be moved into evidence, unless tactical or other consideration dictate otherwise.

E. Counsel are to advise the Clerk of any agreements they have with respect to the proposed exhibits and as to those exhibits that may be received so that no further motion to admit need be made.

F. When referring to an exhibit, counsel should refer to its exhibit number whenever possible. Witnesses should be asked to do the same.

G. Exhibit Binders.

1. Where the volume of exhibits is less than ten binders, Counsel are to prepare exhibits for trial by placing them in three ring binders that are indexed by exhibit number with tabs or dividers on the right side and indicating on the spine of the binder the exhibit numbers contained and the volume number. The exhibits must be numbered in accordance with Fed. R. Civ. P. 16, 26 and the Local Rules. Counsel shall have the original set (with the exhibit tags affixed to the upper or lower right hand corner) and a bench copy on the exhibits, three (3) copies of the exhibit list and three (3) copies of the witness list to the Courtroom Deputy Clerk on the first day of trial.

2. Where the volume of exhibits is greater than ten binders Counsel are to prepare one (1) full set of the exhibits in three ring binders that are indexed by exhibit number with tabs or dividers on the right side and indicating on the spine of the binder the exhibit numbers contained and the volume number. Each exhibit shall have an exhibit tag placed in the upper or lower right hand corner of the first page of the exhibit. (These are the exhibits that will go to the jury during deliberations). With regard to exhibits for the Judge and witnesses, there should be a book for each witness that contains only the exhibits needed for that specific witness with dividers on the right side. This book should be presented to the witness when the witness is called. A copy of this book should be provided to the Judge at the time the witness is called. The Court requires counsel to submit the full set of exhibits, three (3) copies of the exhibit list and three (3) copies of the witness list to the Courtroom Deputy Clerk on the first day of trial.

Depositions

A. All depositions that are to be used in the trial, either as evidence or for impeachment, must be signed and lodged with the Courtroom Deputy on the first day of trial or such earlier date as the Court may order. For any deposition in which counsel is interested, counsel should check with the clerk to confirm that the clerk has the transcript and that the transcript is properly signed.

B. In using depositions of an adverse party for impeachment, either one of the following procedures may be adopted:

(1) If counsel wishes to read the questions and answers as alleged impeachment and ask the witness no further questions on that subject, counsel shall first state the page and line where the reading begins and the page and line where the reading ends, and allow time for any objection. Counsel may then read the portions of the deposition into the record.

(2) If counsel wishes to ask the witness further questions on the subject matter, the deposition is placed in front of the witness and the witness is told to read silently the pages and lines involved. Then counsel may either ask the witness further questions on the matter and thereafter read the quotations or read the quotations and thereafter ask the further questions. Counsel should have an extra copy of the deposition for this purpose.

C. Where a witness is absent and the witness' testimony is offered by deposition, please inquire whether the Court prefers to (1) have a reader occupy the witness chair and read the testimony of the witness while the examining lawyer asks the questions, or, (2) read the deposition in chambers without the questions and answers being repeated for the record. In such instances, the deposition may be offered in evidence as an exhibit.

D. Evidentiary objections should be made with the same thoughtfulness and care as if the objections were being made in open court during the examination of the witness. The Court is unlikely to give consideration to blanket or rote objections.

Using Numerous Answers to Interrogatories and Requests for Admissions

Whenever counsel expects to offer a group of answers to interrogatories or requests for admissions, extracted from one or more lengthy documents, counsel should prepare a new document listing each question and answer and identifying the document from which it has been extracted. Copies of this new document should be given to the Court and opposing counsel. This procedure is intended to save time.

Advance Notice of Evidentiary or Difficult Questions

If any counsel has reason to anticipate that a difficult question of law or evidence will raise legal argument, requiring research and/or briefing, counsel must give the Court advance notice. Counsel are directed to notify the Clerk at the day's adjournment if an unexpected legal issue arises that could not have been foreseen and addressed by a motion *in limine* (*see* Fed. R. Evid. 103).

IV.

The Clerk is ordered to serve a copy of this Order on counsel/parties in this action.

DATED: ________________ ________________

JAMES V. SELNA
United States District Judge

C. *Order Regarding Criminal Trial*

IN THE UNITED STATES DISTICT COURT
FOR THE CENTRAL DISTRICT OF CALIFORNIA

UNITED STATES OF AMERICA, Plaintiff,	)	Case No. _______________
v.	)	**ORDER RE CRIMINAL TRIAL**
Defendant(s).	)	

The above matter is set for trial before the Honorable James V. Selna, Courtroom 10C, Ronald Reagan Federal Building, 411 W. Fourth Street, Santa Ana, CA 92701. All aspects of the preparation and trial of this matter shall be conducted with dignity and civility to all, whether in the court room or elsewhere.

FILINGS

1. All pleadings shall be served electronically on opposing counsel or faxed to opposing counsel no later than 4:30 p.m. on the day of filing.
2. Counsel are ORDERED to list their e-mail address and facsimile transmission numbers along with their address and telephone numbers on all papers submitted to the Court in order to facilitate communication by the Court.

MOTION PRACTICE

4. Memoranda of Points and Authorities in support of or in opposition to motions shall not exceed 25 pages. Replies shall not exceed 12 pages. Only in rare instances and for good cause shown will the Court grant an application to extend these page limitations. No supplemental brief shall be filed without prior leave of court. Typeface shall comply with Local Rule 11-3.1.1. (Civil). NOTE: If Times Roman font is used, the size must be no less than 14; if Courier is used, the size must be no less than 12. Footnotes shall be in the same size as text and no more than five lines. Filings which do not conform to the Local Rules and this Order will not be considered.
5. Before filing any motion for discovery, a party shall consult with opposing counsel to ascertain what discovery will be provided. Any discovery motion shall state with particularity what is requested, the basis for such requested production, whether such discovery has been formally requested, and whether such discovery has been declined. Motions made without prior consultation with opposing counsel or which fail to include the above information will not be heard.

DISCOVERY & NOTICE

6. Counsel for the government and counsel for defendant shall comply promptly with discovery and notice pursuant to Fed. R. Crim. P. , Rules 12, 12.1, 12.2, 12.3, 15, and 16. Upon government counsel's discovery of any evidence within the scope of Brady v. Maryland, 373 U.S. 83 (1963), such evidence shall be produced forthwith to counsel for the defendant. Counsel for the government shall also disclose to counsel for defendant the existence or nonexistence of: (1) evidence obtained by electronic surveillance; (2) testimony by a government informer.

TRIAL

7. Counsel for the government shall file with the Court in camera (under seal) all statements of all witnesses to be called by the government in its case-in-chief. Such

statements shall be filed at least five (5) calendar days before trial.

8. Counsel shall arrive at the Courtroom promptly at 8:30 a.m. on the first day of trial.

9. Counsel for the government shall present the Courtroom Deputy with the following documents on the first day of trial:

   a. THREE copies of the government's witness list.

   b. THREE copies of the government's exhibit list in the form specified in Local Rule 9.9 (Civil).

   c. ALL of the government's exhibits, with official exhibit tags attached and bearing the same number shown on the exhibit list.

   Defendant's counsel does not have to deliver his or her exhibits to the Courtroom Deputy on the first day of trial; however, Defendant's counsel is responsible for affixing completed exhibit tags with the case name and case number to his or her exhibits which are intended to be used in the defendant's case. Exhibit tags can be obtained from the receptionist in the Clerk's Office.

   Exhibits shall be numbered 1, 2, 3, 4, etc., NOT 1.1, 1.50 etc. If a blow up is an enlargement of an existing exhibit, it shall be designated with the number of the original exhibit followed by an "A."

   Counsel for the government should be aware that the Court will order that exhibits such as firearms, narcotics, etc., remain in the custody of the agents during the pendency of the trial. The agent will be required to sign the appropriate form in order to take custody of such exhibits. It shall be the responsibility of the agents to produce said items for court, secure them at night and guard them at all times while in the courtroom.

   d. A bench book containing a copy of all exhibits that can be reproduced. Each exhibit shall be tabbed with the exhibit number for easy referral. Defendant's counsel shall provide the Court with a copy of their exhibits as they are introduced during trial.

   e. If not previously e-mailed to the Courtroom Deputy prior to trial, a 3 1/2-inch diskette in WordPerfect 9 or higher containing the exhibit list.

   A copy of the exhibit list with all admitted exhibits will be given to the jury during deliberations. Government and defense counsel shall review and approve the exhibit list with the Courtroom Deputy prior to it being given to the jury.

10. If counsel need to arrange for the installation of their own additional equipment, such as video monitors, overhead projectors, etc., notify the Courtroom Deputy no later than 4:30 p.m. two court days before trial so that the necessary arrangements can be made.

11. At least four court days prior to trial, each counsel shall file with the Clerk and serve on opposing counsel any special questions requested to be put to prospective jurors on voir dire.

12. Trials commence on Tuesday at 8:30 a.m., with jury selection beginning at 9:00 a.m., or as soon thereafter as possible. Trials are conducted Tuesday through Friday from 9:00 a.m. to 4:30 p.m., with two fifteen (15) minute breaks, and a lunch recess from 12:00 p.m. to 1:30 p.m.

13. Before trial commences, the Court will give counsel an opportunity to discuss administrative matters and anticipated procedural or legal issues. During the trial, if there are any matters you wish to discuss, please inform the Courtroom Deputy.

14. The Court reserves the time from 8:30 a.m. to 9:00 a.m. to handle legal and administrative matters outside of the presence of the jury. The trial before the jury will commence promptly at 9:00 a.m. Counsel are urged to anticipate matters which may need discussion or hearing outside of the presence of the jury and to raise them during this period, during breaks or at the end of the day. The Court places a high priority on making efficient use of jurors' time during the trial day.

JURY INSTRUCTIONS & VERDICT FORMS

15. No later than one week before trial, jury instructions in the form described below are to be submitted. Where possible, counsel are to use the instructions from the Manual of Model Criminal Jury Instructions for the Ninth Circuit, West Publishing, latest edition, modified, as necessary, to fit the facts of the case (e.g., inserting names of defendant(s) to whom instruction applies). Where language appears in brackets in the model instruction, counsel shall select the appropriate text and eliminate the inapplicable bracketed text. Where no applicable Ninth Circuit model instruction is available, counsel are directed to use the instructions from O'Malley, Grenig & Lee (formerly Devitt, et al.), Federal Jury Practice and Instructions, West Publishing Co., current edition. Counsel shall include both general and substantive instructions. If not previously e-mailed to the Courtroom Deputy, Counsel shall submit a 3½-inch diskette, compatible with Word Perfect 9.0 or higher containing the proposed instructions and a "clean" set of such instructions, as set forth below.

16. The parties must submit JOINT jury instructions and a JOINT proposed verdict form (if a special verdict is desired). In order to produce these joint instructions, the parties shall meet and confer sufficiently in advance of the required submission date with the goal of agreeing upon instructions and verdict forms. The jury instructions shall be submitted as follows: 1) JOINT jury instructions, those instructions which are agreed to by all parties; and 2) DISPUTED jury instructions, those instructions propounded by a party to which another party objects. Objections to disputed instructions shall be filed no later than the Friday before the trial. Each requested jury instruction shall be numbered and set forth in full on a separate page, citing the authority or source of the requested instruction.

17. An index page shall accompany all jury instructions that are submitted to the Court. The index page shall indicate the following:

a. The number of the instruction;
b. A brief title of the instruction;
c. The source of the instruction; and
d. The page number of the instruction.

EXAMPLE:

Number	Title	Source	Page Number
#1	Duty of the Jury	9th Cir. 1.01	1

INSTRUCTIONS GOVERNING PROCEDURE DURING TRIAL

18. Counsel shall not refer to their clients or any witness over 14 years of age by the person's first name during trial.

19. Do not discuss the law or argue the case in opening statements.

20. When objecting, state only that you are objecting and the legal ground of the objection, e.g., hearsay, irrelevant, etc. Do not argue an objection before the jury.

21. Do not approach the Courtroom Deputy or the witness box without the Court's permission. Please return to the lectern when your purpose has been accomplished. Do not enter the well of the Court without the Court's permission.

22. Please rise when addressing the Court. In jury cases, please rise when the jury enters or leaves the courtroom.

23. Address all remarks to the Court. Do not directly address the Courtroom Deputy, the reporter or opposing counsel. If you wish to speak with opposing counsel, ask permission to talk to counsel off the record. All requests for the re-reading of questions or answers, or to have an exhibit placed in front of a witness, shall be addressed to the Court.

24. Do not make an offer of stipulation unless you have conferred with opposing counsel and reached an agreement. Any stipulation of fact will require the defendant's personal concurrence and shall be submitted to the Court in writing for approval. A proposed stipulation should be explained to him or her in advance.

25. While court is in session, do not leave the counsel table to confer with investigators, secretaries, or witnesses unless permission is granted in advance.

26. When a party has more than one lawyer, only one may conduct the examination of a given witness and only that same lawyer may handle objections during the testimony of that witness.

27. If a witness was on the stand at a recess or adjournment, have the witness back on the stand and ready to proceed when court resumes.

28. Do not run out of witnesses. If you are out of witnesses and there is more than a brief delay, the Court may deem that you have rested.

29. The Court attempts to cooperate with doctors and other professional witnesses and will, except in extraordinary circumstances, accommodate them by permitting them to be put on out of sequence. Anticipate any such possibility and discuss it with opposing counsel. If there is an objection, confer with the Court in advance.

30. Counsel are advised to be on time; the Court starts promptly.

SENTENCINGS

31. Position papers with respect to sentencing shall be filed not later than two weeks prior to the date of sentencing. Any replies shall be filed no later than one week prior to sentencing.

32. The Court generally makes available a draft Sentencing Memorandum fifteens minute prior to the sentencing hearing.

SPECIAL APPEARANCES.

33. The Court does not entertain special appearances.

* * * * * * * * * * * *

34. The Court thanks counsel in advance for their cooperation.

DATED: ____________

JAMES V. SELNA
United States District Judge

D. Order Regarding Jury Trial

IN THE UNITED STATES DISTICT COURT
FOR THE CENTRAL DISTRICT OF CALIFORNIA

)	Case No. ______________
Plaintiff(s),)	
v.)	**I. ORDER FOR JURY TRIAL SETTING DATES FOR:**
Defendant(s).)	Discovery Cut-Off: ______________
______________________________)	Pre-Trial Conference: _____ at 11:00 A.M.
	Trial: __________ at 8:30 A.M.
	II. Order for Preparation for JURY TRIAL
	III. Order Governing Attorney & Party Conduct at Trial

I.
ORDER FOR JURY TRIAL – SETTING DATES
SCHEDULING

1. **In General:** All motions to join other parties or to amend the pleadings shall be filed and served within sixty (60) days of the date of this order and noticed for hearing within ninety (90) days hereof. All unserved parties shall be dismissed no later than the date set for the Final Pre-Trial Conference.

2. **Motions for Summary Judgment or Partial Summary Judgment:** Motions for summary judgment or partial summary judgment shall be heard no later than the last day for hearing motions, as set forth in the accompanying minute order. Please note the extended notice requirements under F. R. Civ. P. 56(c) which are longer than provided in the Local Rules.

3. **Discovery Cut-Off:** The Court has established a cut-off date for discovery in this action. All discovery is to be completed on, or prior to, the cutoff date. Accordingly, the following discovery schedule shall apply to this case:

A. Depositions: All depositions shall be scheduled to commence at least five (5) working days prior to the discovery cut-off date. All original depositions to be used in trial shall be lodged with the Courtroom deputy on the first day of trial or such earlier date as the Court may order.

B. Interrogatories: All interrogatories must be served at least forty-five (45) days prior to the discovery cut-off date. The Court will not approve stipulations between counsel that permit responses to be served after the cut-off date except in extraordinary circumstances.

C. Production of Documents, *etc.*: All requests for production, etc., shall be served at least forty-five (45) days prior to the discovery cut-off date. The Court will not approve stipulations between counsel that permit responses to be served after the cut-off date except in extraordinary circumstances.

D. Request for Admissions: All requests for admissions shall be served at least forty-five (45) days prior to the discovery cut-off date. The Court will not approve stipulations between counsel that permit responses to be served after the cut-off date except in extraordinary circumstances.

E. Discovery Motions: Any motion respecting the inadequacy of responses to discovery must be filed and served not later than ten (10) days after the discovery cut-off date. Whenever possible, the Court expects counsel to resolve discovery problems among themselves in a courteous, reasonable, and professional manner. Repeated resort to the Court for guidance in discovery is unnecessary and may result in the Court appointing a Special Master at the joint expense of the parties to resolve discovery disputes. The Court expects that counsel will strictly adhere to the Civility and Professional Guidelines adopted by the United States District Court for the Central District of California.

F. <u>Disclosure of Expert Testimony:</u> The above discovery cutoff date includes expert discovery, unless otherwise ordered by Court, and the Court orders the sequence of disclosures provided by Fed. R. Civ. Proc. 26(a)(2)(C), unless the parties otherwise stipulate in writing and obtain the Court's approval.

FINAL PRE-TRIAL CONFERENCE

This case has been placed on calendar for a Final Pre-Trial Conference pursuant to Fed. R. Civ. P. 16. Strict compliance with the requirements of the Fed. R. Civ. P. and Local Rules are required by the Court.

II.

ORDER FOR PREPARATION FOR JURY TRIAL AND SCHEDULING EXHIBIT CONFERENCE FRIDAY BEFORE TRIAL: MOTIONS, INSTRUCTIONS, AND EXHIBITS

The Court ORDERS that all counsel comply with the following in their preparation for trial:

1. MOTIONS IN LIMINE: All motions *in limine* must be filed and served a minimum of four (4) weeks prior to the scheduled pretrial date in accordance with Local Rule 6. Each motion should be separately filed and numbered. All opposition documents must be filed and served at least three (3) weeks prior to the scheduled pretrial date. All reply documents must be filed and served at least two (2) weeks prior to the scheduled pretrial date. Motions *in limine* should be used to raise legitimate evidentiary issues, and not as veiled motions for summary adjudication.

The Court limits the number of *in limine* motions which a party or group of affiliated parties may file to four, not including (1) any *in limine* motion which seeks an exclusionary sanction under Rule 37(c)(1) of the Federal Rules of Civil Procedure and (2) any *in limine* motion which invokes the Court's power under Rule 702 of the Federal Rules of Evidence and *Daubert v. Merrell Dow Pharmaceuticals*, 509 U.S. 579, 597 (1993), to exclude or limit expert testimony. Motions made on the latter two grounds shall prominently state the basis for the motion in the title of the motion on the caption page. Any party desiring to tender any other *in limine* motions shall file an *ex parte* application no later than seven days prior to the due date for such motions, attaching the proposed motion and making a showing why it is imperative that the issue be dealt with by a motion *in limine.*

The Court deems the following motions to have been made and granted:

- Exclusion of evidence of settlement talks, offers of compromise and similar evidence excludable under Federal Rule of Evidence 408 without an offer of proof first made outside the presence of the jury.
- Exclusion of expert opinions not disclosed under Rule 26(a)(2) of the Federal Rule of Civil Procedure or otherwise subjected to examination at the expert's deposition.

All motions *in limine* will be heard on the scheduled pretrial date, unless the Court otherwise orders.

2. **JURY INSTRUCTIONS, VERDICT FORMS, and *VOIR DIRE*:** Plaintiff shall serve plaintiff's proposed jury instructions and verdict form on defendant. Defendant shall serve on plaintiff defendant's objections to plaintiff's instructions and verdict form, together with any alternative verdict form and any additional instructions defendant intends to offer. Counsel are ordered to meet and confer to attempt to come to agreement on the proposed jury instructions and verdict forms.

Counsel shall file with the Court a JOINT set of jury instructions on which there is agreement. Defendant's counsel has the burden of preparing the joint set of jury instructions. At the same time each party shall file its proposed jury instructions which are objected to by any other party, accompanied by points and authorities in support of those instructions.

Jury instructions are to be filed with the Clerk at the Southern Division in Santa Ana and served on opposing counsel as soon as possible. The Court recommends that jury instructions be submitted at least four (4) court days prior to trial, but not later than the first day of trial.

At the same time, counsel must furnish to the assigned Courtroom Deputy Clerk an electronic copy of the proposed jury instructions compatible with WordPerfect® 6.0 or later generations of WordPerfect®. E-mailing the electronic copy to the Courtroom Deputy is the most convenient to accomplish this.

Objections to proposed jury instructions must be filed in writing at the Southern Division in Santa Ana.

***Voir Dire*:** At least four (4) court days prior to trial, each counsel shall file with the Clerk at the Southern Division in Santa Ana and serve on opposing counsel any special questions requested to be put to prospective jurors on *voir dire*.

3. **TRIAL EXHIBITS**

Counsel are to prepare their exhibits for presentation at the trial by placing them in binders that are indexed by exhibit number with tabs or dividers on the right side. Counsel shall submit to the Court an original and one copy of the binders. The exhibits shall be in a three-ring binder labeled on the spine portion of the binder showing both the volume number and the exhibit numbers and contain an index of each exhibit included in the volume. Exhibits must be numbered in accordance with Fed. R. Civ. P. 16, 26, and the Local Rules.

The Court requires that the following be submitted to the Courtroom Deputy Clerk on the first day of trial:

A. The original exhibits with the Court's exhibit tags shall be stapled to the front of the exhibit on the upper right-hand corner with the case number, case name, and exhibit number placed on each tag.

B. One bench book with a copy of each exhibit for use by the Court, tabbed with numbers as described above. (Court's exhibit tags not necessary.)

C. Three (3) copies of exhibit lists, plus an electronic copy in WordPerfect® 6.0 or later generations of WordPerfect®. E-mailing the electronic copy to the Courtroom Deputy is the most convenient to accomplish this.

D. Three (3) copies of witness lists.

E. A joint statement of the case suitable for reading by the Court to the prospective panel of jurors prior to the commencement of jury selection. Counsel are ordered to confer and agree to a one-page joint statement of the case no later than five (5) days prior to the trial date.

All counsel are to meet not later than ten (10) days before trial and to stipulate so far as is possible as to foundation, waiver of the best evidence rule, and to those exhibits which may be received into evidence at the start of trial. The exhibits to be so received will be noted on the extra copies of the exhibit lists.

III.
ORDER GOVERNING ATTORNEY AND PARTY CONDUCT AT TRIAL

Opening Statements, Examining Witnesses, and Summation

A. Unless otherwise ordered, the trial day will be 9:00 a.m. to noon and 1:30 p.m. to 4:30 p.m. with a 15 minute break during each session.

B. At the end of each day, counsel presenting his or her case shall advise opposing counsel of the witnesses anticipated the following day with an estimate of the length of direct examination. Opposing counsel shall provide an estimate of the length of cross–examination. Cooperation of counsel will ensure a smooth flow of witnesses.

C. Opening statements, examination of witnesses, and summation will be from the lectern only. Counsel must not consume time by writing out words or drawing charts or diagrams. Counsel may do so in advance and explain that the item was prepared earlier as ordered by the Court to save time.

D. In final argument of jury cases, counsel must avoid addressing any juror by name and avoid any appeal to a juror to put himself or herself in the position of a party, such as "What would you take for such pain?" or "What would you expect your son or daughter to do in the same circumstances?"

E. In criminal cases, defense counsel should avoid asking their client self-serving questions such as whether the client is married, has children, has a war record or has ever been arrested. Such questions are almost always irrelevant. Where such information would be relevant in counsel's opinion, counsel should obtain permission from the Court prior to making such inquiries.

F. Never strike the lectern for emphasis.

G. The Court will honor reasonable time estimates for opening and closing addresses to the jury. Please be advised this Court will not require a jury to sit longer than 60 minutes in any one session during counsel' summation.

Objections to Questions

A. Counsel must not use objections for the purpose of making a speech, recapitulating testimony, or attempting to guide the witness.

B. When objecting, counsel must rise to state the objection and state only that counsel objects and the legal ground of objection. If counsel wishes to argue an objection further, counsel must ask for permission to do so; the Court may or may not grant a request for conference at sidebar. **The Court strongly discourage sidebars because they represent an inefficient use of jury time when matters can be anticipated.**

General Decorum

A. Please keep the trial low-key. It is not a contest of dramatic ability or an oratorical contest. It is to be a dignified search for the truth.

B. Counsel must not approach the Clerk or the witness box without specific permission. When permission is given, please return to the lectern when the purpose of the permission is finished. Counsel must not engage in questioning a witness at the witness stand.

C. Please rise when addressing the Court and rise when the jury enters or leaves the courtroom.

D. Counsel must address all remarks to the Court. Counsel are not to address the Clerk, the Reporter, persons in the audience, or opposing counsel. If counsel wishes to speak with opposing counsel, counsel must ask permission to talk off the record. Any request for the re-reading of questions or answers shall be addressed to the Court.

E. Counsel must not address or refer to witnesses or parties by first names alone. Young witnesses (under 14) may, however, be addressed and referred to by their first name.

F. Counsel must not make an offer of stipulation unless counsel has conferred with opposing counsel and has reason to believe the stipulation will be acceptable.

G. While Court is in session, counsel must not leave counsel table to confer with any personnel or witnesses in the back of the courtroom unless permission has been granted in advance.

H. Counsel should not by facial expression, nodding or other conduct exhibit any opinion, adverse or favorable, concerning any testimony being given by a witness. Counsel should admonish counsel's own client(s) and witnesses to avoid such conduct.

I. Where a party has more than one lawyer, only one may conduct the direct or cross-examination of a given witness.

Promptness of Counsel and Witnesses

A. The Court makes every effort to commence proceedings at the time set. Promptness is expected from counsel and witnesses. It is counsel's duty of the first day of trial to advise the Court on the first day of any commitments that may result in counsel's absence or late arrival.

B. If a witness is on the stand when a recess is taken, it is counsel's duty to have the witness back on the stand, ready to proceed, when the court session resumes.

> **(1)** If a witness was on the stand at adjournment, it is counsel's duty to have the witness adjacent to, but not on, the stand, ready to proceed when the court session resumes.
>
> **(2)** It is counsel's duty to notify the courtroom deputy clerk in advance if any witness should be accommodated by use of the witness stand's automated platform which lowers and raises to accommodate witnesses who are unable to otherwise take the witness stand.

C. No presenting party may be without witnesses. If counsel has no more witnesses to call and there is more than a brief delay, the Court may deem that the party has rested.

D. The Court attempts to cooperate with physicians, scientists, and all other professional witnesses and will, except in extraordinary circumstances, accommodate them by permitting them to be put on out of sequence. Counsel must anticipate any such possibility and discuss it with opposing counsel. If there is objection, confer with the Court in advance.

Exhibits

A. Each counsel should keep counsel's own list of exhibits and should keep track when each has been admitted in evidence.

B. Each counsel is responsible for any exhibits that counsel secures from the Clerk and, during all recesses and noontime and afternoon adjournments, counsel must return all exhibits in counsel's possession to the Clerk.

C. An exhibit not previously marked should, at the time of its first mention, be accompanied by a request that the Clerk mark it for identification. To save time, counsel must show a new exhibit to opposing counsel before it is mentioned in Court.

D. Whenever in counsel's opinion a particular exhibit is admissible, it should be offered unless tactical considerations dictate otherwise. The motion to admit will be dealt with at the next available recess if there is objection. **No exhibit shall be read or displayed to the jury until admitted.**

E. The Court regards admissibility of exhibits as a legal issue for the Court to rule on unless there is agreement among counsel. Counsel are admonished to make no motion to introduce an exhibit while the jury is present unless counsel has previously conferred with opposing counsel and knows that there will be no objection to the motion to admit.

F. When referring to an exhibit, counsel should refer to its exhibit number whenever possible. Witnesses should be instructed to do the same.

G. The Court resists taking time to pass an exhibit among the jury for viewing when it is admitted. A request to do so should be made to the Court in a recess period preceding introduction of the exhibit.

H. Absent unusual circumstances, counsel must not ask witnesses to draw charts or diagrams nor ask the Court's permission for a witness to do so. If counsel wishes to question a witness in connection with graphic aids, the material must be fully prepared before the court session starts.

I. Exhibit Binders.

1. Where the volume of exhibits is less than ten binders, Counsel are to prepare exhibits for trial by placing them in three ring binders that are indexed by exhibit number with tabs or dividers on the right side and indicating on the spine of the binder the exhibit numbers contained and the volume number. The exhibits must be numbered in accordance with Fed. R. Civ. P. 16, 26 and the Local Rules. Counsel shall have the original set (with the exhibit tags affixed to the upper or lower right hand corner) and a bench copy on the exhibits, three (3) copies of the exhibit list and three (3) copies of the witness list to the Courtroom Deputy Clerk on the first day of trial.

2. Where the volume of exhibits is greater than ten binders Counsel are to prepare one (1) full set of the exhibits in three ring binders that are indexed by exhibit number with tabs or dividers on the right side and indicating on the spine of the binder the exhibit numbers contained and the volume number. Each exhibit shall have an exhibit tag placed in the upper or lower right hand corner of the first page of the exhibit. (These are the exhibits that will go to the jury during deliberations). With regard to exhibits for the Judge and witnesses, there should be a book for each witness that contains only the exhibits needed for that specific witness with dividers on the right side. This book should be presented to the witness when the witness is called. A copy of this book should be provided to the Judge at the time the witness is called. The Court requires counsel to submit the full set of exhibits, three (3) copies of the exhibit list and three (3) copies of the witness list to the Courtroom Deputy Clerk on the first day of trial.

Depositions

A. All depositions that will be used in the trial, either as evidence or for impeachment, must be signed and lodged with the Courtroom Deputy on the first day of trial or such earlier date as the Court may order. For any deposition in which counsel is interested, counsel should check with the clerk to confirm that the clerk has the transcript and that the transcript is properly signed.

B. In using depositions of an adverse party for impeachment, counsel shall first announce the page and line reference of the passage desired to be read, and allow opposing counsel an opportunity to state any objection. Counsel shall use either of the following procedures:

> **(1)** If counsel wishes to read the questions and answers as alleged impeachment and ask the witness no further questions on that subject, counsel may merely read the relevant portions of the deposition into the record.
>
> **(2)** If counsel wishes to ask the witness further questions on the subject matter, the deposition is placed in front of the witness and the witness is told to read silently the pages and lines involved. Then counsel may either ask the witness further questions on the matter and thereafter read the quotations or read the quotations and thereafter ask further questions. Counsel should have an extra copy of the deposition for this purpose.

C. Where a witness is absent and the witness' testimony is offered by deposition, please observe the following procedure. A reader should occupy the witness chair and read the testimony of the witness while the examining lawyer asks the questions.

Using Numerous Answers to Interrogatories and Requests for Admissions

Whenever counsel expects to offer answers to interrogatories or requests for admissions, the desired discovery shall be read to the jury. Any objections shall be resolved in advance.

Advance Notice of Evidentiary or Difficult Questions

If counsel has reason to anticipate that a difficult question of law or evidence will raise legal argument, requiring research and/or briefing, counsel must give the Court advance notice. Counsel are directed to notify the Clerk at the day's adjournment if an unexpected legal issue arises that could not have been foreseen and addressed by a motion *in limine* (*see* Fed. R. Evid. 103). To the maximum extent possible such matters shall be taken outside normal jury hours (*e.g.*, recess, before or after the trial day).

Juror Questionnaires

The Court discourages the use of juror questionnaires except in complex cases or cases involving juror privacy issues. If a party intends to propose a questionnaire, the party shall meet and confer with all parties with the goal of arriving at a joint questionnaire. Any proposed questionnaire shall be submitted to the Court not later than thirty days prior to trial. The particulars for administering a questionnaire will be discussed at the pretrial conference.

IV.

The Clerk is ordered to serve a copy of this Order on counsel/parties in this action.

DATED: ________________

____
JAMES V. SELNA
United States District Judge

E. Order Regarding RICO Case Statement

IN THE UNITED STATES DISTICT COURT
FOR THE CENTRAL DISTRICT OF CALIFORNIA

Plaintiff(s),	Case No. ______________
v.	**ORDER RE RICO CASE STATEMENT**
Defendant(s).	

In this action, claims have been asserted under the Racketeer Influenced and Corrupt Organizations provisions of the Organized Crime Control Act of 1970 ("RICO"), 18 U.S.C. § 1961 *et seq*. Accordingly,

IT IS HEREBY ORDERED as follows:

Plaintiff[1] shall file, within twenty (20) days hereof, a RICO case statement. The statement shall include the facts relied upon to initiate this RICO complaint as a result of the reasonable inquiry required by Rule 11 of the Federal Rules of Civil Procedure. It shall use the caption numbers and letters set forth below, and shall state in detail and with specificity the following information.

1. **RICO Provision.** State whether the alleged unlawful conduct is in violation of 18 U.S.C. §§ 1962(a), (b) (c), and/or (d).

2. **Defendants.** List each RICO defendant and state the alleged misconduct and basis of liability of each defendant.

3. **Other RICO Violators.** List all alleged RICO violators, other than the defendants listed above, and state the alleged misconduct of each wrongdoer.

4. **Victims.** List the alleged victims and state how each victim was allegedly injured.

5. **Pattern of Racketeering Activity.** Describe in detail the pattern of racketeering activity or collection of unlawful debts alleged for each RICO claim. A description of the pattern of racketeering shall include the following information:

a. List the alleged predicate acts and the specific statutes which were allegedly violated;

b. Provide the dates of the predicate acts, the participants in the predicate acts, and a description of the facts surrounding the predicate acts;

c. If the RICO claim is based on the predicate offenses of mail fraud, wire fraud or fraud in the sale of securities, the "circumstances constituting fraud or mistake shall be stated with particularity." Fed. R. Civ. P. 9(b). Identify the time, place and contents of the alleged failures to disclose and/or misrepresentations, and the identity of persons to whom and by whom the alleged misrepresentations and/or failures to disclose were made;

d. State whether there has been a criminal conviction for violation of the predicate acts and if so, provide particulars;

e. State whether civil litigation has resulted in a judgment with respect to the predicate acts and if so, provide particulars;

f. Describe how the predicate acts are both "related" and "continuous" within

---

[1] If the party asserting a RICO violation is not the plaintiff, such as a counter-claimant, this requirement applies to such party as well.

the meaning of *H.J. Inc. v. Northwestern Bell Telephone Co.*, 492 U.S. 229, 239, 109 S.Ct. 2893, 2900 (1989) and its progeny, including *Allwaste, Inc. v. Hecht*, 65 F.3d 1523, 1527 (9th Cir. 1995).

6. Enterprise. Describe in detail the alleged enterprise for each RICO claim and specify just what structure it had. A description of the enterprise shall include the following information:

a. The names of the individuals, partnerships, corporations, associations or other legal entities that allegedly constitute the enterprise;

b. The purpose, function and course of conduct of the enterprise, and whether its usual and daily activities were part of or separate from the pattern of racketeering activity. *See Chang v. Chen*, 80 F.3d 1293, 1298 (9th Cir. 1996.)

c. Whether any named defendants are or were employees, officers or directors of the alleged enterprise;

d. Whether you are alleging that the defendants are or were separate from the alleged enterprise, collectively constitute the enterprise itself, or are or were members of the enterprise; and

e. Whether (and if so how) the enterprise was affected by or benefited from the pattern of racketeering activity.

7. Interstate or Foreign Commerce. Describe the effect of the activities of the enterprise on interstate or foreign commerce.

8. Section 1962(a). If the complaint alleges a violation of 18 U.S.C. § 1962(a), provide the following information:

a. State who received the income derived from the pattern of racketeering activity or through the collection of an unlawful debt; and

b. Describe the use or investment of such income.

9. Section 1962(b). If the complaint alleges a violation of 18 U.S.C. § 1962(b), describe in detail the acquisition or maintenance of any interest in or control of the alleged enterprise.

10. Section 1962(c). If the complaint alleges a violation of 18 U.S.C. § 1962(c), provide the following information:

a. State who is employed by or associated with the enterprise; and

b. State whether the same entity is both the liable "person" and the "enterprise" under § 1962(c).

11. Section 1962(d). If the complaint alleges a violation of 18 U.S.C. § 1962(d), describe in detail the alleged conspiracy.

12. Injury to Business or Property.

a. Describe the alleged injury to business or property;

b. Describe the direct causal relationship between the alleged injury and the violation of the RICO statute.

13. Damages. List the damages sustained for which each defendant is allegedly liable.

14. State Claims. List all supplemental state claims, if any.

Dated: ________________

____
JAMES V. SELNA
United States District Judge

F. Order Setting Rule 26(f) Scheduling Conference

IN THE UNITED STATES DISTICT COURT
FOR THE CENTRAL DISTRICT OF CALIFORNIA

Plaintiff(s),	Case No. ______________
v.	**ORDER SETTING RULE 26(f) SCHEDULING CONFERENCE**
Defendant(s).	
	Date: ___________
	Time: 1:30 p.m.

This case has been assigned to Judge James V. Selna. If plaintiff has not already served the complaint (or any amendment thereto) on all defendants, plaintiff shall promptly do so and shall file proofs of service within three days thereafter. Defendants also shall timely serve and file their responsive pleadings and file proofs of service within three days thereafter.

This matter is set for a scheduling conference on the above date. The conference will be held pursuant to Fed.R.Civ.P., Rule 16(b). The parties are reminded of their obligations under Fed.R.Civ.P., Rule 26(a)(1) to disclose information (without awaiting a discovery request) and under Rule 26(f) to confer on a discovery plan not later than twenty-one (21) days prior to the scheduling conference and to file a report with the Court entitled "Joint Rule 26(f) Report" not later than fourteen (14) days after they confer. Failure to comply with the following requirements or to cooperate in the preparation of the Joint Rule 26(f) Report may lead to the imposition of sanctions.

Unless there is a likelihood that upon motion by a party the Court would order that any or all discovery is premature, it is advisable for counsel to begin to conduct discovery actively before the Scheduling Conference. At the very least, the parties shall comply fully with the letter and spirit of Rule 26(a) and thereby obtain and produce most of what would be produced in the early stage of discovery, because at the Scheduling Conference the Court will impose tight deadlines to complete discovery.

1. Joint Rule 26(f) Report

The Joint Rule 26(f) Report, which shall be filed not later than one week before the scheduling conference, shall be drafted by plaintiff (unless the parties agree otherwise), ***but shall be submitted and signed jointly. "Jointly" contemplates a single report, regardless of how many separately-represented parties there are. The Joint Rule 26(f) Report shall report on all matters enumerated below, which include*** those required to be discussed by Rule 26(f) and Local Rule 26:

a. Synopsis: a short synopsis (not to exceed two pages) of the main claims, counterclaims, and/or affirmative defenses.

b. Legal issues: a brief description of the **key legal issues**.

c. Damages: the realistic range of provable damages.

d. Insurance: whether there is insurance coverage, the extent of coverage, and whether there is a reservation of rights.

e. Motions: a statement of the likelihood of motions seeking to (i) add other parties or claims or (ii) file amended pleadings or (iii) transfer venue.

f. Discovery and experts: pursuant to Rule 26(f), state what, if any, changes in the disclosures under R. 26(a) should be made; the subjects on which discovery may be needed and whether discovery should be conducted in phases or otherwise be limited; what discovery has been conducted thus far; whether applicable limitations should be changed or other limitations imposed; and whether the Court should enter other orders. Please state how many depositions each side will conduct. Also discuss the proposed time of expert witness disclosures under F.R.Civ.P. 26(a)(2).

g. Dispositive motions: a description of the issues or claims that any party believes may be determined by motion for summary judgment or motion *in limine*.

h. Settlement and settlement mechanism: a statement of what settlement discussions and/or written communications have occurred (**specifically excluding any statement of the terms discussed**) and a statement pursuant to the Local Rule 16-14.4 selecting a settlement mechanism under that rule.

i. Trial estimate: a realistic estimate of the time required for trial and whether trial will be by jury or by court. Each side should specify (by number, not by name) how many witnesses it contemplates calling. If the time estimate for trial given in the Rule 26(f) Joint Report exceeds eight court days, counsel shall be prepared to discuss in detail the estimate.

j. Timetable: **complete of the Presumptive Schedule of Pretrial Dates form attached as Exhibit A to this Order and attach it to the Rule 26(f) report.** ***Submission of a completed Exhibit A is mandatory.*** The current entries in the "Weeks Before Trial" column merely reflect what the Court believes are appropriate for many, if not most, cases; those entries are not necessarily applicable to this case, and the form is designed to enable counsel to request the Court to set different last dates by which the key requirements must be completed. Each side should write in the month, day and year it requests for each event. *E.g.*, for the expert discovery cut-off it might be "10/7/02" for plaintiff and "10/28/02" for defendant, if they cannot agree. At the conference, the Court will review this form with counsel. Each entry proposing dates shall fall on a Monday, except the trial date which is a Tuesday. In appropriate cases the Court will order different dates after it hears from Counsel. The proposed non-expert and expert discovery cut-off date means: the last day by which all depositions must be completed and responses to all previously-served written discovery must be provided. The proposed cut-off date for motions means: the last date on which motions may be heard, not noticed.

k. Other issues: a statement of any other issues affecting the status or management of the case (*e.g.*, unusually complicated technical or technological issues, disputes over protective orders, extraordinarily voluminous document production, non-English speaking witnesses, discovery in foreign jurisdictions, *etc.*).

l. Conflicts: for conflict purposes, corporate parties must identify all subsidiaries, parents and affiliates.

m. Patent cases: propose dates and methodology for claim construction and *Markman* hearings. The Court intends to follow the process outlined in the rules for patent cases which have been adopted by the Northern District of California.[1] At a minimum, the Court will require the exchange of Proposed Terms and Claim Elements for Construction, preparation and filing of a Joint Claim Construction and Prehearing Statement, and

---

[1] The rules can be found on the internet at http://www.cand.uscourts.gov/CAND/LocalRul.nsf/fec20e529a5572f0882569b6006607e0/4735a1c69bd18b418825695f00730cdd?OpenDocument

simultaneous opening and reply briefs. *See* Local Patent Rules, Northern District of California, Rules 4-2, 4-3, 4-5.

n. Magistrates: Do the parties wish to have a Magistrate Judge preside? Under 28 U.S.C. § 636, the parties may consent to have a Magistrate Judge preside over all the proceedings, not just discovery. They may pick *any* Magistrate Judge (not just the one assigned to this case) from among those Magistrate Judges who accept these designations. (They are identified on the Central District's website, which also contains the consent form.)

The Joint Rule 26(f) Report should set forth the above enumerated information under section headings corresponding to this Order.

2. Scheduling Conference

Scheduling Conferences will be held in the Ronald Reagan Building, 411 West Fourth Street, Court Room 10C, Santa Ana. Counsel shall comply with the following:

a. Participation. The lead trial attorney **must** attend the Scheduling Conference, unless excused for good cause shown in advance of the Scheduling Conference.

b. Continuance. A continuance of the Scheduling Conference will be granted only for good cause.

3. Protective Orders

If you seek a protective order, propose it to opposing counsel before the Scheduling Conference, if at all possible. Protective Order should be submitted to the assigned Magistrate Judge for consideration.

4. Notice to be Provided by Counsel

Plaintiff's counsel or, if plaintiff is appearing *pro se*, defendant's counsel, shall provide this Order to any parties who first appear after the date of this Order and to parties who are known to exist but have not yet entered appearances.

5. Disclosures to Clients

Counsel are ordered to deliver to their respective clients a copy of this Order and of the Court's Scheduling and Case Management Order, which contains the schedule that the Court sets at the Scheduling Conference.

6. Court's Website

Copies of this and all other orders of this Court that may become applicable to this case are available on the Central District of California website, at "www.cacd.uscourts.gov," under "Judge's Procedures and Schedules." Copies of the Local Rules are available on the website.[2]

The Court thanks the parties and their counsel for their anticipated cooperation in carrying out these requirements.

IT IS SO ORDERED.

Dated: ____________________

JAMES V. SELNA
United States District Judge

---

[2] They may also be purchased from one of the following:

Los Angeles Daily Journal	West Publishing Company	Metropolitan News
915 East First Street	50 West Kellogg Blvd.	210 South Spring Street
Los Angeles, CA 90012	St. Paul, MN 55164-9979	Los Angeles, CA 90012

ERISA Addendum to Scheduling Conference Order

Where the plaintiff's claim is predicated in whole or in part on denial of benefits under a plan regulated by the Employee Retirement Income Security Act of 1974, 29 U.S.C. § 1000 *et seq.* (ERISA), the parties shall address the following additional issues in their Joint Report:

1. Standard of Review. What standard of review is applicable? If the parties are in disagreement, they shall propose a schedule for early briefing and decision of this issue on Motion.

2. Pre-Emption. Is there any contention that any state–law claim asserted by plaintiff is preempted by ERISA? If so, the parties shall propose a schedule for early briefing and decision of the issue on Motion.

EXHIBIT A
PRESUMPTIVE SCHEDULE OF PRETRIAL DATES

Matter	Time	Weeks before trial	Plaintiff's Request (Insert specific date)	Defendant's Request (Insert specific date)	Court Order
Trial date (jury) (court) Estimated length: _____ days	8:30 a.m.				
[Court trial:] File Findings of Fact and Conclusions of Law and Summaries of Direct Testimony		-1			
Final Pretrial Conference; Hearing on Motions *in Limine*; File Agreed Upon Set of Jury Instructions and Verdict Forms and Joint Statement re Disputed Instructions and Verdict Forms; File Proposed *Voir Dire* Qs and Agreed-to Statement of Case	11:00 a.m. (Mondays)	-2			
Lodge Pretrial Conf. Order File Memo of Contentions of Fact and Law; Exhibit List; Witness List; Status Report re Settlement		-3			
Last day for hand-serving Motions *in Limine*		-6			
Last day for hearing motions	1:30 p.m. (Mondays)	-7			
Last day for hand-serving motions and filing (other than Motions *in Limine*). Please note extended notice requirements for motions for summary judgment under F.R.Civ. P. 56(c).		-11			
Non-expert Discovery cut-off		-15			

ADDITIONAL MATTERS TO BE DETERMINED AT SCHEDULING CONFERENCE

L.R. 16-15 Settlement Choice: (1) CT/USMJ (2) Atty (3) Outside ADR

Expert discovery cut-off					
Rebuttal Expert Witness Disclosure					
Opening Expert Witness Disclosure [*See* F.R.Civ.P. 26(a)(2)]					
Last day to conduct Settlement Conference					
Last Day to Amend Pleadings or Add Parties					

Hon. Christina A. Snyder

District Judge

Chambers Information

U.S. District Court, Central District of California
Courtroom 5, 2nd Floor
312 N. Spring Street
Los Angeles, CA 90012

Scheduling Information

Courtroom Deputy: (213) 894-3433

Civil Law and Motion	Mondays at 10:00 a.m.
Criminal Law and Motion	Mondays at 1:30 p.m.

Biographical Information

Born 1947 in Los Angeles, CA

Federal Judicial Service:

-Judge, U. S. District Court, Central District of California
-Nominated by William J. Clinton on January 7, 1997, to a seat vacated by Edward Rafeedie; Confirmed by the Senate on November 7, 1997, and received commission on November 10, 1997.

Education:

-Pomona College, B.A., 1969
-Stanford Law School, J.D., 1972

Professional Career:

-Private Practice, California, 1972-1997

I. Judge Snyder's Procedures and Practices

A. *Procedures and Schedules*

The best way to contact the Judge's Courtroom Deputy Clerk is by calling 213-894-3433; if the clerk does not answer the phone, be sure to leave a voicemail message. Due to this Court's heavy caseload, hearings and trials it is engaged in, the Courtroom Deputy Clerk will return all voicemail messages at the earliest possibility. Information regarding the status of civil motions, civil stipulations or civil proposed orders are not available by telephone. Counsel shall check status on Pacer follow Local Rules and Federal Rules of Civil Procedure (Local Rule 11-4.5).

1. SCHEDULING AND PROCEDURES

If counsel have received a "Notice of Parties of Alternate Dispute Resolution (ADR) Program" - forms ADR-08, ADR-10, or ADR-11 with an attached "ADR Program Questionnaire" form ADR-09, please see General Order 02-07, which is located in the "General Orders" section on the homepage of the Court's website. The Attorney Settlement Officer information is located in the section "Attorney Information > ADR."

a. LOCAL RULES

Counsel are advised the Court expects strict compliance with the provisions of the Local Rules and the Federal Rules of Civil Procedure. Copies of the Local Rules may be purchased from one of the following:

Los Angeles Daily Journal	Metropolitan News	West Group
915 East 1st Street	210 South Spring Street	610 Opperman Drive
Los Angeles, CA 90012	Los Angeles, CA 90012	Egan, Minnesota 55123

The Local Rules may also be found on the United States District Court's website at the following address: http://www.cacd.uscourts.gov. Please note that certain Local Rules have recently been amended.

The attention of counsel is particularly directed to Local Rules 16 and 26 for the conduct of mandatory pretrial and settlement proceedings.

b. INTERROGATORIES

Refer to the Local Rules.

c. MOTIONS IN CIVIL AND CRIMINAL CASES

Motions shall be heard on each Monday of the month at 10:00 a.m., unless otherwise ordered by the Court. If Monday is a national holiday, the succeeding Monday shall be the motion day and all matters noticed for such Monday stand for hearing on the following Monday without special order or notice. The Court provides oral or written tentative rulings on most motions. Counsel are encouraged to direct oral argument to the matters raised in the tentative ruling and to submit to any part of the ruling that is not in genuine dispute, where appropriate. The Court will notify counsel if it does not require oral argument on any specific motion.

Motion papers should comply with the Local Rules. Briefs should not exceed the page limits authorized by the Local Rules. The Court will rarely grant leave to file briefs that exceed the authorized page limits. Counsel are admonished not to circumvent page limits by filing multiple motions which purport to address separate issues in a case. Such motions will not be considered unless counsel obtains leave to file more than one motion or to file a brief that exceeds the page limits authorized by the Local Rules.

Motions in criminal cases shall be heard on each Monday of the month at 1:30 p.m, unless otherwise ordered by the Court. If Monday is a national holiday, the succeeding Monday shall be the motion day and all matters noticed for such Monday stand for hearing on the following Monday without special order or notice.

Special Note: The Court does not reserve hearing dates for any motions. Counsel refer to the applicable rules regarding notice of any matter being set upon the Court's calendar (See, e.g., Local Rule 7).

d. STATUS CONFERENCES, PRETRIAL CONFERENCES

Counsel are reminded of their obligations to disclose information and confer on a discovery plan not later than 21 days prior to the date of the Fed. R. Civ. P. 16(b) scheduling conference and to report to the Court not later than 14 days after they confer on a discovery plan and the other matters required by Fed. R. Civ. P. 26(f) and the Local Rules of this Court. The following issues will be considered at the scheduling conference: the last date by which parties and claims for relief may be added, the discovery cutoff, as well as any issues relating to the discovery plan, the last date for filing motions, the time for the pretrial conference and the trial date. Scheduling conferences are generally held on Monday at 11:00 a.m.

Status conferences and pretrial conferences in civil cases are held on Mondays at 11:00 a.m., unless they have previously been scheduled to take place at a different time. Counsel are reminded to comply fully with Local Rule 16 in preparing for pretrial conferences. Motions in limine shall be noticed to be heard on the same date and time the pretrial conference is scheduled for. Briefing on the motions in limine must comply with the Local Rules. However, no replies are to be filed as the Court will not consider such filings.

Status conferences in criminal cases are held on Mondays at 1:30 p.m., unless they have previously been scheduled to take place at a different time. Motions in limine shall be noticed to be heard on the same date and time the status conference is scheduled for. Briefing on the motions in limine must comply with the Local Rules. However, no replies are to be filed as the Court will not consider such filings.

Judge Snyder will permit oral argument on calendared motions to be heard telephonically if (a) all involved parties consent to the telephone hearing, (b) the parties anticipate presenting limited argument, and © the Court's calendar permits such telephonic oral argument to be heard. Arrangements for telephonic hearings must be made by communicating in writing or by telephone with Judge Snyder's Courtroom Deputy Clerk, Catherine Jeang.

The Courtroom Deputy Clerk must be notified by the moving party of all counsels' intention to participate in a telephonic hearing by the Wednesday prior to the Monday hearing date.

The telephonic hearing will be scheduled at a time convenient for the Court and the parties, on the Monday originally scheduled for the hearing of the motion pursuant to the Federal Rules of Civil Procedure and the Local Rules. The party bringing the motion will initiate the conference call, and when all counsel are present on the line, will contact the Court. Callers will hold on the line until their motion is ready to be heard, at which time they will be connected with the Court, the case will be called, and the telephonic hearing will commence.

2. **DISCOVERY CUTOFF**

Generally, the Court will set a discovery cutoff date at the scheduling conference. The Court expects that by the date of the discovery cutoff, all discovery and responses thereto shall have been served, and all motions to compel will be on file and have been argued (but not necessarily decided). The only discovery that may be conducted after the discovery cutoff date without leave of Court is discovery ordered by the Magistrate Judge for which a timely-filed motion was pending and argued before the discovery cutoff date. Unless the Court has issued a contrary order, all discovery motions should be set before the Magistrate Judge to whom this case is assigned. Furthermore, Judge Snyder has a blanket referral of all discovery matters to be handled by the Magistrate Judge to whom the case is assigned.

3. **ARE TENTATIVE RULINGS ISSUED?**

Generally, prior to argument, written tentative rulings are provided to counsel on the date of the scheduled hearing. The courtroom is open to the public twenty (20) minutes before calendar call, upon which counsel may obtain such written tentative rulings, if available. In some cases, counsel will be notified that the motion has been taken under submission and that counsel need not appear for oral argument.

4. **ARE COPIES REQUIRED BY THE COURT?**

Counsel shall deliver mandatory chambers courtesy copies of all filed motions, responses, and replies in motion matters to Judge Snyder's chambers (Local Rule 11-4). Mandatory chambers copies of motions, oppositions and replies thereto shall be delivered to chambers in conformity with the Local Rules relating to electronic filing. However, the Court requires that mandatory chambers copies of reply memoranda be delivered to chambers no later than 12:00 p.m. on the first court day following the date when reply memoranda are required to be filed. **Furthermore, mandatory chambers copies shall be 2-hole punched and the efile notification date shall be *visible* on or as the first page.** Moreover, in all cases asserting claims under the antitrust laws, the patent laws or federal securities laws, and in such specific cases as may be designated by the Court, counsel must deliver to chambers two (2) mandatory chambers copies of all documents that are electronically filed. The Court will also accept any fax courtesy copies not exceeding five (5) pages in length total. The Courtroom Deputy Clerk's fax number is 213-894-0249.

In addition, counsel shall email any and all proposed orders to the Courtroom Deputy Clerk in "Word" or "WordPerfect" format to CAS_Chambers@cacd.uscourts.gov.

5. **PROCEDURES FOR FILING AN EX PARTE APPLICATION**

The parties' and counsels' attention is directed to Local Rule 7-19. The moving party shall inform the opposing party or parties that such party or parties shall have 48 hours from the date of delivery of the moving papers to file and serve their opposition papers, if any.

No hearing will be held on any ex parte application unless deemed necessary by the Court and in such case counsel will be notified by the Courtroom Deputy Clerk.

6. **TO REQUEST A CONTINUANCE OF ANY SCHEDULED COURT APPEARANCE**
Continuances will only be granted based upon a showing of good cause. Stipulations, including second and subsequent extensions of time to respond to the complaint, are effective ONLY when approved by the Court. (See Local Rule 16-8).

7. **NO COMMUNICATION WITH CHAMBERS STAFF**
Unless counsel have been expressly authorized to communicate with chambers (e. g., for a telephone status conference with all counsel participating), all oral and written communications must be submitted only to the Courtroom Deputy, Catherine Jeang with copies to all counsel of record. Please do not attempt to communicate in writing or by telephone with chambers. (See Local Rule 83-2.11).

8. **CALENDAR CONFLICTS**
Any person appearing before the Court must check in with the Courtroom Deputy Clerk prior to calendar call, and advise the Courtroom Deputy Clerk of the calendar conflict. The Court will provide a priority position on the calendar or, hold the matter until the end of the calendar or permit a party to submit on the tentative ruling.

9. **ELECTRONIC OR PHOTOGRAPHIC EQUIPMENT**
The Local Rules prohibit the recording of federal proceedings, either by electronic recording means or by camera. Video cassette recorders, monitors, computers, overhead projectors, and silent copiers, and the like for presentation of evidence are permitted, only by approval. Counsel shall contact the Courtroom Deputy Clerk by telephone to request leave to bring electronic equipment into the courtroom. Counsel will be advised by the Courtroom Deputy Clerk that such a request shall be made by a letter addressed to the U.S. Marshal's Office, carbon copied to the Court Coordinator and prepared for the Courtroom Deputy Clerk's signature, along with the case name and case number, the purpose, and on what date or for what duration equipment is needed. Counsel may fax the letter listing the equipment that he or she intends utilize to the Courtroom Deputy Clerk for signature, in advance of the trial or hearing, for approval and authorization. Upon approval, counsel shall present the letter to Court Security on the day(s) of the hearing, for admission.
    - Arrangements for bringing voluminous exhibits into the courtroom may be made through the Space and Facilities Help Desk, at (213) 894-1400.
    - ELMO reservations/tutorials may be made by first referring to the court website at www.cacd.uscourts.gov , under "Attorney Information," and then "Attorney Services." Alternatively, you can contact the Courtroom Technology Help Desk at 213-894-3061.

10. **TO ORDER A TRANSCRIPT OF A PROCEEDING**
For general information on how to order a transcript of any reported or digitally recorded proceeding, please contact 213-894-3015 or visit www.cacd.uscourts.gov > General Information > Court Reporter/Recorder Transcripts. If you require an estimate of cost for the preparation of a transcript, contact the court reporter/recorder for the desired proceeding.

    To determine the court reporter/recorder for a particular proceeding, go to the Court Reporter Schedule web page and click on View by Date. Once you've determined the correct court reporter/recorder for the desired session, click on Court Reporter Phone and Email List for contact information.

11. TRIAL CALENDAR AND REQUIRED PREPARATION

Court hours: 9:00 a.m. to 5:00 p.m. The Court may conduct bench trials to 6:30 p.m. and specifically schedule hearings after 5:00 p.m. if convenient for the parties. Luncheon recess is 12:00 p.m. (Noon) to 1:30 p.m.

a. **EXHIBITS:** Two (2) Sets (original and Bench copy) are to be submitted to the Courtroom Deputy Clerk at the beginning of trial - in the form specified in Local Rule 16-5. When applicable, the Court prefers all written exhibits to be placed in 3-ring binders (no larger than 2-1/2 inches), with numbered tabs and, volume numbers identified on the outside spine of the exhibit book. Good photographs of physical exhibits are to be inserted into the bench book, and the actual physical exhibit with the appropriate evidence tag may be tendered to the Courtroom Deputy Clerk. If the physical exhibit is to be returned at the conclusion of trial, a photograph of same is to be provided to the Courtroom Deputy Clerk.

b. **EXHIBIT LISTS:** Three (3) copies are to be submitted to the Courtroom Deputy Clerk at the beginning of trial.

c. **WITNESS LISTS:** Three (3) copies are to be submitted to the Courtroom Deputy Clerk at the beginning of trial.

d. **DEPOSITIONS:** If counsel plans to use deposition transcripts during trial for any purpose, including impeachment, counsel should arrange to have the original lodged on the first day of trial. If the original is not available, please lodge a certified copy in lieu or the original or, counsel may stipulate to the use of an uncertified copy. The use of depositions at trial will not be permitted if the original or a copy has not been lodged.

   Where witnesses testify by deposition, counsel for the parties should do the following: Prepare and file with the Court a stipulated summary of what the witness' testimony will be, and mark those portions of the deposition transcripts that will be offered. Plaintiffs shall use blue markings and defendants shall use red markings. Other colors, clearly identified as to the designating party, shall be used if there are multiple defendants. If there are objections to testimony upon which counsel seeks a ruling from the Court, counsel must indicate the request for a ruling in the margin of the deposition transcript.

e. **VOIR DIRE:** Ordinarily the Court will conduct voir dire. Counsel should submit proposed voir dire examination no later than the Wednesday of the week prior to trial.

f. **JURY INSTRUCTIONS:** Jury instructions in the form described below are to be submitted not later than the Wednesday of the week prior to trial. Counsel need only submit proposed substantive instructions. The Court will propound its own general instructions and will essentially follow the format set out in the Manual of Model Criminal Jury Instructions for the Ninth Circuit (West Publishing, latest edition). In those cases where a special verdict is desired, counsel shall submit a proposed verdict form with the jury instructions Counsel shall submit a floppy disk or compact disc containing the proposed joint and disputed instructions and special verdict.

   The parties must submit JOINT jury instructions and a JOINT proposed verdict form (if a special verdict is requested). In order to produce these joint instructions, the parties shall meet and confer sufficiently in advance of the required submission date with the goal of agreeing upon instructions and verdict forms. The jury instructions shall be submitted as follows: 1) JOINT jury instructions, those instructions which are agreed to be all parties; and 2) DISPUTED jury instructions, those instructions propounded by a party to which another party objects. Objections to disputed instructions shall be filed no later than the Friday before the commencement of trial. Each requested jury instruction shall be numbered and set forth in full on a separate page, citing the case authority or other source of the requested instruction.

The Court prefers counsel to use the instructions from the Manual of Model Criminal Jury Instructions for the Ninth Circuit, West Publishing, latest edition. Another suggested source is Federal Jury Practice and Instructions, Devitt, Blackmar, Wolff and O'Malley, West Publishing Co., current edition.

An index page shall accompany all jury instructions that are submitted to the Court. The index page shall indicate the following:

(1) The number of the instruction;
(2) A brief title of the instruction;
(3) The source of the instruction; and
(4) The page number of the instruction.

EXAMPLE:

Number	Title	Source	Page Number
#1	Duty of the Jury	9th Cir. 1.01	1

Ninth Circuit Model Jury Instruction are preferred. Counsel may discuss the matter with the Court before the commencement of trial proceedings.

12. PROCEDURES FOR OBTAINING THE SERVICES OF A COURT INTERPRETERS

CIVIL CASES: Counsel are responsible for providing federal court certified interpreters at their expense.

CRIMINAL CASES: The Court will provide interpreters at no charge to the parties. The Courtroom Deputy Clerk requires advance notice of no less than 24 hours for Spanish language, and 48 hours for any other language. The more notice the better, as the Courtroom Deputy Clerk cannot guarantee an interpreter on less than one (1) day's notice. You may fax your notice to the Courtroom Deputy Clerk at the telephone number given above.

13. OTHER

Any questions regarding law clerk/extern positions shall be directed to chambers at (213) 894-8551.

II. Judge Snyder's Case Management Orders

A. *Notice to Counsel*

IN THE UNITED STATES DISTICT COURT
FOR THE CENTRAL DISTRICT OF CALIFORNIA

Plaintiff(s),)	Case No. CV [illegible] CAS ([illegible]x)
v.)	**NOTICE TO COUNSEL**
Defendant(s).)	

This case has been assigned to the calendar of Judge Christina A. Snyder. This Notice to Counsel shall be to all parties appearing in propria persona, and for purposes of this notice, the term "counsel" shall include any person appearing in pro per.

Counsel are advised that the Court expects strict compliance with the provisions of the Local Rules and the Federal Rules of Civil Procedure. Copies of the Local Rules may be purchased from one of the following:

Los Angeles Daily Journal 915 E. 1st Street Los Angeles, CA 90012	Metropolitan News 210 South Spring St. Los Angeles, CA 90012	West Group 610 Opperman Drive Egan, Minnesota 55123

The Local Rules and **Judge's Procedures and Schedules** may also be found on the United States District Court's website at the following address: HTTP://WWW.CACD.USCOURTS.GOV. Please note that certain Local Rules have recently been amended.

The attention of counsel is particularly directed to Local Rules 16 and 26 for the conduct of mandatory pretrial and settlement proceedings.

Counsel are reminded of their obligations to disclose information and confer on a discovery plan not later than 21 days prior to the date of the Fed. R. Civ. P. 16(b) scheduling conference and to report to the Court not later than 14 days after they confer on a discovery plan and the other matters required by Fed. R. Civ. P. 26(f) and the Local Rules of this Court. The following issues will be considered at the scheduling conference: the last date by which parties and claims for relief may be added, the discovery cutoff, as well as any issues relating to the discovery plan, the last date for filing motions, the time for the pretrial conference and the trial date. Scheduling conferences are generally held on Monday at 11:00 a.m.

Counsel should also be guided by the following requirements when litigating cases assigned to Judge Snyder:

1. INTERROGATORIES: Refer to the Local Rules.

2. MOTIONS: Motions shall be heard on each Monday of the month at 10:00 a.m., unless otherwise ordered by the Court. If Monday is a national holiday, the succeeding Monday shall be the motion day and all matters noticed for such Monday stand for hearing on the following Monday without special order or notice. The Court provides oral or written tentative rulings on most motions. Counsel are encouraged to direct oral argument to the matters raised in the tentative ruling and to submit to any part of the ruling that is not in genuine dispute, where appropriate. The Court will notify counsel if it does not require oral argument on any specific motion.

Motion papers should comply with the Local Rules. Briefs should not exceed the page limits authorized by the Local Rules. The Court will rarely grant leave to file briefs that exceed the authorized page limits. Counsel are admonished not to circumvent page limits by filing multiple motions which purport to address separate issues in a case. Such motions will not be considered unless counsel obtains leave to file more than one motion or to file a brief that exceeds the page limits authorized by the Local Rules.

3. EX PARTE APPLICATIONS:
   - **A.** NOTICE: The parties' and counsels' attention is directed to Local Rule 7-19. The moving party shall inform the opposing party or parties that such party or parties shall have 48 hours from the date of delivery of the moving papers to file and serve their opposition papers, if any.
   - **B.** HEARING: No hearing will be held on any ex parte application unless deemed necessary by the Court and in such case counsel will be notified by the Courtroom Deputy Clerk.
4. DISCOVERY CUTOFF: Generally, the Court will set a discovery cutoff date at the scheduling conference. The Court expects that by the date of the discovery cutoff, all discovery and responses thereto shall have been served, and all motions to compel will be on file and have been argued (but not necessarily decided). The only discovery that may be conducted after the discovery cutoff date without leave of Court is discovery ordered by the Magistrate Judge for which a timely-filed motion was pending and argued before the discovery cutoff date. Unless the Court has issued a contrary order, all discovery motions should be set before the Magistrate Judge to whom this case is assigned.
5. MANDATORY CHAMBERS COPIES: The Court requires that mandatory copies of electronically filed documents be delivered to chambers no later than 12:00 p.m. on the first court day following the date when the documents are required filed. **Furthermore, mandatory chambers copies shall be 2-hole punched and the efile notification date shall be visible on or as the first page.** Moreover, in all cases asserting claims under the antitrust laws, the patent laws or federal securities laws, and in such specific cases as may be designated by the Court, counsel must deliver to chambers two (2) mandatory chambers copies of all documents that are electronically filed. Mandatory copy documents shall include tabs to separate exhibits, declarations, etc., where applicable. The Court will also accept any fax courtesy copies not exceeding five (5) pages in length total. The Courtroom Deputy Clerk's fax number is 213-894-0249. In addition, counsel shall email any and all proposed orders to the Courtroom Deputy Clerk in "Word" or "WordPerfect" format to CAS_Chambers@cacd.uscourts.gov.
6. CONTINUANCES: Continuances will only be granted based upon a showing of good cause. Stipulations, including second and subsequent extensions of time to respond to the complaint, are effective ONLY when approved by the Court. (See Local Rule 16-8).
7. REMOVED ACTIONS: Any answers filed in state court must be refiled with the Court as a supplement to the petition. Any pending motions must be renoticed in accordance with Local Rule 37-3.

8. TELEPHONIC HEARINGS: Judge Snyder will permit oral argument on calendared motions to be heard telephonically if (a) all involved parties consent to the telephone hearing, (b) the parties anticipate presenting limited argument, and (c) the Court's calendar permits such telephonic oral argument to be heard. Arrangements for telephonic hearings must be made by communicating in writing or by telephone with Judge Snyder's Courtroom Deputy Clerk, Catherine Jeang.

   The Courtroom Deputy Clerk must be notified by the moving party of all counsels' intention to participate in a telephonic hearing by the Wednesday prior to the Monday hearing date.

   The telephonic hearing will be scheduled at a time convenient for the Court and the parties, on the Monday originally scheduled for the hearing of the motion pursuant to the Federal Rules of Civil Procedure and the Local Rules. The party bringing the motion will initiate the conference call, and when all counsel are present on the line, will contact the Court. Callers will hold on the line until their motion is ready to be heard, at which time they will be connected with the Court, the case will be called, and the telephonic hearing will commence.

9. COMMUNICATIONS WITH THE COURT: Unless counsel have been expressly authorized to communicate with chambers (e. g., for a telephone status conference with all counsel participating), all oral and written communications must be submitted only to the Courtroom Deputy, Catherine Jeang with copies to all counsel of record. Please do not attempt to communicate in writing or by telephone with chambers. (See Local Rule 83-2.11).

NOTICE OF THIS ORDER: Counsel for plaintiff is responsible for promptly serving a copy of this Order on all defendants' counsel. If this case came to the Court via removal, the removing defendant shall promptly serve a copy of this Order on all parties of record.

Date: November 4, 2010

CHRISTINA A. SNYDER
United States District Judge

Hon. Alicemarie H. Stotler
District Judge

Chambers Information
U.S. District Court, Central District of California
Courtroom TBD
411 West Fourth Street
Santa Ana, CA 92701

Scheduling Information
Courtroom Deputy: (714) 338-4730

Civil Law and Motion	Mondays (except 5th Monday of the month) at 10:00 a.m.
Criminal Law and Motion	Fridays, as scheduled by clerk

Biographical Information
Born 1942 in Alhambra, CA

Federal Judicial Service:
-Judge, U. S. District Court, Central District of California
-Nominated by Ronald Reagan on April 4, 1984, to a seat vacated by Robert J. Kelleher; Confirmed by the Senate on May 1, 1984, and received commission on May 3, 1984.
-Served as chief judge, 2005-2009. Assumed senior status on January 5, 2009.

Education:
-University of Southern California, B.A., 1964
-University of Southern California Law School, J.D., 1967

Professional Career:
-Deputy District Attorney, Orange County, California, 1967-1973
-Private Practice, Tustin, California, 1973-1976
-Municipal Court Judge, Harbor Judicial District, Newport Beach, California, 1976-1978
-Justice Pro Tempore, Fourth District Court of Appeal, Division Two, San Bernardino, CA, 1977
-Judge, Orange County Superior Court, California, 1978-1983
-Private Practice, Newport Beach, California, 1983-1984

I. Judge Stotler's Procedures and Practices

A. Procedures and Schedules

ALL CRIMINAL MOTION DATES MUST BE CLEARED WITH COURT CLERK PRIOR TO FILING MOTIONS.

1. COURT PROCEEDINGS

A. Scheduled times: CIVIL

Proceeding	Day (M-F)	Time
Motions It is not necessary to clear or reserve a motion date with the court clerk prior to filing the motion.	**Mondays, except 5th Monday of the month.** If Monday is a holiday, set on next available Monday	10:00 a.m. Most motions are adjudicated without oral argument. A separate, proposed order is required.
Discovery motions	to be scheduled before the Magistrate Judge assigned to the case	
Scheduling Orders pursuant to Fed. R. Civ. P. 16(b) and 26(f)		Scheduling orders are issued based on the pleadings and the parties' Joint Report usually without a court hearing.
Final Pretrial Conferences	Fridays	2:00 p.m.
Trials	Tuesday start otherwise, Tues.-Thurs. 9:00 a.m. - 12:00 p.m., 1:00 p.m. - 5:00 p.m.	9:00 a.m.
Bankruptcy Appeals	Fridays	1:30 p.m. Most appeals are adjudicated without oral argument.
Ex Parte Applications	Call Court Clerk to notify of ex parte application. Clerk may hold for opposition. Submitted on the papers unless otherwise scheduled by the Court. **A separate proposed order must be submitted.**	
Trial preparation**	See Judge's order regarding Court or Jury Trials issued with Scheduling Order. The order contains information re: jury instructions, conduct at trial, Exhibit Conference Friday before trial, etc.	
**Court's Order For Jury Trial is attached as Attachment A. **Court's Order for Court Trial is attached as Attachment B.		

B. Scheduled times: CRIMINAL

Proceeding	Day (M-F)	Time
Motions	Fridays **	As scheduled by clerk
Motions in Limine	1st day of trial	9:00 a.m.
Motions to Suppress	Fridays**	As scheduled by clerk
Change of plea	As scheduled by clerk	As scheduled by clerk
Rule 20 plea	As scheduled by clerk	As scheduled by clerk
Sentencing	As scheduled by clerk	As scheduled by clerk
Bail hearings	As scheduled by clerk	As scheduled by clerk
Revocation hearing	As scheduled by clerk	As scheduled by clerk
Trial	Tuesday start otherwise, Tues.-Thurs. 9:00 a.m. - 12:00 p.m., 1:00 p.m. - 5:00 p.m.	9:00 a.m.
Ex Parte Applications	Call Court Clerk to notify of ex parte application. Clerk may hold for opposition. Submitted on the papers unless otherwise scheduled by the Court. **A separate proposed order must be submitted.**	
**All criminal motions are to be filed and served not later than twenty-eight (28) days after arraignment and set for hearing not later than the Monday eight (8) days prior to trial at 1:30 p.m. and date cleared by Court Clerk. Counsel's estimate of time required for presentation of motion must be set forth adjacent to caption. (Court's Order Governing Pretrial Motions, Trial, and Sentencing issued @ PIA by Magistrate Judge. Attachment C.)		

II. COURT PROCEDURES - MOST FREQUENTLY ASKED QUESTIONS

Are tentative rulings issued?	Yes, in some cases. Distributed at the hearing prior to calling the case.
Are counsel allowed to contact the Judge's law clerks or executive assistant?	No, unless initiated by the law clerk or executive assistant.
Questions regarding law clerk/extern positions.	Directed to the Judge's executive assistant.
How to order a transcript of Court proceedings	For general information on how to order a transcript of any reported or digitally recorded proceeding, please contact 213-894-3015 or visit www.cacd.uscourts.gov > General Information > Court Reporter/Recorder Transcripts. If you require an estimate of cost for the preparation of a transcript, contact the court reporter/recorder for the desired proceeding. To determine the court reporter/recorder for a particular

	proceeding, go to the Court Reporter Schedule web page and click on View by Date. Once you've determined the correct court reporter/recorder for the desired session, click on Court Reporter Phone and Email List for contact information.
Questions regarding trial preparation.	Please review the Court's Orders for Jury or Court Trial. (Attachment A or B)
Are appearances permitted by telephone?	No, unless specially set by Court.
Method used to impanel a jury:	"Arizona blind strike" method. Court clerk seats all prospective jurors by random draw. Jurors are handed trial calendar [optional] and a sheet of paper that calls for their later recitation of personal information, such as city of residence, place and type of work, etc. Court conducts voir dire of entire panel, not just jurors in jury box. The Judge may invite counsel to ask questions. After challenges for cause are heard at sidebar, counsel submit their written peremptory challenges. The Clerk collects the forms from counsel and gives forms to the Judge. Judge and Clerk confer so as to assign the unstruck, unchallenged jurors selected by the parties. At sidebar, the Court confirms peremptory challenges as submitted. Judge names first 6-8 unstruck, unchallenged jurors (civil) or first 12-14 unstruck, unchallenged jurors plus alternates (criminal) who constitute the jury. In criminal cases, an alternate pool can be reserved. Alternates are not identified as alternate jurors.
Proper submission of mandatory chambers copies	Mandatory Chambers Copies of all e-filed documents shall be delivered to the mandatory chambers copy box on the 10th Floor. It is imperative that the mandatory chambers copies be delivered by noon following the date of filing as required by General Order 10-07.IV.D. Failure to deliver timely mandatory chambers copies may result in a delay in hearing a motion or ordering the matter off calendar.

II. Judge Stotler's Case Management Orders

A. Order for Court Trial

IN THE UNITED STATES DISTICT COURT
FOR THE CENTRAL DISTRICT OF CALIFORNIA

)	Case No. ______________
Plaintiff(s),)	
v.)	**I. ORDER FOR COURT TRIAL SETTING DATES FOR:**
Defendant(s).)	Discovery Cutoff: ____________
______________________________)	Final Pretrial Conference: ____at 2:00 p.m.
	Trial: _______ at 9:00 a.m.
	II. ORDER FOR PREPARATION FOR COURT TRIAL, PROPOSED FINDINGS OF FACT & CONCLUSIONS OF LAW, AND SCHEDULING AN EXHIBIT CONFERENCE FRIDAY BEFORE TRIAL
	III. ORDER GOVERNING ATTORNEY AND PARTY CONDUCT AT TRIAL

I.
ORDERS FOR PRETRIAL PROCEEDINGS

A. Scheduling

1. Parties and Pleadings: All motions to join other parties or to amend the pleadings shall be filed and served **within sixty (60) days of the date of this order**. All unserved parties shall be dismissed no later than the date on which the Final Pretrial Conference is held.

2. Motions for Summary Judgment or Partial Summary Judgment: No motions for summary judgment or partial summary judgment may be filed later than **fourteen (14) days after the discovery cutoff date**, unless otherwise ordered by Court.

3. Discovery Cutoff: All discovery is to be completed on, or before, the cutoff date. The following discovery schedule shall apply to this case.

a. Depositions: All depositions shall be scheduled to commence at least **seven (7) days** before the discovery cutoff date. All depositions to be used in trial shall be lodged with the Courtroom Deputy Clerk at least **seven (7) days** before trial or such earlier date as the Court may order.

b. Interrogatories: All interrogatories must be served at least **forty-five (45) days** before the discovery cutoff date.

c. Production of Documents, *etc.*, as Among Parties: All requests for production, etc., among parties, shall be served at least **forty-five (45) days** before the discovery cutoff date.

d. Request for Admissions: All requests for admissions shall be served at least **forty-five (45) days** before the discovery cutoff date.

e. Discovery Motions: Any motion respecting the inadequacy of responses to discovery must be filed and served **not later than fourteen (14) days** after the discovery cutoff date. Counsel are reminded to adhere to the Civility and Professional Guidelines adopted by the United States District Court for the Central District of California.

f. Disclosure of Expert Testimony: The above discovery cutoff date includes expert discovery, unless otherwise ordered by Court.

B. Final Pretrial Conference

This case has been placed on calendar for a Final Pretrial Conference pursuant to Fed. R. Civ. P. 16. The Court requires strict compliance with the requirements of the Federal Rules of Civil Procedure and Local Rules, including the format in Appendix A.

II.
ORDER FOR PREPARATION FOR COURT TRIAL, PROPOSED FINDINGS OF FACT AND CONCLUSIONS OF LAW, AND SETTING EXHIBIT CONFERENCE FRIDAY BEFORE TRIAL

A. Counsel shall comply with the following orders in preparing for trial.

1. Motions *in Limine*: All motions *in limine* must be filed and served a minimum of forty-two (42) days before the originally scheduled trial date. Each motion should be separately filed and numbered. All opposition documents must be filed and served at least twenty-one (21) days before the scheduled trial date. All reply documents must be filed and served at least fourteen (14) days before the scheduled trial date.

All motions *in limine* will be heard on the scheduled trial date, unless the parties proceed under the noticed motion provisions of Local Rule 7, or the Court otherwise orders.

2. Finding of Fact and Conclusions of Law: Findings of facts and Conclusions of Law shall be prepared, lodged, and served in accordance with Local Rule 52-1.

At the same time, counsel must furnish to the assigned Courtroom Deputy Clerk a diskette of proposed Findings of Fact and Conclusions of Law.

3. Stipulations: All counsel shall confer no later than five (5) days before trial and stipulate so far as is possible as to foundation, waiver of the best evidence rule, and to those exhibits which may be received into evidence at the start of trial.

B. Counsel Shall Attend An Exhibit Conference.

A special conference regarding trial exhibits and other trial matters, which requires the attendance of trial counsel, will be held on the FRIDAY BEFORE THE SCHEDULED TRIAL DATE AT 3:00 P.M. IN COURTROOM 10-A, UNLESS THE COURT OTHERWISE ORDERS.

The Court requires the following submitted to the Courtroom Deputy Clerk at the time of the Exhibit Conference:

1. Trial Exhibits: Counsel shall prepare the original trial exhibits in either three-ring binders indexed by exhibit number with right-sided divider tabs, or in separately marked file folders inserted within redwells. Original exhibits must have affixed to the upper right-hand corner of the first page of each exhibit the Court's exhibit tag. If using binders, counsel shall label the front and spine of each binder with the respective volume number and exhibits contained within that binder. A binder bench book shall also be provided for use by the Court. Exhibits must be numbered in accordance with the Local Rules and Fed. R. Civ. P. 16 and 26, and shall be internally paginated.

2. Exhibit Lists: Counsel shall provide three (3) conformed copies of the joint or parties' exhibit list(s).

3. Witness Lists: Counsel shall provide three (3) conformed copies of the witness lists.

III.
ORDER GOVERNING ATTORNEY AND PARTY CONDUCT AT TRIAL

A. Opening Statements, Examining Witnesses, and Summation

1. Opening statements, examination of witnesses, and summation will be from the lectern only.

2. Counsel must not consume time by writing out words or drawing charts or diagrams. Counsel may do so in advance and explain that the item was prepared earlier as ordered by the Court to save time.

3. Never strike the lectern for emphasis.

B. Objections to Questions

1. Counsel must not use objections for the purpose of making a speech, recapitulating testimony, or attempting to guide the witness.

2. When objecting, counsel must rise to state only that counsel objects and the legal grounds for the objection.

C. General Decorum

1. Please keep the trial low-key. It is to be a dignified search for the truth.

2. Counsel must not approach the Courtroom Deputy Clerk or the witness box without specific permission. When permission is given, please return to the lectern when the purpose of the permission is completed. Counsel must not question a witness while at the witness stand.

3. Please rise when addressing the Court.

4. Counsel must address all remarks to the Court. Counsel are not to address the Courtroom Deputy Clerk, the reporter, persons in the audience, or opposing counsel. If counsel wishes to speak with opposing counsel, counsel must ask permission to talk off the record. Any request for the rereading of questions or answers shall be addressed to the Court.

5. Counsel must not address or refer to witnesses or parties by first names alone. Young witnesses (under 14) may, however, be addressed and referred to by first names.

6. Counsel must not make an offer of stipulation unless counsel has conferred with opposing counsel and has reason to believe the stipulation is acceptable.

7. While Court is in session, counsel must not leave counsel table to confer with investigators, secretaries, witnesses or other persons in the back of the courtroom unless permission has been granted in advance.

8. Counsel should not by facial expression, nodding, or other conduct exhibit any opinion, adverse or favorable, concerning any testimony being given by a witness. Counsel must admonish counsel's own clients and witnesses to avoid such conduct.

9. Where a party has more than one lawyer, only one may object to the testimony or conduct the direct or cross-examination of a given witness.

D. Promptness of Counsel and Witnesses

1. The Court makes every effort to commence proceedings at the time set. Promptness is expected from counsel and witnesses. It is counsel's duty to tell the Court on the

first day of any commitments in any other court on a subsequent day that may result in absence or late arrival.

2. If a witness was on the stand at adjournment, it is counsel's duty to have the witness adjacent to, but not on, the witness stand, ready to proceed, when the court session resumes. If a witness was on the stand at a recess, it is counsel's duty to have the witness back on the stand, ready to proceed, when the court session resumes.

a. It is counsel's duty to have the next witness in the courtroom after a recess if the last witness was excused at the time of the recess.

b. It is counsel's duty to notify the Courtroom Deputy Clerk in advance if any witness should be accommodated by use of the witness stand's automated platform which lowers and raises to aid witnesses who are unable to otherwise take the witness stand.

3. No presenting party may be without witnesses. If counsel has no more witnesses to call and there is more than a brief delay, the Court may deem that the party has rested.

4. The Court attempts to cooperate with physicians, scientists, and all other professional witnesses and will, except in extraordinary circumstances, accommodate them by permitting them to testify out of sequence. Counsel must anticipate the possibility and discuss it with opposing counsel. If there is objection, Counsel must confer with the Court in advance.

E. <u>Exhibits</u>

1. Each counsel should keep counsel's own list of exhibits and should note when each exhibit has been admitted in evidence.

2. Each counsel is responsible for any exhibits that counsel secures from the Courtroom Deputy Clerk and, at all recesses, at noontime, and afternoon adjournments, must return all exhibits in counsel's possession to the Courtroom Deputy Clerk.

3. An exhibit not previously marked should, at the time of its first mention and assuming that counsel intends for that item to become an exhibit, be accompanied by a request that the Courtroom Deputy Clerk mark it for identification. To save time, counsel must show a new exhibit to opposing counsel before it is mentioned in Court. If an item is meant for non-evidentiary purposes, such as refreshing recollection, no numbering or marking for identification is needed.

4. Whenever a particular exhibit is admissible, in counsel's opinion, it may be moved into evidence at the next available recess if the motion to admit it is opposed. (Counsel should consider waiting, however, until cross-examination concerning the proposed exhibits is concluded.) In the alternative, counsel may hold exhibits until the end of counsel's case and move them all into evidence at that time.

5. Counsel shall advise the Courtroom Deputy Clerk of any agreements they have with respect to the proposed exhibits that may be received so that no further motion to admit need be made.

6. When referring to an exhibit, counsel should refer to its exhibit number whenever possible. Witnesses should be asked to do the same.

7. Counsel must not ask witnesses to draw charts or diagrams nor ask the Court's permission for a witness to do so. If counsel wishes to question a witness in connection with graphic aids, the material must be fully prepared before the court session starts. (*See* Part III, A, 2, *supra*).

F. Depositions

1. All depositions that are to be used in the trial, either as evidence or for impeachment, must be signed and filed before the trial commences. (*See* Part I, A, 3, (a), *supra*). Counsel should check with the Courtroom Deputy Clerk to learn whether the Court already has any deposition, properly signed, in which counsel is interested.

2. In using depositions of an adverse party for impeachment, either one of the following procedures may be adopted:

> **a.** If counsel wishes to read the questions and answers as alleged impeachment and ask the witness no further questions on that subject, counsel may merely read the relevant portions of the deposition into the record, stating the page and line where the reading began and the page and line where the reading ended.
>
> **b.** If counsel wishes to ask the witness further questions on the subject matter, the deposition is placed in front of the witness and the witness is told to read silently the pages and lines involved. Then counsel may either ask the witness further questions on the matter and thereafter read the quotations or read the quotations and thereafter ask the further questions. Counsel should have an extra copy of the deposition for this purpose.

3. Where a witness is absent and the witness' testimony is offered by deposition, please observe the following procedures:

A reader should occupy the witness chair and read the testimony of the witness while the examining lawyer asks the questions. All colloquy among counsel or parties on the deposition record, except relevant stipulations, should be omitted from the reading, thereby presenting only the relevant evidence.

The Court should be asked whether it wishes the above procedure followed or merely wishes to read the deposition in chambers without the questions and answers being repeated for the record. In such instances, the deposition may be offered in evidence as an exhibit.

G. Using Numerous Answers to Interrogatories and Requests for Admissions

Whenever counsel expects to offer a group of answers to interrogatories or requests for admissions, extracted from one or more lengthy documents, counsel should prepare a new document listing each question and answer and identifying the document from which it has been extracted. Copies of this new document should be given to the Court and opposing counsel.

H. Advance Notice of Evidentiary or Difficult Questions

If any counsel has reason to anticipate that a difficult question of law or evidence will raise legal argument, requiring research and/or briefing, counsel must give the Court advance notice.

IT IS SO ORDERED.

Dated: ________________

ALICEMARIE H. STOTLER
United States District Judge

B. Order for Jury Trial

IN THE UNITED STATES DISTICT COURT
FOR THE CENTRAL DISTRICT OF CALIFORNIA

Plaintiff(s), v. Defendant(s).	Case No. ______________ **I. ORDER FOR JURY TRIAL SETTING DATES FOR:** Discovery Cutoff: ____________ Final Pretrial Conference: ___ at 2:00 p.m. Trial: ________ at 9:00 a.m. **II. ORDER FOR PREPARATION FOR JURY TRIAL AND JURY INSTRUCTIONS AND SETTING EXHIBIT CONFERENCE FRIDAY BEFORE TRIAL** **III. ORDER GOVERNING ATTORNEY AND PARTY CONDUCT AT TRIAL**

I.
ORDERS FOR PRETRIAL PROCEEDINGS

A. Scheduling

1. Parties and Pleadings: All motions to join other parties or to amend the pleadings shall be filed and served within **sixty (60) days of the date of this order**. All unserved parties shall be dismissed no later than the date on which the Final Pretrial Conference is held.

2. Motions for Summary Judgment or Partial Summary Judgment: No motions for summary judgment or partial summary judgment may be filed later than **fourteen (14) days after the discovery cutoff date**, unless otherwise ordered by Court.

3. Discovery Cutoff: All discovery is to be completed on, or before, the discovery cutoff date. The following discovery schedule shall apply to this case.

a. Depositions: All depositions shall be scheduled to commence at least **seven (7) days** before the discovery cutoff date. All depositions to be used in trial shall be lodged with the Courtroom Deputy Clerk at least **seven (7) days** before trial or such earlier date as the Court may order.

b. Interrogatories: All interrogatories must be served at least **forty-five (45) days** before the discovery cutoff date.

c. Production of Documents, *etc.*, as Among Parties: All requests for production, *etc.*, among parties, shall be served at least **forty-five (45) days** before the discovery cutoff date.

d. Requests for Admissions: All requests for admissions shall be served at least **forty-five (45) days** before the discovery cutoff date.

e. Discovery Motions: Any motion respecting the inadequacy of responses to discovery must be filed and served **not later than fourteen (14) days** after the discovery cutoff date. Counsel are reminded to adhere to the Civility and Professional Guidelines adopted by the United States District Court for the Central District of California.

f. Disclosure of Expert Testimony: The above discovery cutoff date includes expert discovery, unless otherwise ordered by Court.

B. Final Pretrial Conference

This case has been placed on calendar for a Final Pretrial Conference pursuant to Fed. R. Civ. P. 16. The Court requires strict compliance with the requirements of the Federal Rules of Civil Procedure and the Local Rules, including use of the format in Appendix A.

II.
ORDER FOR PREPARATION FOR JURY TRIAL AND JURY INSTRUCTIONS AND SETTING EXHIBIT CONFERENCE FRIDAY BEFORE TRIAL

A. Counsel shall comply with the following orders in preparing for trial by jury.

1. Motions *in Limine*: All motions *in limine* must be filed and served a minimum of forty-two (42) days before the originally scheduled trial date. Each motion should be separately filed and numbered. All opposition documents must be filed and served at least twenty-one (21) days before the scheduled trial date. All reply documents must be filed and served at least fourteen (14) days before the scheduled trial date.

All motions in limine will be heard on the first day of trial, unless the parties proceed under the noticed motion provisions of Local Rule 7, or the Court otherwise orders.

2. Jury Instructions, Verdict Forms, and *Voir Dire*: Plaintiff shall serve proposed jury instructions and a proposed verdict form on defendant. Defendant shall serve objections to plaintiff's instructions and verdict form, together with any alternative verdict form and any additional instructions defendant intends to offer. Counsel shall confer in an effort to reach agreement on the proposed jury instructions and verdict forms.

a. Joint Jury Instructions: Counsel shall file with the Court a JOINT set of jury instructions on which there is agreement. Defendant's counsel is charged with the preparation of the joint set of jury instructions. At the same time, each party shall file its proposed jury instructions to which there are objections, accompanied by a memorandum of points and authorities in support of those instructions.

b. Filing Jury Instructions: Jury instructions are to be filed and served on opposing counsel in compliance with Local Rule 51-1.

c. Objections to Jury Instructions: Objections to proposed jury instructions must be filed and served in compliance with Local Rules 51-5 and 51-5.1.

3. *Voir Dire*: At least seven (7) days before trial, as recommended in Appendix A to the Local Rules, each counsel shall file and serve on opposing counsel any special questions that counsel requests to be asked of prospective jurors on *voir dire*.

4. Joint Statement of the Case: No later than seven (7) days before the trial date or by the time of the Exhibit Conference, whichever is later, counsel must confer and agree on a joint statement of the case, not to exceed one page, to be submitted to the Courtroom Deputy Clerk.

5. Stipulations: All counsel shall confer no later than seven (7) days before trial and stipulate so far as is possible as to foundation, waiver of the best evidence rule, and to those exhibits which may be received into evidence at the start of trial.

B. Counsel Shall Attend an Exhibit Conference.

A special conference regarding trial exhibits and other trial matters, which requires the attendance of trial counsel, will be held on the FRIDAY BEFORE THE SCHEDULED TRIAL DATE AT 3:00 P.M. IN COURTROOM 10A, UNLESS THE COURT OTHERWISE ORDERS.

The Court requires the following submitted to the Courtroom Deputy Clerk at the time of the Exhibit Conference:

1. Trial Exhibits: Counsel shall prepare the original trial exhibits in either three-ring binders indexed by exhibit number with right-sided divider tabs, or in separately marked file folders inserted within redwells. Original exhibits must have affixed to the upper right-hand corner of the first

page of each exhibit the Court's exhibit tag. If using binders, counsel shall label the front and spine of each binder with the respective volume number and exhibits contained within that binder. A binder bench book shall also be provided for use by the Court. Exhibits must be numbered in accordance with the Local Rules and Fed. R. Civ. P. 16 and 26, and shall be internally paginated.

2. Exhibit Lists: Counsel shall provide five (5) conformed copies of the joint or parties' exhibit list(s).

3. Witness Lists: Counsel shall provide five (5) conformed copies of the witness lists.

III.
ORDER GOVERNING ATTORNEY AND PARTY CONDUCT AT TRIAL

A. Opening Statements, Examining Witnesses, and Summation

1. Opening statements, examination of witnesses, and summation will be from the lectern only.

2. Counsel must not consume time by writing out words or drawing charts or diagrams. Counsel may do so in advance and explain that the item was prepared earlier as ordered by the Court to save time.

3. In final argument, counsel shall not address any juror by name and must avoid any appeal to a juror putting the juror in the position of a party, such as "What would you take for such pain?" or "What would you expect your son or daughter to do in the same circumstances?"

4. Never strike the lectern for emphasis.

5. The Court will honor reasonable time estimates for opening and closing statements to the jury. The Court will not require a jury to sit longer than sixty-five (65) minutes in any one session during counsel's summation. (*See* para. J, *infra.*)

B. Objections to Questions

1. Counsel must not use objections for the purpose of making a speech, recapitulating testimony, or attempting to guide the witness.

2. When objecting, counsel must rise and state only that counsel objects and the

legal grounds for the objection.

C. General Decorum

1. Please keep the trial low-key. It is to be a dignified search for the truth.

2. Counsel must not approach the Courtroom Deputy Clerk or the witness box without specific permission. When permission is given, please return to the lectern when the purpose of the permission is completed. Counsel must not question a witness while at the witness stand.

3. Please rise when addressing the Court and when the jury enters or leaves the courtroom.

4. Counsel must address all remarks to the Court. Counsel are not to address the Courtroom Deputy Clerk, the reporter, persons in the audience, or opposing counsel. If counsel wishes to speak with opposing counsel, counsel must ask permission to talk off the record. Any request for the rereading of questions or answers shall be addressed to the Court.

5. Counsel must not address or refer to witnesses or parties by first names alone. Young witnesses (under 14) may properly be addressed and referred to by first names.

6. Counsel must not make an offer of stipulation unless counsel has conferred with opposing counsel and has reason to believe the stipulation is acceptable.

7. While Court is in session, counsel must not leave counsel table to confer with investigators, secretaries, witnesses or other persons in the back of the courtroom unless permission has been granted in advance.

8. Counsel should not by facial expression, nodding, or other conduct, exhibit any opinion, adverse or favorable, concerning any testimony being given by a witness. Counsel must admonish counsel's own clients and witnesses to avoid such conduct.

9. Where a party has more than one lawyer, only one may object to the testimony or conduct the direct or cross-examination of a given witness.

D. Promptness of Counsel and Witnesses

1. The Court makes every effort to commence proceedings at the time set. Promptness is expected from counsel and witnesses. It is counsel's duty to tell the Court on the first day of any commitments in any other court on a subsequent day that may result in absence or late arrival.

2. If a witness was on the stand at adjournment, it is counsel's duty to have the witness adjacent to, but not on, the witness stand, ready to proceed, when the court session resumes. If a witness was on the stand at a recess, it is counsel's duty to have the witness back on the stand, ready to proceed, when the court session resumes.

> **a.** It is counsel's duty to have the next witness in the courtroom after a recess if the last witness was excused at the time of the recess.
>
> **b.** It is counsel's duty to notify the Courtroom Deputy Clerk in advance if any witness should be accommodated by use of the witness stand's automated platform, which lowers and raises to aid witnesses who are unable to otherwise take the witness stand.

3. No presenting party may be without witnesses. If counsel has no more witnesses to call and there is more than a brief delay, the Court may deem that the party has rested.

4. The Court attempts to cooperate with physicians, scientists, and all other professional witnesses and will, except in extraordinary circumstances, accommodate them by permitting them to testify out of sequence. Counsel must anticipate this possibility and discuss it with opposing counsel. If there is objection, counsel must confer with the Court in advance.

E. <u>Exhibits</u>

1. Each counsel should keep counsel's own list of exhibits and should note when each exhibit has been admitted in evidence.

2. Each counsel is responsible for any exhibits that counsel secures from the Courtroom Deputy Clerk and, at all recesses, at noontime, and afternoon adjournments, must return all exhibits in counsel's possession to the Courtroom Deputy Clerk.

3. An exhibit not previously marked should, at the time of its first mention and assuming that counsel intends for that item to become an exhibit, be accompanied by a request that the Courtroom Deputy Clerk mark it for identification. To save time, counsel must show a new exhibit to opposing counsel before it is mentioned in Court. If an item is meant for non-evidentiary purposes, such as refreshing recollection, no numbering or marking for identification is needed.

4. Whenever a particular exhibit is admissible, in counsel's opinion, it may be moved into evidence at the next available recess if the motion to admit it is opposed. (Counsel should consider waiting, however, until cross-examination concerning the proposed exhibits is concluded.) In the alternative, counsel may hold exhibits until the end of counsel's case and move them all into evidence at that time.

5. The Court regards admissibility of exhibits as a legal issue for the Court to rule on, absent agreement among counsel. Counsel are admonished to make no motion to introduce an exhibit while the jury is present <u>unless</u> counsel has previously conferred with opposing counsel and knows that there will be no objection to the motion to admit. When the Court hears a motion to admit an exhibit before the jury, the Court assumes that counsel has already cleared admission of the exhibit with opposing counsel and will grant the motion. If any objection is lodged, the Court will expect a satisfactory explanation from counsel who moved to admit an exhibit while the jury was present.

6. Counsel shall advise the Courtroom Deputy Clerk of any agreements they have with respect to proposed exhibits that may be received so that no further motion to admit need be made.

7. When referring to an exhibit, counsel should refer to its exhibit number whenever possible. Witnesses should be asked to do the same.

8. The Court resists taking time to pass an exhibit among the jury for viewing when it is admitted. A request to do so should be made to the Court in a recess period preceding introduction of the exhibit.

9. Counsel must not ask witnesses to draw charts or diagrams nor ask the Court's permission for a witness to do so. If counsel wishes to question a witness in connection with graphic aids, the material must be fully prepared before the court session starts. (*See* Part III, A, 2, *supra.*)

F. <u>Depositions</u>

1. All depositions that are to be used in the trial, either as evidence or for impeachment, must be signed and filed before the trial commences. (*See* Part I, A, 3, (a), *supra.*) Counsel should check with the Courtroom Deputy Clerk to learn whether the Court already

has any deposition, properly signed, in which counsel is interested.

2. In using depositions of an adverse party for impeachment, either one of the following procedures may be adopted:

> **a.** If counsel wishes to read the questions and answers as alleged impeachment and ask the witness no further questions on that subject, counsel may merely read the relevant portions of the deposition into the record, stating the page and line where the reading began and the page and line where the reading ended.
>
> **b.** If counsel wishes to ask the witness further questions on the subject matter, the deposition is placed in front of the witness and the witness is told to read silently the pages and lines involved. Then counsel may either ask the witness further questions on the matter and thereafter read the quotations or read the quotations and thereafter ask the further questions. Counsel should have an extra copy of the deposition for this purpose.

3. Where a witness is absent and the witness' testimony is offered by deposition, please observe the following procedures:

A reader should occupy the witness chair and read the testimony of the witness while the examining lawyer asks the questions. All colloquies among counsel or parties on the deposition record, except relevant stipulations, should be omitted from the reading, thereby presenting only the relevant evidence.

G. Using Numerous Answers to Interrogatories and Requests for Admissions

Whenever counsel expects to offer a group of answers to interrogatories or requests for admissions, extracted from one or more lengthy documents, counsel should prepare a new document listing each question and answer and identifying the document from which it has been extracted. Copies of this new document should be given to the Court and opposing counsel.

H. Jury Instructions

All requested instructions must be filed and served in accordance with the Local Rules of this District or this Court's Order served on the parties at the criminal arraignment or other pretrial hearing. Supplemental instructions must be filed and served as soon as the need for them becomes apparent. (*See also*, Part II, A, 2, *supra.*)

I. Advance Notice of Evidentiary or Difficult Questions

If any counsel has reason to anticipate that a difficult question of law or evidence will raise legal argument, requiring research and/or briefing, counsel must give the Court advance notice. Counsel are directed to notify the Courtroom Deputy Clerk at the day's adjournment of unexpected legal issues that could not have been foreseen and addressed by a motion *in limine* (*see* F. R. Evid. 103.) The Court will customarily order counsel to appear one-half hour earlier the next morning of trial to discuss the matter before the jury's return.

J. Final Phase of Jury Trials

1. Time for Arguments: Counsel will be asked to provide reasonable estimates for the time needed to present closing summation. Each counsel will be held to those estimates to within five (5) and no more than ten (10) minutes. Counsel should keep track of time consumed in argument.

After fifty (50) minutes and before sixty-five (65) minutes, counsel may ask the Court if this would be a "convenient time" to take a short break before going on to the next topic. Counsel's request for a break will be honored. After sixty-five (65) minutes of summation, the Court will declare a recess.

2. Exhibits Referred to During Argument: The Courtroom Deputy Clerk is not available to supply exhibits during summation. Exhibits can be arranged and made available to counsel at the lectern before summation if they are needed. Counsel must advise the Courtroom Deputy Clerk of this need at least one day before closing arguments begin.

3. Court Reporter Transcripts: Counsel are admonished to not state in summation, "I am reading from the reporter's transcript." Counsel may, however, refer to "notes" (which may be a partial transcript) and proceed to deliver the recounted evidence in a "question and answer" format. Counsel are not to suggest to the jury that they may request re-reading of testimony.

The Court will provide the jury with the following instruction on the subject of re-reading testimony:

> Re-reading of testimony is possible, but I must review all of what is to be re-read – *there is no transcript for the jury to review.* And, even if there were, I would have to have it re-read due to objections, sidebars, and other proceedings outside the jury's presence. Moreover, I or the attorneys might feel that other matters should be included in the same read-back. Preparing for a re-read of testimony takes time. Please understand that, so that if a request is made, we will gladly arrange to do so, but the jury should keep deliberating until we are able to make sure that we have everything ready.

4. Presence of counsel, parties, and agents at adjournment once deliberations start: Since another trial will likely have started while the jury in the parties' case is deliberating, the following options are suggested for the day's adjournment in lieu of convening a separate session of Court.

a. Counsel may stipulate that the Court sitting alone may admonish the jury at the adjournment and the Court will inform the jury that counsel and parties have been excused; or,

b. Counsel may stipulate that the Courtroom Deputy Clerk may admonish the jurors and excuse them for the evening; or,

c. Counsel may waive the necessity of an evening admonition at adjournment in light of admonitions made to the jury as trial progressed.

IT IS SO ORDERED.

Dated: ________________

____
ALICEMARIE H. STOTLER
United States District Judge

C. *Order Governing Pretrial and Post-Trial Motions, Trials, and Sentencing*

IN THE UNITED STATES DISTICT COURT
FOR THE CENTRAL DISTRICT OF CALIFORNIA

UNITED STATES OF AMERICA, Plaintiff, v. Defendant(s).	Case No. SA CR ___________ AHS **ORDER GOVERNING PRETRIAL AND POST-TRIAL MOTIONS, TRIALS, AND SENTENCINGS; ORDER SETTING EXHIBIT CONFERENCE ON FRIDAY BEFORE TRIAL AT 3:00 P.M.**

I.
MOTIONS

Motions; time estimates required. Unless the Local Rules prescribe a different time for filing a particular motion, all pretrial motions, including motions *in limine*, must be filed and served not later than twenty-eight (28) days after arraignment and set for hearing not later than the Friday (10) days prior to trial at 11:00 a.m., with the date approved in advance by the Courtroom Deputy Clerk. Nothing in this Order precludes counsel from filing motions at an earlier time. Post-trial motions shall be filed in accordance with the requirements of the Federal Rules of Criminal Procedure unless the Court otherwise orders. Dates for hearing on the post-trial motionsmust be approved in advance by the Courtroom Deputy Clerk and set for hearing at 11:00 a.m. ***Counsel's estimate of the time required for presentation of the motion must be set forth adjacent to the caption of the motion.***

A party opposing a motion must file and serve a response not later than seven (7) days after service of the motion or as otherwise ordered by the Court. ***Responding counsel's estimate of the time required for presentation of opposition to the motion must be set forth adjacent to the caption of the responding papers.***

II.
TRIALS

Trials begin at 9:00 a.m.

Exhibit Conference to be held on Friday before trial.

A special conference regarding trial exhibits will be held on the Friday before the scheduled trial date at 3:00 p.m. in a Courtroom to be determined.

Voir Dire. At least seven (7) days prior to trial, each counsel shall file with the Clerk and serve on opposing counsel any special questions requested to be put to prospective jurors on voir dire.

Jury instructions. ***The Court orders that proposed jury instructions be filed and served no later than seven (7) days prior to trial. Objections shall be filed and served no later than the commencement of trial.***

III.
SENTENCING PROCEEDINGS

Sentencing proceedings are conducted pursuant to Fed. R. Crim. P. 32(a) and the Local Rules. If any party wishes to present material to the Court related to the sentencing, such party must file, or otherwise make available to, and serve opposing counsel/parties and the assigned United States Probation Officer such information or evidence no later than **fourteen (14) days** before the scheduled sentencing hearing. The foregoing notwithstanding, a statement of each party's position concerning sentencing shall be filed, or otherwise made available, and served no later than two weeks before the sentencing hearing, and the proof of service shall reflect service on the Probation Officer. Failure to timely file or present and serve such information or evidence or statement of position may result in such information not being considered by the Court in imposing a defendant's sentence.

IV.
SERVICE OF ORDER

The Clerk is directed to serve this Order on all counsel at the time of post-indictment arraignment proceedings.

DATED: ____________________

____
ALICEMARIE H. STOTLER
United States District Judge

Hon. Robert J. Timlin

District Judge

Chambers Information

U.S. District Court, Central District of California
Courtroom N/A
312 N. Spring Street
Los Angeles, CA 90012

Scheduling Information

Courtroom Deputy: (213) 894-0539

Civil Law and Motion	Mondays at 10:00 a.m.
Criminal Law and Motion	Mondays at 1:30 p.m.

Biographical Information

Born 1932 in Buffalo, NY

Federal Judicial Service:

-Judge, U. S. District Court, Central District of California
-Nominated by William J. Clinton on April 26, 1994, to a new seat created by 104 Stat. 5089; Confirmed by the Senate on September 14, 1994, and received commission on September 15, 1994. Assumed senior status on February 1, 2005.
-U.S. Magistrate, U.S. District Court for the Central District of California, 1971-1975

Education:

-Georgetown University, A.B., 1954
-Georgetown University Law Center, J.D., 1959
-Georgetown University Law Center, LL.M., 1964

Professional Career:

-U.S. Army Private First Class, 1955-1957
-Law Clerk and Attorney, Pennsylvania Railroad Company, 1959-1960
-Private Practice, 1960-1961
-Trial Attorney, Criminal Division, U.S. Dept. of Justice, Washington, DC, 1961-1964
-Assistant U.S. Attorney, Central District of California, 1964-1966
-Private Practice, 1966-1967
-City Attorney, Corona, California, 1967-1970
-Teacher, Chaffey Union Jr. College, California, 1970
-Private Practice, California, 1971-1976
-Judge, Municipal Court, Corona Judicial District, 1976-1980
-Judge, Riverside County Superior Court, State of California, 1980-1990
-Associate Justice, Fourth District Court of Appeals, Division 2, CA, 1990-1994

I. Judge Timlin's Procedures and Practices

A. Procedures and Schedules

You may contact the judge's courtroom deputy clerk by calling 213-894-0539; if the clerk does not answer the phone, be sure to leave a voice-mail message.

1. Civil motions are set for hearing on **MONDAY**. Time:**10 A.M.** The court does not hold hearings on civil motions unless it is required by law or it meets the exceptions stated in the Court's Standing Order (below).

   Criminal motions are set for hearing on **MONDAY**. Time: **1:30 P.M.**

   (If Monday is a holiday, next motion hearing date is **the next available Monday**.)

   It is not necessary to clear a motion date with the Courtroom Deputy prior to filing the motion.

2. Discovery motions are to be scheduled before the district judge.

3. Are tentative rulings issued? Not normally

4. Mandatory chambers copies -
   CR - must be dropped in courtesy box on chambers' door, Room 233, not later than noon the day following electronic filing.

   CV - must be conformed FIRST then dropped off immediately after filing.

5. Procedures for filing an Ex parte Application: Follow Federal Rules of Civil Procedure or Federal Rules of Criminal Procedure and the Local Rules.

6. To request a continuance of any scheduled court proceeding: Contact the Courtroom Deputy Clerk.

7. Are counsel allowed to contact the Judge's law clerk or judicial assistant? NO.

8. Inquiries regarding the status of a motion, stipulation or proposed order:
   - **A.** Motion - "See Court's Standing Order (below)"
   - **B.** Stipulation - Comply with Local Rule 52-9
   - **C.** Proposed Order - "See Local Rule 52-9"

9. Calendar conflicts: (Procedures for attorneys to follow if they have a calendar conflict). Send calendar conflict in writing one week prior to scheduled hearing. Leave a follow-up voice mail.

10. Procedure for bring electronic equipment into the courtroom: See Local Civil Rules, then contact Courtroom Deputy.

11. To order an audio tape or transcript For general information on how to order a transcript of any reported or digitally recorded proceeding, please contact 213-894-3015 or visit www.cacd.uscourts.gov > General Information > Court Reporter/Recorder Transcripts. If you require an estimate of cost for the preparation of a transcript, contact the court reporter/recorder for the desired proceeding.

    To determine the court reporter/recorder for a particular proceeding, go to the Court Reporter Schedule web page and click on View by Date. Once you've determined the correct court reporter/recorder for the desired session, click on Court Reporter Phone and Email List for contact information.

12. Questions regarding law clerk positions - Contact Judge. The court no longer needs externs.

13. Trial preparation:

A. Court hours 8:30 A.M - 5:00 P.M.

B. Exhibit preparation - See Local Rules

C. Jury instructions - See Local Rules

14. Procedures for obtaining the services of an interpreter on a civil case. Contact the Court's Interpreter Department, (213) 894-4599.

If counsel has received a "Notice to Parties of Alternate Dispute Resolution (ADR) Program" - forms ADR-08, ADR-10, or ADR-11 with an attached "ADR Program Questionnaire" form ADR-09, please see General Order 02-07 which is located in the "General Orders" section on the home page of the Court's website. The Attorney Settlement Officer information is located in the section "Attorney Information, ADR."

B. Standing Order Regarding Oral Argument in Civil Motions

ORDER (1) AMENDING ORDER, DATED DECEMBER 19, 2000 AND (2) DIRECTING NO ORAL ARGUMENT ON MOTIONS IN CIVIL ACTIONS

The undersigned ORDERS his previous order of December 19, 2000, be amended to read as follows:

The undersigned believes that for most civil law and motion matters, oral argument is generally unnecessary and wasteful of time and resources of both counsel and the Court. Well researched moving and responding papers with thoughtful analysis are usually adequate to allow the Court to make a fully informed and reasoned decision. Nevertheless, the Court recognizes that in some cases oral argument may be valuable or even necessary. Therefore, pursuant to Federal Rules of Civil Procedure 78 and Civil Local Rule 7-15,

IT IS ORDERED that oral argument on motions in civil actions shall not be heard, unless required by law and subject to the following exceptions:

(1) If the Court deems oral argument necessary on certain issues raised in a particular motion or opposition, argument will be heard on the hearing date calendared by the moving party. The Court will notify the parties as far in advance as possible that oral argument will be heard, but no later than 5:00 p.m. on the Wednesday preceding the calendared hearing date.

(2) If the moving and/or responding party believes that oral argument is necessary, such party must file and serve a written request for oral argument. This request should show why oral argument is necessary under the particular circumstances of the case, and why the moving and responding papers are inadequate to present the party's argument to the Court. The fact that the ruling on the motion may be dispositive of the entire action or certain causes of action or claims or that the moving party has raised a new issue in its reply[1] is not, in and of itself, sufficient to establish that oral argument is necessary. This request shall be filed not later than six (6) days before the calendared hearing date. The Court will notify the appropriate parties of its ruling on the request no later than 5:00 p.m. on the Wednesday preceding the calendared hearing date.

A motion will be deemed submitted without oral argument upon expiration of the time for filing a reply brief. Counsel (or parties proceeding pro se) should not appear in Court on the date the motion is calendared unless the Court has ordered that there be oral argument.

DATED: October 1, 2001

ROBERT J. TIMLIN
United States District Judge

---

1 The Court will not base its decision on any new facts or new legal arguments raised in reply papers without the Court giving the respondent an opportunity to respond. *See* Schwarzer, et al., Federal Civil Procedure Before Trial, §§ 12:106-12:107 (2000).

Hon. Josephine Staton Tucker

District Judge

Chambers Information

U.S. District Court, Central District of California
Courtroom 10A
411 West Fourth Street,
Santa Ana, CA 92701

Scheduling Information

Courtroom Deputy: (714) 338-4738

Civil Law and Motion	Mondays at 10:00 a.m.
Criminal Law and Motion	Mondays at 2:30 p.m.

Biographical Information

Born 1961 in St. Louis, MO

Federal Judicial Service:

-Judge, U. S. District Court, Central District of California
-Nominated by Barack Obama on February 4, 2010, to a seat vacated by Alicemarie H. Stotler; Confirmed by the Senate on June 21, 2010, and received commission on June 22, 2010.

Education:

-William Jewell College, B.A., 1983
-Harvard Law School, J.D., 1986

Professional Career:

-Law clerk to the Hon. John R. Gibson, U.S. Court of Appeals for the Eighth Circuit, 1986-87
-Private practice, San Francisco, California, 1987-94
-Private practice, Irvine, California, 1995-2002
-Judge, Superior Court of California, County of Orange, 2002-10

I. Judge Tucker's Procedures and Schedules

A. *Procedures and Schedules*

Some information regarding procedures and schedules is provided below. Additional and more detailed information is contained in the .pdf attachment(s) at the bottom of this page. Counsel should review and strictly comply with all provisions of the Local Rules (unless specifically superseded by an order of this Court) and the Federal Rules of Civil Procedure. Copies of the Local Rules can be found at http://www.cacd.uscourts.gov/LocalRules or purchased from one of the following:

Los Angeles Daily Journal	Metropolitan News	West Group
915 East 1st Street	210 South Spring Street	610 Opperman Drive
Los Angeles, CA 90012	Los Angeles, CA 90012	Eagan, Minnesota 55123

1. **Scheduling Motions.**
   Civil motions are heard on Mondays at 10:00 a.m.

   Criminal motions are heard on Mondays at 2:30 p.m.

   When Monday is a holiday, the next motion date is the following Monday.

   It is not necessary to reserve a motion date with the court clerk prior to filing the motion, but counsel must comply with all Local and Federal Rules regarding service and must review the Court's Closed Motion Dates. If the Court does not believe that oral argument will be helpful, the Court will advise the parties in advance.

2. **Telephone Appearances.** The Court does not entertain telephone appearances for hearings except in exceptional circumstances.

3. **Discovery Motions.** All discovery motions are to be calendared before the magistrate judge.

4. Tentative Rulings. Tentative rulings may be issued. If issued, they will be available either by clicking on the "Tentative Rulings" link above or in the courtroom on the morning of the hearing.

5. **Mandatory Chambers Copies.** Mandatory Chambers Copies of all e-filed documents shall be delivered to the mandatory chambers copy box on the 10th Floor. It is imperative that the mandatory chambers copies be delivered by noon following the date of filing as required by General Order 10-07.IV.D. Failure to deliver timely mandatory chambers copies may result in a delay in hearing a motion or ordering the matter off calendar.

   The Court does not accept mandatory chambers copies of documents sought to be filed under seal pursuant to Local Rule 79-5.1.

6. **Ex Parte Applications.** Ex parte applications are for extraordinary relief only. Ex parte applications are considered on the papers and are rarely set for hearings. The moving party shall serve the opposing party by facsimile or personal service and shall notify the opposing party that any opposition must be filed no later than 24 hours after such facsimile or personal service. If counsel do not intend to oppose the ex parte application, counsel must inform the Courtroom Deputy by telephone as soon as possible.

7. **Status Inquiries.** Do not inquire by phone regarding the status of a motion, stipulation, or proposed order. Please follow Local Rule 11-4.5.

8. **Contact with Chambers.** Counsel shall not initiate telephone calls to Judge Tucker's chambers, law clerks, or judicial assistant.

9. **Calendar Conflicts.** Counsel shall notify the Courtroom Deputy Clerk for each judge prior to the date of the conflict. Counsel should appear before the most senior judge and request priority.

10. **Continuances.** Continuances are granted only upon a showing of good cause, particularly focusing upon evidence of diligent work by the party seeking delay and of prejudice that may result from the denial of the continuance. Counsel requesting a continuance, whether by application or stipulation, must submit a detailed declaration as to the reason(s). The Court will not consider any request that does not comply with the Local Rules or the Initial Standing Order attached below. The Court sets firm trial dates and will not change them without good cause having been shown. Requests should be submitted well in advance of the relief requested. Counsel is not to assume the request is granted unless approved by the Court. See Local Rule 40-1. Any request shall be accompanied by a separate proposed order.

11. **Alternative Dispute Resolution (ADR).** This Court participates in the Court-Directed ADR Program. If counsel have received a Notice to Parties of Court-Directed ADR Program (ADR-08), the case will be presumptively referred to the Court's Mediation Panel or to private mediation. See General Order 11-10, §5.1 and Local Rule 26-1(c). This Court generally does not refer settlement conferences to magistrate judges.

12. **Electronic Equipment.** Counsel should contact the courtroom deputy clerk at the earliest possible date concerning procedures for bringing electronic equipment into the courtroom.

13. Transcripts. For general information on how to order a transcript of any reported or digitally recorded proceeding, please contact 213-894-3015 or visit www.cacd.uscourts.gov > General Information > Court Reporter/Recorder Transcripts. If you require an estimate of cost for the preparation of a transcript, contact the court reporter/recorder for the desired proceeding.

    To determine the court reporter/recorder for a particular proceeding, go to the Court Reporter Schedule web page and click on View by Date. Once you've determined the correct court reporter/recorder for the desired session, click on Court Reporter Phone and Email List for contact information.

14. Law Clerk/Extern Positions. Questions regarding law clerk/extern positions should be directed to Judge Tucker's chambers.

II. Judge Tucker's Case Management Orders

A. *Initial Standing Order for Cases Assigned to Judge Josephine Staton Tucker*

IN THE UNITED STATES DISTICT COURT
FOR THE CENTRAL DISTRICT OF CALIFORNIA

Plaintiff(s),	Case No. ____________ -JST (x)
v.	**INITIAL STANDING ORDER FOR CASES ASSIGNED TO JUDGE JOSEPHINE STATON TUCKER**
Defendant(s).	

PLEASE READ THIS ORDER CAREFULLY. IT GOVERNS THIS CASE AND DIFFERS IN SOME RESPECTS FROM THE LOCAL RULES.

This case has been assigned to the calendar of Judge Josephine Staton Tucker. Both the Court and counsel bear responsibility for the progress of this litigation in federal court. To "secure the just, speedy, and inexpensive determination" of this case, as called for in Fed. R. Civ. P. 1, all parties or their counsel are ordered to become familiar with the Federal Rules of Civil Procedure, the Local Rules of the Central District of California, and this Court's standing orders.

THE COURT ORDERS AS FOLLOWS:

1. Service of the Complaint

The plaintiff shall promptly serve the complaint in accordance with Fed. R. Civ. P. 4 and file the proofs of service pursuant to Local Rule 5-3.1. Although Fed. R. Civ. P. 4(m) does not require the summons and complaint to be served for 120 days, the Court expects service much sooner. The Court will require plaintiffs to show good cause to extend the service deadline beyond 120 days.

2. Presence of Lead Counsel

Lead trial counsel shall attend any scheduling, pretrial, or settlement conference set by the Court. The Court does not entertain special appearances; only counsel of record may appear.

3. Ex Parte Applications

Ex parte applications are solely for extraordinary relief and should be used with discretion. *See Mission Power Engineering Co. v. Continental Casualty Co.*, 883 F. Supp. 488 (C.D. Cal. 1995). Ex parte applications that fail to conform to Local Rule 7-19 and 7-19.1, including a statement of opposing counsel's position, will not be considered except on a specific showing of good cause. Concurrently with service of the ex parte papers by electronic service, facsimile, or personal service, the moving party shall notify the opposition that opposing papers must be filed no later than twenty-four (24) hours (or one court day) following service. On the day the documents are e-filed, a conformed courtesy copy of moving, opposition, or notice of non-opposition papers are to be hand-delivered to the courtesy box on the 10th floor. If counsel do not intend to oppose the ex parte application, counsel must inform the Courtroom Deputy by telephone as soon as possible.

4. Continuances or Extensions of Time

This Court has a strong interest in keeping scheduled dates certain. Changes in dates are disfavored. Trial dates set by the Court are firm and will rarely be changed. Therefore, any request, whether by application or stipulation, to continue the date of any matter before this Court **must** be supported by a sufficient basis that demonstrates good cause why the change in the date is essential. Without such compelling factual support, requests to continue dates set by this Court will not be approved. Counsel requesting a continuance must electronically file any application or stipulation and lodge a proposed order including a **detailed** declaration of the grounds for the requested continuance or extension of time. The Court will not consider any request that does not comply with the Local Rules and this Order. Proposed stipulations extending scheduling dates do not become effective unless and until this Court so orders. Counsel should avoid submitting requests for continuance less than at least five (5) court days prior to the expiration of the scheduled date.

5. TROs and Injunctions

Parties seeking emergency or provisional relief shall comply with Fed. R. Civ. P. 65 and Local Rule 65. The Court will not rule on any application for such relief for at least twenty-four hours after the party subject to the requested order has been served, unless service is excused. Such party may file opposing or responding papers in the interim.

6. Cases Removed from State Court

All documents filed in state court, including documents appended to the complaint, answers, and motions, must be refiled in this Court as a supplement to the notice of removal. *See* 28 U.S.C. § 1447(a) and (b). If the defendant has not yet answered or moved, the answer or responsive pleading filed in this Court must comply with the Federal Rules of Civil Procedure and the Local Rules. If, before the case was removed, a motion was pending in state court, it must be re-noticed in accordance with Local Rule 7. Counsel shall file with their first appearance an original and two copies of a Notice of Interested Parties in accordance with Local Rule 7.1.

If an action is removed to this Court that contains a form pleading, i.e., a pleading in which boxes are checked, the party or parties utilizing the form pleading must file an appropriate pleading with this Court within thirty (30) days of receipt of the Notice of Removal. The appropriate pleading referred to must comply with the requirements of Fed. R. Civ. P. 7, 7.1, 8, 9, 10 and 11.

7. Status of Fictitiously Named Defendants

This Court intends to adhere to the following procedures where a matter is removed to this Court on diversity grounds with fictitiously named defendants. See 28 U.S.C. §§ 1441(a) and 1447.

a. Plaintiff is normally expected to ascertain the identity of and serve any fictitiously named defendants within 120 days of the removal of the action to this Court.

b. If plaintiff believes (by reason of the necessity for discovery or otherwise) that fictitiously named defendants cannot be fully identified within the 120-day period, an ex parte application requesting permission to extend that period to effectuate service may be filed with this Court. Such application shall state the reasons therefore, and may be granted upon a showing of good cause. The ex parte application shall be served upon all appearing parties, and shall state that appearing parties may comment within seven (7) days of the filing of the ex parte application.

c. If plaintiff wants to substitute a defendant for one of the fictitiously named defendants, plaintiff shall first seek the consent of counsel for all defendants (and counsel for the fictitiously named party, if that party has separate counsel). If consent is withheld or denied, plaintiff should file a motion on regular notice. The motion and opposition should address whether the matter should thereafter be remanded to the superior court if diversity of citizenship is destroyed by the addition of the newly substituted party. *See* U.S.C. § 1447(c), (d).

8. Discovery

a. Discovery Matters Referred to Magistrate Judge

All discovery matters have been referred to the assigned United States Magistrate Judge, who will hear all discovery disputes. The Magistrate Judge's initials follow the District Judge's initials next to the case number. All discovery-related documents must include the words "DISCOVERY MATTER" in the caption to ensure proper routing. Counsel are directed to contact the Magistrate Judge's courtroom deputy clerk to schedule matters for hearing. Please deliver mandatory chambers copies of discovery-related papers to the Magistrate Judge assigned to this case rather than to this Court.

In accordance with 28 U.S.C. § 636(b)(1)(A), the Court will not reverse any order of the Magistrate Judge unless it has been shown that the Magistrate Judge's order is clearly erroneous or contrary to law.

Any party may file and serve a motion for review and reconsideration before this Court. See Local Rule 72-2. The moving party must file and serve the motion within fourteen (14) days of service of a written ruling or within fourteen (14) days of an oral ruling that the Magistrate Judge states will not be followed by a written ruling. The motion must specify which portions of the ruling are clearly erroneous or contrary to law and support the contention with points and authorities. Counsel shall deliver a conformed copy of the moving papers and responses to the Magistrate Judge's courtroom deputy clerk at the time of filing.

b. Compliance with Fed. R. Civ. P. 26(a)

Unless there is a likelihood that upon motion by a party the Court would order that any or all discovery is premature, it is advisable for counsel to begin to conduct discovery actively before the Scheduling Conference. At the very least, the parties shall comply fully with the letter and spirit of Fed. R. Civ. P. 26(a) and thereby obtain and produce most of what would be produced in the early stage of discovery, because at the Scheduling Conference the Court will impose firm deadlines to complete discovery.

9. Applications to Seal

a. Standard

In accordance with Local Rule 79-5.1, absent authorization by rule or statute, no case or document may be filed under seal without written application to, and prior approval by, the Court. The existence of a Protective Order issued by the assigned Magistrate Judge relating to the treatment of documents produced during discovery does not constitute a court order permitting an under seal filing. There is a strong presumption that the public has a right of access to records in civil cases. For non-dispositive motions, the party seeking to maintain the confidentiality of the document(s) or portions thereof must show good cause. For dispositive motions, the party seeking protection must articulate compelling reasons for maintaining the confidentiality of the document(s) and must seek relief that is narrowly tailored to the protected interest. *See Pintos v. Pacific Creditors Ass'n*, 605 F.3d 665, 677-79 (9th Cir. 2010). Reliance upon the parties' designation of documents as "Confidential" or "Highly Confidential" or "Attorneys' Eyes Only" is insufficient. Rather, the party must provide competent evidence to support any application. **No document will be filed under seal in its entirety unless it is shown in the application that it is not feasible to file a redacted version for public viewing.** Any proposed redactions must be highlighted in the under seal version of the document so that the Court may readily determine what information the party or parties seek to maintain as confidential.

10. Motions

a. Time for Filing and Hearing Motions

Motions shall be filed in accordance with Local Rule 7. This Court hears motions on Mondays, beginning at 10:00 a.m. If Monday is a national holiday, motions will be heard on the next Monday. It is not necessary to clear a hearing date with the Court Clerk before filing a motion. If the motion date selected is not available, the Court will issue a minute order continuing the date. Counsel should check the Court's website for Closed Motion Dates.

b. Pre-Filing Requirement To Meet and Confer

Counsel must comply with Local Rule 7-3, which requires counsel to engage in a pre-filing conference "to discuss thoroughly . . . the substance of the contemplated motion and any potential resolution." Counsel should discuss the issues to a sufficient degree that if a motion is still necessary, the briefing may be directed to those substantive issues requiring resolution by the Court. Counsel should resolve minor procedural or other non-substantive matters during the conference. The *in propria persona* status of one or more parties does not negate this requirement.

c. Length and Format of Motion Papers

Memoranda of points and authorities shall not exceed 25 pages and all footnotes shall be in the same type size as text. *See* Local Rules 11-6 and 11-3.1.1. Only in rare instances and for good cause shown will the Court grant an application to extend these page limitations. No supplemental brief shall be filed without prior leave of Court. If documentary evidence in support of or in opposition to a motion exceeds 50 pages,the evidence must be separately bound and tabbed and include an index. If such evidence exceeds 200 pages, the documents shall be placed in a Slant D-Ring binder, with an index and with each item of evidence separated by a tab divider on the right side.

d. Citations to Case Law

Citations to case law must identify not only the case cited, but the specific page referenced.

e. Citations to Other Sources

Statutory references should identify with specificity the sections and subsections referenced. Citations to treatises, manuals, and other materials should include the volume, section, and pages being referenced.

f. Oral Argument

If the Court deems a matter appropriate for decision without oral argument, the Court will notify the parties in advance.

11. Specific Motions

a. Motions Pursuant to Rule 12

Many motions to dismiss or to strike can be avoided if the parties confer in good faith (as required by Local Rule 7-3), especially for perceived defects in a complaint, answer, or counterclaim that could be corrected by amendment. *See Chang v. Chen*, 80 F.3d 1293, 1296 (9th Cir. 1996) (where a motion to dismiss is granted, a district court should provide leave to amend unless it is clear that the complaint could not be saved by any amendment). Moreover, a party has the right to amend the complaint "once as a matter of course at any time before a responsive pleading is served." Fed. R. Civ. P. 15(a). A Rule 12(b)(6) motion is not a responsive pleading and therefore plaintiff might have a right to amend. *See, e.g., St. Michael's Convalescent Hospital v. California*, 643 F.2d 1369, 1374 (9th Cir. 1981). Even after a complaint has been amended or a responsive pleading has been served, the Federal Rules provide that leave to amend should be "freely given when justice so requires." Fed. R. Civ. P. 15(a). The Ninth Circuit requires that this policy favoring amendment be applied with "extreme liberality." *Morongo Band of Mission Indians v. Rose*, 893 F.2d 1074, 1079 (9th Cir. 1990).

These principles require that plaintiff's counsel carefully evaluate defendant's contentions as to the deficiencies in the complaint. In most instances, the moving party should agree to any amendment that would cure the defect.

b. Motions to Amend

All motions to amend pleadings shall: (1) state the effect of the amendment and (2) identify the page and line number(s) and wording of any proposed change or addition of material. The proposed amended pleading shall be serially numbered to differentiate it from previously amended pleadings.

In addition to the requirements of Local Rule 15-1, counsel shall attach as an appendix to the moving papers a "redlined" version of the proposed amended pleading indicating all additions and deletions of material.

c. Summary Judgment Motions

Parties need not wait until the motion cutoff date to bring motions for summary judgment or partial summary judgment. Whenever possible, the party moving for summary judgment should provide more than the minimum twenty-eight (28) day notice for motions. *See* Local Rule 6-1. The parties should prepare papers in a fashion that will assist the Court in absorbing the facts (e.g., generous use of tabs, tables of contents, headings, indices, etc.). The parties are to comply precisely with Local Rules 56-1 through 56-4.

i. Statements of Uncontroverted Facts and Genuine Issues

The Statement of Uncontroverted Facts and Conclusions of Law ("Statement of Uncontroverted Facts"), as required by Local Rule 56-1 shall separately identify each claim for relief on which the moving party seeks summary judgment and the legal grounds for summary judgment. In a two-column format beneath the identified claim for relief, the left-hand column shall set forth, sequentially numbered, each allegedly uncontroverted material fact as to that claim for relief, and the right-hand column shall set forth the evidence that supports the factual statement. Citation to the supporting evidence shall be specific, including reference to the exhibit, page, and line number. The Statement of Uncontroverted Facts shall be formatted based on the following examples:

Plaintiff's Claim for Relief for _________ is Barred by the Applicable Statute of Limitations. (Cite)

1. (Moving party's first undisputed fact)	(Supporting evidence citation)
2. (Moving party's second undisputed fact)	(Supporting evidence citation)

The opposing party's statement of genuine issues must be in two columns and track the movant's separate statement exactly as prepared. The left-hand column must restate the allegedly undisputed fact and the alleged supporting evidence, and the right-hand column must state either that it is undisputed or disputed. The opposing party may dispute all or only a portion of the statement, but if disputing only a portion, it must clearly indicate what part is being disputed, followed by the opposing party's evidence controverting the fact. To demonstrate that a fact is disputed, the opposing party must briefly state why it disputes the moving party's asserted fact, cite to the relevant exhibit or other piece of evidence, and describe what it is in that exhibit or evidence that refutes the asserted fact. No legal argument should be set forth in this document.

The opposing party may submit additional material facts that bear on or relate to the issues raised by the movant, which shall follow the format described above for the moving party's separate statement. These additional facts shall continue in sequentially umbered paragraphs and shall set forth in the right hand column the evidence that supports that statement.

ii. Supporting Evidence

No party shall submit evidence other than the specific items of evidence or testimony necessary to support or controvert a proposed statement of undisputed fact. For example, entire deposition transcripts, entire sets of interrogatory responses, and documents that do not specifically support or controvert material in the separate statement shall not be submitted in opposition to a motion for summary judgment.

Evidence submitted in support of or in opposition to a motion should be submitted either by way of stipulation or as exhibits to declarations sufficient to authenticate the proffered evidence, and should not be attached to the memorandum of points and authorities. Documentary evidence as to which there is no stipulation regarding foundation must be accompanied by the testimony, either by declaration or properly authenticated deposition transcript, of a witness who can establish authenticity.

iii. Objections to Evidence

If a party disputes a fact based in whole or in part on an evidentiary objection, the ground of the objection should be succinctly stated in a separate statement of evidentiary objections in a two-column format. The left column should identify the items objected to (including page and line number if applicable) and the right column should set forth a concise objection (e.g., hearsay, lacks foundation, etc.) with a citation to the Federal Rules of Evidence or, where applicable, a case citation.

12. Notice of This Order

Plaintiff's counsel or plaintiff (if appearing on his or her own behalf) shall immediately serve this Order on all parties, including any new parties to the action. If this case came to the Court by a Petition for Removal, the removing defendant(s) shall serve this Order on all other parties.

B. Order Court on Court/Jury Trial

IN THE UNITED STATES DISTICT COURT
FOR THE CENTRAL DISTRICT OF CALIFORNIA

Plaintiff(s),	Case No. ____________ -JST (x)
v.	**ORDER ON COURT/JURY TRIAL**
Defendant(s).	Final Pretrial Conference: ___ at 1:30 p.m. Exhibit Conference: _____ at 3:00 p.m. Trial: _________at 9:00 a.m.

A. **SCHEDULING:**

1. **In General:** The last day for hearing on any motion to join other parties or to amend the pleadings shall be specified in the Scheduling Order. All unserved parties shall be dismissed no later than the date set for the Final Pretrial Conference.

2. **Motions for Summary Judgment or Partial Summary Judgment:** Motions for Summary Judgment or Partial Summary Judgment shall be heard no later than the last day for hearing motions, as set forth in the Scheduling Order.

3. **Settlement Procedures:** It is the policy of the Court to encourage disposition of civil litigation by settlement when such is in the best interest of the parties. The Court favors any reasonable means to accomplish this goal. All settlement discussions shall be conducted in compliance with Local Rule 16-15. Consistent with Local Rule 16-15.2, the Scheduling Order establishes a deadline for participation in settlement proceedings. The parties must elect one of the settlement procedures outlined in Local Rule 16-15.4. Note, however, that the parties may not choose a settlement conference before the magistrate judge. If the parties do not timely file a Notice of Settlement Procedure Selection, the Court may order the parties to participate in any of the settlement procedures set forth in the Local Rule.

4. **Discovery Cut-Off:** The Scheduling Order establishes a cut-off date for discovery in this action. This is not the date by which discovery requests must be served; it is the date by which all discovery is to be completed. The Court will not approve stipulations between counsel that permit responses to be served after the cut-off date except in extraordinary circumstances.

5. **Discovery Motions:** Any motion respecting the inadequacy of responses to discovery must be filed and served not later than ten (10) days after the discovery cut-off date. Whenever possible, the Court expects counsel to resolve discovery problems among themselves in a courteous, reasonable, and professional manner. The Court expects that counsel will strictly adhere to the Civility and Professional Guidelines adopted by the United States District Court for the Central District of California.

6. **Expert Discovery:** The above discovery cut-off date includes expert discovery, unless otherwise ordered by the Court.

B. <u>FINAL PRETRIAL CONFERENCE:</u>

This case has been placed on calendar for a Final Pretrial Conference pursuant to Fed. R. Civ. P. 16. Strict compliance with the requirements of the Federal Rules of Civil Procedure and the Local Rules is mandatory. Counsel will lodge carefully prepared Memoranda of Contentions of Fact and Law (which may also serve as the trial briefs) and a Final Pretrial Conference Order in accordance with the provisions of Local Rules 16-4 and 16-7. The Memoranda of Contentions of Fact and Law will be served no later than twenty-one (21) calendar days before the Pretrial Conference. The Final Pretrial Conference Order will be lodged no later than eleven (11) calendar days before the Pretrial Conference. The form of the Final Pretrial Conference Order will be in conformity with the form set forth in Appendix A to the Local Rules.

C. **<u>PREPARATION FOR TRIAL AND SCHEDULING EXHIBIT CONFERENCE FRIDAY BEFORE TRIAL</u>**

The Court ORDERS that all counsel comply with the following in their preparation for trial:

1. **<u>Motions In Limine:</u>** All motions *in limine* will be heard at the Pretrial Conference. The purpose of these motions is to alert the Court to significant evidentiary issues that can be addressed and resolved prior to trial. All motions *in limine* must be filed and served in compliance with Local Rule 6-1. Opposition papers must be filed and served in compliance with Local Rule 7-9. Reply papers must be filed and served in compliance with Local Rule 7-10.

2. **<u>Statement of the Case (Jury Trials):</u>** Counsel will prepare a joint statement of the case which will be read by the Court to the prospective panel of jurors prior to the commencement of voir dire. The statement should not be more than two or three paragraphs. The statement will be filed with the Court five (5) court days before the Pretrial Conference.

3. _ At least five (5) court days before the Pretrial Conference, each counsel shall file with the Court any special questions requested to be put to prospective jurors on voir dire.

4. **<u>Witness List:</u>** The witness list will be filed no later than five (5) court days prior to the Pretrial Conference. Counsel will submit the names of the witnesses in the order that they are expected to testify, and provide, to the extent possible, an accurate estimate of the time needed for each witness for direct, cross, redirect and re-cross. Counsel will also provide a brief summary of each witness' testimony. If more than one witness is offered on the same subject, the summary should be sufficiently detailed to allow the Court to determine if the testimony is cumulative. A joint witness list will be prepared in compliance with the example below and Local Rule 16-5.

<table>
<tr><td colspan="6"><u>JOINT WITNESS LIST</u></td></tr>
<tr><td colspan="6">Case Name:</td></tr>
<tr><td colspan="6">Case Number:</td></tr>
<tr><td>No. of Witness</td><td>Witness Name</td><td>Party Calling Witness and Estimate</td><td>X-Examiner's Estimate</td><td>Description of Testimony</td><td>Comment s</td></tr>
<tr><td></td><td></td><td></td><td></td><td></td><td></td></tr>
</table>

Instructions: (1) List witnesses (last name first); (2) For description, be extremely brief, e.g., "eyewitness to accident." Or "expert on standard of care." (3) Use estimates within fractions of an hour, rounded off to closest quarter of an hour. E.g., if you estimate 20 minutes, make it .25. An estimate of one and one-half hours would be 1.5. An estimate of three-quarters of an hour would be .75; (4) Note special factors in "Comments" column. E.g., "Needs interpreter." (5) Entries may be in handwriting if very neat and legible.

5. **Jury Instructions (Jury Trials):** In a jury trial, jury instructions are to be filed no later than five (5) court days prior to the Pretrial Conference. The parties must submit joint jury instructions. The parties will meet and confer sufficiently in advance of the required submission date, in order to prepare the joint jury instructions. The instructions should be submitted in the order in which the parties wish to have the instructions read. This order should reflect a single organized sequence agreed to by all of the parties.

   In the event that agreement cannot be reached, counsel will submit three (3) sets of instructions (with an extra set for the Court's law clerks) in the following format: (1) the agreed upon instructions; (2) the instructions proposed by plaintiff and opposed by defendant; and (3) the instructions proposed by defendant and opposed by plaintiff. In addition, counsel must submit electronic versions (in Word format) to the Court at the following email address: JST_Chambers@cacd.uscourts.gov. Instructions upon which agreement cannot be reached should reflect the basic disagreements among the parties as to the law. For disputed instructions, a party should note its objections to a proposed instruction and its reasons for putting forth its alternative on pages placed after its own alternative instruction.

6. **Special Verdict in Jury Trials:** At least five (5) court days prior to the Pretrial Conference, each counsel shall file with the Court any requested special verdict forms.

7. **Exhibits and Exhibit Conference:**

   a. **Exhibit List:** A joint exhibit list will be prepared in compliance with the example below and Local Rule 16-6.

JOINT EXHIBIT LIST					
Case Name:					
Case Number:					
No. of Exhibit	Description	Stip. To Authen.	Stip. To Admiss.	Date Identified	Date Admitted

The joint exhibit list will contain the information required by F.R.Civ.P. 26(a)(3)(A). The joint exhibit list will be filed no later than five (5) court days prior to the Pretrial Conference. In order to produce the joint exhibit list, the parties will meet and confer sufficiently in advance of the required submission date. As part of the meet and confer process, counsel will stipulate so far as is possible as to foundation, waiver of the best evidence rule, and to those exhibits which may be received into evidence at the start of trial. The exhibits to be so received will be noted on the extra copies of the exhibit lists.

   b. **Exhibit Preparation:** All exhibits will be placed in loose leaf binders which are tabbed down the right side with exhibit numbers. The spine of the notebook is to be marked with the case name and number and the numbers of the exhibits contained therein. The notebooks are to be prepared with an original for the Clerk, which will be tagged with the appropriate exhibit tags in the upper right-hand corner of the first page of each exhibit, and one copy for the Court. Each notebook will contain a list of the included exhibits. The exhibits are to be numbered in accordance with Local Rule 26-3.

c. **Exhibit Conference:** AN EXHIBIT CONFERENCE REQUIRING THE ATTENDANCE OF TRIAL COUNSEL WILL BE HELD AT 3:00 P.M. ON THE FRIDAY BEFORE THE SCHEDULED TRIAL DATE IN COURTROOM 10A, UNLESS THE COURT ORDERS OTHERWISE. Exhibits are to be submitted to the Courtroom Deputy Clerk at the time of the exhibit conference.

8. **Findings of Fact and Conclusions of Law (Court Trials):** For any matter requiring findings of fact and conclusions of law, counsel for each party shall lodge and serve proposed findings of fact and conclusions of law as promptly as possible in compliance with Local Rule 52. In addition, counsel must submit electronic versions (in Word format) to the Court at the following email address: JST_Chambers@cacd.uscourts.gov.

D. **ATTORNEY AND PARTY CONDUCT AT TRIAL:**

1. **Trial Schedule:** Unless otherwise ordered, trials will be held on Tuesdays through Thursdays from 9:00 a.m. to 12:00 p.m. and 1:30 p.m. to 4:30 p.m. with a 15-minute break during each session, and on Fridays from 8:00 a.m. to 2:00 p.m. With two 15-minute breaks and no lunch recess.

2. **Trial Conduct:**

a. **Jury Selection**

1. The Court utilizes the "Arizona blind strike" method. *See United States v. Harper*, 33 F.3d 1143, 1145 (9th Cir. 1994). Under that method, the Court conducts voir dire of the entire jury panel, then permits limited voir dire by counsel. After potential jurors are excused for cause, counsel for each side simultaneously submit their peremptory challenges in writing. The Court then eliminates the subjects of the peremptory challenges and selects the eight lowest numbered remaining panel members as the jury.

2. Prior to the voir dire examination of the jury venire, counsel for each side will give a "mini opening" statement lasting no longer than three to five minutes that summarizes the case.

b. **Opening Statements, Examining Witnesses, and Summation**

1. At the end of each day, counsel presenting his or her case shall advise opposing counsel of the witnesses anticipated the following day with an estimate of the length of direct examination. Opposing counsel shall provide an estimate of the length of cross-examination. Cooperation of counsel will ensure a smooth flow of witnesses. It is the responsibility of all counsel to arrange the appearance of witnesses in order to avoid delay.

2. Opening statements, examination of witnesses, and summation will be from the lectern only. Counsel must not consume time by writing out words or drawing charts or diagrams. Counsel may do so in advance and explain that

the item was prepared earlier as ordered by the Court to save time.

3. The Court will honor reasonable time estimates for opening and closing addresses to the jury.

4. In jury trials, where a party has more than one lawyer, only one may conduct the direct or cross-examination of a given witness.

5. If a witness is on the stand when a recess is taken, it is counsel's duty to have the witness back on the stand, ready to proceed, when the court session resumes.

6. If a witness was on the stand at adjournment, it is counsel's duty to have the witness adjacent to, but not on, the stand, ready to proceed when the court session resumes.

7. It is counsel's duty to notify the Courtroom Deputy Clerk in advance if any witness should be accommodated by use of the witness stand's automated platform to accommodate witnesses who otherwise are unable to take the witness stand.

8. The Court attempts to accommodate physicians, scientists, and all other professional witnesses and will, except in extraordinary circumstances, permit them to testify out of sequence. Counsel must anticipate any such possibility and discuss it with opposing counsel. If there is objection, counsel shall confer with the Court in advance.

c. Objections and General Decorum

1. When objecting, counsel must rise to state the objection and state only that counsel objects and the legal ground of objection. If counsel wishes to argue an objection further, counsel must ask for permission to do so; the Court may or may not grant a request for conference at sidebar. The Court strongly discourages sidebars because they represent an inefficient use of jury time when matters can be anticipated.

2. Counsel must not approach the Clerk or the witness stand without specific permission. When permission is given, please return to the lectern when the purpose of the permission is finished. Counsel must not engage in questioning a witness at the witness stand.

3. Counsel must address all remarks to the Court. Counsel are not to address the Clerk, the Reporter, persons in the audience, or opposing counsel. If counsel wishes to speak with opposing counsel, counsel must ask permission to talk off the record. Any request for the re-reading of questions or answers shall be addressed to the Court.

4. Counsel must not make an offer of stipulation unless counsel has conferred with opposing counsel and has reason to believe the stipulation will be acceptable.

5. It is counsel's duty of the first day of trial to advise the Court of any commitments that may result in counsel's absence or late arrival.

d. Exhibits

1. Each counsel should keep counsel's own list of exhibits and should keep

track when each has been admitted in evidence.

2. Each counsel is responsible for any exhibits that counsel secures from the Clerk and, during all recesses and noontime and afternoon adjournments, counsel must return all exhibits in counsel's possession to the Clerk.

3. An exhibit not previously marked should, at the time of its first mention, be accompanied by a request that the Clerk mark it for identification. To save time, counsel must show a new exhibit to opposing counsel before it is mentioned in Court.

4. Counsel should move exhibits into evidence as soon as admissibility is established, while they are freshly in the minds of all participants. If there is an objection, the motion to admit will be dealt with at the next available recess. In jury trials, no exhibit shall be read or displayed to the jury until admitted.

5. Absent unusual circumstances, counsel must not ask witnesses to draw charts or diagrams nor ask the Court's permission for a witness to do so. If counsel wishes to question a witness in connection with graphic aids, the material must be fully prepared before the court session starts.

e. Depositions:

1. All depositions that will be used in the trial, either as evidence or for impeachment, must be signed and lodged with the Clerk on the first day of trial or such earlier date as the Court may order. For any deposition in which counsel is interested, counsel should check with the Clerk to confirm that the Clerk has the transcript and that the transcript is properly signed.

2. In using depositions of an adverse party for impeachment, counsel shall first announce both the beginning and ending page and line references of the passage desired to be read, and allow opposing counsel an opportunity to state any objection. Counsel shall use either of the following procedures:

3. If counsel wishes to read the questions and answers as alleged impeachment and ask the witness no further questions on that subject, counsel may merely read the relevant portions of the deposition into the record.

4. If counsel wishes to ask the witness further questions on the subject matter, the deposition is placed in front of the witness and the witness is told to read silently the pages and lines involved. Then counsel may either ask the witness further questions on the matter and thereafter read the quotations or read the quotations and thereafter ask further questions. Counsel should have an extra copy of the deposition for this purpose.

5. Where a witness is absent and the witness' testimony is offered by deposition, please observe the following procedure. A reader should occupy the witness chair and read the testimony of the witness while the examining lawyer asks the questions.

f. Advance Notice of Evidentiary or Difficult Questions

If counsel has reason to anticipate that a difficult question of law or evidence will raise legal argument, requiring research and/or briefing, counsel must give the Court advance notice. Counsel are directed to notify the Clerk at the day's adjournment if an unexpected legal issue arises that could not have been foreseen and addressed by a motion *in limine* (*see* Fed. R. Evid. 103). To the maximum extent possible such matters shall be taken outside normal trial hours (*e.g.*, recess, before or after the trial day).

The Clerk is ordered to serve a copy of this Order on counsel/parties in this action.

IT IS SO ORDERED.

DATED: ____________________

JOSEPHINE STATON TUCKER
United States District Judge

C. *Order Regarding Criminal Pretrial Motions, Trials, and Sentencing*

IN THE UNITED STATES DISTICT COURT
FOR THE CENTRAL DISTRICT OF CALIFORNIA

UNITED STATES OF AMERICA, Plaintiff,	))	Case No. ____________
v.	)	**ORDER RE CRIMINAL PRE-TRIAL**
Defendant(s).	)	**MOTIONS, TRIALS, AND**
______________________________	)	**SENTENCING**

The above matter is set for trial before the Honorable Josephine Staton Tucker, United States District Judge, Courtroom 10A, Ronald Reagan Federal Building and United States Courthouse, 411 West Fourth Street, Santa Ana, CA 92701. Counsel preparing for trial before this Court shall comply with this Order. Failure to comply with this order may subject counsel to sanctions.

MOTION PRACTICE

1. Unless the Local Criminal Rules prescribe a different time for filing a particular motion, pre-trial motions must be filed and served not later than twenty-eight (28) days after arraignment and set for hearing not later than the Monday eight (8) days prior to the trial date at 2:30 p.m. Counsel's estimate of the time required for presentation of the motion must be set forth adjacent to the caption.

2. A party opposing a motion must file and serve an opposition not later than seven (7) days after service of the motion or as otherwise permitted by the Court. Counsel's estimate of the time required for presentation of the opposition to the motion must be set forth in the caption of the opposition.

3. Memoranda of Points and Authorities in support of or in opposition to motions shall not exceed 25 pages. Replies shall not exceed 12 pages. Only in rare instances and for good cause shown will the Court grant an application to extend these page limitations. No supplemental briefs shall be filed without prior leave of court.

4. Before filing any motion for discovery, counsel shall confer with opposing counsel to ascertain what discovery will be provided. Any discovery motion shall state with particularity what is requested, and whether such discovery has been declined. Motions made without prior consultation with opposing counsel or which fail to include the above information will not be heard.

DISCOVERY AND NOTICE

5. Counsel for the government and counsel for the defendant shall comply promptly with discovery and notice pursuant to Fed. R. Crim. P., Rules 12, 12.1, 12.2, 12.3, 15 and 16. Upon government counsel's discovery of any evidence within the scope of *Brady v. Maryland*, 373 U.S. 83 (1963), such evidence shall be produced forthwith to counsel for the defendant. Counsel for the government shall also disclose to counsel for the defendant the existence or non-existence of: (1) evidence obtained by electronic surveillance; and (2) testimony by a government informant.

TRIAL

8. Trials are held Tuesdays through Thursdays, 9:00 a.m. to 1:30 p.m. And Fridays, 8:00 a.m. to 2:00 p.m.

9. Counsel shall arrive at the Courtroom at 8:30 a.m. on the first day of trial and present the Courtroom Deputy with the following documents:

a. Three copies of the government's witness list;

b. Three copies of the government's exhibit list;

c. All of the government's exhibits with official exhibit tags attached;

d. Two binders containing a copy of all reproducible exhibits, tabbed with exhibit numbers along the right hand side;

10. Defense counsel need not deliver the exhibits to the Courtroom Deputy on the first day of trial; however, defense counsel is responsible for affixing completed exhibit tags to the exhibits which are intended for use in defendant's case. Defense counsel shall provide the Court with two copies of their exhibits as they are introduced during trial.

11. Voir Dire: At least four (4) court days prior to trial, each counsel shall file and serve on opposing counsel any special questions requested to be put to prospective jurors by the Court during voir dire.

12. Jury Instructions and Verdict Forms: In a jury trial, no later than one (1) week before trial, counsel shall submit **JOINT** jury instructions and a **JOINT** proposed verdict form (if a special verdict is desired). In order to produce these joint documents, counsel shall meet and confer sufficiently in advance of the required submission date with the goal of agreeing upon instructions and a verdict form. The instructions should be submitted in the order in which the parties wish to have the instructions read. This order should reflect a single organized sequence agreed to by all of the parties.

The jury instructions shall be submitted as follows:

a. Agreed upon JOINT jury instructions;

b. Instructions propounded by the government to which the defendant(s) objects; and

c. Instructions propounded by defendant(s) to which the government objects.

Instructions upon which agreement cannot be reached should reflect the basic disagreements among the parties as to the law. Counsel shall include both general and substantive instructions. In addition, counsel must submit electronic versions (either Word or WordPerfect format) to the Court at the following email address: JST_Chambers@cacd.uscourts.gov.

Attribution and case citation for each instruction should be placed on pages following a proposed instruction. For disputed instructions, a party should note its objections to a proposed instruction and its reasons for putting forth its alternative on pages placed after its own alternative instruction.

SENTENCING PROCEEDINGS

13. If a defendant is convicted, the sentencing proceedings will be conducted pursuant to Fed. Crim. Pro. Rule 32 and the Local Rules. If any party wishes to present material to the Court which has (a) not been previously filed with the Court or presented at trial, or (b) not been previously provided to the opposing party and the assigned United States Probation Officer, such party must file and serve the information or evidence no later than two (2) weeks before the scheduled sentencing hearing. Notwithstanding the foregoing, a statement

of each party's position concerning sentencing shall be filed and served no later than two (2) weeks before the sentencing hearing, and the proof of service shall reflect service on the assigned United States Probation Officer. Timely filing is important to enable the Probation Officer sufficient time to prepare and disclose any addendum to the Probation Report that may be required in response to new information and/or evidence and/or a party's sentencing position. Failure to timely file and serve such information, evidence, or statement of position may result in such information not being considered by the Court in imposing defendant's sentence.

The Clerk is directed to serve this Order on all counsel at the time of postindictment arraignment proceedings.

IT IS SO ORDERED.

DATED: ____________________

JOSEPHINE STATON TUCKER
United States District Judge

Hon. John F. Walter

District Judge

Chambers Information

U.S. District Court, Central District of California
Courtroom 16, Spring Street Floor
312 N. Spring Street
Los Angeles, CA 90012

Scheduling Information

Courtroom Deputy: (213) 894-5396

Civil Law and Motion	Mondays at 1:30 p.m.
Criminal Law and Motion	Mondays at 9:00 a.m.

Biographical Information

Born 1944 in Buffalo, NY

Federal Judicial Service:

-Judge, U. S. District Court, Central District of California
-Nominated by George W. Bush on January 23, 2002, to a seat vacated by John G. Davies; Confirmed by the Senate on April 25, 2002, and received commission on May 1, 2002.

Education:

-Loyola University of Los Angeles, B.A., 1966
-Loyola University of Los Angeles School of Law, J.D., 1969

Professional Career:

-Private Practice, California, 1969-1970, 1972-2002
-Assistant U.S. Attorney for the Central District of California, 1970-1972

I. Judge Walter's Procedures and Practices

A. *Procedures and Schedules*

The Courtroom Deputy Clerk ("CRD") prefers to be contacted via e-mail. Phone or e-mail messages without case name, number and a brief message will not be returned. Due to the high volume of calls and e-mails, not all e-mails/phone calls can be returned. Requests that can be answered by reviewing the local rules, Orders issued by the Court, or the Court's website will not be returned. Do not leave multiple messages regarding the same issue.

Criminal

- Criminal matters are heard on: **Monday at 9:00 a.m.**
- The Court will not consider any stipulation or application to continue any hearing unless such stipulation or application is properly filed with a separate proposed order at least three court days prior to the date of the hearing. If the stipulation/application for continuance was not filed at least three court days prior to the date of the hearing, or if the Court has not ruled on the stipulation/application, counsel and the defendant(s) shall appear on the scheduled hearing date.
- Filing criminal documents under seal: Refer to the Local Rules.

Civil

- Civil motions are heard on: **Monday at 1:30 p.m.**
- Tentative rulings are not issued.
- It is not necessary to clear a motion date with the CRD prior to filing the motion. Any Monday that is not a federal holiday shall be considered an available date.
- If Monday is a holiday, the next motion date is the next available Monday.
- Discovery motions are to be calendared before the Magistrate Judge.
- Continuances are granted only upon a showing of good cause. Requests for continuances must be made by motion, stipulation, or application with a separate proposed order accompanied by a declaration setting forth the reasons for the requested continuance. The declaration should also state whether there have been any prior requests for continuances and whether these requests were granted or denied by the Court and shall include all pending dates set by the Court. Stipulations extending dates set by this Court are not effective unless approved by the Court. Requests for continuance should be submitted well in advance of the requested relief. Requests for continuance not in compliance with the Court's Standing Order or the Local Rules will be denied.
- Filing civil documents under seal: Refer to the Local Rules and the Court's Standing Order.

General Information

- All documents which are required to be filed in an electronic format pursuant to General Order **Authorizing Electronic Filing** shall be filed electronically no later than 4:00 p.m. on the date due unless otherwise ordered by the Court. Any documents filed electronically after 4:00 p.m. on the date due will be considered late and may be [illegible] by the Court. Any documents which counsel attempt to file electronically which are improperly filed will not be accepted by the Court.
- When a proposed order accompanies a filing, a WordPerfect or Word copy of the

proposed order, along with a copy of the PDF electronically filed main document, shall be e-mailed to the Chamber's e-mail address listed on the ECF Website. The subject line of the e-mail shall be in the following format: court's divisional office, year, case type, case number, document control number assigned to the main document at the time of filing, judge's initials and filer (party) name. Failure to comply with this requirement may result in the denial or striking of the request or the Court may withhold ruling on the request until the Court receives the required documents.

- Counsel are ORDERED to deliver 2 copies of all documents filed electronically to Chambers. For each document filed electronically, one copy shall be marked "CHAMBERS COPY" and the other copy shall be marked "COURTESY COPY." The copies of each electronically filed document must include on each page the running header created by the ECF system. In addition, on the first page of each copy, in the space between lines 1-7 to the right of the center, counsel shall include the date the document was e-filed and the document number. The copies shall be delivered to Chambers no later than 10:00 a.m. on the next business day after the document was electronically filed. For any document that is not required to be filed electronically, counsel are ORDERED to deliver 1 conformed copy of the document, which shall be marked "COURTESY COPY" to Chambers at the time of filing.
- The CRD will not file documents in Court.
- All filed documents must contain counsel's "E-mail Address of Record."
- Telephonic appearances for hearings in Court are not permitted.
- *Ex parte* Applications, Temporary Restraining Orders and Injunctions: Refer to the Local Rules and the Court's Standing Order.
- Calls or e-mails will not be returned regarding the status of submitted motions, stipulations, or proposed orders. Counsel may determine the status of any submitted motion, stipulation, or proposed order by accessing the docket through PACER.
- Counsel are not permitted to contact the judge's law clerks or secretary unless responding to an inquiry they initiated.
- For general information on how to order a transcript of any reported or digitally recorded proceeding, please contact 213-894-3015 or visit www.cacd.uscourts.gov > General Information > Court Reporter/Recorder Transcripts. If you require an estimate of cost for the preparation of a transcript, contact the court reporter/recorder for the desired proceeding.
  To determine the court reporter/recorder for a particular proceeding, go to the Court Reporter Schedule web page and click on View by Date. Once you've determined the correct court reporter/recorder for the desired session, click on Court Reporter Phone and Email List for contact information.
- The following trial preparation will be discussed at the Scheduling Conference and Pretrial Conference:
  - Court hours
  - Motions in Limine
  - Exhibit preparation
  - Jury Instructions and Verdict Forms
- Counsel are directed to the Court's website for information related to reserving courtroom equipment.
- The Court requires the following to be submitted to the CRD on the first day of trial:

  - The original exhibits with the Court's exhibit tags. Plaintiff shall use yellow tags; defendant shall use blue tags. Each tag shall be affixed to the front of the exhibit as detailed in the Court's Civil and Criminal Trial Orders. Exhibit tags can be obtained from the Clerk's Office.
  - One bench book with a copy of each exhibit for the Court's use, tagged as described above.
  - Three (3) copies of exhibit lists (CRD will instruct at pretrial conference as to format).
  - Three (3) copies of witness lists in the order in which the witnesses will be called to testify (CRD will instruct at pretrial conference as to format).
- All exhibits will be returned to counsel at the end of trial and will not be kept by the Court. Counsel shall keep the lodged and admitted exhibits in their possession pursuant to Local Rules.
- It is the responsibility of counsel in a civil case to arrange for the services of an Interpreter. Interpreter's Office: (213) 894-4599.
- Other information: Counsel are directed to comply with all Local Rules and all Orders issued by the Court.
- Law clerk/extern positions: Submit resume.

Hon. Stephen V. Wilson

District Judge

Chambers Information

U.S. District Court, Central District of California
Courtroom 6, 2nd Floor
312 N. Spring Street
Los Angeles, CA 90012

Scheduling Information

Courtroom Deputy: (213) 894-2881

Civil Law and Motion	Mondays at 1:30 p.m.
Criminal Law and Motion	Mondays at 11:00 a.m.

Biographical Information

Born 1941 in New York, NY

Federal Judicial Service:

-Judge, U. S. District Court, Central District of California
-Nominated by Ronald Reagan on September 9, 1985, to a new seat created by 98 Stat. 333; Confirmed by the Senate on October 16, 1985, and received commission on October 17, 1985.

Education:

-Lehigh University, B.A., 1963
-Brooklyn Law School, J.D., 1967
-George Washington University Law School, LL.M., 1973

Professional Career:

-Trial attorney, Tax Division, U.S. Department of Justice, 1968-1971
-Assistant U.S. Attorney, Los Angeles, California, 1971-1977
-Chief, Fraud and Special Prosecutions Section, 1973-1977
-Private Practice, Beverly Hills, California, 1977-1985
-Adjunct Professor of Law, Loyola University, 1975-1979
-Chairman, Federal Indigent Defense Panel Committee of District Court in Los Angeles, 1979-1980
-Adjunct Professor of Law, University of San Diego, 1984

I. Judge Wilson's Procedures and Practices

A. Procedures and Schedules

1. Civil motions are heard on **Mondays**, Time: **1:30 p.m.**

   Criminal motions are heard on: **Mondays**, Time: **11:00 a.m.**

   (If Monday is a holiday, next motion date is the following Monday.)

   It is not necessary to clear a motion date with the court clerk prior to filing the motion.

2. Discovery motions are to be calendared before the magistrate judge.

3. Tentative rulings are not issued.

4. E-FILING: All electronic filing shall comply with General Order No. 10-07, or any other superseding order. Mandatory chambers copies shall be delivered must be delivered to the chambers of the assigned judge no later than 12:00 noon the following business day.

5. Procedures for filing an ex parte application: Ex parte applications are considered on the papers and are not set for hearing. Counsel are advised to file and serve their ex parte applications as soon as they realize that extraordinary relief is necessary. Counsel are advised that this Court allows ex parte applications solely for extraordinary relief - sanctions may be imposed for misuse of ex parte applications. *See In Re: Intermagnetics America, Inc., 101 Bankr. 191 (C.D. Cal. 1989).* The requesting party shall notify the responding party that opposing papers must be filed not later than 3:00 p.m. on the first business day succeeding the day the ex parte was served. If counsel are not going to oppose an ex parte application, they must inform the clerk at 213-894-2881. Counsel will be notified by the clerk of the Court's ruling.

6. To request a continuance of any scheduled court proceeding: Continuances are granted only upon a showing of good cause, particularly focusing upon evidence of diligent work by the party seeking delay and of prejudice that may result from the denial of a continuance. Counsel requesting a continuance MUST submit a DETAILED declaration as to the reason. Any continuances requested not accompanied by said declaration will be rejected without notice to the parties. The Court sets FIRM trial dates and will not change them without good cause having been shown.

   NO stipulations extending scheduling dates set by this Court are effective unless approved by this Court. All stipulations must be accompanied by a DETAILED declaration explaining the reason for the stipulation. Any stipulation not in compliance with this Order or the Local Rules of the Central District of California will automatically be rejected without notice to the parties. Stipulations shall be submitted well in advance of the relief requested. Counsel wishing to know whether or not a stipulation has been signed shall comply with Local Rule 7-1.

7. Counsel are not allowed to contact the judge's law clerk or secretary.

8. Inquiries regarding the status of a motion, stipulation or proposed order: See Local Rule 7-1.

9. Calendar conflicts: Counsel shall notify both of the judges court clerks. Counsel

should go to the most senior of the judges. A priority before that judge should be requested.

10. Procedures for bringing electronic equipment into the courtroom: Equipment such as a video tape player, tape recorder, projector, shadow box, large drawing paper, etc. are no longer provided by the Court. You must arrange to bring your own equipment. You may bring the equipment into the courthouse, but courthouse regulations require a property pass to remove the equipment from the building. A property pass may be obtained by calling the Space & Facilities Help Desk at 213-894-1400.

11. For general information on how to order a transcript of any reported or digitally recorded proceeding, please contact 213-894-3015 or visit www.cacd.uscourts.gov > General Information > Court Reporter/Recorder Transcripts. If you require an estimate of cost for the preparation of a transcript, contact the court reporter/recorder for the desired proceeding.

    To determine the court reporter/recorder for a particular proceeding, go to the Court Reporter Schedule web page and click on View by Date. Once you've determined the correct court reporter/recorder for the desired session, click on Court Reporter Phone and Email List for contact information.

12. Questions regarding law clerk/extern positions, please call 213-894-4327.

13. Trial preparation:
    a. Court hours: Tuesday - Friday, 9:00 a.m. - 12:00 p.m. and 1:30 p.m. to 5:00 p.m.

    b. Exhibit preparation: **ALL** of your exhibits, with **official** exhibit tags attached, bearing the same number shown on your exhibit list, must be delivered to the Courtroom Deputy Clerk not later than 8:30 a.m. on the first day of trial. Official exhibit tags are available from the receptionist in the main Clerk's Office, Room G-8. Exhibits shall be marked in accordance with Local Rule 11-5.3 and 16-5. A separate number is NOT given to each page of a single document.

    c. Jury instructions: In a jury trial, jury instructions and a verdict form are to be **submitted not later than 2 court days prior to the pretrial conference or 1 week prior to the trial if pretrial conference is waived**. Counsel need only submit proposed substantiative jury instructions, the Court propounds its own **general instructions** and essentially follows the format set out in the Ninth Circuit Model Jury Instructions.

       Form of Jury Instructions and Verdict Forms: The parties MUST submit JOINT jury instructions and a joint proposed verdict form. In order to produce these joing instructions, the parties **SHALL MEET AND CONFER** sufficiently in advance of the required submission date. The instructions should be submitted in the order in which the parties wish to have the instructions read. This order should reflect a single organized sequence agreed to by all of the parties. **The Court INSISTS upon receiving lucid and accurate instructions setting forth the elements of each party's claim and defenses.** the instructions should be tailored to the facts of each case. **Procedures for Instructions Upon Which Agreement Cannot be Reached.**

       Instructions shall be submitted in three (3) sets (with an extra copy for the Court's law clerks) in the following form:

1. The agreed upon instructions.
2. Those instructions propounded by plaintiff, opposed by defendant.
3. Those instructions propounded by defendant, opposed by plaintiff.

Instructions upon which agreement cannot be reached should reflect the basic disagreements among the parties as to the law. While the Court recognizes that such disagreements arise in almost every case, the Court also recognizes that parties ultimately disagree over only a limited number of issues. The disputed instructions should be equally so limited.

The disputed instructions should be presented to the Court within the framework of the overall set of instructions. The parties should put forth differing versions of disputed instructions, and the Court will select one version (as outlined above).

The instructions and verdict form submitted to the Court MUST be numbered, and the parties must also **submit an un-numbered index**. Attribution and case citation for each instruction shall be placed on pages following a proposed instruction. For disputed instructions, a party should note its objections to a proposed instruction and its reasons for putting forth its alternative on pages placed after **its own** alternative instruction.

INSTRUCTIONS SHALL BE BRIEF, CLEAR, CONCISE, WRITTEN IN PLAIN ENGLISH, FREE OF ARGUMENT AND SHALL BE ORGANIZED IN A LOGICAL FASHION SO AS TO AID JURY COMPREHENSION. Standard or form instructions, if used, must be revised to address the particular facts and issues of this case.

The following list contains some suggested sources for jury instructions:

1. **Ninth Circuit Model Jury Instructions** (updated yearly)
2. **Federal Jury Practice and Instructions** (Devitt and Blackmar (4th Edition))
3. **Modern Federal Jury Instructions** (Mathew Bender)
4. California Forms of Jury Instructions (Mathew Bender)

d. Verdict forms: Counsel are to prepare and submit verdict form(s) at the start of trial.

14. Procedures for obtaining the services of an interpreter on a civil case. Counsel are to make the arrangements. Contact the Interpreters Office at 213-894-4370 or 213-894-4599.

Hon. Otis D. Wright II
District Judge

Chambers Information
U.S. District Court, Central District of California
Courtroom 11, Spring Street Floor
312 N. Spring Street
Los Angeles, CA 90012

Scheduling Information
Courtroom Deputy: (213) 894-8266

Civil Law and Motion	Mondays at 1:30 p.m.
Criminal Law and Motion	Mondays at 10:00 a.m.

Biographical Information
Born 1944 in Tuskegee, AL

Federal Judicial Service:
-Judge, U. S. District Court, Central District of California
-Nominated by George W. Bush on January 9, 2007, to a seat vacated by Gary L. Taylor; Confirmed by the Senate on March 15, 2007, and received commission on April 16, 2007.

Education:
-California State University at Los Angeles, B.A., 1976
-Southwestern School of Law, J.D., 1980

Professional Career:
-United States Marine Corps, 1963-1966
-United States Marine Corps Reserve, 1966-1969
-Deputy Sheriff, Los Angeles County Sheriff's Department, California, 1969-1980
-Deputy Attorney General, Office of the Attorney General, California Department of Justice, 1980-1983
-Private Practice, Los Angeles, California, 1983-2005
-Judge, Superior Court of California, Los Angeles County, 2005-2007

I. Judge Wright's Procedures and Practices

A. *Procedures and Schedules*

I. COURT HOURS:

A. Trials -- Generally 9:00 a.m. to 5:00 p.m. with a 90 minute lunch break and short breaks in the morning and afternoon. Alternatively, jurors are given the option of a court day beginning at 8:30 a.m. ending around 2:30 p.m. with no lunch break but periodic breaks for the reporter.

B. Criminal Motions -- Mondays at 10:00 a.m. Only.

C. Civil Motions -- Mondays at 1:30 p.m. Only. (When Monday is a holiday, the next motion date is the following Monday.)

D. Civil Pre-Trial Conferences -- Mondays at 2:30 p.m.

II. CONTACT WITH CHAMBERS: Counsel are not to communicate with chambers unless first contacted by a law clerk or Judge Wright's Courtroom Deputy Clerk, (CRD).

III. CALENDAR CONFLICTS: If counsel has an appearance with another district judge, please leave a voice mail message with the Court Clerk at 213-894-8266 indicating the time of the appearance and the name of the other judge. On the day of the appearance, if possible, request the other judge's Court Clerk to update Judge Wright's Court Clerk as to when counsel will be appearing in Judge Wright's courtroom.

If counsel cannot make a court appearance, good cause must be shown.

IV. CONTINUANCES: Continuances and special requests must be approved by the Court. Good cause must be shown. Refer to Local Rule 52.9 for the proper format.

If a stipulation cannot be reached, counsel must submit an ex parte application and proposed order. (See Section X, infra.). The written opposition to the ex parte application must be submitted within 24 hours for consideration by the Court.

Time does not permit the Court Clerk to respond to questions regarding whether the Court has approved requests, or to confirm a message left for counsel.

V. ORDERS: Any request shall be accompanied by a separate proposed order. Then emailed to the Judges chambers email ODW_chambers@cacd.uscourts.gov. in word or word perfect. Failure to do so may cause your filing stricken.

VI. MANDATORY CHAMBERS COPIES: The Court requires delivery of one non-blue backed Mandatory Chambers Copy* delivered by 3:00 p.m. the following business day of only the following manual and electronically filed documents to Judge Wright's document box outside the entrance to chambers near courtrooms 10 and 12.

1. All noticed motions and related documents;
2. All ex parte *applications* and related documents; and
3. *All exhibits and attachments must be separately tabbed.*
   *[Refer to the Court's General Order No. 10-07 regarding ECF Courtesy Paper Copies.]

VII. FILINGS: Follow the local rules and federal rules of procedure.

It is not necessary to clear a motion date with the Court Clerk prior to filing the motion. The Court hears motions only on Mondays (civil at 1:30 p.m. and criminal at 10:00 a.m.).

Motions in limine are to be noticed for hearing no later than the Monday eight days prior to the trial date. If the hearing date falls on a legal holiday, notice the motion-in-limine hearing fifteen days prior to the trial date. Motions in limine are heard at 2:30 p.m.

Discovery motions are to be scheduled before the magistrate judge assigned to the case (the magistrate judge's initials, followed by a small "x," are in the parenthetical in the case number). All discovery motion papers must include "DISCOVERY MATTER" in the caption.

VIII. **TELEPHONIC HEARINGS:** At least one week prior to the scheduled hearing, counsel located outside the Central District may arrange to appear telephonically. Contact the Court Clerk at 213-894-8266 for the Court's permission. The requesting attorney is responsible for coordinating and initiating the telephone call. No cellular or speaker telephones may be used.

IX. **DISCOVERY MOTIONS:** All discovery motions must be heard prior to the discovery cut-off date.

X. **TRIAL EXHIBITS:** Three non-blue backed copies each of exhibit lists and witness lists are to be delivered to the Court Clerk on the morning of the first day of trial.

Two exhibit notebooks (an original and the Judge's copy) are required to be delivered to the Court Clerk on the morning of the first day of trial. No additional notebook is needed for witnesses. Counsel are to prepare their exhibits by placing them in 3-ring binders. The holes are to be 3/8" in diameter. The notebooks are to be tabbed down the right side with numeric tabs separating each exhibit. The exhibits are to be numbered in accordance with Local Rule 26.4. Each exhibit must have an exhibit tag stapled to the upper right-hand corner of its first page. The spine on the exhibit notebook must reflect the exhibit numbers contained within that volume. For example: Trial Exhibit Notebook 1, Exh. Nos. 1-25.

The following documents are to be submitted to the court three-hole punched, with 3/8" holes: (Proposed) Pretrial conference order, joint witness list, joint exhibit list, memoranda of fact and law, joint statement of the case to be read to the jury and jury instructions.

A. **Exhibit Tags:** The Court requires the large exhibit tags, which may be obtained from the Clerk's Office, Room G-19, 312 North Spring Street, Los Angeles.

Each exhibit should have an exhibit tag stapled to the lower right-hand corner of its first page. The plaintiff's exhibits shall be tagged with yellow tags; and the defendant's exhibits shall be tagged with blue tags. The tags shall indicate the case number, case name, and exhibit number. All exhibits are to be sequentially numbered regardless of which party produces the exhibit. The joint exhibit list must be in substantially the following format:

Exh No.	Description	Date I.D.	Admitted

XI. JURY INSTRUCTIONS:

A. Civil Jury Trials – Local Rule 16.2 requires that counsel meet at least forty (40) days in advance of the date set for the final Pre-Trial Conference for the purpose of accomplishing various tasks in preparation for trial. In addition to the tasks set forth in Local Rule 16.2, the parties shall meet with the goal of reaching agreement to one set of joint jury instructions and one verdict form. The set of joint jury instructions must be filed at least five (5) court days before the final Pre-Trial Conference. The parties may submit another set of jury instructions containing the instructions upon which the parties disagree and the objections to those instructions.

Where the parties disagree on an instruction, the party opposing the instruction must attach a short (i.e., one to two paragraphs) statement supporting the objection and the party submitting the instruction must attach a short statement supporting the instruction. Each statement should be on a separate page and should follow directly after the disputed instruction.

The parties ultimately will submit one document or, if the parties disagree to any proposed jury instructions, two documents. If the parties submit two documents, those documents should consist of: (1) a set of agreed upon jury instructions and (2) a set of disputed jury instructions along with reasons supporting and opposing each disputed instruction.

The Court orders the parties to make every attempt to agree upon the jury instructions before submitting them to the Court. In addition, where the Manual of Model Civil Jury Instructions for the Ninth Circuit (2007 edition) provides a version of a requested instruction, the parties shall submit the Model instruction. Where California law applies, the Court prefers counsel to use California Jury Instructions -- Civil ("BAJI") or CACI. If neither of the above sources is applicable, counsel are directed to use the instructions from O'Malley-Grenig-Lee, et al., Federal Jury Practice and Instructions(Fifth Edition). Each requested jury instruction shall cover only one subject or principle of law and shall be numbered and set forth in full on a separate page, citing the authority or source of the requested instruction (except for the jury copy discussed below).

The Court will send a copy of the jury instructions into the jury room for use by the jury during deliberations. Accordingly, in addition to the filed copies described above, the parties shall file with the Courtroom Deputy Clerk the day before closing arguments a "clean set" of the final jury instructions which contain only the text of each instruction set forth in full on each page, with the caption "Court's Instruction Number" (eliminating titles, supporting authority, indication of party proposing, etc.). This will be referred to as the "Jury Copy" of the jury instructions.

An index page shall accompany all jury instructions submitted to the Court. The index page shall indicate the following:

a. The number of the instruction;
b. A brief title of the instruction;
c. The source of the instruction or the relevant case citation, and
d. The page number of the instruction.

EXAMPLE:

Number	Title	Source	Page
1	Burden of Proof	9th Cir. 12.02	7

Counsel will also prepare and submit to the court a joint statement to be read to the prospective panel of jurors prior to the commencement of voir dire. The statement should not be longer than two or three paragraphs. The statement shall be filed with the Court five (5) court days before the Pre-Trial Conference. The statement is to be a non-argumentative neutral recitation of the basic facts of the case and the parties' positions.

B. Criminal Jury Trials – At least five (5) court days prior to the final Pre-Trial Conference, the parties shall meet with the goal of reaching agreement to one set of joint jury instructions.

Where the parties disagree on an instruction, the party opposing the instruction must attach a short (i.e., one to two paragraphs) statement supporting the objection and the party submitting the instruction must attach a short statement supporting the instruction. Each statement should be on a separate page and should follow directly after the disputed instruction.

The parties ultimately will submit one document or, if the parties disagree over any proposed jury instructions, two documents. If the parties submit two documents, those documents should consist of: (1) a set of agreed upon jury instructions and (2) a set of disputed jury instructions along with reasons supporting and opposing each disputed instruction.

The Court orders the parties to make every attempt to agree upon the jury instructions before submitting them to the Court. In addition, where the Manual of Model Criminal Jury Instructions (2010) for the Ninth Circuit provides a version of a requested instruction, the parties shall submit the Model instruction. The only exception to the above is that the Court prefers the instruction from Edward J. Devitt, et al., Federal Jury Practice and Instructions on the burden of proof. If a Model instruction does not exist for a particular subject, counsel may submit an instruction from Devitt (supra). Each requested jury instruction shall cover only one subject or principle of law and shall be numbered and set forth in full on a separate page, citing the authority or source of the requested instruction (except for the jury copy discussed below).

The Court will send a copy of the jury instructions into the jury room for use by the jury during deliberations. Accordingly, in addition to the filed copies described above, the parties shall file with the Courtroom Deputy Clerk the day before closing arguments a "clean set" of the final jury instructions which contain only the text of each instruction set forth in full on each page, with the caption "Court's Instruction Number" (eliminating titles, supporting authority, indication of party proposing, etc.). This will be referred to as the "Jury Copy" of the jury instructions.

An index page shall accompany all jury instructions submitted to the Court. The index page shall indicate the following:

a. The number of the instruction;
b. A brief title of the instruction;
c. The source of the instruction and any relevant case citations; and

d. The page number of the instruction.

EXAMPLE:

Number	Title	Source	Page
1	Burden of Proof	9th Cir. 12.02	7

Counsel will also prepare and submit to the court a joint statement to be read to the prospective panel of jurors prior to the commencement of voir dire. The statement should not be longer than two or three paragraphs. The statement shall be filed with the Court five (5) court days before the Pre-Trial Conference. The statement is to be a non-argumentative neutral recitation of the basic facts of the case and the parties' positions.

XII. **EX PARTE APPLICATIONS AND TEMPORARY RESTRAINING ORDERS:** Do not attempt to schedule a hearing date and time for ex parte applications and temporary restraining orders. Follow the local rules and federal rules of procedure. Judge Wright will review your papers. If a hearing is necessary, counsel will be notified as soon as possible. Ex parte applications are solely for extraordinary relief and should be used sparingly. Sanctions may be imposed for misuse of the ex parte application process. See Mission Power Engineering Co. v. Continental Cas.. Co., 883 F.Supp. 488 (C.D. Cal.1995.)

XIII. **TRANSCRIPT ORDERS:** For general information on how to order a transcript of any reported or digitally recorded proceeding, please contact 213-894-3015 or visit www.cacd.uscourts.gov > General Information > Court Reporter/Recorder Transcripts. If you require an estimate of cost for the preparation of a transcript, contact the court reporter/recorder for the desired proceeding.

To determine the court reporter/recorder for a particular proceeding, go to the Court Reporter Schedule web page and click on View by Date. Once you've determined the correct court reporter/recorder for the desired session, click on Court Reporter Phone and Email List for contact information.

XIV. **INTERPRETERS:** Procedures for obtaining the services of an interpreter on a civil case are the responsibility of counsel. Interpreters must be certified. For information, dial 213-894-4599.

XV. **OTHER INFORMATION:** General information:213-894-3535 or 213-894-1565 (recording).

XVI. **LAW CLERK and EXTERN APPLICANTS:** Applicants may submit applications to Judge Otis D.Wright, II Room #155, 312 North Spring Street, Los Angeles, California 90012. Applications are to include a cover letter, resume, transcript, and writing sample. Letters of recommendation are to be directed to this address.

XVII. **PURCHASING COPIES OF LOCAL RULES:**

Los Angeles Daily Journal, 915 East First Street, Los Angeles, California 90012;
Metropolitan News, 210 South Spring Street, Los Angeles, California 90012;
West Publishing Company, 50 West Kellogg Boulevard, St. Paul, Minnesota 55164-9979.

II. Judge Wright's Case Management Orders

A. *Criminal Motion and Trial Order*

IN THE UNITED STATES DISTICT COURT
FOR THE CENTRAL DISTRICT OF CALIFORNIA

UNITED STATES OF AMERICA, Plaintiff, v. Defendant(s).	Case No. ________________ **CRIMINAL MOTION AND TRIAL ORDER**

This matter is set for trial before the Honorable Otis D. Wright II, United States District Judge, Courtroom 11, United States Courthouse, 312 N. Spring Street, Los Angeles, California 90012.

A. PRETRIAL AND TRIAL DATES AND MOTIONS

1. Pretrial motions shall be filed on or before __________ (Monday preceding four weeks before trial). Motions expected to take more than one hour of court time must include a time estimate beneath the hearing date on the face page of the motion.

Oppositions (or notices of non-opposition) shall be filed on __________ (Monday preceding three weeks before trial.)

Replies (optional) shall be filed on __________ (Monday one week before trial).

Local Rule 7-12 will apply to papers not timely filed by a party.

Adherence to these timing requirements is essential to chambers' preparation of motion matters.

2. Memoranda of Points and Authorities in support of or in opposition to motions shall not exceed 25 pages. Replies shall not exceed 12 pages. Only in rare instances and for good cause shown will the Court grant an application to extend these page limitations. No supplemental brief shall be filed without prior leave of court. **Typeface shall comply with Local Rule 11-3.1.1. (Civil). NOTE: Times New Roman font must be used; the size must be no less than 14.** Footnotes shall be in typeface no less than two sizes smaller than text size and shall be used sparingly.

3. Filings that do not conform to the Local Rules and this Order may not be considered.

4. Before filing any motion for discovery, a party shall consult with opposing counsel to ascertain whether the requested discovery will be provided. All discovery motions shall state with particularity what is requested, the basis for the request, whether the discovery has been requested from opposing counsel, and whether the discovery has been declined, in whole or in part. Motions made without prior consultation with opposing counsel or that fail to include the above information may not be heard.

5. A Status Conference/Motions Hearing is set for ________at ___ p.m.

6. **Trial is set for Tuesday, ________________ at 9:00 a.m.**

7. All documents shall be e-filed and served on opposing counsel at approximately the same time.

8. Courtesy copies of all filed motions, oppositions or notice of non-opposition, and replies must be delivered to Judge Wright's chambers on the Spring Street level of the U.S. Courthouse, 312 North Spring Street not later than 12:00 noon the following business day. For security reasons, courtesy copies should be removed from envelopes or folders before placing them in the courtesy-copy drop box.

9. All Counsel are to list e-mail addresses, facsimile transmission numbers, along with street address (no Post Office box numbers) and telephone numbers, on all papers submitted to the Court.

B. DISCOVERY & NOTICE

Counsel shall comply promptly with discovery and notice pursuant to Rules 12, 12.1, 12.2, 12.3, 12.4, 15, and 16 of the Federal Rules of Criminal Procedure. On government counsel's discovery of any evidence within the scope of *Brady v. Maryland*, 373 U.S. 83 (1963), such evidence shall be produced forthwith to counsel for the defendant. Counsel for the government shall also disclose to counsel for defendant the existence or non-existence of: (1) evidence obtained by electronic surveillance; and (2) testimony by a government informer.

C. TRIAL REQUIREMENTS

1. **No later than one week before trial**, counsel for the government shall file with the Court:

a. *In camera* (under seal) all statements of all witnesses to be called by the Government in its case-in-chief;

b. A Trial Memorandum setting forth a factual summary of the government's case, a statement of the charges and the elements of each charge, an estimate of the length of the government's case in chief, including anticipated cross-examination, the names of witnesses the government intends to call, and a discussion of relevant legal and evidentiary issues as applied to the facts of the particular case. Counsel for the government shall attempt to obtain defense counsel's agreement to the factual summary, statement of the charges, time estimate for cross-examination of the government's witnesses, and legal and evidentiary issues.

2. Counsel shall arrive at the Courtroom no later than 8:30 a.m. on the first day of trial.

3. Counsel for the government shall present the courtroom deputy clerk (CRD) with the following documents on the first day of trial:

a. Three copies of the government's witness list;

b. Three copies of the government's exhibit list in the form specified in Local Rule 16-5 (Civil);

c. A bench book containing a copy of the indictment/ information, a copy of all exhibits that can be reproduced, and a copy of the witness list. Each exhibit shall be tabbed with the exhibit number for easy referral;

d. All of the government's exhibits, with official exhibit tags attached and bearing the same number shown on the exhibit list. Exhibit tags may be obtained from the receptionist in the Public Intake Section, located on the Main Street level of the courthouse at 312 North Spring Street, Room G-19. Exhibits shall be numbered 1, 2, 3, *etc.*, NOT 1.1, 1.2, *etc.* If a "blow-up" is an enlargement of an existing exhibit, it shall be designated with the number of the original exhibit followed by an "A."

4. The Court orders that exhibits such as firearms, narcotics, etc., remain in the custody of a law enforcement agent during the pendency of the trial. It shall be the responsibility of the agent to produce any such items for court, secure them at night and guard them at all times while in the courtroom.

5. Defense counsel need not deliver defense exhibits to the CRD on the first day of trial; however, defense counsel is responsible for affixing completed exhibit tags with the case name and case number to all exhibits to be used in Defendant's case.

6. Defense counsel shall provide a three ring binder, if possible, tabbed with numbers to correspond to the exhibits counsel expects to introduce. Defense counsel shall provide the Court with a copy of defense exhibits as they are introduced during trial.

7. Defense counsel shall provide the CRD and the court reporter with the defense witness list and defense exhibit list.

8. A copy of the exhibit list with all **admitted exhibits** will be given to the jury during deliberations. Government and defense counsel shall review and approve the exhibit list with the CRD before the list is given to the jury.

9. If any counsel wishes to arrange for the use of additional equipment, such as video monitors, overhead projectors, etc., counsel shall notify the CRD no later than 4:00 p.m. at least one week before trial so that the necessary arrangements may be made.

10. Counsel shall not attempt to display or use any charts or enlargements of exhibits unless all counsel have agreed to their use or objections have been heard and a ruling has been made by the Court.

11. On the day of jury selection, trial will begin at 9:00 a.m. Counsel will appear at 8:30 a.m. Thereafter, trial days are Tuesday through Friday, 9:00 a.m. to 4:30 p.m., with two fifteen-minute breaks during the morning and afternoon sessions. If counsel contemplate that this schedule will be problematic due to the unavailability of witnesses, counsel should provide details to the Court at the Status Conference.

12. Before trial begins, the Court will give counsel an opportunity to discuss administrative matters and anticipated procedural or legal issues. Before trial begins, and as soon as the information becomes available to counsel, counsel should advise the court of any concerns or accommodations that are requested for parties or witnesses. During trial, if there are any matters to be discussed outside the presence of the jury, counsel shall advise the CRD of the request. The Court discourages sidebars during trial.

13. On the day of jury selection, the Court reserves the time from 8:30 a.m. to 9:00 a.m. to handle legal and administrative matters. Jury selection will commence promptly at 9:00 a.m. or as soon as jurors are available. Thereafter, legal and administrative matters shall be addressed between 8:30 a.m. and 9:00 a.m. All counsel are urged to anticipate matters that may need to be addressed outside of the presence of the jury and to raise them during this period, during breaks, or at the end of the day. The Court does not make jurors wait while counsel discuss matters that should have been addressed previously. Counsel are urged to consider any unusual substantive or evidentiary issues that may arise, and to advise the Court of such issues. Short briefs addressing such disputed issues are welcome.

14. Should counsel for the government wish to order transcripts, they shall

provide agency authorization to the court reporter at the time the request is made.

15. NOTE: Counsel for both parties are instructed not to bring excessive exhibits to trial, but only those exhibits that will actually be used.

D. JURY INSTRUCTIONS, VERDICT FORMS & QUESTIONNAIRES

1. **No later than one week before trial**, counsel shall submit both general and substantive jury instructions in the form described below. If possible, all instructions should be taken from the *Manual of Model Criminal Jury Instructions for the Ninth Circuit* (West Publishing, current edition). In those cases where a special verdict is requested, counsel shall submit a proposed verdict form with the jury instructions. Counsel shall submit the proposed instructions and a "clean" set of such instructions, as set forth below.

2. The parties must submit JOINT jury instructions and a JOINT proposed verdict form (if a special verdict is requested). In order to produce these joint instructions, the parties shall meet and confer sufficiently in advance of the required submission date, with the goal of agreeing on instructions and verdict forms. Where the parties cannot agree, disputed instructions shall be submitted one week before trial as follows: 1) JOINT jury instructions (those instructions agreed to by all parties), and 2) DISPUTED jury instructions (those instructions propounded by a party to which another party objects). On a separate page following each disputed jury instruction, the party opposing the instruction shall briefly state the basis for the objection, any authority in support thereof and, if applicable, an alternative instruction. On the following page, the party proposing the disputed instruction shall briefly state its response to the objection, and any authority in support of the instruction. Each requested jury instruction shall be numbered and set forth in full on a separate page, citing the authority or source of the requested instruction.

3. Jury instructions should be modified as necessary to fit the facts of the case (*e.g.*, inserting names of defendant(s) to whom instruction applies). Where language appears in brackets in the model instruction, counsel shall select the appropriate text and eliminate the inapplicable bracketed text. Where no applicable Ninth Circuit model instruction is available, counsel are directed to use the instructions from O'Malley, Grenig & Lee (formerly Devitt, et al.), *Federal Jury Practice and Instructions* (West Publishing Co., current edition).

4. An index page shall accompany all jury instructions submitted to the Court. The index page shall indicate the following:

a. The number of the instruction;
b. A brief title of the instruction;
c. The source of the instruction; and
d. The page number of the instruction.

EXAMPLE:

Number	Title	Source	Page Number
#1	Conspiracy-Elements	9th Cir.8.5.1	1

5. One or more copies of the instructions will be given to the jury during deliberations. Accordingly, counsel shall summit a "clean" set of all instructions, containing only the text of each instruction, set forth in full on each page, with the caption "Court's Instruction No. __" (eliminating titles, supporting authority, indication of party proposing, *etc.*)

6. If counsel wish to submit a written questionnaire to prospective jurors, a motion shall be made in writing, with the proposed questionnaire attached, no later than eight weeks before the trial date. The Court does not routinely use questionnaires. Counsel should

attempt to discuss this issue and reach a proposed agreement before submitting the motion to the Court.

7. At least one week before trial, each counsel must file with the CRD and serve on opposing counsel any proposed questions to be asked of prospective jurors. Counsel shall also file a Joint Statement of the Case which the Court will read to prospective jurors prior to the commencement of voir dire. The statement shall not exceed one page

E. INSTRUCTIONS GOVERNING PROCEDURE DURING TRIAL

1. Counsel shall not refer to any witness – including a client – over 14 years of age by his/her first name.

2. Counsel shall not discuss the law or argue the case in opening statements.

3. Counsel shall not use objections for the purpose of making a speech, recapitulating testimony, or attempting to guide the witness. When objecting, counsel shall stand, state only the legal ground of the objection, *e.g.*, hearsay, irrelevant, *etc.* Counsel shall not argue an objection before the jury. Requests to approach sidebar to further argue an objection should be made sparingly, and may not be granted.

4. Counsel shall not make facial expressions, nod, or shake their heads, comment or otherwise exhibit in any way any agreement, disagreement or other opinion or belief concerning the testimony of a witness. Counsel shall admonish their clients and witnesses not to engage in such conduct.

5. Counsel should not talk to jurors at all, and should not talk to co-counsel, opposing counsel, witnesses or clients where the conversation can be overheard by jurors. Each counsel should admonish counsel's own clients and witnesses to avoid such conduct.

6. Counsel shall question witnesses from the lectern. Counsel shall not approach the witness box or enter the well without the Court's permission, and shall return to the lectern when counsel's purpose has been accomplished.

7. Counsel should speak clearly when questioning witnesses, making objections, etc.

8. No document shall be placed before a witness unless a copy has been provided to the Court. Counsel may consider such devices as overhead projectors, jury notebooks for admitted exhibits, or enlargements of important exhibits. The Court has an Elmo and other equipment available for use during trial. Call the CRD if you wish to visit when the Court is not in session to practice using the equipment. The Court does not permit exhibits to be "published" by passing them up and down the jury box. Exhibits may be displayed using the screen in the courtroom.

9. Water will be provided at counsel table. Water cups are not to be brought to the lectern. No other beverages are permitted in the courtroom. Food is not permitted in the courtroom.

10. Counsel shall rise when addressing the Court. In jury trials, counsel and the defendant shall rise when the jury enters or leaves the courtroom. [Special procedures or exceptions may apply when the defendant is in custody or restrained.]

11. In trial, all remarks shall be addressed to the Court. Counsel shall not directly address the CRD, the court reporter or opposing counsel. All requests for rereading of questions or answers, or to have an exhibit placed in front of a witness, shall be addressed to the Court

12. Counsel should not offer a stipulation without having first conferred and reached an agreement with opposing counsel. Any stipulation of fact will require defendant's personal concurrence and shall be submitted to the Court in writing for approval. A proposed stipulation should be explained to defendant in advance.

13. While court is in session, counsel shall not leave counsel table to confer with investigators, paralegals, or witnesses unless permission is granted in advance.

14. When a party has more than one lawyer, only one lawyer may conduct the examination of a given witness, and only that same lawyer may handle objections during the testimony of that witness.

15. If a witness was on the stand at a recess or adjournment, counsel who called the witness shall ensure the witness is back on the stand and ready to proceed when court resumes.

16. Counsel are directed to have witnesses available throughout the court day. If no witnesses are available and there is more than a brief delay, the Court may deem counsel to have rested.

17. The Court attempts to cooperate with expert witnesses and other professionals, and will, except in extraordinary circumstances, accommodate them by permitting them to be called out of sequence. Counsel are urged to anticipate any such possibility and to discuss it with opposing counsel. If there is an objection, counsel shall confer with the Court in advance.

18. Counsel must notify the CRD in advance if any witness should be accommodated based on the Americans with Disabilities Act or for other reasons.

19. Counsel are advised to be on time, as the Court makes every effort to start promptly.

IT IS SO ORDERED.

Dated: ________________

____
OTIS D. WRIGHT II
United States District Judge

B. Scheduling and Case Management Order

IN THE UNITED STATES DISTICT COURT
FOR THE CENTRAL DISTRICT OF CALIFORNIA

)	Case No. ______________
Plaintiff(s),)	
v.)	**SCHEDULING AND CASE**
Defendant(s).)	**MANAGEMENT ORDER FOR**
____________________)	**CASES ASSIGNED TO**
	JUDGE OTIS D. WRIGHT II

This Order is to advise the parties and counsel of the schedule that will govern this case. **THE SCHEDULING CONFERENCE IS VACATED. SEE THE LAST PAGE OF THIS ORDER FOR THE SPECIFIED DATES.** Ordinarily, the dates set forth on the last page are determined after consultation with the parties at the Fed. R. Civ. P. 16(b) Scheduling Conference. The dates and requirements are firm. The Court is unlikely to grant continuances, even if stipulated by the parties, unless the parties establish good cause through a concrete showing.

IT IS HEREBY ORDERED:

1. To secure the just, speedy and inexpensive determination of every action, all counsel are ordered to familiarize themselves with and follow the Federal Rules of Civil Procedure and the Local Rules of the Central District of California. This Court follows these rules and they will govern this litigation.

2. Because this Order in some respects modifies or adds to the Local Rules, counsel are advised to read it carefully. Counsel are advised to pay particular attention to the requirements of the Court with respect to the filing of motions for summary judgment and documents to be submitted at the Final Pretrial Conference and Trial.

3. The attorney attending any proceeding before this court must be an attorney who is thoroughly knowledgeable about the case, responsible for the conduct of the litigation, and who has authority to enter into stipulations and to make admissions regarding all matters that the participants reasonably anticipate may be discussed. Lead counsel who will actually try the case must attend the Pretrial Conference. A party who is not represented must attend all proceedings in person.

4. **<u>COURTESY COPIES:</u>** Courtesy copies of all electronically filed documents are to be delivered to the courtesy box outside chambers by 3:00 p.m. the following business day. ***Any original filings (such as under seal documents) are to be filed at the filing window (Clerk's Office, Room G-19), NOT in chambers and NOT in the courtroom.***

   Courtesy copies DO NOT need to be blue-backed. All courtesy copies of pretrial documents (e.g. witness lists, exhibit lists, pretrial conference orders, jury instructions, etc.) shall be three-hole punched.

5. **<u>DISCOVERY CUT-OFF:</u>** All discovery shall be completed by the discovery cut-off date specified on the last page of this Order. **THIS IS NOT THE DATE BY WHICH DISCOVERY REQUESTS MUST BE SERVED; IT IS THE DATE BY WHICH ALL DISCOVERY IS TO BE COMPLETED.**

Any motion challenging the adequacy of responses to discovery must be heard sufficiently in advance of the discovery cut-off date to permit the responses to be obtained before that date if the motion is granted. In an effort to provide further guidance to the parties, the Court notes the following:

a. **Depositions:** All depositions shall be scheduled to commence sufficiently in advance of the discovery cut-off date to permit their completion and to permit the deposing party enough time to bring any discovery motions concerning the deposition prior to the cut-off date.

b. **Written Discovery:** All interrogatories, requests for production of documents, and requests for admissions shall be served sufficiently in advance of the discovery cut-off date to permit the discovering party enough time to challenge (via motion practice) responses deemed to be deficient.

c. **Discovery Motions:** Whenever possible, the Court expects the parties to resolve discovery issues among themselves in a courteous, reasonable and professional manner. The Magistrate Judge assigned to this case will rule on discovery motions. (The Magistrate Judge's initials follow the district judge's initials next to the case number on the first page of this Order.) Counsel are directed to contact the Magistrate Judge's courtroom deputy clerk (CRD) to schedule a hearing on any discovery related matters. Counsel should not deliver courtesy copies of these discovery documents to this court.

d. **Expert Discovery:** If expert witnesses are to be called at trial, the parties shall designate affirmative experts to be called at trial and provide reports required by Fed. R. Civ. P. 26(a)(2)(B) not later than eight weeks prior to the discovery cut-off date. Rebuttal expert witnesses shall be designated and reports provided as required by Fed. R. Civ. P. 26(a)(2)(B) not later than five weeks prior to the discovery cut-off date. Failure to timely comply with deadlines may result in the expert being excluded as a trial witness.

6. MOTIONS AND MOTION CUT-OFF DATE

a. **General Provisions:** All law and motion matters, except for motions in limine, must be set for hearing (not filing) by the motion cut-off date specified on the last page of this Order.

This Court hears motions in civil matters on Mondays, beginning at 1:30 p.m.

The parties must adhere to the requirements of the Local Rules. See Local Rules 7-1 et seq. If any party does not oppose a motion, that party shall submit a written statement that it does not oppose the motion in accordance with Local Rule 7-9. The parties should note that failure to meet the time limits for filing an opposition set forth in Local Rule 7-9 shall be deemed consent to the granting of the motion. See Local Rule 7-12.

The title page of all motions must state the Pre-Trial Conference date and the Trial date. Counsel must comply with Local Rule 7-3, which requires counsel to engage in a pre-filing conference "to discuss thoroughly . . . the substance of the contemplated motion and any potential resolution."

Issues left undetermined after the passage of the motion cut-off date should be listed as issues for trial in the Final Pre-Trial Conference Order. As an exception to the above, motions in limine dealing with evidentiary matters may be heard pursuant to the schedule specified on the last page of this Order.

Ex parte practice is discouraged. *See Mission Power Eng'g v Co. vs . Continental Cas. Co.*, 883 F. Supp. 488 (C.D. Cal. 1995). The Court will require strict adherence to proper ex parte procedures for any ex parte application filed with the Court. *Id.* at 492; *see also* Judge Wright's Standing Order and Local Rule 7-19.

b. **Applications and Stipulations to Extend Time:** Applications to extend the time to file any required document or to continue any hearing, Pre-Trial Conference or Trial date must set forth the following:

(i) the existing due date or hearing date, as well as the discovery cut-off date, the Pre-Trial Conference date, and the Trial date;

(ii) specific, concrete reasons supporting good cause for granting the extension; and

(iii) whether there have been prior requests for extensions, and

(iv) whether these requests were granted or denied by the Court.

c. **Joinder of Parties and Amendment of Pleadings:** The deadline for joining parties and amending pleadings is ninety days after the date of this Order. Any motions to join other parties or for leave to amend the pleadings shall be filed within sixty days of the date of this Order so that they can be heard and decided prior to the deadline.

In addition to the requirements of Local Rule 15-1, all motions to amend the pleadings shall: (1) state the effect of the amendment; (2) be serially numbered to differentiate the amendment from previous amendments; and (3) state the page, line number(s), and wording of any proposed change or addition of material..

The parties shall deliver to Chambers a redlined version of the proposed amended pleading indicating all additions and deletions of material.

d. **Summary Judgment Motions:** Parties need not wait until the motion cutoff to bring motions for summary judgment or partial summary judgment. However, the court expects that the party moving for summary judgment will provide more than the minimum twenty-eight (28) day notice for motions. Because summary judgment motions are fact-dependent, parties should prepare papers in a fashion that will assist the court in absorbing the mass of facts (e.g., generous use of tabs, tables of contents, headings, indices, etc.). The parties are to comply precisely with Local Rule 56-1 through 56-4. The Court will also require adherence to the following requirements:

(i) Statement of Uncontroverted Facts and Statement of Genuine Issues of Material Fact.

The Separate Statement of Uncontroverted Facts is to be prepared in a two column format. The left-hand column should set forth the allegedly undisputed fact. The right-hand column should set forth the evidence that supports the factual statement. The factual statements should be set forth in sequentially numbered paragraphs. Each paragraph should contain a narrowly focused statement of fact. Each numbered paragraph should address a single subject in as concise a manner as possible.

The opposing party's Statement of Genuine Issues of Material Fact must be in two columns and track the movant's Separate Statement exactly as prepared. The document must be in two columns; the left-hand column must restate the allegedly undisputed fact, and the right-hand column must indicate either undisputed or disputed. The opposing party may dispute all or only a portion of the statement, but if disputing only a portion, must clearly indicate what part is being disputed. Where the opposing party is disputing the fact in whole or part, the opposing party must, in the right-hand column, label and restate the moving party's evidence in the support of the fact, followed by the opposing party's evidence controverting the fact. Where the opposing party is disputing the fact on the basis of an evidentiary objection, the party must cite the evidence alleged to be objectionable and state the ground of the objection and nothing more. **No argument should be set forth in this document.**

The opposing party may submit additional material facts that bear on or relate to the issues raised by the movant, which shall follow the format described above for the moving party's Separate Statement. These additional facts shall follow the movant's facts, shall continue in sequentially numbered paragraphs (i.e. if movant's last statement of fact was set forth in paragraph 30, then the first new fact will be set forth in paragraph 31), and shall set forth in the right-hand column the evidence that supports that statement.

The moving party, in its reply, shall respond to the additional facts in the same manner and format that the opposing party is required to adhere to in responding to the Statement of Uncontroverted Facts, as described above.

(ii) Supporting Evidence. No party should submit any evidence other than the specific items of evidence or testimony necessary to support or controvert a proposed statement of undisputed fact. Thus, for example, the entire transcripts of depositions and/or entire sets of interrogatory responses should generally not be submitted in support of or in opposition to a motion for summary judgment.

Evidence submitted in support of or in opposition to a motion for summary judgment should be submitted either by way of stipulation or as exhibits to a declaration sufficient to authenticate the proffered evidence, and should not be attached to the memorandum of points and authorities. The Court will accept counsel's authentication of deposition transcripts, written discovery responses, and the receipt of documents in discovery *if the fact that the document was in the opponent's possession is of independent significance.* Documentary evidence as to which there is no stipulation regarding foundation must be accompanied by the testimony, either by declaration or properly authenticated deposition transcript, of a witness who can establish its authenticity.

All evidence in support of or in opposition to a motion for summary judgment, including declarations and exhibits to declarations, shall be separated by a tab divider on the bottom of the page. If evidence in support of or in opposition to a motion for summary judgment exceeds twenty pages, the evidence must be in a separately bound volume and include a Table of Contents. If the supporting evidence exceeds fifty pages, the documents shall be placed in a Slant D-Ring binder with each item of evidence separated by a tab divider on the right side. All documents contained in the binder should be three-hole-punched.

(iii) Objections to Evidence. If a party disputes a fact based in whole or in part on an evidentiary objection, the ground for the objection, as indicated above, should be stated in the Separate Statement, but not argued in that document. Evidentiary objections should be addressed in a separate memorandum to be filed with the opposition or reply brief of the party. This memorandum should be organized ***to track the paragraph numbers of the Separate Statement in sequence***. It should identify the specific item of evidence to which objection is made, the ground for the objection, and a very brief argument with citation to authority as to why the objection is well taken. The following is an example of the format contemplated by the Court:

Separate Statement Paragraph 1: Objection to the supporting deposition transcript of Jane Smith at 60:1-10 on the grounds that the statement constitutes inadmissible hearsay and no exception is applicable. To the extent it is offered to prove her state of mind, it is irrelevant since her state of mind is not in issue. Fed. R. Evid. 801, 802.

DO NOT SUBMIT BLANKET OR BOILERPLATE OBJECTIONS TO THE OPPONENT'S STATEMENTS OF UNDISPUTED FACT. THESE WILL BE DISREGARDED AND OVERRULED.

(iv) The Memorandum of Points and Authorities. The movant's memorandum of points and authorities should be in the usual form required under Local Rule 7 and should contain a narrative statement of facts as to those aspects of the case that are before the Court. All facts should be supported with citations to the paragraph number in the Separate Statement that supports the factual assertion.

Unless the case involves some unusual twist, the motion need only contain a brief statement of the Fed. R. Civ. P. 56 standard; the Court is familiar with the Rule and with its interpretation under *Celotex* and its progeny. If at all possible, the argument should be organized to focus on the pertinent elements of the claim(s) for relief or defense(s) in issue, with the purpose of showing the existence or non-existence of a genuine issue of material fact for trial on that element of the claim or defense.

Likewise, the opposition memorandum of points and authorities should be in the usual form required by Local Rule 7. Where the opposition memorandum sets forth facts, the memorandum should cite to paragraphs in the Separate Statement if they are not in dispute, to the evidence that contravenes the fact where the fact is in dispute, or, if the fact is contravened by an additional fact in the Statement of Genuine Issues of Material Fact, the citation should be to such fact by paragraph number.

(v) Proposed Statement of Decision. Each party shall file and serve a Proposed Statement of Decision, which shall contain a statement of the relevant facts and applicable law with citations to case law and the record. The Proposed Statement of Decision shall not exceed five pages and shall be in a form that would be appropriate for the Court to enter as its final order on the motion.

(vi) Timing. In virtually every case, the Court expects that the moving party will provide more than the minimum twenty-one day notice for such motions. **[NOTE: Parties need not wait until the motion cut-off to bring motions for summary judgment or partial summary judgment. Early completion of non-expert discovery and filing of motions for summary judgment may eliminate or reduce the need for expensive expert depositions that are normally conducted in the last stages of discovery.]**

e. **Avoid Composite Motions.** Unless clearly justified under the circumstances of the case, "motions to dismiss or in the alternative for summary adjudication" are discouraged. These composite motions tend to blur the distinctions between the two motions.

f. **Motions in Limine.** Before filing any motion in limine, counsel for the parties shall confer pursuant to Local Rule 7-3 in a good faith effort to eliminate the necessity for hearing the motion in limine or to eliminate as many of the disputes as possible. It shall be the responsibility of counsel for the moving party to arrange for this conference. The motion papers must include a declaration showing a good faith meet and confer effort. The conference shall take place in person within ten calendar days of service upon opposing counsel of a letter requesting such a conference, but in no event later than twenty-one days before the Pre-Trial Conference. If both counsel are not located in the same county in the Central District, the conference may take place by telephone.

If counsel are unable to resolve their differences, they shall prepare a separate, sequentially numbered Motion in Limine for each issue in dispute which contains a clear caption which identifies the moving party and the nature of the dispute (i.e., "Plaintiff's Motion in Limine #1 to exclude the testimony of Defendant's expert"). The Motion in Limine shall contain a clear identification of the testimony, exhibits, or other specific matters alleged to be inadmissible and/or prejudicial and a statement of the specific prejudice that will be suffered by the moving party if the motion is not granted. The identification of the matters in dispute shall be followed by the moving party's contentions and memorandum of points and authorities. The title page of the Motion in Limine must state the Pre-Trial Conference date, hearing date for the motions in limine, and the trial date.

Motions in Limine made for the purpose of precluding the mention or display of inadmissible and/or prejudicial matter in the presence of the jury shall be accompanied by a declaration that includes the following: (1) a clear identification of the specific matter alleged to be inadmissible and/or prejudicial; (2) a representation to the Court that the subject of the motion in limine has been discussed with opposing counsel, and that opposing counsel has either indicated that such matter will be mentioned or displayed in the presence of the jury before it is admitted in evidence or that counsel has refused to stipulate that such matter will not be mentioned or displayed in the presence of the jury unless and until it is admitted in evidence; and (3) a statement of the specific prejudice that will be suffered by the moving party if the motion in limine is not granted. Unless ordered otherwise, the Court will only consider the moving papers and any opposition thereto. No replies are necessary.

All evidence in support of or in opposition to a motion in limine, including declarations and exhibits to declarations, shall be separated by a tab divider on the bottom of the page. If evidence in support of or in opposition to a motion in limine exceeds twenty pages, the evidence must be in a separately bound volume and include a Table of Contents. Though strongly discouraged, if by necessity the supporting evidence exceeds fifty pages, the documents shall be placed in a Slant D-Ring binder with each item of evidence separated by a tab divider on the right side. All documents contained in the binder should be three-hole-punched.

Unless otherwise ordered by the Court, motions in limine will be heard on the date specified on the last page of this Order. The moving party shall file with the Court and serve its Motion in Limine on the responding party on or before the date for filing of motions in limine indicated in the Schedule of Trial and Pre-trial Dates. The responding party shall then file with the Court and serve an opposition to the Motion in Limine on the moving party at least seven (7) days prior to the date for the hearing on motions in limine. Neither party's submissions with respect to a Motion in Limine shall exceed eight (8) pages.

7. **FINAL PRE-TRIAL CONFERENCE AND LOCAL RULE 16 FILINGS**
Please read this portion carefully, as there are some differences between the Court's requirements and the Local Rules.

a. **General Provisions.** The Final Pre-Trial Conference ("PTC") will be held on the date specified on the last page of this Order, unless the Court expressly waived the PTC at the Scheduling Conference. (In the rare cases where the Court waives a PTC, the parties must follow Local Rule 16-10.) If adjustments in the Court's calendar to accommodate congestion become necessary, the Court may re-schedule the PTC instead of the trial date. Therefore, the parties should assume that if the PTC goes forward, the trial will go forward without continuance, although some brief period of trailing may prove necessary.

The lead trial attorney on behalf of each party shall attend both the PTC and all meetings of the parties in preparation for the PTC, unless excused for good cause shown in advance of the PTC.

A continuance of the PTC at the parties' request or by stipulation is highly unlikely. **Specifically, failure to complete discovery is not a ground for continuance.** In the unlikely event that the Court agrees to continue the PTC, the trial date is likely to be delayed as a result. If a change to the trial date is necessitated or likely because of the Court's calendar or otherwise, modifications of that date will be discussed at the PTC.

At the PTC, the parties should be prepared to discuss means of streamlining the trial, including, but not limited to the following: bifurcation; presentation of foundational and non-critical testimony and direct testimony by deposition excerpts; narrative summaries and/or stipulations as to the content of testimony; presentation of testimony on direct examination by affidavit or by declaration subject to cross-examination; and qualification of experts by admitted resumes. The Court will also discuss settlement.

b. **Final Pretrial Conference Order ("PTCO").** The proposed PTCO shall be lodged seven calendar days before the PTC. Adherence to this time requirement is necessary for in-chambers preparation of the matter. The form of the proposed PTCO shall comply with Appendix A to the Local Rules and the following:

1. Place in "ALL CAPS" and in "**bold**" the separately numbered headings for each category in the PTCO (e.g., "**1. <u>THE PARTIES</u>**" or "**7. <u>CLAIMS AND DEFENSES OF THE PARTIES</u>**").

2. <u>Include a table of contents at the beginning.</u>

3. In specifying the surviving pleadings under section 1, state which claims or counterclaims have been dismissed or abandoned, *e.g.*, "Plaintiff's second cause of action for breach of fiduciary duty has been dismissed." Also, in multiple party cases where not all claims or counterclaims will be prosecuted against all remaining parties on the opposing side, please specify to which party each claim or counterclaim is directed.

4. In specifying the parties' claims and defenses under section 7, each party shall closely follow the examples set forth in Appendix A of the Local Rules.

5. In drafting the PTCO, the court expects that the parties will attempt to to agree on and set forth as many non-contested facts as possible. The court will usually read the uncontested facts to the jury at the start of trial. A carefully drafted and comprehensively stated stipulation of facts will reduce the length of trial and increase jury understanding of the case. It is unacceptable for the parties to indicate in the Proposed Pretrial Conference Order that they are not able to stipulate to any facts whatever.

6. In drafting the factual issues in dispute for the PTCO, the parties should attempt to state issues in ultimate fact form, not in the form of evidentiary fact issues. The issues of fact should track the elements of a claim or defense on which the jury will be required to make findings.

7. Issues of law should state legal issues on which the court will be required to rule during the trial, and should not list ultimate fact issues to be submitted to the trier of fact.

8. The Court may submit fact issues to the jury in the form of findings on a special verdict. The issues of fact should track the elements of a claim or defense on which the jury will be required to make findings.

9. If expert witnesses are to be called at trial, each party must list and identify its respective expert witnesses, both retained and non-retained. Failure of a party to list and identify an expert witness in the PTCO could result in a court order which precludes the party from calling that expert witness at trial.

c. **<u>Rule 16 Filings; Memoranda; Witness Lists; Exhibit Lists.</u>** Unless otherwise indicated, the parties must comply fully with the requirements of Local Rule 16. See the last page of this Order for applicable dates.

<u>Memorandum of Contentions of Fact and Law:</u> Memoranda of Contentions of Fact and Law shall be filed by the date listed in this Scheduling Order, and shall comply with the requirements set forth in Local Rule 16-4.

Witnesses: Counsel shall prepare a **joint** list of their witnesses, including a brief summary (two to three paragraphs) of each witness's expected testimony, **what makes the testimony unique** from any other witness testimony, an estimate of the length of time needed for direct examination of each side's own witnesses and an estimate for the cross examination of opposing witnesses, and whether the witness will testify by deposition or in person. The joint witness list shall be filed at the same time counsel lodge the PTC Order. If a party intends to offer deposition testimony into evidence at trial, the party shall designate the relevant portions of the deposition testimony to be read at trial and advise opposing counsel of same. Opposing counsel shall then designate any additional portions of such deposition testimony which counsel intends to offer in evidence. All objections to any such testimony shall be made in writing and filed at the same time counsel lodge the PTC Order so that the Court may consider whether ruling on the objections will facilitate trial or result in the disposition of evidentiary matters that may assist continuing settlement negotiations.

If expert witnesses are to be called at trial, each party shall list and identify their respective expert witnesses. Failure of a party to list and identify an expert witness may preclude a party from calling that expert witness at trial. If expert witnesses are to be called at trial, the parties shall exchange at the PTC short narrative statements of the qualifications of the expert and the testimony expected to be elicited at trial. Previously prepared and exchanged expert reports shall not substitute for the narrative statements required.

Exhibits: The parties shall prepare a Pre-Trial Exhibit Stipulation that shall contain each party's numbered list of all trial exhibits, with objections, if any, to each exhibit including the basis of the objection and the offering party's response. All exhibits to which there is no objection shall be deemed admitted. The parties shall stipulate to the authenticity of exhibits whenever possible, and the Pre-Trial Exhibit Stipulation shall identify any exhibits for which authenticity has not been stipulated to and the specific reasons for the party's failure to stipulate.

The Stipulation shall be substantially in the following form:

Pre-Trial Exhibit Stipulation

Plaintiff(s)'/Defendant(s)' Exhibits

Number	**Description**	**If Objection, State Grounds**	**Response to Objection**

The Pre-Trial Exhibit Stipulation shall be filed at the same time counsel lodge the (Proposed) PTC Order. Failure to comply with this paragraph could be deemed to constitute a waiver of all objections. Do not submit blanket or boilerplate objections to the opposing party's exhibits. These will be disregarded and overruled. NOTE: Counsel are instructed not to bring excessive exhibits to trial, but only those exhibits that are reasonably expected to actually be used.

Jury Instructions/Special Verdict Forms. The parties shall make every attempt to agree upon the jury instructions before submitting them to the Court. It is expected that counsel will agree on the substantial majority of jury instructions. This is in addition to the standard cautionary and introductory instructions regarding duties of the jury, the order of the trial, etc. found in Chapters 1, 2 & 3 of the *9th Circuit Manual of Model Jury Instructions.* The court requires little or no assistance in the preparation of these instructions. Counsels' attention should be focused on reaching agreement on the instructions covering the substantive legal issues. It is anticipated that working diligently and cooperatively counsel will be able to reach agreement on the vast majority of the substantive instructions. Judicial involvement will be limited to resolving disputes on only a few instructions on which the parties are unable to agree.

On the date listed in this Scheduling Order, counsel shall file with the Court a JOINT set of jury instructions on which there is agreement. Defendant's counsel has the burden of preparing the joint set of jury instructions. At the same time each party shall file its proposed jury instructions which are objected to by any other party, accompanied by points and authorities in support of those instructions.

When the parties disagree on an instruction, the party opposing the instruction must attach a short statement (one to two paragraphs) supporting the objection, and the party submitting the instruction must attach a short reply supporting the instruction. Each statement should be on a separate page and should follow directly after the disputed instruction.

The parties ultimately must submit one document, or if the parties disagree over any proposed jury instructions, three documents. The three documents shall consist of: (1) a set of Joint Proposed Jury Instructions; (2) Plaintiff's Disputed Jury Instructions; and (3) Defendant's Disputed Jury Instructions. Any disputed Jury Instructions shall include the reasons supporting and opposing each disputed instruction in the format set forth in the previous paragraph.

The Court directs counsel to use the instructions from the *Manual of Model Jury Instructions for the Ninth Circuit* where applicable. Where California law is to be applied and the above instructions are not applicable, the Court prefers counsel to use the California Jury Instructions in CACI. If none of these sources is applicable, counsel are directed to use the instructions in Devitt, Blackmar and Wolff, *Federal Jury Practice and Instructions.*

Modifications of instructions from the foregoing sources (or any other form instructions) must specifically state the modification made to the original form instruction and the authority supporting the modification.

Each requested instruction shall be in the format specified by Local Rule 51-2 and shall be set forth in full; be on a separate page with the caption "COURT'S INSTRUCTION NUMBER"; be numbered; cover only one subject or principle of law; not repeat principles of law contained in any other requested instructions; and cite the authority for a source of the requested instruction. In addition to the foregoing, each party shall file with the Courtroom Deputy Clerk (CRD) on the first day of trial a "clean set" of the aforesaid requested duplicate jury instructions. The "clean set" shall not cite the authority for a source of the requested instruction.

An index page shall accompany all jury instructions submitted to the Court. The index page shall indicate the following:

- the number of the instruction;
- a brief title of the instruction;
- the source of the instruction and any relevant case citation; and

- the page number of the instruction.

EXAMPLE:

NO.	TITLE	SOURCE	PAGE NO.
5	Evidence for Limited Purpose	9th Cir. 1.5	9

During the trial and again before argument, the Court will meet with counsel and settle the instructions. Strict adherence to time requirements is necessary for the Court to examine the submissions in advance so that there will be no delay in starting the jury trial, or the final instructions to the jury and the closing arguments of counsel. **Failure of counsel to strictly follow the provisions of this section may subject the non-complying party and/or its attorney to sanctions and SHALL CONSTITUTE A WAIVER OF JURY TRIAL in all civil cases.**

Joint Statement of the Case and Requests for Voir Dire. At the PTC, the parties shall file their proposed voir dire questions and their joint Statement of the Case which the Court will read to all prospective jurors prior to the commencement of voir dire. The statement should not be longer than two or three paragraphs, and contain no argument nor an excessive amount of information. The Statement of the Case is merely to advise the prospective jurors of the general nature of the case, i.e. securities law violations, bank robbery, copyright infringement, etc.

The Court conducts voir dire of all prospective jurors. The parties need not submit requests for standard voir dire questions such as education, current occupations, marital status, prior jury service, etc., but should include only proposed questions specifically tailored to the parties and issues of the case.

Trial Exhibits: Counsel are to prepare their exhibits for presentation at the trial by placing them in binders which are indexed by exhibit number with tabs or dividers on the right side. Counsel shall submit to the Court an original and one copy of the binders. The exhibits shall be in a three-ring binder labeled on the spine portion of the binder as to the volume number and contain an index of each exhibit included in the volume. Exhibits must be numbered in accordance with Fed. R. Civ. P. 16, 26 and the Local Rules. **NOTE:** Counsel are instructed not to bring excessive exhibits to trial, but only those exhibits that will actually be used.

The exhibit list shall indicate which exhibits are objected to, the reason for the objection, and the reason it is admissible. Failure to object will result in a waiver of objection.

The Court requires that the following be submitted to the Courtroom Deputy Clerk on the first day of trial:

- The original exhibits with the Court's exhibit tags, which shall be stapled to the front of the exhibit on the upper right-hand corner with the case number, case name, and exhibit number placed on each tag. Exhibit tags can be obtained from the Clerk's Office, Room G-8, 312 North Spring Street, Los Angeles, CA 90012.
- One bench book with a copy of each exhibit for use by the Court, tabbed with numbers as described above. (Court's exhibit tags not necessary.)

- Three (3) copies of the exhibit list.
- Three (3) copies of the witness list, which shall include the names of the witness in the approximate order in which the they may be called to testify.
- All counsel are to meet not later than ten (10) days before trial and to stipulate so far as is possible as to foundation, waiver of the best evidence rule, and to those exhibits which may be received into evidence at the start of trial. The exhibits to be so received will be noted on the copies of the exhibit lists.
- Any items that have not been admitted into evidence and are left in the courtroom overnight without prior approval will be discarded.

Real-Time Reporting Requirement: Each party must file with the Court, at the same time counsel lodges the PTCO, a document for the Court Reporter that contains proper names, unusual or scientific terms, or any other foreign or uncommon words that are likely to be used by the parties during the FPTC and the Trial.

d. Court Trials

Declarations of Witness Direct Testimony: Counsel in non-jury trials may submit the direct testimony of their witnesses in writing in a declaration executed under penalty of perjury. These declarations shall be in admissible form with appropriate foundation established for the declarant's statements. Paragraphs in each declaration shall be numbered consecutively to facilitate the identification of paragraphs for evidentiary objections.

Counsel are to exchange and file these declarations with the Court at least eleven calendar days before trial, unless otherwise ordered by the Court. Seven calendar days before trial, counsel may file evidentiary objections to those declarations. Counsel shall prepare a separate document for each declaration for which they have an evidentiary objection in which they shall quote the specific language from the declaration to which they object, followed by the objection and any relevant argument. Counsel shall file any reply or response to the objections by noon on the fourth calendar day before trial. Courtesy copies of the declarations and evidentiary objections shall be deposited in the drop box located in the entrance way to Chambers on the date due. Do not submit blanket or boilerplate objections to the opposing party's witness declarations. These will be disregarded and overruled.

At trial, the Court will rule on the evidentiary objections and, depending upon the ruling, the declarations will be received in evidence, either in whole or in part, or rejected. Counsel will then conduct the cross-examination and re-direct examination at trial.

Failure to comply with the literal terms of this Order will result in sanctions or the Court may refuse to allow that witness to testify.

Trial Briefs: Counsel for each party shall file and serve a trial brief, not to exceed 15 pages in length, at least seven (7) days before the scheduled final pretrial conference.

Findings of Fact and Conclusions of Law: Counsel for each party shall lodge and serve initial proposed findings of fact and conclusions of law with the trial brief. Counsel shall then:

(1) Underline in red the portions which it disputes;
(2) Underline in blue the portions which it admits; and
(3) Underline in yellow the portions which it does not dispute, but deems irrelevant.

Counsel may agree with a part of a finding or conclusion, disagree with a part of it, and/or consider a part of it irrelevant.

Two marked copies of opposing counsel's proposed findings of fact and conclusions of law shall be lodged with Court no later than seven (7) days after the final pretrial conference.

8. SETTLEMENT

This court will not conduct settlement conferences in non-jury cases unless counsel for all parties and their respective clients agree either in writing or on the record. In jury cases, the Court will conduct a settlement conference at the parties' joint request if three conditions exist:

a. The parties are satisfied that the fact issues in the case will be tried by a jury;

b. All significant pre-trial rulings which the Court must make have been made; and

c. The parties desire the Court to conduct the conference, understanding that if settlement fails, the Court will preside over trial of the case.

The parties must file a Status Report regarding settlement at the time they lodge the Proposed Final Pre-Trial Conference Order. This Report shall not disclose the parties' settlement positions, i.e., the terms of any offers or demands. It shall merely describe the efforts made by the parties to resolve the dispute informally, i.e., the occasions and dates when the parties participated in mediation or settlement conferences. The Status report shall also include the name and phone number of the Settlement Officer who assisted the parties with their settlement conference.

Caveat: If counsel fail to file the required Pre-Trial documents or fail to appear at the Pre-Trial Conference and such failure is not otherwise satisfactorily explained to the Court: (a) the cause shall stand dismissed for failure to prosecute if such failure occurs on the part of the plaintiff; (b) default judgment shall be entered if such failure occurs on the part of the defendant; or (c) the Court may take such action as it deems appropriate.

Dated: March 13, 2012

OTIS D. WRIGHT II
United States District Judge

JUDGE OTIS D. WRIGHT II
SCHEDULE OF TRIAL AND PRE-TRIAL DATES

Event	Date
Jury Trial at **9:00 a.m.** Estimated length: _________	
Last Date to File Final Pretrial Exhibit Stipulation	
Hearing on Motions in Limine at **2:30 p.m.**	
Pre-Trial Conference at **2:30 p.m.**; Deadline to File Motions In Limine, Proposed Voir Dire Questions and an Agreed-to Statement of Case	
Deadline to: Lodge Proposed Pretrial Conference Order & Pretrial Exhibit Stipulation; File Contentions of Fact and Law, Exhibit and Witness Lists, Status Report Regarding Settlement, Agreed Upon Set of Jury Instructions and Verdict Forms, Joint Statement Re Disputed Jury Instructions, Verdicts, etc.	
Last date for hearing motions at **1:30 p.m.**	
Last date to conduct Settlement Conference	
Discovery cut-off	
Last date to amend pleadings or add parties	

* Motions for class certification shall be filed in accordance with Local Rule 23-3.

C. *Scheduling Conference Order*

IN THE UNITED STATES DISTICT COURT
FOR THE CENTRAL DISTRICT OF CALIFORNIA

Plaintiff(s),)	Case No. ____________
v.)	**SCHEDULING MEETING OF COUNSEL [FRCP 16, 26(f)]**
Defendant(s).)	
____________________________________)	**SCHEDULING CONFERENCE** set for ______, at 1:30 p.m. **[FRCP 26(f)]**

This case has been assigned to the calendar of United States District Judge Otis D. Wright II. The responsibility for the progress of litigation in the federal courts falls not only upon the attorneys in the action, but upon the court as well.

In order "to secure the just, speedy, and inexpensive determination of every action," (Fed. R. Civ. P. 1), all counsel are hereby ordered to familiarize themselves with the Federal Rules of Civil Procedure and the Local Rules of the Central District of California.

Counsel please note the changes made to former Local Rule 6, now superseded by Fed. R. Civ. P. 16 and 26(f), effective December 1, 2000. A Scheduling Conference is set for the date and time set forth in the caption.[1] Counsel shall meet at least twenty-one (21) days in advance of the Scheduling Conference to prepare a jointly signed report for the court to be submitted no less than fourteen (14) days before the Scheduling Conference. The report is to contain the items set forth below. Pursuant to Fed. R. Civ. P. 16(c), the parties shall be represented by counsel with authority to enter into stipulations regarding all matters pertaining to conduct of the case.

The joint report to be submitted shall contain the items listed in Fed. R. Civ. P. 26(f), the parties' recommendations and agreements, if any, about the final scheduling order as listed in Fed. R. Civ. P. 16(b)(1) through (6), and those items listed in Fed. R. Civ. P. 16(c) which counsel believe will be useful to discuss at the Scheduling Conference. Items which must be listed are the following:

(1) a listing and proposed schedule of written discovery, depositions, and a proposed discovery cut-off date;

(2) a listing and proposed schedule of law and motion matters, and a proposed dispositive motion cut-off date;

(3) a statement of what efforts have been made to settle or resolve the case to date and what settlement procedure is recommended pursuant to Local Rule 16-15.4 (specifically excluding any statement of the terms discussed);

(4) an estimated length of trial and a proposed date for the Final Pretrial Conference and for Trial;

---

1 Unless there is a likelihood that upon motion by a party the Court would order that any or all discovery is premature, it is advisable for counsel to begin to conduct discovery actively before the Scheduling Conference required by Fed. R. Civ. P. 16(b). At the very least, the parties shall comply fully with the letter and spirit of Fed. R. Civ. P. 26(a) and thereby obtain and produce most of what would be produced in the early stage of discovery, because at the Scheduling Conference the Court will impose tight deadlines to complete discovery.

(5) a discussion of other parties likely to be added;

(6) whether trial will be by jury or to the court;

(7) any other issues affecting the status or management of the case; and

(8) proposals regarding severance, bifurcation or other ordering of proof.

In addition, the Scheduling Conference Report shall contain the following:

(1) a short synopsis of the principal issues in the case;

(2) a statement of whether pleadings are likely to be amended;

(3) a statement as to issues which any party believes may be determined by motion.[2]

At the Scheduling Conference, the court will set a date for discovery cutoff,[3] a final date by which dispositive motions must be set for hearing, a Final Pretrial Conference date, and a trial date. A continuance of the Scheduling Conference will be granted only for good cause. (Counsel are informed that continuance of the Scheduling Conference causes commensurate delay in the trial date.) **The failure to submit a joint report in advance of the Scheduling Conference or the failure to attend the Scheduling Conference may result in the dismissal of the action, striking the answer and entering a default, and/or the imposition of sanctions.**

A settlement procedure appropriate to the particular case will be used in every civil action pursuant to Local Rule 16-15.1. In the Scheduling Conference Report, counsel are to recommend a specific settlement procedure provided for in Local Rule 16-15 which will be utilized in this case. Available alternatives for consideration, not to the exclusion of others, include:

(1) a settlement conference before the magistrate or district judge assigned to this case (Local Rule 16-15.4(1));

(2) appearance before an attorney selected from the Attorney Settlement Officer Panel (Local Rule 16-15.4(2));

(3) appearance before a retired judicial officer or other private or non-profit dispute resolution body for non-judicial settlement or mediation proceedings (Local Rule 16-15.4(3));

(4) such other settlement mechanism proposed by the parties and approved by the court.

The report to the court as to the above items should be preceded by a thorough and

---

[2] Where the Plaintiff's claim is predicated in whole or in part on denial of benefits under a plan regulated by the Employee Retirement Income Security Act of 1974, 29 U.S.C. § 1000 et seq. (ERISA), the parties shall address the following additional issues in their Joint Report: (1) Standard of Review: What standard of review is applicable? If the parties are in disagreement, they shall propose a schedule for early briefing and decision of this issue on Motion; and (2) Pre-emption: Is there any contention that any state-law claim asserted by Plaintiff is pre-empted by ERISA? If so, the parties shall propose a schedule for early briefing and decision of the issue on Motion.

[3] This is not the date by which discovery requests must be served; but the date by which all discovery is to be completed. Any motion challenging the adequacy of discovery responses must be filed timely, served and calendared sufficiently in advance of the discovery cutoff date to permit the responses to be obtained before that date, if the motion is granted. The Court requires compliance with Local Rule 37-1 and 37-2 in the preparation and filing of discovery motions. Except in the case of an extreme emergency which was not created by the lawyer bringing the motion, discovery motions may not be heard on an ex parte basis.

frank discussion among the attorneys for the parties. A Joint Scheduling Report which does not comply with FRCP 16, 26(f) and this Order may cause continuance of the Scheduling Conference and possible award of sanctions under FRCP 16(f) against the party or parties responsible. **A conformed courtesy** copy of the Joint Report shall be delivered to the courtesy box on the wall outside the entrance to chambers on the Spring Street level of the U.S. Courthouse, 312 North Spring Street, **by 3:00 p.m. the following business day**.

Motions shall be filed in accordance with Local Rule 7; the next available motion date can be found on the Court's motion calendar, which can be viewed on the Court's website.[4] This Court hears motions on **Mondays, commencing at 1:30 p.m. No supplemental brief shall be filed without prior leave of Court.** Conformed courtesy copies of **opposition and reply papers** shall be delivered to the courtesy box on the wall outside the entrance to chambers on the Spring Street level of the U.S. Courthouse, 312 North Spring Street, **by 3:00 p.m. the following business day**. Adherence to the timing requirements is mandatory for chambers' preparation of motion matters.

Counsel should take note of the changes to the Local Rules affecting motion practice in the Central District. Among other things, Local Rule 7-3 requires counsel to engage in a pre-filing conference "to discuss thoroughly . . . the substance of the contemplated motion and any potential resolution." Counsel should discuss the issues sufficiently that if a motion is still necessary, the briefing may be directed to those substantive issues requiring resolution by the Court. Counsel should resolve minor procedural or other nonsubstantive matters during the conference.

Memoranda of Points and Authorities in support of or in opposition to motions shall not exceed 25 pages. Replies shall not exceed 12 pages. Only in rare instances and for good cause shown will the Court grant an application to extend these page limitations. **Typeface shall comply with Local Rule 11-3.1.1. NOTE: Times New Roman font must be used and the size must be no less than 14.** Footnotes shall be in typeface no less than two sizes smaller than text size and shall be used sparingly. Filings which do not conform to the Local Rules and this Order will not be considered.

Each party filing or opposing a motion or seeking the determination of any matter shall serve and lodge a Proposed Order setting forth the relief or action sought and a brief statement of the rationale for the decision with appropriate citations.

Counsel are reminded ex parte applications are solely for extraordinary relief. *See Mission Power Engineering Co. v. Continental Casualty Co.*, 883 F.Supp. 488 (C.D. Cal. 1995).

Counsel for plaintiff shall immediately serve this Order on all parties, including any new parties to the action.

IT IS SO ORDERED.

DATED: ________________

____
OTIS D. WRIGHT II
United States District Judge

4 All law and motion matters, except for motions in limine, must be set for hearing (not filing) by the motion cutoff date.

D. *Self-Representation Order*

IN THE UNITED STATES DISTICT COURT
FOR THE CENTRAL DISTRICT OF CALIFORNIA

Plaintiff(s),	)	Case No. _______________
v.	)	**SELF-REPRESENTATION ORDER**
Defendant(s).	)	
______________________________	)	

One or more of the parties to this action has elected to appear *pro se*. Persons appearing before this Court are not required to retain the services of a lawyer or obtain the advice of counsel. Individual litigants may represent themselves *pro se*, but corporations and associations must be represented by counsel. *See Church of the New Testament v. United States*, 783 F.2d 771, 773 (9th Cir. 1986) (unincorporated associations); *In re Highley*, 459 F.2d 554, 555 (9th Cir. 1972) (corporations). In addition, non-attorney litigants may not represent other individual litigants or trusts for which they serve as trustee. *See Johns v. County of San Diego*, 114 F.3d 874, 876 (9th Cir. 1997) (minor children); *C.E. Pope Equity Trust v. United States*, 818 F.2d 696, 697-98 (9th Cir. 1987) (trust); *McShane v. United States*, 366 F.2d 286, 288 (9th Cir. 1996) (other litigants). A partner may not represent his or her own interest in a partnership *pro se*, and a sole shareholder may not represent a corporation. *See In re Am. West Airlines*, 40 F.3d 1058, 1059 (9th Cir. 1994) (*per curiam*) (partner); *United States v. High Country Broad. Co., Inc.*, 3 F.3d 1244, 1245 (9th Cir. 1993) (*per curiam*) (shareholder).

Proceeding *pro se* is not without its pitfalls, and this Court wishes to make those pitfalls known at the outset of this proceeding:

- Generally speaking, non-attorney litigants are less likely to be victorious than those assisted by counsel.
- The opposing party may have a lawyer, and that lawyer will show you no mercy. That lawyer's duty is to achieve victory for his or her client. He or she will take every step legally permissible to that end.
- The Court is a neutral adjudicator of the law. The role of the judge is to resolve disputes arising between the parties in accordance with the law. As such, the judge cannot assist you, cannot answer your legal questions, and cannot take sides in the dispute. Nor can any members of the judge's staff.
- You will be proceeding alone in a complex area where experience and professional training are greatly desired.

Simply put, when you elect to proceed *pro se*, you are on your own and become personally responsible for litigating your action in accordance with the rules. Practice in the federal courts is governed by the Federal Rules of Civil Procedure. You **must** become familiar with these rules. You will be held to the same standards as a lawyer as far as complying with court procedures and the rules and regulations of the court system.

As litigating an action in federal court often requires a great deal of time, preparation, knowledge, and skill, this Court highly recommends against proceeding without the assistance of counsel. Some attorneys will represent clients on a contingency fee basis, whereby the fees associated with representation are subtracted from a judgment in favor of the client.[1] However, should you wish to continue without counsel – fully understanding the risks – you are hereby ordered to carefully review the remainder of this Order, as it contains instructions for proceeding in this Court which **must** be followed.

This Order, while not comprehensive – and not a substitute for fully familiarizing yourself with the Federal Rules of Civil Procedure, the Federal Rules of Evidence, the Local Rules of Practice for the United States District Court for the Central District of California, the orders of this Court, including the Court's Standing Order, Scheduling Order, and Civil Trial Order, as well as federal and state case law applicable to this action – is intended to bring certain aspects of law and motion practice to your attention at an early stage in the litigation to remedy problems commonly associated with *pro se* pleadings.[2]

Communications with Chambers: Pursuant to Local Rule 83-2.11, parties **shall refrain** from writing letters to the judge, making telephone calls to chambers, or otherwise communicating with a judge unless opposing counsel is present. You may contact the Courtroom Deputy, at (213) 894-8266, with **appropriate** inquiries. The Courtroom Deputy is **not** an attorney, and will not provide you with any legal advice. The Courtroom Deputy cannot waive any of the requirements of this, or any other, Order. Should you wish to bring any matter to the attention of the Court, you **must** do so in writing, and file it and serve it on the opposing party.

Jurisdiction: The Federal Rules of Civil Procedure require that "[a] pleading which sets forth a claim for relief ... shall contain (1) a short and plain statement of the grounds upon which the court's jurisdiction depends." Fed. R. Civ. P. 8(a). This District's Local Rules further provide that "[t]he statutory or other basis for the exercise of jurisdiction by this Court shall be plainly stated in . . . any document invoking this Court's jurisdiction." Local Rule 8-1. A copy of Fed. R. Civ. P. 8 is attached.[*]

This is extremely important. Unlike state courts, federal courts are not courts of general jurisdiction, and can only preside over matters authorized by the Constitution and Congress. *Bender v. Williamsport Area Sch. Dist.*, 475 U.S. 534, 541, 106 S. Ct. 1326, 1331, 89 L. Ed. 2d 501 (1986). In other words, the party filing the action must **prove** to the Court that jurisdiction over the action exists **before** the Court can reach the merits of the complaint. *See Smith v. McCullough*, 270 U.S. 456, 459, 46 S. Ct. 338, 339, 70 L. Ed. 682 (1926) (A "plaintiff, suing in federal court, must show in his pleading, affirmatively and distinctly, the existence of whatever is essential to federal jurisdiction . . . .").

Federal jurisdiction may be alleged either pursuant to 28 U.S.C. section 1331 for actions "arising under the Constitution, laws, or treaties of the United States," otherwise known as "federal question" jurisdiction, or 28 U.S.C. section 1332 as an action "between citizens of different States," otherwise known as "diversity" jurisdiction.

To allege federal question jurisdiction, the complaint should identify which right(s) the plaintiff(s) claim(s) have been violated, and which law, statute, or constitutional amendment provides that right. *See Keniston v. Roberts*, 717 F.2d 1295, 1298 (9th Cir. 1983).

---

[1] The Los Angeles County Bar Association Lawyer Referral and Information Services may be able to refer you to a lawyer who may or may not be willing to take your case on a contingency basis. The lawyer referral service may be reached at (213) 243-1525.

[2] This Court's orders and the Local Rules of Practice for the United States District Court for the Central District of California are available on the district court's website: www.cacd.uscourts.gov.

[*] [*Editor's Note*: *See* current Rule 8 of the Federal Rules of Civil Procedure.]

Diversity jurisdiction has **two** requirements. First, diversity jurisdiction requires complete diversity of citizenship, that is, all plaintiffs must have a different citizenship from all defendants. *See Owen Equipment & Erection Co. v. Kroger*, 437 U.S. 365, 373, 98 S. Ct. 2396, 2402, 57 L. Ed. 2d 274 (1978). Residence and citizenship are distinct concepts, with significantly different jurisdictional ramifications: "[i]n order to be a citizen of a State within the meaning of the diversity statute, a natural person must both be a citizen of the United States and be domiciled within the State." *Newman-Green, Inc. v. Alfonzo-Larrain*, 490 U.S. 826, 828, 109 S. Ct. 2218, 2221, 104 L. Ed. 2d 893 (1989). "A person's domicile is her permanent home, where she resides with the intention to remain or to which she intends to return. A person residing in a given state is not necessarily domiciled there, and thus is not necessarily a citizen of that state." *Kanter v. Warner-Lambert Co.*, 265 F.3d 853, 857 (9th Cir. 2001) (citations omitted). Corporations are citizens of both their state of incorporation and the state in which they have their principal place of business. 28 U.S.C. § 1332(c)(1); *see also New Alaska Dev. Corp. v. Guetschow*, 869 F.2d 1298, 1300-01 (9th Cir. 1989). Unincorporated associations are citizens of the states of each member. *See Fifty Associates v. Prudential Ins. Co. of Am.*, 446 F.2d 1187, 1190 (9th Cir. 1970). Second, when jurisdiction is based on diversity of citizenship, district courts do not have original jurisdiction unless a party alleges an amount in controversy exceeding $75,000. 28 U.S.C. § 1332(a).

Finally, you should understand that it is **insufficient** for a party to merely claim that jurisdiction exists. Sufficient **facts** must be alleged to allow the Court to assess whether it has jurisdiction over the action.

Service: Service is the formal delivery of a legal pleading. The Federal Rules of Civil Procedure have different requirements for service to be effective depending on the type of entity to be served: service on an individual within the United States is governed by Fed. R. Civ. P. 4(e), corporations and associations must be served in conformity with Rule 4(h), the United States and it agencies must be served pursuant to Fed. R. Civ. P. 4(i), and state and local governmental units require service under Fed. R. Civ. P. 4(j).

Time limits for service of the complaint are set forth in Fed. R. Civ. P. 4(m). It is important to promptly and properly serve the opposing party, especially with the summons and complaint when initiating an action, because **failure to serve within the time limits specified by the Federal Rules may result in the dismissal of your action for lack of prosecution**. You **must** always inform the Court whenever you serve a filing on an opposing party; this is done by filing a proof of service. *See* Fed. R. Civ. P. 4(l).

Discovery: Discovery is the mechanism by which the parties to an action collect evidence relating to the case from one another. Certain information is expected to be provided to the other side without a request. *See* Fed. R. Civ. P. 26(a). If the other side seeks to obtain discovery from you, you must cooperate and provide the information sought on "any matter, not privileged, that is relevant to the claim or defense of any party." Fed. R. Civ. P. 26(b)(1). The principal forms of discovery envisioned by the Federal Rules are the production and inspection of documents, requests for admissions, depositions and interrogatories. Discovery disputes are resolved by, and should be brought to the attention of, the magistrate judge assigned to the action. Discovery should begin early in the litigation and may commence prior to the Scheduling Conference.

Motions: Motions are requests to this Court to make a specified ruling or order. The opposing party may file a motion to dismiss your action, pursuant to Fed. R. Civ. P. 12, or a motion for summary judgment pursuant to Fed. R. Civ. P. 56. If the opposing party files and serves a motion on you, you **must** oppose it if you disagree with the requested relief. **Failure**

to oppose an otherwise properly supported motion may result in the Court granting that motion. *See* Local Rule 7-12. **Depending on the motion, this *may result in the dismissal of your case.***

To oppose a motion, you **must** present the Court with a statement explaining the basis of your opposition and the legal authority supporting your contentions. You **must** also file any evidence upon which you intend to base your opposition to a motion for summary judgment. Pursuant to Local Rule 7-9, your opposition is due **not later** than twenty-one (21) days before the date designated for the hearing of the motion. If you need additional time to oppose the motion, you **must** file and serve an *ex parte* application requesting an extension of time **prior** to the date on which your opposition is due, and must demonstrate that the additional time you seek is warranted and that the requested extension is not a crisis of your creation, thus precluding you from seeking *ex parte* relief. *See Mission Power Eng'g Co. v. Continental Cas. Co.*, 883 F. Supp. 488, 492 (C.D. Cal. 1995).

Motion to Dismiss: A Fed. R. Civ. P. 12(b)(6) motion to dismiss for failure to state a claim tests the legal sufficiency of the claims asserted in the complaint. Under Fed. R. Civ. P. 12(b)(6), a motion to dismiss can be made and granted when the complaint fails "to state a claim upon which relief can be granted." Dismissal under Rule 12(b)(6) is appropriate where the complaint lacks a cognizable legal theory or sufficient facts to support a cognizable legal theory. *Balistreri v. Pacifica Police Dep't*, 901 F.2d 696, 699 (9th Cir. 1990).

To sufficiently state a claim to relief and survive a 12(b)(6) motion, a complaint's "[f]actual allegations must be enough to raise a right to relief above the speculative level." *Bell Atl. Corp. v. Twombly*, 550 U.S. 544, 555 (2007). Mere "labels and conclusions" or a "formulaic recitation of the elements of a cause of action will not do." *Id.* Rather, "[t]o survive a motion to dismiss, a complaint must contain sufficient factual matter, accepted as true, to state a claim to relief that is plausible on its face." *Ashcroft v. Iqbal*, __ U.S. __, 129 S.Ct. 1937, 1949, 173 L. Ed. 2d 868 (2009) (internal quotation marks omitted). "The plausibility standard is not akin to a probability requirement, but it asks for more than a sheer possibility that a defendant has acted unlawfully. Where a complaint pleads facts that are merely consistent with a defendant's liability, it stops short of the line between possibility and plausibility of entitlement to relief." *Id.* (internal citation and quotation marks omitted).

In deciding whether to grant a motion to dismiss, the court must accept as true all "well-pleaded factual allegations." *Iqbal*, 129 S. Ct. at 1950. A court is not, however, "required to accept as true allegations that are merely conclusory, unwarranted deductions of fact, or unreasonable inferences." *Sprewell v. Golden State Warriors*, 266 F.3d 979, 988 (9th Cir. 2001); *see, e.g., Doe I v. Wal-Mart Stores, Inc.*, __F.3d __, 2009 WL 1978730, at *3 (9th Cir. July 10, 2009) ("Plaintiffs' general statement that Wal-Mart exercised control over their day-today employment is a conclusion, not a factual allegation stated with any specificity. We need not accept Plaintiffs' unwarranted conclusion in reviewing a motion to dismiss.").

Thus, the Ninth Circuit has summarized the governing standard, in light of Twombly and Iqbal, as follows: "In sum, for a complaint to survive a motion to dismiss, the non-conclusory factual content, and reasonable inferences from that content, must be plausibly suggestive of a claim entitling the plaintiff to relief." *Moss v. U.S. Secret Service*, 572 F.3d 962, 969 (9th Cir. 2009) (internal quotation marks omitted).

Motion for Summary Judgment: Summary judgment may be granted when there are no material facts in dispute between the parties, making a trial unnecessary. To resist summary judgment under Fed. R. Civ. P. 56, you **must** submit affidavits or other documentary evidence, such as depositions and answers to interrogatories, which set forth specific facts showing there is a genuine issue for trial. *Klingele v. Eikenberry*, 849 F.2d 409, 411-12 (9th Cir. 1988). Failure to do so may result in the entry of summary judgment against you. You should also note that Rule 56(e) requires that affidavits or declarations shall be made on personal knowledge, set forth facts that are admissible as evidence, and show affirmatively that the affiant is competent to testify to the matters stated therein. A copy of Fed. R. Civ. P. 56 is attached.[**] **Should you fail to contradict the moving party with counter-affidavits, declarations or other evidence, the moving party's evidence may be taken as the truth, and final judgment may be entered against you without a trial, thus ending your case.** *Rand v. Rowland*, 154 F.3d 952, 960-61 (9th Cir. 1998).

To effectively address a summary judgment motion, you should be aware of, and familiar with, the following United States Supreme Court cases on summary judgment: *Celotex v. Catrett*, 477 U.S. 317, 106 S. Ct. 2548, 91 L. Ed. 2d 265 (1986); *Anderson v. Liberty Lobby, Inc.*, 477 U.S. 242, 106 S. Ct. 2505, 91 L. Ed. 2d 202 (1986); *Matsushita Elec. Indus. Co. v. Zenith Radio Corp.*, 475 U.S. 574, 106 S. Ct. 1348, 89 L. Ed. 2d 538 (1986).

IT IS SO ORDERED.

DATED: ________________

____
OTIS D. WRIGHT II
United States District Judge

** [*Editor's Note*: *See* current Rule 56 of the Federal Rules of Civil Procedure.]

E. *Standing Order Regarding Patent Cases*

IN THE UNITED STATES DISTICT COURT
FOR THE CENTRAL DISTRICT OF CALIFORNIA

Plaintiff(s),	)	Case No. CV ODW (x)
v.	)	
Defendant(s).	)	**STANDING ORDER REGARDING PATENT CASES**

UNLESS OTHERWISE ORDERED BY THE COURT, THE FOLLOWING RULES SHALL APPLY TO ALL PATENT CASES ASSIGNED TO JUDGE OTIS D. WRIGHT II:

1. Patent Local Rules

The Court adopts the Patent Local Rules of the United States District Court for the Northern District of California, Rev. 12/01/2009. Parties are expected to familiarize themselves with and closely adhere to these rules. A copy of the rules may be found at http://www.cand.uscourts.gov/localrules.

2. Motions for Summary Judgment

Prior to filing any summary judgment motion, the parties must submit letter briefs requesting permission to file the motion. The opening letter brief shall be no longer than five (5) pages and shall be filed with the Court on or before the discovery cut-off date. The letter brief must state the basis for the summary judgment motion and reasons why the motion is not premature. Opposition letter briefs shall be no longer than five (5) pages and shall be filed with the Court no later than seven (7) days after the opening letter brief. No reply letter briefs may be filed without the Court's permission. No hearing will be held unless otherwise ordered by the Court. The last day to file an opening letter brief shall be the discovery cut-off date.

The Court typically schedules the motion deadline eight (8) weeks after the discovery cutoff. Because motions must be noticed twenty-eight (28) days before the hearing date under L.R. 6-1, parties are advised to file the opening letter briefs well in advance of the discovery cut-off date.

The Court reminds counsel of their obligation to meet and confer prior to filing the letter briefs. *See* L.R. 7-3.

3. *Markman* Claim Construction Hearing

Parties must notice a *Markman* hearing in accordance with the timeframe specified in the Patent Local Rules. See Patent L.R. 4-6. To allow for sufficient discovery after the *Markman* hearing, the Court contemplates holding the *Markman* hearing sooner than the maximum allotted time of 199 days after the initial case scheduling conference under the Patent Local Rules. The Court will not entertain requests to continue the discovery cut-off date absent good cause. Thus, if parties desire more time for discovery after—rather than before—the *Markman* hearing, parties should take less than the maximum allotted time under Patent L.R. 3-1–3-5, 3-7, and 4-1–4-5.

The *Markman* hearing is scheduled for a maximum of four (4) hours. Each side shall have a maximum of two (2) hours to present evidence and argument in support of its position. Subject to the Court's approval, parties will jointly agree to the format of the *Markman* hearing.

The claim construction briefs have the following page limits—twenty-five (25) for opening and response, twelve (12) for reply. Copies of all exhibits shall be premarked, bound, and tabbed. In addition to memoranda, parties shall also submit the following: 1) Final Joint Claim Chart, which includes citations to intrinsic evidence to be filed on the same day as the opening brief; 2) Joint Appendix of Intrinsic Evidence, which contains all intrinsic evidence relied upon in the claim construction briefing—to be filed on the same day as the reply brief.

If a party intends to present expert testimony at the *Markman* hearing, whether as a witness or by way of affidavit, a statement of the expert's qualifications shall be submitted as an additional attachment to any memorandum submitted.

Each party shall prepare three bound volumes of exhibits, one for the Court, one for opposing counsel, and one to be kept on the witness stand. The copies for the Court and opposing counsel shall be delivered seven days prior to the *Markman* hearing.

Parties are further reminded of the ten (10) term limit for construction. Patent L.R. 4-3(c). Failure to make a good faith effort to narrow the instances of disputed terms may expose counsel to sanctions. Patent L.R. 4-7.

4. Tutorial

The Court may request a tutorial on the subject matter of the patents-in-suit, to be conducted approximately six (6) weeks prior to the *Markman* hearing. The parties, in consultation with the Court, will jointly agree to the format of the tutorial. The length of the tutorial will be determined on a case by case basis. The tutorial shall be conducted *solely* as an objective presentation of the technology at issue. Visual aids and demonstrative exhibits are strongly encouraged.

5. Discovery

The Court expects the parties to resolve discovery issues among themselves in a courteous, reasonable, and professional manner. Unless otherwise directed, this Court will rule on all discovery motions.

The Court's Scheduling Order states the discovery cut-off date for *all* discovery, both fact and expert. Expert discovery shall be initiated so that it will be completed on or before the discovery cut-off date. If necessary, parties shall, in good faith, stipulate to a fact discovery cut-off date.

Because patent cases tend to involve significant discovery concerning confidential documents, parties are encouraged to file a stipulated protective order as soon as possible. If one was not filed earlier, the Court requires parties to lodge a stipulated protective order along with the parties' joint scheduling conference report under Fed. R. Civ. P. 26(f), unless the parties deem such a protective order unnecessary in this case.

6. Patent File Histories

Concurrently with the parties' filing of the Joint Claim Construction and Prehearing Statement under Patent L.R. 4-3, patentees are required to file with the Court a certified copy of the patent file history for each asserted patent.

The patent file history shall be printed double-sided and compiled in a 3-ring binder. Prior art references[1] should not be included in the paper copy. In addition to the paper copy of the patent file history, the patentee shall submit an electronic copy on a CD-ROM or DVD. Each patent file history shall be a single electronic file in PDF format. All prior art references shall also be included on the CD-ROM or DVD, with each prior art reference appearing as a separate, identifiable PDF file.

---

[1] The documents listed under the "References Cited" section of the patent.

7. Jury Instructions and Special Jury Verdict Form

Although not mandatory, the Court favors the adoption of the Model Patent Jury Instructions for the Northern District of California, Rev. 11/03/2011. Further, prior to the pre-trial conference, the Court requires Parties to file, among other documents, a proposed special jury verdict form substantially based on the Sample Verdict Form, Appendix C.3 of the Model Patent Jury Instructions for the Northern District of California, Rev. 11/03/2011. A copy of Model Patent Jury Instructions may be found at http://www.cand.uscourts.gov/juryinstructions.

IT IS SO ORDERED.

DATED: ______________

____
OTIS D. WRIGHT II
United States District Judge

Hon. George H. Wu

District Judge

Chambers Information

U.S. District Court, Central District of California
Courtroom 10, Spring Street Floor
312 N. Spring Street
Los Angeles, CA 90012

Scheduling Information

Courtroom Deputy: (213) 894-0191

Civil Law and Motion	Mondays and Thursdays at 8:30 a.m.
Criminal Law and Motion	Mondays and Thursdays at 8:00 a.m.

Biographical Information

Born 1950 in New York, NY

Federal Judicial Service:

-Judge, U. S. District Court, Central District of California
-Nominated by George W. Bush on January 9, 2007, to a seat vacated by Ronald S.W. Lew; Confirmed by the Senate on March 27, 2007, and received commission on April 17, 2007.

Education:

-Pomona College, B.A., 1972
-University of Chicago Law School, J.D., 1975

Professional Career:

-Private Practice, Los Angeles, California, 1975-1976, 1977-1979, 1989-1991
-Law clerk, Hon. Stanley N. Barnes, U.S. Court of Appeals for the Ninth Circuit, 1976-1977, 1979
-Assistant Professor of Law, University of Tennessee College of Law, 1979-1982
-Assistant U.S. Attorney, U.S. Attorney's Office, Central District of California, 1982-1989, 1991-1993
-Judge, Los Angeles Municipal Court, California, 1993-1996
-Judge, Los Angeles Superior Court, California, 1996-2007

I. Judge Wu's Procedures and Practices

A. Procedures and Schedules

Criminal

- Criminal matters are heard on: **Thursday and Monday at 8:00 a.m.**
- All documents which are required to be filed in an electronic format pursuant to General Order No. 10-07 shall be filed electronically, on the date due unless otherwise ordered by the Court. Any documents which counsel attempt to file electronically which are improperly filed will not be accepted by the Court.
- Counsel shall deliver 1 conformed mandatory chambers copy of all documents filed in the action (electronically or with the Clerk's office) directly to Chambers by no later than noon the next business day following the due date. If the document is filed on a matter to be heard by the Court within two business days of the filing, the conformed copy must be delivered to chambers on the day of filing before 4:00 p.m.
- The Court will not consider any stipulation or application to continue any hearing unless such stipulation or application is properly filed with a separate proposed order at least three calendar days prior to the date of the hearing. If the stipulation/application for continuance was not filed at least three days prior to the date of the hearing, or if the Court has not ruled on the stipulation/application, counsel and the defendant(s) shall appear on the scheduled hearing date.
- Filing criminal documents under seal: Refer to General Order No. 10-07.

Civil

- Civil motions are heard on: **Monday and Thursday at 8:30 a.m.**
- Tentative rulings are not issued in advance of the hearing date but may be available with the clerk on the day of the hearing.
- It is not necessary to clear a motion date with the court clerk prior to filing the motion, except motions for summary judgment, to dismiss, or preliminary injunctions. Any Monday or Thursday that is not a federal holiday shall be considered an available date.
- If Monday or Thursday is a holiday, the next motion date is the next available Monday or Thursday.
- Discovery motions are to be calendared before the Magistrate Judge.
- Mandatory chambers copies: One conformed mandatory chambers copy of all documents filed in the action (electronically or with the Clerk's Office) shall be delivered directly to Chambers no later than noon of the following business day.
- Continuances are granted only upon a showing of good cause. Requests for continuances must be made by motion, stipulation, or application with a separate proposed order accompanied by a declaration setting forth the reasons for the requested continuance. The declaration should also include whether there have been any prior requests for continuances and whether these requests were granted or denied by the Court. Stipulations extending dates set by this Court are not effective unless approved by the Court. Requests for continuance should be submitted well in advance of the requested relief. Requests for continuance not in compliance with the Court's Standing Order or the Local Rules for the Central District of California will be denied.
- Filing civil documents under seal: Refer to "Preparing Sealed Documents for Filing"

located under Filing Procedures on the Court's website.

General Information

- All filed documents must contain counsel's e-mail address (pursuant to Local Rule 11-3.8).
- Telephonic appearances for hearings in Court are permitted only if matter need not be reported or if the attorneys do not wish to make any oral argument. Request shall be submitted in writing no later than one (1) week prior to scheduled hearing.
- Ex parte applications are for extraordinary relief. (*See Mission Power Engineering Co. v. Continental Casualty Co., 883 F. Supp. 488 (C.D. Cal. 1995*). Ex parte applications are normally considered on the papers and are rarely set for hearing. If a hearing is necessary, the parties will be notified. The moving party shall immediately serve the opposing party by fax or hand service and shall notify the opposing party that any opposition must be filed not later than 24 hours after the filing of the ex parte application. A conformed mandatory chambers copy of moving, opposition, or notice of non-opposition papers are to be hand-delivered to the courtesy box outside the entrance to chambers on the Spring Street level of the U.S. Courthouse, 312 North Spring Street. Clerk of the Court's ruling will notify counsel. Sanctions may be imposed for misuse of ex parte applications.
- Counsel is not permitted to contact the judge's law clerks or secretary unless responding to an inquiry they initiated.
- Calls will not be returned regarding the status of submitted motions, stipulations, or proposed orders. Sufficient copies of any forms of order should be provided for conforming along with a self-addressed, stamped envelope (not more than two). Counsel may also determine the status of any submitted motion, stipulation, or proposed order by accessing the docket sheet through PACER.
- For general information on how to order a transcript of any reported or digitally recorded proceeding, please contact 213-894-3015 or visit www.cacd.uscourts.gov > General Information > Court Reporter/Recorder Transcripts. If you require an estimate of cost for the preparation of a transcript, contact the court reporter/recorder for the desired proceeding.
  To determine the court reporter/recorder for a particular proceeding, go to the Court Reporter Schedule web page and click on View by Date. Once you've determined the correct court reporter/recorder for the desired session, click on Court Reporter Phone and Email List for contact information.
- Counsel is directed to the section under "Services" on the Court's website for reserving equipment for trial. Prior to calling Space & Facilities to set up an appointment, counsel shall contact the Courtroom Deputy Clerk to arrange for a date and time for any training or set up of equipment in the Courtroom.
- Counsel who need to make special arrangements to bring in equipment or voluminous materials in to Court for trial shall contact the Space & Facilities Help Desk at (213) 894-1400.
- The Court requires the following to be submitted to the Courtroom Deputy Clerk on the first day of trial.
- The original exhibits with the Court's exhibit tags for the Court Clerk. One (1) copy for the Judge, One (1) copy for the witness and one (1) copy for opposing party. Plaintiff shall use yellow tags; defendant shall use blue tags. Each tag shall be affixed

to the front of the exhibit. Exhibit tags can be obtained from the Clerk's Office.

- One bench book with a copy of each exhibit for the Court's use, tagged as described above.
- Three (3) copies of exhibit lists (Courtroom Deputy Clerk will instruct at pretrial conference as to format).
- Three (3) copies of witness lists in the order in which the witnesses will be called to testify (Courtroom Deputy Clerk will instruct at pretrial conference as to format).
- All exhibits will be returned to counsel at the end of trial and will not be kept by the Court. Counsel shall keep the lodged and admitted exhibits in their possession pursuant to Local Rules 79-3 and 79-4.
- It is the responsibility of counsel in a civil case to arrange for the services of an Interpreter. Interpreter's Office: (213) 894-4599.
- Other information: Counsel is directed to comply with all Local Rules.
- If counsel has received a "Notice to Parties of Alternate Dispute Resolution (ADR) Program" - forms ADR-08, ADR-10, or ADR-11 with an attached "ADR Program Questionnaire" form ADR-09, please see General Order 07-01, which is located in the "General Orders" section on the home page of the Court's website. The Attorney Settlement Officer information is located in the section "Attorney Information > ADR."

II. Judge Wu's Case Management Orders

A. *Order for Discovery and Inspection in Criminal Cases*

IN THE UNITED STATES DISTICT COURT
FOR THE CENTRAL DISTRICT OF CALIFORNIA

)	Case No. _______________
Plaintiff(s),)	
v.)	**ORDER FOR DISCOVERY AND**
Defendant(s).)	**INSPECTION IN CRIMINAL CASES**
______________________________)	**BEFORE JUDGE GEORGE H. WU**

In order to obviate unnecessary motions for discovery in criminal actions, proceedings, or cases assigned to the undersigned court for trial,

IT IS ORDERED:

1. Within seven (7) days of the initial arraignment before the Magistrate Judge, the Assistant United States Attorney assigned to the trial of the case and the defendant's attorney shall meet and confer on the issue of discovery in this case including, but not limited, the items referenced in Federal Rules of Criminal Procedure 12, 12.1, 12.2, 12.3, 15 and 16. Further, upon request of the attorney for the defendant, the Government shall:

(a) Permit defendant's attorney to inspect and copy or photograph any relevant written or recorded statements or confessions made by the defendant, or copies thereof, within the possession, custody, or control of the Government, the existence of which is known, or may become known, to the attorney for the Government;

(b) Permit defendant's attorney to inspect and copy or photograph any relevant results or reports of physical or mental examinations, and of specific tests or experiments made in connection with the case, or copies thereof, within the possession, custody, or control of the Government, the existence of which is known, or may become known, to the attorney for the Government, and which are material to the defendant's case;

(c) Permit defendant's attorney to inspect and copy or photograph any relevant recorded testimony of the defendant before a grand jury;

(d) Permit defendant's attorney to inspect and copy or photograph books, papers, documents, tangible objects, buildings, or places which are the property of the defendant and which are within the possession, custody, or control of the Government;

(e) Make known to the defendant's attorney the defendant's prior criminal record in the possession of the attorney for the Government;

(f) Permit defendant's attorney to inspect, copy, or photograph any evidence favorable to the defendant;

(g) Advise defendant's attorney of the existence or non-existence of any evidence in the possession of the Government obtained as the result of any electronic surveillance or wiretap;

(h) Advise defendant's attorney of the contemplated use of informer testimony (fact of informer only, not name or testimony);

(i) Disclose to defendant's attorney its intent to use any statements or confessions made by the defendant. If defendant questions the admissibility of such statement or confession, the hearing required by *Jackson v. Denno*, 378 U.S. 368 (1964), shall be scheduled at the first status conference with the court; and

(j) Give to defendant's counsel a copy of the statements of all witnesses the government intends to call in its case in chief.

2. If, in the judgment of the United States Attorney, it would not be in the interests of justice to make any one or more disclosures set forth in paragraph (1) and requested by defendant's counsel, disclosure may be specifically declined, and this matter shall be addressed at the first status conference with the court which will normally be set ten days after the initial arraignment.

3. At the meet and confer, counsel for the defendant shall notify the attorney for the Government whether the defendant intends to raise an alibi defense under Rule 12.1, insanity under Rule 12.2, or a public authority defense under Rule 12.3. Counsel shall also discuss any motion(s) which they are then contemplating and confer in a good faith effort to eliminate the necessity for a hearing on said motion(s).

4. Upon completion of the meet and confer referenced in paragraph 1 above, no later than the Friday before the status conference, the parties shall file (with a courtesy copy to Chambers at Room 128, Spring Street Courthouse) a joint statement that includes the following information:

(a) That the prescribed meet and confer was held;

(b) The date of said conference;

(c) The names of the Assistant United States Attorney and the defense counsel with whom the conference was held;

(d) The time estimate, in days, that the criminal trial is expected to take;

(e) The contested matters of discovery and inspection, if any, plus any additional discovery or inspection desired by either party;

(f) Any contemplated motions in the lawsuit; and

(g) The fact of disclosure of all material favorable to the defendant or the absence thereof within the meaning of *Brady v. Maryland*, 373 U.S. 83 (1963) and related cases.

5. Any duty of disclosure and discovery set forth herein is a continuing one.

6. This order is not intended to preclude discovery by the defendant or the Government pursuant to Rule 16(b).

7. It shall be the joint duty of counsel for the defendant and the United States Attorney to schedule and hold the meet and confer contemplated herein. The United States Attorney shall assure time and availability for such conference within the deadlines herein provided unless the discovery conference is waived in writing by defendant and his/her/its counsel, and such waiver is filed with the court.

8. Counsel for defendant shall have (1) reviewed all disclosures made and discovery received, and (2) had sufficient discussion with his/her client and the United States Attorney by the time of the first status conference with the court to enable counsel to meaningfully discuss with the court at said conference the likelihood of trial/disposition of this case.

9. The government shall be represented at all status conferences with the court by the Assistant United States Attorney who is assigned to the trial of the case, and who is most knowledgeable about the aforesaid matters, as well as any other matters scheduled for discussion with the court at the status conferences.

DATED: ________________

____
GEORGE H. WU
United States District Judge

B. *Standing Order Regarding Final and Pretrial Conferences for Civil Jury Trials*

IN THE UNITED STATES DISTICT COURT
FOR THE CENTRAL DISTRICT OF CALIFORNIA

)	Case No. ________________
Plaintiff(s),)	
v.)	**STANDING ORDER RE FINAL**
Defendant(s).)	**PRE-TRIAL CONFERENCES FOR**
____________________________________)	**CIVIL JURY TRIALS BEFORE**
	JUDGE GEORGE H. WU

1. You are instructed to read and to follow (unless otherwise superseded herein) the Central District of California Local Rules (henceforth "Local Rules") 16-1 through 16-15 regarding pre-trial requirements.

2. At least twenty-one (21) days prior to the Final Pre-Trial Conference (henceforth "FPTC"), counsel for each party and pro per litigants[1] must have prepared and exchanged with each other all of the following:

a) a list of pre-marked exhibits which that party intends to use at trial,[2]

b) copies of the exhibits which are on the list (except that exhibits previously provided during discovery and Bates-stamped need not be produced again),

c) a list of witnesses which that litigant intends to call at trial,

d) marked deposition transcripts as required by paragraph 7, below,

e) an initial version of the short statement of the case to be read to the jury panel,

f) proposed jury instructions, and

g) any verdict forms that a party wishes to utilize.

3. At least ten (10) days before the FPTC, all counsel and *pro se* litigants will meet and confer in person so that at least five (5) days before the FPTC, the parties will have filed and provided to the Court "joint" versions of the following:

a) joint statement of the case,

b) joint exhibit list (with any concomitant objections),

c) joint witness list,

---

1 While the Court does not expect pro per litigants to have any legal training or experience, most of the requirements in this Order either do not require legal knowledge *per se* or are matters which the pro per litigant will have to address anyway at the trial (*e.g.*, knowing what witnesses and exhibits he or she will be presenting, selecting the jury instructions that he or she will be asking the Court to read to the jury, *etc.*). This Court believes that it would be as helpful for pro per litigants, as it is for attorneys, to address those matters prior to trial in order for all of the trial participants to be better prepared and the trial to proceed more smoothly. Therefore, contrary to Local Rule 16-12(c), this Court will require pro per litigants, to the extent they are able, to participate in meeting the pre-trial conference obligations for civil jury trials delineated in this Order.

2 Rebuttal exhibits need not be placed on the list. However, actual rebuttal exhibits are (like hen's teeth) extremely rare. If the court determines that an undisclosed exhibit is not in fact a rebuttal exhibit, said item will be excluded from the trial.

d) joint proposed jury instructions,

e) joint special verdict forms (if any), and

f) stipulation(s) of facts as per Local Rule 16-2.2.

By "joint," the Court means that the materials will be contained in a single document signed by all counsel and pro per litigants. In the preparation of said document, no party shall have the right to veto (i.e., exclude from the document) material proffered by any other party. However, areas of dispute or other differences shall be noted. For example, as to the joint statement of the case, the sections which are agreed upon by all parties would be in regular type while the portions submitted by one litigant and contested by one or more of the others would be denoted by different fonts, *italicized*, underlined, or in **bold**. Further, where there are disagreements, the bases for each dispute will be noted in a brief footnote to the relevant section of the joint submission in question.

In addition to supplying the Court with a paper copy of the documents, all "joint" submissions are to be placed on a cd-rom disc using "Word Perfect" (7.0 or above) or "Word" and provided to the Court.

4. As to the joint exhibit list, the parties are to employ the following format:[3]

Exhibit Number	Party Offering	Description	If objection(s), briefly state the ground(s)	Response to objection(s)

If all the parties stipulate to the admissibility of an exhibit or if there are no objections to it on the exhibit list, it may be used by either side at any point in the trial after jury selection including the opening statements and closing arguments.

Any and all objections to an exhibit must be included in the joint exhibit list. Any objections not so included will be deemed by this Court to have been waived. Do not submit blanket or boilerplate objections as they will be disregarded and overruled.

In numbering and marking the exhibits, the parties are to follow L.R. 16-6 and 26-3.

5. As to each witness on the joint witness list, the parties shall state the name of the witness, the party(s) calling the witness, and provide an estimate of the amounts of time for the witness's direct and cross-examinations. If there is an objection to the witness's being called at trial, the opposing party must file a motion *in limine* to resolve the dispute in advance of trial or the objection will be deemed to have been waived, unless the Court finds that the basis for the objection arose after the FPTC.

6. The proposed jury instructions are to be placed in the order in which they are to be read to the jury and printed in booklet form (*i.e.*, fitting multiple instructions sequentially on each page). Normally, there should be: 1) a "Preliminary Instructions" section with items such as Ninth Circuit Manual of Model Jury Instructions – Civil (henceforth "9th Cir. Jury Instructions") Nos. 1.1C, 1.6, 1.7, 1.9 through 1.11, *etc.*;[4] 2) a "Cause(s) of Action/Affirmative

[3] In order to fit all of the necessary information into the limited spaces on the form, for this document the parties can utilize as low as 9 point font, if they so desire.

[4] The Court will usually give the jury an initial set of instructions (henceforth "Initial Set"), after the *voir dire* is completed and the actual panel is sworn in, just before opening statements of counsel. In addition to the standard instructions (such as 9th Cir. Jury Instruction Nos. 1.1A, 1.2, *etc.*), the parties may request that the Court include in the Initial Set those instructions which state the essential elements of the cause(s) of action or affirmative defenses on which the respective parties bear the burden of proof.

Defense(s)" section which delineates the elements of each claim and defense; 3) a "Damages" section which describes the types of damages (*e.g.*, economic, non-economic, future, punitive, *etc.*), and 4) a "Closing Instructions" section with items such as 9th Cir. Jury Instructions Nos. 3.1 through 3.4.

This Court has a preference for established/published jury instructions (such as the 9th Cir. Jury Instructions) over those specially prepared by counsel in the instant case because the former have usually survived some appellate review. As to the established form jury instructions, where the claim arises under federal law, counsel should initially refer to the applicable provisions in the 9th Cir. Jury Instructions. Where the claim is based on California law, either the Judicial Council of California Civil Jury Instructions (henceforth ("CACI") or California Jury Instructions – Civil (henceforth "BAJI") may be used. The Court has no objection to the parties' selection of various items from the different publications (i.e., mixing and matching) so long as each instruction is identified by its source and there are no overlaps or discrepancies. Where there is no applicable form instruction on a particular matter and counsel are drafting specific language, they are to include reference to the statutory, regulatory or case law which supports that language.

The most recent version of any form instruction is to be utilized. Any blanks or spaces are to be filled in by the parties. Modifications of established jury instructions from the various sources must specifically indicate the change(s) made to the original form instruction and cite to the authority supporting the modification(s).

In addition to the joint proposed jury instruction booklet, the parties are to provide the court with a table listing each proposed instruction and the following information (at the time of the FPTC, only the first two columns need to be filled out):

Jury Instruction Number and Source/Identification/Description	Party(s) Offering	Rejected	Given	Given as Modified	Date

Each juror will receive a written copy of the jury instructions at the close of the evidentiary phase of the trial. The jury will be instructed prior to closing arguments.

Before giving the instructions and/or verdict forms to the jury, the Court will meet with counsel and pro per litigants near the close of trial to finalize the versions of those documents.

7. Where a party seeks to present a witness's testimony at trial by way of a deposition, at least twenty-one (21) days prior to the FPTC, that party will provide the opposing side with a copy of the witness's deposition transcript with the parts it seeks to proffer marked in blue. Seven (7) days later, the opposing side will return the transcript indicating in red any objections it has to the parts selected by the originating party and also designating any portions which the opposing side wishes to have read to the jury. At least ten (10) days before the FPTC, the parties will meet and confer to resolve any differences regarding the deposition testimony. Should there be any disputes which the parties cannot resolve, at least five (5) days before the FPTC, the parties will lodge with the court: 1) a marked copy of the deposition transcript indicating the portions agreed upon and the parts in dispute, and 2) a joint filing delineating the parties' respective positions on the disputed parts. The Court will resolve those disputes at the FPTC.

At the trial, the marked deposition will be read to the jury by counsel unless some other method is agreed upon. If the deposition was taken by way of video, the edited videotape can be played to the jury.

8. The parties are requested to reach as many stipulations of fact as they can before trial in order to reduce trial time, simplify the proceedings, and make the process more intelligible to the jurors. Such stipulations can be read to the jury or handed out in written form at the start of the trial if requested by the parties.

9. All motions *in limine* are to be filed and personally served no later than twenty-one (21) days before the FPTC. Any oppositions to said motions are to be filed and personally served ten (10) days before the FPTC. Any replies are to be filed and personally served four (4) days before the FPTC and courtesy copies are to be delivered to Court chambers.

Motions *in limine* would include making requests: 1) to exclude an item of evidence or a witness from the trial, 2) to bifurcate issues, 3) for the court to take judicial notice, or 4) for any unusual procedure during the trial such as having the jury visit a particular location or conducting an experiment in court, *etc.*[5] However, do not waste the Court's and your opponent's time by making general boilerplate motions *in limine* such as a "Motion to Exclude at Trial All Evidence Not Previously Produced During Discovery."[6]

Remember, motions *in limine* are covered by the meet and confer requirements of Local Rule 7-3.

10. On the first day of trial, parties will jointly present sets of binders containing all of the pre-marked documentary and photographic exhibits for: 1) the court, 2) the court clerk (who receives the originals), and 3) the witness box. Each exhibit shall be separated by a tabbed divider indicating the exhibit number on the right hand side.

If the trial revolves around a limited set of key documents/exhibits and if the parties have stipulated to the admissibility of those items, the parties can request the jurors be provided with their own exhibit binders at the start of the trial.

Also, if any party potentially intends to use deposition testimony to impeach a witness (or for any other purpose), a copy of the deposition transcript is to be lodged with the court clerk on the first day of trial.

11. Courtroom 10 has an available Samsung SDP-950STA Digital Presenter (an "ELMO" like device with laptop computer connections), two 40 inch flat screen monitors for the jury, and concomitant desk top monitors for the judge, witness box and attorney tables. If a party elects to utilize the court's equipment, counsel are advised to learn how to operate the equipment before trial begins. If counsel are bringing their own audio/visual apparatus (or have any other logistical issue, *e.g.*, a large number of boxes or exhibits), they must make arrangements with the court clerk at least three (3) business days in advance of trial.

If interpreters are required for any witness, the party calling that witness bears the burden of supplying an interpreter.

---

5 Motions *in limine* are not meant to serve as a vehicle for resolving discovery disputes which should have already been decided before the close of discovery or for attempting to re-litigate prior judicial decisions. Further, motions *in limine* are not a substitute for a timely made motion for summary judgment or adjudication.

6 Any motion to exclude evidence not produced during discovery would have to specify the particular exhibit(s) or witness(es) to be excluded, the exact discovery requests which required their revelation, and the opposing party's purported deficient response.

12. At the FPTC, an inquiry will also be made as to any scheduling problems and an attempt will be made to accommodate parties, attorneys and witnesses at trial.[7] However, the failure to raise such a scheduling issue at the FPTC will normally mean that the problem will not be later considered by the Court.

During the trial, each party must advise its opponent(s) at least 24 hours in advance of the witnesses which it plans to call for the next day. Likewise, any chart or other item of demonstrative evidence (which is otherwise not a pre-marked exhibit) must be shown to the opponent(s) at least 48 hours before its intended use so that a hearing can conveniently be heard outside the presence of the jury, if necessary.

The parties are expected to have their witnesses stacked such that there will be no delay between the time one witness is excused and the next one is called. Should there be any instance where a party is unable to call a witness for more than thirty (30) minutes, the Court will deem that side to have rested.

13. At the FPTC, the Court will discuss with the parties which of the causes of action and affirmative defenses will, in fact, need to be tried to the jury. At that time, the Court will review the time estimate for the trial and, if necessary, set a specified time table for each party to present its claims/defenses (including the imposition of time limits on opening statements and closing arguments). Since the Court's allotment of time to try the case will inevitably be less than the parties' estimate, the Court will allocate the time generally giving the plaintiff's side 55% to 60% and the defendant's side 45% to 40%.[8] The Court will keep track of the time taken by each side.

14. *Voir dire* examinations will primarily be conducted by the Court. *See* Federal Rules of Civil Procedure ("FRCP") 47(a). Each side will be allowed a brief period to ask follow-up questions. Parties are to submit at the FPTC any questions that they want the Court to ask the jurors. Prior to the *voir dire*, the Court will indicate if any of the proposed questions are objectionable or if the Court will decline to ask particular question(s) but will allow the counsel to ask it/them during their allotted time.

If the case is complex or raises "delicate issues" and if the parties stipulate in advance, they can submit a proposed written jury questionnaire form at the FPTC.

15. It is this Court's normal practice to allow jurors to ask questions of witnesses during the trial using the procedure set forth in 9th Cir. Jury Instruction No. 1.15. If any party objects to such juror questioning, it should raise that issue at the FPTC.

16. Other Trial Matters

a) No speaking objections. If an attorney wishes to make an objection, say the word "objection" and the word or phrase that delineates its basis (*e.g.*, "hearsay," "lack of foundation," *etc.*). The challenged attorney is not to give a response unless specifically asked to do so by the Court.

---

7 Because trials are set with lengthy advance notice, it is expected that the parties, counsel and witnesses will have cleared their calendars for purposes of the trial. Nevertheless, it is understood that certain situations (*e.g.*, a non-party doctor witness who is not a retained expert) may arise where accommodations will be necessary. At the FPTC, the parties should be knowledgeable as to their witnesses' schedules. Upon a proper showing, the Court will allow witnesses to be taken out of order.

8 Because plaintiffs have the initial burden of proof and they also have to establish the factual background for the disputes, the Court normally will give them a little more than half the trial time to present their case. The Court will deviate from that normal course in such situations as where the defendants' counterclaims predominate or where there is only one plaintiff and a multitude of defendants.

b) Court hours. Judge Wu hears motions on Mondays and Thursdays and therefore the starting time for those days will vary depending upon the number and nature of the matters on his morning calendar. Normal trial hours are from 8:30 a.m. to 12:00 p.m. and 1:15 p.m. To 5:00 p.m. There will be one morning and one afternoon break of about 10 to 15 minutes.

c) Punctuality. The first time a party's counsel is late, the Court will verbally admonish. The second time, the Court will have brought the jury into the courtroom and counsel can explain their whereabouts/tardiness directly to the jury. The third time, the court will sanction monetarily.

d) Use of podium. Counsel are expected to use the podium when questioning witnesses and may not approach the jury or witness boxes unless counsel has asked and obtained permission from the Court beforehand.

e) Moving exhibits. Counsel should move an exhibit into the record at the time the exhibit is initially shown to a witness (unless the exhibit list indicates that no party has objected to its admissibility). The Court will not allow parties to recall witnesses to remedy defects in the initial testimony as to the admissibility of exhibits.

f) Advising parties and witnesses. Counsel and pro per litigants are ordered to advise their parties and witnesses that, during the trial, they are not to have any contact either directly or indirectly with any juror. Should counsel fail to so advise those persons and one of them attempts to interface with a juror, the Court will hold the attorney in violation of this order.

Counsel are also instructed to advise their witnesses of any of this Court's applicable evidentiary rulings, so that witnesses do not blurt out previously excluded evidence in front of the jury. Counsel will also admonish their clients, witnesses and related persons that they are not to respond to particular testimony or to any ruling of this Court with observable facial expressions, body movements (such as head nodding or shaking) or commentary indicating their agreement or non-agreement.

g) Multiple counsel. If a party has more than one trial counsel, the Court will start/resume the trial once any one of the attorneys is present. Also, only one attorney may question or cross-examine a witness, and/or make objections to questions or answers of a particular witness. "Double teaming" will not be allowed.

17. The Court will re-address the topic of settlement at the FPTC.

IT IS SO ORDERED.

DATED: ________________

____
GEORGE H. WU
United States District Judge

This page intentionally left blank.

This page intentionally left blank.

Visiting Judges

Hon. Visiting Judges

Chambers Information
U.S. District Court, Central District of California
Courtroom 1
3470 Twelfth Street
Riverside, CA 92501
Courtroom Deputy: (951) 328-4464

I. Visiting Judges' Procedures and Practices

1. **Procedures:** Many visiting judges have issued minute orders regarding procedures in their cases. If you have received a minute order in your case outlining the visiting judge's procedures, such as courtesy/chambers copies, filings, etc., please follow the outlined procedures. The minute order indicates who to contact and where to send chambers/courtesy copies, if required. If the minute order does not address a question you might have, please contact the courtroom deputy designated in the minute order.

   If you have not received a minute order in your case outlining the visiting judge's procedures, please contact the above listed courtroom deputy.

2. **Electronic Filings:** Counsel shall e-file all criminal and civil filings pursuant to Federal Rules of Civil Procedure 5(d)(3), Local Rule 5-4, and General Order 08-02, as follows:

   Step 1: All non-signature items shall be E-FILED in pdf format. All proposed signature items shall be E-FILED as an attachment to the main document in pdf format.

   Step 2: All proposed signature items shall be E-MAILED to the email address indicated in the minute order issued in your case. If no minute order has been issued with an email address, send your documents to sgl_chambers@cacd.uscourts.gov in Word or Word Perfect format. ONLY proposed signature items should be emailed to the chambers' email address. Please do NOT email other associated documents, and DO NOT use this email address for communication with the Court or the court clerk.

3. **Motion Dates:** If you would like to file a motion, many visiting judges have issued orders outlining what procedures to follow. Please follow those instructions - If you have not received an order with instructions on filing motions, please follow the Federal Rules of Civil Procedure and the Local Rules of the Central District of California. It is not necessary to clear a hearing date with the court clerk prior to filing a motion, except for motions for summary judgment or preliminary injunction. Moving papers are to be filed and served at least twenty-eight (28) days before the hearing date. Opposition papers are to be filed and served no later than twenty-one (21) days before the hearing date, and any reply papers are to be filed and served at least fourteen (14) days before the hearing date. See Local Rules 6-1, 7-9, 7-10. The only closed dates for visiting judges are holidays. You may select any Monday. If Monday should fall on a holiday, please select the next available Monday. No hearing

time or courtroom number is required. The Court will notify counsel if a hearing is to be scheduled. If you have further questions, please contact the above listed courtroom deputy.

4. **Discovery:** Unless you have been notified otherwise, all discovery motions will be handled by the Magistrate Judge assigned to the case.

5. **Ex Partes:** When it is necessary to file an ex parte application, counsel shall submit with the application a declaration indicating the necessity of the ex parte, that the opposing party(ies) have been notified and whether they oppose the application. The Court will notify counsel if a hearing is to be scheduled.

6. **Filed Under Seal:** See Local rule 79-5.

7. **Continuances:** Contact the courtroom deputy as designated on the Court's minute order issued in your case regarding continuance practice. If there is not a designated courtroom deputy, contact the above listed courtroom deputy.

8. **Case Status:** Status of motions, stipulations or proposed orders should be made by checking the docket sheet through PACER which you may find at www.pacer.uscourts.gov or by calling, 1-800-676-6856.

9. **Settlement:** Please e-file a Notice of Settlement and notify the courtroom deputy as soon as a settlement of your case has been reached. Include in your notice the anticipated length of time needed to file a stipulated dismissal.

10. **Telephonic Appearance:** Many of the visiting judges hold telephonic conferences. If an in-person appearance is ordered, the Court may permit appearances by telephone for status conferences, scheduling conferences, and for oral argument on motions upon a showing that a personal appearance will cause undue hardship. If such a request is necessary, notify the above listed courtroom deputy.

11. **Conflicts:** Contact the courtroom deputy as designated on the Court's minute order issued in your case with any conflict in schedules. If there is not a designated courtroom deputy, contact the above listed courtroom deputy.

12. **Trials:** Court will notify counsel of trial dates and procedures by order or minute order.

13. **Calendars:** Court will notify counsel of hearings dates by order or minute order.

14. **Transcripts:** For general information on how to order a transcript of any reported or digitally recorded proceeding, please contact 213-894-3015 or visit www.cacd.uscourts.gov>General Information>Court Reporter/Recorder Transcripts. If you require an estimate of cost for the preparation of a transcript, contact the court reporter/recorder for the desired proceeding.

    To determine the court reporter/recorder for a particular proceeding, go to the Court Reporter Schedule web page and click on View by Date. Once you've determined the correct court reporter/recorder for the desired session, click on Court Reporter Phone and Email List for contact information.

This page intentionally left blank.

This page intentionally left blank.

Magistrate Judges

Hon. Paul L. Abrams

Magistrate Judge

Chambers Information

U.S. District Court, Central District of California
Courtroom G, 9th Floor
312 N. Spring Street
Los Angeles, CA 90012

Scheduling Information

Courtroom Deputy: (213) 894-7103

Civil Law and Motion	Tuesdays at 10:00 a.m.
Criminal Law and Motion	As scheduled.

Biographical Information

[Not available]

I. Judge Abrams' Procedures and Practices

A. *Procedures and Schedules*

1. Civil motions are heard on **Tuesdays** at **10:00 a.m.** It is not necessary to clear a civil motion date with the court clerk prior to filing the motion. Criminal motions are scheduled as required.

2. Discovery motions are to be scheduled before the magistrate judge, if referred by the district court judge. Strict compliance with Local Rule 37 is required.

3. Tentative rulings are usually not issued.

4. Mandatory chambers copies of all e-filed documents must be provided to chambers no later than 12 noon the following day.

5. Procedures for filing an ex parte application: Strict compliance with Local Rule 7-19 is required. A FILED stamped, mandatory chambers copy of the application and any opposition must be delivered directly to the judge's chambers. Any opposition must be served and filed within 24 hours of applicant's oral notice. Court will notify parties if a telephonic hearing is desired. Please note that, absent an emergency, ex parte applications may not be used to obtain a ruling on a discovery dispute.

6. To request a continuance of any scheduled court proceeding, parties should submit a signed stipulation and proposed order. If it is necessary to file an ex parte application to request a continuance, the application must, in addition to complying with Local Rule 7-11 and paragraph 5 above, set forth the opposing counsel's position.

7. Counsel are not allowed to contact the judge's law clerks.

8. Inquiries regarding the status of a motion, stipulation or proposed order should be made to the court's clerk. Also, please refer to Local Rule 11-4.5.

9. Calendar conflicts: Advise the court clerk in advance about a calendar conflict and attempt to stipulate to an alternative date and time with opposing counsel after clearing the alternative date and time with the court's clerk.

10. Counsel should contact the court's clerk regarding procedures for bringing electronic equipment into the courtroom.

11. Arrangements for bringing voluminous exhibits into the courtroom may be made through the Space and Facilities Help Desk, at (213) 894-1400.

12. ELMO reservations/tutorials may be made by first referring to the court website at www.cacd.uscourts.gov, under "Attorney Information," and then "Attorney Services." Alternatively, you can contact the Courtroom Technology Help Desk at 213 894-3061.

13. For general information on how to order a transcript of any reported or digitally recorded proceeding, please contact 213-894-3015 or visit www.cacd.uscourts.gov> General Information>Court Reporter/Recorder Transcripts. If you require an estimate of cost for the preparation of a transcript, contact the court reporter/recorder for the desired proceeding.

    To determine the court reporter/recorder for a particular proceeding, go to the Court Reporter Schedule web page and click on View by Date. Once you've determined the correct court reporter/recorder for the desired session, click on Court Reporter Phone and Email List for contact information.

14. Questions regarding law clerk/extern positions: Communicate via letter to the judge.

15. Trial preparation: Counsel should comply with Local Rule 16 et seq.

16. Procedures for obtaining the services of an interpreter on a civil case: If the government is the moving party, contact the court clerk. All others may contact the Interpreter's Section at 213-894-4599.

17. Other Information: All Settlement conference papers should be delivered directly to the judge's chambers, 9th Floor, Spring Street Courthouse.

II. Judge Abrams' Case Management Orders

A. *Case Management Order for Social Security Cases*

IN THE UNITED STATES DISTICT COURT
FOR THE CENTRAL DISTRICT OF CALIFORNIA

Plaintiff(s),	)	Case No. ______________
v.	)	
______________, Commissioner of	)	**CASE MANAGEMENT ORDER**
Social Security Administration,	)	**[Social Security]**
Defendant.	)	
______________________________	)	

In accordance with General Order 05-01, this case is designated for electronic filing.

In order to facilitate the just, speedy, and inexpensive determination of this case, the parties shall comply with the following instructions.

I. Service of the Summons and Complaint

Plaintiff shall promptly serve the summons and complaint on the Commissioner in the manner required by Rule 4(i) of the Federal Rules of Civil Procedure. Such service shall consist of sending a copy of the summons and complaint by registered or certified mail to each of the following: (a) the United States Attorney for the Central District of California, or his or her authorized agent, addressed to the civil process clerk at the Office of the United States Attorney, Civil Division, Room 7516, Federal Building, 300 North Los Angeles Street, Los Angeles, California 90012; (b) the Commissioner of Social Security in Washington, D.C.; and (c) the Attorney General of the United States in Washington, D.C. Plaintiff shall electronically file a proof of service showing compliance with this paragraph within twenty-eight (28) days after the filing of the complaint.[1] Failure to comply with this paragraph may result in dismissal of this case.

II. Motion to Dismiss

Any motion to dismiss the complaint shall be electronically filed in accordance with the rules governing noticed motions; provided, however, that the motion shall be deemed submitted on the basis of the papers timely filed as of the hearing date, without oral argument, unless the Court orders otherwise. *See* Fed.R.Civ.P. 7 and 12; C.D. Cal. Local Rules 7 and 12. **Courtesy copies of the motion and supporting papers, the opposition papers, and the reply papers, with the Notice of Electronic Filing attached, shall either (a) be delivered to the Magistrate Judge's chambers (Room 926, Spring Street Courthouse) no later than 4:00 pm on the next court day, or (b) shall be mailed to the Magistrate Judge at 312 N. Spring Street, Los Angeles, CA 90012, no later than the next court day.**

III. Service of Administrative Record and Notice Thereof

The Commissioner shall have one hundred and twenty (120) days from the date of service of the complaint in which to serve a complete copy of the certified administrative

---

1 If this Case Management Order is electronically filed prior to service of the summons and complaint, plaintiff shall serve a copy of this order concurrently with the summons and complaint. If this order is electronically filed after the service of the summons and complaint, plaintiff shall serve a copy of it by first-class mail on the Office of the United States Attorney within fourteen (14) days from the date the order is electronically filed, and plaintiff shall promptly electronically file a proof of service with the Court.

record on plaintiff and electronically file a notice of service with the Court.

IV. Discovery and Pre-trial Proceedings

No discovery or other pre-trial proceedings not authorized by this order shall be conducted without leave of court. In particular, no motion for summary judgment shall be filed. The decision in this case will be made on the basis of the pleadings, the administrative record, and the Joint Stipulation filed by the parties. In accordance with Rule 12(c) of the Federal Rules of Civil Procedure, the Court will determine which party is entitled to judgment under the standards set forth in 42 U.S.C. § 405(g).

V. Mandatory Settlement Procedures

The parties shall engage in good faith settlement negotiations to resolve the matter, according to the following schedule.

A. Within twenty-one (21) days of the date of service of a copy of the administrative record, plaintiff shall prepare and deliver to the Assistant United States Attorney ("AUSA") representing the Commissioner a written and detailed proposal of settlement. Plaintiff shall transmit a copy of the settlement proposal to:

Social Security Administration
Office of the General Counsel
Office of the Regional Chief Counsel, Region IX
Attn: Early Review Program
333 Market Street, Suite 1500
San Francisco, CA 94105
Telephone: (415) 977-8943
Facsimile: (415) 744-0134

B. Within twenty-eight (28) days of receipt of the written settlement proposal, the Commissioner shall evaluate the merits of plaintiff's contentions and confer with plaintiff's counsel in writing by mail or facsimile transmission.

C. Within seven (7) days after the service on plaintiff of the Commissioner's written response to the settlement proposal, one of the following actions shall occur:

1. The parties shall electronically file a stipulation dismissing, remanding, or otherwise resolving the case;

2. The parties shall electronically file a Joint Status Report advising the Court that they are exercising their option to extend the due dates an additional fourteen (14) days for continued settlement discussions (such extension is automatic upon filing of the Joint Status Report). Within fourteen (14) days after the electronic filing of a Joint Status Report, the parties shall comply with either paragraph 1 or 3; or,

3. The Commissioner shall electronically file an answer (or a noticed motion to remand).

4. The certified administrative record shall be manually filed with the Clerk and served upon the parties in the traditional manner. A Notice of Manual Filing and Service of the Administrative Record, Form G-92, shall be electronically filed.

VI. Joint Stipulation

If the parties cannot resolve the matter in settlement discussions (and there is no motion to dismiss or motion to remand pending before the Court), the parties shall electronically file a Joint Stipulation in the manner, and according to the schedule, set forth below. The parties shall cooperate in preparing the Joint Stipulation, and sanctions may be imposed for any failure to cooperate. A Joint Stipulation that is not signed by counsel for both parties may be rejected and stricken by the Court. A Joint Stipulation that is electronically filed, but that is not prepared in the manner required by this order, may be stricken, in which event the parties will be required to cure the defects by electronically filing an Amended Joint Stipulation.

VII. Content of Joint Stipulation

The Joint Stipulation shall include a brief summary of the case, the parties' positions with respect to the Administrative Law Judge's ("ALJ") summary of the material medical evidence and testimony of record, a statement of the disputed issues, the parties' contentions with respect to each disputed issue, and the parties' statements of the relief requested. Any issue not raised in the Joint Stipulation may be deemed to have been waived. The Court is familiar with the standard of review and the sequential evaluation process, so the parties should avoid boilerplate discussions of the governing legal standards. Rather, the parties should focus on applying relevant and controlling legal authority to the facts germane to each disputed issue.[2] When citing cases, statutes, regulations, Social Security Rulings, medical and vocational reference sources, or other legal authority to support their legal arguments, the parties shall provide complete and accurate citations to the portions of those authorities relied upon. The parties shall also specify the evidence upon which they rely to support their contentions, and provide accurate page citations to the administrative record for all evidence relied upon ["AR ___"]. In addition, all medical terminology (including medical conditions, diagnoses, procedures, tests, anatomical references, and pharmaceuticals) shall be defined in terms understandable to a layperson, preferably by citation to a medical dictionary or glossary from a standard reference work. The parties may not supplement the record beyond definition of technical terms.

VIII. Form of Joint Stipulation

The Joint Stipulation shall be prepared in the following format, and shall comply with the local rules governing form and typeface:

A. Summary of the Case

Plaintiff shall provide a brief summary of the background facts and procedural history. The Commissioner need not respond to plaintiff's summary, unless the Commissioner believes that plaintiff's summary misstates, mischaracterizes or omits any material facts or proceedings.

B. Medical Evidence

1. Plaintiff shall state whether plaintiff will stipulate that the ALJ's decision fairly and accurately summarizes the material medical evidence and testimony of record. If not, plaintiff shall either (a) specify the respects in which plaintiff contends the ALJ's decision misstates, mischaracterizes, or omits any of the material medical evidence and/or testimony of record, or (b) state that the contentions of misstatement, mischaracterization, or omission are addressed in the argument in support of the Joint Stipulation.

2. The Commissioner shall state whether the Commissioner will stipulate that the ALJ's decision fairly and accurately summarizes the material

[2] The parties should cite only controlling case authority (*i.e.*, decisions of the United States Supreme Court or the Ninth Circuit Court of Appeals). If there is no controlling authority, the decisions of other courts may be cited.

medical evidence and testimony of record. If not, the Commissioner shall either (a) specify the respects in which the Commissioner contends that the ALJ's decision misstates, mischaracterizes, or omits any of the material medical evidence and/or testimony of record, or (b) state that the contentions of misstatement, mischaracterization, or omission are addressed in the argument in support of the Joint Stipulation.

C. Statement of Disputed Issues

Plaintiff shall identify and frame, in a neutral fashion, each of the disputed issues that plaintiff is raising as the grounds for reversal and/or remand. [Example: "Issue No. 1 – Whether the ALJ properly evaluated plaintiff's subjective complaints of pain."]

D. Issues and Contentions

1. Issue No. 1 [The heading shall conform to the first issue listed in the Statement of Disputed Issues.]

a. Plaintiff's Contentions Regarding Issue No. 1 [Plaintiff shall concisely set forth plaintiff's contentions (including citations to the page(s) of the administrative record where cited evidence is found, complete citations to relevant legal authority, and definitions of medical terminology).]

b. The Commissioner's Contentions Regarding Issue No. 1 [The Commissioner shall concisely set forth The Commissioner's contentions (including citations to the page(s) of the administrative record where cited evidence is found, complete citations to relevant legal authority, and definitions of medical terminology).]

c. Plaintiff's Reply Regarding Issue No. 1 [Plaintiff may, but is not required to, reply to the contentions actually raised by the Commissioner; provided, however, that any such reply does not exceed 56 continuous lines of text per issue.]

2. Issue No. 2, etc. [Repeat the foregoing format as needed.]

E. Relief Requested

1. Plaintiff's statement of relief requested.

2. The Commissioner's statement of relief requested.

IX. Schedule for Preparation and Filing of Joint Stipulation

The Joint Stipulation shall be prepared and electronically filed according to the following schedule:

A. Within twenty-one (21) days of the filing of the answer, plaintiff's counsel shall prepare and deliver to the AUSA a draft of plaintiff's portions of the Joint Stipulation (prepared as described in section VIII, paragraphs A, B, C, D subparagraph a, and E). Plaintiff's counsel shall provide the AUSA and the Office of Regional Counsel with a printed copy of plaintiff's portions of the Joint Stipulation and a computer-readable copy on diskette or via e-mail. The draft of plaintiff's portions of the Joint Stipulation shall comply with the format and content requirements set forth elsewhere in this order.

B. Within twenty-eight (28) days of the date on which plaintiff's counsel provides the AUSA and the Office of Regional Counsel with the draft of plaintiff's portions of the Joint Stipulation, the Commissioner shall provide to plaintiff's counsel the

Commissioner's portions of the Joint Stipulation and shall deliver a printed and computer-readable copy of the Commissioner's portions of the Joint Stipulation to plaintiff's counsel. [The Court recognizes that differing word-processing platforms make incorporation of the entire Joint Stipulation into a single electronic document difficult. If the parties do not use the same word-processing platform, the parties may break the Joint Stipulation into different sections on different pages as necessary.]

C. Within fourteen (14) days after the Commissioner provides plaintiff's counsel with the Commissioner's portions of the Joint Stipulation, plaintiff's counsel shall incorporate into the Joint Stipulation any reply that plaintiff may wish to make to the Commissioner's contentions, and shall deliver a completed copy of the Joint Stipulation signed by plaintiff to the AUSA for review, signature and electronic filing. [See paragraph B regarding incorporation and breaking of document.] Plaintiff shall not use the reply to raise new issues that the Commissioner has not had an opportunity to address.

D. Within three (3) days of delivery by plaintiff's counsel of the signed Joint Stipulation, the AUSA shall sign and electronically file the Joint Stipulation. **A courtesy copy of the Joint Stipulation, with the Notice of Electronic Filing attached, shall either (a) be delivered to the Magistrate Judge's chambers (Room 926, Spring Street Courthouse) no later than 4:00 pm on the next court day, or (b) shall be mailed to the Magistrate Judge at 312 N. Spring Street, Los Angeles, CA 90012, no later than the next court day.**

X. Requests for Extensions of Time

The deadlines set forth in this order are designed to give parties exercising reasonable diligence sufficient time to perform the required acts without seeking extensions of time. Accordingly, requests for extensions of time are discouraged. Any such request shall set forth specific facts showing that additional time is needed despite diligent attempts to meet a deadline. Requests for extensions of time shall be electronically filed at least three (3) days before the deadline that is the subject of the request. Whenever possible, a request for extension of time should be made in the form of a proposed stipulated order.

XI. Oral Argument

Unless otherwise ordered, the issues presented in any Joint Stipulation shall be deemed submitted for decision without oral argument.

XII. Motions and Petitions for Attorney Fees

A. Equal Access to Justice Act

1. Any motion or petition for attorney fees, costs, and expenses shall be made in accordance with 28 U.S.C. § 2412 (EAJA). Plaintiff shall electronically file a notice of any motion or petition for attorney fees, costs, and expenses under the EAJA and manually serve a copy on the Office of Regional Counsel. **A courtesy copy of the motion or petition and supporting papers, with the Notice of Electronic Filing attached, shall either (a) be delivered to the Magistrate Judge's chambers (Room 926, Spring Street Courthouse) no later than 4:00 pm on the next court day, or (b) shall be mailed to the Magistrate Judge at 312 N. Spring Street, Los Angeles, CA 90012, no later than the next court day.**

2. The Commissioner shall have a period of twenty-one (21) days from the date of electronic filing of the motion or petition within which to electronically file the Commissioner's opposition to the motion or petition. **A courtesy copy of the Commissioner's opposition papers, with the**

Notice of Electronic Filing attached, shall either (a) be delivered to the Magistrate Judge's chambers (Room 926, Spring Street Courthouse) no later than 4:00 pm on the next court day, or (b) shall be mailed to the Magistrate Judge at 312 N. Spring Street, Los Angeles, CA 90012, no later than the next court day.

3. If the Commissioner believes that there is a possibility of arriving at a settlement with plaintiff of the fees, costs and expenses issue, the parties shall electronically file a stipulation to extend the time for the Commissioner to file an opposition for the purpose of affording the parties an opportunity to discuss settlement. Any such stipulated extension shall be electronically filed prior to the date the Commissioner's opposition is due, and the stipulated extension shall be for no more than thirty (30) days.

4. Assuming either that there is no extension to discuss settlement or that no settlement is reached after such an extension, plaintiff may electronically file a reply to the Commissioner's opposition within ten (10) days of service thereof. **A courtesy copy of the reply papers, with the Notice of Electronic Filing attached, shall either (a) be delivered to the Magistrate Judge's chambers (Room 926, Spring Street Courthouse) no later than 4:00 pm on the next court day, or (b) shall be mailed to the Magistrate Judge at 312 N. Spring Street, Los Angeles, CA 90012, no later than the next court day.**

5. The matter will stand submitted pursuant to Local Rule 7-15 as of the date of the last filing.

B. 42 U.S.C. § 406(b)

1. Any motion or petition for attorney fees pursuant to 42 U.S.C. § 406(b) shall be made by plaintiff's counsel within a reasonable time after the publication of a notice by the Commissioner allowing the Court to determine the maximum allowable fee under that provision. The motion or petition shall include a statement by plaintiff's counsel indicating the amount of EAJA fees and/or 42 U.S.C. § 406(a) fees awarded and/or requested.

2. Plaintiff's counsel shall electronically file a motion or petition for attorney fees pursuant to 42 U.S.C. § 406(b) and manually serve copies on the Office of Regional Counsel and on the plaintiff. Plaintiff's counsel shall state in any notice that plaintiff may file any statement or opposition with the Court not more than fourteen (14) days after service of the motion [petition], and that any statement or opposition filed by plaintiff shall be served on both plaintiff's counsel and the AUSA. **A courtesy copy of the motion or petition and supporting papers, with the Notice of Electronic Filing attached, shall either (a) be delivered to the Magistrate Judge's chambers (Room 926, Spring Street Courthouse) no later than 4:00 pm on the next court day, or (b) shall be mailed to the Magistrate Judge at 312 N. Spring Street, Los Angeles, CA 90012, no later than the next court day.**

3. The Commissioner shall electronically file any statement or opposition not more than fourteen (14) days after service of the motion or petition, and also manually serve a copy on the plaintiff. **A courtesy copy of**

the Commissioner's statement or opposition papers, with the Notice of Electronic Filing attached, shall either (a) be delivered to the Magistrate Judge's chambers (Room 926, Spring Street Courthouse) no later than 4:00 pm on the next court day, or (b) shall be mailed to the Magistrate Judge at 312 N. Spring Street, Los Angeles, CA 90012, no later than the next court day.

4. Plaintiff's counsel may electronically file a reply in support of the motion or petition within seven (7) days of service of any statement or opposition, and also manually serve a copy on the plaintiff. **A courtesy copy of the reply papers, with the Notice of Electronic Filing attached, shall either (a) be delivered to the Magistrate Judge's chambers (Room 926, Spring Street Courthouse) no later than 4:00 pm on the next court day, or (b) shall be mailed to the Magistrate Judge at 312 N. Spring Street, Los Angeles, CA 90012, no later than the next court day.**

5. The matter will stand submitted pursuant to Local Rule 7-15 as of the date the last filing is due.

IT IS SO ORDERED.

DATED: June ____, 2005

____
PAUL L. ABRAMS
United States Magistrate Judge

Hon. Robert N. Block

Magistrate Judge

Chambers Information

U.S. District Court, Central District of California
Courtroom 6D
411 West Fourth Street
Santa Ana, CA 92701

Scheduling Information

Courtroom Deputy: (714) 338-4754

Civil Law and Motion	Tuesdays at 9:30 a.m.

Biographical Information

[Not available]

I. Judge Block's Procedures and Practices

A. Procedures and Schedules

1. Civil motions are heard on **Tuesdays at 9:30 a.m.**

   It is not necessary to clear a motion date with the court clerk prior to filing the motion, although the Judge reserves the right to sua sponte continue motions or decide them on the papers without oral argument. The Judge does not permit telephonic appearances for hearings absent exceptional circumstances.

2. Discovery motions are to be set before the district judge unless the district judge to whom the case is assigned has a blanket referral of all discovery matters to the magistrate judge or already has issued a case specific order referring all discovery matters to the magistrate judge. (See Discovery Referral Sheet.) Strict compliance with Local Rules 37-1 and 37-2 is required. It is the Judge's general practice to decline requests by counsel for telephonic conferences to resolve discovery disputes that arise during pending depositions.

3. If there is a tentative ruling, it will be provided to counsel at the time counsel checks in with the court clerk

4. E-Filing: Failure to strictly comply with General Order 10-07 will result in a party's papers not being considered. Courtesy paper copies of e-filed documents shall be delivered to the courtesy copy box outside chambers, 6th Floor, Santa Ana, no later than 12:00 noon the following business day after filing. It is the Judge's general practice to take no action on e-filed documents until after the courtesy copies are received.

5. Procedures for filing an ex parte application: Strict compliance with Local Rule 7-19 and 7-19.1 will be required. An ex parte application is usually considered on the papers only. If the application is opposed, opposition papers should be filed no later than noon on the first court day following electronic filing of the application. In most cases, the Court will wait until that time before ruling. If needed, the Court will schedule a hearing.

6. Continuances of any scheduled court proceeding will be granted only on a showing of good cause. To request a continuance, the parties should submit a signed stipulation and proposed order. If opposing counsel will not agree to a continuance, the request should be made by ex parte application.

7. Counsel are not allowed to call chambers, the Judge's law clerk, or his judicial assistant, unless specifically directed to do so by the Judge or the court clerk.

8. Calls will not be returned regarding the status of a motion, stipulation, or proposed order. Counsel should check the docket sheet to ascertain the status.

9. Calendar conflicts: (Procedures for attorneys to follow if they have a calendar conflict). Immediately advise the court clerk telephonically; attempt to secure other counsel's agreement to stipulate to a new date.

10. Electronic equipment: Permission to bring in or use audio, video, or electronic equipment should be requested from the court clerk in advance of the date of the court proceeding.

11. For general information on how to order a transcript of any reported or digitally

recorded proceeding, please contact 213-894-3015 or visit www.cacd.uscourts.gov > General Information > Court Reporter/Recorder Transcripts. If you require an estimate of cost for the preparation of a transcript, contact the court reporter/recorder for the desired proceeding.

To determine the court reporter/recorder for a particular proceeding, go to the Court Reporter Schedule web page and click on View by Date. Once you've determined the correct court reporter/recorder for the desired session, click on Court Reporter Phone and Email List for contact information.

12. Questions regarding law clerk/extern positions: Communicate via letter to the Judge.

13. Trial preparation:

a. Court hours: The Judge generally conducts bench trials from 8:30 a.m. to 2:30 p.m. with no lunch break. For jury trials, the hours generally are from 9:00 a.m. to 12:00 noon and 1:30 p.m. to 4:30 p.m. for short cases (i.e., less than 5 days), and from 8:30 a.m. to 2:30 p.m. with no lunch break for longer cases. The final determination of trial hours will be made at the final pretrial conference.

b. Other instructions: see exemplars of bench trial order and jury trial order below.

14. It is the responsibility of the parties to obtain the services of an interpreter on a civil case if one is needed.

15. Settlement conferences: The parties should contact the court clerk about dates available for settlement conferences. The proposed date(s) should be at least two weeks in advance. The Judge has its own settlement conference order, which differs in some respects from Local Rule 16-14.5. (See exemplar of settlement conference order below). All settlement conference papers should be delivered directly to the Judge's chambers, Room 6166, 6th floor. In lieu of personal delivery, settlement conference papers may be faxed to chambers at 714-338-2895, but only if the total number of pages being faxed is 15 or less.

16. Stipulated protective orders: see list of recurring mistakes below.

17. Other information: The Judge does not permit special appearances. Counsel of record shall appear at all court proceedings.

B. Recurring Mistakes in Stipulated Protective Orders

RECURRING MISTAKES IN STIPULATED PROTECTIVE ORDERS

1. Frequently, the parties do not make a sufficient showing of good cause as required by Fed. R. Civ. P. 26(c). Such showing should be made separate from the parties' stipulation regarding the terms of the proposed protective order.

2. Frequently, the proposed protective order does not define with sufficient particularity the kinds of information which will qualify a document for designation as "Confidential" and subject to protection under the terms of the protective order. For example, the proposed protective order does not limit the designation to information which has not been made public, or limit the designation to information which the party in good faith believes will, if disclosed, have the effect of causing harm to its competitive position. Sometime, the proposed protective order even purports to provide blanket protection for all documents, material and information produced or disclosed during discovery.

3. Proposed two-tiered proposed protective orders also need to define with sufficient particularity the kinds of information that will qualify a document for designation as or "Attorneys Eyes Only."

4. The proposed protective order invariably contains provisions identifying the classes of persons to whom protected information may be disclosed, and requiring that all persons to whom protected information is disclosed sign a confidentiality agreement. Frequently, the listing of persons to whom protected information may be disclosed includes the Court and court personnel, and the proposed protective order fails to exclude the Court and court personnel from the requirement to sign a confidentiality agreement. The parties need to make clear that such a requirement does not apply to the Court or court personnel.

5. It is the custom and practice of the Central District of California for the assigned Magistrate Judge to issue protective orders relating to discovery. Sometimes the proposed protective order speaks in terms of what the parties and persons to whom protected information is disclosed are "enjoined" from doing. The proposed protective order should not use the word "enjoined" since Magistrate Judges lack jurisdiction to issue injunctive relief under 28 U.S.C. § 636(b)(1)(A).

6. Frequently, the proposed protective order purports to authorize in advance the filing under seal of documents containing protected information. However, neither the fact that counsel have stipulated to an under seal filing nor the fact that a proposed filing contains information that one of the parties elected to designate as "Confidential" or "Attorneys Eyes Only" in accordance with the terms of the protective order is sufficient in itself for the Court to find that good cause exists to file the papers or the portion containing the designated information under seal. At the very least, the parties will need to convince the Court in their application that protection clearly is warranted for the designated information or documents. For declarations with exhibits, this means making the requisite showing on an exhibit by exhibit basis. In accordance with Local Rule 79-5.1, the provision in question should provide that, if any papers to be filed with the Court contain protected information, the proposed filing shall be accompanied by an application to file the papers or the portion thereof containing the protected information (if such portion is segregable) under seal; and that the application shall be directed to the judge to whom the papers are directed. For motions, the parties should also file a redacted version of the motion and supporting papers.

7. Sometimes, the proposed protective order purports also to apply to evidence presented at court proceedings and/or trial. The proposed protective order should not include any provisions relating to evidence presented at court proceedings and/or trial. The parties will need to take up that matter with the judicial officer conducting the proceeding at the appropriate time.

8. Sometimes (most likely when lead counsel for both sides are non-local attorneys), the proposed protective order specifies a procedure for resolving disputes over the designation of documents which does not comport with the requirements under Local Rules 37-1 and 37-2 governing discovery disputes (including the requirement that the parties file a Joint Stipulation concerning the matters in dispute).

9. Sometimes, the proposed protective order contains a provision that purports to restrict or limit the rights of the parties in another action to conduct discovery or the subpoena power of another court (*e.g.*, a provision that contains a 21-day no disclosure requirement). The proposed protective order should contain a provision to the following effect: "Nothing in this Order shall be construed as authorizing a party to disobey a lawful subpoena issued in another action."

10. Sometimes, the proposed protective order specifies that any violation of its terms "**will**" constitute contempt of Court," as opposed to "**may** constitute contempt of Court."

11. Frequently, the proposed protective order contains a provision which provides that it may be modified on the stipulation of the parties. The proposed protective order needs to make clear that no modification by the parties shall have the force or effect of a Court order unless the Court approves the modification.

II. Judge Block's Case Management Orders

A. *Civil Bench Trial Order*

IN THE UNITED STATES DISTICT COURT
FOR THE CENTRAL DISTRICT OF CALIFORNIA

Plaintiff(s), v. Defendant(s).	Case No. ______________ **CIVIL BENCH TRIAL ORDER**

This case is set for a bench trial before the Honorable Robert N. Block, in Courtroom No. 6D, Ronald Reagan Federal Building and United States Courthouse, 411 West Fourth Street, Santa Ana, California.

To facilitate the efficient conduct of the trial in this matter, all parties shall review carefully the following Order and instructions, as well as the Court's Scheduling and Case Management Order.

I. Proposed Findings of Fact and Conclusions of Law

On the date specified in the schedule attached as Exhibit A to the Scheduling and Case Management Order, each party shall lodge its proposed Findings of Fact and Conclusions of Law. Concurrently, each party shall also deliver to chambers a copy of this document on disk in either Microsoft Word or WordPerfect® 6.0 or higher format.

II. Witness Declarations

Concurrently with the filing of their proposed Findings of Fact and Conclusions of Law, counsel for each party shall either (a) file and serve by e-mail, fax, or personal delivery an executed declaration in lieu of direct testimony for each witness that party intends to call at trial, or (b) if, and only if, such testimony is contained in discrete portions of a deposition, lodge a copy of the deposition provided it has been marked in accordance with the Local Rules (including with the opposing party's objections to the proffered evidence).

Not later than five (5) court days prior to trial, each party shall file and serve by e-mail, fax, or personal delivery its written objections (if any) to the testimony contained in the opposing party's declarations. Failure to timely file such written objections will be deemed by the Court as a waiver of any evidentiary objections.

The Court expects to read the declarations and/or pertinent portions of the lodged depositions in chambers prior to trial. At trial, the Court will rule on any timely-filed objections, and permit "live" questioning only for cross-examination and re-direct of each such witness.

These provisions do not apply to adverse or hostile witnesses; rather, counsel may call such witnesses to the stand for live examination during their case-in-chief.

III. Trial Times

The Court generally conducts bench trials Tuesday through Friday, from 8:30 a.m. to 2:30 p.m., with two 15-minute breaks, normally at 10:00 a.m. and 12:00 p.m. This schedule is subject to change.

IV. Exhibits

A. Format

The parties shall prepare their exhibits for presentation at trial by placing them in 3-ring binders in the following format.

1. Each binder shall be divided by tabs down the side with corresponding exhibit numbers.

2. In the original set of exhibits to be filed with the Court and maintained by the Courtroom Deputy during trial, each exhibit shall be tagged with the appropriate filled-out exhibit tags in the lower or upper right hand corner of the first page of each exhibit.

3. The exhibits shall be numbered in accordance with Local Rule 26-3.

4. The front of each binder shall contain a list of each exhibit included, with a notation indicating whether the parties have stipulated to the admission of the exhibit.

B. Filing

Each party shall file an original and one copy of their exhibit binder(s) on the first day of trial. The parties shall also present to the Courtroom Deputy three (3) extra copies of the joint exhibit list.

V. Deposition Transcripts

The Court expects strict compliance with Local Rules 16-2.7 and 32-1. If not already lodged, an extra copy of each deposition transcript anticipated to be used at trial for any purpose shall also be presented to the Courtroom Deputy on the first day of trial, when counsel check in.

VI. Extra copies of Witness Lists

When counsel check in on the first day of trial, they shall also present to the Courtroom Deputy three (3) copies of their witness list, in the order in which the witnesses are anticipated to testify. If a witness is not going to be testifying live, then the words "By deposition" shall be added in parentheses and underlined in red after the witness' name.

VII. Opening Statements, Closing Argument, and Post-Trial Briefs

It is the Court's general practice to dispense with opening statements in bench trials.

For an overview and review of the evidence, the Court will rely exclusively on closing argument. It will not accept or read post-trial briefs, unless specifically authorized in advance. In delivering their closing arguments, counsel should use their respective proposed findings of fact and conclusions of law as a "checklist," and should identify the evidence that supports each proposed finding.

VIII. Rules of Courtroom Etiquette

A. Examination of Witnesses

1. Counsel should examine witnesses from the lectern only, and speak audibly and clearly when examining a witness or interposing an objection. Counsel should instruct their witnesses to speak audibly and clearly as well.

2. Counsel should not approach a witness without securing permission in advance from the Court. The Court will only grant permission for the limited purpose of placing a document (after showing it first to opposing counsel) before the witness. If necessary to direct the witness' attention to something particular in the document, counsel may remain adjacent to the witness box for that limited purpose. Otherwise, counsel shall return to the lectern when the purpose of the approach is finished.

3. If a party is represented by more than one lawyer, only one lawyer may conduct the direct or cross-examination of a given witness, or argue a given motion.

4. At the end of each trial day, counsel for the party presenting its case shall advise opposing counsel of the witnesses anticipated to be called the following trial day with an estimate of the length of direct-examination. Opposing counsel shall then provide an estimate of the length of cross-examination.

B. Objections to Questions

1. Counsel should rise when making an objection.

2. Counsel should not use objections for the purpose of making speeches, recapitulating testimony or attempting to coach the witness.

3. When objecting, counsel should rise to state the objection, and then state only that counsel is objecting and the legal ground of the objection (*e.g.*, hearsay, irrelevant, *etc.*). If counsel wishes to argue an objection further, counsel should ask for permission to do so.

C. Use of Depositions

1. In using depositions of an adverse party for impeachment, counsel shall use either one of the following procedures:

a. If counsel wishes to read the questions and answers as alleged impeachment and ask the witness no further questions on that subject, counsel shall first state the page and line where the reading begins and the page and line where the reading ends, and allow time for any objection. Counsel may then read the portions of the deposition into the record.

b. If counsel wishes to ask the witness further questions on the subject matter, the deposition shall be placed in front of the witness and the witness shall be instructed to read silently the pages and lines involved. Then counsel may ask the witness further questions on the matter and thereafter read the quotations, or counsel may read the quotations and thereafter ask the further questions. Counsel should have an extra copy of the deposition for this purpose.

2. Where a witness is absent and the witness' testimony is offered by deposition, a reader should occupy the witness chair and read the testimony of the witness while the examining lawyer asks the questions. However, if the offered testimony is relatively short in length (i.e., less than one transcript page), then the Court will permit counsel to read both the questions and the answers.

D. Use of numerous answers to interrogatories and/or requests for admission

Whenever counsel expects to offer a group of answers to interrogatories or requests for admission extracted from one or more lengthy documents, counsel should prepare a new document listing each question and/or request for admission and each answer, and identifying the document from which the answer has been extracted. Copies of this new document should be given to the Court and opposing counsel. This procedure is intended to conserve time.

E. Exhibits

1. Each counsel should keep his/her own list of exhibits and keep track of which exhibits have been admitted into evidence.

2. Each counsel shall be responsible for any exhibits that he/she secures from the Courtroom Deputy and, at all recesses and at the afternoon adjournment, shall return all exhibits in his/her possession to the Courtroom Deputy.

3. An exhibit not previously marked should, at the time of its first mention, be accompanied by a request that the Courtroom Deputy mark it for identification. To save time, counsel should show a new exhibit to opposing counsel before it is mentioned in Court.

4. When referring to an exhibit, counsel should refer to its exhibit number whenever possible. Witnesses should be instructed to do the same.

5. Absent unusual circumstances, counsel shall not ask witnesses to draw charts or diagrams nor ask the Court's permission to do so. If counsel wishes to question a witness in connection with graphic aids, the material should be fully prepared before the court session begins.

F. Promptness of Counsel and Witnesses

1. Counsel are expected to arrive on time and be prepared to proceed, as the Court intends to start on time. Promptness also is expected from witnesses. It shall be counsel's duty to advise the Court on the first day of trial of any commitments in any other court on subsequent trial days that may result in absence or late arrival. However, the Court reserves the right to insist that, once trial has commenced, it shall be counsel's first priority.

2. If a witness was on the stand at a recess or adjournment, it is the duty of counsel who called the witness to have the witness back on the stand, ready to proceed, when Court resumes.

3. Counsel should not run out of witnesses. If counsel has no more witnesses to call and there is more than a brief delay, the Court may deem that party to have rested.

4. The Court attempts to cooperate with doctors and other professional witnesses and will, except in extraordinary circumstances, accommodate them by permitting them to be called out of sequence. Counsel should anticipate any such possibility and discuss it with opposing counsel in advance. If there is an objection, this should be brought to the Court's attention in advance.

G. Advance Notice of Unusual or Difficult Issues

If any counsel has reason to anticipate that a difficult question of law or evidence will necessitate legal argument regarding research or briefing, counsel must give the Court advance notice. Counsel shall notify the Courtroom Deputy at the day's adjournment if an unexpected legal issue has arisen that could not have been foreseen and addressed by a motion *in limine*. See Fed. R. Evid. 103.

H. General Decorum

1. The trial is not an oratorical contest. The trial should be a quiet, dignified search for the truth.

2. Counsel should rise when addressing the Court.

3. All remarks by counsel should be addressed to the Court. While the judge is present, counsel should not address the Courtroom Deputy, the Reporter or opposing counsel. If counsel wishes to say something to opposing counsel, permission from the Court to speak off the record should be requested. All requests for the re-reading of questions or answers, or to have an exhibit placed in front of a witness, should be addressed to the Court.

4. Counsel should not address or refer to witnesses by their first names, unless they are children.

5. The maintenance of personal dignity requires care in the pronunciation of a person's surname. If necessary, counsel should inquire privately, in advance of the first reference to the name in court, how a person pronounces his or her name and how he or she prefers to be addressed (e.g., whether Maria Lopez Garcia prefers to be referred to as Ms. Garcia or Mrs. Lopez Garcia).

6. While Court is in session, counsel should not leave the counsel table to confer with investigators, secretaries or witnesses in the back of the Courtroom unless permission has been secured in advance from the Court.

7. Counsel should not by facial expression, nodding or other conduct exhibit any opinion (adverse or favorable) concerning any testimony being given by a witness. Counsel should admonish their own clients and witnesses to avoid such conduct.

IT IS SO ORDERED.

DATED: ________________

ROBERT N. BLOCK
United States Magistrate Judge

B. *Civil Jury Trial Order*

IN THE UNITED STATES DISTICT COURT
FOR THE CENTRAL DISTRICT OF CALIFORNIA

	)	Case No. ______________
Plaintiff(s),	)	
v.	)	**CIVIL JURY TRIAL ORDER**
Defendant(s).	)	
______________________________	)	

This case is set for a jury trial before the Honorable Robert N. Block, in Courtroom No. 6D, Ronald Reagan Federal Building and United States Courthouse, 411 West Fourth Street, Santa Ana, California.

To facilitate the efficient conduct of the trial in this matter, all parties shall review carefully the following Order and instructions, as well as the Court's Scheduling and Case Management Order.

I. Jury Instructions, Verdict Forms and Special Interrogatories

Fourteen (14) days before the Rule 16 meeting of counsel, the parties shall exchange proposed jury instructions, verdict forms and special interrogatories. Seven (7) days before the meeting, the parties shall exchange written objections, if any, to each other's proposed jury instructions, verdict forms and special interrogatories. At the Rule 16 meeting, counsel shall confer with the objective of submitting one set of agreed-upon substantive jury instructions, verdict forms and, if necessary, special interrogatories.

"Substantive jury instructions" means all instructions relating to the elements of all claims and defenses in the case.[1] The parties need not submit general instructions. Each jointly requested instruction shall be typed and set forth in full; be on a separate page; cover only one subject or principle of law; and not repeat principles of law contained in any other jointly requested instructions.

If the parties are unable to agree upon one complete set of substantive instructions, verdict forms and special interrogatories, they shall file two documents with the Court on the date specified in the schedule attached as Exhibit A to the Scheduling and Case Management Order: first, a joint document reflecting the agreed-upon instructions, verdict forms and special interrogatories, if any; and second, a joint statement regarding the disputed instructions, verdict forms and special interrogatories. The second document (the joint statement) shall be prepared in the following format for each disputed instruction, verdict form and special interrogatory:

a. A separate page containing the text of the disputed instruction, verdict form, or special interrogatory with an identification of the party proposing it;

---

[1] The parties are advised that the Court prefers the use of Ninth Circuit model instructions as modified or supplemented to fit the circumstances of the case. Where California law is to be applied and the Ninth Circuit model instructions are inapplicable, counsel are directed to use California Civil Jury (BAJI) and/or the Judicial Council of California Civil Jury Instructions (CACI). If none of these sources is applicable, counsel are directed to use the instructions in O'Malley, Grenig & Lee, *Federal Jury Practice and Instructions, Fifth*, to the extent applicable. Modifications of instructions from the foregoing sources (or any other form instructions) must specifically state the modification made to the original form instructions, and cite the authority supporting the modification.

b. Following the text, the opposing party's statement of objections, along with legal authority in support of the objections (not to exceed one page) and proposed alternative language where appropriate;

c. The proposing party's response to the objection with legal authority supporting the proposed language (not to exceed one page).

A table of contents shall be included with all jury instructions submitted to the Court. The table of contents shall set forth the following:

a. The number of the instruction;
b. A brief title of the instruction;
c. The source of the instruction; and
d. The page number of the instruction.

For example:

Number	Title	Source	Page Number
7	Trademark-Defined	9th Cir. 15.3.2	8

Concurrently, the parties shall also deliver to chambers a copy of these filings on disk in either Microsoft Word or WordPerfect® 6.0 or higher format.

During the course of the trial and before closing arguments, the Court will meet with counsel and settle disputes regarding the submitted instructions, verdict forms and special interrogatories. The Court also will address any other instructions deemed warranted by unexpected developments during the course of the trial.

Unless all counsel agree to have the Court instruct the jury before closing argument, the Court will instruct the jury after closing argument. The Court also will send copies of the jury instructions, verdict forms and special interrogatories into the jury room for use by the jury during deliberations.

II. Joint Statement of the Case

Concurrently with the filing of their jury instruction document(s), the parties shall also file a joint statement generally describing the action, to be read to the jury by the Court prior to the commencement of voir dire. This statement shall include the names of the parties and a brief description of plaintiff(s)' claims. It should not exceed two pages in length, and ordinarily two or three paragraphs should suffice.

III. *Voir Dire* Questions

Concurrently with the filing of their jury instruction document(s), each party shall also file its separate proposed *voir dire* questions. The parties need not submit requests for standard *voir dire* questions (e.g., education, current occupation, marital status, prior jury service, etc.), but rather should include only proposed questions tailored to the parties and issues of the case.

IV. Trial Times

On the first day of trial, court will commence at 8:30 a.m., and conclude at approximately 4:30 p.m., with a lunch break. The Court initially will meet with counsel to ensure that all matters necessary for resolution prior to trial have been resolved. The jury panel will be called when the Court is satisfied that the matter is ready for trial. Jury selection usually can be accomplished in a few hours, so counsel should be prepared to proceed with their opening statements and witness examination immediately after jury selection.

After the first day of trial, trial days will be Tuesday through Friday, from 8:30 a.m. to

2:30 p.m., with two 15-minute breaks, normally at 10:00 a.m. and 12:00 p.m. As necessary, the Court will meet with counsel before and/or after each day's regular trial session to deal with such matters as anticipated evidentiary problems and jury instructions. This schedule is subject to change.

V. <u>Jury Selection</u>

The Court will conduct *voir dire* of all prospective jurors, after taking into consideration each party's timely filed proposed *voir dire* questions.

In selecting a jury, the following procedures will most likely be followed. The Courtroom Deputy initially will sit the entire group of prospective jurors in the

visitors benches of the Courtroom. The Court then will read the agreed-upon joint statement of the case and determine whether any prospective jurors should be excused for cause because, for example, they know a lawyer, party or prospective witness. The Court also will determine whether the length of the trial requires that other prospective jurors be excused for "undue hardship." From the remaining pool of prospective jurors, the Courtroom Deputy will select at random 13 or 14 jurors. Each of these

prospective jurors will then answer in turn some general questions (e.g., occupation, education, prior jury experience). The Court then will ask more specific *voir dire* questions that have been individually tailored for the case.

Following the questioning of each of the 13-14 prospective jurors, the Court will entertain challenges for cause. The parties are advised that the Court will not necessarily accept a stipulation to a challenge for cause. The prospective jurors excused for cause will be replaced by jurors selected at random from the remaining pool. The new jurors will then be questioned, and the process will be repeated until the Court determines that none of prospective 13 or 14 jurors should be excused for cause.

Each side then will be permitted up to three (3) peremptory challenges, on an alternating basis.[2] To avoid the potential embarrassment of a disallowed peremptory challenge on the grounds set forth in *Batson v. Kentucky*, 476 U.S. 79, 106 S. Ct. 1712, 90 L. Ed. 2d 69 (1986), the party making a *Batson* objection shall request a side bar. At side bar, the party making the *Batson* objection will be required to make the requisite *prima facie* showing, before the Court will ask opposing counsel to provide an explanation for striking the prospective juror(s) in question.

Following the resolution of all challenges, the first seven (7) of the remaining randomly-called prospective jurors will constitute the jury panel for trials estimated to last four (4) days or less. For trials estimated to last more than four (4) days, the first eight (8) of the remaining randomly-called prospective jurors will constitute the jury panel.

VI. <u>Exhibits</u>

A. <u>Format</u>

The parties shall prepare their exhibits for presentation at trial by placing them in 3-ring binders in the following format.

1. Each binder shall be divided by tabs down the side with corresponding exhibit numbers.

2. In the original set of exhibits to be filed with the Court and

---

2 The Court may allow up to three (3) peremptory challenges per party where there are multiple parties with adverse interests on one or both sides.

maintained by the Courtroom Deputy during trial, each exhibit shall be tagged with the appropriate filled-out exhibit tags in the lower or upper right hand corner of the first page of each exhibit.

3. The exhibits shall be numbered in accordance with Local Rule 26-3.

4. The front of each binder shall contain a list of each exhibit included, with a notation indicating whether the parties have stipulated to the admission of the exhibit.

B. Filing

Each party shall file an original and one copy of their exhibit binder(s) on the first day of trial. The parties shall also present to the Courtroom Deputy three (3) extra copies of the joint exhibit list.

C. Presentation to the Jury

In jury cases where a significant number of exhibits are to be admitted, the Court encourages counsel, preferably by prior agreement, to consider ways in which testimony about exhibits may be clarified for the jury while it is being presented. Counsel should consider the use of such devices as overhead or ELMO projectors, jury notebooks for admitted exhibits, and/or blow-ups of important exhibits. Where appropriate, counsel should take advantage of Fed. R. Evid. 1006 ("Summaries") to present voluminous evidence. Only in rare circumstances will the Court permit counsel to pass exhibits up and down the jury box.

VII. Deposition Transcripts

The Court expects strict compliance with Local Rules 16-2.7 and 32-1. An extra copy of each deposition transcript anticipated to be used at trial for any purpose shall also be presented to the Courtroom Deputy on the first day of trial, when counsel check in.

VIII. Extra copies of Witness Lists

When counsel check in on the first day of trial, they shall also present to the Courtroom Deputy three copies (3) of their witness list, in the order in which the witnesses are anticipated to testify. If a witness is not going to be testifying live, then the words "By deposition" shall be added in parentheses and underlined in red after the witness' name.

IX. Rules of Courtroom Etiquette

A. Opening Statements and Closing Arguments

1. Opening statements and closing arguments should be delivered from the lectern only.

2. Counsel should keep in mind that the purpose of an opening statement is to inform the jurors of the nature of the case, the facts they expect to be proved in the trial and the issues in the case. An opening statement is not an argument to the jury, and it is not permissible to attempt to argue to the jury about the application of the law to the facts at this stage of the case.

B. Examination of Witnesses

1. Counsel should examine witnesses from the lectern only, and speak audibly and clearly when examining a witness or interposing an objection. Counsel should instruct their witnesses to speak audibly and clearly as well.

2. Counsel should not approach a witness without securing permission in advance from the Court. The Court will only grant permission for the limited purpose of placing a document (after showing it first to opposing counsel) before the witness. If necessary to direct the witness' attention to something particular in the document, counsel may remain adjacent to the witness box for that limited purpose. Otherwise, counsel shall return to the lectern when the purpose of the approach is finished.

3. If a party is represented by more than one lawyer, only one lawyer may conduct the direct or cross-examination of a given witness, or argue a given motion.

4. At the end of each trial day, counsel for the party presenting its case shall advise opposing counsel of the witnesses anticipated to be called the following trial day with an estimate of the length of direct-examination. Opposing counsel shall then provide an estimate of the length of cross-examination.

C. Objections to Questions

1. Counsel should rise when making an objection.

2. Counsel should not use objections for the purpose of making speeches, recapitulating testimony or attempting to coach the witness.

3. When objecting, counsel should rise to state the objection, and then state only that counsel is objecting and the legal ground of the objection (e.g., hearsay, irrelevant, etc.). If counsel wishes to argue an objection further, counsel should ask for permission to do so. Only rarely will the Court permit side-bar conferences about evidentiary issues during a jury trial. Most unusual or complex evidentiary issues can be foreseen and disposed of in advance; those that cannot ordinarily will be disposed of at the next recess, with the witness retained until the issue is resolved.

D. Use of Depositions

1. In using depositions of an adverse party for impeachment, counsel shall use either one of the following procedures:

> **a.** If counsel wishes to read the questions and answers as alleged impeachment and ask the witness no further questions on that subject, counsel shall first state the page and line where the reading begins and the page and line where the reading ends, and allow time for any objection. Counsel may then read the portions of the deposition into the record.
>
> **b.** If counsel wishes to ask the witness further questions on the subject matter, the deposition shall be placed in front of the witness and the witness shall be instructed to read silently the pages and lines involved. Then counsel may ask the witness further questions on the matter and thereafter read the quotations, or counsel may read the quotations and thereafter ask the further questions. Counsel should have an extra copy of the deposition for this purpose.

2. Where a witness is absent and the witness' testimony is offered by deposition, a reader should occupy the witness chair and read the testimony of the witness while the examining lawyer asks the questions. However, if the offered testimony is relatively short in length (i.e., less than one transcript page), then the Court will permit counsel to read both the questions and the answers.

E. Use of numerous answers to interrogatories and/or requests for admission

Whenever counsel expects to offer a group of answers to interrogatories or requests for admission extracted from one or more lengthy documents, counsel should prepare a new document listing each question and/or request for admission and each answer, and identifying the document from which the answer has been extracted. Copies of this new document should be given to the Court and opposing counsel. This procedure is intended to conserve time.

F. Exhibits

1. Each counsel should keep his/her own list of exhibits and keep track of which exhibits have been admitted into evidence.

2. Each counsel shall be responsible for any exhibits that he/she secures from the Courtroom Deputy and, at all recesses and at the afternoon adjournment, shall return all exhibits in his/her possession to the Courtroom Deputy.

3. An exhibit not previously marked should, at the time of its first mention, be accompanied by a request that the Courtroom Deputy mark it for identification. To save time, counsel should show a new exhibit to opposing counsel before it is mentioned in Court.

4. No exhibit shall be read or displayed to the jury before it is admitted. The Court regards admissibility of exhibits as a legal issue for the Court to rule on unless there is agreement among counsel. Counsel are admonished to make no motion to admit an exhibit while the jury is present unless counsel previously has conferred with opposing counsel and knows that there will be no objection to the admission of the exhibit. Whenever the Court hears a motion to admit an exhibit while the jury is present, the Court will assume that counsel already has cleared admission of the exhibit with opposing counsel and grant the motion. If opposing counsel does interpose an objection, the Court will expect a full explanation from counsel who made the motion to admit the exhibit why he/she did so in the jury's presence.

5. When referring to an exhibit, counsel should refer to its exhibit number whenever possible. Witnesses should be instructed to do the same.

6. Absent unusual circumstances, counsel shall not ask witnesses to draw charts or diagrams nor ask the Court's permission to do so. If counsel wishes to question a witness in connection with graphic aids, the material should be fully prepared before the court session begins.

7. Counsel should not attempt to use or display any enlargements of exhibits or charts unless all counsel agree to such use, or the Court has ruled on any objections in advance. This applies to opening arguments as well.

G. Advance Notice of Unusual or Difficult Issues

If any counsel has reason to anticipate that a difficult question of law or evidence will necessitate legal argument regarding research or briefing, counsel must give the Court advance notice. Counsel shall notify the Courtroom Deputy at the day's adjournment if an unexpected legal issue has arisen that could not have been foreseen and addressed by a motion *in limine*. *See* Fed. R. Evid. 103. To the maximum extent possible, the Court will address such issues either before or after a day's regular trial session.

H. Promptness of Counsel and Witnesses

1. Counsel are expected to arrive on time and be prepared to proceed, as the Court makes every effort to start on time. Promptness also is expected from witnesses. Once trial has commenced, it shall be counsel's first priority. The Court will not delay a jury trial or inconvenience jurors except under extraordinary circumstances. On request, the Court will advise other courts that counsel are engaged in a jury trial in this Court.

2. If a witness was on the stand at a recess or adjournment, it is the duty of counsel who called the witness to have the witness back on the stand, ready to proceed, when Court resumes.

3. Counsel shall notify the Courtroom Deputy in advance if any witness needs to be accommodated based on the Americans with Disabilities Act or for other reasons.

4. The Court attempts to cooperate with doctors and other professional witnesses and will, except in extraordinary circumstances, accommodate them by permitting them to be called out of sequence. Counsel should anticipate any such possibility and discuss it with opposing counsel in advance. If there is an objection, it should be brought to the Court's attention in advance.

5. Counsel should not run out of witnesses. If counsel has no more witnesses to call and there is more than a brief delay, the Court may deem that party to have rested.

I. General Decorum

1. The trial is not an oratorical contest. The trial should be a quiet, dignified search for the truth.

2. Counsel should rise when addressing the Court. Counsel and the parties also should rise when the jury enters or leaves the Courtroom.

3. All remarks by counsel should be addressed to the Court. While the judge is present, counsel should not address the Courtroom Deputy, the Reporter or opposing counsel. If counsel wishes to say something to opposing counsel, permission from the Court to speak off the record should be requested. All requests for the re-reading of questions or answers, or to have an exhibit placed in front of a witness, should be addressed to the Court.

4. Counsel should not address or refer to witnesses by their first names, unless they are children.

5. The maintenance of personal dignity requires care in the pronunciation of a person's surname. If necessary, counsel should inquire privately, in advance of the first reference to the name in court, how a person pronounces his or her name and how he or she prefers to be addressed (e.g., whether Maria Lopez Garcia prefers to be referred to as Ms. Garcia or Mrs.

Lopez Garcia).

6. Counsel should not make an offer of stipulation in the presence of the jury unless counsel already has conferred with opposing counsel and has been advised by opposing counsel that the stipulation is acceptable.

7. While Court is in session, counsel should not leave the counsel table to confer with investigators, secretaries or witnesses in the back of the Courtroom unless permission has been secured in advance from the Court.

8. Counsel should not by facial expression, nodding or other conduct exhibit any opinion (adverse or favorable) concerning any testimony being given by a witness. Counsel should also admonish their own clients and witnesses to avoid such conduct.

9. Counsel should not talk to jurors at all, and should not talk to co-counsel, opposing counsel, witnesses or clients where the conversation can be overheard by any jurors. Counsel should also admonish their own clients and witnesses to avoid such conduct.

IT IS SO ORDERED.

DATED: ________________

____
ROBERT N. BLOCK
United States Magistrate Judge

C. *Order Regarding Settlement Conference*

IN THE UNITED STATES DISTICT COURT
FOR THE CENTRAL DISTRICT OF CALIFORNIA

	)	Case No. ______________
Plaintiff(s),	)	
v.	)	**ORDER RE SETTLEMENT**
Defendant(s).	)	**CONFERENCE**
______________________________	)	

PLEASE READ THIS ORDER CAREFULLY!

This case has been referred to Magistrate Judge Robert N. Block for settlement proceedings.

The Settlement Conference is placed on calendar for ___________, **at 9:00 a.m., Ronald Regan Federal Building and U.S. Courthouse, 411 West Fourth Street, Courtroom 6D, Santa Ana, California**.

The Magistrate Judge will not be involved in the actual trial of the case, but rather will assist the parties in an objective appraisal and evaluation of the case. The following are guidelines for the parties in preparing for the Settlement Conference.

1. The purpose of the Settlement Conference is to permit an informal discussion between the attorneys, parties, non-party indemnitors or insurers, and the settlement judge, of every aspect of the case bearing on its settlement value.

2. Pursuant to Local Rule 16-15.8, all settlement proceedings shall be confidential and no statement made therein shall be admissible in any proceeding in the case, unless the parties otherwise agree. No part of a settlement proceeding shall be reported or otherwise recorded, without the consent of the parties, except for any memorialization of a settlement.

3. In addition to counsel who will try the case being present, a person with full settlement authority should likewise be present for the conference. This requirement contemplates the physical presence of your client or, if a corporate or governmental entity, of an authorized and knowledgeable representative of your client.[1] The plaintiff's representative must have full and final authority, **<u>in the representative's sole discretion</u>**, to authorize dismissal of the case with prejudice, or to accept a settlement amount recommended by the settlement judge down to the defendant's last offer made prior to the settlement conference. The defendant's representative must have final settlement authority to commit the defendant to pay, **<u>in the representative's sole discretion</u>**, a settlement amount recommended by the settlement judge up to the plaintiff's prayer (excluding punitive damage prayers), or up to the plaintiff's last demand made prior to the settlement conference, whichever is **<u>lower</u>**.

The purpose of this requirement is to have representatives present who can settle the case during the course of the conference without consulting a superior.

4. If Board approval is required to authorize settlement, the attendance of at least one sitting and knowledgeable member of the Board (preferably the Chairman) is

---

[1] However, unless otherwise ordered by the Court, if this matter is a lawsuit in which the United States or any of its agencies is a party, the Assistant United States Attorney who will try the case may appear without a representative, provided that he or she comes armed with the full measure of authority conveyed by his or her superiors within the United States Attorney's Office after appropriate consultation.

absolutely required.

5. Subject to paragraph 7 below, counsel appearing without their clients (whether or not counsel purportedly have been given settlement authority) will cause the settlement conference to be cancelled and rescheduled. The noncomplying party, attorney, or both, may be assessed the costs and expenses incurred by other parties as a result of such cancellation and rescheduling.

6. Any insurance company that is a party to the case or is contractually required to defend or to pay damages assessed within policy limits, should have a settlement representative present at the conference. Such representative must have final settlement authority to commit the company to pay, **in the representative's sole discretion**, an amount recommended by the settlement judge within the policy limits. The purpose of this requirement is to have an insurance representative present who can settle the outstanding claim or claims during the course of the conference without consulting a superior. An insurance representative authorized to pay, **in his or her sole discretion**, up to the plaintiff's last demand made prior to the settlement conference will also satisfy this requirement. Counsel of record will be responsible for timely advising any involved non-party insurance company of the requirements of this Order.

7. When a person whose personal attendance would otherwise be required pursuant to the foregoing paragraphs resides outside the District, the Court will consider excusing the personal attendance of such person, so long as such person can and will be available by telephone during the entire settlement conference. ***If a party desires to avail itself of this excuse from personal attendance, counsel should so request in such party's Settlement Conference Statement*** (and specify where such person will be located during the settlement conference). After the party's Settlement Conference Statement is submitted, counsel should contact Magistrate Judge Block's courtroom deputy clerk to ascertain whether the request has been granted. **Frequently, such requests are not granted.**

8. The Magistrate Judge may, in his discretion, converse with the lawyers, the parties, the insurance representatives, or any one of them outside of the hearing of the others. The comments of the judge during such separate sessions are not to be used by counsel in settlement negotiations with opposing counsel. This is a necessary requirement in order to avoid intentional or unintentional misquotation of the judge's comments. If all counsel and parties are not present to hear the Court's opinions, it is all too easy for counsel to misrepresent the Court's comments in an effort to obtain a tactical advantage with opposing counsel. Violation of this policy may be misleading and therefore a hindrance to settlement.

9. Prior to the Settlement Conference, the attorneys are directed to discuss settlement with their respective clients and insurance representatives, so that the parameters of possible settlement will have been explored well in advance of the Settlement Conference. At the Settlement Conference, each party shall be fully prepared to discuss all economic and non-economic factors relevant to a full and final settlement of the case.

10. In order to avoid the unnecessary expenditure of resources if the case is not ripe for settlement, and in order to provide the parties with a starting point for their settlement discussions with the Magistrate Judge if the case is ripe for settlement, plaintiff shall advise defendant(s) of the terms upon which plaintiff then is prepared to settle the case, in a letter delivered or faxed no later than ten (10) **court days** prior to the Settlement Conference. Within forty-eight (48) hours of receipt of plaintiff's settlement offer, each defendant shall respond to the same by letter advising plaintiff of the terms upon which such defendant is prepared to

settle the case.[2] **If, following this exchange of settlement offers, counsel for any of the parties believes that the case is not ripe for settlement and/or that proceeding with the settlement conference as scheduled will not be a productive use of the Magistrate Judge's and the parties' time, then counsel for the parties shall immediately contact the courtroom deputy and arrange for a telephonic conference with the Magistrate Judge to discuss the advisability of proceeding with the settlement conference as scheduled.**

11. Assuming the settlement conference remains on calendar, no later than 4:00 p.m. five (5) **court days** prior thereto, each party shall ***submit a Settlement Conference Statement directly to the chambers of Magistrate Judge Block*** (*i.e.*, Ronald Regan Suite 6165) or fax to (714) 338-2895. The parties shall exchange the Statements on the same date. The Statements should not be filed with the Clerk of the Court, and they will not be made part of the case file. The Statements shall be double-spaced and shall not exceed ten (10) pages in length.

The parties' respective Settlement Conference Statements shall include the following:

A. A brief statement of the facts of the case, and of the claims and defenses remaining to be tried, including the statutory or other grounds upon which the claims are founded. This statement should identify the major factual and legal issues in dispute, and cite any controlling authorities.

B. An itemized statement of the damages claimed, and of any other relief sought.

C. A summary of the proceedings to date, including any case management dates/deadlines already set by the District Judge.

D. A history of past settlement discussions, offers and demands, including the most recent settlement offers exchanged pursuant to ¶ 10 above. A copy of such party's letter sent pursuant to ¶ 10 above should be attached to such party's Settlement Conference Statement.

12. ***Each party shall also prepare a Confidential Addendum to Settlement Conference Statement, which shall be delivered (or faxed) directly to Magistrate Judge Block only, along with the Settlement Conference Statement.*** The Confidential Addendum shall not be filed with the Court or served upon the other parties. The Confidential Addendum shall contain:

A. A forthright evaluation of the party's likelihood of prevailing on each of its claims and/or defenses.

B. The approximate amount of attorney's fees, time and costs expended to date, and an estimate of the fees, time and costs to be expended for (i) further discovery, (ii) pretrial and (iii) trial.

C. The party's evaluation of the terms on which the other side is prepared to settle the case.

D. The party's evaluation of the terms on which the case could be settled **fairly,**

---

[2] The Court expects the parties to exchange good faith settlement offers. For the plaintiff, this means offering to settle on terms less favorable than those which the plaintiff reasonably could expect to achieve if plaintiff prevailed at trial, taking into account plaintiff's non-recoupable costs of litigation. For each defendant, this means offering to settle on terms less favorable to such defendant than those such defendant reasonably could expect to achieve if such defendant prevailed at trial, taking into account such defendant's non-recoupable costs of litigation.

<u>taking into account the litigation position and settlement position of the other side</u>.

13. If it does not appear to the Court from its review of the parties' Settlement Conference Statements and Confidential Addenda that a Settlement Conference at this juncture in the proceedings is likely to result in a settlement of the matter, the Court may order the Settlement Conference off calendar or defer it to a later juncture in the proceedings (e.g., after a pending or anticipated dispositive summary judgment motion is decided).

14. At the commencement of the conference, counsel for each party should be prepared to make the equivalent of a mini-opening statement and/or to respond to the Court's questions regarding the relevant facts and law, in the presence of all parties and counsel. Counsel should have available for the Court's perusal copies of all key documents in the case, as well as copies of all important witnesses' deposition transcripts.

15. Any failure of the trial attorneys, parties or persons with authority to attend the conference may result in sanctions to include the fees and costs expended by the other parties in preparing for and attending the conference. The failure of any party to timely submit a Settlement Conference Statement and Confidential Addendum in compliance with this Order, or otherwise comply strictly with this Order, may result in the Settlement Conference being ordered off calendar and sanctions being imposed.

16. If settlement between any or all parties is reached as a result of the Settlement Conference, it is the responsibility of counsel to immediately report the settlement to the District Judge's courtroom deputy clerk, as well as to timely memorialize the settlement. <u>See</u> Local Rule 16-15.7.

17. All papers submitted for the Settlement Conference will either be returned to the parties or destroyed by the Magistrate Judge, after the settlement proceedings are concluded, unless the parties agree otherwise.

DATED: ________________

ROBERT N. BLOCK
United States Magistrate Judge

D. Scheduling and Case Management Order

IN THE UNITED STATES DISTICT COURT
FOR THE CENTRAL DISTRICT OF CALIFORNIA

)	Case No. ______________
Plaintiff(s),)	
v.)	**SCHEDULING AND CASE**
Defendant(s).)	**MANAGEMENT ORDER**
______________________________)	[See Exh. A for Pretrial and Trial dates]

The purpose of this Order is to enable the parties and their counsel to know well in advance the schedule to which they will be expected to adhere, and the procedures which they will be expected to follow. **Because this Order in some respects modifies the applicable Local Rule of Court, counsel are advised to read it carefully to avoid default on the obligations established herein.**

I. Applicable Schedule

This case shall be litigated according to the schedule in Exhibit A hereto. **To the extent that the timing and dates set forth in Exhibit A differ from the timing and dates set forth in Local Rule 16, the timing and dates set forth in Exhibit A shall govern.** Ordinarily, those dates are determined after consultation with the parties at the Rule 26(f) Scheduling Conference, and this Order is issued after that Conference. Accordingly, the dates are firm and the Court is very unlikely to grant continuances, even if stipulated by the parties, unless the parties establish good cause through a strong, concrete showing.

II. Cut-off Date for Joining Parties or Amending Pleadings

The Court has established a cut-off date for adding parties or amending pleadings. All motions to add other parties or amend the pleadings shall be noticed for hearing on or before the cut-off date. All unserved parties will be dismissed at the time of the Final Pretrial Conference pursuant to Local Rule 16-8.1.

III. Discovery

The Court has established a cut-off date for discovery, including expert discovery if applicable.[1]

All depositions shall be scheduled to commence at least one (1) week prior to the discovery cut-off date, and shall be completed on or before the cut-off date. A deposition which was commenced prior to the discovery cut-off date may continue beyond the cut-off date, as necessary. Written discovery (e.g., interrogatories, requests for admission, requests for production) shall be served at least forty-five (45) days in advance of the discovery cut-off date; and counsel are advised that the Court will be disinclined to approve any stipulations between counsel which permit the response to any written discovery to be served after the discovery cut-off date.

1 If expert witnesses are to be called at trial, the plaintiff (including any counter-claimant, cross-claimant and third-party plaintiff) shall designate experts to be called by plaintiff and provide the reports required by Fed. R. Civ. P. 26(a)(2)(B), not later than eight (8) weeks prior to the discovery cut off date. Defendant shall designate experts to be called by defendant and provide the reports required by Fed. R. Civ. P. 26(a)(2)(B), not later than five (5) weeks prior to the discovery cut-off date. Failure to timely comply with this rule will likely result in the expert being excluded at trial as a witness. Expert testimony intended solely for impeachment or rebuttal shall be disclosed as required by Fed. R. Civ. P. 26(a)(2)(C).

Any motion relating to discovery shall be filed not later than one (1) week after the discovery cut-off date, and set for hearing not later than four (4) weeks after the discovery cut-off date. **The Court expects strict compliance with Local Rule 37 in the preparation and filing of discovery motions, including a good faith effort by counsel to eliminate the necessity for hearing the motion or to eliminate as many of the disputes as possible. Further, the Court expects counsel to comply with the Central District's Civility and Professional Guidelines.**

For counsel's information, the Court hears law and motion matters on Tuesdays at 9:30 a.m. Frequently, the Court decides discovery motions on the papers without oral argument. If the motion is left on calendar, it is the general practice of the Court to provide a written tentative ruling before the call of the calendar.

IV. Motions

A. General Provisions

All law and motion matters, except for discovery motions and *in limine* motions, shall be noticed for hearing on or before the motion hearing cut-off date. *In limine* motions dealing with evidentiary matters may be heard at the Final Pretrial Conference or (at the Court's discretion) at the start of trial; however, the Court will not hear or resolve any summary judgment motions disguised as motions *in limine.*

The Court expects strict compliance with Local Rule 7 in the preparation and filing of motions, including the pre-filing conference of counsel requirement of Local Rule 7-3.

If any party does not oppose a motion, that party shall submit a written statement that it does not oppose the motion, in accordance with Local Rule 7-16.

Reply papers shall be limited to argument and/or authorities responsive to the opposition papers. The Court will ignore any new matter that is improperly introduced in a party's reply papers.

B. Summary Judgment Motions

Parties need not, and in many cases should not, wait until the motion hearing cut-off date to bring motions for summary judgment or summary adjudication. However, in virtually every case, the Court expects the moving party to provide more than the minimum twenty-one (21) days of notice. Summary judgment motions are, of course, very fact-dependent. All parties should prepare their papers in a fashion that will assist the Court in absorbing the mass of facts (e.g., generous use of tabs, tables of contents, headings, indices, etc.). **The Court expects strict compliance with Local Rules 56-1 through 56-4.**

1. *Statement of Uncontroverted Facts and Conclusions of Law*

The uncontroverted facts shall be set forth in a two column format. The left hand column shall set forth the allegedly undisputed fact. The right hand column shall set forth the evidence that supports the factual statement. The fact statements shall be set forth in sequentially numbered paragraphs. Each paragraph should contain a narrowly focused statement of fact, and address a single subject in as concise a manner as possible.

2. *Statement of Genuine Issues*

The first part of the opposing party's Statement of Genuine Issues shall track the moving party's Statement of Uncontroverted Facts. It shall be set forth in a two-column format. The left hand column shall restate the allegedly undisputed fact, and the right hand column shall state either that the fact is undisputed or disputed. The opposing party may dispute all or only a portion of the allegedly undisputed fact, but if disputing only a portion, the opposing party must specify clearly what portion is being disputed. To demonstrate that a fact is disputed, the opposing party shall briefly state why it disputes the moving party's allegedly undisputed fact, cite to the relevant exhibit or other evidence controverting the allegedly undisputed fact, and describe what it is in that exhibit or evidence that controverts the allegedly undisputed fact. No legal argument shall be set forth in this document.

The opposing party may also specify additional material facts that bear on or relate to the issues raised by the moving party, which shall follow the same two column format described above for the moving party's Statement of Uncontroverted Facts. These additional facts shall continue in sequentially numbered paragraphs (i.e., if the moving party's last allegedly undisputed fact was set forth as ¶ 30, then the first new allegedly undisputed fact specified by the opposing party shall be set forth as ¶ 31).

The moving party, in its reply, shall respond to the additional allegedly undisputed facts in the same manner and format that the opposing party is required to adhere to in responding to the moving party's Statement of Uncontroverted Facts, as described above.

3. *Supporting Evidence*

No party shall submit any evidence other than the specific items of evidence or testimony necessary to support or controvert an allegedly undisputed fact. Thus, for example, the entire transcript of a deposition, entire sets of interrogatory responses, and documents that do not specifically support or controvert material in the separate statements should not be submitted in support of or in opposition to a summary judgment motion. The Court will not consider such material.

Evidence submitted in support of or in opposition to a summary judgment motion should be submitted either by way of stipulation or as exhibits to declarations sufficient to authenticate the proffered evidence, and should not be attached to the party's Memorandum of Points and Authorities. The Court will accept counsel's authentication of deposition transcripts, of written discovery responses, and of the receipt of documents in discovery if the fact that the document was in the opponent's possession is of independent significance. Documentary evidence as to which there is no stipulation regarding foundation must be accompanied by the testimony, either by declaration or properly authenticated deposition transcript, of a witness who can establish authenticity. The parties should use colored markers to highlight the testimony of portions of exhibits on which they are relying.[2]

4. *Objections to Evidence*

If a party disputes a fact based in whole or in part on an evidentiary objection, the ground of the objection should be stated in that party's separate statement but not argued in that document. Evidentiary objections should be addressed in a separate memorandum to be filed with the opposition or reply brief of the party. The memorandum should be organized to track the paragraph numbers of the other party's separate statement in sequence. It should identify the specific item of evidence to which objection is made, the ground of the objection, and a very brief argument with citation to authority as to why the objection is well taken.[3]

---

2 When a party relies on deposition testimony in a summary judgment motion without citing to page and line numbers, the Court in its discretion may exclude or disregard the supposed "evidence." *See Orr v. Bank of America*, 275 F.3d 764, 775 (9th Cir. 2002).

3 Blanket or boilerplate objections will be disregarded and summarily overruled.

For example:

> Statement of Uncontroverted Facts, ¶ 3: Objection to the supporting deposition transcript of Jane Smith at 60:1-10 on the ground that the statement constitutes inadmissible hearsay and no exception is applicable. To the extent that the statement is offered to prove her state of mind, it is irrelevant since her state of mind is not in issue. Fed. R. Evid. 801, 802.

5. *The Memorandum of Points and Authorities*

The moving party's Memorandum of Points and Authorities should be in the usual form required under Local Rule 7 and should contain a narrative statement of facts as to those aspects of the case that are before the Court. All facts should be supported with citations to the paragraph number in the moving party's Statement of Uncontroverted Facts that supports the factual assertion and not to the underlying evidence.

Unless the case involves some unusual twist on Fed. R. Civ. P. 56, the motion need only contain a brief statement of the Rule 56 standard; the Court is familiar with the interpretation of Rule 56 under *Celotex* and its progeny. If at all possible, the argument should be organized to focus on the pertinent elements of the cause(s) of action or defense(s) in issue, with the purpose of showing the existence or nonexistence of a genuine issue of material fact for trial on that element of the claim or

defense.

Likewise, the opposing party's Memorandum of Points and Authorities should be in the usual form required by Local Rule 7, and where the opposition memorandum sets forth facts, the memorandum should cite to paragraphs in the moving party's Statement of Uncontroverted Facts if the facts are not in dispute, to the evidence that contravenes the fact where the fact is in dispute, or if the fact is contravened by an additional fact in the opposing party's Statement of Genuine Issues, the citation should be to such fact by paragraph number.

C. Motions *in Limine*

Parties often do not focus on evidentiary and related issues until the last stages of trial preparation. This is a mistake. *In limine* motions can be very helpful in narrowing issues, limiting or allowing evidence and promoting settlement. With these benefits in mind, the Court encourages the parties to consider carefully filing such motions before the last stages of trial preparation. In any event, the parties shall file and serve *in limine* motions in accordance with Local Rule 7 by the date specified in Exhibit A hereto. The Court will make every effort to rule upon *in limine* motions at or before the Final Pretrial Conference.

D. Oral Argument

Sometimes the Court will not hear oral argument. When that is the case, the Court will notify the parties in advance. If there is a hearing, tentative rulings will often be available in the courtroom approximately fifteen (15) minutes before the call of the calendar. The Court expects the parties to be familiar with the tentative ruling at the time of argument.

V. Applications and Stipulations for Extensions of Time

A. Applications or Stipulations to Extend the Time to File Any Required Document or to Continue Any Pretrial or Trial Date

No stipulations extending scheduling requirements or modifying applicable rules shall be effective unless and until the Court approves them. Both applications and stipulations must set forth:

1. The existing due date or hearing date.

2. Specific, concrete reasons supporting good cause for granting the extension. In this regard, a statement to the effect that an extension "will promote settlement" will be insufficient. The requesting party or parties must indicate the status of ongoing negotiations (e.g., whether written proposals have been exchanged, whether counsel is in the process of reviewing a draft settlement agreement, whether a private mediator has been selected).

3. Whether there have been any prior requests for extensions, and whether these were granted or denied by the Court.

B. *Ex Parte* Applications

The Court strongly discourages *ex parte* applications. *See Mission Power Engineering Co. v. Continental Cas. Co.*, 883 F. Supp. 488 (C.D. Cal. 1995). **The Court expects strict compliance with Local Rule 7-19.**

VI. Final Pretrial Conference; Scheduling; Management

A. Meeting of Counsel Before Final Pretrial Conference

The Court expects strict compliance with Local Rules 16-2 and 16-3.

B. Memorandum of Contentions of Fact and Law

Each party's Memorandum of Contentions of Fact and Law should conform with Local Rule 16-4.

C. Witness List

The Court expects strict compliance with Local Rule 16-5. In addition, the witness lists must include a brief (one or two paragraph) description of each witness' anticipated testimony, and a time estimate for both direct and cross-examination (separately stated).

The obligation of listing such witnesses is a continuing one, and except for good cause shown, the testimony of any such witness proffered at trial who is not listed upon a party's witness list shall be precluded.

D. Exhibits

The Court expects strict compliance with Local Rule 16-6.

In addition to the Joint Exhibit List contemplated by Local Rule 16-6.1, the parties shall prepare and file a Pretrial Exhibit Stipulation which shall contain each party's numbered list of all trial exhibits, with objections (if any) to each exhibit including the basis of the objection and the offering party's response. All exhibits to which there is no objection shall be deemed admitted. All parties shall stipulate to the authenticity of exhibits whenever possible, and the Pretrial Exhibit Stipulation shall identify any exhibits whose authenticity has not been stipulated to and the specific reasons for the party's failure to stipulate (as well as the offering party's response).

The Stipulation shall be substantially in the following form:

Plaintiff's Exhibits

No. of Exhibit	Description	If objection, state grounds	Response to objection

Defendant's Exhibits

No. of Exhibit	Description	If objection, state grounds	Response to objection

The Pretrial Exhibit Stipulation shall be filed at the same time counsel lodge the Final Pretrial Conference Order. Failure to comply with this paragraph shall constitute a waiver of all objections to the other party's exhibits.

E. Final Pretrial Conference Order

Plaintiff shall lodge the Final Pretrial Conference Order on the date specified in Exhibit A hereto.

In accordance with Local Rule 16-7.2, the Final Pretrial Conference Order shall be substantially in the form shown in Pretrial Form No. 1 set forth in Appendix A to the Local Rules. In drafting Section 5 of the Final Pretrial Conference Order, the Court expects the parties to attempt to agree on and set forth as many non-contested facts as possible.[4]

F. Final Pretrial Conference

The Final Pretrial Conference will be held at 10:00 a.m. on the date specified in Exhibit A hereto, unless the Court expressly waives a Final Pretrial Conference at the Scheduling Conference. If the Court does waive a Final Pretrial Conference, the Court will expect strict compliance with Local Rule 16-11.

The lead trial attorney on behalf of every party shall attend both the Final Pretrial Conference and all meetings of counsel in preparation for the Final Pretrial Conference. Unless counsel has been excused for good cause shown in advance of the Final Pretrial Conference, the Court reserves the right to designate the attorney attending the Final Pretrial Conference as lead trial counsel.

Counsel should presume that a continuance of the Final Pretrial Conference at the parties' request or by stipulation is unlikely. Specifically, failure to complete discovery does not constitute good cause for a continuance. In the unlikely event that the Court agrees to a continuance of the Final Pretrial Conference, the trial date is likely to be delayed as a result, possibly for several months.

At the Final Pretrial Conference, the parties should be prepared to discuss means of streamlining the trial, including, but not limited to: bifurcation; presentation of foundational and non-critical testimony and direct testimony by deposition excerpts, narrative summaries and/or stipulations as to the content of the testimony; presentation of testimony on direct examination by declaration subject to cross-examination; and qualification of experts by admitted resumes. The Court will attempt to rule upon previously-filed *in limine* motions at the Final Pretrial Conference. The Court also will discuss settlement at the Final Pretrial Conference.

For jury trials, the Court also will set a date at the Final Pretrial Conference, generally several days before the trial date, for a final status conference. The purpose of the final status conference will be to rule on any remaining motions *in limine*, discuss *voir dire* and jury selection procedures with counsel, resolve anticipated evidentiary and foundational issues to the extent possible, and address any other issues that may impact the efficient trial of the case.

G. Consequences of Noncompliance

If counsel fail to file the required pretrial documents or fail to appear at the Final Pretrial Conference and such failure is not otherwise satisfactorily explained to the Court, (a) the case shall be dismissed for failure to prosecute if such failure occurs

[4] The Court will usually read the uncontested facts to the jury at the start of a jury trial. A carefully drafted and comprehensively stated stipulation of facts will reduce the length of trial and increase jury understanding of the case.

on the part of the plaintiff, (b) default judgment shall be entered if such failure occurs on the part of the defendant, and/or (c) the Court may take such action as it deems appropriate (including the imposition of monetary sanctions against counsel).

VII. Settlement

The Court believes that, in most cases, the completion of all or substantially all discovery and the determination of dispositive motions will help the parties assess their positions before they embark on the costly pretrial process. However, the Court recognizes that parties sometimes find it more difficult to settle after they have incurred the cost of all discovery and motion practice. The Court therefore strongly encourages counsel and the parties to pursue settlement earlier, and if the parties believe that a settlement more likely would be reached if their mandatory settlement conference were held earlier than the last day specified in Exhibit A hereto, they should arrange to hold it earlier. In any event, as indicated in Exhibit A hereto, the parties must file a Status Report re Settlement concurrently with the filing of the parties' memoranda of contentions of fact and law, witness lists, and exhibit lists.

The Court will not conduct settlement conferences itself in its non-jury cases. In its jury cases, the Court will conduct a settlement conference at the parties' joint request if the following three conditions exist:

1. The parties are satisfied that the fact issues in the case will be tried to a jury.

2. All significant pretrial rulings which the Court must make have already been made.

3. The parties desire the Court to conduct the settlement conference, understanding that if a settlement is not reached, the Court will try the case.

If the Court conducts a settlement conference, the Court will expect strict compliance with its Order re Settlement Conference (a copy of which can be secured in advance from the Courtroom Deputy Clerk).

VIII. Trial Brief

At least seven (7) calendar days before trial is scheduled to commence, each party may serve and file a trial brief in accordance with Local Rule 16-10.

IX. Trial Date

This case has been set for trial on the date specified in Exhibit A hereto at 8:30 a.m. Please review the Court's separately-issued Civil Trial Order for additional procedures and requirements.

X. Conclusion

The Court thanks the parties and their counsel for their anticipated cooperation in carrying out these requirements.

IT IS SO ORDERED.

DATED: ________________

____
ROBERT N. BLOCK
United States Magistrate Judge

EXHIBIT A
Presumptive Schedule of Pretrial Dates

Matter	Time	Weeks before trial	Pl's Request	Def's Request	Court Order
Trial Date (jury)	8:30 a..m.				
Estimated length: ___ days					
For jury trial: date of final status conference	10:00 a.m.				
Last day to file Trial Brief		-1			
Date of Final Pretrial Conference; hearing on *in limine* motions	10:00 a.m.	-2			
For jury trial: file agreed-upon set of jury instructions, verdict forms and special interrogs, and Joint Statement re disputed instructions, verdict forms and special interrogs; file proposed *voir dire* questions and agreed-upon Statement of Case		-2			
For court trial: lodge proposed Findings of Fact and Conclusions of Law, and Witness Declarations		-2			
Lodge Final Pretrial Conference Order; File Memos of Contentions of Fact and Law, Joint Exhibit List, Pretrial Exhibit Stip, Witness Lists, and Joint Status Report re Settlement		-4			
Last day for hand serving and filing motions *in limine*		-5			
Last day to hold Mandatory Settlement Conference		-8			
Last day for hearing motions other than *in limine* and discovery motions	9:30 a.m.	-9			
Last day for hearing discovery motions	9:30 a.m.	-11			
Discovery cut-off date		-15			
Last day to amend pleadings or add parties					

Hon. David T. Bristow
Magistrate Judge

Chambers Information
U.S. District Court, Central District of California
Courtroom 4
3470 Twelfth Street
Riverside, CA 92501

Scheduling Information
Courtroom Deputy: (951) 328-4466

Civil Law and Motion	Thursdays at 10:00 a.m.

Biographical Information
[Not available]

I. <u>Judge Bristow's Procedures and Practices</u>

A. *<u>Procedures and Schedules</u>*

1. Civil motions are heard on **Thursdays at 10:00 a.m.**

   It is not necessary to clear a motion date with the court clerk prior to filing the motion, although the Judge reserves the right to sua sponte continue motions or decide them on the papers without oral argument. The Judge does not permit telephonic appearances for hearings absent exceptional circumstances.

2. Discovery motions are to be set before the district judge unless the district judge to whom the case is assigned has a blanket referral of all discovery matters to the magistrate judge or already has issued a case specific order referring all discovery matters to the magistrate judge. Strict compliance with Local Rules 37-1 and 37-2 is required. It is the Judge's general practice to decline requests by counsel for telephonic conferences to resolve discovery disputes that arise during pending depositions.

3. If there is a tentative ruling, it will be provided to counsel at the time counsel checks in with the court clerk.

4. E-Filing: Mandatory Chambers Copies of all e-filed documents shall be delivered to the courtesy copy box on the 3rd Floor. It is imperative that mandatory chambers copies be delivered by noon following the date of filing as required by General Order 08-11.IV.D. Failure to deliver timely mandatory chambers copies may result in a delay in hearing a motion or ordering the matter off calendar.

5. Procedures for filing an ex parte application: Strict compliance with Local Rule 7-19 is required. Any opposition shall be served and filed within 24 hours of receipt of the applicant's oral notice. Conformed paper copies of the filed application and any opposition should be delivered directly to the Judge's chambers. Ex parte applications will generally be decided on the papers without oral argument. The Judge will notify the parties if a telephonic hearing is desired.

6. Continuances of any scheduled court proceeding will be granted only on a showing of good cause. To request a continuance, the parties should submit a signed stipulation and proposed order. If opposing counsel will not agree to a continuance, the request should be made by ex parte application.

7. Inquiries concerning the status of a motion, stipulation or proposed order should be made to the Court's deputy clerk. Counsel are not allowed to contact the Judge's law clerk or secretary, or to communicate with the Court or Chambers by means of the Court's email address other than to email proposed orders.

8. Calendar conflicts: (Procedures for attorneys to follow if they have a calendar conflict) Immediately advise the court clerk telephonically; attempt to secure other counsel's agreement to stipulate to a new date.

9. Electronic equipment: Permission to bring in or use audio, video, or electronic equipment should be requested from the court clerk in advance of the date of the court proceeding.

10. For general information on how to order a transcript of any reported or digitally recorded proceeding, please contact 213-894-3015 or visit www.cacd.uscourts.gov > General Information > Court Reporter/Recorder Transcripts. If you require an

estimate of cost for the preparation of a transcript, contact the court reporter/recorder for the desired proceeding.

To determine the court reporter/recorder for a particular proceeding, go to the Court Reporter Schedule web page and click on View by Date. Once you've determined the correct court reporter/recorder for the desired session, click on Court Reporter Phone and Email List for contact information.

11. Questions regarding law clerk/extern positions: Communicate via letter to the Judge.

12. It is the responsibility of the parties to obtain the services of an interpreter on a civil case if one is needed.

13. Settlement conferences: The parties should contact the court clerk about dates available for settlement conferences. The proposed date(s) should be at least two weeks in advance. All settlement conference papers should be delivered directly to the Judge's chambers, Room 390, 3rd floor. In lieu of personal delivery, settlement conference papers may be faxed to chambers at 951-328-4448, but only if the total number of pages being faxed is 15 or less.

14. Stipulated protective orders: Parties must comply with Fed. R. Civ. P. 26(c).

Hon. Jacqueline Chooljian
Magistrate Judge

Chambers Information
U.S. District Court, Central District of California
Courtroom 20, 3rd Floor
312 N. Spring Street
Los Angeles, CA 90012

Scheduling Information
Courtroom Deputy: (213) 894-2921

Civil Law and Motion	Tuesdays at 9:30 a.m.

Biographical Information
[Not available]

I. Judge Chooljian's Procedures and Practices

A. *Procedures and Schedules*

1. Where should mandatory chambers copies be delivered?
   a. Criminal Duty Documents: Criminal Duty Chambers, Roybal Federal Building, 3rd Floor.
   b. Regular filings: Judge's courtesy box outside chambers, Spring Street Courthouse, 3rd Floor, Room 339.
2. Civil motions and discovery motions are heard on **TUESDAY at 9:30 a.m.**, in Courtroom 20 - 3rd Floor of the Spring Street Courthouse.
3. All parties must deliver courtesy copies to Chambers (Room 339, Spring Street) of **all** documents filed in the Judge's civil cases (JC) and all discovery-related documents filed in the Judge's discovery cases (JCx). The "mandatory Chambers copy" shall be delivered to the drop box in the hall outside Chambers no later than noon of the court day following the e-filing of the document.
4. For general information on how to order a transcript of any reported or digitally recorded proceeding, please contact 213-894-3015 or visit www.cacd.uscourts.gov > General Information > Court Reporter/Recorder Transcripts. If you require an estimate of cost for the preparation of a transcript, contact the court reporter/recorder for the desired proceeding.

   To determine the court reporter/recorder for a particular proceeding, go to the Court Reporter Schedule web page and click on View by Date. Once you've determined the correct court reporter/recorder for the desired session, click on Court Reporter Phone and Email List for contact information.

Hon. Charles F. Eick

Magistrate Judge

Chambers Information

U.S. District Court, Central District of California
Courtroom 20, 3rd Floor
312 N. Spring Street
Los Angeles, CA 90012

Scheduling Information

Courtroom Deputy: (213) 894-5234

Civil Law and Motion	Fridays at 9:30 a.m.

Biographical Information

[Not available]

I. Judge Eick's Procedures and Practices

A. *Procedures and Schedules*

1. Civil motions customarily are heard on **Fridays** at **9:30 a.m.**

   If a motion is to be noticed for hearing on a Friday at 9:30 a.m., it is not necessary to clear a motion date with the court's deputy clerk prior to filing the motion. The provision of Local Rule 6 governing the service of a notice of motion served personally shall govern a notice of motion served electronically.

2. "Mandatory chambers copies" of e-filed documents are not required unless the document relates to an ex parte application, a TRO or an injunction, or unless the Court requests "mandatory chambers copies" in a particular case. If a "mandatory chambers copy" is required, it shall be delivered to the drop box in the hall outside Chambers no later than noon of the court day following the e-filing of the document.

3. Inquiries concerning the status of a motion, stipulation or proposed order should be made to the Court's deputy clerk. Counsel are not allowed to contact the Judge's law clerk or secretary, or to communicate with the Court or Chambers by means of the Court's email address other than to email proposed orders.

4. Settlement conferences may be heard any day of the week, usually at 1:30 p.m. Counsel should select a date for the settlement conference in consultation with the Court's deputy clerk. Counsel should select the date at least two weeks in advance. After the date is selected, the Court usually will issue an order regarding settlement conference procedures.

5. For general information on how to order a transcript of any reported or digitally recorded proceeding, please contact 213-894-3015 or visit www.cacd.uscourts.gov> General Information>Court Reporter/Recorder Transcripts. If you require an estimate of cost for the preparation of a transcript, contact the court reporter/recorder for the desired proceeding.

   To determine the court reporter/recorder for a particular proceeding, go to the Court Reporter Schedule web page and click on View by Date. Once you've determined the correct court reporter/recorder for the desired session, click on Court Reporter Phone and Email List for contact information.

6. It is the responsibility of the parties to obtain the services of an interpreter in a civil case if an interpreter is needed. Counsel may contact the Court Interpreter Coordinator at (213) 894-4599 to arrange for such services.

7. Questions concerning law clerk or extern positions should be communicated via letter to the Magistrate Judge.

Hon. Rita Coyne Federman

Magistrate Judge

Chambers Information

U.S. District Court, Central District of California
Courtroom N/A
1415 State Street
Santa Barbara, CA 93101

Scheduling Information

Courtroom Deputy: (213) 894-3787

Criminal Law and Motion	On scheduled days at 1:30 p.m.

Biographical Information

[Not available]

I. <u>Judge Federman's Procedures and Practices</u>

A. *<u>Procedures and Schedules</u>*

<u>Motion Procedures for Misdemeanor and Petty Offenses:</u>

1. Motions are heard at 1:30 p.m. A calendar of hearing dates may be obtained from the courtroom deputy.
2. Motions in criminal matters that have been electronically filed also shall be electronically filed. In criminal matters that have not been electronically filed, motions shall be filed in open court or with the Clerk of Court at the Roybal Federal Building. In the alternative, papers may be filed by mail, addressed to the Court as follows:

   CRD to Judge Federman
   255 East Temple Street, Suite 181-L
   Los Angeles, CA 90012

   with a mandatory chambers copy to be emailed to chambers.
3. The caption of the motion shall include the date, time, and location of the hearing under the case number, and the initials "RCF" after the case number.
4. Pre-trial motions shall be filed and served fourteen (14) calendar days before the hearing date.
5. Opposition shall be filed and served seven (7) calendar days before the hearing date. In all criminal matters, a mandatory chambers copy of the opposition shall be emailed to chambers on the day of filing.
6. Replies shall be filed and served three (3) calendar days before the hearing date. In all criminal matters, a mandatory chambers copy of the reply shall be emailed to chambers on the day of filing.
7. All papers filed with the Court shall comply with the Local Rules of Practice of the Central District of California, including Local Rules 7 and 11, and Local Criminal Rule 12.

<u>Ex Parte Applications in Misdemeanor and Petty Offense Cases:</u>

1. Ex-parte applications in criminal matters that have been electronically filed also shall be electronically filed. In criminal matters that have not been electronically filed, motions shall be filed in open court or with the Clerk of Court at the Roybal Federal Building. In the alternative, papers may be filed by mail, addressed to the Court as follows:

   CRD to Judge Federman
   255 East Temple Street, Suite 181-L
   Los Angeles, CA 90012

   with a mandatory chambers copy emailed to chambers.
2. Ex parte applications shall comply with Local Rule 7-19. The moving party shall inform the opposing party that any opposition is due the next business day by 4:00 p.m.
3. Opposition papers are to be filed, on the first business day following service of

the application. In all criminal matters, a mandatory chambers copy of the opposition shall be emailed to chambers. If counsel does not intend to oppose the ex parte application, counsel must inform the courtroom deputy by telephone.

4. Ex parte applications normally are considered on the papers. If the Court determines a hearing is necessary, the courtroom deputy will notify the parties of the hearing date and time.

5. Counsel and parties should note that ex parte applications are for extraordinary relief. *See Mission Power Engineering Co. V. Continental Casualty Co., 883 F. Supp. 488 (C.D. Cal. 1995).*

Interpreters:

6. For initial proceedings in misdemeanor and petty offense cases, interpreting services will be provided for Spanish speaking defendants. Parties requiring interpreting services for other languages should notify the courtroom deputy at least 48 hours before the hearing date.

General:

7. Judge Federman conducts hearings in Courtroom 202 of the United States Bankruptcy Court, 1415 State Street, Santa Barbara, CA 93101.

8. **No papers should be filed or sent to the courthouse when Judge Federman is not in session.**

9. When court is not in session, papers may be filed with the Clerk of Court at the Roybal Federal Building. In the alternative, papers may be filed by mail, addressed to the Court as follows:

   CRD to Judge Federman
   255 East Temple Street, Suite 181-L
   Los Angeles, CA 90012

4. Hearings are scheduled for select days of the month. A calendar may be obtained by contacting the courtroom deputy.

5. Judge Federman's courtroom deputy may be contacted at 213-894-3787.

6. As soon as an attorney or party is aware of a calendar conflict, or that a request for a continuance will be made, the attorney or party should advise the courtroom deputy.

7. Additional information concerning misdemeanor and petty offense cases may be available by contacting the Central Violations Bureau (CVB) as follows: www.cvb.uscourts.gov or (800) 827-2982.

Hon. Jay C. Gandhi

Magistrate Judge

Chambers Information

U.S. District Court, Central District of California
Courtroom A, 8th Floor
312 N. Spring Street
Los Angeles, CA 90012

Scheduling Information

Courtroom Deputy: (213) 894-5369

Civil Law and Motion	Tuesdays at 2:00 p.m.

Biographical Information

[Not available]

I. Judge Gandhi's Procedures and Practices

A. *Procedures and Schedules*

1. Civil motions are heard on **Tuesdays** at **2:00 p.m.** It is not necessary to clear a motion date with the deputy clerk prior to filing the motion, although the Judge reserves the right to *sua sponte* continue motions or decide them on the papers without oral argument. The Judge does not permit telephonic appearances for hearings absent good cause.
2. Discovery motions are to be set before the district judge unless the district judge to whom the case is assigned has a blanket referral of all discovery matters to the magistrate judge or already has issued a case specific order referring all discovery matters to the magistrate judge. Strict compliance with Local Rules 37-1 and 37-2 is required.
3. If a tentative ruling is issued, it will be provided to counsel at the time counsel checks in with the deputy clerk.
4. E-Filing: Mandatory Chambers Copies of all e-filed documents shall be delivered to the courtesy copy box on the 8th Floor. It is imperative that mandatory chambers copies be delivered by noon following the date of filing as required by General Order 08-11.IV.D. Failure to deliver timely mandatory chambers copies may result in a delay in hearing a motion or ordering the matter off calendar.
5. Procedures for filing an *ex parte* application: Strict compliance with Local Rule 7-19 is required. Any opposition shall be filed and served within 24 hours of receipt of the applicant's oral notice. Conformed paper copies of the filed application and any opposition should be delivered directly to the Judge's chambers. *Ex parte* applications will generally be decided on the papers without oral argument. The Judge will notify the parties if a hearing is desired.
6. Continuances of any scheduled court proceeding will be granted only on a showing of good cause. To request a continuance, the parties should submit a signed stipulation and proposed order. If opposing counsel will not agree to a continuance, the request should be made by *ex parte* application.
7. Inquiries concerning the status of a motion, stipulation or proposed order should be made to the Court's deputy clerk. Counsel are **not** allowed to contact the Judge's law clerk or administrative law clerk, or to communicate with the Court or chambers.
8. Calendar conflicts: Immediately advise the deputy clerk telephonically and attempt to secure in good faith opposing counsel's agreement to stipulate to a new date.
9. Electronic equipment: Permission to bring in or use audio, video, or electronic equipment should be requested from the deputy clerk in sufficient advance of the date of the court proceeding.
10. For general information on how to order a transcript of any reported or digitally recorded proceeding, please contact 213-894-3015 or visit www.cacd.uscourts.gov > General Information > Court Reporter/Recorder Transcripts. If you require an estimate of cost for the preparation of a transcript, contact the court reporter/recorder for the desired proceeding.

    To determine the court reporter/recorder for a particular proceeding, go to the Court

Reporter Schedule web page and click on View by Date. Once you've determined the correct court reporter/recorder for the desired session, click on Court Reporter Phone and Email List for contact information.

11. Questions regarding law clerk/extern positions: Communicate via letter with the Judge.

12. It is the responsibility of the parties to obtain the services of an interpreter on a civil case should one be needed.

13. Settlement conferences: Settlement conferences are to be scheduled on **Wednesdays** or **Thursdays** at **10:00 a.m.** The proposed date(s) should be cleared at least fourteen (14) calendar days in advance. All settlement conference papers shall be confidential and should be submitted at least seven (7) calendar days prior to the conference. All settlement conference papers shall be delivered directly to the Judge's chambers, Suite 829/831, 8th floor of the Spring Street Courthouse.

14. Stipulated protective orders: Parties must comply strictly with F.R.Civ. P. 26(c).

15. Other information: The Judge does not permit special appearances. Counsel of record shall appear at all court proceedings and, in certain circumstances, the Court may specifically instruct parties and/or lead trial counsel to appear at proceedings or conferences.

Hon. Marc L. Goldman

Magistrate Judge

Chambers Information

U.S. District Court, Central District of California
Courtroom 6A
411 West Fourth Street
Santa Ana, CA 92701

Scheduling Information

Courtroom Deputy: (714) 338-4755

Civil Law and Motion	Tuesdays at 10:00 a.m.

Biographical Information

[Not available]

I. Judge Goldmans' Procedures and Practices

A. Procedures and Schedules

1. Unless otherwise directed by the Court, civil motions are heard on **Tuesday** at **10:00 a.m.** in Santa Ana. Counsel should anticipate that the Court may decide the motion on the pleadings. Telephonic appearances are not permitted. Court requires oral argument be heard on civil motions. Counsel may not waive oral argument.

2. Unless otherwise directed by the Court, settlement conferences will be held on **Wednesday** at **9:30 a.m.** in Santa Ana. Counsel must contact the Court's deputy clerk to schedule a settlement conference after the filing of the ADR-01 form: Settlement Procedure Selection - Notice, Request and Order or Order from the District Judge assigned. Telephonic appearances are not permitted.

3. Discovery motions are to be calendared before the magistrate judge unless otherwise ordered by the district judge. Strict compliance with Local Rule 37-3 is required. Mandatory chambers copies are required by the Court on all e-filed discovery motions. It is not necessary to clear a motion date with the court clerk prior to filing the motion.

   Mandatory Chambers Copies of all e-filed documents shall be delivered to the mandatory chambers copy box on the 6th Floor. It is imperative that the mandatory chambers copies be delivered by noon following the date of filing as required by General Order 10-07.IV.D. Failure to deliver timely mandatory chambers copies may result in a delay in hearing a motion or ordering the matter off calendar.

4. Tentative rulings are not issued.

5. Use of ELMO (Electronic Visual Evidence Presenter) is available to all counsel. The Court encourages the use of this technology. Please notify the judge's deputy clerk, Terri Steele at (714) 338-4755 at least five working days prior to the hearing if you wish to use this system.

6. *Ex parte* applications are an unacceptable method of bringing a discovery dispute to the attention of the Court in the absence of an extreme emergency. In the event of such an extreme emergency, the applicant must comply with Local Rule 7-19. *Ex parte* applications will ordinarily be decided without a hearing.

7. To request a continuance of a scheduled court proceeding, counsel should first contact the Court's deputy clerk and then file a stipulation and proposed order or an application and a proposed order.

8. In the event of calendar conflicts, counsel should file a stipulation after obtaining an alternate date from the deputy clerk

9. Counsel should contact the deputy clerk prior to bringing electronic equipment into the courtroom. The deputy clerk will inform counsel of the appropriate procedures.

10. For general information on how to order a transcript of any reported or digitally recorded proceeding, please contact 213-894-3015 or visit www.cacd.uscourts.gov > General Information > Court Reporter/Recorder Transcripts. If you require an estimate of cost for the preparation of a transcript, contact the court reporter/recorder for the desired proceeding.

    To determine the court reporter/recorder for a particular proceeding, go to the Court

Reporter Schedule web page and click on View by Date. Once you've determined the correct court reporter/recorder for the desired session, click on Court Reporter Phone and Email List for contact information.

11. Pretrial proceedings shall conform with the requirements of Local Rule 16. The Court shall issue a supplemental order governing trial proceedings.

12. Counsel shall make their own arrangements for the presence of an interpreter in civil cases.

Hon. Stephen J. Hillman

Magistrate Judge

Chambers Information

U.S. District Court, Central District of California
Courtroom 550
255 East Temple Street
Los Angeles, CA 90012

Scheduling Information

Courtroom Deputy: (213) 894-6487

Civil Law and Motion	Mondays at 2:00 p.m. or as scheduled
Criminal Law and Motion	As scheduled

Biographical Information

[Not available]

I. Judge Hillman's Procedures and Practices

A. *Procedures and Schedules*

1. Civil motions are heard on **Mondays** at **2:00 p.m.** or as scheduled by Court Clerk upon special request of counsel. If Monday is a holiday, the next motion date is: **As scheduled.** It is not necessary to check a Monday motion date with the Court Clerk prior to filing the motion.

2. Criminal motions are heard on: **As scheduled**, Time: **As scheduled**.

3. In cases where all parties have consented to Judge Hillman for all purposes, discovery motions are to be calendared before him.

   For all other cases, discovery motions are to be calendared before the District Judge or Magistrate Judge (as determined by the policy of the District Judge assigned to the case).

   The title page of the Joint Stipulation must state the discovery cutoff date, the motion cutoff date, the pretrial conference date, and the trial date. In addition, a copy of the Order establishing the initial case schedule, as well as any amendments, must be attached to the Joint stipulation or to the declaration filed in support of the motion.

4. Tentative rulings are often, but not always, issued on discovery motions. Discovery motions may be taken under submission without oral argument. Out-of-town counsel may request a telephonic hearing on a discovery motion. Such requests will be carefully considered on a motion-by-motion basis.

5. Mandatory chambers copies of e-filed documents are to be delivered to chambers, 5th Floor, Roybal. Counsel must comply with General Order 10-07, II S.

6. Procedures for filing an Ex Parte Application: Follow Local Rule 7-19.

7. To request a continuance of any scheduled hearing, counsel should contact opposing counsel, then contact the Court Clerk for direction.

   To request an extension of a court-ordered filing deadline, counsel should contact opposing counsel (if possible), then contact the Court Clerk for direction.

8. Counsel are not allowed to contact the Judge's law clerk or secretary.

9. Inquiries regarding the status of a motion, stipulation or proposed order: Counsel should check the Central District's Pacer site. Alternatively, if necessary, counsel should contact the Court Clerk.

10. Calendar conflicts (procedures for attorneys to follow if they have a calendar conflict): If there is a calendar conflict, counsel should contact the Court Clerk by phone and/or e-mail as soon as the conflict is known.

11. Procedures for bringing electronic equipment into the courtroom: Contact the Court Clerk.

12. For general information on how to order a transcript of any reported or digitally recorded proceeding, please contact 213-894-3015 or visit www.cacd.uscourts.gov > General Information > Court Reporter/Recorder Transcripts. If you require an estimate of cost for the preparation of a transcript, contact the court reporter/recorder for the desired proceeding.

To determine the court reporter/recorder for a particular proceeding, go to the Court Reporter Schedule web page and click on View by Date. Once you've determined the correct court reporter/recorder for the desired session, click on Court Reporter Phone and Email List for contact information.

13. Questions regarding extern positions: Mail cover letter and resume to chambers.

14. Trial Preparation:

  a. Court Hours: **9:00 a.m. to 4:30 p.m.**

  b. Exhibit preparation: **Follow Local Rules**

  c. Jury Instructions: Local Rules

  d. Verdict forms: Local Rules

  e. other:

15. Procedures for obtaining the services of an interpreter in a civil case: Counsel are responsible for obtaining the services of an interpreter if one is needed.

16. Counsel must promptly schedule a settlement conference after referral to the Magistrate Judge pursuant to Local Rule 16-14.

17. Filing or Lodging Documents Under Seal: No document(s) may be filed or lodged under seal absent Court Order pertinent to the specific document(s).

Proposed Protective Orders containing contrary language will be rejected.

If any party seeks to file or lodge with the Court any documents which Confidential Information (as defined in a previously entered Protective Order), such materials shall be submitted to the Court in accordance with the procedures set forth in Local Rule 79-5.1. If one party wishes to file or lodge documents under seal, the other party shall not unreasonably withhold agreement to such procedure. If an agreement is reached, the parties shall submit to the Court a Stipulation and Proposed Order for such filing or lodging under seal. If no such agreement is reached, then the proponent of lodging or filing under seal shall submit an Application and Proposed Order pursuant to Local Rule 79-5.1.

II. Judge Hillman's Case Management Orders

A. *Case Management Order in General Order 08-09 Cases (Magistrate Judge Pilot Project)*

IN THE UNITED STATES DISTICT COURT
FOR THE CENTRAL DISTRICT OF CALIFORNIA

)	Case No. ______________
Plaintiff(s),)	
v.)	**CASE MANAGEMENT ORDER IN GENERAL ORDER 08-09 CASES (MAGISTRATE JUDGE PILOT PROJECT)**
Defendant(s).)	
______________________________)	(See LAST PAGE FOR FORM RE: PRETRIAL AND TRIAL DATES)

This case has been assigned to the calendar of Magistrate Judge Stephen J. Hillman, and the parties have agreed to the magistrate judge's exercise of jurisdiction in cases randomly assigned pursuant to General Order 08-09.

The magistrate judge is located in Courtroom 550, which is on the 5th floor of the Edward R. Roybal Federal Building and Courthouse, 255 E. Temple Street, Los Angeles, CA 90012. The courtroom deputy clerk ("CRD"), Ms. Sandra Butler, can be reached at (213) 894-6487. The magistrate judge expects full compliance with the Federal Rules of Civil Procedure, the Local Rules for the Central District of California ("the Local Rules"), and the scheduling order in this case. Ambiguities, if any, will be construed to secure the just, speedy, and inexpensive determination of each action.

The purpose of this order is to enable counsel[1] to know well in advance the schedule and requirements to which they will be expected to adhere.

I. SCHEDULING CONFERENCE AND/OR ORDER

The magistrate judge may set a scheduling conference, or issue a scheduling order without a scheduling conference. In either event, at least twenty-one (21) days in advance of the time limits set forth in Fed. R. Civ. P. 16(b)(2), counsel shall file the joint report required by Fed. R. Civ. P. 26(b) and Local Rule 26. A form for suggested pre-trial and trial dates is attached to this order. **Counsel must jointly complete this form and attach it to the joint report.**

At the time of the filing of the joint report, counsel shall also file a separate document entitled "joint notice of scheduling status conference," which shall schedule the conference on the magistrate judge's calendar on the first Monday three weeks thereafter at 1:30 p.m. If that Monday is a holiday, the joint notice shall designate the immediately following Tuesday at 1:30 p.m.. The magistrate judge will consider the dates suggested by counsel on the form attached to the joint report. A scheduling order with specific dates for pre-trial events and trial will be issued after the magistrate judge's review of the completed form and, if necessary, a scheduling conference.

II. DISCOVERY CUT-OFF

All discovery shall be completed by the discovery cutoff date. **THIS IS NOT THE**

1 "Counsel" as used in this order also applies to persons appearing *in propia persona.*

DATE BY WHICH DISCOVERY REQUESTS MUST BE SERVED; IT IS THE DATE BY WHICH ALL DISCOVERY, INCLUDING EXPERT DISCOVERY, IS TO BE COMPLETED.

Any motion challenging the adequacy of responses to discovery must be filed timely, served, and calendared sufficiently in advance of the discovery cutoff date to permit additional discovery to be obtained before that date, if the motion is granted. The magistrate judge requires compliance with Local Rule 37-1 and 37-2 in the preparation and filing of discovery motions. Except in the case of an extreme emergency which was not created by the lawyer briefing the motion, discovery motions may not be heard on *ex parte* application. Discovery motions are frequently decided on the papers without a hearing.

III. MOTIONS AND MOTION CUTOFF DATE

A. GENERAL PROVISIONS

All law and motion matters, except for discovery motions (which are subject to the time limits set forth in the preceding paragraph) and motions *in limine*, must be filed by the motion cut-off date specified on the attached schedule of trial and pre-trial dates after this schedule is approved by the magistrate judge.

The parties must adhere to the requirements of the Local Rules. See Local Rules 7-1 *et seq*. If any party does not oppose a motion, that party shall submit a written statement in accordance with Local Rule 7-16 that it does not oppose the motion. The parties should note that failure to meet the time limits set forth in Local Rule 7 may be deemed consent to the granting of the motion. Local Rule 7-12.

To insure that the magistrate judge receives oppositions and replies in a timely fashion, chambers copies conformed to reflect that they have been e-filed must be delivered to Chambers by leaving them in the courtesy/chambers copy box located outside chambers.

Motions are heard on Mondays at 2:00 p.m. unless otherwise ordered by the Court. Even if a motion is still necessary after a good faith pre-filing conference, counsel should have sufficiently discussed the issues so that the briefing will be directed to those substantive issues which require resolution by the Court.

Unless clearly justified under the circumstances of the case, "motions to dismiss or in the alternative for summary adjudication" are discouraged. Such composite motions tend to blur the legitimate distinction[s] between the two motions, which have different purposes. Moreover, Fed. R. Civ. P. 12(b)(6) motions are discouraged unless moving counsel has a legitimate belief after a good faith conference that such motion will likely result in dismissal, without leave to amend, of all or at least some of the claims under applicable law. In most cases, the prospective moving party should agree to any amendment that would cure the defect.

B. *EX PARTE* APPLICATIONS

Ex parte practice is strongly discouraged. *See Mission Power Eng. Co. v. Continental Casualty Co.*, 883 F. Supp. 488 (C.D. Cal. 1995). Counsel must adhere to proper *ex parte* procedures for any *ex parte* application filed with the magistrate judge. *Id.*, at 492; *see also* Local Rule 7-19.

C. SIZE OF PLEADINGS AND CITATION

Memoranda of points and authorities in support of or in opposition to any motion **shall not exceed 25 pages**. Replies **shall not exceed 12 pages**. Only in rare instances and for good cause shown will the Court grant an application to extend these page limitations.

Citations to case law must identify not only the case cited, but the specific page referenced. Statutory and other references should identify with specificity the sections and subsections referenced.

D. APPLICATIONS AND STIPULATIONS TO EXTEND TIME

Extensions of time are rarely granted and no stipulations extending the magistrate judge's scheduling dates shall be effective unless approved by the magistrate judge. Applications to extend the time to file any required document or to continue any pre-trial or trial date must set forth:

(i) the existing due date or hearing date;

(ii) specific, concrete reasons supporting good cause for granting the extension. This information must be presented in a sworn declaration;

(iii) whether there have been prior requests for extensions, and whether these were granted or denied by the magistrate judge.

The party(ies) requesting the extension must provide the magistrate judge with a proposed order setting forth the proposed new dates and/or proposed new schedule.

E. SUMMARY JUDGMENT MOTIONS

No party may file more than one motion pursuant to Fed. R. Civ. P. 56 regardless of whether such motion is denominated as a motion for summary judgment or summary adjudication.

To increase efficiency and to assist counsel in structuring and focusing these motions, the following requirements apply when filing motions for summary judgment.

1. Separate Statement of Undisputed Facts and Statement of Genuine Issues

The separate statement of undisputed facts is to be prepared in a two-column format. The left-hand column should set forth the allegedly undisputed fact. The right-hand column should set forth the evidence that supports the factual statement. The fact statements should be set forth in sequentially numbered paragraphs. Each paragraph should contain a narrowly focused statement of fact. Each numbered paragraph should address a single subject in as concise a manner as possible.

The opposing party's statement of genuine issues must be in two columns and track the moving party's separate statement exactly as prepared. The document must be in two columns; the left-hand column must restate the allegedly undisputed fact, and the right-hand column must indicate either undisputed, or disputed. The opposing party may dispute all or only a portion of the statement, but if disputing only a portion, must clearly indicate what part is being disputed.

Where the opposing party is disputing the fact in whole or part, the opposing party must, in the right-hand column, label and restate the moving party's evidence in support of the fact, followed by the opposing party's evidence controverting the fact. Where the opposing party is disputing the fact on the basis of an evidentiary objection, the party must cite to the evidence alleged to be objectionable and state the ground of the objection and nothing more. **No argument should be set forth in this document.**

The opposing party may submit additional material facts that bear on or relate to the issues raised by the moving party, which shall follow the format described above for the moving party's separate statement. These additional facts shall follow the moving party's facts, shall continue in sequentially numbered paragraphs (*e.g.*, if the moving party's last statement of fact was set forth in paragraph 30, then the first new fact will be set forth in paragraph 31), and shall set forth in the right hand column the evidence that supports that statement. The moving party, in its reply, shall respond to the additional facts in the same manner and format that the opposition party is required adhere to in responding to the statement of undisputed facts, as described above.

2. Supporting Evidence

No party should submit any evidence other than the specific items of evidence or testimony necessary to support or controvert a proposed statement of undisputed fact. Thus, for example, the entire transcript of a deposition, entire sets of interrogatory responses, and documents that do not specifically support or controvert material in the separate statements, should not be submitted in support or opposition to a motion for summary judgment.

Evidence submitted in support or opposition to a motion should be submitted either by way of stipulation or as exhibits to declarations sufficient to authenticate the proffered evidence and should not be attached to the memorandum of points and authorities. The magistrate judge will accept counsel's authentication of deposition transcript, of written discovery responses, and of the receipt of documents in discovery if the fact that the document was in the opponent's possession is of independent significance. Documentary evidence as to which there is no stipulation regarding foundation must be accompanied by the testimony, either by declaration or properly authenticated deposition transcript, of a witness who can establish its authenticity.

3. Objections to Evidence

If a party disputes a fact based in whole or in part on an evidentiary objection, the ground of the objection, as indicated above, should be stated in the separate statement but not argued in that document. Evidentiary objections are to be addressed in a separate memorandum to be filed with the opposition or reply brief of the party. This memorandum should be organized ***to track the paragraph numbers of the separate statement in sequence***. It should identify the specific item of evidence to which objection is made, identify the ground of the objection, and make a very brief argument with citation to authority as to why the objection is well taken. The following is an example of the format contemplated by the magistrate judge:

> Separate Statement Paragraph 1: Objection to the supporting deposition transcript of Jane Smith at 60:1-10 on the grounds that the statement constitutes inadmissible hearsay and no exception is applicable. To the extent it is offered to prove her state of mind, it is irrelevant since her state of mind is not in issue. Fed. R. Evid. 801, 802.

DO NOT SUBMIT BLANKET OR BOILERPLATE OBJECTIONS TO THE OPPONENT'S STATEMENTS OF UNDISPUTED FACT: THESE WILL BE DISREGARDED AND OVERRULED.

4. The Memorandum of Points and Authorities

The moving party's memorandum of points and authorities should be in the usual form required under Local Rule 7 and should contain a narrative statement of facts as to those aspects of the case that are before the magistrate judge. All facts should be supported with citation to the paragraph number in the separate statement that supports the factual assertion and not to the underlying evidence.

Unless the case involves some unusual application of Fed. R. Civ. P. 56, the motion need only contain a brief statement of the Fed. R. Civ. P. 56 standard. The argument should be organized to focus on the pertinent elements of the claim(s) or defense(s) in issue, with the purpose of showing the existence or non-existence of a genuine issue of material fact for trial on that element of the claim or defense.

Likewise, the opposition memorandum of points and authorities should be in the usual form required by Local Rule 7, and where the opposition memorandum sets forth facts, the memorandum should cite to paragraphs in the separate statement if they are not in dispute, to the evidence that contravenes the fact where the fact is in dispute, or, if the fact is contravened by an additional fact in the statement of genuine issues, the citation should be to such fact by paragraph number.

5. Timing

The magistrate judge expects that the moving party will provide more than the minimum twenty-one (21) day notice for such motions. The moving party should deliver to the CRD a copy of a diskette or USB flash drive, in WordPerfect format (9.0 or earlier versions), containing the statement of uncontroverted facts and conclusions of law.

F. ORAL ARGUMENT

If the Court concludes that a motion can be resolved without argument, the magistrate judge will notify the parties in advance.

G. MOTIONS IN LIMINE

The parties must file motions in limine addressing the admissibility of evidence in accordance with Local Rule 7-3 by the date specified in the scheduling order, guidelines for which are on the last page. The parties shall file their opposing and reply papers in accordance with Local Rules 7-9 and 7-10 respectively.

IV. PRE-TRIAL CONFERENCE FILINGS

A. GENERAL PROVISIONS

The pre-trial conference ("PTC") will be held at 1:30 p.m. on the date on the last page, unless the magistrate judge expressly waived a PTC at the status conference. (In the rare cases where the magistrate judge waives a PTC, the parties must follow Local Rule 16-10.)

The lead trial attorney on behalf of each party shall attend both the PTC and all meetings of the parties in preparation of the PTC, unless excused for good cause shown in advance of the PTC.

At the PTC, the parties should be prepared to discuss means of streamlining the trial, including, but not limited to: bifurcation; presentation of foundational and non-critical testimony and direct testimony by deposition excerpts; narrative summaries and/or stipulations as to the content of testimony; presentation of testimony on direct examination by affidavit or by declaration subject to crossexamination; and, qualification of experts by admitted resumes.

B. FORM OF PRE-TRIAL CONFERENCE ORDER ("PTCO")

The proposed PTCO shall be lodged fourteen (14) calendar days before the PTC. Adherence to this time requirement is necessary for in-chambers preparation of the matter. The form of the proposed PTCO shall comply with Appendix A to the Local Rules.

C. LOCAL RULE 16 FILINGS; MEMORANDA; WITNESS LISTS; EXHIBIT LISTS

The parties must comply fully with the requirements of Local Rule 16. They shall file carefully prepared memoranda of contentions of fact and law (which may also serve as the trial brief), along with their respective witness lists and exhibit lists, all in accordance with Local Rules 16-3, 16-4, 16-5 and 16-6.

D. JURY INSTRUCTIONS, VERDICT FORMS, SPECIAL INTERROGATORIES

1. Thirty (30) days before the Fed. R. Civ. P. 16 meeting, the parties shall exchange proposed jury instructions, verdict forms, and special interrogatories. Twenty one (21) days before the meeting, counsel shall exchange written objections, if any, to proposed jury instructions, verdicts, and special interrogatories. At the meeting, the parties shall confer with the objective of submitting one set of agreed upon substantive instructions, verdict forms and, if necessary, special interrogatories. "Substantive jury instructions" means all instructions relating to the elements of all claims and defenses in the case. The Court will appreciate the parties delivering to the CRD a courtesy copy of these filings in an electronic format compatible with WordPerfect at the time the documents are filed.

2. If the parties cannot agree upon one complete set of substantive instructions, verdict forms, and/or special interrogatories, they shall file two documents with the magistrate judge: a joint document reflecting the agreed upon instructions, verdict forms, and/or special interrogatories, and a second document in the form of a joint statement regarding the disputed instructions, verdicts, and interrogatories in the following format for each instruction, verdict, or interrogatory in issue:

(a) A separate page containing the text of the disputed language with an identification of the party proposing it;

(b) Following the instruction, the opposing party's statement of objections to the instruction along with legal authority in support of the argument (**not to exceed <u>one</u> page**) and proposed alternative language where appropriate;

(c) The proposing party's response to the objection with legal authority supporting the proposed language (**not to exceed <u>one</u> page**).

Both the agreed on set, and the joint statement re disputed instructions are to be filed with the pre-trial conference order and other Fed. R. Civ. P. 16 documents fourteen (14) days before the pre-trial conference.

3. All proposed jury instructions shall be in the format specified by Local Rule 51-2.

4. A table of contents shall be included with all jury instructions submitted to the magistrate judge. The table of contents shall set forth the following:

(a) The number of the instruction;
(b) A brief title of the instruction;
(c) The source of the instruction; and,
(d) The page number of the instruction.

<u>For example:</u>

Number	Title	Source	Page Number
1	Burden of Proof	9th Cir. 12.2	5

5. The Court directs counsel to use the instructions from the <u>Manual of Model Jury Instructions for the Ninth Circuit</u> (West 1997) where applicable. Where California law is

to be applied and the above instructions are not applicable, the Court prefers counsel to use the Judicial Council of California Civil Jury Instructions ("CACI") forms. If neither of these sources is applicable, counsel are directed to use the instructions in Devitt, Blackmar and Wolff, Federal Jury Practice and Instructions.

6. Modifications of instructions from the foregoing sources (or any other form instructions) must specifically state the modification made to the original form instruction and the authority supporting the modification.

E. JOINT STATEMENT OF THE CASE AND REQUESTS FOR *VOIR DIRE*

At the pre-trial conference, the parties shall lodge their proposed *voir dire* questions and their joint statement of the case which the magistrate judge shall read to all prospective jurors prior to the commencement of *voir dire*. The statement should be not longer than two or three paragraphs.

The Court conducts *voir dire* of all prospective jurors. The parties need not submit requests for standard *voir dire* questions, such as education, current occupation, marital status, prior jury service, etc., but should include only proposed questions specifically tailored to the parties and issues of the case.

F. FINDINGS OF FACT AND CONCLUSIONS OF LAW

For a non-jury trial, the parties shall lodge their proposed findings of fact and conclusions of law in accordance with Local Rule 52-1 not later than one week before trial. The Court will appreciate the parties delivering to the CRD a copy of these findings on disk or USB flash drive in WordPerfect 9.0 format.

V. SETTLEMENT

Local Rule 16-15.2 provides that the settlement conference shall be concluded not later than forty-five (45) days before the pre-trial conference. In any event, the parties must file a status report re settlement at the time that they lodge the proposed PTCO, indicating that they have conducted the Local Rule 16 settlement conference.

The magistrate judge will not conduct settlement conferences in non-jury cases which are to be tried before him. In jury cases, the magistrate judge will personally conduct a settlement conference at the parties' joint request if three conditions exist:

1. The parties are satisfied that the fact issues in the case will be tried to a jury;

2. All significant pre-trial rulings which the magistrate judge must make have been made; and,

3. The parties desire the magistrate judge to conduct the conference, understanding that if settlement fails, the magistrate judge will preside over trial of the case.

VI. SERVICE OF THIS ORDER

Counsel for plaintiff(s), in an action commenced in this court, and counsel for defendant(s) in a removed action, shall serve a copy of this order on all other parties or their counsel at the earliest possible time. Counsel, or any party required to give notice of this order, shall file proof of service of such notice within 48 hours of the service of such notice.

IT IS SO ORDERED.

DATED. ________________

____
STEPHEN J. HILLMAN
United States Magistrate Judge

SUGGESTED SCHEDULE OF PRETRIAL AND TRIAL DATES

CASE NAME: ______________________
CASE NO: __________________________

Matter	Time	Weeks before trial	Plaintiff(s) Request	Defendant(s) Request	Court Order
Trial (jury)(court) (length ___days) (**Tuesday**)	9:00 a.m.				
For Court Trial Lodge Findings of Fact and Conclusions of Law, LR 52, and Summaries of Direct Testimony		3			
Pretrial Conference, LR 16; Hearing on Motions *in Limine*	2:00 p.m.	4			
For Jury Trial Lodge Pretrial Conference Order, LR 16-7; File Agreed Set of Jury Instructions and Verdict Forms; File Statement Regarding Disputed Instructions, Verdicts, *etc.*; File Oppositions to Motions *in Limine*		6			
For Jury Trial File Memo of Contentions of Fact and Law, LR 16-4; Exhibit & Witness Lists, LR 16-5, 6; File Status Report Regarding Settlement; File Motions *in Limine*		7			
Last date to conduct Settlement Conf., LR 16-15		12			
Last day for **hearing** motions, LR 7		14			
Non-expert Discovery Cut-off					
Expert Disclosure (initial)					
Expert Disclosure (rebuttal)					
Expert Discovery Cut-off					
Last Date to Amend Pleadings or Add Parties					

LR 16-15 Settlement Choice:

1. ______ Attorney Settlement Panel
2. ______ Outside ADR
3. ______ Judge Hillman

Hon. Victor B. Kenton

Magistrate Judge

Chambers Information

U.S. District Court, Central District of California
Courtroom 590
255 East Temple Street
Los Angeles, CA 90012

Scheduling Information

Courtroom Deputy: (213) 894-1831

Civil Law and Motion	Tuesdays at 10:00 a..m. or as scheduled
Criminal Law and Motion	As scheduled

Biographical Information

[Not available]

I. Judge Kenton's Procedures and Practices

A. *Procedures and Schedules*

1. Civil motions are heard on: **TUESDAYS** Time: **10:00am or as scheduled**

   Criminal motions are heard on: **As scheduled.** Time: **As scheduled.**

   (If Tuesday is a holiday, next motion date is **as scheduled**.)

   It is/**is not** necessary to clear a motion date with the court clerk prior to filing the motion.

2. Discovery motions are to be calendared before the district judge/magistrate judge. Determined by policy of the District Judge assigned to the case.

3. Are tentative rulings issued? Often on discovery motions, but not always. Discovery motions may be taken under submission without oral argument.

4. Electronic Filings: Counsel shall e-file all criminal and civil filings for MAGISTRATE JUDGE KENTON pursuant to Federal Rules of Civil Procedure 5(d)(3), Local Rule 5-4, and General Order 10-07, as follows:

   Step 1: All non-signature items shall be E-FILED in .pdf format. All proposed signature items shall be E-FILED as a separate document in pdf format.

   Step 2: All **proposed** signature items shall be E-MAILED to the chambers email address at vbk_chambers@cacd.uscourts.gov in Word or Word Perfect format. ONLY proposed signature items should be emailed to the chambers' email address. Please do NOT email other associated documents, and do NOT use this email address for communication with the Court or the Clerk.

   Step 3: A MANDATORY CHAMBERS COPY of all e-filed documents shall be delivered to the COURTESY COPY DROP BOX NEAR CHAMBERS IN THE ROYBAL BUILDING, ROOM 5100, 5TH FLOOR **within 24 hours or on the same day, if priority processing is being requested**. All copies delivered to the courtesy bin shall have the notice of E-filing attached.

5. Procedures for filing an ex parte application: Follow local rules. Opposition or Non-opposition due within 24 hours.

6. To request a continuance of any scheduled court proceeding: Contact opposing counsel, then court clerk for an acceptable date. Stipulation or Ex Parte Application in compliance with local rules must be filed with a proposed order.

7. Are counsel allowed to contact the judge's law clerk or secretary? NO.

8. Inquiries regarding the status of a motion, stipulation or proposed order. Contact court clerk.

9. Calendar conflicts: (Procedures for attorneys to follow if they have a calendar conflict) Timely conflict calendar should be provided to court clerk.

10. Procedures for bringing electronic equipment into the courtroom: Contact court clerk.

11. For general information on how to order a transcript of any reported or digitally recorded proceeding, please contact 213-894-3015 or visit www.cacd.uscourts.gov >

General Information > Court Reporter/Recorder Transcripts. If you require an estimate of cost for the preparation of a transcript, contact the court reporter/recorder for the desired proceeding.

To determine the court reporter/recorder for a particular proceeding, go to the Court Reporter Schedule web page and click on View by Date. Once you've determined the correct court reporter/recorder for the desired session, click on Court Reporter Phone and Email List for contact information.

12. Questions regarding law clerk/extern positions. Contact judge's secretary.

13. Trial preparation:

- **a.** Court hours: **9:00am – 4:30pm**
- **b.** Exhibit preparation: **Follow local rules.**
- **c.** Jury instructions: **Follow local rules.**
- **d.** Verdict forms: **Follow local rules.**
- **e.** Other

14. Procedures for obtaining the services of an interpreter on a civil case Contact court clerk.

II. Judge Kenton's Case Management Orders

A. Order Regarding Civil Trial

IN THE UNITED STATES DISTICT COURT
FOR THE CENTRAL DISTRICT OF CALIFORNIA

Plaintiff(s),	Case No. ______________
v.	**ORDER RE CIVIL TRIAL**
Defendant(s).	

1. Cut-Off Date for Joining Parties or Amending Pleadings: __________
2. Cut-Off Date for Election of Jury Trial: __________
3. Discovery Cut-Off Date: __________
4. Settlement Procedure Selection Date Cut-Off: ______________
5. Expert Witness Disclosure Cut-Off Date: ______________
6. Settlement Conference Cut-Off Date: ______________
7. Expert Discovery Cut-Off Date: ____________
8. Dispositive Motion Cut-Off Date: ____________
9. Motion Hearing Date: _______, 20011 at 10:00 a.m.
10. Pre-Trial Conference Date: _________, 2011 at 10:00 a.m.
11. Trial Date: _______, 2011 at 9:00 a.m.

This action has been assigned to the calendar of the Honorable Victor B. Kenton, Courtroom 590, Roybal Federal Building, 255 East Temple Street, Los Angeles, California 90012.

In accordance with General Order 10-07, this case is designated for electronic filing. Counsel are to familiarize themselves with General Order 10-07 and must comply with all requirements. [Counsel shall electronically file all documents by 4:00 pm on or before the due date.] [Courtesy copies of the following electronically filed documents, with the Notice of Electronic Filing attached, shall either (a) be delivered to the Magistrate Judge's Chambers no later than 1:00 pm on the next court day, or (b) shall be mailed to Magistrate Judge Victor B. Kenton at the Roybal Federal Building, 255 East Temple Street, Los Angeles, CA 90012 no later than the next court day.]:

1. For any motion to dismiss the Complaint or motion for summary judgment: the motion and supporting papers, the opposition papers, and the reply papers.
2. The Answer.
3. For any other dispositive motion and supporting papers, the opposition papers, and the reply papers.

In order to facilitate the just, speedy, and inexpensive determination of this case, the parties shall comply with the following instructions.

Contents

Pre-Trial and Trial Dates

1. The Court has ordered the dates as indicated above and described as follows:

a. Joining Parties or Amending Pleadings. The Court has established a cut-off date for joining parties or amending pleadings. All motions to join other parties or to amend the pleadings shall be filed and served on, or prior to, the cut-off date. All motions to join other parties or amend the pleadings shall be noticed for hearing. All unserved parties are subject to dismissal at the time of the Pre-Trial Conference pursuant to Local Rule 16-7.1.

b. Discovery Cut-Off. This is the last date to complete discovery.

c. Motion Filing Cut-Off. The Court hears motions on Tuesdays at 10:00 a.m. The motion cut-off date is the last day motions may be filed. The cut-off date applies to all motions except motions in limine.

Motions in limine, i.e., those pertaining only to evidentiary matters, shall be filed in accordance with the requirements of Local Rule 7. Parties must notice motions in limine for hearing no later than the Monday eight days before the Tuesday trial date. If that Monday is a holiday, the motions must be noticed for hearing on the preceding Monday. Motions in limine may not be used as a substitute for a summary judgment motion.

d. Dates for hearing on motions in limine will be set after dispositive motions have been heard or notice has been given that no motions will be filed. Each party appearing in this action shall be represented at the Pre-Trial Conference and at all pre-trial meetings by the lead trial counsel. Counsel should be prepared to discuss streamlining the trial, including bifurcation, presentation of testimony by deposition excerpts, time limits, stipulations as to undisputed facts, and qualification of experts by admitted resumes.

e. Trial. Trials are conducted Tuesday through Friday, from 9:30 a.m. to 4:30 p.m. Counsel should plan to meet with the Court at 9:00 a.m. on the first day of trial. Jury selection generally takes two hours. Counsel must be ready to proceed with opening statements immediately thereafter.

Discovery

2. Counsel shall initiate all discovery other than depositions at least forty-five (45) days prior to the cut-off date. The Court will not approve stipulations between counsel which permit responses to be served after the cut-off date, except in unusual circumstances and for good cause shown.

3. Counsel shall commence all depositions at least five (5) working days prior to the cut-off date. **Counsel shall lodge all original depositions to be used in trial with the Courtroom Deputy Clerk on the first day of trial.**

Settlement

In conformity with the Local Rules, counsel shall file the settlement procedure selection by the date given by the Court. Available settlement alternatives for consideration include:

(1) a settlement conference before an available Magistrate Judge willing to conduct the conference. Parties should contact the Courtroom Deputy Clerk, Roxanne Horan, at 213-894-1831, and provide the name of the requested Magistrate Judge. The Courtroom Clerk will then contact the requested Magistrate Judge's Courtroom Clerk to determine availability and dates. (Note: the Court does not participate in settlements of cases on its own docket.)

(2) a settlement conference or mediation before an attorney selected from the Attorney Settlement Panel (list available from the Court's Website);

(3) the employment by the parties of a private judge, mediator or arbitrator.

The parties in every case must elect a settlement procedure, pursuant to Local Rule 16-14.4. Given the high costs of litigation and the enormous commitment of resources that a trial requires, the Court urges the parties to explore every option for resolving their disputes short of trial.

Preparation for the Pre-Trial Conference

6. Compliance with the requirements of Local Rule 16 is mandatory. Counsel shall submit carefully prepared Memoranda of Contentions of Fact and Law (which may also serve as the trial briefs) and Proposed Pre-Trial Conference Order in accordance with the provisions of Local Rules 16-2.8 through 16-6. The Proposed Pre-Trial Conference Order shall conform to the example set forth in Appendix A to the Local Rules, modified as necessary to comply with this order.

7. The Memoranda of Contentions of Fact and Law, Exhibit Lists, and Witness Lists shall be served and filed no later than twenty-one (21) calendar days before the Pre-Trial Conference. The Proposed Pre-Trial Conference Order shall be lodged fourteen (14) calendar days before the Pre-Trial Conference. Adherence to time limits is essential to in-chambers preparation.

8. **Proposed Pre-Trial Conference Order.**

   a. The Proposed Pre-Trial Conference Order must contain a Table of Contents.

   b. Under paragraph 1, list each claim, counterclaim, or defense that has been dismissed or abandoned.

   c. The factual issues in dispute should track the elements of a claim or defense upon which the jury would be required to make findings. Counsel should state issues in ultimate fact form, not as evidentiary fact issues (i.e., "was the defendant negligent," "was defendant's negligence the proximate cause of plaintiff's injury;"

not "was the plaintiff standing on the corner of 5th and Spring at 10:00 a.m. on May 3").

d. Issues of law should state legal issues upon which the Court will be required to rule after the Pre-Trial Conference, including during the trial, and should not list ultimate fact issues to be submitted to the trier of fact.

e. If expert witnesses are to be called at trial, each party must list and identify its respective expert witnesses. Failure of a party to list and identify an expert witness in the Proposed Pre-Trial Conference Order shall preclude a party from calling that expert witness at trial.

9. **Summary of Witness Testimony and Time Estimates**
Counsel shall prepare a list of their witnesses, including a brief summary (two to three paragraphs) of each witness's expected testimony and an estimate of the length of time needed for direct examination. Counsel shall exchange these lists with opposing counsel. **Counsel shall jointly file a single list of witness testimony summaries, including estimates for direct examination of their own witnesses and estimates for cross-examination of opposing witnesses.** These statements shall be filed at the time counsel lodge the Proposed Pre-Trial Conference Order, i.e., fourteen (14) days before the Pre-Trial Conference.

Exhibits

10. Counsel are to assemble their exhibits by placing them in 3-ring binders, with each exhibit separated by a tabbed divider on the right side. Counsel shall provide original exhibits for the Courtroom Deputy Clerk and a duplicate set for the judge. The original exhibits shall be tagged with the appropriate exhibit tags in the upper and lower right corner of the first page of each exhibit. Each binder shall contain a Table of Contents.

Counsel must comply with Local Rule 26-4 when numbering the exhibits. The Clerk's Office, Room G-8, 312 North Spring Street, Los Angeles, can supply counsel with appropriate exhibit tags.

11. The Court requires the following to be submitted to the Courtroom Deputy Clerk on the first day of trial:

a. The original exhibits with the Court's exhibit tags. Plaintiff shall use yellow tags; defendant shall use blue tags. Each tag shall be stapled to the front of the exhibit on the upper right corner and include the case number, case name, and exhibit number.

b. One bench book with a copy of each exhibit for the Court's use, tabbed as described above; a copy of the witness list(s).

c. Three (3) copies of exhibit lists.

d. Three (3) copies of witness lists in the order in which the witnesses will be called to testify.

12. All counsel are to meet no later than ten (10) calendar days before trial to discuss and agree to the extent possible on issues including foundation, waiver of the best evidence rule, and which exhibits may be received into evidence at the start of trial.

Trial Preparation for Jury Trials

13. Fourteen (14) calendar days prior to counsel's Rule 16-2 pretrial meeting, counsel shall exchange proposed jury instructions (general and special) and special verdict forms (if applicable). Seven (7) calendar days prior to the Rule 16-2 meeting, counsel shall exchange any objections to the instructions and special verdict forms. Prior to, or at the time of the Rule 16-2 meeting, counsel shall meet and confer with the goal of reaching agreement on one set of joint jury instructions and one special verdict form.

14. The Court directs the parties to make every attempt to agree upon the jury instructions before submitting them to the Court. The Court expects counsel to agree on the substantial majority of jury instructions, particularly when pattern instructions provide a statement of applicable law. When the *Manual of Model Civil Jury Instructions for the Ninth Circuit* provides a version of an applicable requested instruction, the parties should submit the most recent version of the model instruction, modified as necessary to fit the facts of the case (e.g., inserting names of parties to whom instruction applies). Where language appears in brackets in the model instruction, counsel shall select the appropriate text and eliminate the inapplicable bracketed text. Where California law applies, counsel are directed to use *California Jury Instructions -- Civil* (8th ed.)("BAJI"). If neither of the above sources is applicable, counsel are directed to use the instructions from O'Malley, Grenig & Lee (formerly Devitt, et al), *Federal Jury Practice and Instructions* (latest edition). Each requested jury instruction shall cover only one subject or principle of law and shall be numbered and set forth in full on a separate page, citing the authority or source of the requested instruction (except for the "clean" jury copy discussed below).

15. When the parties disagree on an instruction, the party opposing the instruction must attach a short statement (one to two paragraphs) supporting the objection, and the party submitting the instruction must attach a short statement supporting the instruction. Each statement should be on a separate page and should follow directly after the disputed instruction.

16. The parties ultimately must submit one document or, if the parties disagree over any proposed jury instructions, two documents. If the parties submit two documents, those documents shall consist of: (1) a set of Joint Proposed Jury Instructions and (2) a set of Disputed Jury Instructions, along with reasons supporting and opposing each disputed instruction in the format set forth in paragraph 15.

17. The parties must file proposed jury instructions seven (7) calendar days before the Pre-Trial Conference. If the court is closed that day, counsel shall file the proposed instructions the preceding Friday. No later than 5:00 p.m. on the date such instructions are due, the parties must submit conformed courtesy copies to Judge Kenton's chambers. Counsel shall also provide the Court with a 3½ inch diskette compatible with WordPerfect 6.1 or 7.0 containing the proposed jury instructions, in accordance with this paragraph and paragraph 18.

18. The Court will send a copy of the instructions into the jury room for the jury's use during deliberations. Accordingly, in addition to the file copies described above, the diskette submitted with the jury instructions shall contain a "clean set" of Joint Proposed and/or Disputed Jury Instructions, containing only the text of each instruction set forth in full on each page, with the caption "Court's Instruction No. __" (eliminating titles, supporting authority, indication of party proposing, etc.).

19. An index page shall accompany all jury instructions submitted to the Court. The index page shall indicate the following:

a. The number of the instruction;

b. A brief title of the instruction;

c. The source of the instruction and any relevant case citations; and

d. The page number of the instruction.

EXAMPLE:

Number	Title	Source	Page
1	Trademark-Defined (15 U.S.C. §1127)	9th Cir. 15.3.2	7

20. Along with the jury instructions, counsel shall submit any necessary special verdict form seven (7) calendar days before the Pre-Trial Conference.

21. Counsel may, but need not, submit brief proposed voir dire questions for the jury seven (7) calendar days before the Pre-Trial Conference. The Court will conduct its own voir dire after consulting any proposed voir dire submitted by counsel.

22. Counsel shall prepare a joint statement of the case for the Court to read to the prospective panel of jurors prior to the commencement of voir dire. The statement should not exceed one page. The statement shall be filed with the Court seven (7) calendar days before the Pre-Trial Conference.

Trial Preparation for Court Trials

23. Fourteen (14) calendar days before the trial date, each party shall prepare and serve on opposing counsel copies of the proposed Findings of Fact and Conclusion of Law. Each party shall review the other party's proposed Findings and Conclusions and make such changes in the party's own proposed Findings and Conclusions as necessary following such review.

24. Seven (7) calendar days before the trial date, each party shall lodge two copies of its proposed Findings of Fact and Conclusions of Law with the Court together with a copy of diskette. Each party shall serve other parties if changes have been made. The parties shall be prepared to submit to the Court, and to exchange among themselves, supplemental Findings of Fact and Conclusions of Law during the course of the trial.

IT IS SO ORDERED.

DATED: ________________

____
VICTOR B. KENTON
United States Magistrate Judge

B. *Standing Order*

IN THE UNITED STATES DISTICT COURT
FOR THE CENTRAL DISTRICT OF CALIFORNIA

Plaintiff(s),	) Case No. ______________
v.	) **STANDING ORDER**
Defendant(s).	)

READ THIS ORDER CAREFULLY. IT CONTROLS THIS CASE AND DIFFERS IN SOME RESPECTS FROM THE LOCAL RULES.

This action has been assigned to the calendar of Judge Victor B. Kenton.

In accordance with General Order 10-07, this case is designated for electronic filing. Counsel are to familiarize themselves with General Order 10-07 and comply with all requirements. [Counsel shall electronically file all documents by 4:00 pm on or before the due date.] [Courtesy copies of the following electronically filed documents, with the Notice of Electronic Filing attached, shall either (a) be delivered to the Magistrate Judge's Chambers no later than 4:00 pm on the next court day, or (b) shall be mailed to Magistrate Judge Victor B. Kenton at the Edward R. Roybal Federal Building, 255 East Temple Street, Los Angeles, CA 90012 no later than the next court day.]:

1. For any motion to dismiss the Complaint, or motion for summary judgment: the motion and supporting papers, the opposition papers, and the reply papers.
2. The Answer.
3. For any other motions: the motion or petition and supporting papers, the opposition papers, and the reply papers.

In order to facilitate the just, speedy, and inexpensive determination of this case, the parties shall comply with the following instructions.

Both the Court and the attorneys bear responsibility for the progress of litigation in the Federal Courts. This order applies to all parties including those appearing pro se. To secure the just, speedy, and inexpensive determination of every action, F.R.Civ.P. 1, all counsel are ordered to familiarize themselves with the Federal Rules of Civil Procedure and the Local Rules of the Central District of California.[1]

IT IS FURTHER ORDERED:

1. **Service of the Complaint:** The Plaintiff shall promptly serve the Complaint in accordance with F.R.Civ.P. 4 and file the proofs of service pursuant to Local Rule

---

[1] Copies of the Local Rules are available on our website at "**http://www.cacd.uscourts.gov**" or they may be purchased from one of the following:

Los Angeles Daily Journal 915 East 1st Street Los Angeles, CA 90012	West Group 610 Opperman Drive Post Office Box 64526 St. Paul, MN 55164-0526	Metropolitan News 210 South Spring Street Los Angeles, CA 90012

5-3.1.

2. **Removed Actions:** Any answers filed in state court must be attached to the Notice of Removal. Any pending motions must be renoticed as required by Local Rule 7.

3. **Presence of Lead Counsel:** Lead trial counsel shall attend any proceeding before this Court, including all status conferences, as well as settlement conferences.

4. **Rule 26(f) Meeting of Counsel:** Counsel for the parties shall meet personally pursuant to FRCP 26(f) and applicable Local Rules in anticipation of the court-ordered scheduling conference. FRCP 16(b).

5. **Joint Report of Rule 26(f) Meeting:** No later than fifteen (15) court days before the Scheduling Conference, counsel shall file a Joint Report of Rule 26(f) Meeting. **A conformed courtesy copy** of the Joint Report shall be delivered to Judge Kenton's chambers on the Fifth Floor of the Edward R. Roybal Federal Building, 255 East Temple Street, Los Angeles, CA 90012, **by 4:00 p.m. on the date due**. A Joint Report which is not timely filed or does not conform with this Order, FRCP 26(f), and applicable Local Rules will interfere with preparation by the Court and its staff, and may result in delays and/or the assessment of sanctions.

   The Joint Rule 26(f) Report shall address the matters set forth in FRCP 26(f) (some of which are enumerated below), and shall also contain the following:

   (a) A brief statement by each party, not to exceed one (1) page, setting forth that party's factual summary of the case, including the basis for any claims, counterclaims, or defenses.

   (b) The basis for the Court's subject-matter jurisdiction.

   (c) A brief description of the key legal issues.

   (d) The realistic range of probable damages.

   (e) The likelihood of appearance of additional parties.

   (f) Whether all or part of the procedures of the Manual for Complex Litigation should be utilized.

   (g) A proposed discovery cut-off date. Note: this means the final day for completion of discovery, including resolution of all discovery motions.

   (h) What motions (other than discovery motions) are contemplated.

   (i) Prospects of settlement based on counsel's discussion at the Rule 26(f) meeting and any other communications.

   (j) Whether the trial will be a court or jury trial.

   (k) The estimated length of trial.

   (l) The name of the attorney(s) who will try the case.

6. **Mandatory Settlement Procedure:**

   a. **ADR Pilot Program:** This Court is part of the Alternative Dispute Resolution (ADR) Pilot Program. For cases referred to ADR, counsel will be required to complete the ADR Questionnaire and file it at the time the Joint Report is filed. Counsel will thereafter have the option of completing a stipulation selecting the agreed-upon Settlement Officer, or having the Program Coordinator randomly select a Settlement Officer for the case.

b. Cases not in the ADR Pilot Program: In conformity with the Local Rules, counsel shall file the settlement procedure selection by the date given by the Court at the time of the Scheduling Conference. Available alternatives for consideration include:

(1) a settlement conference before an available Magistrate Judge willing to conduct the conference. Parties should contact the Courtroom Deputy Clerk, Roxanne Horan, at 213-894-1831, and provide the name of the requested Magistrate Judge. The Courtroom Clerk will then contact the requested Magistrate Judge's Courtroom Clerk to determine availability and dates. (Note: the Court does not participate in settlements of cases on its own docket unless the parties elect to proceed to a jury trial);

(2) a settlement conference or mediation before an attorney selected from the Attorney Settlement Panel (list available from the Court's Website);

(3) the employment by the parties of a private judge, mediator or arbitrator.

7. Discovery: All discovery matters will be heard by Judge Kenton.

The decision of the Magistrate Judge shall be final.

8. Motions:

a. Time for Filing and Hearing Motions: Motions shall be filed in accordance with Local Rule 7; the next available motion date can be obtained from the Courtroom Deputy or the Filing Window. This Court customarily hears motions on **Tuesdays, commencing at 10:00 a.m.** Opposition and Reply Briefs, including all declarations and supporting documentation, will be rejected if not timely filed in accordance with the Local Rules. **No supplemental brief shall be filed without prior leave of Court. Local Rule 7-10.**

Adherence to the timing requirements is essential for the Court's preparation of motion matters.

b. Pre-filing Requirement: Counsel should take note of the changes to the Local Rules affecting motion practice in the Central District. Among other things, Local Rule 7-3 requires counsel to engage in a pre-filing conference "to discuss thoroughly... the substance of the contemplated motion and any potential resolution," and to confirm in the notice of motion that such conference has taken place. Local Rule 7-3. Counsel should discuss the issues sufficiently that if a motion is still necessary, the briefing may be directed to those substantive issues requiring resolution by the Court. Counsel should resolve minor procedural or other non-substantive matters during the conference. **Failure to comply with Local Rule 7-3 and to set forth such compliance in the notice of motion will result in the motion being vacated.**

c. Length and Format of Motion Papers: Memoranda of Points and Authorities in support of or in opposition to motions shall not exceed 25 pages. Replies shall not exceed 12 pages. Only in rare instances and for good cause shown will the Court grant an application to extend these page limitations.

Typeface shall comply with Local Rule 11-3.1.1. NOTE: If Times Roman

font is used, the size must be no less than 14; if Courier is used, the size must be no less than 12. Footnotes shall be in typeface no less than one size smaller than text size and shall be used sparingly.

Filings that do not conform to the Local Rules and this Order will not be considered.

d. **Courtesy Copies:** Counsel shall deliver a conformed courtesy copy to all reply papers to Judge Kenton's chambers **by 4:00 p.m. on the date due**.

e. **Motions for Summary Judgment:** Before filing a motion for summary judgment, counsel are strongly encouraged to review Chapter 14 of Schwarzer, Tashima & Wagstaffe, *California Practice Guide: Federal Civil Procedure Before Trial* (1998). To assist the Court, the moving party shall submit the required Statement of Uncontroverted Facts and Conclusions of Law as set forth in Form 14:C. The opposing party shall submit the required Statement of Genuine Issues as set forth in Form 14:D, responding first to each of the moving party's alleged uncontroverted facts, then listing any material facts in dispute, and citing to supporting evidence. **Note: Separate statements that fail to comply with the above format will not be considered.**

9. **Proposed Orders:** Each party filing or opposing a motion or seeking the determination of any matter shall serve and lodge a Proposed Order setting forth the relief or action sought and a brief statement of the rationale for the decision with appropriate citations. If the Proposed Order exceeds two pages, the proposing party shall also submit the document on a 3½-inch diskette compatible with WordPerfect 11.

10. **Telephonic Hearings:** The Court will conduct status conferences by telephone if any party outside the district so requests and all involved parties consent. The attorney requesting the telephonic hearing shall contact the Courtroom Deputy Clerk, Roxanne Horan, at 213-894-1831, at least one week prior to the date scheduled for the motion or conference to make the necessary arrangements. A member of the Court's staff will place the conference call.

11. **Ex Parte Applications:** Counsel are reminded that ex parte applications are solely for extraordinary relief. *See Mission Power Engineering Co. v. Continental Casualty Co.*, 883 F.Supp. 488 (C.D. Cal. 1995). Applications that fail to conform with Local Rules 7-19 and 7-19.1, **including a statement of opposing counsel's position**, will not be considered. The Court considers ex parte applications on the papers and usually does not set these matters for hearing. In addition to the requirements of Local Rules 7-19 and 7-19.1, counsel for the moving party shall serve opposing counsel by facsimile transmission and shall notify opposing counsel that opposition papers must be filed no later than 24 hours following such facsimile service. Counsel shall deliver a conformed courtesy copy of moving, opposition, or notice of non-opposition papers to Judge Kenton's chambers. The Courtroom Deputy Clerk will notify counsel of the Court's ruling or a hearing date and time, if the Court determines a hearing is necessary.

12. **Continuances:** Counsel requesting a continuance must lodge — prior to the date to be continued — a Proposed Stipulation and Order including a detailed declaration of the grounds for the requested continuance or extension of time. Local Rule 7-11. The Court grants continuances only upon a showing of good cause, focusing on the

diligence of the party seeking the continuance and any prejudice that may result if the continuance is denied. Failure to comply with the Local Rules and this Order will result in rejection of the request without further notice to the parties. **Proposed stipulations to continue scheduling dates shall address the effect of such continuance on any other dates previously set by the Court. Such stipulations do not become effective unless and until signed by the Court. Parties requesting conformed copies shall comply with Local Rule 11-4.5.**

13. <u>Communications with Chambers:</u> Counsel shall not attempt to contact the Court or its chambers staff by telephone, letter, facsimile, e-mail or by any other <u>ex parte</u> means. Local Rule 83-2.11. Counsel may contact the **Courtroom Deputy, Roxanne Horan, at 213-894-1831**, with appropriate inquiries. To facilitate communication with the Courtroom Deputy, counsel should list their facsimile transmission numbers along with their telephone numbers on all papers.

14. <u>Notice of this Order:</u> Counsel for Plaintiff shall immediately serve this Order on all parties, including any new parties to the action. If this case came to the Court by noticed removal, Defendant shall serve this Order on all other parties.

DATED: ________________

____
VICTOR B. KENTON
United States Magistrate Judge

Hon. John E. McDermott
Magistrate Judge

Chambers Information
U.S. District Court, Central District of California
Courtroom C, 8th Floor
312 N. Spring Street
Los Angeles, CA 90012

Scheduling Information
Courtroom Deputy: (213) 894-0216

Civil Law and Motion	Tuesdays at 10:00 a.m.
Criminal Law and Motion	Heard on Criminal Duty Days or as set by the Court.

Biographical Information
[Not available]

I. Judge McDermott's Procedures and Practices

A. *Procedures and Schedules*

1. Civil motions are heard on **Tuesdays** at **10:00 a.m.** or such other time as set by the court after consultation with counsel. You do not need to contact the clerk for a date. Counsel should make sure that all motions comply with the Local Rules. Counsel should anticipate the possibility that a motion will be submitted on the papers. Please check the motion calendar to make certain that the date chosen is a date available on the Judge's calendar.

   Criminal motions are heard on Criminal Duty Days or as set by the Court.

2. Discovery motions are to be scheduled before the magistrate judge, if referred by the district judge. Strict compliance with Local Rule 37, et seq. is required. Counsel should pay particular attention to Local Rules 7-3, 37-1 and 37-2.4. Motions not in complete compliance with the Local Rules are subject to being rejected.

3. Mandatory chambers copies of e-filed documents are to be delivered to chambers, 8th Floor, Spring Street. Counsel must comply with General Order 10-07.

4. Procedures for filing and *Ex Parte* Application: Follow Local Rule 7-19.

5. To request a continuance of any scheduled court proceeding, counsel should first attempt to file a stipulation and proposed order.

6. Counsel should only contact the court clerk and never chambers unless directed to do so by the Court.

7. Inquiries regarding the status of a motion, stipulation or proposed order: Counsel should check the Central District's Pacer site. Alternatively, if necessary, counsel should contact the court clerk.

8. Other than Confidential Settlement Statements in letter form, all other letters are an unacceptable method of contact with the Court. All matter to be brought to the Court's attention must comply with Local Rule 83-2.11. All letters will be rejected.

9. Please advise the court's deputy clerk in advance about a calendar conflict and attempt to stipulate to an alternative date and time with opposing counsel after clearing the alternative date and time with the court's deputy clerk.

10. Counsel should contact the court's deputy clerk, regarding procedures for bringing electronic equipment into the courtroom. As a general rule, electronic equipment will not be allowed in the courtroom.

11. For general information on how to order a transcript of any reported or digitally recorded proceeding, please contact 213 894 3015 or visit www.cacd.uscourts.gov > General Information > Court Reporter/Recorder Transcripts. If you require an estimate of cost for the preparation of a transcript, contact the court reporter/recorder for the desired proceeding.

    To determine the court reporter/recorder for a particular proceeding, go to the Court Reporter Schedule web page and click on View by Date. Once you've determined the correct court reporter/recorder for the desired session, click on Court Reporter Phone and Email List for contact information.

12. Trial preparation: Counsel should comply with the local rules.

13. Procedures for obtaining the services of an interpreter in a civil case: Counsel are responsible for obtaining the services of an interpreter if one is needed.

14. Counsel must **promptly** schedule a settlement conference after referral to the Magistrate Judge pursuant to Local Rules 16-14 and 16-5.5.

The Court appreciates compliance by counsel with these procedures.

Hon. Frederick F. Mumm

Magistrate Judge

Chambers Information

U.S. District Court, Central District of California
Courtroom E, 9th Floor
312 N. Spring Street
Los Angeles, CA 90012

Scheduling Information

Courtroom Deputy: (213) 894-3046

Civil Law and Motion	Tuesdays at 10:00 a.m.

Biographical Information

[Not available]

I. Judge Mumm's Procedures and Practices

A. *Procedures and Schedules*

The best way to contact the judge's courtroom deputy clerk is by calling (213) 894-3046; if the clerk does not answer the phone, be sure to leave a voice-mail message.

- Civil motions are heard on **Tuesdays** at **10:00 a.m.**
    - It is not necessary to clear a motion date with the court clerk prior to filing the motion, although the Judge reserves the right to continue motions sua sponte.
- Discovery motions are to be set before the district judge unless the district judge to whom the case is assigned has a blanket referral of all discovery matters to the magistrate judge or already has issued a case specific order referring all discovery matters to the magistrate judge, in which case discovery motions are set before the magistrate judge. (See Discovery Referral Sheet.) Strict compliance with Local Rules 37-1 and 37-2 is required. It is the Court's policy to decline requests by counsel for telephonic conferences to resolve discovery disputes which arise during pending depositions.
- Mandatory chambers copies of filings are requested by the Court. **Pursuant to General Order 10-07, mandatory chambers copies are required for documents filed electronically and shall be delivered to the courtesy copy box outside chambers, 9th Floor, Spring Street not later than noon on the day following the electronic filing of the document. Mandatory chambers copies must comply with Local Rule 11-3.**
- Procedures for filing an ex parte application: Strict compliance with Local Rule 7-19 is required. A FILED stamped mandatory chambers copy should be delivered directly to the Judge's chambers. Any opposition should be served and filed within 24 hours of applicant's oral notice. Court will notify parties if a telephonic hearing is desired.
- To request a continuance of any scheduled court proceeding, parties should submit a signed stipulation and proposed order.
- Counsel are not allowed to contact the judge's secretary or law clerk.
- Inquiries regarding the status of a motion, stipulation or proposed order: Counsel should check the docket sheet before inquiring of the court clerk. The Court discourages the practice of calling the court clerk.
- Calendar conflicts: (Procedures for attorneys to follow if they have a calendar conflict). Immediately advise the court clerk telephonically; attempt to secure other counsel's agreement to stipulate to a new date.
- For general information on how to order a transcript of any reported or digitally recorded proceeding, please contact 213-894-3015 or visit www.cacd.uscourts.gov > General Information > Court Reporter/Recorder Transcripts. If you require an estimate of cost for the preparation of a transcript, contact the court reporter/recorder for the desired proceeding.

  To determine the court reporter/recorder for a particular proceeding, go to the Court Reporter Schedule web page and click on View by Date. Once you've determined the correct court reporter/recorder for the desired session, click on Court Reporter Phone and Email List for contact information.
- Other information: Parties should contact court clerk about dates available for settlement conferences. The parties should comply with Local Rule 16-14.5. All settlement conference papers should be delivered directly to the Judge's chambers, Room 931, 9th floor.

Hon. Margaret A. Nagle
Magistrate Judge

Chambers Information
U.S. District Court, Central District of California
Courtroom 580
255 East Temple Street
Los Angeles, CA 90012

Scheduling Information
Courtroom Deputy: (213) 894-8285

Civil Law and Motion	Tuesdays at 10:00 a.m. or as set by the court.
Criminal Law and Motion	Heard on Criminal Duty Days or as set by the Court.

Biographical Information
[Not available]

I. Judge Nagle's Procedures and Practices

A. *Procedures and Schedules*

1. All Civil Motions are heard on TUESDAY at **10:00 A.M.** or such other time as set by the court. Counsel should anticipate the possibility that a motion will be submitted on the papers.

   Criminal motions are heard on: **CRIMINAL DUTY DAYS** or as set by the court.

   It **is not** necessary to clear a motion date with the court clerk prior to filing the motion.

2. Discovery motions are to be scheduled before the magistrate judge, if referred by the district court judge. Strict compliance with Local Rule 37-1 and 37-2 is required.

3. Mandatory chambers copies should be delivered to chambers. **Mandatory chambers copies of e-filed documents are to be delivered to courtesy copy box outside of chambers, 5th floor, Roybal.**

4. Ex Parte applications are an unacceptable method of bringing a discovery dispute to the attention of the court, absent an extreme emergency. If an ex parte application is filed, the application shall be personally served on opposing counsel, and the opposition shall be due within 24 hours of the service of the application. If an extension of the filing of the opposition is necessary, please contact the court clerk. If an ex parte request seeking a continuance is filed, opposing counsel's position should be set forth. Refer to Local Rule 7.19.

5. To request a continuance of a scheduled proceeding before this court, counsel should file a joint stipulation and proposed order.

6. Unless otherwise directed to do so, counsel should not contact the judge's law clerk or judicial assistant, except when a conference call has been set on calendar. In that event, the judicial assistant should be contacted.

7. Inquiries regarding the status of a motion, stipulation or proposed order should be made to the court clerk.

8. Calendar conflicts: Advise the court clerk in advance about a calendar conflict and attempt to stipulate to an alternative date and time with opposing counsel after clearing the alternative date and time with the court clerk.

9. Counsel should contact the court clerk regarding procedures for bringing electronic equipment into the courtroom.

10. Counsel should contact the court clerk to order an audio tape or transcript of any proceeding.

11. Questions regarding law clerk/extern positions should be directed to the judge's judicial assistant.

12. Trial preparation: Counsel should comply with F.R. Civ. P. 16 et seq.

13. Counsel should contact the court clerk regarding procedures for obtaining services of an interpreter on a civil case.

14. Settlement conferences will be scheduled by the court clerk after a conference has been referred to the magistrate judge pursuant to Local Rule 16-14. If counsel have an

agreeable date, that date must be cleared with the court clerk.

15. The court appreciates the compliance of counsel with these procedures.

16. For general information on how to order a transcript of any reported or digitally recorded proceeding, please contact 213-894-3015 or visit www.cacd.uscourts.gov > General Information > Court Reporter/Recorder Transcripts. If you require an estimate of cost for the preparation of a transcript, contact the court reporter/recorder for the desired proceeding.

To determine the court reporter/recorder for a particular proceeding, go to the Court Reporter Schedule web page and click on View by Date. Once you've determined the correct court reporter/recorder for the desired session, click on Court Reporter Phone and Email List for contact information.

Hon. Arthur Nakazato

Magistrate Judge

Chambers Information
U.S. District Court, Central District of California
Courtroom 6B
411 West Fourth Street
Santa Ana, CA 92701

Scheduling Information
Courtroom Deputy: (714) 338-4756

Civil Law and Motion	Thursdays at 10:00 a.m.

Biographical Information
[Not available]

I. Judge Nakazato's Procedures and Practices

A. *Procedures and Schedules*

1. Unless otherwise directed by the Court, Civil motions are normally heard on **Thursdays** at **10:00 a.m.** in Santa Ana.

   Unless otherwise directed by the Court, Settlement Conferences are held on **Thursdays** at **1:30 p.m.** or Fridays at **10:00 a.m.** and **1:30 p.m.** in Santa Ana. Counsel must contact Stephen Ybarra in order to secure an available date.

2. Discovery motions are to be scheduled directly before the Magistrate Judge on cases where the District Judge has a blanket referral policy or unless the District Judge's clerk has directed counsel to do so. Parties are directed to review and follow the form and substance of the sample Local Rule 37-1. Letter, Joint Stipulation, and Notice of Motion are available for download below.

3. Mandatory Chambers Copies of all e-filed documents shall be delivered to the mandatory chambers copy box on the 6th Floor. It is imperative that the mandatory chambers copies be delivered by noon following the date of filing as required by General Order 10-07.IV.D. Failure to deliver timely mandatory chambers copies may result in a delay in hearing a motion or ordering the matter off calendar.

4. Ex Parte Procedure - See L.R. 7-19 - The Ex Parte Application must be for a **true** emergency. The papers should be filed without a hearing date but **must** comply with the notice requirements set forth in L.R. 7-19.1. After a review of the papers, the court clerk will contact the moving counsel to give appropriate notice to all parties and a briefing schedule if the Magistrate Judge determines that a hearing should be held.

5. Counsel may NOT contact the judge's law clerk or secretary.

6. Counsel may contact the court clerk if the status of a motion, stipulation or proposed order is not yet docketed.

7. Calendar conflicts: Counsel should file a stipulation to reschedule.

8. Procedures for bringing electronic equipment into the courtroom: Parties should comply with the Local Rules and follow the courthouse rules.

9. For general information on how to order a transcript of any reported or digitally recorded proceeding, please contact 213-894-3015 or visit www.cacd.uscourts.gov > General Information > Court Reporter/Recorder Transcripts. If you require an estimate of cost for the preparation of a transcript, contact the court reporter/recorder for the desired proceeding.

   To determine the court reporter/recorder for a particular proceeding, go to the Court Reporter Schedule web page and click on View by Date. Once you've determined the correct court reporter/recorder for the desired session, click on Court Reporter Phone and Email List for contact information.

10. Trial preparation: See Local Rules.
    - **a.** Court hours - currently 9:00 a.m. to 5:00 a.m. or 8:00 a.m. to 1:00 p.m. if the jury is amenable, or if counsel are amenable in a bench trial.
    - **b.** Exhibit preparation - See Local Rules/contact court clerk – counsel should

prepare 3 sets/binders:

1. one which contains the original tagged exhibits for the clerk,
2. one with copies for the Magistrate Judge,
3. one with copies for the witness stand.

11. It is the responsibility of the requesting party to secure its own interpreter for a particular matter on a civil case. The requesting party may arrange for an outside interpreter or may make an arrangement with Lenne Rosen-Kabe, Court Interpreter Services Manager at 213-894-4559 to secure an interpreter. The requesting party will bear the cost.

II. Judge Nakazato's Forms

A. *Joint Stipulation on Motion to Compel Discovery*

[Firm Name and address]
[Telephone]
[Fax]

Attorneys for defendants B and C

IN THE UNITED STATES DISTICT COURT
FOR THE CENTRAL DISTRICT OF CALIFORNIA

Plaintiff(s), v. Defendant(s).	Case No. ________________ **JOINT STIPULATION ON MOTION OF DEFENDANT C TO COMPEL PLAINTIFF 2 TO ANSWER INTERROGATORIES 9, 17, AND 21-23** Hearing Date: ______________ Time: ______________ Place: Courtroom 6B Before Magistrate Judge Nakazato

Defendant C's Introduction:

[State only enough about the case so that it will be reasonably apparent why the particular discovery sought in the interrogatories is needed to litigate the case.]

[Avoid argument, hyperbole, and attempts to evoke sympathy.]

[Leave out statements about meeting and conferring unless opposing party refused to meet. It is assumed that counsel did meet and confer.]

Plaintiff 2's Introduction:

[If you agree with above, simply say so. Otherwise, correct any erroneous statements and add any additional information that is needed to understand what the case is about that is not clear from

the above and is needed to understand the general context of your resistance to the discovery.]

[If there are inconsistent statements between defendant's introduction and plaintiff's introduction, a declaration is necessary to prove the point. The Court will not assume one attorney is correct and the other is not.]

The Interrogatories in Issue:

Interrogatory 9 from defendant C to plaintiff 2:

[Quote interrogatory as served. If parties agreed at the meet-and-confer to construe certain language in the interrogatory, the agreed-upon construction should follow the interrogatory.]

Plaintiff 2's response to Interrogatory 9:

[Quote response as served.]

Defendant C's contentions:

"Defendant C offered at the meet-and-confer to resolve the dispute over the interrogatory by ________________________."

[State contentions and legal authorities why the information sought is discoverable.]

Plaintiff 2's contentions:

"Plaintiff 2 offered at the meet-and-confer to resolve the dispute over this interrogatory by ________________________."

The interrogatory is objectionable because: [contentions]

[If undue burden or the like is contended, a declaration must be attached quantifying the expected burden.]

Interrogatory 17 from defendant C to plaintiff 2:

[Same format as above.]

Interrogatory 21 from defendant C to plaintiff 2:

[Same format as above.]

Interrogatory 22 from defendant C to plaintiff 2:

[Same format as above.]

Interrogatory 23 from defendant C to plaintiff 2:

[Same format as above.]

Defendant C's conclusion:

Plaintiff 2 should be ordered to respond forthwith, without objections, to interrogatories 9, 17, and 21-23.

Plaintiff 2's conclusion:

Defendant C's motion should be denied.

Alternatively, plaintiff 2 should not be compelled to respond beyond what it offered at the meet-and-confer and it should be permitted at least 10 days to gather the information.

Respectfully submitted,

[Dated:] [FIRM NAME]

By:

____

Attorney
Attorneys for defendants B and C

[Dated:] [FIRM NAME]

By:

____

Attorney
Attorneys plaintiff 2

B. *Local Rule 37-1 Letter*

Local Rule 37-1 Letter

[DATE]

BY FAX

[TIP: Fax the L.R. 37-1 Letter as early in the day as possible so as to give the opposing party the maximum amount of notice; keep a transmission record and attach it along with a copy of your letter to your declaration of non-cooperation.]

Name of Each Opposing Party or Counsel
Address of Each Opposing Party or Counsel
Re: Case Name, correct case number

Dear [Opposing Party/Counsel]:

Pursuant to Local Rule 37-1, please be advised that I am requesting a conference in order to eliminate the need for a hearing, or to eliminate as many of our disputes, regarding the following discovery matters.

Request For Production Of Documents

Response To Request No. 1

In your client's written responses, [s/he][it] objects to this particular request on the ground(s) that [identify specific ground(s)]. Please be advised your client's objection(s) is[are] without merit because [discuss specific points and authorities supporting your client's position; be objective and avoid any unnecessary characterizations or accusations that would be counter-productive to achieving an informal resolution.]

[TIP: If done correctly, your discussion of the specific points and authorities supporting your client's position can be copied with little, if any, revision into the joint stipulation or motion itself if the opposing party fails to cooperate in the preparation of the joint stipulation. The time spent in researching and explaining your position will be worthwhile since it will help in evaluating your position, and will either result in an informal resolution of the dispute or substantially reduce the time needed to prepare and finalize the joint stipulation and/or motion.]

[TIP: If a legitimate dispute exists and your own research discloses the chance of prevailing is questionable or remote, give serious thought about whether the time and expense is worth the battle, particularly if the items being sought are of questionable evidentiary value. A good idea is to suggest a compromise position.]

Pursuant to Local Rule 37-1, please be advised that we are required to conduct our conference [in my office][telephonically] no later than ten days from today's date. I am available to meet on the following three dates at the times indicated:

1. Date & Time
2. Date & Time
3. Date & Time

[TIP: Give opposing party at least three dates and times, the third date being set on the tenth or last date, preferably at a time one would reasonably be expected to be available. For example, setting dates on the third, fifth, and tenth day, either in the early morning, noontime, or late afternoon, would make it difficult for opposing counsel to argue that you did not provide reasonable notice or times to meet.]

[TIP: If the opposing counsel is being represented by a law firm that is staffing the case with several lawyers in the law firm, request that at least one of the opposing counsel be available and demand an explanation if none of them are ostensibly available to meet with you.]

Since your client's foregoing objections are set forth in written responses, which you signed in accordance with Rule 11(a) of the Federal Rules of Civil Procedure, I will presume they "are warranted by existing law" or constitute "nonfrivolous arguments" and you are already, or will be, fully prepared to engage in a meaningful discussion of the legal points and authorities for your client's objections and our aforementioned contentions at our conference.

Consequently, and in a further effort to expedite matters, enclosed please find a draft of the joint stipulation with our portion of the stipulation that includes, in the form required by Local Rule 37-2.1: (1) the disputed discovery requests, (2) your client's objections, (3) my client's contentions for each disputed request, and (4) a space to insert your client's contentions for each disputed request. If possible, please [bring a 3 1/2" standard sized floppy diskette to our conference with][e-mail] your client's contentions for each disputed request so we can finalize and sign the joint stipulation if we are unable to resolve all of our disputes. Please have the computer file formatted in [identify your firm's word processing program] or ASCII.

[TIP: Your opposing party or counsel, at least in theory, should already know the legal basis for the written objections to your discovery requests. Accordingly, requesting the party to prepare and bring its contentions to the conference is not unreasonable. Further, by including a draft of the joint stipulation with your client's contentions with your letter, the opposing party will know you are serious and may back down from some or all of its objections.]

Where we agree with your contentions or you agree with ours, we will simply delete the corresponding issues from the motion. At the least, by having each other's detailed contentions at the meeting, we should be able to greatly narrow the issues. I will call you within the next two hours to confirm your receipt of this fax letter and set a date and time for our discovery conference. If none of the foregoing dates and times are convenient, please be prepared to give me at least three alternative dates and times that are convenient to you.

If you are not in or available to speak when I call, and I do not hear from you [or your colleague/co-counsel] **by 5:OO p.m. tomorrow** with alternative dates, I will assume you will be available to meet on the third proposed date and time set forth above; the last available meeting date. Accordingly, a [nonappearance][failure to participate in a telephone conference] on the last proposed date will be construed as a refusal to comply with Local Rule 37-1, after which my client will bring the motion to compel without the benefit of a joint stipulation. Copies of this letter and the enclosed draft of the joint stipulation will be attached as Exhibits A, and B, respectively, to my declaration of non-cooperation accompanying the motion. A request for other forms of appropriate relief under Local Rules 37-4, 27, F.R.Civ.P. 37, and 28 U.S.C. §1927 will also be made.

[TIP: BE REASONABLE AND OVERLY ACCOMMODATING IF NECESSARY!!! If, for example, the opposing party fails to call until the sixth day and then asks to meet within a reasonable time after the tenth day deadline, the moving party should make every effort to accommodate this request, especially if the opposing counsel has a reasonable, good-faith excuse for failing to respond by the time requested. Remember, the goal is to avoid the need for a hearing at all and, if all of the disputed issues cannot be resolved, obtain a joint stipulation so its easier for the Court to understand the contentions and issue a correct ruling. The more courteous, flexible, and accommodating the moving party appears to have been, the more credibility that party will have with the Court; conversely, the Court is more likely to take the appropriate measures against an opposing party whose unreasonable lack of cooperation is perceived to be the cause for the discovery dispute and lack of a joint stipulation.]

Please do not hesitate to call if you have any questions or comments. Meanwhile, I hope to hear from you before 5:00 p.m. tomorrow.

Sincerely,

Moving Party

cc: [Opposing co-counsel]

C. *Notice of Motion and Motion to Compel Discovery*

[Firm Name and address]
[Telephone]
[Fax]

Attorneys for defendants B and C

IN THE UNITED STATES DISTICT COURT
FOR THE CENTRAL DISTRICT OF CALIFORNIA

Plaintiff(s),	Case No. __________
v.	**NOTICE OF MOTION AND MOTION BY DEFENDANT C TO COMPEL PLAINTIFF 2 TO ANSWER INTERROGATORIES 9, 17 AND 21-23; JOINT STIPULATION; DECLARATION OF JOHN DOE; DECLARATION OF JANE ROE**
Defendant(s).	Hearing Date: __________ Time: __________ Place: Courtroom 6B Before Magistrate Judge Nakazato

TO ALL PARTIES AND THEIR ATTORNEYS OF RECORD:

PLEASE TAKE NOTICE that at the above time and place defendant C will move to compel plaintiff 2 to answer interrogatories 9, 17, and 21-23.

This motion is made pursuant to Local Rule 37-1 and is based on the attached joint stipulation, the declarations of John Doe and Jane Roe, any supplemental memoranda filed under Local Rule 37-2.3, and such arguments as may be presented at the hearing.

[Dated:] [FIRM NAME]

By:

____

Attorney
Attorneys for defendants B and C

Hon. Fernando M. Olguin
Magistrate Judge

Chambers Information
U.S. District Court, Central District of California
Courtroom F, 9th Floor
312 N. Spring Street
Los Angeles, CA 90012

Scheduling Information
Courtroom Deputy: (213) 894-0215

Civil Law and Motion	Wednesdays at 10:00 a.m.
Criminal Law and Motion	Scheduled as required.

Biographical Information
[Not available]

I. Judge Olguin's Procedures and Practices

A. *Procedures and Schedules*

1. Civil motions are heard on **Wednesdays** at **10:00 a.m.** It is not necessary to clear a civil motion date with the court clerk prior to filing the motion. Criminal motions are scheduled as required.
2. Discovery motions are to be scheduled before the magistrate judge, if referred by the district court judge. Strict compliance with Local Rule 37-1 et seq is required. Discovery motions are heard on **Wednesdays** at **10:00 a.m.** It is not necessary to clear a discovery motion date with the court's clerk prior to filing the motion.
3. Tentative rulings may be issued.
4. A mandatory chambers copy of all e-filed documents shall be delivered to the courtesy copy box outside chambers (9th Floor of Spring Street Courthouse) **no later than noon the day following the electronic filing of the document**.

   All proposed signature items shall be e-mailed to the chambers email address at fmo_chambers@cacd.uscourts.gov [fmo(underscore)chambers@cacd.uscourts.gov] in Word or Word Perfect format.

   The mandatory chambers copy must be clearly marked MANDATORY CHAMBERS COPY.
5. Ex parte applications are not heard unless ordered by the court. Counsel should refer to Local Rules 7-19 and 7-20. Oppositions (with a mandatory chambers copy delivered to chambers), if any, are due no later than 5:00 p.m. on the first business day following the service of the ex parte application. For example, if an ex parte application is served on a Wednesday at 2:00 p.m., the opposition must be filed and served (with a mandatory chambers copy delivered to chambers) no later than Thursday at 5:00 p.m.
6. **Ex parte applications are an unacceptable method of bringing a discovery dispute to the attention of the court absent an extreme emergency.**
7. To request a continuance of any scheduled court proceeding, parties should submit a signed stipulation and proposed order. If it is necessary to file an ex parte application to request a continuance, the application should, in addition to complying with Local Rule 7-11 and number 5 above, set forth the opposing counsel's position.
8. Counsel are not allowed to contact the judge's law clerks.
9. Information regarding the status of civil motions, civil stipulations or civil proposed orders are not available by telephone. Counsel shall follow the Local Rules and Federal Rules of Civil Procedure. (Local Rule 11-4.5).
10. Calendar conflicts: Advise the court clerk in advance about a calendar conflict and attempt to stipulate to an alternative date and time with opposing counsel after clearing the alternative date and time with the court's clerk.
11. Counsel should contact the court's clerk regarding procedures for bringing electronic equipment into the courtroom.
12. For general information on how to order a transcript of any reported or digitally recorded proceeding, please contact 213-894-3015 or visit www.cacd.uscourts.gov >

General Information > Court Reporter/Recorder Transcripts. If you require an estimate of cost for the preparation of a transcript, contact the court reporter/recorder for the desired proceeding.

To determine the court reporter/recorder for a particular proceeding, go to the Court Reporter Schedule web page and click on View by Date. Once you've determined the correct court reporter/recorder for the desired session, click on Court Reporter Phone and Email List for contact information.

13. Questions regarding law clerk/extern positions: Communicate via letter to the judge.

14. Trial preparation: Counsel should comply with Local Rule 16 et seq.

15. Procedures for obtaining the services of an interpreter on a civil case: If the government is the moving party, contact the court's clerk. All others may contact the Interpreter's Section at (213) 894-4599.

16. Other Information: All Settlement conference papers should be delivered directly to the judge's chambers (drop box provided outside chambers) in the Spring Street Courthouse, 312 N. Spring St., Suite 901.

Hon. Oswald Parada

Magistrate Judge

Chambers Information

U.S. District Court, Central District of California
Courtroom 3
3470 Twelfth Street
Riverside, CA 92501

Scheduling Information

Courtroom Deputy: (951) 328-4463

Civil Law and Motion	Wednesdays at 9:30 a.m.
Criminal Law and Motion	Scheduled as required.

Biographical Information

[Not available]

I. Judge Parada's Procedures and Practices

A. *Procedures and Schedules*

1. Civil motions are heard on **Wednesdays** at **9:30 a.m.** It is not necessary to clear a civil motion date with the Court Room Deputy Clerk (CRD) prior to filing the motion. The Court may take any motion under submission without oral argument. See Local Rule 7-15. Criminal motions are scheduled as required.

2. Discovery motions are to be scheduled before the magistrate judge, if referred by the district judge. Strict compliance with Local Rule 37 is required. The Court may take any motion under submission without oral argument. See Local Rule 7-15.

3. Tentative rulings are usually but not always issued at the time counsel checks in with the CRD.

4. Mandatory chambers copies may be delivered to the CRD. Mandatory chambers copies of e-filed documents are to be delivered to chambers.

5. Procedures for filing an ex parte application: Strict compliance with Local Rule 7-19 is required. A file-stamped mandatory chambers copy should be delivered to chambers. Any opposition should be served and filed within 24 hours of applicant's oral notice. Ex parte applications ordinarily will be decided without a hearing. The Court will notify parties if a hearing is desired. Please note that, absent an emergency, ex parte applications are an unacceptable method of bringing a discovery dispute to the attention of the Court.

6. To request a continuance of any scheduled court proceeding, the parties should submit a signed stipulation and proposed order at least three business days prior to the scheduled hearing date. If it is necessary to file an ex parte application to request a continuance, the application must, in addition to complying with Local Rule 7-11 and paragraph 5 above, set forth the opposing counsel's position.

7. Counsel are not allowed to contact the Judge's assistant or law clerk(s).

8. Inquiries regarding the status of a motion, stipulation, or proposed order should be made by checking the docket sheet. If the information is unavailable, counsel may contact the CRD. Also, please refer to Local Rule 11-4.5.

9. Calendar conflicts: The parties are to advise the CRD in advance about a calendar conflict and attempt to stipulate to an alternative date and time with opposing counsel. The alternative date and time should be cleared in advance with the CRD.

10. Counsel should contact the CRD regarding procedures for bringing electronic equipment into the courtroom.

11. For general information on how to order a transcript of any reported or digitally recorded proceeding, please contact 213-894-3015 or visit www.cacd.uscourts.gov > General Information > Court Reporter/Recorder Transcripts. If you require an estimate of cost for the preparation of a transcript, contact the court reporter/recorder for the desired proceeding.

    To determine the court reporter/recorder for a particular proceeding, go to the Court Reporter Schedule web page and click on View by Date. Once you've determined the correct court reporter/recorder for the desired session, click on Court Reporter Phone and Email List for contact information.

12. For questions regarding law clerk/extern positions, please communicate via letter to the Judge.

13. Trial preparation. Counsel should comply with Local Rule 16 et seq.

14. Procedures for obtaining the services of an interpreter on a civil case: If the government is the moving party, contact the CRD. All other parties may contact the Interpreter's Section at (213) 894-4599.

15. Other Information: Parties should contact the CRD about available dates for settlement conferences. All settlement conference papers should be delivered directly to the Judge's chambers located at 3470 Twelfth Street, 3rd Floor, Riverside, California.

II. Judge Parada's Case Management Orders

A. *Order Regarding Settlement Conference*

**IN THE UNITED STATES DISTICT COURT
FOR THE CENTRAL DISTRICT OF CALIFORNIA**

Plaintiff(s), v. Defendant(s).	Case No. _______________ **ORDER RE: SETTLEMENT CONFERENCE** Location: Courtroom Number 3 3470 Twelfth Street, Riverside, California

This case has been referred to the Honorable Oswald Parada, United States Magistrate Judge, for settlement proceedings. A Settlement Conference will be held on _________, **at 9:30 a.m.**

The Magistrate Judge will not be involved in the actual trial of the case and will assist the parties in an objective appraisal and evaluation of the case. The following are guidelines for the parties in preparing for the Settlement Conference:

1. The purpose of the Settlement Conference is to permit an informal discussion between the attorneys, parties, non-party indemnitors or insurers, and the settlement judge, of every aspect of the case bearing on its settlement value.

2. Pursuant to Local Rule 16-14.8, all settlement proceedings shall be confidential and no statement made therein shall be admissible in any proceeding in the case, unless the parties otherwise agree. No part of a settlement proceeding shall be reported or otherwise recorded, without the consent of the parties, except for any memorialization of a settlement.

3. In addition to counsel who will try the case being present, a person with full settlement authority must likewise be present for the conference. This requirement contemplates the physical presence of your client or, if a corporate or governmental entity, of an authorized and knowledgeable representative of your client.[1] This requirement applies even if the representative resides outside of the Central District. The plaintiff's representative must have full and final authority, in the representative's sole discretion, to authorize dismissal of the case with prejudice, or to accept a settlement amount recommended by the settlement judge down to the defendant's last offer made prior to the settlement conference. The defendant's representative must have final settlement authority to commit the defendant to pay, in the representative's sole discretion, a settlement amount recommended by the settlement judge up to the plaintiff's prayer (excluding punitive damage prayers), or up to the plaintiff's last demand made prior to the settlement conference, whichever is lower. The purpose of this requirement is to have representatives present who can settle the case during the course of the conference without consulting a superior.

4. If Board approval is required to authorize settlement, the attendance of at least one sitting and knowledgeable member of the Board (preferably the Chairman) is required.

5. Counsel appearing without their clients (whether or not counsel purportedly

---

1 However, if this matter is a lawsuit in which the United States or any of its agencies is a party, the Assistant United States Attorney who will try the case may appear without a representative, provided that he or she comes armed with the full measure of authority conveyed by his or her superiors within the United States Attorney's Office after appropriate consultation.

have been given settlement authority) may cause the settlement conference to be canceled and rescheduled. The noncomplying party, attorney, or both, may be assessed the costs and expenses incurred by other parties as a result of such cancellation and rescheduling.

6. Any insurance company that is a party to the case or is contractually required to defend or to pay damages assessed within policy limits, shall have a settlement representative present at the conference. Such representative must have final settlement authority to commit the company to pay, in the representative's sole discretion, an amount recommended by the settlement judge within the policy limits. The purpose of this requirement is to have an insurance representative present who can settle the outstanding claim or claims during the course of the conference without consulting a superior. An insurance representative authorized to pay, in his or her sole discretion, up to the plaintiff's last demand made prior to the settlement conference will also satisfy this requirement. Counsel of record will be responsible for timely advising any involved non-party insurance company of the requirements of this Order.

7. The settlement judge may, in his discretion, converse with the lawyers, the parties, the insurance representatives, or any one of them outside of the hearing of the others. The comments of the judge during such separate sessions are not to be used by counsel in settlement negotiations with opposing counsel. This is a necessary requirement in order to avoid intentional or unintentional misquotation of the judge's comments. If all counsel and parties are not present to hear the Court's opinions, it is all too easy for counsel to misrepresent the Court's comments in an effort to obtain a tactical advantage with opposing counsel. Violation of this policy may be a hindrance to settlement.

8. Unless otherwise excused by the Court, no later than fifteen (15) days before the date of the settlement conference, counsel for plaintiffs shall fax or hand-deliver a written settlement demand to counsel for defendants. Counsel for defendants shall fax or hand-deliver a response to counsel for plaintiffs no later than twelve (12) days before the date of the settlement conference; if plaintiffs' demand is not accepted, defendants' written response must include a counter-settlement offer. Plaintiffs must then fax or hand-deliver a reply to defendants' counter-offer no later than nine (9) calendar days before the date of the settlement conference; if defendants' counter-offer is rejected, plaintiffs' reply must contain a counter-settlement demand. All demands and counter-offers must be accompanied by a brief explanation of the party's settlement proposal. At the Settlement Conference, each party shall be fully prepared to discuss all economic and non-economic factors relevant to a full and final settlement of the case.[2]

9. No later than seven (7) days prior to hearing, each party shall submit a Confidential Settlement Conference Statement directly to the chambers of Magistrate Judge Parada or fax to (951) 328-4438. The statement shall be submitted in a sealed envelope clearly marked confidential, and shall not be filed with the Clerk of the Court or given to opposing counsel; it will not be made part of the case file. The Statement shall be in the form of a letter, and shall not exceed five (5) pages in length. The Statement shall include the following:

A. A brief statement of the facts of the case, and of the claims and

---

[2] The Court expects the parties to exchange good faith settlement offers. For the plaintiff, this means offering to settle on terms less favorable than those which the plaintiff reasonably could expect to achieve if plaintiff prevailed at trial, taking into account plaintiff's non-recoupable costs of litigation. For each defendant, this means offering to settle on terms less favorable to such defendant than those such defendant reasonably could expect to achieve if such defendant prevailed at trial, taking into account such defendant's non-recoupable costs of litigation. The Court also expects that counsel for each party has discussed with his or her client the estimated attorneys' fees, time and costs to be expended if a settlement is not reached.

defenses remaining to be tried, including the statutory or other grounds upon which the claims are founded. This statement should identify the major factual and legal issues in dispute, and cite any controlling authorities.

B. An itemized statement of the damages claimed, and of any other relief sought.

C. A history of past settlement discussions, offers and demands.

D. A forthright evaluation of the party's likelihood of prevailing on each of its claims and/or defenses.

E. The approximate amount of attorney's fees, time and costs expended to date, and an estimate of the fees, time and costs to be expended for (I) further discovery, (ii) pretrial and (iii) trial.

F. The party's evaluation of the terms on which the case could be settled fairly, taking into account the litigation position and settlement position of the other side.

10. If it does not appear to the Court from its review of the parties' Statements that a Settlement Conference at this juncture in the proceedings is likely to result in a settlement of the matter, the Court may order the Settlement Conference off calendar or defer it to a later juncture in the proceedings (e.g., after a pending or anticipated dispositive summary judgment motion is decided). In the event any party believes, in good faith, after the above described steps have been completed, that a settlement conference at this point in the litigation would not be meaningful, the party may contact Magistrate Judge Parada's courtroom deputy clerk at (951) 328-4463 and provide him with this information. The Court will then contact the parties to discuss with them how to proceed.

11. Any failure of the trial attorneys, parties or persons with authority to attend the conference may result in sanctions to include the fees and costs expended by the other parties in preparing for and attending the conference. The failure of any party to timely submit a Confidential Settlement Conference Statement in compliance with this Order, or otherwise comply strictly with this Order, may result in the Settlement Conference being ordered off calendar and sanctions being imposed.

12. Counsel for each party should be prepared to respond to the Court's questions regarding the relevant facts and law, in the presence of all parties and counsel.

13. If settlement between any or all parties is reached as a result of the Settlement Conference, it is the responsibility of all counsel to immediately report the settlement to the District Judge's courtroom deputy clerk, as well as to timely memorialize the settlement. *See* Local Rule 16-14.7.

14. All papers submitted for the Settlement Conference will either be returned to the parties or destroyed by the Magistrate Judge, after the settlement proceedings are concluded, unless the parties agree otherwise.

DATED. _______________

____
OSWALD PARADA
United States Magistrate Judge

Hon. Sheri Pym

Magistrate Judge

Chambers Information

U.S. District Court, Central District of California
Courtroom 3 or 4, 3rd Floor
3470 Twelfth Street
Riverside, CA 92501

Scheduling Information

Courtroom Deputy: (951) 328-4467

Civil Law and Motion	Tuesdays at 10:00 a.m.
Criminal Law and Motion	Contact the Courtroom Deputy Clerk

Biographical Information

[Not available]

I. Judge Pym's Procedures and Practices

A. *Procedures and Schedules*

1. Civil motions are heard on **Tuesdays at 10:00 a.m.** It is not necessary to clear a civil motion date with the Court Room Deputy Clerk (CRD) prior to filing the motion. The Court may take any motion under submission without oral argument. See Local Rule 7-15. The parties shall contact the CRD to schedule all motions in criminal cases.
2. Discovery motions are to be scheduled before the magistrate judge only if referred by the district judge. Counsel are advised to review the procedures and standing orders of the assigned district judge before filing any discovery motion. Strict compliance with Local Rule 37 is required. The Court may take any motion under submission without oral argument. See Local Rule 7-15.
3. If there is a tentative ruling, it will be provided to counsel at the time counsel checks in with the CRD.
4. Mandatory chambers copies of all e-filed documents must be delivered to the chambers copy box on the 3rd Floor by noon on the court day following the date of filing as required by General Order 10-07.IV.D. Electronic copies of proposed orders shall be emailed to the Court at SP_chambers@cacd.uscourts.gov. Proposed orders shall be in WordPerfect (preferred) or Microsoft Word format.
5. Procedures for filing an ex parte application: Strict compliance with Local Rule 7-19 is required. Any opposition should be served and filed within 24 hours of applicant's oral notice. Conformed paper copies of the filed application and any opposition should be delivered directly to chambers. Ex parte applications will ordinarily be decided on the papers without oral argument. The Court will notify the parties if it desires a hearing. Please note that, absent an emergency, ex parte applications are not an acceptable method of bringing a discovery dispute to the attention of the Court.
6. To request a continuance of any scheduled court hearing, the parties should submit a signed stipulation and proposed order at least three court days prior to the scheduled hearing date. If it is necessary to file an ex parte application to request a continuance, the application must set forth opposing counsel's position. In addition, the parties should notify the CRD as soon as the need to reschedule a hearing is discovered.
7. Any party who wishes to appear at a hearing by telephone shall make such a request at least two court days before the hearing. Telephonic appearances are not allowed absent permission of the Court given on showing of good cause.
8. The parties are to advise the CRD in advance about any calendar conflict and attempt to stipulate to an alternative date and time with opposing counsel. The alternative date and time should be cleared in advance with the CRD.
9. Inquiries regarding the status of a motion, stipulation, or proposed order should be made by checking the docket. If the information is unavailable, counsel may contact the CRD. Also, please refer to Local Rule 11-4.5. Counsel are not allowed to contact the magistrate judge's law clerks, or to communicate with chambers by means of the Court's email address other than to email proposed orders.
10. Counsel should contact the CRD regarding procedures for using or bringing electronic equipment into the courtroom.

11. For general information on how to order a transcript of any reported or digitally recorded proceeding, please contact 213-894-3015 or visit www.cacd.uscourts.gov > General Information > Court Reporter/Recorder Transcripts. If you require an estimate of cost for the preparation of a transcript, contact the court reporter/recorder for the desired proceeding.

To determine the court reporter/recorder for a particular proceeding, go to the Court Reporter Schedule web page and click on View by Date. Once you've determined the correct court reporter/recorder for the desired session, click on Court Reporter Phone and Email List for contact information.

12. It is the responsibility of the parties to obtain the services of an interpreter in a civil case if one is needed. If the government is the moving party, contact the CRD. All other parties may contact the Interpreter's Section at 213-894-4599.

13. Settlement Conferences: Parties should contact the CRD about available dates for settlement conferences. All settlement conference papers should be delivered directly to the magistrate judge's chambers located at 3470 Twelfth Street, 3rd Floor, Riverside, California. In lieu of personal delivery, settlement conference papers may be faxed to chambers at 951-328-2249, provided that the total number of pages being faxed is 15 or less.

14. For inquiries regarding law clerk positions, please visit https://oscar.uscourts.gov . For inquiries regarding extern positions, please communicate via letter to the magistrate judge.

Hon. Alicia G. Rosenberg
Magistrate Judge

Chambers Information

U.S. District Court, Central District of California
Courtroom D, 8th Floor
312 N. Spring Street
Los Angeles, CA 90012

Scheduling Information

Courtroom Deputy: (213) 894-5419

Civil Law and Motion	Tuesdays at 10:00 a.m.
Criminal Law and Motion	Scheduled as required.

Biographical Information

[Not available]

I. Judge Rosenberg's Procedures and Practices

A. Procedures and Schedules

1. Civil motions are heard on Tuesdays at 10:00 a.m. It is not necessary to clear a civil motion date with the court clerk prior to filing the motion. Criminal motions are scheduled as required.
2. Discovery motions are to be scheduled before the magistrate judge, if referred by the district court judge. Strict compliance with Local Rule 37 is required.
3. Tentative rulings usually are not issued.
4. Mandatory chambers copies may be delivered to the court's clerk. Mandatory chambers copies of e-filed documents are to be delivered to chambers no later than noon the following business day. Mandatory chambers copies of e-filed documents need not be blue backed.
5. Procedures for filing an ex parte application: Strict compliance with Local Rule 7-19 is required. A FILED, stamped , mandatory chambers copy must be delivered directly to the judge's chambers. The opposition shall be due within 24 hours after service of the ex parte application. If an extension of time for filing the opposition is necessary, please contact the court clerk. The Court will notify the parties if a telephonic hearing is desired. Please note that, absent an emergency, ex parte applications may not be used to obtain a ruling on a discovery dispute.
6. To request a continuance of any scheduled court proceeding, parties should submit a signed stipulation and proposed order. If it is necessary to file an ex parte application to request a continuance, the application must, in addition to complying with Local Rule 7-11 and paragraph 5 above, set forth the opposing counsel's position.
7. Counsel are not allowed to contact the judge's secretary or law clerk.
8. Inquires regarding the status of a motion, stipulation or proposed order should be made to the court's clerk. Also, please refer to Local Rule 11-4.5.
9. Calendar conflicts: Advise the court clerk in advance about a calendar conflict and attempt to stipulate to an alternative date and time with opposing counsel after clearing the alternative date and time with the court's clerk.
10. Counsel should contact the court's clerk regarding procedures for bringing electronic equipment into the courtroom.
    - Arrangements for bringing voluminous exhibits into the courtroom may be made through the Space and Facilities Help Desk, at (213) 894-1400.
    - ELMO reservations/tutorials may be made by first referring to the court website at www.cacd.uscourts.gov , under "Attorney Information," and then "Attorney Services." Alternatively, you can contact the Courtroom Technology Help Desk at 213-894-3061.
11. For general information on how to order a transcript of any reported or digitally recorded proceeding, please contact 213-894-3015 or visit www.cacd.uscourts.gov > General Information > Court Reporter/Recorder Transcripts. If you require an estimate of cost for the preparation of a transcript, contact the court reporter/recorder for the desired proceeding.

To determine the court reporter/recorder for a particular proceeding, go to the Court Reporter Schedule web page and click on View by Date. Once you've determined the correct court reporter/recorder for the desired session, click on Court Reporter Phone and Email List for contact information.

12. Trial preparation: Counsel should comply with Local Rule 16 et seq.

13. Procedures for obtaining the services of an interpreter on a civil case: If the government is the moving party, contact the court clerk. All others may contact the Interpreter's Section at 213-894-4599.

14. Other Information: All settlement conference papers should be delivered directly to chambers.

Hon. Jean P. Rosenbluth

Magistrate Judge

Chambers Information

U.S. District Court, Central District of California
Courtroom 6A
411 West Fourth Street
Santa Ana, California 92701

Scheduling Information

Courtroom Deputy: (714) 338-4776

Civil Law and Motion	Thursdays at 10:30 a.m.

Biographical Information

[Not available]

I. Judge Rosenbluth's Procedures and Practices

A. Procedures and Schedules

1. Unless otherwise directed by the Court, civil motions are heard on **Thursdays at 10:30 a.m.** It is not necessary to clear a motion date with the Court's clerk prior to filing the motion, although the Court reserves the right to sua sponte continue motions or decide them on the papers without oral argument. The Court does not permit telephonic appearances for hearings absent exceptional circumstances.

2. Unless otherwise directed by the Court, settlement conferences will be held on **Fridays at 10:30 a.m.** in Santa Ana. Counsel must contact the Court's clerk to schedule a settlement conference after the filing of the ADR-01 form: Settlement Procedure Selection - Notice, Request and Order or Order from the District Judge assigned. The Court does not permit telephonic appearances for settlement conferences absent exceptional circumstances.

3. Discovery motions are to be calendared before the magistrate judge unless otherwise ordered by the district judge. Strict compliance with Local Rule 37 is required. Mandatory chambers copies are required by the Court on all e-filed discovery motions. It is not necessary to clear a motion date with the Court's clerk prior to filing the motion. It is the Court's general practice to decline requests by counsel for telephonic conferences to resolve discovery disputes that arise during depositions. Mandatory Chambers Copies of all e-filed documents shall be delivered to the chambers copy box on the 9th floor. It is imperative that mandatory chambers copies be delivered by noon the day following the date of filing as required by General Order 10-07.IV.D. Failure to deliver timely mandatory chambers copies may result in a delay in hearing a motion or ordering the matter off calendar.

4. If there is a tentative ruling, it will be provided to counsel at the time counsel check in with the Court's clerk.

5. Procedures for filing an ex parte application: Strict compliance with Local Rule 7-19 and 7-19.1 are required. An ex parte application is usually considered on the papers only. If the application is opposed, opposition papers should be filed no later than noon on the first court day following service of the application. In most cases, the Court will wait until that time before ruling. If needed, the Court will schedule a hearing. Discovery disputes should generally not be brought to the Court's attention in an ex parte application.

6. Continuances of any scheduled court proceeding will be granted only on a showing of good cause. To request a continuance, the parties should submit a signed stipulation and proposed order. If opposing counsel will not agree to a continuance, the request should be made by ex parte application.

7. Counsel are not allowed to call chambers or the Court's law clerks unless specifically directed to do so by the Court or the Court's clerk.

8. Calls will not be returned regarding the status of a motion, stipulation, or proposed order. Counsel should check the docket sheet to ascertain the status.

9. In the event of calendar conflicts, counsel should immediately advise the Court's clerk telephonically and attempt to secure other counsel's agreement to stipulate to a new date.

10. Counsel should contact the Court's clerk prior to bringing electronic equipment into the courtroom. The clerk will inform counsel of the appropriate procedures. The use of ELMO (Electronic Visual Evidence Presenter) is available to all counsel Please notify the Court's clerk, Joe Roper, at 714-338-4776 at least five (5) working days prior to the hearing if you wish to use this system.

11. To order an audiotape or transcript, click on Ordering tapes/transcripts.

12. It is the responsibility of the parties to obtain the services of an interpreter on a civil case if one is needed.

13. Other information: The Court does not permit special appearances. Counsel of record shall appear at all court proceedings.

Hon. Suzanne H. Segal
Chief Magistrate Judge

Chambers Information
U.S. District Court, Central District of California
Courtroom 23, 3rd Floor
312 N. Spring Street
Los Angeles, CA 90012

Scheduling Information
Courtroom Deputy: (213) 894-0958

Civil Law and Motion	Tuesdays at 10:00 a.m.

Biographical Information
[Not available]

I. Judge Segal's Procedures and Practices

A. *Procedures and Schedules*

1. Civil motions are heard on **Tuesdays** at **10:00 a.m.**

   It is not necessary to clear a motion date with the court clerk prior to filing the motion.

   If Tuesday is a holiday, next motion date is the following Tuesday.

2. Discovery motions are to be calendared before the magistrate judge after checking if the assigned district judge has a blanket referral policy. Strict compliance with Local Rules 37-1 and 37-2 is required.

3. No tentative rulings are issued.

4. Mandatory chambers copies are to be delivered to chambers.

   Mandatory chambers copies of e-filed documents are to be delivered to courtesy copy box outside chambers, 3rd Floor, Spring Street.

5. Procedures for filing an ex parte application: Strict compliance with Local Rule 7-19 is required. A **FILED** stamped mandatory chambers copy should be delivered directly to the Judge's chambers. Any opposition should be served and filed within 24 hours of applicant's oral notice. Court will notify parties if a telephonic hearing is desired.

6. To request a continuance of any scheduled court proceeding: Submit stipulation no less than **3 business days** before hearing.

7. Counsel are not allowed to contact the judge's secretary or law clerk.

8. Inquiries regarding the status of a motion, stipulation or proposed order: Counsel should check the docket sheet before inquiring of the court clerk. The Court discourages the practice of calling the court clerk.

9. Calendar conflicts: (Procedures for attorneys to follow if they have a calendar conflict) - Contact opposing counsel then CRD.

10. Procedures for bringing electronic equipment into the courtroom: Contact the CRD.

11. For general information on how to order a transcript of any reported or digitally recorded proceeding, please contact 213-894-3015 or visit www.cacd.uscourts.gov > General Information > Court Reporter/Recorder Transcripts. If you require an estimate of cost for the preparation of a transcript, contact the court reporter/recorder for the desired proceeding.

    To determine the court reporter/recorder for a particular proceeding, go to the Court Reporter Schedule web page and click on View by Date. Once you've determined the correct court reporter/recorder for the desired session, click on Court Reporter Phone and Email List for contact information.

12. Questions regarding law clerk/extern positions: Submit letter, resume and writing samples to chambers.

13. **Stipulated Protective Orders:** Parties frequently file stipulated protective orders that do not satisfy Rule 26 and the Ninth Circuit's standards for protective orders. All proposed protective orders must describe the documents to be protected with

particularity. *See Rivera v. Nibco, Inc., 364 F.3d 1057, 1063 n. 3 (9th Cir. 2004).* Therefore, the documents, information, items or materials that are subject to the protective order shall be described in a meaningful fashion (for example, "personnel records," or "market surveys," etc.). It is not sufficient to use only conclusory terms such as "confidential or proprietary information." Also, the Court cannot agree to "seal all confidential documents." If confidential material is included in any papers to be filed in Court, such papers shall be accompanied by an application, pursuant to Local Rule 79-5.1, to file the papers – or the confidential portion thereof – under seal. The application shall be directed to the judge to whom the papers are directed. Pending the ruling on the application, the papers or portions thereof subject to the sealing application shall be lodged under seal. In the event of a dispute regarding the designation of confidential information, the procedure for obtaining a decision from the Court is that set forth in Local Rule 37. All proposed protective orders must include a statement establishing the requisite good cause. *Foltz v. State Farm Mut. Auto Ins. Co., 331 F.3d 1122, 1130 (9th Cir. 2003) (court's protective order analysis requires examination of good cause) (citing Phillips v. Gen. Motors Corp., 307 F.3d 1206, 1210-11, 1212 (9th Cir. 2002); San Jose Mercury News, Inc. v. United States Dist. Court, 187 F.3d 1096, 1102 (9th Cir. 1999); Beckman Indus., Inc. v. Int'l Ins. Co., 966 F.2d 470, 476 (9th Cir.1992).*

The Court may only enter a protective order upon a showing of good cause. K*amakana v. City and County of Honolulu, 447 F.3d 1172, 1176 (9th Cir. 2006)* (parties must make a "particularized showing" under Rule 26(c)'s good cause showing for court to enter protective order); *Phillips, 307 F.3d at 1210-11 (Rule 26(c) requires a showing of good cause for a protective order); Makar-Wellbon v. Sony Electrics, Inc., 187 F.R.D. 576, 577 (E.D. Wis. 1999)* (even stipulated protective orders require good cause showing). The Court recommends that a separate paragraph be included in each protective order and that paragraph should be labeled "GOOD CAUSE STATEMENT." The parties should then set forth the reasons establishing good cause. Finally, in all proposed protective orders and other filings pertaining to discovery, the parties shall include the following in the caption: "[Discovery Document: Referred to Magistrate Judge Suzanne H. Segal]."

14. Trial preparation:

a. Court hours: Tuesday - Friday - 9:00 a.m. to 5:00 p.m.

b. Exhibit preparation: Original Exhibit +4 copies (1 for judge, 1 for opposing counsel, 1 for themselves, 1 extra copy) of exhibit list/witness list on the first day of trial. Submit copies of **all** exhibits (both sides) except for exhibits used for impeachment/cross examination.

c. Jury Instructions (form, when they're to be submitted, whether counsel need to submit general or substantiative instructions or both) general 7 days before trial on computer disc to CRD.

d. Verdict forms - Follow Local Rules.

15. Procedures for obtaining the services of an interpreter on a civil case - contact the Interpreter's Office.

16. Other Information: Parties should contact CRD about dates available for settlement conferences. Settlement Conferences will generally be held on **Mondays, Tuesdays or Fridays at 2:00 p.m.**

Counsel should review and follow procedures set forth in the court's own settlement conference order (available for download below) which differs in some respects from Local Rule 16-14.5. All settlement conference papers should be delivered directly to the Judge's chambers, Room 324, 3rd floor.

17. Refer to the instructions specific to e-filing in Social Security Cases in the Case Management Order for Social Security cases.

II. Judge Segal's Case Management Orders

A. *Order Regarding Settlement Conference*

IN THE UNITED STATES DISTICT COURT
FOR THE CENTRAL DISTRICT OF CALIFORNIA

Plaintiff(s),	)	Case No. CV _______________
v.	)	
Defendant(s).	)	**Referred for settlement proceedings to Magistrate Judge Suzanne H. Segal**
	)	**ORDER RE SETTLEMENT CONFERENCE**

DATE: ____________
TIME: 2:00 p.m.
PLACE: COURTROOM 23

PLEASE READ THIS ORDER CAREFULLY - PLEASE REVIEW PARAGRAPHS 3, 4,6, 8, 9, 10 AND 11 WHICH INCLUDE MANDATORY REQUIREMENTS FOR ALL PARTIES WHO PARTICIPATE IN THIS CONFERENCE

This case has been referred to Magistrate Judge Suzanne H. Segal for settlement proceedings.

The Settlement Conference is placed on calendar for Monday, November 13, 2006 at 2:00 p.m., Courtroom 23, Third Floor, 312 N. Spring Street, Los Angeles, California 90012.

The Magistrate Judge will not be involved in the actual trial of the case and will assist the parties in an objective appraisal and evaluation of the case. The following are guidelines for the parties in preparing for the Settlement Conference.

1. The purpose of the Settlement Conference is to permit an informal discussion between the attorneys, parties, non-party indemnitors or insurers, and the settlement judge, of every aspect of the case bearing on its settlement value.

2. Pursuant to Local Rule 16-14.8, all settlement proceedings shall be confidential and no statement made therein shall be admissible in any proceeding in the case, unless the parties otherwise agree. No part of a settlement proceeding shall be reported or otherwise recorded, without the consent of the parties, except for any memorialization of a settlement.

3. Counsel who will try the case must be present. In addition, a person with full settlement authority should likewise be present for the conference. ***This requirement contemplates the physical presence of your client or, if a corporate or governmental entity, of an authorized and knowledgeable representative of your client. The plaintiff's representative must have full and final authority, in the representative's discretion, to authorize dismissal of the case with prejudice, or to accept a settlement amount recommended by the settlement judge down to the defendant's last offer made prior to the settlement conference. The defendant's representative must have final settlement authority to commit the defendant to pay, in the representative's discretion, a settlement amount recommended by the settlement judge up to the plaintiff's prayer (excluding punitive damage prayers), or up to the plaintiff's last demand made prior to***

the settlement conference, whichever is lower.[1]

The purpose of this requirement is to have representatives present who can settle the case during the course of the conference without consulting a superior. ***ANY VIOLATION OF THIS REQUIREMENT WILL CAUSE THE COURT TO CANCEL THE SETTLEMENT CONFERENCE. IN ADDITION, COUNSEL AND/OR THE PARTY WHO VIOLATE THIS ORDER MAY BE SUBJECT TO SANCTIONS.***

Either at a telephonic conference prior to the date of the settlement conference (which will only take place if the Court requests such a telephonic conference) or at the beginning of the settlement conference, the Court will ask each counsel to identify who will appear on behalf of the party. Even if your client is located outside the Central District of California, the client will be expected to appear in person.

Any relief from this requirement may only be granted by the Court, following a motion or ex parte application from the party seeking relief. Relief from this requirement will rarely, if ever, be granted and only upon a showing of exceptional good cause.[2]

4. If Board approval is required to authorize settlement, the attendance of at least one sitting and knowledgeable member of the Board (preferably the Chairman) is absolutely required.

5. Counsel appearing without their clients (whether or not counsel purportedly have been given settlement authority) will cause the settlement conference to be canceled and rescheduled. The noncomplying party, attorney, or both, may be assessed the costs and expenses incurred by other parties as a result of such cancellation and rescheduling.

6. Any insurance company that is contractually required to defend or to pay damages assessed within policy limits also should have a settlement representative present at the conference. Such representative must have final settlement authority to commit the company to pay, in the representative's discretion, an amount recommended by the settlement judge within the policy limits. The purpose of this requirement is to have an insurance representative present who can settle the outstanding claim or claims during the course of the conference without consulting a superior. An insurance representative authorized to pay, ***in his or her discretion***, up to the plaintiff's last demand made prior to the settlement conference will also satisfy this requirement. Counsel of record will be responsible for timely advising any involved non-party insurance company of the requirements of this Order.

7. The settlement judge may, in her discretion, converse with the lawyers, the parties, the insurance representatives, or any one of them outside of the hearing of the others. The comments of the judge during such separate sessions are not to be used by counsel in settlement negotiations with opposing counsel. This is a necessary requirement in order to avoid intentional or unintentional misquotation of the judge's comments. Violation of this policy may be misleading and therefore a hindrance to settlement.

8. Prior to the Settlement Conference, the attorneys are directed to discuss settlement with their respective clients and insurance representatives, so that the parameters of possible settlement will have been explored well in advance of the Settlement Conference. At the

---

1 This rule does not apply to cases involving pro se plaintiffs. However, Defendant must have a representative present with appropriate authority to settle the case.

2 The provisions of Local Rule 16-14.5(b) are inapplicable to this Order. Parties may only appear by telephone with prior approval of the Court. Only the United States, its agencies or employees are entitled to rely upon Local Rule 16-15.5(b).

Settlement Conference, each party shall be fully prepared to discuss all economic and non economic factors relevant to a full and final settlement of the case.

In addition, the Court ORDERS that the following occur prior to the settlement conference:

20 days prior to the date of the conference, Plaintiff must serve a detailed written demand on Defendant[s];

15 days prior to the date of the conference, Defendant[s] must serve a detailed written counter offer to Plaintiff[s];

12 days prior to the date of the conference, Plaintiff[s] must serve a written Reply to the Counter Offer;

The settlement statements of each party must include a summary of the history of these exchanges. Parties who fail to timely serve written demands and counter offers will very likely be subject to sanctions.

9. **No later than five (5) court days prior to the conference, each party shall *submit a Settlement Conference Statement directly to the chambers of Magistrate Judge Segal* (312 N. Spring St., Room 324) or fax to (213) 894-4368. *The parties shall serve the Statements on all relevant parties in the action on the same date.* The Statements should not be filed with the Clerk of the Court and they will not be made part of the case file. The Statements shall be double-spaced and shall not exceed ten (10) pages in length.** Parties may attach exhibits that are relevant to settlement discussions.

The parties respective Settlement Conference Statements shall include the following:

A. A brief statement of the facts of the case, including the party's claims and defenses. The statement should include citations to the applicable statutory or other grounds upon which claims or defenses are based. This statement should identify the major factual and legal issues in dispute, and cite any controlling authorities.

B. ***An ITEMIZED STATEMENT OF THE DAMAGES claimed, and of any other relief sought.*** This is one of the most **critical** aspects of the party's statement. ***Any statement which omits an itemized statement of damages will be considered a violation of this Order and may subject the party to sanctions.***

C. A summary of the proceedings to date, including any case management dates/deadlines already set by the District Judge.

D. A history of past settlement discussions, offers and demands, **INCLUDING THE DEMANDS/OFFERS DESCRIBED IN PARAGRAPH 8.**

10. ***Each party shall also prepare a Confidential Addendum to Settlement Conference Statement, which shall be delivered directly to Magistrate Judge Segal only, along with the Settlement Conference Statement.*** The Confidential Addendum shall not be filed with the Court or served upon the other parties. The Confidential Addendum shall contain:

A. A forthright evaluation of the party's likelihood of prevailing on each of its claims and/or defenses.

B. The approximate amount of attorney's fees, time and costs expended to date, and an estimate of the fees, time and costs to be expended for (i) further discovery, (ii) pretrial and (iii) trial.

C. The party's evaluation of the terms on which the case could be settled fairly, taking into account the litigation position and settlement position of the other side.

11. In the event both parties agree that a settlement conference at this point in the litigation would not be meaningful, after the above described steps are completed, the parties are instructed to telephone Judge Segal's courtroom deputy clerk at (213) 894-0958 and inform her of this information. The Court will then hold the settlement conference telephonically and will notify the parties of the date of the telephonic conference.

12. Any failure of the trial attorneys, parties or persons with authority to attend the conference will result in sanctions to include the fees and costs expended by the other parties in preparing for and attending the conference. Failure to timely deliver a Settlement Conference Statement and Confidential Addendum, or otherwise comply with this Order, will also result in sanctions being imposed.

13. At the commencement of the conference, each party through counsel may be required to make an oral presentation (not to exceed 10 minutes) of the relevant facts and law, in the presence of all parties and counsel. Counsel should have available for the Court's review copies of all critical documents (i.e., pleadings, declarations or witness statements, business records, personnel files, etc.) in the case, as well as copies of all important witnesses' deposition transcripts, if a party believes such documents will assist in the evaluation of the case. If a party's settlement position is predicated on the recoupment or recovery of attorney's fees and/or costs, then its counsel should have available for the Court's review copies of billing records substantiating both the time expended and the expenses incurred.

14. If settlement between any or all parties is reached as a result of the Settlement Conference, it is the responsibility of all counsel to immediately report the settlement to the District Judge's courtroom deputy clerk, as well as to timely memorialize the settlement. See Local Rule 16-14.7.

15. All papers submitted for the Settlement Conference will either be returned to the parties or destroyed by the Magistrate Judge, after the settlement proceedings are concluded, unless the parties agree otherwise.

DATED: ________________

____

SUZANNE H. SEGAL
United States Magistrate Judge

B. *Order Setting Scheduling Conference*

IN THE UNITED STATES DISTICT COURT
FOR THE CENTRAL DISTRICT OF CALIFORNIA

Plaintiff(s),	)	Case No. CV ______ -SS
v.	)	**ORDER SETTING SCHEDULING CONFERENCE**
Defendant(s).	)	
______________________________	)	Date: ____________ Time: __________

The parties have consented to have this case assigned to Magistrate Judge Suzanne H. Segal. All counsel are hereby ordered to familiarize themselves with the Federal Rules of Civil Procedure and the Local Rules of the Central District of California.

This matter is set for a scheduling conference on the above date. If plaintiff has not already served the operative complaint on all defendants, plaintiff shall promptly do so and shall file proofs of service within three days thereafter. Defendants also shall timely serve and file their responsive pleadings, and file proofs of service within three days thereafter. For record-keeping purposes, the Court will dismiss all remaining fictitiously-named defendants (i.e., those who have not been named) at the scheduling conference. The Court will also set a date by which motions to amend the pleadings or add parties must be heard.

The conference will be held pursuant to Rule 16(b) of the Federal Rules of Civil Procedure. The parties are reminded of their obligations under Rule 26(a)(1) of the Federal Rules of Civil Procedure to disclose information without awaiting a discovery request, and under Rule 26(f) to confer on a discovery plan not later than 21 days before the scheduling conference. Counsel must file a "Joint Rule 26(f) Report" with the Court not later than 14 days before the conference. Counsel should deliver mandatory chambers copies of the Joint Rule 26(f) Report to Judge Segal's chambers. Failure to comply with the following requirements or to cooperate in the preparation of the Joint Rule 26(f) Report may lead to the imposition of sanctions.

Unless, upon motion by a party, the Court finds that any or all discovery is premature, counsel should begin to conduct discovery before the Scheduling Conference. At the very least, the parties shall comply fully with the letter and spirit of Rule 26(a) and obtain and produce most of what would be produced in the early stages of discovery, because at the Scheduling Conference the Court will impose strict deadlines to complete discovery.

This Court does not exempt parties appearing *in propria persona* from compliance with any of the Local Rules, including Local Rule 16. "Counsel," as used in this order, includes parties appearing *in propria persona*.

A continuance of the Scheduling Conference will be granted only for good cause.

1. Joint Rule 26(f) Report

The Joint Rule 26(f) Report, which shall be filed not later than 14 days before the scheduling conference, shall be drafted by plaintiff (unless the parties agree otherwise), but shall be submitted and signed jointly. "Jointly" contemplates a single report, regardless of how many separately-represented parties there are. The Joint Rule 26(f) Report shall specify the date of the scheduling conference on the caption page. It shall report on all matters described below, which include those required to be discussed by Rule 26(f) and Local Rule 26:

a. Statement of the case: a short synopsis (not to exceed two pages) of the main claims, counterclaims, and affirmative defenses.

b. Subject matter jurisdiction: a statement of the specific basis of federal jurisdiction, including supplemental jurisdiction.

c. Legal issues: a brief description of the **key legal issues**, including any unusual substantive, procedural, or evidentiary issues.

d. Parties, evidence, *etc.*: a list of parties, percipient witnesses, and key documents on the main issues in the case. For conflict purposes, corporate parties must identify all subsidiaries, parents, and affiliates.

e. Damages: the realistic range of provable damages.

f. Insurance: whether there is insurance coverage, the extent of coverage, and whether there is a reservation of rights.

g. Motions: a statement of the likelihood of motions seeking to add other parties or claims, file amended pleadings, transfer venue, *etc.*

h. Manual for Complex Litigation: whether all or part of the procedures of the Manual for Complex Litigation should be utilized.

i. Status of Discovery: a discussion of the present state of discovery, including a summary of completed discovery.

j. Discovery Plan: a detailed discovery plan, as contemplated by Rule 26(f), including the identity of all anticipated deponents and dates by which their depositions are to be completed (if possible), anticipated written discovery requests, including requests for admission, document requests, and interrogatories, and a schedule for completion of all discovery. State what, if any, changes in the disclosures under Rule 26(a) should be made, the subjects on which discovery may be needed and whether discovery should be conducted in phases or otherwise be limited, **any issues about disclosure or discovery of electronically stored information, including the form or forms in which it should be produced**, whether applicable discovery limitations should be changed or other limitations imposed, and whether the Court should enter other orders.

k. Discovery cut-off: a proposed discovery cut-off date. This means the final day for completion of discovery, including production of all documents, completion of depositions and resolution of all discovery motions.

l. Expert discovery: proposed dates for expert witness disclosures (initial and rebuttal) and expert discovery cutoff under Rule 26(a)(2).

m. Dispositive motions: a description of the issues or claims that any party believes may be determined by motion for summary judgment or other dispositive motion.

n. Settlement: a statement of what settlement discussions or written communications have occurred (**excluding any statement of the terms discussed**) and a statement pursuant to Local Rule 16-14.4 selecting a settlement mechanism under that Rule. Note, If a case is selected for the ADR Pilot Program, the parties may choose private mediation (at their own expense) instead. No case will proceed to trial unless all parties, including the principals of all corporate parties, have appeared personally at a settlement conference.

o. Trial estimate: a realistic estimate of the time required for trial and whether trial will be by jury or by court. Each side should specify (by number, not by name) how many witnesses it contemplates calling. If the time estimate for trial given in the Joint Rule 26(f) Report exceeds eight court days, counsel shall be prepared to discuss in detail the estimate.

p. Trial counsel: the name(s) of the attorney(s) who will try the case.

q. Independent expert: whether this is a case where the Court should consider appointing an independent scientific expert.

r. Timetable: counsel should complete the Schedule of Pretrial and Trial Dates form attached to this Order and attach it to the Joint Rule 26(f) Report. The entries in the "Weeks Before Trial" column reflect what the Court believes are appropriate for most cases and will allow the Court to rule on potentially dispositive motions sufficiently in advance of the pretrial conference. The form is designed to enable counsel to ask the Court to set different last dates by which the key requirements must be completed. Each side should write in the month, day and year it requests for each event. *E.g.*, for the expert discovery cut-off it might be "10/7/07" for plaintiff and "10/28/07" for defendant, if they cannot agree. At the conference, the Court will review this form with counsel. Each entry proposing Court dates shall fall on a Tuesday. In appropriate cases, the Court may order different dates after it hears from counsel. The discovery cut-off date is the last day by which all depositions must be completed, responses to previously-served written discovery must be provided, and motions concerning discovery disputes must have been heard, not filed. The cut-off date for motions is the last date on which motions may be heard, not filed.

s. Other issues: a statement of any other issues affecting the status or management of the case (e.g., unusually complicated technical or technological issues, disputes over protective orders, extraordinarily voluminous document production, non-English speaking witnesses, ADA-related issues, discovery in foreign jurisdictions, etc.) and any proposals concerning severance, bifurcation, or other ordering of proof.

The Joint Rule 26(f) Report should set forth the above described information under section headings corresponding to those in this Order.

2. Scheduling Conference

Scheduling conferences will be held in Courtroom 23 on the 3rd Floor of the Spring Street Courthouse. Counsel shall comply with the following:

a. Participation: the lead trial attorney must attend the scheduling conference, unless excused by the Court for good cause shown in advance of the scheduling conference. When seeking permission not to attend, lead counsel must identify the person who will appear by name and bar number, and specify that person's involvement in the case. The Court may choose to postpone the scheduling conference rather than permit counsel other than lead counsel to attend. Local counsel may not appear at a scheduling conference in place of lead counsel. Counsel should not purport to be "co-lead" counsel as a means of avoiding this requirement.

b. Continuance: a continuance of the scheduling conference will be granted only for good cause.

3. Notice to be Provided by Counsel

Plaintiff's counsel or, if plaintiff is appearing *pro se*, defendant's counsel, shall provide this Order to any parties who first appear after the date of this Order and to parties who are known to exist but have not yet entered appearances.

4. **Disclosures to Clients**

Counsel are ordered to deliver to their respective clients a copy of this Order and of the Court's trial order, which will contain the schedule that the Court sets at the scheduling conference.

5. **Court's Website**

Copies of this and all other orders of this Court that may become applicable to this case are available on the Central District of California website, at www.cacd.uscourts.gov, under "Judge's Procedures and Schedules." Copies of the Local Rules are available on the website. If counsel fail to file the required Joint Rule 26(f) Report, or the required pretrial documents, or if counsel fail to appear at the scheduling conference, the pretrial conference or any other proceeding scheduled by the Court, and such failure is not satisfactorily explained to the Court: (a) the cause shall stand dismissed for failure to prosecute, if such failure occurs on the part of the plaintiff; (b) default judgment shall be entered if such failure occurs on the part of the defendant; or (c) the Court may take such action as it deems appropriate.

The Court thanks the parties and their counsel for their anticipated cooperation in complying with these requirements.

IT IS SO ORDERED.

Dated: ________________

____
SUZANNE H. SEGAL
United States Magistrate Judge

Schedule of Pretrial and Trial Dates

Case Name: ______________
Case No. ______________

Matter	Date/ Time	Weeks before trial	Pl's Request	Def's Request	Court's Order
Trial date (Court/Jury) Length of trial: __ days	9:00 a.m. (Tuesday)				
Pretrial Conference, LR 16	10:00 a.m. (Tuesday)	4			
Hearing on Motions *in Limine*	10:00 a.m. (Tuesday)	2			
Court Trial Lodge Findings of Fact and Conclusions of Law, LR 52, and Summaries of Direct Testimony		3			
Jury Trial Lodge Final Pretrial Conference Order, LR 16-7; File Proposed and Disputed Jury Instructions and Verdict Forms		(*See* LR 16-7.1)			
Jury Trial File Memo of Contentions of Fact and Law, LR 16-4; Exhibit and Witness Lists, LR 16-5, 16-6 File Status Report Regarding Settlement		7			
Trial Brief, LR 16-10		1			
Last date to conduct Settlement Conference, LR 16-14		10			
Last date for hearing dispositive motions, LR 7	10:00 a.m. (Tuesday)	12			
Non-Expert Discovery cut-off					
Expert Disclosure (Initial)					
Expert Disclosure (Rebuttal)					
Expert Discovery cut-off					
Last day to amend pleadings					

Hon. Patrick J. Walsh

Magistrate Judge

Chambers Information

U.S. District Court, Central District of California
Courtroom 23, 3rd Floor
312 N. Spring Street
Los Angeles, CA 90012

Scheduling Information

Courtroom Deputy: (213) 894-8958

Civil Law and Motion	Wednesdays, Thursdays, and Fridays at 11:00 a.m.
Criminal Law and Motion	As scheduled.

Biographical Information

[Not available]

I. Judge Walsh's Procedures and Practices

A. *Procedures and Schedules*

1. Civil motions are heard on: **Wednesday, Thursdays and Fridays at 11:00 a.m.**

   Criminal motions are heard on: **As scheduled.**

   It is not necessary to clear a motion date with the court clerk prior to filing the motion.

2. Discovery motions are to be calendared before the magistrate judge after checking if the assigned district judge has a blanket referral policy. **Strict Compliance with Local Rule 37 is required.**

3. Are tentative rulings issued? As appropriate.

4. **Mandatory chambers copies:**
   a. Mandatory chambers copies of criminal e-filed documents are to be delivered to criminal duty chambers, 3rd Floor, Roybal.

   b. Regular filings are to be delivered to courtesy copy box outside chambers, 3rd Floor, Spring String Courthouse.

5. Procedures for filing an ex parte application: Must comply with local rules, obtain opposing side's position and phone number.

6. To request a continuance of any scheduled court proceeding: Submit stipulation no less than 3 business days before hearing.

7. Are counsel allowed to contact the judge's law clerk or secretary? Do not contact the secretary. Counsel may contact the law clerk, but they are not allowed to discuss the merits of the case.

8. Inquiries regarding the status of a motion, stipulation or proposed order: Contact the CRD.

9. Calendar conflicts: (Procedures for attorneys to follow if they have a calendar conflict) Contact opposing counsel then CRD.

10. Procedures for bringing electronic equipment into the courtroom: Contact the CRD.

11. For general information on how to order a transcript of any reported or digitally recorded proceeding, please contact 213-894-3015 or visit www.cacd.uscourts.gov > General Information > Court Reporter/Recorder Transcripts. If you require an estimate of cost for the preparation of a transcript, contact the court reporter/recorder for the desired proceeding.

    To determine the court reporter/recorder for a particular proceeding, go to the Court Reporter Schedule web page and click on View by Date. Once you've determined the correct court reporter/recorder for the desired session, click on Court Reporter Phone and Email List for contact information.

12. Questions regarding law clerk/extern positions: Submit letter, resume, and writing sample to chambers.

13. Trial preparation:
    a. Court hours: Tuesday (or Monday) - Friday - 9 a.m.-5 p.m.

Break - 10:30 - 10:45 a.m. & 3:15 - 3:30 p.m.

Lunch - 12 - 1:30 p.m.

b. Exhibit preparation: Original Exhibits + 4 copies (1 for judge, 1 for opposing counsel, 1 for themselves, 1 extra); 3 copies of exhibit list/witness list on the first day of trial.

Submit copies of all exhibits (both sides) except for exhibits used for impeachment/cross examination.

c. Jury instructions (form, when they're to be submitted, whether counsel need to submit general or substantiative instructions or both) general 7 days before trial on computer disc to CRD.

d. Verdict forms - Follow local rules.

e. Other

14. Procedures for obtaining the services of an interpreter on a civil case - Call Interpreter's Office

15. Other information: Parties are required to read and follow local rules. No sidebars are allowed.

Hon. Michael R. Wilner
Magistrate Judge

Chambers Information
U.S. District Court, Central District of California
Courtroom H, 9th Floor
312 N. Spring Street
Los Angeles, CA 90012

Scheduling Information
Courtroom Deputy: (213) 894-5496

Civil Law and Motion	Wednesdays at 9:30 a.m.

Biographical Information
[Not available]

I. Judge Wilner's Procedures and Practices

A. *Procedures and Schedules*

1. Civil motions are heard on **Wednesdays** at 9:30 a.m. Please check the Closed Motion Dates link above before filing a motion. It is not necessary to clear a civil motion date with the Court before filing the motion. The parties shall contact the courtroom deputy clerk to schedule all motions in criminal cases.
2. If any party is in federal or state custody, the moving party shall file the motion ***without*** requesting a hearing date. The Court will review the pleadings to determine whether a hearing is necessary.
3. The parties may file discovery motions with Judge Wilner only if the assigned district judge has so directed. Counsel are advised to review the procedures and standing orders of the assigned district judge before filing any discovery motion. Strict compliance with all local rules regarding motion practice is required.
4. Mandatory chambers copies of all e-filed documents must be delivered to chambers (by hand or overnight courier) by noon on the following day. Chambers copies do not need to be blue backed. Electronic copies of proposed orders shall be e-mailed to the Court at MRW_chambers@cacd.uscourts.gov. Proposed orders shall be in WordPerfect (preferred) or Microsoft Word format.
5. Requests to reschedule a hearing, conference, or other proceeding must be submitted in writing. The parties shall contact the courtroom deputy clerk as soon as the need to reschedule a proceeding is discovered.
6. Any party who wishes to appear at a hearing by telephone shall make such a request at least two court days before the hearing.
7. Federal law enforcement agents and the U.S. Attorney's Office are encouraged to advise the courtroom deputy clerk in advance of the anticipated submission of warrants, criminal complaints, and other applications for the Court's review.
8. The parties are not allowed to contact or communicate with the judge's law clerks in any manner without express authorization from the Court. Letters to chambers are strictly forbidden and may lead to sanctions against the offending party.
9. For general information on how to order a transcript of any reported or digitally recorded proceeding, please contact 213-894-3015 or visit www.cacd.uscourts.gov > General Information > Court Reporter/Recorder Transcripts. If you require an estimate of cost for the preparation of a transcript, contact the court reporter/recorder for the desired proceeding.

   To determine the court reporter/recorder for a particular proceeding, go to the Court Reporter Schedule web page and click on View by Date. Once you've determined the correct court reporter/recorder for the desired session, click on Court Reporter Phone and Email List for contact information.

Hon. Andrew J. Wistrich
Magistrate Judge

Chambers Information

U.S. District Court, Central District of California
Courtroom 690
255 East Temple Street
Los Angeles, CA 90012

Scheduling Information

Courtroom Deputy: (213) 894-6509

Civil Law and Motion	Mondays at 10:00 a.m.
Criminal Law and Motion	Specially set by Court Clerk

Biographical Information

[Not available]

I. Judge Wistrich's Procedures and Practices

A. *Procedures and Schedules*

1. Civil motions are heard on: **Mondays at 10:00 a.m.**

   If Monday is a holiday, the next motion date is the following Monday. It is not necessary to clear a motion date with the court clerk prior to filing the motion.

   Criminal motions are heard on: **contact court clerk to specially set on calendar.**
2. Discovery motions are to be calendared before the magistrate judge unless otherwise ordered by the district judge.
3. Tentative rulings are issued occasionally.
4. Mandatory chambers copies should be delivered to chambers, Room 6100, Roybal Federal Building and Courthouse.

   Mandatory chambers copies of e-filed documents are to be delivered to courtesy copy box outside of Roybal Clerk's Office.
5. Procedures for filing an ex parte application: Follow the local rules. Ex parte applications are generally decided without a hearing.
6. To request a continuance of any scheduled court proceeding: Contact court clerk to reschedule and follow up with a stipulation and proposed order, or application and proposed order.
7. Counsel are not allowed to contact the judge's law clerk or secretary.
8. Inquiries regarding the status of a motion, stipulation or proposed order: All inquiries are to be directed to the court clerk. Generally, rulings will be mailed to the parties. Rulings on ex parte applications will usually be disseminated by fax or telephone call.
9. Calendar conflicts: Notify the court clerk.
10. Procedures for bringing electronic equipment into the courtroom: Contact the court clerk.
11. For general information on how to order a transcript of any reported or digitally recorded proceeding, please contact 213-894-3015 or visit www.cacd.uscourts.gov > General Information > Court Reporter/Recorder Transcripts. If you require an estimate of cost for the preparation of a transcript, contact the court reporter/recorder for the desired proceeding.

    To determine the court reporter/recorder for a particular proceeding, go to the Court Reporter Schedule web page and click on View by Date. Once you've determined the correct court reporter/recorder for the desired session, click on Court Reporter Phone and Email List for contact information.
12. Law clerk/extern positions: Submit a cover letter, resume, writing sample and law school transcript to the magistrate judge.
13. Trial preparation: The Court will issue an order advising counsel of what is required. The court hours during trial are 9:00 a.m. to 5:00 p.m.
14. Procedures for obtaining the services of an interpreter on a civil case: Counsel are to make their own arrangements to have a court interpreter present.

Hon. Carla Woehrle
Magistrate Judge

Chambers Information
U.S. District Court, Central District of California
Courtroom 640
255 East Temple Street
Los Angeles, CA 90012

Scheduling Information
Courtroom Deputy: (213) 894-6825

Civil Law and Motion	Tuesdays at 10:00 a.m.
Criminal Law and Motion	As required.

Biographical Information
[Not available]

I. Judge Woehrle's Procedures and Practices

A. *Procedures and Schedules*

1. Civil motions are heard on **Tuesdays**, Time: **10:00 a.m.**

   Criminal motions are heard on: **as required**.

   (If Monday is a holiday, next motion date is **Wednesday**.

   It is not necessary to clear a motion date with the court clerk prior to filing the motion, but it is necessary to check the court's website for closed motion dates prior to filing.
2. Tentative rulings are not always available but they may be issued either prior to the hearing date or possibly on the morning of the hearing.
3. Mandatory chambers copies:
   1. Mandatory chambers copies of criminal e-filed documents are to be delivered to criminal intake, 1st floor, Roybal.
   2. Regular e-filings courtesy copy box outside chambers, 6th Floor, Roybal and chambers e-mail box in word or wordperfect format with proposed order.
4. Procedures for filing an ex parte application: E-file documents. Notify the opposing side that opposition papers shall be filed within 24 hours. The court clerk will notify counsel if a hearing is required. Otherwise, the Court will rule on the papers.
5. To request a continuance of any scheduled court proceeding: File a request for continuance, state the reason(s) for the continuance and attach Proposed Order.
6. Counsel are not allowed to contact the judge's chambers unless specifically directed by the court.
7. Inquiries regarding the status of a motion, stipulation or proposed order may be checked via the website, or through the computer at the courthouse, or in the Records Section.
8. Calendar conflicts: Notify the magistrate clerk.
9. Procedures for bringing electronic equipment into the courtroom: Contact the magistrate clerk.
10. For general information on how to order a transcript of any reported or digitally recorded proceeding, please contact 213-894-3015 or visit www.cacd.uscourts.gov > General Information > Court Reporter/Recorder Transcripts. If you require an estimate of cost for the preparation of a transcript, contact the court reporter/recorder for the desired proceeding.

    To determine the court reporter/recorder for a particular proceeding, go to the Court Reporter Schedule web page and click on View by Date. Once you've determined the correct court reporter/recorder for the desired session, click on Court Reporter Phone and Email List for contact information.
11. Questions regarding law clerk/extern positions: Contact chambers.
12. Trial preparation: Orders governing trial procedures will be issued by the court in cases where the parties have consented to jurisdiction of the Magistrate Judge.
13. Procedures for obtaining the services of an interpreter on a civil case: If the government is the moving party, the Court will pay for an interpreter. If sign language is required, the Court will also pay for the services of an interpreter. Contact the Interpreter's Section at 213-894-4459.

Hon. Ralph Zarefsky
Magistrate Judge

Chambers Information
U.S. District Court, Central District of California
Courtroom 540
255 East Temple Street
Los Angeles, CA 90012

Scheduling Information
Courtroom Deputy: (213) 894-8256

Civil Law and Motion	Mondays at 10:00 a.m.
Criminal Law and Motion	Contact court clerk.

Biographical Information
[Not available]

I. Judge Zarefsky's Procedures and Practices

A. Procedures and Schedules

The best way to contact the judge's courtroom deputy clerk is by calling (213) 894-8256; if the clerk does not answer the phone, be sure to leave a voice-mail message.

1. Civil motions are heard on: Mondays Time: 10:00 a.m.

Criminal motions are heard on: contact court clerk.

It is not necessary to clear a motion date with the court clerk prior to filing the motion.

2. Discovery motions are to be calendared before the district judge if the case does not have a blanket referral for discovery.

3. Tentative rulings not issued.

4. Mandatory chambers copies are not desired, except as ordered, as to documents filed traditionally over the intake counter. Mandatory chambers copies are required for documents filed electronically and shall be delivered to the courtesy copy drop box located outside of the Court Clerk's office, Room 181L at the Roybal Terrace Clerk's Office, within 24 hours after e-filing.

5. Procedures for filing an ex parte application: Refer to the Local Rules and Federal Rules; the clerk will notify the parties if a hearing will be necessary.

6. To request a continuance of any scheduled court proceeding: Refer to the Local Rules and Federal Rules.

7. Counsel are not allowed to contact the judge's law clerk or secretary.

8. Inquiries regarding the status of a motion, stipulation or proposed order: Refer to the Local Rules and Federal Rules.

9. Calendar conflicts: Contact the clerk.

10. Procedures for bringing electronic equipment into the courtroom: Except as barred by Local Rules or Federal Rules, contact the clerk.

11. For general information on how to order a transcript of any reported or digitally recorded proceeding, please contact 213-894-3015 or visit www.cacd.uscourts.gov > General Information > Court Reporter/Recorder Transcripts. If you require an estimate of cost for the preparation of a transcript, contact the court reporter/recorder for the desired proceeding.

To determine the court reporter/recorder for a particular proceeding, go to the Court Reporter Schedule web page and click on View by Date. Once you've determined the correct court reporter/recorder for the desired session, click on Court Reporter Phone and Email List for contact information.

12. Questions regarding law clerk/extern positions: Applications not accepted at this time.

13. Trial preparation: (varies)

14. Exhibit preparation: 1 book of original exhibits and 1 duplicate book for the court. All exhibits shall be numbered and tabbed.

15. Procedures for obtaining the services of an interpreter on a civil case: contact the clerk.

16. For other information, contact the clerk.

www.ingramcontent.com/pod-product-compliance
Lightning Source LLC
LaVergne TN
LVHW082001200926
848481LV00010B/2779
9780983830207